Author Note

Correspondence concerning this text should be addressed to:

James C. Brown

Department of Economic Crime, Justice Studies and Cybersecurity

Utica College

1600 Burrstone Road

Utica, New York 13502

E-mail: jbrown@utica.edu or jcbrown1980@yahoo.com

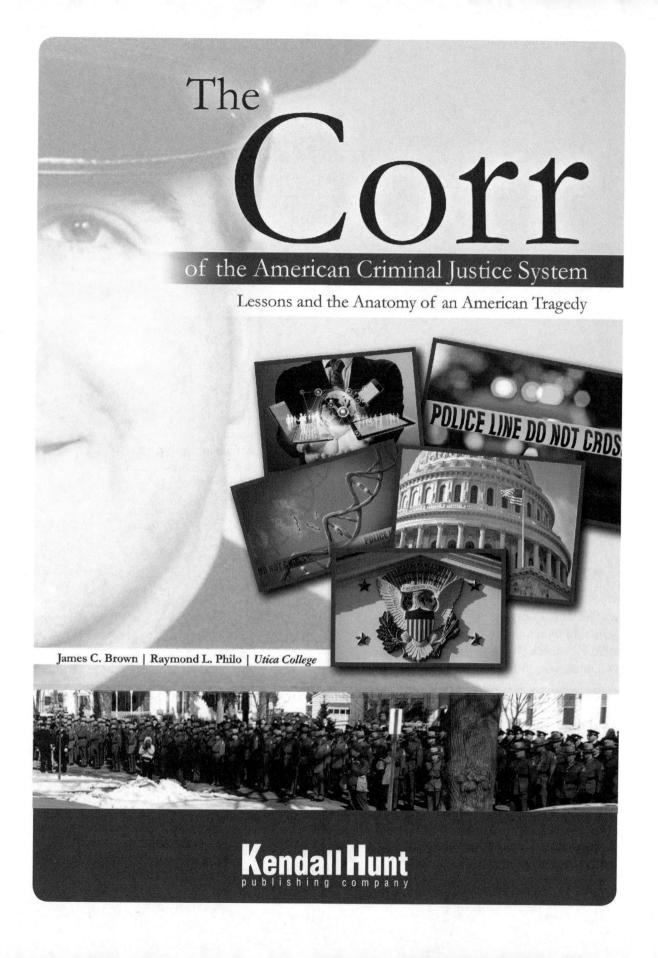

The Corr

of the American Criminal Justice System

Lessons and the Anatomy of an American Tragedy

POLICE LINE DO NOT CROSS

James C. Brown | Raymond L. Philo | *Utica College*

Kendall Hunt
publishing company

COVER PHOTO(s): Photo of Officer Joseph D. Corr (credit: Fraternal Composite Service, Inc.), Photo of Funeral detail (credit: Nancy L. Ford Photography); reprinted with permission

www.kendallhunt.com
Send all inquiries to:
4050 Westmark Drive
Dubuque, IA 52004-1840

Published in the United States of America

Contents

Preface

This work presents a picture of the American Criminal Justice System through the lens of the many unique facets surrounding the February 27, 2006 murder of New Hartford, New York Police Officer Joseph D. Corr. This work is not a step-by-step accounting of the crimes that occurred in 2006 and their aftermath. This work is also not an exhaustive analysis of the American Criminal Justice System. Rather, this enhanced case study uses the historical record and accounts of the crimes that occurred, the ensuing investigation, and its aftermath, as the lens to bring focus to the foundations of our American Criminal Justice System and the many lessons learned from this true American tragedy. Where possible, the reader has access to video news footage of the time, and radio transmissions that chronicle the moments leading up to the first reports of the robbery through the aftermath of Officer Corr's murder. Actual state and federal trial transcripts and related documents are also included and related images that help to frame the overall context of the research. In addition, readers have access both in text and online to copies of foundational documents, such as our United States Constitution, that further frame the research and provide additional context to the work.

This work is not a novel or a biography of Officer Corr's life. There are no formal interviews with family, friends, co-workers, or other victims of the crimes committed on February 27, 2006; only a concise analysis of the official records of the time. Two trials took place in our American courts: one for the robbery-homicide in Oneida County, New York against defendant John T. Healy (a.k.a. Toussaint Davis, a.k.a. Toussaint Martin), and one in the United States District Court for the Northern District of New York against the three surviving defendants: Toussaint Davis, Robert Ward, and Marion Pegese. Appeals also took place in New York State, and in our federal appeals courts, and at the United States Supreme Court.

According to the United States Court of Appeals for the Second Circuit, a brief overview of the facts of the case are as follows:

On August 26, 2005, at 3:45 p.m., the three defendants and another man, Eric Lane, entered Ballew Jewelers in Freehold, New Jersey, forced the store's employees into a back room at gunpoint, bound their hands and feet, and robbed the store of approximately $1.8 million dollars worth of diamonds and Rolex watches. Nearly six months later, in late February, 2006, the defendants conducted Internet research on jewelry stores in Utica, New York and took a daylong trip from Philadelphia, Pennsylvania to New Hartford, a suburb of Utica. On February 27, 2006, the defendants again traveled to New Hartford, this time accompanied by a fourth man, Walter Richardson ("Richardson"). While en route to New Hartford, the four men, traveling in two vehicles, pulled into a gas station and asked two other customers, Louis and Julie Shkane, for directions to Commercial Drive, some four miles away. Within about a half hour, a number of masked men entered Lennon's Jewelers, on Commercial Drive, and robbed it at gunpoint. At trial, Gary Lennon ("Lennon"), one of the store owners, testified to the presence of at least three men, but was unsure of the exact number. Lennon also testified that one of the men held a gun a few feet from his head and handcuffed his left wrist to his right ankle. Leslie Liesch ("Liesch"), another employee, testified that she alerted the police by phone, after which two of the robbers discovered her lying on the floor, and stood over her while one pointed a gun at her head and the other repeatedly yelled, "shoot the bitch in the head." At this time, Liesch heard someone else shout, "the cops are here," and the robbers fled the store in two separate vehicles, absconding with nearly a million dollars worth of merchandise. Two officers responding to the robbery, Joseph Corr and Ronald Fontaine, pursued one of these vehicles until it crashed, at a high speed, into a gasoline pump. Davis and Richardson then exited the vehicle and fled on foot. Officer Fontaine testified at trial that as he pursued and arrested Davis, Officer Corr was shot and killed by Richardson. Evading arrest, Richardson then hijacked a truck at gunpoint and fled to Chester, Pennsylvania. Richardson was killed the next morning in a firefight with law enforcement agents who had tracked him to that location and attempted to arrest him. Ward and Pegese, who fled from the robbery in a separate vehicle [a Cadillac], were arrested later in 2006. While incarcerated pending trial, Ward and Pegese approached a fellow inmate, David Carroway ("Carroway"), and discussed the Lennon robbery with him. Carroway later approached law enforcement agents with the details of these conversations. At trial, the government presented the testimony of fifty-six witnesses and introduced more than 150 exhibits into evidence. Among the witnesses were Carroway, and Louis and Julie Shkane. On November 5, 2010, the jury returned a verdict finding the defendants guilty on all counts. (*Pegese v. United States of America*, U.S. Dist. Ct. Case 5:09-cr-00390-NAM, Document 278, November 30, 2015, p. 2–3)

We wrote this work to address a significant gap in the literature of justice studies and public administration that fails to prepare our high school and college students, graduate students, criminal justice practitioners, and other public administrators with the foundational knowledge necessary to thrive in their profession. Today's instructional materials in this space are overly dense with facts and figures that strive to keep pace with real-time news events in this space, but are void of the fundamental knowledge needed to arm professionals with the tools necessary to intelligently write well, speak well, critically think, and perform effectively in a team environment. This work preserves key elements of the Corr case for historical purposes and for future public safety professionals, and associates those elements with companion segments of our American Criminal Justice System through the lens of a single case.

James C. Brown and Raymond L. Philo

About the Authors

James C. Brown

Dr. James C. Brown is an Assistant Professor of Criminal Justice in the School of Business & Justice Studies at Utica College in Utica, New York; joining the full-time faculty in January of 2014 after serving multiple senior administrative roles at Utica College since 2005. Most recently Dr. Brown served as the Vice President for the School of Online & Extended Studies and an adjunct instructor in the School of Arts and Sciences and School of Business and Justice Studies at Utica College. Dr. Brown has also served as Assistant Vice President for Marketing & Communications, Assistant Vice President for Academic Affairs & Dean of the School of Graduate & Extended Studies, and Vice President for Strategic Initiatives.

Dr. Brown holds a bachelor's degree in criminal justice from Utica College (1988), a master's degree in public administration from Sage Graduate School in Albany (1994), where he was awarded the Outstanding Public Administration Student, and a doctorate in education from the University of Phoenix School of Advanced Studies in educational leadership (2007). Dr. Brown's diverse background includes a 16 year full and part-time career as a police officer, police commander, and police administrator, serving as Oneida County, New York's first and youngest ever, Chief Deputy of Law Enforcement & Civil Division Operations with the Oneida County Sheriff's Office. Dr. Brown also served as a police officer and Assistant Chief of Police for the Village of Frankfort, NY and the City of Sherrill, NY. Dr. Brown also served as the Oneida County STOP-DWI Program Administrator for eight years and as vice president for public relations, security and facilities for the former Herkimer County Trust.

Dr. Brown has also served as the assistant director and director of security for the Boilermaker Roadrace and National Distance Running Hall of Fame. In 1996 he served as a volunteer police supervisor for the Security Team Program at the Centennial Olympic Games in Atlanta, Georgia, responsible for security at the Rhythmic Gymnastics, Volleyball, and Olympic Village at the University Georgia at Athens (UGA). Although unable to attend during the Games period, Dr. Brown was also selected as a member of the volunteer police force for the Utah Public Safety Command during the 2002 Winter Olympic Games in Salt Lake City, Utah.

Most recently Dr. Brown was sworn in as a Police Commissioner/Member of the New Hartford Police Commission in January of 2014, having been duly appointed by the Town Board, and reappointed to a five-year term in January of 2015. Dr. Brown also served as the chairman of the transition team for Oneida County Sheriff Robert M. Maciol; leading the team responsible for preparing then Sheriff-Elect Maciol to recruit and select his senior management team and prepare all related aspects of assuming the office of the Sheriff on January 1, 2011.

Dr. Brown actively teaches on ground and online in the areas of Criminal Justice & Public administration. His research interests include public administration and criminal justice command leadership, traffic safety and impaired driving, and United States Constitutional law and history. He most recently served as lead author and principal investigator on a 2016 *Springer Briefs in Policing* article titled "Command Transitions in Public Administration: A Quantitative and Qualitative Analysis of Proactive Strategies" (Brown, Philo, Callisto, & Smith, 2016).

Dr. Brown is a member of the Academy of Criminal Justice Sciences and the Northeastern Association of Criminal Justice Sciences, as well as a Fellow with the Criminal Justice Educators Association of New York State. Dr. Brown is also a member of the American Society of Public Administration. He also serves as an active member of the International Association of Chiefs of Police (IACP), and the New York State Association of Chiefs of Police (NYSACOP). He is also a proud associate member of the United States Marine Corps League. Dr. Brown resides in New Hartford, New York with his wife and three children.

Raymond L. Philo

Raymond L. Philo is a Professor of Practice in Criminal Justice at Utica College and is the Executive Director of the Economic Crime and Cybersecurity Institute. He also served as Director of Research for the Department of Economic Crime, Justice Studies and Cybersecurity at Utica College. Professor Philo has served as a faculty member at Utica College since 2001, teaching both at the undergraduate and graduate levels. Prior to joining Utica College, he served as a law enforcement administrator, retiring as Chief of Police for the New Hartford, N.Y. Police

© Larry Pacilio, Utica College, reprinted with permission

Department. Professor Philo received his bachelor's degree in Political Science from Utica College, and his master's degree in Public Administration from Marist College.

He holds numerous state and federal certifications in law enforcement operations and management. Philo is currently a licensed consultant with the New York State Division of Criminal Justice Services and is a member of The Association of Certified Fraud Examiners, The International Association of Chiefs of Police and the New York State Association of Chiefs of Police. Professor Philo also serves as a member of the Supervisory Committee at First Source Federal Credit Union, and serves on the Board of Directors at the Griffiss Institute.

Professor Philo has taught courses in Criminal Evidence, Modern Methods of Criminal Investigation, Criminalistics, Senior Seminar, Counterterrorism and Homeland Security, and Introduction to Intelligence Studies. He has also taught the Graduate Capstone Course in the Financial Crime & Compliance Management Program, and Ethical Leadership and Public Budgeting in the Criminal Justice Administration Graduate Program. He most recently served as an author and investigator on a 2016 *Springer Briefs in Policing* article titled "Command Transitions in Public Administration: A Quantitative and Qualitative Analysis of Proactive Strategies" (Brown, Philo, Callisto, & Smith, 2016).

Dedication

For my Wife, Susan, and my Children, Kaitland, Walker, and Zoe.

~ James C. Brown

Dedicated to the memory of Officer Joseph D. Corr and in salute to the dedicated law enforcement officers and prosecutors who pass through these pages.

~ Raymond L. Philo

Acknowledgement(s)

1. Kathleen Aiello, Chief Clerk III, Oneida County Combined Courts, Utica, NY

2. The Honorable Michael A. Arcuri, Esq., Member of Congress (ret.), Utica, NY

3. President Laura M. Casamento, Utica College, Utica, NY

4. The Family of Officer Joseph D. Corr, New Hartford, NY

5. John Duncan, Esq, (ret.), Executive Assistant United States Attorney, Office of the United States Attorney for the Northern District of New York, Syracuse, NY

6. Nancy L. Ford, Nancy L. Ford Photography, Utica, NY

7. Fraternal Composite Service, Inc., Utica, NY

8. Keith Henry, Utica College, Utica, NY

9. Jodi L. Hibbard, RPR, CRR, CSR, Official Court Reporter, United States District Court, Northern District of New York

10. Keith Hunt, WKTV Television, Utica, NY

11. President Todd S. Hutton, President Emeritus, Utica College, Utica, NY

12. The Honorable Robert M. Maciol, Oneida County Sheriff (2010-present)

13. Steve McMurray, General Manager, WKTV Television, Utica, NY

14. The Honorable Scott D. McNamara, Oneida County District Attorney, Utica, NY

15. Richard Miller, Rome Sentinel, Rome, NY

16. Members of the New Hartford Fire Department, New Hartford, NY

17. Members of the New Hartford Police Department, New Hartford, NY

18. Investigator Richard Salamone, (ret.), New Hartford Police Department, New Hartford, NY

19. Chief Gregory Pflieger, Oneida County Sheriff's Office, Oriskany, NY

20. Investigator Michael Simmons, Oneida County Sheriff's Office, Oriskany, NY

21. Richard R. Southwick, Esq., Assistant United States Attorney, Office of the United States Attorney for the Northern District of New York, Syracuse, NY

22. Undersheriff Robert S. Swenszkowski, Oneida County Sheriff's Office, Oriskany, New York

23. Utica College, Utica, NY

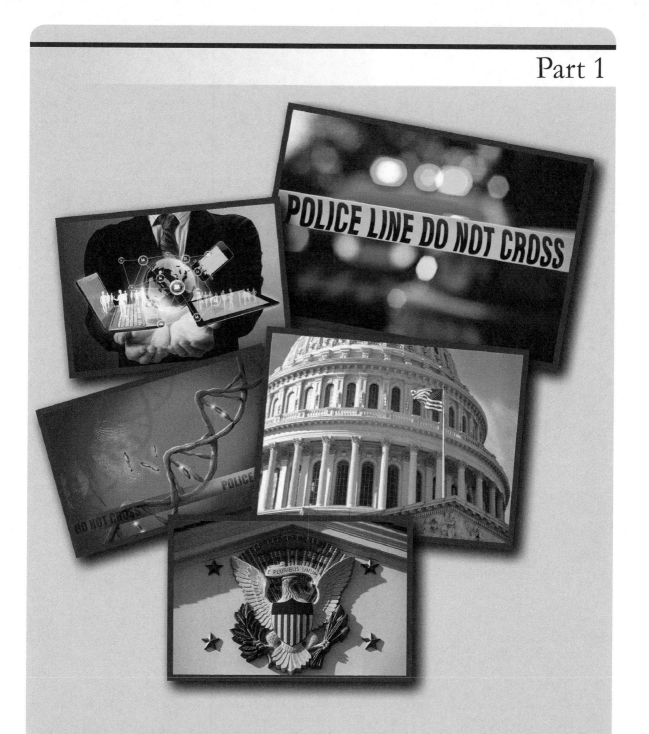

Part 1

The Public Administration of Justice in America

Chapter 1

Our American Government and Public Administration

~James C. Brown

Outline

Keywords

1. Felony hearing

   (preliminary hearing)

2. Jurisdiction

3. Stare decisis

People

1. Oliver Wendel Holmes, Jr.

2. Honorable Norman A. Mordue

Expected Learning Outcomes

After reading this chapter and supplemental online materials, the reader will be able to:

1. Explain the foundations of our three branches of government in the United States.

2. Explain the importance and role of our three branches of government in our American Government, the Criminal Justice System and The Corr Case.

3. Articulate the differences, similarities, and critical relationships between our three branches of government at the local, county, state, and federal levels of government.

1 – 1 – The Premise and the Preamble

1 – 2 – The Corr Structure of Our Government and the Founders

1 – 3 – Corr Legislation – Our Legislative Branch of Government

1 – 4 –Corr Enforcement and Prosecution – Our Executive Branch of Government

1 – 5 – Corr Judiciary – Our Judicial Branch of Government

1 – 1 – The Premise and the Preamble

© Shutterstock.com

READ

See the full official text of the United States Constitution in the back matter of this text, or at our online companion site.

At this early stage of reading one might ask themselves what an enhanced case study surrounding the robbery of a jewelry store, murder of a police officer, and kidnapping of a tow truck operator in a small upstate New York town has anything to do with broad philosophical concepts such as the Founding Fathers, the **United States Constitution**, and public administration. The answer is quite rudimentary; everything. At first glance one could see the murder of Officer Joseph Corr as any other homicide; an initial robbery that lead to a murder that lead to a kidnapping that lead to an investigation, arrests, arraignments, trials, convictions and eventually appeals. The aforementioned approach, however, is overly simplistic on its face, yet much deeper upon careful reflection and analysis. Those in the public service, in public administration, and in particular in the criminal justice profession are guided by their training, both at the outset of their careers and through continual in-service training experiences. Only by learning in a disciplined manner from the actions of others can the criminal justice profession continue to become more refined and grow to the benefit of those few who serve in this noble profession. Those in public service are ultimately guided by the law, which emanates in the United States from our Constitution. Only through the collective actions and reactions by our colleagues can we truly continue to refine our guiding principles, much in the same way in which our United States Constitution continues to evolve over time since first being crafted in 1787.

In 1880, more than two decades before sitting on the United States Supreme Court, and after his service to the Union during the Civil War, **Justice Oliver Wendell Holmes, Jr.** remarked during one of a series of 12 lectures at the Lowell Institute in Boston, Massachusetts,

> *The life of the law has not been logic; it has been experience. The felt necessities of the time, the prevalent moral and political theories, intuitions of public policy, avowed or unconscious, even the prejudices which judges*

share with their fellow men, have had a good deal more to do than the syllogism in determining the rules by which men should be governed. The law embodies the story of a nation's development through many centuries, and it cannot be dealt with as if it contained only the axioms and corollaries of a book of mathematics. (Holmes & White, 2009)

Therefore, it is our experiences that help to form our future actions. The tragedy, in too many cases involving a law enforcement officer who is murdered in the line of duty, is that the collective experiences of those involved in the case too often fade over time, left to the memories of those who will one day pass and with them leave their collective experiences undocumented and unavailable for future generations. America's Founding Fathers left future generations a living, breathing, evolving document in our Constitution and companion writings that firmly establish a framework for order, in the form of our Union, justice, through the establishment of the rule of law, and the general welfare. The Preamble to our United States Constitution reads:

We the People of the United States, in Order to form a more perfect Union, establish Justice, insure domestic Tranquility, provide for the common defence, promote the general Welfare, and secure the Blessings of Liberty to ourselves and our Posterity, do ordain and establish this Constitution for the United States of America. (U.S. Const. Preamble)

The premise of this work, much like the Preamble to our United States Constitution, establishes the overarching context, structure and purpose of each historical document; this work on the murder of Officer Joseph D. Corr, and the United States Constitution. No matter how chaotic an event may at first appear, the presence of a guiding foundational document and/or resource is essential to a more successful event outcome. Absent structure and order, there is chaos and anarchy.

Since the document's original signing on September 17, 1787 as the Constitutional Convention closed at Independence Hall in Philadelphia, Pennsylvania, and the subsequent ratification by the states, our United States Constitution continues to serve as the foundation of our uniquely American system

© Shutterstock.com

of government and public administration. Now more than 10 years since Officer Corr's murder on February 27, 2006, a firm understanding of our Constitutional form of government at all levels is essential to better understanding how the Corr case evolved and to preserving the many important lessons for future generations to follow. Without an understanding of the history of the United States of America through the lens of such archived and codified works and experiences including the drafting and execution of the Declaration of Independence in 1776, the Constitutional Convention in 1787, and the many thoughts of the founders of our Nation in *The Federalist Papers*, authored in 1787 by James Madison, Alexander Hamilton, and John Jay, collectively known by their pen name of Publius, our United States Constitution would stand only as a collection of words without the proper historical context. Likewise, without the proper archiving, codification and context of the Corr case, Officer Corr's memory and all of the critical lessons and interrelationships that resulted from the case would fade like print on a page left in the sunlight; hence this work and the need for the meticulous review and connection between the Corr case and the fundamental aspects and interrelationships of our three branches of government as so eloquently articulated in our United States Constitution. This next section discusses in detail the Corr structures of our government at all levels through the lens of history, and the Corr case.

1 – 2 – The Corr Structure of Our Government and the Founders

The Federalist Papers (also known as *The Federalist*) were series of 85 letters/essays written by James Madison, Alexander Hamilton, and John Jay starting on October 27, 1787 and published in various New York papers/periodicals (Kramnick, 1987). The 85 letters were penned with the purpose of persuading New Yorkers to ratify the United States Constitution drafted during the summer of 1787. Cornell University political scientist Clinton Lawrence Rossiter III observed of *The Federalist*, that it was

> *The most important work in political science that has ever been written, or has likely ever to be written, in the United States. It is, indeed…*
>
> *The one product of the American mind that is rightly counted among the classics of political theory.*
>
> *(Kramnick, 1987, p. 11)*

Federalist No. 10: "The Same Subject Continued: The Union as a Safeguard Against Domestic Faction and Insurrection." [Publius] James Madison. New York Packet, November 23, 1787

The Federalist Papers are arguably one of, if not the most comprehensive assessment of what was in the minds of the Framers of our United States Constitution as the document was being developed. At the heart of the Corr case are the fundamental relationships first envisioned by our Founding Fathers, articulated through the passionate prose of Madison, Hamilton, and Jay, and finally codified in the United States Constitution, the Bill of Rights, and related amendments throughout history. These relationships, through the establishment of our three branches of government, and the relationships between local and state governments, and our national government form the framework for the entire Corr case, as well as our American criminal justice system. A case that started with a local robbery, kidnapping, and murder, benefited from the historically tightly woven interrelationships between the branches of government and the various levels of government; each acting independently as they were designed, as well as harmoniously as one unit toward the goal of justice for Officer Corr and the victims of this senseless tragedy. Publius (Hamilton) in *Federalist XVII* (17) perhaps most eloquently captured the relationship(s) and differences between local/state government and our federal government when he said:

> *The superiority of influence in favor of the particular governments would*
> *result partly from the diffusive construction of the national government,*
> *but chiefly from the nature of the objects to which the attention of the State*
> *administrations would be directed. It is a known fact in human nature,*
> *that its affections are commonly weak in proportion to the distance or*
> *diffusiveness of the object. Upon the same principle that a man is more*
> *attached to his family than to his neighborhood, to his neighborhood than*
> *to the community at large, the people of each State would be apt to feel a*

stronger bias towards their local governments than towards the government

of the Union; unless the force of that principle should be destroyed by a much

better administration of the latter. This strong propensity of the human

heart would find powerful auxiliaries in the objects of State regulation.

The variety of more minute interests, which will necessarily fall under the

superintendence of the local administrations, and which will form so many

rivulets of influence, running through every part of the society, cannot be

particularized, without involving a detail too tedious and uninteresting to

compensate for the instruction it might afford. There is one [transcendent]

advantage belonging to the province of the State governments, which alone

suffices to place the matter in a clear and satisfactory light,—I mean the

ordinary administration of criminal and civil justice. This, of all others,

is the most powerful, most universal, and most attractive source of popular

obedience and attachment. It is that which, being the immediate and

visible guardian of life and property, having its benefits and its terrors

in constant activity before the public eye, regulating all those personal

interests and familiar concerns to which the sensibility of individuals is

more immediately awake, contributes, more than any other circumstance,

to impressing upon the minds of the people, affection, esteem, and reverence

towards the government. This great cement of society, which will diffuse

itself almost wholly through the channels of the particular governments,

independent of all other causes of influence, would insure them so decided

an empire over their respective citizens as to render them at all times

a complete counterpoise, and, not unfrequently, dangerous rivals to the

power of the Union. (Kramnick, 1987, p. 157)

The unique and differentiating aspect and lessons of the Corr case is the seemingly accidental, yet harmoniously perfect alignment of local, state, and federal law enforcement officers and agencies (executive branch), local, state, and federal legislation (legislative branch), and local, state, and federal judicial oversight (judicial branch). Understanding these interrelationships is the key to unlocking how the Corr case was executed and why each and every aspect of the case and the foundational underpinnings are transferable to all future related cases in our American criminal justice system.

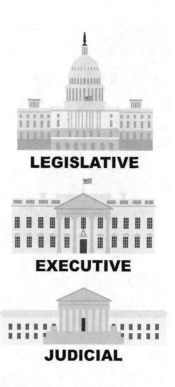

LEGISLATIVE

EXECUTIVE

JUDICIAL

© *Shutterstock.com*

1 – 3 – Corr Legislation – Our Legislative Branch of Government

With seven articles, 27 amendments, and 4,543 words, including signatures, our Founding Fathers sought fit to align the first three articles around arguably the most significant functions of government at any level; the legislative, executive, and judicial functions. While the Federal government tends to garner the most attention when there is discussion surrounding our three branches of government, critical to this conversation is understanding that our three branches of government exist at all levels of government, from local towns and villages to counties, states, and our federal system. While the essential functions of each of the branches are identical at all levels of government, the interrelationships between local, county, state, and federal branches of government are often times at odds. Therefore, a fundamental understanding of these functions is critical to understanding how the Corr case initially evolved, and continues to live on

Chambers of the New York State Assembly

Oneida County

more than a decade after Officer Corr's murder.

Article I, §1 of the Constitution of the United States of America reads, "All legislative Powers herein granted shall be vested in a Congress of the United States, which shall consist of a Senate and House of Representatives" (U.S. Const. art. I, § 1). At the federal level, the legislative function is represented by the United States Congress; made up of the House of Representatives, and Senate. There are 435 members of the House of Representatives, and 100 Senators, to Senators representing each state. The federal government was responsible for the passage of the Hobbs Act legislation, critical to the ultimate prosecution of the Corr case, and discussed in later parts of this work. At the state level in New York State, the legislative function is represented by the New York State Assembly, and Senate. At present, there are 150 members of the Assembly, and 63 members of the Senate. In Oneida

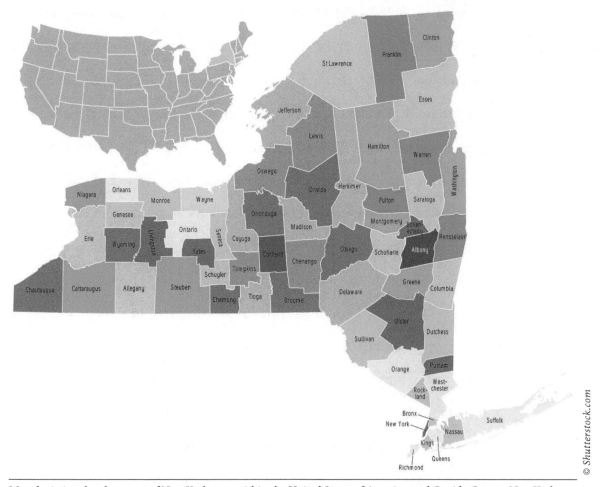

Map depicting the placement of New York state within the United States of America, and Oneida County, New York, within the state of New York.

County, New York, the county in which the murder of Officer Corr occurred, the legislative function is represented by the Oneida County Board of Legislators, consisting currently of 23 members representing the cities, towns and villages throughout Oneida County. At the micro/local level, the legislative function of the Town of New Hartford, the jurisdiction where Officer Corr was employed, and where the initial robbery occurred, is comprised of the Town Board of the Town of New Hartford and consists of four members representing wards throughout the town, and one town supervisor who serves as a quasi-fifth member of the legislative arm of the town, but who also serves as the towns chief executive.

According to the official transcript of the Oneida County Court Trial of *People v. John T. Healy* (a.k.a. Toussaint Davis, a.k.a., Toussaint Martin), the defendant (one of four accomplices) was "charged with one count of murder in the second degree, he's been charged with 12 counts of robbery in the first degree, and six counts of robbery in the second degree" (Indictment 06-113, p. 20, January 8, 2007). In the State of New York, these offenses are all pieces of legislation/laws that were passed by the New York State Assembly and Senate, and signed into law by the governor at their time of passage, thus being the law of the land throughout the State of New York.

In New York State, as the legislature drafted the Penal Law, they codified the general purpose of the law when they said:

The general purposes of the provisions of this chapter are:

1. To proscribe *conduct* which unjustifiably and inexcusably causes or threatens substantial harm to individual or public interests;

2. To give *fair warning* of the nature of the conduct proscribed and of the sentences authorized upon conviction;

3. To define the *act or omission* and the accompanying mental state which constitute each offense;

4. To differentiate on reasonable grounds between *serious and minor offenses* and to prescribe *proportionate penalties* therefor;

5. To provide for an *appropriate public response* to particular offenses, including consideration of the consequences of the offense for the victim, including the victim's family, and the community; and

6. To *insure the public safety* by preventing the commission of offenses through the *deterrent influence* of the sentences authorized, the

rehabilitation of those convicted, the promotion of their successful and productive reentry and reintegration into society, and their *confinement* when required in the interests of *public protection*. (N.Y. Penal Law, § 1.05, McKinneys, 2016 [emphasis added])

Similar purposes exist in the creation of any section of the law and typically appear at the front end of a volume of statutes. The legislature, representing the people of a particular jurisdiction, codify what is most relevant at the time that laws are enacted and/or amended. Frequently when courts are required to rule on a particular statute or interpret some other section of the law or a Constitution, courts will often times referred to legislative intent when rendering their decisions; what was in the mind of the legislators/legislature at the time a particular law was passed. When Constitutions are under consideration, courts will often look to historical documentation and ask themselves what was in the mind of the framers of a particular document when it was created at the time. For example, not only will courts look at their prior decisions when rendering opinions (**stare decisis**), but they will also look to documents such as *The Federalist Papers*, and other documents of the time to better understand the original intent of the legislature when a particular law was passed. This process is

Stare decisis: Latin, "to standby things decided." The doctrine of precedent, under which a court must follow earlier judicial decisions when the same points arise again in litigation (Garner, 2014; Black's Law Dictionary 10th ed., reprinted with permission, Thomson Reuters).

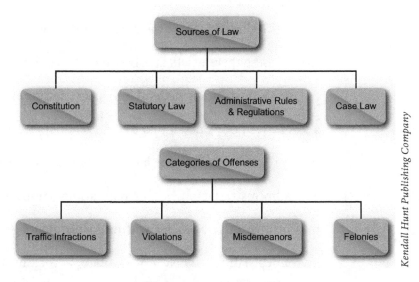

Kendall Hunt Publishing Company

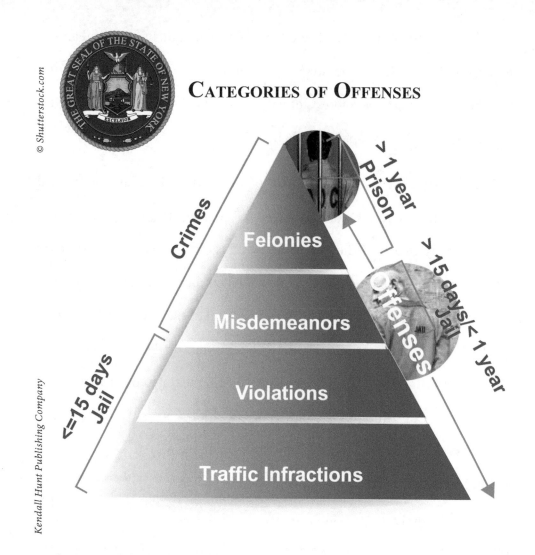

CATEGORIES OF OFFENSES

© Shutterstock.com

Kendall Hunt Publishing Company

another part of the built-in checks and balances in our American Constitutional system of government.

In the United States of America, and in other civilized countries around the world where there exists a stable rule of law, there are traditionally four sources of law; a Constitution (federal and state), statutory law (initially promulgated by a legislative body and signed by an executive; federal, state, and local), case law (interpretations of current laws by courts, sometimes called judge made law), and administrative rules and regulations (rules and regulations promulgated by administrative agencies within governments generally given their authority by the legislature). In New York State, according to the Penal Law, categories of offenses include traffic infractions, violations, misdemeanors, and felonies. Only misdemeanors and felonies, however, are crimes (N.Y. Penal Law § 10, McKinneys, 2016). Within each offense, various elements of those offenses must be carefully reviewed and proven by prosecutors to enable them to obtain a conviction for a particular offense. Whether the offense is a violation of the vehicle and traffic law, or murder, understanding the various elements of offenses is critical to developing a successful case against any individual charged with an offense. In addition to legislatures acting at a state-level, federal legislation often times can result in dual-jurisdiction resulting in dual-prosecutions.

At the federal level, three of the four surviving defendants involved in the initial robbery at Lennon's W.B. Wilcox Jewelers, resulting in the murder of Officer Corr were also tried through violations of federal law at the United States District Court for the Northern District of New York, located in Syracuse, New York. According to the Memorandum-Decision and Order of the **Honorable Norman A. Mordue**, Senior U.S. District Judge,

> *On November 5, 2010, a jury convicted petitioner Marion Pegese ("Pegese") and codefendants Robert Ward and Toussaint Davis on all counts of a three-count indictment charging conspiracy to interfere with interstate commerce by robbery, in violation of the Hobbs*

PEOPLE: The Honorable Norman A. Mordue

was born in Elmira, NY in 1942. As a Syracuse University Economics student, he was part of the ROTC program and commissioned as a Second Lieutenant upon graduation. After completing Basic Training, the new First Lieutenant heroically led his platoon during the Vietnam War. He was awarded the Distinguished Service Cross after his selfless efforts to relieve another platoon that had come under heavy artillery fire. Armed with a machine gun, First Lieutenant Mordue rescued two of his men who had been injured from enemy fire. Though he was severely injured after the incident, he refused to accept medical help until his men could withdraw and they could order artillery strikes on enemy positions. Following his distinguished military service, Norman returned to Syracuse University in 1971 to earn a degree in law. After graduating with his J.D., he served as the district attorney for Onondaga County. He eventually worked his way up to the bench, serving as the State Supreme Court justice in the county from 1986 until 1998. Nominated by President Bill Clinton and confirmed in only sixteen days, he was appointed to the Northern District of New York, serving [as] the chief judge of the court until 2011 when he became the Senior Judge on the bench. (Adapted from Syracuse University Institute for Veterans and Military Families, 2016; reprinted with permission)

Act, 18 U.S.C. § 1951(a); interference with interstate commerce by robbery, in violation of 18 U.S.C. §§ 1951(a) and 2; and murder as a result of possession and discharge of a firearm in furtherance of a crime of violence, in violation of 18 U.S.C. § 924(c)(1) and (j)(1), and pursuant to Pinkerton v. United States, *328 U.S. 640 (1946). The Court sentenced each defendant to concurrent terms of 240 months' imprisonment on the two robbery counts and life imprisonment on the murder count. The Second Circuit affirmed the conviction and sentence,* United States v. Ward (Pegese), *505 F.App'x 18 (2d Cir. 2012), and the Supreme Court denied certiorari.* Pegese v. United States, *133 S.Ct. 1512 (2013). (*Pegese v. United States of America, *U.S. Dist. Ct. Case 5:09-cr-00390-NAM, Document 278, November 30, 2015, p. 1–2)*

Whether at the federal, state, or local level of government, the legislative branch in our American Constitutional system of government remains the closest branch of government to the people of the country. Article I powers granted to the legislature through the United States Constitution and mirrored by state Constitutions have appropriately permeated the American landscape of public administration first envisioned by our Founding Fathers in 1787.

1 – 4 – Corr Enforcement and Prosecution – Our Executive Branch of Government

The laws promulgated by legitimate legislatures serve no purpose if some enforcement mechanism does not exist to back up the words articulated by representatives of the people through the legislature. In the creation of our American Constitution, the Founding Fathers were very careful and deliberate to clearly articulate the three branches of government in the context of ensuring that no one branch would be more powerful than the other. From the Declaration of Independence forward, the founders appropriately feared ever creating an all-powerful executive such that existed with the kings of our British past; hence the creation of our balanced three branches of government. Article II, §1 of the Constitution of the United States of America reads, "The executive Power shall be vested in a President of the United States of America" (U.S. Const. art. II, § 1). In *Federalist LXIX* (69), Publius (Hamilton) articulated a powerful comparison and contrast of the American presidency/executive versus the old British rule/monarchy when he noted:

> *The President of the United States would be an officer elected by the people for four years; the king of Great Britain is a perpetual and hereditary prince. The one would be amenable to personal punishment and disgrace; the person of the other is sacred and inviolable. The one would have a qualified negative upon the acts of the legislative body; the other has an absolute negative. The one would have a right to command the military and naval forces of the nation; the other, in addition to this right, possesses that of declaring war, and of raising and regulating fleets and armies by his own authority. The one would have a concurrent power with a branch of the legislature in the formation of treaties; the other is the sole possessor of the power of making treaties. The one would have a like concurrent authority in appointing to offices; the other is the sole author of all appointments. The one can confer no privileges whatever; the other can make denizens of aliens, noblemen of commoners; can erect corporations with all the rights incident to corporate bodies. The one can prescribe no rules concerning the commerce or currency of the nation;*

the other is in several respects the arbiter of commerce, and in this capacity

can establish markets and fairs, can regulate weights and measures, can lay

embargoes for a limited time, can coin money, can authorize or prohibit the

circulation of foreign coin. The one has no particle of spiritual jurisdiction;

the other is the supreme head and governor of the national church! What

answer shall we give to those who would persuade us that things so unlike

resemble each other? The same that ought to be given to those who tell us that

a government, the whole power of which would be in the hands of the elective

and periodical servants of the people, is an aristocracy, a monarchy, and a

despotism. (Kramnick, 1987, p. 401–402)

At the local, state, and federal level of government, Article II powers are granted to duly elected and appointed executives with such titles as president, governor, mayor, county executive, administrator, or supervisor. These individuals and their duly appointed executive subordinates are charged with the enforcement authority of the law. In the Corr case, dozens of executive level enforcement agencies collaborated to navigate this complex multi-state, multi-jurisdictional investigation and prosecution. Some of these agencies included local, county, state, and federal law enforcement agencies as well as county/state and federal prosecutors. In addition to formal executive/enforcement agencies involved in the case, numerous other non-governmental organizations (NGO) supported the efforts as well. The magnitude and scale of the Corr investigation demanded the collaboration of many public and private sector agencies and organizations, relationships that can sometimes hinder an investigation or prosecution if not carefully executed. Later sections of this work further articulate the importance and success of task force policing and related strategies to yield successful investigations and prosecutions of these types of cases.

1 – 5 – Corr Judiciary – Our Judicial Branch of Government

In no area of the Corr case was the importance of understanding our three branches of government and the relationships between the branches more evident than in the activities that took place through the judiciary (prosecution and appeals). Article III, §1 of the Constitution of the United States of America reads in part,

> *The judicial Power of the United States, shall be vested in one supreme Court, and in such inferior Courts as the Congress may from time to time ordain and establish. The Judges, both of the supreme and inferior Courts, shall hold their Offices during good Behaviour, and shall, at stated Times, receive for their Services, a Compensation, which shall not be diminished during their Continuance in Office. (U.S. Const. art. III, § 1)*

The Corr case seemingly started at first glance with a robbery and related offenses that occurred in the jurisdiction of the Town of New Hartford, New York. Four men participated in the robbery of Lennon's W.B. Wilcox Jewelers; in violation of the New York State Penal Law, § 160.15 et. al. From the scene of the robbery, a police chase ensued that traveled through multiple jurisdictions, ending with a vehicle crash and foot chase by law enforcement officers in the Town of Kirkland, New York. The foot chase resulted in the murder of Officer Corr by Walter Richardson in the Town of Kirkland, located in Oneida County, New York, a felony offense under the New York State Penal Law in violation of § 125.25. After murdering Officer Corr, Walter Richardson car jacked/kidnapped a tow truck operator at Kirkland Auto, nearby the murder scene, and began a several hour trip from Oneida County, New York, through many jurisdictions back to the State of Pennsylvania.

Read the full transcript of the felony hearing in New Hartford Town Court (*People of the State of New York v John T. Healy*, March 6, 2006) in our online companion.

Read the full Oneida County Grand Jury Indictment (*People of the State of New York v. John T. Healy*) in the Appendix of this work.

At the time of the murder, only one individual, Toussaint Davis, (a.k.a. John T. Healy et al), was caught by local law enforcement officers at the scene of the murder. Walter Richardson, who was also in the vehicle with Davis, fled to Pennsylvania and was subsequently killed by law enforcement officers after an exchange of gunfire. The remaining two defendants involved in the case, Robert Ward (a.k.a. "RB"), Marion Pegese (a.k.a. "Dump," "Bill," "Amin"), were captured at a later time in the investigation (*U.S. v. Ward*, 505 Fed.Appx. 18 (2012)). For defendant Toussaint Davis, an initial **felony hearing (preliminary hearing)** took place at the local criminal court in the Town of New Hartford. Thereafter, the case was transferred to Oneida County Court for trial, whereupon Davis was convicted of all of the original 19 counts in his indictment, including murder and robbery.

However, while the State of New York, through the Oneida County District Attorney's Office had chosen to initially prosecute Davis (and Ward and Pegese) under New York State law, additional work was well underway to prosecute Davis, Ward, and Pegese under a variety of federal laws that were far more reaching than those in New York State. While typically an act is prosecuted within the sole geographical **jurisdiction** of where the offense(s) occurred, the expansiveness of the crimes and associated actions of Davis, Pegese, Ward, and Richardson necessitated the expansion of jurisdiction and related resources of the United States Attorney for the Northern District of New York, and those related

Felony hearing (preliminary hearing): a criminal hearing (often conducted by a magistrate) to determine whether there is sufficient evidence to prosecute an accused person; specif., A proceeding before a judge or magistrate held soon after a criminal defendant is taken into custody, usu. on felony charges, the typical prosecution having the burden to establish reasonable cause to believe that the defendant has committed a felony. If sufficient evidence exists, the case will be set for trial or bound over for grand jury review, or information will be filed in the trial court. Also termed preliminary examination; probable cause hearing; bind overhearing; examining trial; felony hearing (Garner, 2014; Black's Law Dictionary 10th ed., reprinted with permission, Thomson Reuters).

Jurisdiction: 1. a government's general power to exercise authority over all persons and things within its territory; esp., a state's power to create interests that will be recognized under common law principles as valid in other states. 2. A court's power to decide a case or issue a decree (Garner, 2014; Black's Law Dictionary 10th ed., reprinted with permission, Thomson Reuters).

local, state, and federal resources contained within the United States Court of Appeals for the Second Circuit.

Questions for Review and Further Discussion

1. Identify and explain the three branches of our government in the United States of America.

2. Where does each branch of government derive their power from?

3. Discuss the three branches of government where you live from the perspective of your local, county, and state branches. Who represents each branch at each level?

4. Explain how someone can be prosecuted for violations of state law, and federal law.

5. What do you think prompted local prosecutors to engage the assistance of the federal government in the Corr case? Explain your thought process.

Chapter 2

The Corr of the American Criminal Justice System

~James C. Brown

Outline

Keywords

24. Subpoena

25. Uniform Crime Report (UCR)

26. United States Court of Appeals

27. United States District Court

28. United States Sentencing Commission

29. United States Supreme Court

People

1. The Honorable Michael L. Dwyer

2. The Honorable Norman A. Mordue

3. Chief Raymond L. Philo (ret.)

Expected Learning Outcomes

After reading this chapter and supplemental online materials, the reader will be able to:

1. Articulate the seven (7) Corr foundations of our American Criminal Justice System.

2. Explain the relationship between criminal justice and public administration.

3. Through the Corr case, articulate the seven (7) Corr foundations of our American Criminal Justice System and the critical interrelationships between each of the foundations.

   2 – 1 – The Corr Foundations of the American Criminal Justice System

   2 – 2 – United States Constitution

   2 – 3 – Jurisdiction

   2 – 4 – Categories of Offenses

   2 – 5 – Elements of Offenses

   2 – 6 – Plea Bargaining

2 – 1 – The Corr Foundations of the American Criminal Justice System

Contemporary scholars have historically viewed and portrayed the American Criminal Justice System as being comprised of three major components: police, courts, and corrections, and all of the sub-related practical, historical, and theoretical underpinnings of each of these areas (Fuller, 2014; Peak, 2017; Schmalleger, 2015). Noted criminal justice scholar Frank Schmalleger sees the criminal justice system as "the aggregate of all operating and administrative or technical support agencies that perform criminal justice functions. The basic divisions of the operational aspects of criminal justice are law enforcement, courts, and corrections" (Schmalleger, 2015). While we would concur with Schmalleger's assessment of the criminal justice system, we suggest, however, that criminal justice is a subcomponent of public administration, the broader parent umbrella, and thus entails a more fundamental approach to viewing American Criminal Justice. By broadening the view of the American Criminal Justice System to incorporate the foundational elements of public administration, criminal justice remains grounded in those foundational elements necessary to maintain both public order, and the public welfare. Raadschelders (1999, p. 288) contends that the:

> *The intrinsic function of public administration is the governance of society. Public administration exists to realize the governance of society.*

CRIMINAL JUSTICE SYSTEM OVERVIEW

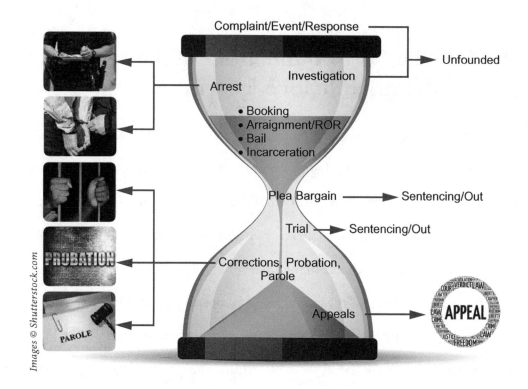

Images © Shutterstock.com

The purpose of public administration is to govern, and thus government and governance are the core concepts that help us to organize the study of Public Administration. Governments exist because they have the resources to translate the citizens' needs into collective action. Whatever era or area, citizens had some kind of government. A government will continue to exist for an undetermined period of time only if it is able to meet the most basic expectations of its population.

© Shutterstock.com

Understanding the criminal justice system through the lens of the Corr case allows the reader to better conceptualize both the system, and the key elements/takeaways of the case.

The shortcomings of some of the current literature in the field are that they attempt to provide fine details about so many diverse aspects of the system that they neglect to provide the reader with a proper foundation to better understand these diverse aspects and elements of the system. In other words, too much information without a proper foundation is merely undigested and un-discernible information. To better conceptualize and adequately navigate both a major case, as well as the American Criminal Justice System, one needs to clearly understand seven key elements that frame the entire system and serve as the foundational knowledge of all aspects of the system:

Corr Foundations of our American Criminal Justice System

1. United States Constitution and our three branches of government

2. Jurisdiction

3. Categories of Offenses

4. Elements of Offenses

5. Plea Bargaining

6. Sentencing

7. Appeals

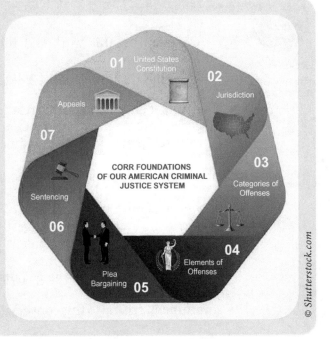

It is a broad solid understanding of these seven Corr foundations of our American Criminal Justice System that provides the reader—whether a student at a high school or college, a police or corrections recruit, law student, or current practicing law enforcement officer/investigator, attorney, public administrator, or community member seeking a better understanding of our American Criminal Justice System—with the knowledge, skills, and abilities to navigate these complex waters. While Chapter 1 of this work provided a cursory overview of these Corr foundations, this chapter provides additional detail. The discussion herein juxtaposes between the facts of the Corr case, along with the underpinnings of each of the seven foundational items. In this way, the reader can follow the logical nexus between theory and practice and develop or further refine their understanding of each of these foundational topics.

2 – 2 – United States Constitution

Read the full transcript of the United States Constitution in the Appendix of this work, and in our online companion.

Chapter 1 of this work laid the initial foundation for understanding our United States Constitution, and most importantly our three branches of government and their specific relationships to the Corr case. As we have eluded to, with seven articles, 27 amendments, and 4,543 words, including signatures, our Founding Fathers sought fit to align the first three articles around arguably the most significant functions of government at any level: the legislative, executive, and judicial functions. While the Federal government tends to garner the most attention when there is discussion surrounding our three branches of government, critical to this conversation is understanding that our three branches of government exist at all levels of government, from local towns and villages to counties, states, and our federal system. While the essential functions of each of the branches are identical at all levels of government, the interrelationships between local, county, state, and federal branches of government are often times at odds. Therefore, a fundamental understanding of these functions is critical to understanding how the Corr case initially evolved, and continues to live on more than a decade after Officer Corr's murder.

While not always at the forefront of the daily activities of an officer working patrol, an investigator analyzing a case, an attorney prosecuting or defending a case, a corrections officer working in the blocks/pods or transporting an inmate, or even the judge handling seemingly mundane cases, our United States Constitution permeates all of those activities. In the Corr case, multiple aspects of the Constitution were on display, from the initial crime, through the appeals more than 10 years after the murder of Officer Corr. Students and practitioners anywhere in the public administration space must have a fundamental understanding of the history, structure/design, and operational aspects of our United States Constitution. This fundamental understanding provides members of the public administration and criminal justice communities with the critical thinking skills necessary to approach simple and complex fact patterns that are presented on a daily basis. These range from seemingly minor vehicle and traffic violations, the regular checking of an inmate, the filing and service of legal process, all the way up to cases as complex as the murder of Officer Corr. Here are some examples of how the United States Constitution comes to life in the Corr case:

1. **Article I – Legislative Branch** The legislative branch is responsible for making the laws. The legislative branch of government in New York State, representing the people of the State of New York, historically determined that the acts of robbery and murder were both codified in the Laws of New York, along with the appropriate punishments for each offense. Likewise,

Our Three Branches of Government at all Levels

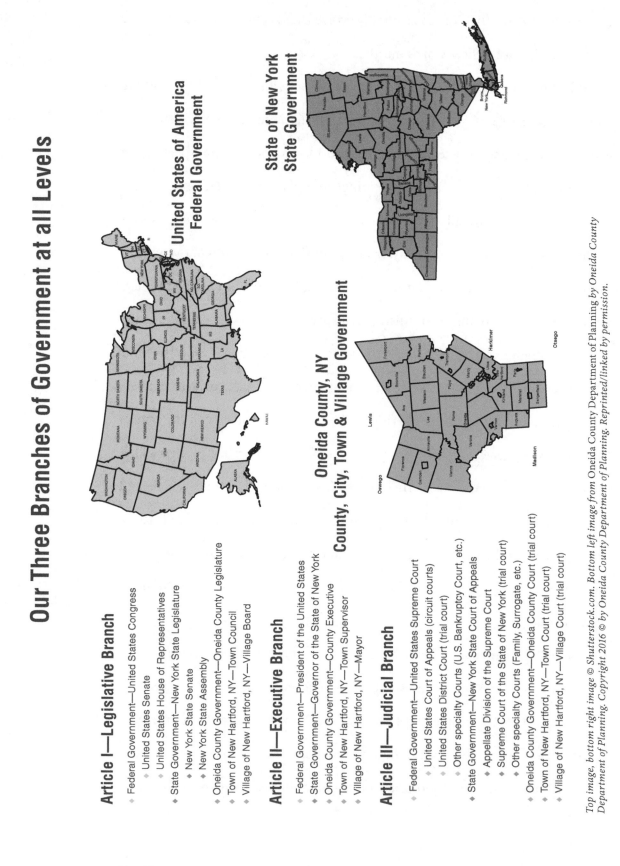

United States of America Federal Government

State of New York State Government

Oneida County, NY
County, City, Town & Village Government

Article I—Legislative Branch

- Federal Government—United States Congress
  - ◇ United States Senate
  - ◇ United States House of Representatives
- State Government—New York State Legislature
  - ◆ New York State Senate
  - ◆ New York State Assembly
- ◆ Oneida County Government—Oneida County Legislature
- ◆ Town of New Hartford, NY—Town Council
- ◆ Village of New Hartford, NY—Village Board

Article II—Executive Branch

- Federal Government—President of the United States
- State Government—Governor of the State of New York
- ◆ Oneida County Government—County Executive
- ◆ Town of New Hartford, NY—Town Supervisor
- ◆ Village of New Hartford, NY—Mayor

Article III—Judicial Branch

- Federal Government—United States Supreme Court
  - ◇ United States Court of Appeals (circuit courts)
  - ◇ United States District Court (trial court)
  - ◇ Other specialty Courts (U.S. Bankruptcy Court, etc.)
- ◆ State Government—New York State Court of Appeals
  - ◆ Appellate Division of the Supreme Court
  - ◆ Supreme Court of the State of New York (trial court)
  - ◆ Other specialty Courts (Family, Surrogate, etc.)
- ◆ Oneida County Government—Oneida County Court (trial court)
- ◆ Town of New Hartford, NY—Town Court (trial court)
- ◆ Village of New Hartford, NY—Village Court (trial court)

Top image, bottom right image © Shutterstock.com. Bottom left image from Oneida County Department of Planning by Oneida County Department of Planning. Copyright 2016 © by Oneida County Department of Planning. Reprinted/linked by permission.

the United States Congress, representing the people of the United States of America, through the passage of the **Hobbs Act** on July 3, 1946, sought to prevent the disruption of interstate commerce by means of robbery and other offenses. The Hobbs Act was a critical piece of legislation used in the Corr case by prosecutors, allowing the further engagement of federal law enforcement members in the investigation, and prosecution of the surviving three defendants.

2. **Article II – Executive Branch** The executive branch is responsible for the final approval of proposed laws from the legislature (through signature of the chief executive or veto) and the enforcement of the law. The four primary sources of law include the United States Constitution, statutory law (promulgated by the legislature), case law (interpretations from the courts), and administrative rules and regulations (promulgated by agencies authorized to enact specific rules and regulations). While dozens of local, county, state, and federal law enforcement officers responded to the initial events that took place in the Corr case on February 27, 2006, the formation of an executive branch task force consisted of a finite group of agencies that would ensure that the investigation and prosecution of the case would be continued to its logical end. These agencies included:

> **HOBBS ACT:** Title 18 of the United States Code (U.S.C) § 1951 has come to be known as The Hobbs Act. The Hobbs Act was enacted in 1946 and takes its name from the sponsor of the legislation Congressman Sam Hobbs of Alabama. The legislation was enacted in an attempt to aggressively address racketeering in labor management disputes. Among other things, the Act prohibits actual or attempted robbery or extortion affecting interstate or foreign commerce. Section 1951 also proscribes conspiracy to commit robbery or extortion without reference to the conspiracy statute at 18 U.S.C. § 371. Although the Hobbs Act was enacted as a statute to combat racketeering in labor-management disputes, the statute is frequently used in connection with cases involving public corruption, commercial disputes, and corruption directed at members of labor unions (United States Department of Justice, 2015, § 9-131.010).

Joseph D. Corr Robbery-Homicide Task Force

1. Federal Bureau of Alcohol, Tobacco, & Firearms, Syracuse, New York

2. Federal Bureau of Investigation – Albany Field Office, Albany, New York

3. Kirkland Police Department, Clark Mills, New York

4. New Hartford Police Department, New Hartford, New York

5. New York State Police – Troop D, Oneida, New York

6. Oneida County District Attorney's Office, Utica, New York

7. Oneida County Sheriff's Office, Oriskany, New York

8. Pennsylvania State Police, Media, Pennsylvania

9. United States Attorney's Office for the Northern District of New York, Syracuse, New York

10. United States Marshals Service, Northern District of New York

11. City of Utica Police Department, Utica, New York

All laws remain dormant once they are codified until they are activated by executive branch/enforcement officials with the appropriate enforcement jurisdiction who act upon fact patterns that fit various elements and categories of offenses in the law. Like so many incidents that preceded the murder of Officer Corr, and so many incidents that tragically followed, and sadly will continue to follow, dozens of agencies/organizations and hundreds of individuals converged on the tiny Town of Kirkland in Oneida County, New York to answer the call of a fallen brother. It is the unique function and power of executive branch agencies that are solely responsible for piecing together the intricate puzzle of the case investigation, and eventual prosecution and appeals that follow such a horrific act.

12. **Article III – Judicial Branch** The judicial branch of our government, constituted under Article III of our United States Constitution, is not only charged with interpreting the laws, but is also responsible for the review and issuance of legal process that allows both government agents, and private citizens to direct certain activities. These include, but are

not limited to such items as the issuance of a **search warrant** under the Fourth Amendment of our United States Constitution, and/or a **subpoena** that can be issued in either criminal or civil proceedings. Much like the executive branch enforcement of laws, the judicial branch lies dormant until activated by some actual case or controversy that falls within their or original or appellate jurisdiction. In the Corr case, local (New Hartford, New York, Town Court), county/state (Oneida County, New York, County Court), and federal (United States District Court for the Northern District of New York and the United States Court of Appeals for the Second Circuit)

> **Search Warrant:** A judge's written order authorizing a law enforcement officer to conduct a search of a specified place and to seize evidence (Garner, 2014; Black's Law Dictionary 10th ed., reprinted with permission, Thomson Reuters).
>
> **Subpoena:** A writ or order commanding a person to appear before a court or other tribunal, subject to a penalty for failing to comply... [also] 1. To serve with a subpoena to appear before a court or other tribunal, <subpoena the material witness>. 2. To order the production of (documents or other things) by subpoena duces tecum <subpoena the corporate records> (Garner, 2014; Black's Law Dictionary 10th ed., reprinted with permission, Thomson Reuters).
>
> **Arraignment:** The initial step in a criminal prosecution whereby the defendant is brought before the court to hear the charges and to enter a plea (Garner, 2014; Black's Law Dictionary 10th ed., reprinted with permission, Thomson Reuters).

courts were all activated in some manner throughout the duration of the case from the initial arraignment of the first defendant caught on the night of the robbery-homicide, Toussaint Davis, to the latest appeal by the three surviving defendants in the fall of 2015, nearly 10 years after robbery-homicide initially occurred. In addition to the **arraignment** of defendants, multiple hearings, trials at the state and federal level, numerous subpoenas, search warrants, and other legal process were obtained through the actions of the judicial branch of government, continually moving the case through the criminal justice system.

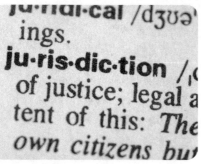

2 – 3 – Jurisdiction

Jurisdiction is

1. Government's general power to exercise authority over all persons and things within its territory; esp., a state's power to create interests that will be recognized under common law principles is valid and other states.

2. A court's power to decide a case or issue a decree.

(Garner, 2014)

Jurisdiction can also be discussed in the context of whether or not a court has **original jurisdiction** over a case, or **appellate jurisdiction** over a case. For the purposes of the Corr case, we focus on geographical jurisdiction, the legislative, executive, and judicial

Original Jurisdiction: A court's power to hear and decide a matter before any other court can review the matter (Garner, 2014; Black's Law Dictionary 10th ed., reprinted with permission, Thomson Reuters).

Appellate Jurisdiction: The power of the court to review and revise a lower court's decision. For example, U.S. Const. art. III, § 2 vests appellate jurisdiction in the Supreme Court, while 28 USCA §§ 1291-1295 grant appellate jurisdiction to lower federal courts of appeals (Garner, 2014; Black's Law Dictionary 10th ed., reprinted with permission, Thomson Reuters). [The same structures/rules apply at the state level as well].

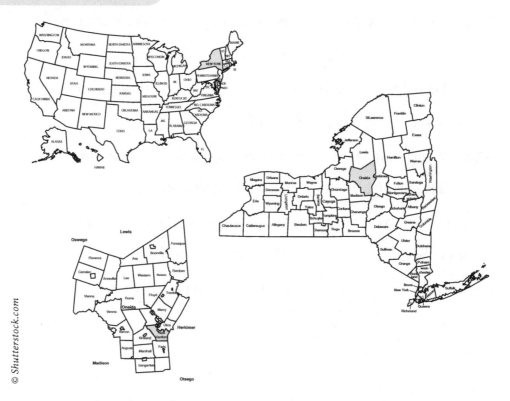

jurisdiction governed by the exercise of authority based upon the geographical boundaries of the legislative, executive, or judicial entity in question. A firm understanding of the basic concept of jurisdiction within each branch of local, county, state, and federal governments is essential to understanding both the benefit, and complexity of overlapping jurisdictions when dealing with such a complex case.

Geographical jurisdiction should be looked at as a funnel, the broadest point represented by the federal government, leading down to the smallest point in the funnel at the local government level. Laws apply only to those within the jurisdiction of the entity promulgating

> **Binding authority:** [also called binding precedent]. A precedent that a court must follow. For example, a lower court is bound by an applicable holding of a higher court in the same jurisdiction.- Also termed authoritative precedent; binding authority (Garner, 2014; Black's Law Dictionary 10th ed., reprinted with permission, Thomson Reuters).

the law. Likewise, court decisions only have **binding authority** on those individuals living within the geographical jurisdiction of the court rendering the decision. Laws passed by the United States Congress have bearing on all individuals living or traveling within the geographical boundaries of the United States of America. Laws in place in New York State only have bearing

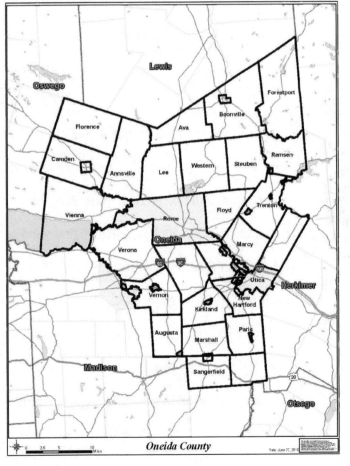

Oneida County

From Oneida County Department of Planning by Oneida County Department of Planning. Copyright 2016 © by Oneida County Department of Planning. Reprinted/linked by permission.

on those individuals within the geographical boundaries of New York State. Moving further down the funnel, laws passed by counties, cities, and towns and villages only have bearing on those individuals living within the geographical boundaries of those jurisdictions, and courts can only typically hear cases for incidents that occur within their jurisdiction.

The three surviving defendants in the Corr case committed offenses that were prohibited both by New York State law, as well as federal law, thus the involvement of county/state prosecutors (Oneida County District Attorney's Office) as well as federal prosecutors (United States Attorney's Office for the Northern District of New York). While the primary laws that were in play during the Corr case were relatively clear as having been promulgated by state (robbery-homicide; New York State Legislature) and federal legislatures (Hobbs Act; United States Congress), the enforcement and judicial aspects of the jurisdiction issue were less clear based upon how the facts of the case unfolded.

Listen to actual radio transmissions and related television news footage from the night of February 27, 2006 in our online companion.

The Corr case seemingly started at first glance with a robbery and related offenses that occurred in the jurisdiction of the Town of New Hartford, New York. Four men participated in the robbery of Lennon's W.B. Wilcox Jewelers; in violation of the New York State Penal Law, § 160.15 et. al. From the scene of the robbery, a police chase ensued that traveled through multiple jurisdictions, ending with a vehicle crash and foot chase by law enforcement officers in the Town of Kirkland, New York. The foot chase resulted in the murder of Officer Corr by Walter Richardson in the Town of Kirkland, located in Oneida County, New York, a felony offense under the New York State Penal Law in violation of § 125.25. After murdering Officer Corr, Walter Richardson car jacked/kidnapped a tow truck operator at Kirkland Auto, nearby the murder scene, and began a several hour trip from Oneida County, New York, through many jurisdictions back to the State of Pennsylvania.

At the time of the murder, only one individual, Toussaint Davis, (a.k.a. John T. Healy et al.), was caught by local law enforcement officers at the scene of the murder. Walter Richardson, who was also in the vehicle with Davis, fled to Pennsylvania and was subsequently killed by law enforcement officers after an exchange of gunfire at a home in Chester, Pennsylvania. The remaining two defendants involved in the case, Robert Ward (a.k.a. "RB"), Marion Pegese (a.k.a. "Dump," "Bill," "Amin"), were captured at a later time in the investigation (*U.S. v. Ward*, 505 Fed.Appx. 18 (2012)). At exactly 8:20:49 p.m. on the evening of February 27, 2006, New Hartford Police Officer Joseph D. Corr (Car 43) and New Hartford Police Officer Shane Yoxall were dispatched to a reported robbery in progress at Lennon's W.B. Wilcox Jewelers on Commercial Drive in the Town of New Hartford, New York. At exactly 8:28:37 p.m., just under eight minutes after the initial radio call for robbery in progress, New Hartford Police Sergeant Paul Colburn radioed an "officer down" transmission from the rear of the Byrne Dairy Convenience Store located in the Town of Kirkland, New York, the time and location where Officer Corr was mortally wounded while in foot pursuit of Walter Richardson. Richardson and Davis had fled the jewelry store in one vehicle, while the other defendants, Pegese and Ward, fled with other proceeds from the robbery in another car. During the eight minutes from the initial radio transmission of the robbery in progress to the "officer down" radio transmission, numerous law enforcement, fire, and emergency medical services personnel from multiple jurisdictions throughout the region were

Chief Raymond L. Philo (ret.), New Hartford Police Department

Credit: Nancy L. Ford Photography (reprinted with permission)

Read the full transcript of the Oneida County indictment in the Appendix of this work, and in our online companion.

Felony hearing (preliminary hearing): A criminal hearing (often conducted by a magistrate) to determine whether there is sufficient evidence to prosecute an accused person; specif., A proceeding before a judge or magistrate held soon after a criminal defendant is taken into custody, usu. on felony charges, the typical prosecution having the burden to establish reasonable cause to believe that the defendant has committed a felony. If sufficient evidence exists, the case will be set for trial or bound over for grand jury review, or information will be filed in the trial court. Also termed preliminary examination; probable cause hearing; bind overhearing; examining trial; felony hearing (Garner, 2014; Black's Law Dictionary 10th ed., reprinted with permission, Thomson Reuters).

Indictment: 1. The formal written accusation of a crime, made by a grand jury and presented to a court for prosecution against the accused person. 2. The act or process of preparing or bringing forward such a formal written accusation (Garner, 2014; Black's Law Dictionary 10th ed., reprinted with permission, Thomson Reuters).

simultaneously activated to respond to this crime in progress. In the face of having just lost one of his officers to this horrific crime, **New Hartford Police Chief Raymond L. Philo**, maintained his composure and professionalism and quickly activated the needed resources to continue the investigation and eventually form a task force operation, eventually housed at the Town of Kirkland Senior Citizen Center in Clark Mills, New York. While multiple local, county, state, and federal law enforcement and other public safety professionals were engaged in the Corr case, Chief Philo maintained the primary lead agency role, heading up the task force and all related operations through the conclusion of the investigation, and subsequent trial and appeals.

For defendant Toussaint Davis, an initial **felony hearing (preliminary hearing)** later took place at the local criminal court in the Town of New Hartford. Thereafter, the case was transferred to Oneida County Court for trial, whereupon Davis was convicted of all of the original 19 counts in his **indictment**, including murder and robbery. However, while the State of New York, through the Oneida County District Attorney's Office had chosen to initially prosecute Davis (and Ward and Pegese) under New York State law, additional work was well underway to prosecute Davis, Ward, and Pegese under a variety of federal laws that were far more reaching than those in New York

State. On July 16, 2009, a multi-count federal **grand jury** indictment was handed down against Pegese, Ward, and Davis, specifically charging "Conspiracy to Interfere with Interstate Commerce by Robbery...Interference with Interstate Commerce by Robbery...Murder as a Result of Possession and Discharge of a Firearm in Furtherance of a Crime of Violence" (*United States of America v. Marion Pegese, Robert Ward & Toussaint Davis*, Indictment, 2009).

While typically an act is prosecuted within the sole local geographical **jurisdiction** of where the offense(s) occurred, the expansiveness of the crimes and associated actions of Davis, Pegese, Ward, and Richardson necessitated the expansion of jurisdiction and related resources of the United States Attorney for the Northern District of New York, and those related local, state, and federal resources contained within the United States Court of Appeals for the Second Circuit. While often times very complex, clearly understanding legislative, executive, and judicial jurisdictional issues, can dramatically and positively change the course of such a complex investigation for all involved.

> **Grand Jury:** A body of [usually 16 to 23] people were chosen to sit permanently for at least a month-and sometimes a year-and who, in ex parte proceedings, decide whether to issue indictments. If the grand jury decides the evidence is strong enough to hold the suspect for trial, it returns the bill of indictment (*a true bill*) charging the suspect with a specific crime.-Also termed *accusing jury; presenting jury; jury of indictment* (Garner, 2014; Black's Law Dictionary 10th ed., reprinted with permission, Thomson Reuters).
>
> **Jurisdiction:** 1. A government's general power to exercise authority over all persons and things within its territory; [especially] a state's power to create interests that will be recognized under common law principles as valid and other states. 2. A court's power to decide a case or issue a decree (Garner, 2014; Black's Law Dictionary 10th ed., reprinted with permission, Thomson Reuters).

Read the full transcript of the federal indictment in the Appendix of this work, and in our online companion.

2 – 4 – Categories of Offenses

The primary sources of law in the United States include the United States Constitution, statutes, enacted by the legitimate authority of the legislature in a particular jurisdiction, case law, and administrative rules and regulations typically promulgated by executive branch agencies. The criminal laws of a jurisdiction are typically codified in volumes with different names. Some of the most common are the penal law, penal code, criminal law, or the criminal code, all volumes containing the same information, but with different names typically chosen by the various jurisdictions enacting the laws. At the federal level, many of our laws are housed within the United States Code (U.S.C). In New York State, criminal laws are primarily codified in the Penal Law of the State of New York.

Warrant: A judge's written order authorizing a law enforcement officer to conduct a search of a specified place and to seize evidence (Garner, 2014; Black's Law Dictionary 10th ed., reprinted with permission, Thomson Reuters).

Subpoena: A writ or order commanding a person to appear before a court or other tribunal, subject to a penalty for failing to comply... [also] 1. To serve with a subpoena to appear before a court or other tribunal, <subpoena the material witness>. 2. To order the production of (documents or other things) by subpoena duces tecum <subpoena the corporate records> (Garner, 2014; Black's Law Dictionary 10th ed., reprinted with permission, Thomson Reuters).

Procedural rules such as **search warrants** and **subpoenas** are codified in the Criminal Procedure Law of the State of New York. Regardless of what state or country the reader is from, it is essential to have a firm understanding of the fundamental structure and related organization of the civil and criminal laws of one's jurisdiction, how the legislature has chosen to organize the laws of their jurisdiction. In New York State, for example, there are currently 104 distinct areas of the law that are codified at the legislature. In addition to the Penal and Criminal Procedure Law of the State of New York, other such sections of the law include: Agriculture and Markets Law, Banking Law, Canal Law, Domestic Relations Law, and Vehicle and Traffic Law, to name a few. Despite the many differences in specific offenses between local, county, state, and federal laws around the United States of America, commonalities nonetheless exist in their general organization and structure not only here in the United States, but around the world in those countries with a relatively stable rule of law.

As a general rule, laws are organized/structured to inform the reader of the name of the law being reviewed, the purpose of the law, definitions applicable to the specific section of law being reviewed, the specific offenses, penalties for committing specific offenses, and the specific elements of each offense. In New York State, for example, when the Penal Law of the State of New York was originally constructed, the legislature established (and amended over time), six main purposes of the law. These include:

The general purposes of the provisions of this chapter are:

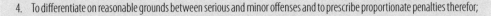

1. To *proscribe conduct* which unjustifiably and inexcusably causes or threatens substantial harm to individual or public interests;

2. To *give fair warning* of the nature of the conduct proscribed and of the *sentences authorized* upon conviction;

© *Shutterstock.com*

3. To *define the act or omission* and the *accompanying mental state* which constitute each offense;

4. To differentiate on reasonable grounds between serious and minor offenses and to prescribe proportionate penalties therefor;

5. To provide for an *appropriate public response* to particular offenses, including *consideration of the consequences of the offense for the victim,* including the victim's family, and the community; and

6. To *insure the public safety* by preventing the commission of offenses through the *deterrent influence of the sentences authorized,* the *rehabilitation of those convicted,* the promotion of their successful and productive reentry and reintegration into society, and their *confinement when required in the interests of public protection.* (N.Y. Penal Law § 10, McKinney's, 2016 [*emphasis added*])

Regardless of the jurisdiction, state legislatures generally provide a section of all of the laws that delineates the purposes of the various section of law being reviewed. For example, the State of Florida closely parallels the six core purposes of the New York State Penal Law when describing the purposes of the Florida Criminal Statutes (Fla. Stat. Ann., § 775.012, West, 2016).

Within the six core purposes of the Penal Law of the State of New York, 13 additional societal imperatives are articulated within this section of the law and each individual purpose. These form the basis of our categories of offenses. The societal imperatives articulated by the legislature include keywords/phrases including:

1. proscribing conduct

2. giving fair warning

3. sentences authorized upon conviction

4. defining acts or omissions

5. defining accompanying mental states

6. differentiating between serious and minor offenses

7. prescribing proportionate penalties

8. providing for an appropriate public response to an offense

9. taking into account the consequences of an offense upon a victim, their family, and the community

10. ensuring public safety

11. deterrent influence of sentences

12. rehabilitation of those convicted

13. confinement of the worst offenders in the interests of public protection

In addition to the aforementioned, categories of offenses then are the official labels assigned by the legislature to differentiate the seriousness of offenses and the accompanying punishments associated with the commission of those offenses when all requisite elements are met. In the Penal Law of the State of New York, an offense

> *Means conduct for which a sentence to a term of imprisonment or to a fine*
>
> *is provided by any law of this state or by any law, local law or ordinance*
>
> *of a political subdivision of this state, or by any order, rule or regulation*
>
> *of any governmental instrumentality authorized by law to adopt the same.*
>
> *(N.Y. Penal Law § 10.00, McKinney's, 2016)*

An offense is a broad, overarching description of four key categories of offenses; traffic infractions, violations, misdemeanors, and felonies. Having a clear understanding of definitions associated with any section of law being reviewed is critical as a member of the criminal justice system. In New York State, the four key categories of offenses are defined as:

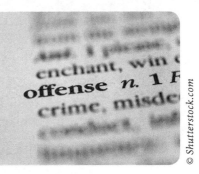

1. "Traffic infraction" means any offense defined as "traffic infraction" by section one hundred fifty-five of the vehicle and traffic law.

2. "Violation" means an offense, other than a "traffic infraction," for which a sentence to a term of imprisonment in excess of fifteen days cannot be imposed.

3. "Misdemeanor" means an offense, other than a "traffic infraction," for which a sentence to a term of imprisonment in excess of fifteen days may be imposed, but for which a sentence to a term of imprisonment in excess of one year cannot be imposed.

4. "Felony" means an offense for which a sentence to a term of imprisonment in excess of one year may be imposed. (N.Y. Penal Law § 10.00, McKinney's, 2016)

In addition, a crime in the State of New York "means a misdemeanor or a felony (N.Y. Penal Law § 10.00, McKinney's, 2016). The definitions provided in most statutes not only define what the category of offense means, but typically also defines ranges of penalties available for violations of specifically delineated offenses. Therefore, while all traffic infractions, violations, misdemeanors, and felonies are offenses, only misdemeanors and felonies in the State of New York are crimes. While seemingly minor, the proper use of language through analysis of purposes and definitions of sections of law are critical to successful navigation of any particular case or related subject matter. In the Corr case, both at the state and federal levels, felony level activity was clearly a foot. Once investigators had initially determined not only the category of offenses that were in play during the investigation, the analysis then turned to assembling the appropriate amount of evidence for prosecutors to lead a successful investigation; proving the elements of the previously identified offenses (robbery-homicide, Hobbs Act violations).

2 – 5 – Elements of Offenses

Elements of offenses are the very exacting ingredients that must be met in order for both initial investigating officers and prosecutors to successfully convict someone of a particular offense. While the elements of various offenses are concrete and generally well defined either through statutory or case law, the fact patterns surrounding various perceived offenses are often times very gray

© Shutterstock.com

and imprecise. Unlike reading a magazine or a novel, or even a short story, reading specific offenses within the law and the various elements/ingredients that comprise those offenses is an extremely precise and deliberate exercise that requires a great deal of care and the ability to draw together all of the previous discussions that we have had related to our three branches of government, the sources of law, and sound critical thinking skills. The adage *words have power* can have no greater meaning than when deciphering the necessary ingredients that go into analyzing an offense in the law, whether a minor traffic infraction, or in the case of the robbery

of Lennon's W.B. Wilcox Jewelers or the murder of Officer Corr.

From the initial dispatch information from New Hartford 911 dispatchers on the evening of February 27, 2006, officers and those listening to the radio communications knew that they were responding to what was reported as a robbery in progress. Trained law enforcement officers immediately know before arriving at the scene that if a robbery is occurring, the safe assumption to make is that certain elements may or may not be present, chief among them, someone or some group is forcibly trying to take something from someone else. Without clearly understanding the elements of an offense, the general public frequently confuses a robbery and a burglary. In New York, the typical burglary elements involve entering or remaining on *premises*, or in a *dwelling* or a *building* with an intent to commit a crime therein; the crime typically being larceny (theft of property). Clearly understanding the fact pattern and the specific Penal Law definitions of the previously italicized words are key to understanding the elements of burglary, and any other offense. This typically requires individuals researching the law to conduct extensive cross-referencing between sections of one particular statutory law book, as well as cross-referencing between statutory law and case law to fully understand the appropriate elements/ingredients that go into an offense.

In the Corr case, officers initially only knew that there was most likely some type of attempt to forcibly steal something from the jewelry store, which was occupied at the time by employees. Had the jewelry store been closed at the time, and the defendants had broken into the store and tried only to steal items within jewelry cases or in other locations, the initial offenses may have been quite different. The facts of the Corr case, however, clearly demonstrated that a robbery was in progress, and not a burglary. In the State of New York, for example,

> *Robbery is forcible stealing. A person forcibly steals property and commits robbery when, in the course of committing a larceny, he uses or threatens the immediate use of physical force upon another person for the purpose of:*
>
> 1. *Preventing or overcoming resistance to the taking of the property or to the retention thereof immediately after the taking; or*
> 2. *Compelling the owner of such property or another person to deliver up the property or to engage in other conduct which aids in the commission of the larceny. (N.Y. Penal Law § 160.00, McKinney's, 2016)*

With most offenses, increased penalties and/or the severity of an offense is often times dictated by the presence (or absence) of particular elements of the offense. Within most laws this differentiation is typically delineated through the use of increasing degrees of seriousness. Thus, in New York State, an individual can be arrested and/or convicted of Robbery in the Third Degree (Class D Felony), Robbery in the Second Degree (Class C Felony), or Robbery in the First Degree (Class B Felony), with first-degree Robbery the most serious offense carrying the most severe penalty. In the Corr case, defendant Toussaint Davis (a.k.a. John T. Healy, a.k.a. Toussaint Martin), was convicted in Oneida County, New York County Court of six counts of Robbery in the First Degree (armed with a deadly weapon), six counts of Robbery in the First Degree (causing serious physical injury to any person who is not a participant in the crime, Officer Corr), six counts of Robbery in the Second Degree (aided by another person actually present), and Murder in the Second Degree. Below we have italicized the key elements/ingredients that make up the offense of Robbery in the First Degree. The reader should also carefully note when reading the law that two of the most significant words are often times overlooked, the operative word *or*, and the operative word *and*. These two words have some of the most significant meaning when dealing with the law in general, and specifically with elements/ingredients of offenses, as they either join sections of the law, or bifurcate sections of the law.

The Elements of the Offense of Robbery in the First Degree

A person is guilty of robbery in the first degree when he *forcibly steals property* **and** when, in the course of the commission of the crime or of immediate flight therefrom, he **or** another participant in the crime:

1. *Causes serious physical injury* to any person who is not a participant in the crime; **or**

2. Is *armed with a deadly weapon*; **or**

3. *Uses* or *threatens the immediate use of a dangerous instrument*; **or**

4. *Displays* what appears to be a pistol, revolver, rifle, shotgun, machine gun or other firearm; except that in any prosecution under this subdivision, it is an affirmative defense that such pistol, revolver, rifle, shotgun, machine gun or other firearm was not a loaded weapon from which a shot, readily capable of producing death or other serious physical injury, could be discharged. Nothing contained in this subdivision shall constitute a defense to a prosecution for, or preclude a conviction of, robbery in the second degree, robbery in the third degree or any other crime.

Robbery in the first degree is a class B felony. (N.Y. Penal Law § 160.15, McKinney's, 2016 [emphasis added])

Elements of offenses are the very exacting ingredients that must be met in order for both initial investigating officers and prosecutors to successfully convict someone of a particular offense. In the Oneida County Court case

© *Shutterstock.com*

New Hartford Police Department/Oneida County Sheriff's Office

involving the first defendant captured and prosecuted in the Corr case, Toussaint Davis, the fact pattern developed by investigators allowed prosecutors to match the elements of the offenses of robbery and murder, thus allowing for a conviction of 18 counts of robbery, and one count of murder. At the federal level, the same fact pattern developed in the Lennon's W.B. Wilcox jewelry store robbery and murder of Officer Corr, along with additional information on the interstate robbery activities of Davis, Pegese, and Ward, allowing federal prosecutors to match that extended fact pattern with other activities to allow for successful federal prosecution as well (Hobb's Act Robbery-Murder).

2 – 6 – Plea Bargaining

The American system of justice, civil or criminal, is adversarial by nature: plaintiffs versus defendants, prosecutors representing the people/state/government versus defendants, and appellants versus appellees in the appeals process. At the state and local level, estimates are as high as 95% or more of all criminal convictions are garnered through plea agreements, with even higher percentages at the federal level (Ross, 2006). The terms *plea* and *bargain* are two separate and distinct words, each with multiple meanings.

Plea: 1. *Criminal law.* An accused person's formal response of "guilty," "not guilty," or "no contest" to a criminal charge – Also termed *criminal plea* (Garner, 2014; Black's Law Dictionary 10th ed., reprinted with permission, Thomson Reuters).

When combined, however, they serve as one of the most powerful tools in the American justice system, and in particular the American Criminal Justice System. In practice, **plea** bargaining is a balancing tool, utilized by prosecutors to obtain convictions for offenses and often times compel defendants to perform certain tasks without most often having to take a matter through the normal court channels of the criminal justice system. While the term *plea* takes on many meanings in the law, and is well codified

in our American jurisprudence, plea bargaining is something that is evolved over time and has developed more in case law rather than in statutory law. According to Garner (2014), a plea bargain is:

> *a negotiated agreement between a prosecutor in a criminal defendant*
>
> *whereby the defendant pleads guilty or no contest to a lesser offense or to*
>
> *one of multiple charges in exchange for some concession by the prosecutor,*
>
> *[usually] a more lenient sentence or dismissal of the other charges.*

The *New York State Criminal Procedure Law* goes on to further statutorily codify a plea and when a plea may be entered by noting in part:

The only kinds of pleas which may be entered to an indictment are those specified in this section:

1. The defendant may as a matter of right enter a plea of "not guilty" to the indictment.

2. Except as provided in subdivision five, the defendant may as a matter of right enter a plea of "guilty" to the entire indictment.

3. Except as provided in subdivision five, where the indictment charges but one crime, the defendant may, with both the permission of the court and the consent of the people, enter a plea of guilty of a lesser included offense.

4. Except as provided in subdivision five, where the indictment charges two or more offenses in separate counts, the defendant may, with both the permission of the court and the consent of the people, enter a plea of:

   a. Guilty of one or more but not all of the offenses charged; or

   b. Guilty of a lesser included offense with respect to any or all of the offenses charged; or

   c. Guilty of any combination of offenses charged and lesser offenses included within other offenses charged.

5. (a)(i) Where the indictment charges one of the class A felonies defined in article two hundred twenty of the penal law or the attempt to commit any such class A felony, then any plea of guilty entered pursuant to subdivision three or four of this section must be or must include at least a plea of guilty of a class B felony…[additional sections omitted] (N.Y. Criminal Procedure Law § 220.10, 2016)

Uniform Crime Report: The FBI's Uniform Crime Reporting (UCR) Program is a nationwide, cooperative statistical effort of nearly 18,000 city, university and college, county, state, tribal, and federal law enforcement agencies voluntarily reporting data on crimes brought to their attention. Since 1930, the FBI has administered the UCR Program and continued to assess and monitor the nature and type of crime in the nation. The program's primary objective is to generate reliable information for use in law enforcement administration, operation, and management; however, its data have over the years become one of the country's leading social indicators. Criminologists, sociologists, legislators, municipal planners, the media, and other students of criminal justice use the data for varied research and planning purposes (FBI Uniform Crime Reporting Statistics, 2016).

According to the Federal Bureau of Investigation's **Uniform Crime Report**, the longitudinal standard for criminal activity in the United States, 11,205,803 arrests (excluding traffic offenses) were made during 2014, the last full year of statistics available (FBI Uniform Crime Report 2014, 2016). It would be unrealistic, and counterproductive to the ends of the criminal justice system if each and every individual arrested had their case proceed to trial, even though that right is guaranteed by the Sixth Amendment to the United States Constitution. The system that has evolved to deal with the millions of arrests that occur annually throughout the United States was plea bargaining. In a 5–4 divided 1978 opinion (for the majority, Justice Stewart et al.; for the dissent, Justice Blackmun, Brennan, Marshall, and Powell), the United States Supreme Court affirmed in case law the long established practice of plea bargaining when they noted in part in their landmark case of *Bordenkircher v. Hayes* (1978):

> *[W]hatever might be the situation in an ideal world, the fact is that the guilty plea and the often concomitant plea bargain are important components of this country's criminal justice system. Properly administered, they can benefit all concerned.* Blackledge v. Allison, *431 U.S. 63, 71, 97 S.Ct. 1621, 1627, 52 L.Ed.2d 136. The open acknowledgment of this previously clandestine practice has led this Court to recognize the importance of counsel during plea negotiations, Brady v. United States, 397 U.S. 742, 758, 90 S.Ct. 1463, 1474, 25 L.Ed.2d 747, the need for a public record indicating that a plea was knowingly and voluntarily made,* Boykin v. Alabama, *395 U.S. 238, 242, 89 S.Ct. 1709, 1711, 23 L.Ed.2d 274, and the requirement that a prosecutor's plea bargaining promise must be kept,* Santobello v. New York, *404 U.S. 257, 262, 92 S.Ct. 495, 498, 30 L.Ed.2d 427. (*Bordenkircher v. Hayes, *(1978), 434 U.S. 357, 98 S.Ct. 663, 54 L.Ed.2d 604*

Plea bargaining not only provides prosecutors and courts with the opportunity to efficiently and expeditiously move massive volumes of cases through the criminal justice system, plea bargaining also provides prosecutors with the opportunity to inject case specific stipulations geared toward preventing future bad acts. For example, an individual arrested for domestic violence related offenses such as assault and endangering the welfare of a child—which are common domestic violence related offenses—may further traumatize/victimize the victims if the case proceeds to trial. The goal of any domestic violence related arrest and/or prosecution is to first stop the related incident from escalating, and then prevent future incidents and related offenses from occurring. Given this scenario, prosecutors and defense attorneys/defendants must perform a careful risk assessment based upon the fact pattern before them. While prosecutors may have a solid fact pattern and believe that they can meet all of the elements of the offenses charged, they nonetheless may wish to engage in plea negotiations in order to not only ensure a conviction, but to attach specific stipulations that may mitigate future occurrences of similar criminal behavior. As a part of a plea agreement, the prosecutor may offer the defense attorney/defendant an opportunity to plead guilty to a lesser offense such as harassment. In exchange for a plea of guilty to the offense of harassment, the defendant (in New York State), would be pleading guilty to a noncriminal offense (a violation), instead of the original misdemeanor offenses originally charged by law enforcement. In exchange for the plea of guilty, the prosecutor may attach certain stipulations such as:

1. the imposition of an order of protection (temporary or permanent)

2. the imposition of mandatory anger management classes

3. the imposition of mandatory alcohol and/or other substance abuse screening/counseling

4. the imposition of restitution to the victim(s) for medical and/or other tangible expenses incurred due to the original criminal offense

5. the imposition of a caveat that if the defendant re-offends that original charges may be reinstated

This is just one scenario of hundreds of permutations where plea bargaining can be utilized as an effective tool in the American Criminal Justice System. Whether the case is murder and robbery, such as the facts presented in the Corr case, domestic violence cases, or simple traffic infractions, prosecutors, courts, and defense attorneys/defendants utilize the past practice of plea bargaining as a critical and effective tool toward arriving at a just conclusion for each case presented in our justice system.

2 – 7 – Sentencing

The pronouncement of a **sentence** by a judge is the final judgment of a court having jurisdiction to hear a particular case. The terms *sentence* or *sentencing* connote a court issuing some type of term of imprisonment, whether in a local jail, or in a state or federal prison facility. While all of the 1,561,500 adult inmates in federal and state prison correctional facilities in 2014 have been sentenced by a court (Carson, 2015), and 744,600 county and city inmates held through the middle of 2014 are either serving a sentence or awaiting a sentence or other court proceeding (Minton & Zeng, 2015), all have found

Sentence: The judgment that a court formally pronounces after finding a criminal defendant guilty; the punishment imposed on a criminal wrongdoer… Also termed *judgment of conviction* (Garner, 2014; Black's Law Dictionary 10th ed., reprinted with permission, Thomson Reuters).

© *Shutterstock.com*

their place in the criminal justice system through initially having been arrested at some point by members of the law enforcement community.

While seemingly simple in its definition, the process of sentencing, and companion sentencing guidelines are very complex at both the local, county, state, and federal levels. Typically, two levels of sentencing guidelines are in existence.

State sentencing guidelines are promulgated by the appropriate legislature and apply to all courts within the jurisdiction of the state in question. When a matter involves a question of federal law, sentencing guidelines are promulgated by the United States Congress as a legislative body, as well as through the lens of an independent judicial branch agency called the **United States Sentencing Commission**. The Commission is responsible for establishing sentencing guidelines for the federal court system, along with recommendations to executive and legislative branch policymakers as sentencing structures are evaluated. The Commission's decisions/guidelines are only recommendations and members of the judiciary at the federal level have the discretion of modifying the guidelines to fit their particular case under review for sentence. According to the Commission (USSC, 2016),

The U.S. Sentencing Commission: is an independent agency in the judicial branch of government created by the Sentencing Reform Act of 1984. Congress enacted the SRA in response to widespread disparity in federal sentencing, ushering in a new era of federal sentencing through the creation of the Commission and the promulgation of federal sentencing guidelines (USSC, 2016).

The Commission's principal purposes are:

1. to establish sentencing policies and practices for the federal courts, including guidelines to be consulted regarding the appropriate form and severity of punishment for offenders convicted of federal crimes;

2. to advise and assist Congress and the executive branch in the development of effective and efficient crime policy; and

3. to collect, analyze, research, and distribute a broad array of information on federal crime and sentencing issues, serving as an information resource for Congress, the executive branch, the courts, criminal justice practitioners, the academic community, and the public.

The functions articulated in the Commission's mission statement provide criminal justice system practitioners and the lay public with a solid framework from which to analyze and better understand the sentencing structure and practices of the federal court system.

On April 19, 2007, defendant Davis was sentenced in Oneida County Court, New York, for 19 counts of the original grand jury indictment, including the robbery of Lennon's W.B. Wilcox Jewelry store, and the murder of Officer Corr. On July 12, 2011, defendants Davis, Pegese, and Ward were all sentenced in United States District Court for the Northern District of New York for the Hobbs Act robbery-homicide involving Lennon's W. B. Wilcox Jewelry store and Officer Corr. Once a conviction is secured at either the state or federal level, the time between the date of conviction and the date of formal sentencing is no less busy than activities surrounding preparations for plea bargaining discussions or a trial. Generally, the interim period between conviction and sentencing is occupied by defense attorneys preparing their appeals, prosecutors preparing to answer appeals, as well as state and federal agents (usually probation officers) preparing **presentence investigation reports** for use by the court as they determine whether or not to accept a plea agreement, or what an actual sentence will be after a trial verdict. In addition, the court will often receive written victim impact statements, providing additional context to the court as they consider final sentencing. In addition to written victim impact statements, some victims may also opt to be heard on the actual day of sentencing in open court where they have an opportunity to both speak to the court, as well as confront the defendant(s) in their case. We discuss this in more detail in other sections of this work. Just prior to pronouncing a final sentence, courts will also entertain final words from the defendants themselves.

Presentence Investigation: A probation officer's detailed account of the convicted defendants educational, criminal, family, and social background, conducted at the courts request as an aid in passing sentence (Garner, 2014; Black's Law Dictionary 10th ed., reprinted with permission, Thomson Reuters).

As noted, at the state and local level, estimates are as high as 95% or more of all criminal convictions are garnered through plea agreements, with even higher percentages at the federal level (Ross, 2006). Therefore, the drama that is normally created through television trials is much more theatrics than reality. Sentences of imprisonment in a local jail, a state prison, or a federal correctional facility are just one sentence that judges have within their toolbox of judicial discretion. While judges do have a great deal of flexibility and discretion at their disposal when considering pronouncement of a sentence, they nonetheless remain constrained by statute and past practice. Depending upon the offense and statutory constraints, judges have the discretion of imposing four broad categories of sentences, and/or a combination of each. These include, but are not limited to:

1. fines (monetary penalty)

2. restitution (payment to victims of an offense in an effort to make them fiscally whole again)

3. probation (depending upon the offense, a period of typically two to six years where a defendant must adhere to a list of conditions specified by the court in lieu of imprisonment)

4. imprisonment (confinement in a correctional facility for a defined period of time)

Multiple permutations and variables that are typically unique to federal or state statutes exist within each of these four broad categories. Whether the offense

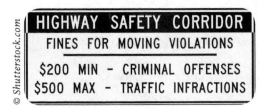

is a traffic infraction, violation, misdemeanor, or felony, statutes typically codify the general range of options available to judges based upon independent fact patterns for each individual case. In New York State, for example, sentencing options and associated parameters are codified in both the New York State Penal Law (PL), and the New York State Criminal Procedure Law (CPL). In addition to case law, readers should look to similar sources in their jurisdiction for specific penalties associated with offenses. Whether the jurisdiction is a local town or village, county, or state government, or the federal government, all laws have companion sections that deal with the range of penalties for violating those laws.

One commonality that does exist across all courts when the time for sentencing arrives is the language utilized by the court when pronouncing sentence. Since a sentence is a judgment of the court, judges are generally very careful and deliberate when pronouncing their sentence. In the Corr case, at both the county/state trial of defendant Davis, and at the federal trial of defendants Davis, Pegese, and Ward, the sentencing judges in those cases utilized similar language when pronouncing their sentence. In the sentencing of defendant Davis at the Oneida County, New York trial, **The Honorable Michael L. Dwyer** pronounced sentence on one of 19 counts in the original indictment when he said:

> *It will be the sentence of this court, as to the defendant's conviction for murder in the second degree, that he will receive the maximum sentence that is 25 years to life in prison. And I want to state for the record right now that I may not be here in 25 years, I may be dead myself, and if that, in fact, does happen, I want the Department of Parole to know,*

PEOPLE: The Honorable Michael L. Dwyer.

Michael L. Dwyer is an elected Oneida County, New York Judge. Judge Dwyer is a former prosecutor/assistant district attorney with the Oneida County, New York District Attorney's Office, serving in that role from 1980 to 1995. Judge Dwyer was first elected to a 10-year term as County Court judge in 1995 and continues to serve in that role today. In 2007, Judge Dwyer was appointed as the Supervising Judge for the Justice Courts in the Fifth judicial District of New York. He is a graduate of St. Lawrence University, and St. John's University School of Law (New York State Unified Court System, 2016). Judge Dwyer was the trial court judge for the case of the *People v. John T. Healy* (a.k.a. Toussaint Davis).

© *Rome Sentinel*

READ

Read the full transcript of the county/state trial and sentencing of *People v. John T. Healy* in our online companion.

and the Department of Corrections, that under no circumstances should you ever be released from confinement in a state prison facility. There would be no excuses, no exceptions for you to be released...I do not agree with all of the rules and regulations concerning concurrent and consecutive sentences that are currently in the New York State Penal Law. And there is ample case law that finds gray areas in many of these statutes. I do not feel that a person should be sentenced to the same sentence whether there's one person in the store or whether there is six people in the store. In my estimation, every one of those six individuals in that Lennon's Jewelry Store on the night of this robbery were separately robbed, threatened, and harassed. And so I am going to order that all of those robbery in the first degree sentences be imposed consecutively. That would be for a total of 150 years. And I will freely admit—I will freely admit that I am not sure, I have great doubts as to whether an Appellate Court will ever approve of this decision, but if anybody deserves it, Mr. Martin, it is—or Mr. Davis, it is you. (Official sentencing transcript of the Oneida County Court Trial of People v. John T. Healy, p. 43–45)

At the sentencing of defendant Davis at United States District Court for the Northern District of New York, **The Honorable Norman A. Mordue** pronounced during his sentencing:

PEOPLE: The Honorable Norman A. Mordue.

was born in Elmira, NY in 1942. As a Syracuse University Economics student, he was part of the ROTC program and commissioned as a Second Lieutenant upon graduation. After completing Basic Training, the new First Lieutenant heroically led his platoon during the Vietnam War. He was awarded the Distinguished Service Cross after his selfless efforts to relieve another platoon that had come under heavy artillery fire. Armed with a machine gun, First Lieutenant Mordue rescued two of his men who had been injured from enemy fire. Though he was severely injured after the incident, he refused to accept medical help until his men could withdraw and they could order artillery strikes on enemy positions. Following his distinguished military service, Norman returned to Syracuse University in 1971 to earn a degree in law. After graduating with his J.D., he served as the district attorney for Onondaga County. He eventually worked his way up to the bench, serving as the State Supreme Court justice in the county from 1986 until 1998. Nominated by President Bill Clinton and confirmed in only 16 days, he was appointed to the Northern District of New York, serving [as] the chief judge of the court until 2011 when he became the Senior Judge on the bench. (Adapted from Syracuse University Institute for Veterans and Military Families, 2016; reprinted with permission)

Now upon your conviction by jury trial of Counts 1, 2, and 3 of the indictment, it is the judgment of the court you are hereby committed to the custody of the Bureau of Prisons to be imprisoned for a term of life. This consists of terms of 240 months on Counts 1 and 2 and a term of life on Count 3, with all terms to be served concurrently...It is further ordered you shall make payments of restitution of $1,003,984 to Ballew Jewelers and 173,200 to Lennon's Jewelers, and $1,240 to Wendy Davis—Daniels, rather. Restitution is to be paid jointly and severally with your co-defendants Marion Pegese and Robert Ward. Payments are to be made in monthly installments of no less than 25 percent of your gross income while you are in custody. Payments shall be forwarded to the United States District Court Clerk. The court finds you are not in a position to pay a fine or interest on the restitution you owe, therefore, both of those items are waived. Now I'm imposing a life sentence with the understanding that you will not be eligible for release. However, in the event you are somehow released, I'm imposing a term of supervised release of five years, and that consists of terms of three years on each of Counts 1 and 2, a term of five years on Count 3, such terms to run concurrently. . . So far as your case is concerned, I've lived with this case for a long time, held hearings on it, I listened to the full trial, and I want you to know that as far as I am concerned, the jury has returned the proper verdict in this case, and I think I imposed the proper sentence in your case and your co-defendants. I think it's not more than is necessary in light of your background, nature of the offense in this case, and that's the order and judgment of the court. You are remanded to the custody of the United States Marshal. That concludes this matter. (Official sentencing transcript,

United States of America v. Marion Pegese, Robert Ward &

Toussaint Davis, p. 32–34)

Read the full transcript of the federal trial, *United States of America v. Marion Pegese, Robert Ward & Toussaint Davis* in our online companion.

Sentencing is a seemingly basic part of our criminal justice. To be effective, laws must not only be well written by a legislature and enforced by an executive branch officer, but have tangible and meaningful consequences handed down by the judicial branch of government when they are violated. The Corr case demonstrated significant differences in state and federal laws and their application to the facts of this case. However, despite the differences, both the process and ultimate disposition/judgment of the county/state and federal courts ultimately shared more similarities than differences.

Judiciary Act of 1789: The Judiciary Act of 1789, officially titled "An Act to Establish the Judicial Courts of the United States," was signed into law by President George Washington on September 24, 1789. Article III of the Constitution established a Supreme Court, but left to Congress the authority to create lower federal courts as needed. Principally authored by Senator Oliver Ellsworth of Connecticut, the Judiciary Act of 1789 established the structure and jurisdiction of the federal court system and created the position of attorney general. Although amended throughout the years by Congress, the basic outline of the federal court system established by the First Congress remains largely intact today (United States Library of Congress, 2016).

Original Jurisdiction: A court's power to hear and decide a matter before any other court can review the matter (Garner, 2014; Black's Law Dictionary 10th ed., reprinted with permission, Thomson Reuters).

Appellate Jurisdiction: The power of the court to review and revise a lower court's decision. For example, U.S. Const. art. III, § 2 vests appellate jurisdiction in the Supreme Court, while 28 USCA §§ 1291-1295 grant appellate jurisdiction to lower federal courts of appeals (Garner, 2014; Black's Law Dictionary 10th ed., reprinted with permission, Thomson Reuters). [The same structures/rules apply at the state level as well].

2 – 8 – Appeals

Although adopted and signed by the delegates to the Constitutional Convention on September 17, 1787, the United States Constitution was not formally ratified by the 13 colonies until June 21, 1788. Thereafter, the first United States Congress enacted *An Act to Establish the Judicial Courts of the United States*, more commonly referred to as the **Judiciary Act of 1789**, passed by the United States Congress on September 24, 1789, and signed that same day by President George Washington. Earlier we noted that jurisdiction can be discussed in the context of whether or not a court has **original jurisdiction** over a case, or **appellate jurisdiction** over a case. The Constitution of the

United States of America was clear when it granted the ultimate appellate jurisdiction to the United States Supreme Court. According to Article III, § 2,

> *...In all Cases affecting Ambassadors, other public Ministers and Consuls, and those in which a State shall be Party, the supreme Court shall have original Jurisdiction. In all the other Cases before mentioned, the supreme Court shall have appellate Jurisdiction, both as to Law and Fact, with such Exceptions, and under such Regulations as the Congress shall make.*

In the landmark United States Supreme Court case of *Marbury v. Madison* (1803), the high court took the opportunity in a seemingly mundane case involving the alleged failure of then Secretary of State, James Madison, to deliver presidential appointments to four justices of the peace in Washington, D.C. In asserting their supremacy, the court said in part:

> *This is the* supreme *court, and by reason of its supremacy must have the superintendance of the inferior tribunals and officers, whether judicial or ministerial. In this respect there is no difference between a judicial and a ministerial officer. From this principle alone the court of king's bench in England derives the power of issuing the writs of mandamus and prohibition. 3. Inst. 70, 71. Shall it be said that the court of king's bench has this power in consequence of its being the supreme court of judicature, and shall we deny it to this court which the constitution makes the* supreme *court? It is a beneficial, and a necessary power; and it can never be applied where there is another* adequate, specific, legal remedy. *The second section*

of the third article of the constitution gives this court appellate jurisdiction in all cases in law and equity arising under the constitution and laws of the United States (except the cases in which it has original jurisdiction) with such exceptions, and under such regulations as congress shall make. The term "appellate jurisdiction" is to be taken in its largest sense, and implies in its nature the right of superintending the inferior tribunals…In the Federalist, vol. 2, p. 239, it is said, that the word "appellate" is not to be taken in its technical sense, as used in reference to appeals in the course of the civil *law, but in its broadest sense, in which it denotes nothing more than the power of one tribunal to review the proceedings of another, either as to law or fact, or both.* Marbury v. Madison, *5 U.S. 137, 146–47, 2 L. Ed. 60 (1803)*

Appeal: … A proceeding undertaken to have a decision reconsidered by a higher court [especially], the submission of a lower court's or agency's decision to a higher court for review and possible reversal (Garner, 2014; Black's Law Dictionary 10th ed., reprinted with permission, Thomson Reuters).

For more than 213 years, the premise of *Marbury* remains the law of the land. The United States Supreme Court is America's court of final appeal in all cases and controversies. Since the enactment by the Congress of the United States of the Judiciary Act of 1789, our local, county, state, and federal courts continue to evolve and adapt to the changing needs of the American landscape. Fundamental in our American Criminal Justice System is an individual's right to **appeal**, the right to have a higher court review various aspects of a lower court's decision. In the United States we have a dual court system comprised of state courts and federal courts. Matters dealing with civil and criminal state affairs originate in local town and village, city, county, and state courts, while matters dealing with civil and

CIVIL COURT STRUCTURE

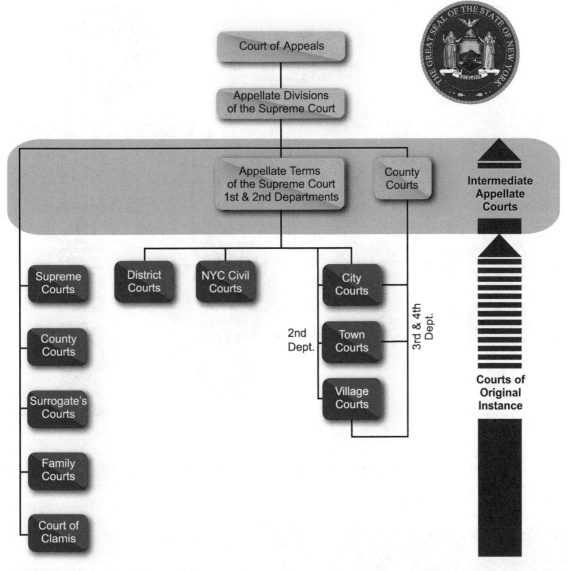

criminal federal offenses originate in the federal court system. While each state and the federal government have different names for their courts, each state and the federal government follows a similar structure in terms of how cases move throughout the court system.

In the first instance, courts that first see a case, whether civil or criminal, are called courts of original jurisdiction. They can also be known as trial courts, or courts of first instance. These are the courts that individuals and/or prosecutors

CRIMINAL COURT STRUCTURE

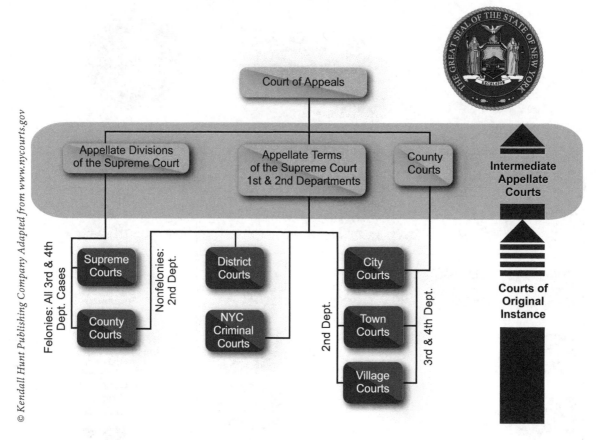

© Kendall Hunt Publishing Company Adapted from www.nycourts.gov

first bring cases or controversies. In New York State, for example, the courts of first instance, or trial courts, can be called by such names as village court, town court, city court, county court, supreme court, and in the City of New York, courts of original jurisdiction/trial courts are structured in a district court format. When matters of law may dictate a case to be appealed from a lower level court, cases in New York State first move to a lower level appellate court

© Shutterstock.com

New York State Court of Appeals, New York's highest court. The Court of Appeals is located in New York State's capitol, Albany, New York.

(cases being appealed from town, city, and village courts). Those cases are heard at the County Court level, broken up by a special appellate term for the areas encompassing the City of New York, and by judicial district for the rest of New York State. All other cases, typically from county court or supreme court move to an intermediate appellate level court. Again, while the name of these courts differs from state to state, in New York State these intermediate appeals courts are called the **Appellate Division of the Supreme Court**. The Appellate Division is broken into four geographical jurisdictions called departments. Each department is responsible for a predetermined number of counties within the State of New York. For example, the Corr case took place in Oneida County, New York. Oneida County falls within the State of New York, within the Fifth Judicial District, and the Fourth Department of the Appellate Division of the Supreme Court. Decisions made by the Appellate Division of the Supreme Court are appealed only to New York's highest court, the **New York State Court of Appeals**, a seven member judicial panel sitting in the state's capitol, Albany, New York. Like the federal system, New York has many specialized courts that deal with specific subject matter. Some of these courts include, but are not limited to, Family Court, Surrogate Court, and the **New York State Court of Claims**, dealing with claims against the State of New York.

Appellate Division of the Supreme Court: There are four Appellate Divisions of the Supreme Court, one in each of the State's four Judicial Departments. These Courts resolve appeals from judgments or orders of the superior courts of original jurisdiction in civil and criminal cases, and review civil appeals taken from the Appellate Terms and the County Courts acting as appellate courts (NYCourts.gov, 2016).

New York State Court of Appeals: The Court of Appeals, New York's highest-level court, hears civil and criminal appeals from the state's intermediate appellate courts, and, in some instances, directly from the trial courts. The Court also hears appeals from determinations by the State Commission on Judicial Conduct, which is responsible for reviewing allegations of misconduct brought against judges (NYCourts.gov, 2016).

New York State Court of Claims: The New York State Court of Claims is the exclusive forum for civil litigation seeking damages against the State of New York or certain other State-related entities such as the New York State Thruway Authority, the City University of New York, the Olympic Regional Development Authority, the Roswell Park Cancer Institute Corporation and the New York State Power Authority (claims for the appropriation of real property only). The Court of Claims has no jurisdiction over any city, county or town government, or over any individual defendant (NYCourts.gov, 2016).

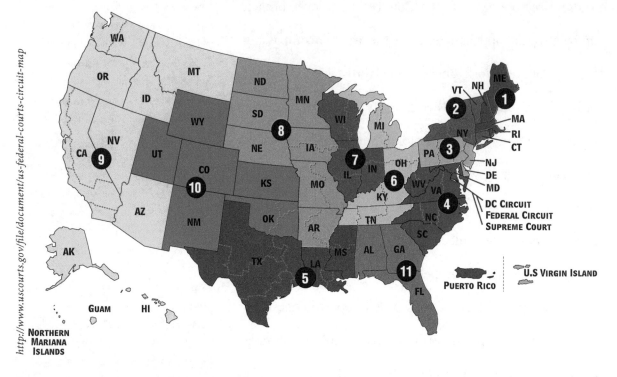

Geographic Boundaries
of United States Courts of Appeals and United States District Courts

http://www.uscourts.gov/file/document/us-federal-courts-circuit-map

United States District Court: The nation's 94 district or trial courts are called U.S. District Courts. District courts resolve disputes by determining the facts and applying legal principles to decide who is right. Trial courts include the district judge who tries the case and a jury that decides the case. Magistrate judges assist district judges in preparing cases for trial. They may also conduct trials in misdemeanor cases. There is at least one district court in each state, and the District of Columbia. Each district includes a U.S. bankruptcy court as a unit of the district court. Four territories of the United States have U.S. district courts that hear federal cases, including bankruptcy cases: Puerto Rico, the Virgin Islands, Guam, and the Northern Mariana Islands. There are also two special trial courts. The Court of International Trade addresses cases involving international trade and customs laws. The U.S. Court of Federal Claims deals with most claims for money damages against the U.S. government (USCourts.gov, 2016).

The federal level court structure mirrors that of most states in the nation. Courts of first instance, or trial courts at the federal level are called district courts. There are 94 district courts at the federal level spread throughout the United States. Like state courts of original jurisdiction, **United States District Courts** hear both civil and criminal action brought to them in the first instance, from private citizens or prosecutors/United States Attorneys (USA). Also like state courts, the federal system has specialized courts dealing with bankruptcy issues, issues of Veterans Affairs, and claims against the United States government. Similar to the state court system, the intermediate appellate court at the federal level is called the **United**

States Court of Appeals, also called the Circuit Court of Appeals. The federal intermediate appellate level courts are broken up into 11 geographical circuits spread across the United States, and two specialized intermediate appellate courts, the Federal Circuit, and the United States Court of Appeals for the District of Columbia, also known as the D.C. Circuit. Final appeals from the lower courts ultimately end up at the nation's highest court, the **United States Supreme Court**. Eight associate justices and one Chief Justice, all appointed for life terms by the President of the United States and confirmed by the United States Senate, serves as this nations court of last resort for all civil and criminal matters.

While more than 10 years has passed since the robbery of Lennon's W.B. Wilcox Jewelry store, and the murder of Officer Corr, the case continues to live in our court system, most recently with the November 30, 2015 *Memorandum-Decision and Order* issued by the United States District Court for the Northern District of New York, denying various motions of defendant Marion Pegese (*Marion Pegese v. United States of America*, 5:09-CR-390-1 [NAM], 5:14-CV-218 [NAM]). Since the original conviction of defendant Davis in Oneida County, New York County Court, and the subsequent conviction of defendants Davis, Pegese, and Ward at the United States District Court for the Northern District of New York, all three defendants and their attorneys have actively pursued appeals at both the state and federal level. With the exception of the Appellate Division, fourth Department, of the New York State Supreme Court

> **United States Court of Appeals:** There are 13 appellate courts that sit below the U.S. Supreme Court, and they are called the U.S. Courts of Appeals. The 94 federal judicial districts are organized into 12 regional circuits, each of which has a court of appeals. The appellate court's task is to determine whether or not the law was applied correctly in the trial court. Appeals courts consist of three judges and do not use a jury. A court of appeals hears challenges to district court decisions from courts located within its circuit, as well as appeals from decisions of federal administrative agencies. In addition, the Court of Appeals for the Federal Circuit has nationwide jurisdiction to hear appeals in specialized cases, such as those involving patent laws, and cases decided by the U.S. Court of International Trade and the U.S. Court of Federal Claims (USCourts.gov, 2016).
>
> **United States Supreme Court:** The Supreme Court is the highest court in the United States. Article III of the U.S. Constitution created the Supreme Court and authorized Congress to pass laws establishing a system of lower courts. In the federal court system's present form, 94 district level trial courts and 13 courts of appeals sit below the Supreme Court (USCourts.gov, 2016).

Read the actual *Memorandum-Decision and Order* issued by the United States District Court for the Northern District of New York, in our online companion.

reversing the County Court's determination to have defendant Davis serve all of his 19 count conviction consecutively, rather than concurrently, all other appeals have failed to date. The following traces some of the more notable appeals made by defendants in the Corr case.

Notice of Appeal: A document filed with the court and served on the other parties, stating in intention to appeal the trial court's judgment or order. In most jurisdictions, filing a notice of appeal is the act by which the appeal is perfected. For instance, the Federal Rules of Appellate Procedure provide that an appeal is taken by filing a notice of appeal with the clerk of the District Court from which the appeal is taken and that the clerk is to send copies of the notice to all of the other party's attorneys, as well as the Court of Appeals (Garner, 2014; Black's Law Dictionary 10th ed., reprinted with permission, Thomson Reuters).

Appellant: A party who appeals a lower court's decision [usually] seeking reversal of that decision (Garner, 2014; Black's Law Dictionary 10th ed., reprinted with permission, Thomson Reuters).

Respondent: 1. The party against whom an appeal is taken; Appellee. In some appellate courts, the parties are designated as petitioner and respondent. In most appellate courts in the United States, the parties are designated as appellant and appellee. Often the designations depend on whether the appeal is taken by writ of certiorari (or writ of error) or by direct appeal. 2. The party against whom a motion or petition is filed.3. At common law, the defendant in an equity proceeding. 4. Civil law. Someone who answers for another or acts as another security (Garner, 2014; Black's Law Dictionary 10th ed., reprinted

Appellee: A party against whom an appeal is taken and whose role is to respond to that appeal [usually] seeking affirmance of the lower court's decision [also known as Respondent] (Garner, 2014; Black's Law Dictionary 10th ed., reprinted with permission, Thomson Reuters).

Defendant Toussaint Davis (a.k.a. John T. Healy, a.k.a. Toussaint Martin)

1. **2007** – Oneida County, New York, County Court – convicted of 18 counts of robbery in the first and second degree, and one count of murder in the second degree. Sentenced on all counts to the maximum penalty of 25 years to life for murder in the second degree, 15 years for each count of robbery in the second degree, and 25 years for each count of robbery in the first degree, to be served consecutively with the murder conviction, as opposed to concurrently. A **Notice of Appeal** to the Appellate Division of the Supreme Court of New York, Fourth Department, was filed by defendant Davis, with the Oneida County, New York, County Clerk on April 23, 2007.

2. **2009** – Tuesday, October 20, 2009, Oral argument before the New York State Supreme Court, Appellate Division, Fourth Department, by the **Appellant** (Toussaint Davis) and **Respondent/Appellee** (People of the State of New York represented by the Oneida County District Attorney). Extensive written briefs on

behalf of the Appellant and Respondent were filed prior to oral argument before the Court. According to the Brief for the Appellant filed with the New York State Supreme Court, Appellate Division, Fourth Department, the Appellant raised eight points in their written and oral argument for the court's consideration on appeal:

a. **Point I:** The repeal of § 511(4) of the Judiciary Law, which had disqualified state judges, including Justices of the Supreme Court of the state of New York, from serving as jurors, including service as grand jurors, constituted a violation of the purpose of Article I, § 6 of the Bill of Rights but the New York Constitution and also denied the defendant due process of law.

b. **Point II:** Since the Justice of the New York Supreme Court, who served not only as a member of the grand jury, but also as its foreperson, had also been the first assistant district attorney in the same office that was prosecuting this matter before the grand jury, and who had received campaign contributions from the owner of the jewelry store that had been robbed in this case, the court should have granted the defendants motion to dismiss the indictment, pursuant to § 210.35 (5) of the CPL [Criminal Procedure Law], on the ground that the integrity of the grand jury proceeding had been impaired and that prejudice to the defendant may have resulted.

c. **Point III:** The court improperly refused to instruct the jury to take into account the fact that the defendant had been taken into custody just before another alleged participant in the robbery had shot the police officer, which was a factor that the jury should have considered in determining whether the shooting had been done in the immediate flight from the robbery, and, therefore the defendant's conviction for felony murder should be reversed.

d. **Point IV:** The black glove found by the police in the rear of the patrol car where the defendant had been sitting, which was later found by the State Police Lab to contain fibers that were consistent with the fibers found on a piece of plastic laminate on a glass case containing Rolex Watches at Lennon's Jewelry Store, should not of been received in evidence at the trial because, as conceded by the prosecutor, there had been mistakes in the chain of custody of the glove, and, as the defense argued, those mistakes had affected its admissibility.

e. **Point V:** The defendant's consecutive sentences for felony murder in the second degree, robbery in the first degree (for causing serious physical injury, i.e., death), robbery in the first degree (for being armed with a deadly weapon, i.e., a loaded firearm), and robbery in the second degree (for being aided by another participant) had all been imposed in violation of § 70.25(2) of the Penal Law, and were required to be run concurrently instead.

f. **Point VI:** The defendant's consecutive sentences for robbery in the first degree (for another participant causing serious physical injury, i.e., death), robbery in the first degree (for another participant being armed with a deadly weapon,, i.e., a loaded firearm), and robbery in the second degree (for being aided by another participant) had all been imposed in violation of § 70.25 (2) of the Penal Law, and were required to run concurrently because there had only been one act of robbery which had allegedly violated three different robbery provisions.

g. **Point VII:** The defendant's consecutive sentences for robbery in the first degree (another participant causing serious physical injury, i.e., death), robbery in the first degree (for another participant being armed with a deadly weapon, i.e., a loaded firearm), and robbery in the second degree (for being aided by another participant) for each of the six victims in this matter should have all run concurrently because there had only been one act of robbery-that of stealing jewelry and Rolex Watches from all six victims at the same time in the store, and it did not involve stealing items from any of the individual victims, and, therefore, the sentence is required by § 70.25 of the Penal Law to run concurrently.

h. **Point VIII:** The defendants indeterminate sentence of twenty-five years to life for his conviction for murder in the second degree and all eighteen determinate sentences for his convictions for robbery in the first and second degrees, totaling 375 years to life, were unduly harsh and severe and should be reduced to lesser sentences. (*The People of the State of New York v. Toussaint Davis*, Brief for Appellant, Docket No. KA 07-01886, 2009 [text originally appeared in all capital letters])

i. **August 30, 2009** - New York State Supreme Court, Appellate Division, Fourth Department rejected all of the Appellant's arguments/points except for agreeing that the sentences handed down by the court should have run concurrently, and not consecutively (*People v. Davis*, 68 A.D.3d 1653, 893 N.Y.S.2d 411 (2009)).

3. **2010** – April 9, 2010 – request to appeal the judgement of the New York State Supreme Court, Appellate Division, Fourth Department to the New York State Court of Appeals denied (*People v. Davis*, 14 N.Y.3d 839 , N.Y. , Apr. 09, 2010

Read the full opinion of the New York State Supreme Court, Appellate Division, Fourth Department, in our online companion.

Defendant(s) Toussaint Davis, Marion Pegese, and Robert Ward

1. **2010** - United States District Court for the Northern District of New York, Syracuse, New York. "Defendants were convicted…of conspiracy to interfere with interstate commerce by robbery, in violation of the Hobbs Act, interference with interstate commerce by robbery, and murder as a result of possession and discharge of a firearm in furtherance of a crime of violence" (*United States v. Ward*, 505 F. App'x 18 (2d Cir. 2012)).

2. **2011** - July 12, 2011, defendants sentenced in United States District Court for the Northern District of New York, Syracuse New York. Defendants appealed various matters to the United States Court of Appeals for the Second Circuit.

3. **2012** - December 11, 2012, United States Court of Appeals for the Second Circuit issued their opinion on the defendants appeal (*United States of America, Appellee, v. Robert WARD (a.k.a. "RB"), Marion Pegese (a.k.a. "Dump," "Bill," "Amin"), and Toussaint Davis (a.k.a. "Toot," "John Healy," "Toussaint Martin")*, Defendants–Appellants. Nos. 11–2989 (L); 11–3058; 11–3172), Argued before the United States Court of Appeals for the Second Circuit, December 4, 2012, (*United States v. Ward*, 505 F. App'x 18 (2d Cir. 2012) [case citation]. In sum, although many arguments were presented by the defendants, the Court of Appeals held that:

Listen to the full oral argument before the United States Court of Appeals for the Second Circuit in our online companion. Case argued December 4, 2012.

Read the full opinion of the United States Court of Appeals for the Second Circuit in our online companion.

a. co-defendant's murder of police officer while fleeing jewelry store robbery was reasonably foreseeable;

b. evidence was sufficient to establish defendants' guilt; and

c. jury was not required to find that robbery of jewelry store had a "substantial effect" on interstate commerce in order to sustain a conviction for conspiracy to interfere with interstate commerce by robbery. *United States v. Ward*, 505 F. App'x 18 (2d Cir. 2012)

4. **2013 – Certiorari** denied by the United States Supreme Court (an effort by the defendants to appeal the judgment of the United States Court of Appeals for the Second Circuit to the United States Supreme Court), *Pegese v. U.S.*, 133 S.Ct. 1512, Mar. 04, 2013, and *Davis v. U.S.*, 133 S.Ct. 1842, Apr. 15, 2013.

> **Certiorari:** An extraordinary writ issued by an appellate court, at its discretion, directing a lower court to deliver the record in the case for review. The writ evolved from one of the prerogative writs of the English Court of Kings Bench, and in the United States it became a general appellate remedy. The US Supreme Court uses certiorari to review most of the cases that it decides to hear. Also termed *writ of certiorari* (Garner, 2014; Black's Law Dictionary 10th ed., reprinted with permission, Thomson Reuters).

5. **2015** – November 30, 2015 – Decision on a Habeas Corpus petition (defendant Pegese only) by The Honorable Norman A. Mordue, United States District Court for the Northern District of New York, Syracuse New York. The court held, in part, "In this *habeas corpus* proceeding under 28 U.S.C. § 2255 ("section 2255") (Dkt. Nos. 250, 255), Pegese, who is represented by counsel, claims he received ineffective assistance of trial counsel. In a separate motion (Dkt. No. 269), he requests investigative services and discovery to support his section 2255 motion. As set forth below, the Court denies the motions, dismisses the proceeding, and denies a certificate of appealability" (*Marion Pegese, Petitioner, v.*

Read the official opinion of Judge Mordue of the United States District Court for the Northern District of New York in our online companion.

United States of America, Respondent, 5:09-CR-390-1 (NAM), 5:14-CV-218 (NAM), Memorandum-Decision and order, November 30, 2015)

Appeals have, and continue to be, one element of the American Criminal Justice System that is essential to ensuring that all individuals in criminal or civil cases are afforded both due process of the law, and all of the protections that the law affords. The law at both the state and federal level does however, limit an individual's rights to appeal in order to provide relative legal closure to a case. In reality, inmates confined to correctional facilities serving lengthy sentences will invariably continue to attempt to appeal aspects of their case in hopes of one day being freed prior to their sentence. Our American Criminal Courts have the responsibility to review these petitions, no matter how seemingly frivolous to the general public, to uniformly ensure that all of our individual rights and due process of law are adhered to consistent with the Constitution of the United States of America.

Questions for Review and Further Discussion

1. Identify and explain the basic elements of the seven (7) Corr foundations of our American Criminal Justice System.

2. Explain how our three branches of government in the United States impact your job/career on a daily basis.

3. Identify and explain how a criminal court case moves from an arrest through the highest court in your jurisdiction, and the highest court in the United States.

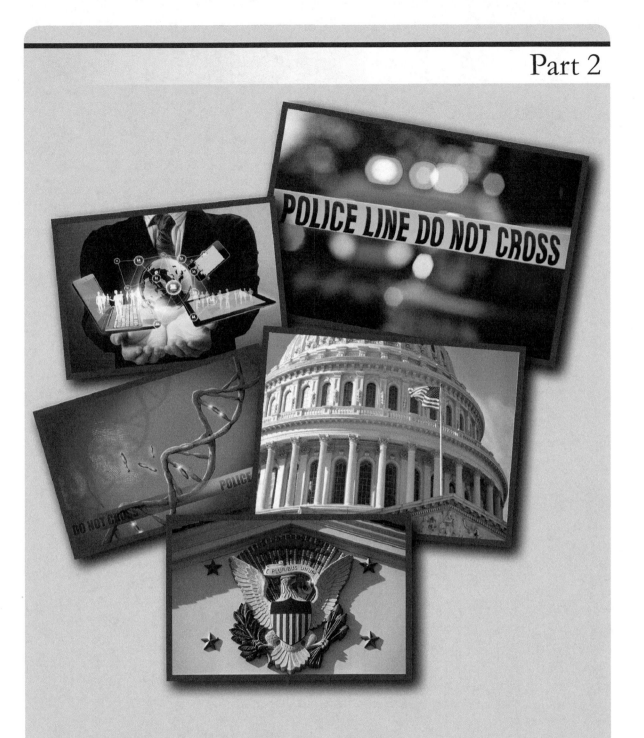

Part 2

Wielding Executive Power – "Officer Down" – Managing the Investigation

Chapter 3

American Law Enforcement

~James C. Brown

Outline

Keywords

1. Arrest

2. District Attorney

3. Oath of Office

People

1. John G. Duncan

2. Kurt D. Hameline

3. Paul J. Hernon

4. The Honorable Scott D. McNamara

5. The Honorable Raymond A. Meier

6. Richard R. Southwick

Expected Learning Outcomes

After reading this chapter and supplemental online materials, the reader will be able to:

1. Explain the evolution of law enforcement authority in America.

2. Articulate where law enforcement officers derive their power(s).

3. Differentiate the role(s) of police and peace officers and the related classifications of the same.

      3 – 1 – "…He Shall Take Care That the Laws Be Faithfully Executed…" – The Development of Executive Authority

      3 – 2 – The Many Faces of Law Enforcement in America and American Policing

      3 – 3 – Prosecutorial Enforcement

3 – 1 – "…He Shall Take Care That the Laws Be Faithfully Executed…" – The Development of Executive Authority

According to BJS (United States Department of Justice, Bureau of Justice Statistics, 2014),

> *'Law enforcement' is the term that describes the individuals and agencies responsible for enforcing laws and maintaining public order and public safety. Law enforcement includes the prevention, detection, and investigation of crime and the apprehension and detention of individuals suspected of law violation. (1)*

The most recent census of state and local law enforcement agencies conducted by BJS indicates that in the United States there are 765,000 sworn law enforcement officers across 17,985 state and local law enforcement agencies (Brown, Philo, Callisto, & Smith, 2016; U.S. Department of Justice, 2011).

As we have discussed, the laws promulgated by legitimate legislatures serve no purpose if some enforcement mechanism does not exist to back up the words articulated by representatives of the people through the legislature. In the creation of our American Constitution, the Founding Fathers were very careful and deliberate to clearly articulate the three branches of government in the context of ensuring that no one branch would be more powerful than the other. From the Declaration of Independence forward, the founders appropriately feared ever creating an all-powerful executive such that existed with the kings of our British past; hence the creation of our balanced three branches of government. Article II, §1 of the Constitution of the United States of America reads, "The executive Power shall be vested in a President of the United States of America" (U.S. Const. art. II, § 1). Article II § 2-4 of the Constitution of the United States of America goes on to articulate additional powers of the president, the nation's chief executive and chief enforcement officer:

© Shutterstock.com

> § 2 - *The President shall be* Commander in Chief *of the Army and Navy of the United States, and of the Militia of the several States, when called into the actual Service of the United States;* he may require the Opinion, in writing, of the principal Officer in each of *the* executive Departments, *upon any Subject relating to the Duties of their respective Offices, and he shall have Power to grant Reprieves and Pardons for Offences against the United States, except in Cases of Impeachment. He shall have Power, by and with the Advice and Consent of the Senate, to make Treaties, provided two thirds of the Senators present concur; and he shall nominate, and by and with the Advice and Consent of the Senate, shall appoint Ambassadors, other public Ministers and Consuls, Judges*

of the supreme Court, and all other Officers *of the United States, whose Appointments are not herein otherwise provided for, and which shall be established by Law:* but the Congress may by Law vest the Appointment of such inferior Officers, as they think proper, in the President alone, in the Courts of Law, or in the Heads of Departments. *The President shall have Power to fill up all Vacancies that may happen during the Recess of the Senate, by granting Commissions which shall expire at the End of their next Session.*

§ 3 – He shall from time to time give to the Congress Information of the State of the Union, and recommend to their Consideration such Measures as he shall judge necessary and expedient; he may, on extraordinary Occasions, convene both Houses, or either of them, and in Case of Disagreement between them, with Respect to the Time of Adjournment, he may adjourn them to such Time as he shall think proper; he shall receive Ambassadors and other public Ministers; he shall take Care that the Laws be faithfully executed, and shall Commission all the Officers of the United States.

§ 4 – The President, Vice President and all civil Officers of the United States, shall be removed from Office on Impeachment for, and Conviction of, Treason, Bribery, or other high Crimes and Misdemeanors. (U.S. Const. art. II, § 2-4, emphasis added*)*

All executive authority, from federal to local law enforcement, derives their genesis from the initial structure of Article II of the United States Constitution. Only 11 years had passed since the issuance and signing of the Declaration of

Independence in 1776 until the final creation of the United States Constitution in 1787. Of the three branches of government, the executive branch was perhaps most controversial, as those who considered the new Constitution were still reeling from the tyranny of the monarchy as clearly expressed in the Declaration of Independence in 1776. Despite this fear, the framers of the United States Constitution knew that a strong executive, perhaps just short of a monarch, was necessary to enforce the laws of this new land and new style of governance.

Publius (Hamilton) in *Federalist LXXII* (72) perhaps most eloquently captured the challenges facing those considering the new Constitution when he said:

Publius (Alexander Hamilton), contributor to *The Federalist Papers*.

> *The administration of government, in its largest sense, comprehends all the operations of the body politic, whether legislative, executive, or judiciary; but in its most usual, and perhaps its most precise signification. It is limited to executive details, and falls peculiarly within the province of the executive department. The actual conduct of foreign negotiations, the preparatory plans of finance, the application and disbursement of the public moneys in conformity to the general appropriations of the legislature, the arrangement of the army and navy, the directions of the operations of war, these, and other matters of a like nature, constitute what seems to be most properly understood by the administration of government. (Kramnick, 1987)*

Publius (Hamilton) in *Federalist LXX* (70) went on to note the inherent conflicts that arise when decisions need to be made in furtherance of the ends of government when he noted:

Men often oppose a thing, merely because they have had no agency in planning it, or because it may have been planned by those whom they dislike. But if they have been consulted, and have happened to disapprove, opposition then becomes, in their estimation, an indispensable duty of self-love. They seem to think themselves bound in honor, and by all the motives of personal infallibility, to defeat the success of what has been resolved upon contrary to their sentiments. Men of upright, benevolent tempers have too many opportunities of remarking, with horror, to what desperate lengths this disposition is sometimes carried, and how often the great interests of society are sacrificed to the vanity, to the conceit, and to the obstinacy of individuals, who have credit enough to make their passions and their caprices interesting to mankind. Perhaps the question now before the public may, in its consequences, afford melancholy proofs of the effects of this despicable frailty, or rather detestable vice, in the human character.

(Kramnick, 1987)

Despite the intense debate that ensued after the Declaration of Independence, and the ratification of the Constitution of the United States of America, perhaps the most significant clause that continues to endure today authorizing executive branch officials/officers to continue to perform their duties in the face of controversy is that, "…he shall take Care that the Laws be faithfully executed…" (U.S. Const. art. II, § 3). Whether police officers responding to and/or investigating the Corr case, or prosecutors continuing to pursue justice in the Corr

case, all the way up to the President of the United States, the many faces of law enforcement in the United States of America all swear a common oath of office that includes the language that they will faithfully execute/uphold the laws of their jurisdiction. This common phraseology, taken directly from our United States Constitution, is the common thread that binds all executive branch/law enforcement officers as one, and distinguishes them from the other branches of government. As he assumed the job of police officer in the Town of New Hartford, New York, Officer Corr took the **oath of office** before the Town Clerk as follows:

Oath of Office: An oath or affirmation taken by a person to enter into the duties of public office, by which the person promises to perform the duties of that office in good faith (Garner, 2014; Black's Law Dictionary 10th ed., reprinted with permission, Thomson Reuters).

I, [Joseph D. Corr], do solemnly swear that I will support the Constitution of the United States, the Constitution of the State of New York, the rules and regulations of the Town of New Hartford, and that I will faithfully discharge the duties of [Police Officer], according to the best of my ability, so help me God. (G. Wolanin-Young, personal communications, August 8, 2016)

© Shutterstock.com

Individuals holding public office are bound to their duties by a historically solemn Oath of Office. Members of the law enforcement community are bound by this common Oath of Office.

Through Article II of our United States Constitution, all members of the executive branch of our local, county, state, and federal governments derive their base power. Unlike Officer Corr and his colleagues in policing, not all executive branch members charged with making sure the laws are executed, possess the powers of **arrest**, usually

Arrest: 1. A seizure or forcible restraint, [especially] by legal authority. 2. The taking or keeping of a person in custody by legal authority, [especially] in response to a criminal charge; [specifically], the apprehension of someone for the purpose of securing the administration of the law, [especially] of bringing that person before a court (Garner, 2014; Black's Law Dictionary 10th ed., reprinted with permission, Thomson Reuters).

uniquely reserved for a special sub classification of executive branch members with peace or police officer status as articulated by the legislature in specific jurisdictions. As a general rule, society sees law enforcement officers and assumes that only means police officers. However, policing is only one aspect of the many faces of law enforcement in America.

3 – 2 – The Many Faces of Law Enforcement in America and American Policing

Always a strong advocate for public safety initiatives, former Oneida County Executive and New York State Senator **Raymond A. Meier** would frequently note in his public appearances that "it is the number one responsibility of government to secure the public safety" (personal communication, R.A. Meier, n.d.). Members of the law enforcement community are responsible for securing the public safety in a multitude of ways, and through a multitude of agencies all under the law enforcement banner. Like our courts that derive their power from Article III of our United States Constitution, and our legislatures that derive their power from Article I of the United States Constitution, executive branch powers derived from Article II of the United States Constitution exist at the local, county, state, and federal levels as well. Executive branch powers then, are dispersed across all different layers of government

throughout the United States. Executive agencies charged with the responsibility of enforcing the laws of a particular jurisdiction all have a similar function, but frequently go by different names, and are individually subject to the different laws established by different jurisdictions, often times with limited authority. For

© *Shutterstock.com*

example, while federal level enforcement agents have geographical jurisdiction to enforce the laws of the federal government throughout the United States of America, their powers of enforcement for non-federal offenses are often times limited by legislation enacted by state governments.

In New York State, the *Criminal Procedure Law* (CPL) provides the guidance to all law enforcement personnel on both their powers and the procedures necessary to perform their duties. Each state in the nation and the federal government has codified similar procedures related to their respective agencies under their jurisdiction. Currently, 29 federal law enforcement agencies are authorized by the New York State Criminal Procedure Law to function as Peace Officers within the state of New York. Some of these agencies include:

1. Federal Bureau of Investigation special agents

2. United States Secret Service special agents

3. Immigration and Customs Enforcement special agents, deportation officers, and detention and deportation officers

4. United States Marshals and Marshals Service deputies

5. Drug Enforcement Administration special agents

6. Federal Protective Officers, including law enforcement security officers, criminal investigators, and police officers of the Federal Protective Service

7. United States Customs and Border Protection Officers and United States Customs and Border Protection Border Patrol agents

8. United States Postal Service police officers and inspectors (N.Y. Criminal Procedure Law § 2.15)

Likewise, within the State of New York, the Criminal Procedure Law authorizes 22 classifications of individuals who could be called Police Officers. Some of these positions/titles include:

34. "Police officer." The following persons are police officers:

a. A sworn member of the division of state police;

b. Sheriffs, under-sheriffs, and deputy sheriffs of counties outside of New York City;

c. A sworn officer of an authorized county or county parkway police department;

d. A sworn officer of an authorized police department or force of a city, town, village, or police district;

e. A sworn officer of an authorized police department of an authority or a sworn officer of the state regional park police in the office of parks and recreation;

f. A sworn officer of the capital police force of the office of general services;

g. An investigator employed in the office of a district attorney; (N.Y. Criminal Procedure Law § 1.20, 2016)

Officer Corr served as a duly authorized Police Officer under the *New York State Criminal Procedure Law* § 1.20 §§ (d), as a sworn member of the New Hartford Police Department. The skill of understanding and accurately mapping ones executive/enforcement authority and related powers and limitations is critical to successful navigation of any case encountered. Just as it is equally important to fully understand the categories of offenses, and elements of offenses within one's jurisdiction, a full appreciation for the level of authority and related limitations within one's jurisdiction is equally important. In the Corr case, the many faces of law enforcement were quickly identified in the early hours of the investigation, and related resources for each enforcement agency were maximized to an optimal outcome.

By virtue of their size in terms of personnel, and their size in terms of fiscal resources, law enforcement agencies must rely on a complex set of legal and sometimes unwritten set of agreements and relationships between agencies and organizations in times of need. The New Hartford Police Department is a relatively small law enforcement agency with fewer than 30 full and part-time sworn officers. Part of their heaviest call activity exists within a densely populated commercial district that is bisected by heavily traveled state and local highways that connect other areas of Oneida County. While primary jurisdiction for the municipality falls to the New Hartford Police Department, police patrols from the Oneida County Sheriff's Office, and the New York State Police are also active within the jurisdiction. Immediately surrounding jurisdictions with police departments include the Town of Kirkland, City of Utica, Town of Whitestown, Village of New York Mills, and the Village of Yorkville. When the first call of a robbery in progress at Lennon's W.B, Wilcox Jewelry Store was dispatched at 8:20:49 p.m. on February 27, 2006, Officers Shane Yoxall (Car 51) and Joseph Corr (Car 43) of the New Hartford Police Department were the first to respond to the call. Additional patrols working the night of the robbery included a patrol supervisor, Sergeant Paul Colburn (ret.) (Car 55), and Officer Ronald Fontaine (Car 49). Moments after Officer Yoxall arrived at the scene he radioed that individuals were exiting the jewelry store heading toward a local Hannaford Supermarket, located adjacent and to the rear of the jewelry store. At the same time, Officer Corr arrived at the scene to observe one of two apparent getaway cars exiting the jewelry store and refusing to yield to his attempt to stop the vehicle. Officer Corr immediately engaged in an effort to follow this vehicle in an attempt to stop the car. As Officer Corr continued his attempt to stop the vehicle subsequently found to be containing defendants Walter Richardson and Toussaint Davis (a.k.a. John T. Healy, Toussaint Martin), the other two New Hartford Police Department vehicles began to respond to both the attempt to stop

Listen to the full actual radio transmissions from the New Hartford Police Department on February 27, 2006 in our online companion.

the defendant's vehicle, as well as to the robbery. Simultaneously, Officer Yoxall entered the jewelry store, discovered bound employees, and not knowing whether or not other suspects were still present, asked for backup law enforcement officers from the Oneida County Sheriff's Office. While additional law enforcement cars responded to the jewelry store to back up Officer Yoxall, the attempt to stop the fleeing vehicle containing suspects/defendants Richardson and Davis continued heading through the jurisdiction of the Town of New Hartford toward the Town of Kirkland.

While attempting to negotiate a turn, the defendant's vehicle crashed into a gas pump located at the Byrne Dairy Convenience Store on Route 233 in the Town of Kirkland, New York. Simultaneously monitoring radio transmissions, law enforcement officers from the Town of Kirkland converged on the crash site. As Officer Corr arrived at the scene he exited his vehicle and began a foot chase in an attempt to apprehend one of the two suspects in the vehicle (later identified as Walter Richardson). Simultaneously, Officers Ronald Fontaine of the New Hartford Police Department, Peter Cania and Vito Sparace of the Kirkland Police Department, Chief Daniel English of the Kirkland Police Department and Sergeant Paul Colburn of the New Hartford Police Department converged on the scene. Unable to flee successfully on snow-covered terrain, officers immediately apprehended defendant Toussaint Davis. As Officer Corr continued his foot chase toward a wooded tree line, he was shot by defendant Walter Richardson and mortally wounded. Officer Peter Cania of the Kirkland Police Department, and Officer Ronald Fontaine of the New Hartford Police Department rushed to Officer Corr's side and rendered him emergency first aid, including cardiopulmonary resuscitation (CPR), until medical personnel arrived to take over the care. Officer Corr was immediately transported to the regions local trauma center, St. Elizabeth's Hospital, where he died a short time later from his injuries, despite the heroic resuscitation efforts of first responders and medical personnel at the hospital.

An immediate manhunt ensued involving dozens of local, county, state, and federal law enforcement agencies for the individual who murdered Officer Corr, as well as for the other individuals who escaped from the jewelry store robbery. Unbeknownst to officers at the scene, defendant Walter Richardson had carjacked/kidnapped a tow truck operator at gunpoint, just a few hundred feet away from the Byrne Dairy Convenience Store, called Kirkland Auto. Richardson then began his journey with the tow truck operator heading south toward his hometown of Philadelphia, Pennsylvania. During the minutes and hours that followed the murder of Officer Corr, dozens of local, county, state, and federal law enforcement agencies and hundreds of officers became immediately engaged in the investigation. Shortly after responding to the scene, Chief of Police Raymond L. Philo of the New Hartford Police Department immediately requested the response of the Oneida County District Attorney. Shortly after his request, Oneida County District Attorney Michael A. Arcuri, arrived at the scene to begin to facilitate the continuing investigation and eventual prosecution of the defendants involved in this case.

At the time, no one knew that four defendants from the Philadelphia, Pennsylvania region (Richardson, Davis, Pegese, and Ward) were a part of an elaborate interstate robbery ring that targeted Rolex Watch dealers in the northeast. At the time, none of the hundreds of law enforcement officers immediately engaged in this case knew that defendant Richardson had carjacked/

kidnapped a tow truck operator and was heading south toward Pennsylvania. In the minutes and hours after the murder of Officer Corr, law enforcement officers only knew that one of their brothers had fallen, that the murderer was still on the loose, one defendant (Toussaint Davis) was in police custody, and at least one of the defendant had fled the initial scene of the robbery in another car. Shortly after the murder of Officer Corr, New Hartford Police Department Chief Raymond L. Philo, and then Oneida County District Attorney Michael A. Arcuri, reached out to the United States Attorney's Office for the Northern District of New York located in Syracuse New York. Both men knew that by activating this critical resource that the full weight and fiscal and personnel resource base of the federal government would be activated to catch Officer Corr's murderer. As a result of the formal and informal relationships established between law enforcement agencies before the Corr robbery-homicide, a more formalized task force was established to continue the investigation and prosecution of the case.

Joseph D. Corr Robbery-Homicide Task Force

Members of the Joseph D. Corr Robbery-Homicide Task Force included:

1. Federal Bureau of Alcohol, Tobacco, & Firearms, Syracuse, New York

2. Federal Bureau of Investigation – Albany Field Office, Albany, New York

3. Kirkland Police Department, Clark Mills, New York

4. New Hartford Police Department, New Hartford, New York

5. New York State Police – Troop D, Oneida, New York

6. Oneida County District Attorney's Office, Utica, New York

7. Oneida County Sheriff's Office, Oriskany, New York

8. Pennsylvania State Police, Media, Pennsylvania

9. United States Attorney's Office for the Northern District of New York, Syracuse, New York

10. United States Marshals Service, Northern District of New York

11. City of Utica Police Department, Utica, New York

It is overly simplistic to think that law enforcement only means police officers. While our police officers tend to be the most public/visual representation of law enforcement, dozens of other local, county, state, and federal law enforcement personnel were not only engaged in the Corr case, but in regular, less serious cases every day. The many faces of law enforcement were all at work in the Corr case. While police officers and those with police/peace officer powers are our first line of defense when crimes occur, the inherent executive branch law enforcement power of our prosecutors is equally as critical to understand and embrace in our American Criminal Justice System.

3 – 3– Prosecutorial Enforcement

Prosecutors are law enforcement officers. Some would argue that they are the chief law enforcement officer of their jurisdiction. Depending upon the jurisdiction, those who are responsible for representing the "people" of a jurisdiction are called many different names. Some of these names in the United States include,

© Shutterstock.com

> **District Attorney:** A public official appointed or elected to represent the state in criminal cases in a particular judicial district; prosecutor [abbreviated DA]-Also termed *public prosecutor; states attorney; prosecuting attorney, United States Attorney* (Garner, 2014; Black's Law Dictionary 10th ed., reprinted with permission, Thomson Reuters).

1. Prosecutor (Assistant Prosecutor)

2. **District Attorney**, DA (Assistant District Attorney [Assistant DA])

3. States Attorney (Assistant States Attorney)

4. Attorney General, AG (Assistant Attorney General [Assistant AG])

5. United States Attorney, USA (Assistant United States Attorney [AUSA].)

Article XIII, § 13 of the Constitution of the State of New York defines a district attorney as both a public officer and as a law enforcement officer. According to the New York State Criminal Procedure Law (CPL),

31. "Prosecutor" means a district attorney or any other public servant who represents the people in a criminal action.

32. "District attorney" means a district attorney, an assistant district attorney or a special district attorney, and, where appropriate, the attorney general, an assistant attorney general, a deputy attorney general, a special deputy attorney general, or the special prosecutor and inspector general for the protection of people with special needs or his or her assistants when

New York's 62 counties each have a district attorney responsible for the prosecution of criminal cases within their jurisdiction. The State of New York has one elected Attorney General, representing all of the people of the State of New York in both civil and criminal matters as well as defending actions against the State of New York and providing legal advice to the executive branch of state government.

In most local and state jurisdictions in the United States, prosecutors are elected officials. For example, in Oneida County, New York, the district attorney is an elected official who runs for office every four years. In New York State there are 62 counties, and thus a district attorney responsible for criminal prosecutions in each county. In the State of New York, the New York State Attorney General is also an elected official and runs for office every four years as well. However, at the federal level, the position of United States Attorney is appointed by the President of the United States and serves at the pleasure of the current presidential administration. There are currently 94 federal districts in the United States, each represented by a different presidentially appointed United States Attorney. ("Find Your U.S. Attorney" https://www.justice.gov/usao/find-your-united-states-attorney)

Throughout the United States, prosecutors' offices at all levels vary in size and resources. Some offices employ only a prosecutor, some part-time assistant prosecutors, and a limited clerical and support staff. Since prosecutors in New York State, for example, each represent their respective counties, resources within a particular county often dictate the size of an office. Readers should explore their own prosecutors in their jurisdiction at all levels of government, local, county, state, and federal, to be well versed in the various resources within each of these offices. Serving the most populated county in the United States in the most populated state in the nation, the Los Angeles County, California District Attorney is responsible for one of the largest prosecutors' offices in the United States, serving just over 10 million people according to the United States

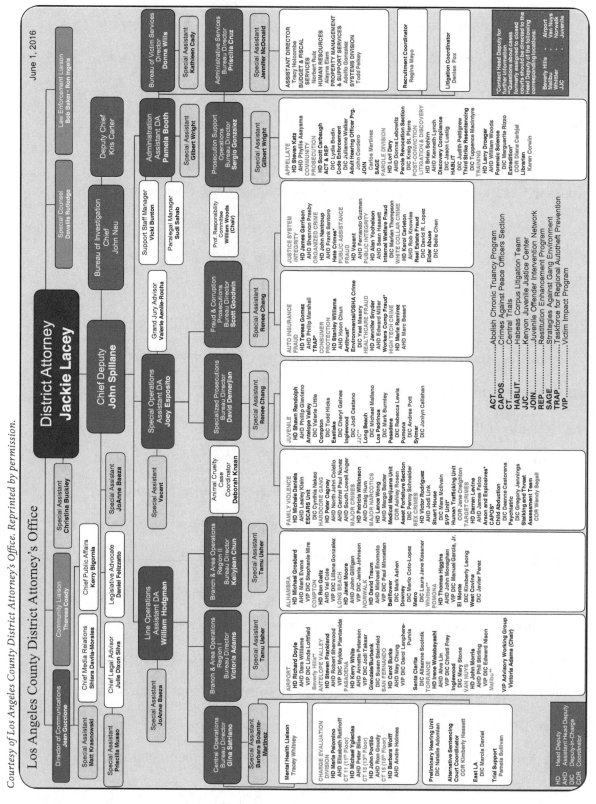

Los Angeles County District Attorney's Office

Census (2016). The District Attorney of Los Angeles County leads a staff of approximately 2,100 members including 1,000 deputy/assistant district attorney's, 300 investigators, and a support staff of nearly 800 (DA.LACounty.gov, 2016). The annual operating budget for the Los Angeles County District Attorney proposed for 2016-2017 was $391,085,000 (CEO. LACOUNTY.gov, 2016).

Conversely, in Oneida County, New York, there is one elected district attorney, currently **Scott D. McNamara**, 21 assistant district attorney's, seven (7) criminal investigators, and seven (7) support staff. The Oneida County District Attorney's Office serves a 2015 estimated county population of 232,500 residents (U.S. Census Bureau, 2016). The annual operating budget for the Oneida County District Attorney for 2016 was $3,527,591 (OCGOV.net/ budget, 2016). Much like a private practice attorney who specializes in one area such as DWI, litigation, appeals, or matrimonial matters, district attorney's offices have likewise needed to develop focused groups of prosecutors who specialize in one area of criminal activity or related functions of the office. Toward that end, District Attorney McNamara has established nine (9) specialized bureau units, each headed by a designated bureau chief or chief investigator.

PEOPLE: The Honorable Scott D. McNamara

Oneida County District Attorney. Scott D. McNamara is the Oneida County District Attorney. He started his career in the office as an Assistant District Attorney in 1992. He has held numerous positions within the office including Bureau Chief of the Narcotics Unit, Chairperson of the Death Penalty Committee, and First Assistant DA. In 2007, McNamara was elected DA and has since been re-elected. During his tenure, McNamara started many initiatives including (1) an economic crime unit; (2) a conviction integrity unit; (3) a second chance program and (4) the addition of a community liaison to his office. McNamara is currently a member of the New York State Commission on Forensic Science and he is the President-elect of the District Attorney's Association of the State of New York (DAASNY), assuming office as President in July, 2017. He recently served on a committee with the National Academy of Sciences that studied eyewitness identification and issued a report titled: *Identifying the Culprit: Assessing Eyewitness Identification* (adapted from the National District Attorney's Association, 2016, as submitted by The Honorable Scott D. McNamara, reprinted with permission).

The Honorable Scott D. McNamara by Karl F. Ermisch

The Honorable Scott D. McNamara, Oneida County District Attorney (2007–present).

Each unit is individually responsible for cases and activities under their domain. In addition, the District Attorney's Office is responsible for staffing all of the local town and village criminal courts throughout Oneida County, as well as staffing a daily caseload in Oneida County Court.

During the Corr case, two prosecutors were dedicated to the assembly of documentation and related evidence for the successful prosecution of the initially captured defendant on February 27, 2006, Toussaint Davis, and the later indictment of the two remaining surviving defendants, Robert Ward and Marion Pegese. **Assistant District Attorney Kurt D. Hameline** (ret.), and **Assistant District Attorney Paul J. Hernon** (ret.) lead the case for the prosecution in the *People of the State of New York vs. John T. Healy* (a.k.a. Toussaint Davis, a.k.a. Toussaint Martin). Ultimately, only defendant Toussaint Davis

PEOPLE: Kurt D. Hameline

Kurt D. Hameline, Esq., is a former Oneida County Assistant District Attorney, and a member of the team responsible for the prosecution in the *People of the State of New York vs. John T. Healy*. Mr. Hameline is now in private law practice.

PEOPLE: Paul J. Hernon

Paul J. Hernon, Esq., is a former Oneida County Assistant District Attorney, and a member of the team responsible for the prosecution in the *People of the State of New York vs. John T. Healy*. Mr. Hernon currently serves as the law clerk for the Honorable Michael L. Dwyer, Oneida County Court Judge.

was prosecuted in Oneida County Court for the robbery of Lennon's W.B. Wilcox Jewelers, and the murder of Officer Corr. Subsequent indictments for defendants Ward and Pegese were dismissed in lieu of prosecution by the United States Attorney's Office for the Northern District of New York for all three defendants (Davis, Ward, & Pegese).

Shortly after the robbery of Lennon's W.B. Wilcox Jewelry Store and the murder of Officer Corr occurred, and with at least one or more felons who had escaped initial capture, federal law enforcement resources quickly became involved in the investigation. Utilizing the cell phone technology available at the time (2006), agents from the Federal Bureau of Alcohol, Tobacco, and Firearms (ATF) were able to quickly determine that calls made from the car jacked/ kidnapped tow truck operator's cell phone were hitting off of cell phone towers heading south into Pennsylvania, thus crossing state lines. While at the federal level, the ATF, FBI, and United States Marshals Service ultimately became a part of the Joseph D. Corr Robbery-Homicide Task Force, federal prosecutorial resources were ultimately coordinated under the banner of the United States Attorney's Office for the Northern District of New York located in Syracuse, New York.

The lead federal prosecutors engaged in the investigation from shortly after the robbery-homicide occurred were **Executive Assistant United States Attorney John G. Duncan** (ret.), and **Assistant United States Attorney Richard R. Southwick**. Effectively leveraging federal prosecutorial financial

Read the original Oneida County, New York & federal grand jury indictments and the full transcript of the Oneida County Court Trial of *People of the State of New York vs. John T. Healy* and the entire transcript of the federal trial, *United States of America v. Marion Pegese, Robert Ward & Toussaint Davis* in our online companion.

PEOPLE: John G. Duncan, Esq. (ret.).

John G. Duncan is the former Executive Assistant United States Attorney for the Northern District of New York, and a member of the team responsible for the prosecution in the case of the *United States of America v. Toussaint Daivs, Marion Pegese & Robert Ward.*

PEOPLE: Richard R. Southwick, Esq.

Richard R. Southwick is an Assistant United States Attorney for the Northern District of New York, and a member of the team responsible for the prosecution in the case of the *United States of America v. Toussaint Daivs, Marion Pegese & Robert Ward.*

and personnel resources became a critical element toward the eventual successful prosecution of the defendants involved in the Corr case. As the investigation progressed, it became clear that the defendant's actions clearly involved criminal activity in multiple states, and at a minimum conspiring together to commit these coordinated jewelry store robberies. With the formation of the Joseph D. Corr Robbery-Homicide Task Force, local law enforcement agencies involved in the investigation were able to expand their jurisdiction through the engagement of federal resources that could seamlessly cross previously restrictive jurisdictional law enforcement boundaries. The synergies created by the formation of the Task Force allowed local and federal prosecutors to build much more complete and effective cases against all three surviving defendants in the Corr case, thus leading to convictions in both the local, and federal court cases.

Questions for Review and Further Discussion

1. Identify all of the local, county, state, and federal law enforcement agencies in your jurisdiction, clearly identifying, by name of the current occupant, the head of each of those agencies.

2. Identify the lead prosecutorial offices within your jurisdiction.

3. Select three police agencies in your region and analyze and compare the fiscal and personnel resources available to those agencies. What differentiates the three?

4. Select a major crime that has occurred in the last five years in your jurisdiction/region and analyze the law enforcement resources expended in that case. How might you have done things differently upon hindsight?

Chapter 4

Prosecution: Reflections of a Prosecutor

~The Honorable Michael A. Arcuri

Outline

Keywords

1. Assigned Counsel

2. Circumstantial Evidence

3. Command Post

4. County Coroner

5. Defense Counsel

6. Defenses

7. District Attorney

8. Evidence Technician

9. Exhibits

10. Foundation

11. Jurisdiction

12. Jury

Courtesy of the Honorable Scott D. McNamara, Oneida County District Attorney.

PEOPLE: The Honorable Michael A. Arcuri

served as a Member of Congress from New York; born in Utica, Oneida County, N.Y., in June 1959; graduated from T.R. Proctor High School, Utica, N.Y.; B.A., State University of New York, Albany, N.Y., 1981; J.D., New York Law School, New York, N.Y., 1984; lawyer, private practice; college instructor; Oneida County, N.Y., district attorney, 1994–2006; elected as a Democrat to the One Hundred Tenth Congress and to the succeeding Congress (January 3, 2007–January 3, 2011)

The Honorable Michael A. Arcuri, reprinted with permission, DeNicola Photography

The Honorable Michael A. Arcuri

13. Lead Desk

14. Lead Index System

15. Medical Examiner

16. Objection

17. Prosecutor

18. Public Defender

19. Task Force

20. Trial

21. United States Attorney for the
    Northern District of New York

People

1. The Honorable Michael A. Arcuri

2. Michael A. Coluzza

3. Chief Daniel J. English

4. Chief Raymond L. Philo

5. Honorable Glenn T. Suddaby

Expected Learning Outcomes

After reading this chapter and supplemental online materials, the reader will be able to:

1. Define terms fundamental to understanding the role of the prosecutor in the People of the State of New York v. Defendant(s) equation.

2. Explain the role of the District Attorney's Office and the importance of their early involvement in a case in progress.

3. Explain the differences between a local (state) prosecution vs. a federal prosecution.

    4 – 1 – Receiving the Call and Response

    4 – 2 – Early Presence/Early Processing

    4 – 3 – Witness to Murder

    4 – 4 – Deploying Prosecutorial Resources and Building the Case

4 – 1 – Receiving the Call and Response

It was a winter night late in the season. I was with a few of my friends getting together to watch a game. I still remember when the call came in; it was around 8:00 or 9:00 p.m. One of the people I was with was a police officer with another local department and he knew from the look on my face as soon as I answered the phone that something bad had happened, only at that time neither of us knew just how bad it was.

I went straight to the scene at the Byrne Dairy on Route 233 in Kirkland, NY. I had been past the gas station hundreds of times and even stopped there a few. Before it was a gas station, it was a miniature golf course. It's funny I remember as I drove up to the scene that was the first thing that popped into my mind—playing miniature golf at that spot. Now it was the scene of a tragic murder.

When I arrived, as is always the case when the **District Attorney** arrives at a crime scene, I was briefed by the

Oneida County Sheriff's Office

Byrne Dairy, State Rt. 233/Clark Mills Road, Town of Kirkland, New York, taken within days of Officer Corr's murder, from the ground and the air.

> **District Attorney:** The district attorney, sometimes referred to as the prosecutor, is the representative of the government, the People of the State of New York (or other state). District Attorney's are typically elected by the people of their jurisdiction (usually a county), as is the case in New York State. A public official appointed or elected to represent the state in criminal cases in a particular judicial district; prosecutor [abbreviated D.A], [also termed *public prosecutor; state's attorney; prosecuting attorney*, and at the federal level, the United States Attorney] (Garner, 2014; Black's Law Dictionary 10th ed., reprinted with permission, Thomson Reuters).

Larry Pacilio, Utica College

senior law enforcement officer. On this night it was New Hartford Police Chief **Raymond L. Philo**. As Chief Philo began to brief me, I could tell he was having a difficult time. This was not some stranger who had unfortunately been at the wrong place at the wrong time. This was one of his own, a young officer whom Chief Philo hired, trained and served with. The New Hartford Police Department was not like most departments. It was a small, very modern and a very proud department with a long history. The officers were a very close-knit group much like a family and all the officers knew each other, socialized together, and knew each other's families. Officer Corr was newly married with a young child; he was a local boy from a local family with a promising future. He was everything you hope for in a public servant. Chief Philo knew Joe and his entire family for many years and now Officer Corr was dead.

New Hartford Police Department/ Oneida County Sheriff's Office

Lennon's W.B. Wilcox Jewelers, New Hartford, NY, February 2006

Chief Philo and I had come on the jobs at roughly the same time, he as Chief of New Hartford and me as District Attorney. We had been through more than our share of difficult and high profile cases together but none like this and I could see in the Chief's face that despite all of his training and abilities this was going to be the most difficult thing professionally he ever had to face.

As Chief Philo began to brief me, he started to tell me how the call came in of a robbery in progress at Lennon's W.B. Wilcox Jewelers. At the time (2006),

Lennon's was one of a few dealers of Rolex Watches in the region. Lennon's was a high end jewelers owed by a local family that had been in business for years. This would later be a consideration in how we handled that part of the crime scene. The jewelry store was in a very high traffic business district within the Town of New

Hartford, NY, which the Chief added was a factor in how the matter evolved. Chief Philo went on to tell me how Officer Corr responded to the scene and pursued the suspects. He explained to me their initial theory of how the vehicular pursuit became a foot chase behind the convenience store on State Route 233 and how one of the suspects was believed to have gotten off a shot over his shoulder, which struck officer Corr. It was this shot that hit Officer Joseph Corr and ultimately killed him, although few of the details were known at that time. The facts at this time, as they usually are early in an investigation, were very inadequate. It's strange when thinking back to the tragic events of that evening, even after all these years, what tends to stick out in ones memory of those tragic events.

4 – 2 – Early Presence/Early Processing

I can still remember, as the night progressed standing on the side of the road with Chief Philo discussing the case. It was after midnight and it started to snow. The snowflakes were the biggest, whitest snowflakes I still to this day have ever seen; beautiful at any other time and in any other setting but not now. When you have an outdoor crime scene such as we had this night any change in weather conditions, like a heavy snow, can not only be a distraction, but can cause serious problems for investigators and prosecutors. A heavy blanketing snow such as the one we were getting that evening can wreak havoc for evidence technicians who must photograph a crime scene and attempt to locate and process evidence. This is difficult at night under normal conditions, but with the added covering of fresh snow the job becomes even more difficult.

A snowfall like the one we were getting that evening creates a number of challenges for evidence technicians processing a crime scene. Whether it is locating footprints, a button to a jacket that might have fallen off during the pursuit, or anything that might help identify the perpetrator, this heavy

Circumstantial Evidence: 1. Evidence based on inference and not on personal knowledge or observation. Also termed indirect evidence; oblique evidence. 2. All evidence that is not given by eyewitness testimony (Garner, 2014; Black's Law Dictionary 10th ed., reprinted with permission, Thomson Reuters).

snow was making that task nearly impossible. A boot footprint can be an extremely helpful piece of **circumstantial evidence** in helping to identify the perpetrator of a crime. These are the kind of things prosecutors and police investigators think about at a crime scene.

Shutterstock.com

A sample photo taken at night with snow falling.

The second problem with the changing weather that evening was snowflakes, making photos, which are critical to a criminal presentation of a case to a jury, far less effective. Instead of clear resonate representations of what the scene looked like at the time of the incident, you get blurry photos and videography often with big white blotches across the pictures. From a prosecutor's perspective, this makes it that much harder to portray to a **jury** what happened on the night in question. I have always believed it is extremely helpful if a prosecutor can

Shutterstock.com

give a jury a sense that they were at the crime scene on the night in question. That is why photographs and video of the crime scene are always so effective in criminal cases. But that night the heavy snow, after the occurrence of the crime, was making the accurate portrayal of the scene that much more difficult.

> **Jury:** A group of persons selected according to law and given the power to decide questions of fact and return a verdict in the case submitted to them. In certain contexts, jury embraces any fact-trier, including an arbitrator or a trial judge sitting in a nonjury proceeding-Also termed *empaneled jury*; *empaneled jury* (Garner, 2014; Black's Law Dictionary 10th ed., reprinted with permission, Thomson Reuters).

There was one more additional problem with the snow from an evidentiary perspective. In presenting a case for trial, a prosecutor has to qualify each photograph, purportedly being offered into evidence as a true and accurate representation of the scene at the time of the crime; yet the snow actually creates a different look from the actual scene. When this occurred we would often show a jury the photos from the night in question, for whatever they were worth, preserve the scene (not allow anyone to contaminate it), then have the original evidence technician return to the scene and take photos at a later time when conditions were similar to the night in question. This is what we did for this investigation in the hope that it would give the jury to a sense of the actual conditions at the time

Objection: A formal statement opposing something that has occurred, or is about to occur, in court and seeking the judge's immediate ruling on the point. The party objecting must [usually] state the basis for the objection to preserve the right to appeal an adverse ruling (Garner, 2014; Black's Law Dictionary 10th ed., reprinted with permission, Thomson Reuters).

Defense Counsel: An attorney hired/appointed to represent a defendant. Typically this individual is a member of a Public Defender's Office, or an assigned attorney, frequently called an assigned counsel. These are typically local members of a Bar Association who are a part of a pool of attorneys available in a rotation to defend accused individuals in criminal matters.

Foundation: The basis on which something is supported; [especially] evidence or testimony that establishes the admissibility of other evidence [laying the foundation] (Garner, 2014; Black's Law Dictionary 10th ed., reprinted with permission, Thomson Reuters).

Exhibit: 1. A document, record, or other tangible object formally introduced as evidence in court. 2. A document attached to and made part of a pleading, motion, contract, or other instrument (Garner, 2014; Black's Law Dictionary 10th ed., reprinted with permission, Thomson Reuters).

of the incident. This of course was subject to an **objection** by **defense counsel** and it was necessary to set the proper foundation for the subsequent photos to be admitted into evidence.

This is done by having follow up photographs taken by an evidence technician who was on the scene on the night in question, preferably the person who took the original photographs. The evidence technician should then take the exact same photographs from the exact same angle as the original photos when the weather conditions were better. We did this on this investigation so the jurors could see the scene the way it looked at the actual moment of the commission of the crime rather than after the snowfall when the pictures were taken.

In order to successfully introduce the second set of photographs into evidence we would be required to lay the proper **foundation** to get them admitted into evidence over objection. To do this it would be necessary to ask the evidence technician who took the photographs a series of questions along these lines:

Q. Officer were you at the crime scene on the night in question?

A. Yes.

Q. Did you take the original photos marked as **Exhibits** 1–25?

A. Yes.

Q. Did you at some point return to the scene to take photos?

A. Yes.

Q. Why did you do that?

A. In reviewing the pictures with you, I could see that some of the images from that night of the incident were blurry because of the heavy snow that started to fall after we began to process the scene. So you asked me to return and retake the photos on a clearer evening.

Q. And when did you do that?

A. Two days later.

Q. And is that when all of these photographs, Exhibits 25–50 were taken?

A. Yes.

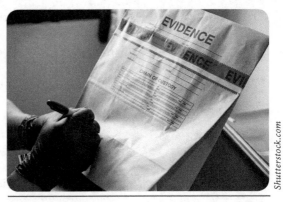

Evidence collected at a crime scene may be introduced as an exhibit in a trial.

Q. Now did you have an opportunity to view the crime scene on the night in question before it started to snow?

A. Yes.

Q. And at what time did you first observe it?

A. As soon as I arrived at the scene, probably a half hour after the incident took place.

Q. And can you describe for the jury the way the scene appeared to you when you first arrived and observed it?

A. It was a typical late winter night.

Q. Was it snowing at that time?

A. No, as I said it was not snowing when I first arrived; it did not start snowing until about midnight.

Q. Was the scene in some way preserved after the first night?

A. Yes, it was.

Q. Can you tell us how it was preserved?

A. Yes, there were two officers there at all times between the time I left the scene the morning after the shooting, until the time I returned to take the photographs marked as Exhibits 25–50 two days later.

Q. And in comparing the images reflected in the second set of photographs you took (Exhibits 25–50) two days later to the way the crime scene appeared to you when you first observed on the night in question what can you tell me?

A. The images in the second set of photos those marked as Exhibits 25–50 exactly reflect the way the scene appeared to me on the night in question, before it started snowing.

Q. And does the second set of photographs, Exhibits 25–50, fairly and accurately depict the scene as you first viewed one-half hour after the incident and before the snow started falling on the night in question?

A. Yes, they do.

Prosecutor: The People would offer People's Exhibits 25–50.

This is one of the many reasons why, from the big picture perspective, it is always important that a representative from the office of the prosecutor that will be handling the case, be present at a major crime scene. It is also helpful in making a smooth transition from investigation to prosecution that the attorney who is handling the case is present during as many aspects of the case as possible.

There are multiple reasons for this, not the least of which is advising investigators as to what evidence you as a prosecutor think might be useful to the ultimate success of the prosecution. Additionally, often when certain evidence that may be relevant to an investigation requires a warrant to be obtained, assisting in preparation and review of the warrant before it is presented to a local judge is very helpful to investigators. As District Attorney I always tried to have the assistant district attorney who I expected to assign the case to present at the scene. In my experience this was the best way to give the prosecuting attorney a sense and feel of the crime scene.

As a prosecutor the one thing you quickly learn is that a prosecutor who is on a crime scene from early in the investigation has a significant advantage. First he or she begins to develop a good working relationship with the investigators assigned to that case, which is always very helpful to a successful prosecution. Second he or she becomes not only personally invested in the case but is able to get a much better perspective and sense of the physical appearance and condition of the scene. The assistant district attorney (ADA) will then not just hear from witnesses at trial what the lighting and weather conditions were like but will have personal knowledge of what the conditions were like at the time of the event. They will know in advance how things were at the time of the crime. This can be a significant advantage to a prosecutor when preparing the case, especially when examining or cross examining a witness at a trial or preliminary hearing.

4 – 3 – Witness to Murder

There is also one other aspect about murder scenes, at least every murder scene I have ever been to, and this one was no different. It is this almost surreal

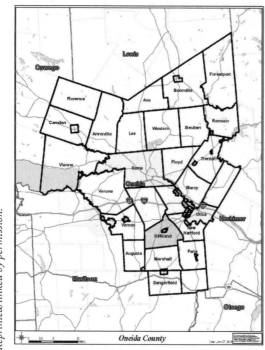

Oneida County

Jurisdiction: 1. a government's general power to exercise authority over all persons and things within its territory; esp., a state's power to create interests that will be recognized under common law principles as valid in other states. 2. A court's power to decide a case or issue a decree (Garner, 2014; Black's Law Dictionary 10th ed., reprinted with permission, Thomson Reuters).

Task Force: A temporary group of people formed to carry out a specific mission or project, or to solve a problem that requires a multi-disciplinary approach (BusinessDictionary.com, 2016).

PEOPLE: Daniel J. English

is the Chief of Police of the Town of Kirkland Police Department. Chief English serves is this capacity presently.

sense, something almost in the air it seems. I think in some cases it may have something to do with the fact that the victim's body is often still on the scene. Perhaps it is because of the sense of the extreme nature of the violence that so recently occurred in that very place. But to me it was always that feeling that a very short time ago there was a living breathing person right here and then just like that they are lying here dead. It always made me feel like it was the job of law enforcement to stop time in an attempt to reconstruct the crime and find the perpetrator. In this case, although Officer Corr had been taken to the hospital, the scene still had that dreamlike surreal feeling to it.

As the evening progressed more and more law enforcement personnel from numerous agencies arrived on the scene. Even though the shooting of Officer Corr actually took place in the Town of Kirkland, NY, and that technically meant it was within their **jurisdiction**, it was agreed that because the initial robbery of the jewelry store occurred in the Town of New Hartford, the investigation would be handled by a **task force** under the direction of New Hartford Police Chief Raymond L. Philo. The Chief of the Kirkland Police Department at the time was **Daniel J. English**. Chief English's experience, his collaborative approach to policing, and his realistic view of the incident would prove to be a mantra for this task force of law enforcement officers.

This interagency cooperation that manifested itself from the first minute of this investigation proved to be a significant advantage to the investigation. It gave investigators an extraordinarily diverse, talented, experienced, and well equipped multi-agency unit well equipped to handle even an investigation as complex as this one. Bringing together and coordinating such a unit however did not happen by itself. Chief Philo of New Hartford took the lead role and acted as the spokesman for the taskforce (task force policing is discussed in detail in other sections of this text). While Chief Philo and the members of the New Hartford Police Department had to attend to duties surrounding the wake and funeral of Officer Corr, the task force nonetheless continued to operate 24 hours a day with seasoned investigators.

4 – 4 – Deploying Prosecutorial Resources and Building the Case

As the night progressed, it became obvious that this was going to be a protracted investigation. Everyone soon realized that this would require long hours, numerous law enforcement officers working 24 hours a day seven days a week, along with significant financial resources. But first the unit needed a large central location to act as a **command post** for the rapidly growing task force. The Town of Kirkland made available the Kirkland Senior Citizen Center. The Kirkland Senior Citizen Center was the logical choice as

> **Command Post:** (also known as an incident command post) is "the field location at which the primary tactical-level, on-scene incident command functions are performed (Federal Emergency Management Agency [FEMA], 2008).

PEOPLE: Michael A. Coluzza, Esq.

Assistant District Attorney with the Oneida County, New York District Attorney's Office. Mr. Coluzza currently serves as the First Assistant District Attorney.

The Arson Strike Force

was a task force of several police departments in Oneida County created several years earlier to help the City of Utica fight its Arson problem. The unit was highly successful and included the New York State Police, the Oneida County Sheriff's Office, the Utica Police Department the New Hartford Police Department, the County of Oneida and The District Attorney's Office.

it was large enough to easily host all of the investigating officers, and associated records close to the murder scene.

I realized early on we needed a number of ADAs involved in the investigation so they would be able to be present at the various crime scenes and headquarters to assist officers with the investigation. The first call I made to my staff that evening was **Michael A. Coluzza**. Mike was one of my two First Assistant District Attorneys; he was very level-headed in high-pressure situations and was also an excellent trial attorney with a number of murder trials to his credit. Having been the ADA in charge of our local **Arson Strike Force** several years earlier, ADA Coluzza certainly had more experience in dealing with law enforcement task forces. Most importantly Mike was the ADA who handled New Hartford Town Court each week so he knew Officer Corr and all of the New Hartford Police Department personnel, which would prove to be very helpful in this investigation.

As soon as Mike got on the scene, his experience working with the New Hartford Police Department, his relationships with other officers and his reputation for hard work and fairness with local police agencies, made the first crucial 12–24 hours of the investigation incredibly effective and productive. As the jewelry store was a major part of this investigation and the one place that could help to quickly solve this case, ADA Coluzza left the scene in Kirkland after a short time and headed over to Lennon's W.B. Wilcox Jeweler's, the scene of the original robbery, to assist in that aspect of the investigation.

At this point in the investigation, the jewelry store aspect was somewhat sensitive to deal with. It was sensitive in that the personnel who worked at the store as well as the owners of the store, all of whom were law-abiding citizens and who probably had never had any dealing whatsoever with law enforcement before this, were all still potential suspects and needed to be questioned, and if need be interrogated, and statements taken before they were cleared to go home. This part of the investigation was somewhat of a challenge from a prosecutor's perspective because it required balancing properly investigating the case, with allowing traumatized members of the community to go home and go to sleep. In the early stage of an investigation, especially one such as this, with such a well-planned and well-carried out robbery, everyone was considered a suspect. Here, as with robberies such as this, there is always the possibility that the robbery was an inside job.

Early on in this case, we had somewhat of a hint that no one on the inside was involved for a couple of reasons; nonetheless no one wanted to chance missing something in an investigation where a police officer had been killed. One fact we were aware of early on in the investigation is that one of the young female clerks at the store was forced to hide in a backroom during the robbery and the door was locked. While hiding under a desk she took out her cell phone and called her boyfriend to tell him what was happening. The boyfriend subsequently contacted law enforcement, which initiated the first response of police officers, including Officer Corr. Officer Corr had been across the street from the jewelry store at the New Hartford Police Department's shopping mall substation when the call was received.

Because the circumstances of the call were so unusual, some investigators were not convinced that the call was legitimate and may have been made as a cover to being an accomplice in helping to set up the job. Additional questions were asked among investigators, as are always asked in situations such as this, as

to whether the store and/or the owners were having any financial troubles and could this have been an inside job to set and bolster an insurance claim. Although looking back at it today, these seem like outlandish and unimaginable scenarios, at the time they all seemed if not plausible certainly aspects that needed to be investigated and cleared.

Defense: A defendant's stated reason why the plaintiff or prosecutor has no valid case; [especially] a defendant's answer, denial, or plea [her defense was that she was 25 miles away in the building at the time of the robbery] (Garner, 2014; Black's Law Dictionary 10th ed., reprinted with permission, Thomson Reuters).

Trial: A formal judicial examination of evidence and determination of legal claims in an adversary proceeding (Garner, 2014; Black's Law Dictionary 10th ed., reprinted with permission, Thomson Reuters).

One aspect in which a prosecutor is helpful in investigating a crime at the early stages is identifying possible **defenses** that might be raised by defense counsel at **trial** and asking the police investigators to rigorously investigate that aspect of the crime. This can prove to be very helpful at trial as it gives the prosecutor the ability to recall an investigator as part of its rebuttal case and demonstrate that a particular defense raised by the defendant's attorney after the People rested, were identified early in the case, thoroughly investigated, and disproved. This is part of the reason investigators needed to be thorough before they cleared anyone at the jewelry store scene.

Very often at a murder scene there can be some overlap and disagreement as to who is in charge of the scene and who has the ultimate authority to make the decisions as to how the scene is processed. It is also often important to an investigation, depending on whether the victim's body is still on the scene, how the body is photographed and when it is ultimately removed from the scene. Obviously if a victim is still alive at the time emergency medical technicians (EMTs) arrive, he or she is administered care and/or rushed to the hospital for further treatment [as was the case with Officer Corr]. However, if the victim were pronounced dead at the scene, evidence technicians and prosecutors generally like to have the scene photographed first with the victim where he or she actually fell and died. The reason for this is, these photographs can often prove to be helpful to a jury in understanding the chain of events leading up to the incident and proving what happened or did not happen.

In New York State at that time, it was customary that the District Attorney was in charge of the crime scene; however if there was a deceased victim at the scene the law provided that the **County Coroner** was responsible for the body and therefore ultimately the most important part of the scene. To an outsider this may seem like petty jurisdictional turf issues, but at 3:00 a.m. on a cold snowy winter morning, in the middle of a murder

Coroner: A public official whose duty it is to investigate the causes and circumstances of any death that occurs suddenly, suspiciously, or violently. [See also Medical Examiner] (Garner, 2014; Black's Law Dictionary 10th ed., reprinted with permission, Thomson Reuters).

investigation, with evidence technicians attempting to properly document the scene and the Corner ordering the body to be removed from the scene and brought to the morgue, it can make for some heated exchanges. This sometimes created conflicts at murder scenes if the Coroner arrived before the DA and made the call to remove the victim before law enforcement had an opportunity to photograph the body or even draw a line or spray paint the outline of the victim, as you often see in old movies. Some counties actually had arrangements where the DA was also the Coroner [Madison County, NY]; this obviously alleviates such a scenario from occurring and can make for a smoother crime scene investigation. Today, many counties have done away with the Coroner system and have adopted a **Medical Examiner** System for taking charge of a deceased victim.

> **Medical Examiner:** A public official who investigates deaths, conduct autopsies, and helps the state prosecute homicide cases. Medical examiners have replaced corners in many states [sometimes shortened to examiner] (Garner, 2014; Black's Law Dictionary 10th ed., reprinted with permission, Thomson Reuters).
>
> **Lead Desk:** A physical location, usually at a law enforcement command post, where all leads and other case management information and activities are received, assigned, and systematically cataloged for a specific investigation.

Jurisdictional issues are not the only factors which can affect the quality of an investigation. Having numerous law enforcement agencies at a crime scene can create a logistical nightmare for the investigation of a single scene routine matter, but for a multi-scene investigation such as this, it can prove to be incredibly challenging. Little did we know at the time, it would turn out to be not only numerous scenes and jurisdictions but an investigation that would take place in three different states (New York, Pennsylvania, and New Jersey). In working through how to

logistically handle the investigation, the various agencies worked out a system for what department would be responsible for what aspect of the investigation. For example, one agency may handle the evidence technician work, while another agency would handle the **Lead Desk** (discussed in detail in other sections of this text).

A lead index system can be compared to a library Dewey Decimal System. The **Lead Index System** (discussed in detail in other sections of this text) is a management tool used in large investigations with

numerous leads. The lead desk is the central point of the lead index system, where incoming leads are recorded and subsequently signed out for follow-up by law enforcement personnel. What the officer managing the lead desk does is essentially assign a number to any relevant piece of evidence or information in the criminal investigation and categorizes it. This relevant information can be the name of an individual who is believed to have witnessed the crime, a serial number on a gun found at the scene, or even a receipt for a donut shop found on the pocket of the victim. If this piece of evidence or information, known as a *lead*, is unknown and deemed to be relevant to the investigation, it is referred to as an *open lead* and it is assigned by the officer in charge of the lead desk, to an officer or team to investigate it. This system has been incredibly enhanced with the use of computers to categorize and keep track of the many leads in an investigation. In all there were an incredible 893 leads investigated and categorized in the Corr investigation.

Before leaving the scene early the next morning, I spoke to ADA Coluzza by phone to get an update from the jewelry store. ADA Coluzza indicated that the investigators had divided up into teams and were beginning the tedious process of interviewing and taking statements from each and every employee as well as owners of the store. It is normally the procedure of law enforcement to keep potential witnesses, and especially individuals who had not been cleared, separate from one another. This is done so that witnesses who might have been involved in the crime do not have a chance to discuss the events with other witnesses before being interviewed. When this is not done, witnesses will often attempt to coordinate their stories. What sometimes also happens even with individuals who are not in any way involved in the crime is they unintentionally tend to adopt the story of someone else, who they believe may have a better memory or different recollection (right or wrong) of the events that occurred.

One of the aspects of this first 24 hours of the investigation I remember best is returning to the command post the first thing the next morning and seeing all of the employees and the owner of the jewelry store still waiting to be questioned or waiting to be sent home. It was more than 15 hours after the robbery and I had completely forgotten they had not yet been cleared and were still there. The police were close to clearing them and letting everyone go home but no one wanted to leave a stone unturned so they were being very thorough and fastidious in the interviewing process and the preparation of statements. I spoke to the owner of the store and he was being as reasonable and cooperative as we could ever have asked for. These victims had been through a very harrowing and traumatic experience themselves, and yet when they finally heard that an officer had been shot, they were not at all worried about their own situation but were concerned with helping police get as much information as they could to solve the crime. I recall it was about 10:00 a.m. the next morning that we all gathered at the command post and decided we had all we were going to get from these individuals and that we were relatively sure no one on the inside had anything whatsoever to do with the crime. We let them all go home about mid-morning.

While police do not actually use the television detective line "Don't make any plans to leave town," we nonetheless did ask them if it would all right if we called them if we had any additional questions or follow up. All without exception answered yes and told us if they thought of anything else they forgot they would give the police a call.

It is at this point in an investigation when supervisors often have to step in and tell investigators and ADAs to go home get some sleep and come back later. What often ends up being the case, however, is everyone is working on adrenaline and caffeine and they don't always realize they have been working for over 24 hours. This is when supervisors have to step in and send people home. Regardless of how well intentioned someone is or how driven they are after 24 straight hours of working a person loses his or her perspective and judgment and that can be detrimental to the investigation. I noticed this that morning as most of the officers had been working the case for over 15 hours and most had already put a full day in before the investigation had even begun. We started ordering our staffs to go home and get some rest. This does not always go over well when a brother police officer is killed in the line of duty, but it is something that is necessary and a component of being a good supervisor. At this point the investigation was progressing well and the first team that had responded had done an incredible job of getting the investigation off the ground and pointed in the right direction. The first step in the investigation was complete, and now the hard, tedious work would begin.

4 – 5 – Leveraging the Laws and Resources – State and Federal Collaboration

Article 1, Section 8 [18] of the United States Constitution gives to Congress the right to make any laws it deems necessary and proper for carrying out the operation of government. Article 1, Section 8 [18] specifically provides:

Congress shall have the power [t]o make all laws which shall be necessary
and proper for carrying into execution the foregoing Powers, and all other
powers vested by this Constitution in the Government of the United States,
or in any department or Officer thereof. (U.S. Const. art. I, § 8, §§ 18).

If however Congress fails to act in a particular area, the 10th Amendment reserves to the states those powers not otherwise given to the Federal Government by the Constitution. The 10th Amendment to the United States Constitution, enacted in 1791 provides: "The powers not delegated to United States by the Constitution, nor prohibited by it to the States, are reserved to the States respectively, or to the people" (U.S. Const. amend. X).

Should there develop any ambiguity or discrepancy as to whether a lawfully enacted state law or federal provision controls, the federal provision always supersedes the state. Article VI Section 2 of the Constitution, which has come to be known as the Supremacy Clause, leaves no question but that the Constitution and the laws made pursuant thereto are the supreme law of the land and supersede those laws made by states that conflict with federal law (U.S. Const. art. VI, § 2).

Under the Federal system of government in the United States however the responsibility for safeguarding and maintaining the health and safety of the local population has always been the primary responsibility of state and local governments. This means that the right and authority to enact penal law statues and prescribe punishments for violations of those statutes rests with the state and local legislatures. Therefore, the day-to-day responsibility for enforcing those state and local statutes rests with the village, town, city, county, or state police department where the crime occurs and the state or local prosecutor responsible for the prosecution of local crimes under state law.

While some states have state prosecutors, which have general statewide criminal prosecutorial authority, New York State has independently elected prosecutors in each of the 57 counties and five boroughs of New York City. This means that in New York State, general jurisdiction to prosecute crimes, such as murder and robbery, rests with the locally elected prosecutor. This jurisdiction and authority to prosecute however is not exclusive.

> In New York State, the State Attorney General also has jurisdiction to prosecute criminal matters in certain selected areas. Section 63(1) of the NY Executive Law sets forth in pertinent part: The attorney-general shall: 1. Prosecute and defend all actions and proceedings in which the state is interested, and have charge and control of all the legal business of the departments and bureaus of the state, or of any office thereof which requires the services of attorney or counsel, in order to protect the interest of the state, but this section shall not apply to any of the military department bureaus or military offices of the state.

Most local prosecutors tend to be conscious of, and very protective of their authority to decide who will be prosecuted and how they will be prosecuted. As with most if not all of the 61 independently elected district attorneys in New York State, this territorial tendency is not about ego or protecting ones prosecutorial turf, but rather about maintaining the sense security, and safety that the local citizens come to expect and rely upon from their elected district attorney. It is more about insuring that those living within the county feel safe, secure and confident in those they had hired and elected to protect them.

There also often is a feeling among most local prosecutors that they can do the job of prosecuting local crimes better that any federal prosecutor's office. Whether or not that is true is of course irrelevant, but what is relevant is that local prosecutors do not like to give the appearance to the public who elected them and pay their salary, that they cannot do the job and must bring in someone from the outside to do the job for them.

The last thing anyone wanted in this investigation was to leave any resource on the table, especially in light of the incredible extent of the cooperation that was being demonstrated by the local police agencies. The decision of whether to call in the **United States Attorney for the Northern District of New York** became very easy early in the investigation when we learned that this case was not isolated to Oneida County or even New York State but rather went across state lines and into the State of Pennsylvania, and by an unrelated crime into the State of New Jersey as well.

United States Attorney for the Northern District of New York: Like a local district attorney, state's attorney, or prosecutor, the United States Attorney and his/her assistant are charged with representing the People of the United States in regards to violations of federal criminal laws/prosecutions. There are 94 federal districts in the United States, each represented by one appointed United States Attorney (USA), and many other Assistant United States Attorneys (AUSA).

Title 18 of the United States Code (U.S.C) § 1951 has come to be known as The Hobbs Act. U.S. Attorney's Handbook: http://www.justice.gov/usam/usam-9-131000-hobbs-act-18-usc-1951 The Hobbs Act was enacted in 1946 and takes its name from the sponsor of the legislation Congressman Sam Hobbs of Alabama. The legislation was enacted in an attempt to aggressively address racketeering in labor management disputes. Among other things, the Act prohibits actual or attempted robbery or extortion affecting interstate or foreign commerce. Section 1951 also proscribes conspiracy to commit robbery or extortion without reference to the conspiracy statute at 18 U.S.C. § 371. Although the Hobbs Act was enacted as a statute to combat racketeering in labor-management disputes, the statute is frequently used in connection with cases involving public corruption, commercial disputes, and corruption directed at members of labor unions (United States Department of Justice, 2015, § 9-131.010).

The Act, in essence, gives the Federal Government, through the United States Attorney, jurisdiction over an inter-state matter that would, under ordinary circumstances, rest within the purview of local law enforcement and prosecutors. While the Federal Prosecutors in the Northern District of New York were always good about not being overly aggressive in stepping on the toes of local prosecutors, there was still always a cautious and deliberate approach when our office asked the federal government for assistance in a case.

Very early in the investigation however, we reached out to the U.S. Attorney for the Northern District of New York for its assistance in several aspects of the investigation. The U.S. Attorney for the Northern District of New York at the time was **Glenn T. Suddaby**. Suddaby himself a former county prosecutor with the Onondaga County District Attorney's Office, was very familiar with and mindful of the occasional jurisdictional conflicts between local prosecutors' offices and the U.S. Attorney's Office. With Suddaby as the U.S. Attorney, and our many years of working together

PEOPLE: The Honorable Glenn T. Suddaby

Glenn T. Suddaby is a United States District Court Judge for the Northern District of New York. At the time of his appointment in September 2008, he was U.S. Attorney for the Northern District of New York. Judge Suddaby earned his B.A. degree from the State University of New York at Plattsburgh in 1980 and his J.D. degree in 1985 from Syracuse University College of Law. Judge Suddaby served as Assistant District Attorney for Onondaga County from 1985–1989. He then became a private legal practitioner with the Menter Law Firm in Syracuse from 1989 to 1992. He was appointed Chief of Homicide for the Onondaga County District Attorney's Office in 1992 and subsequently served as First Chief Assistant District Attorney until October, 2002 when he was appointed U.S. Attorney for the Northern District of New York (United States District Court; Northern District of New York, 2015).

in the past, we in the Oneida County District Attorney's Office felt a certain level of comfort in calling in the U.S. Attorney's Office for assistance knowing they would not attempt to take the case over or insist on making all of the decisions in the direction the case would go. This level of comfort stemmed from the sense that Suddaby would understand the pressure on our office to keep the primary prosecution local and work with our office to direct the maximum resources of all of the organizations involved in the case into making arrests of the guilty parties and getting convictions.

Once the U.S. Attorney became involved in and more importantly interested in the case we were able to bring the significant resources of the Department of Justice to bear on case. Although the cost of the investigation remained the primary responsibility of local law enforcement and the Oneida County District Attorney's Office, having the resources of the U.S. Attorney's Office and the national network of law enforcement and prosecutors, which it had at its disposal, would prove to be and incredible asset to the ultimate success of this investigation, and eventual prosecutions at both the state and federal levels.

Ultimately, two prosecutions ensued; one at the local (Oneida County) level, and one at the federal level (all defendants). A careful orchestration of local, state, and federal resources that ultimately led to the conviction of all of those associated with the murder of Officer Joseph D. Corr; a truly textbook exercise of both understanding and leveraging state and federal laws, as well as state and federal resources all in the name of preserving justice. Although I had already moved on in my career at the time of the initial state prosecution of one of the defendants in this case, I remain enormously proud that in the immediate aftermath of Officer Corr's murder, prosecutors in collaboration with hundreds of others played an integral role in laying the foundation for getting justice for Officer Corr, his family, and the larger Oneida County and public safety community at large.

Questions for review and further discussion

1. Why should prosecutors be called/consulted when there is a major crime?

2. How can conflict between agencies be mitigated when there are multiple jurisdictions involved?

3. What are some of the differences in resources between local District Attorney's offices and the office of the United States Attorney?

4. What is The Hobbs Act?

Chapter 5

Managing Large Scale Investigations

~Raymond L. Philo

Outline

Keywords

1. Concurrent jurisdiction

2. Jurisdiction

3. Task Force Policing

4. Unity of Command

Expected Learning Outcomes

After reading this chapter and supplemental online materials, the reader will be able to:

1. Explain the concept of task force policing and its value to small and large-scale investigations.

2. Explain the concept of unity of command and why the same is critical to effective task force operations.

3. Differentiate between the use of normal operating fund sources and contingency fund sources and their use in emergency situations.

5 – 1 – Task Force Policing

© *Shutterstock.com*

When studying how law enforcement agencies conduct investigations, especially large scale investigations, it is important to understand and evaluate what manpower resources the "average" agency has at its disposal. Law enforcement agencies in the United States vary greatly in size and collateral resources such as specialized investigative units and equipment. According to data maintained by the United States Department of Justice (USDOJ), Bureau of Justice Statistics (2013), local police departments in the United States employ an estimated 605,000 individuals on a full-time basis. This figure includes 477,000 sworn law enforcement officers and approximately

Concurrent Jurisdiction: 1. Jurisdiction that might be exercised simultaneously by more than one court over the same subject matter and within the same territory, a litigant having the right to choose the court in which to file the action. 2. Jurisdiction shared by two or more states, [especially] over the physical boundaries (such as rivers or other bodies of water) between them [also termed coordinate jurisdiction; overlapping jurisdiction]. (Garner, 2014; Black's Law Dictionary 10th ed., reprinted with permission, Thomson Reuters).

128,000 non-sworn employees. While these resources may initially seem significant, it is important to note that about half (40%) of the 15,388 police departments in the United States employ fewer than 10 sworn officers. Often these small agencies do not have specialized investigative units and are fully engaged in performing the "patrol" function. While larger agencies might have **concurrent jurisdiction** with smaller agencies such as a state police organization, often that "larger" agency is disbursed to such an extent that they may not be able to provide much assistance to the smaller agency. The question remains, how does an agency lacking manpower and other collateral resources necessary for large scale comprehensive criminal investigations handle such a task? The answer lies in the concept of **Task Force Policing**.

> **Task Force Policing:** A temporary group of law enforcement and other related practitioners whose mission is directed at a specific public safety need that requires focused attention.

Simply defined, a task force is a "temporary group of people formed to carry out a specific mission or project, or to solve a problem that requires a multi-disciplinary approach" (BusinessDictionary.com, 2016). The concept of using task forces is nothing new to government operations, especially the military and law enforcement. Primarily, law enforcement task forces have been used as a crime control tool such as narcotics investigations, youth crime abatement, etc. with much success. Using the concept of a task force for specific large-scale investigations is not as common.

Multi-disciplined refers to "combining several usually separate branches of learning or fields of expertise (Dictionary.com, 2016). Modern policing, like many disciplines, has evolved into domain areas requiring very specialized equipment and practices. These domain areas require qualified individuals to administer the functions of those areas and to be uniquely educated and trained therein. An example would be a computer forensic or a crime scene processing unit within a law enforcement agency. Additionally, an investigation may require individual law enforcement officers who are highly trained and experienced in a "process," such as drafting search warrant applications, interpreting data (data analysis), language skills, etc. A task force engaged in a large-scale investigation will also require an individual who has experience in administering an organizational infrastructure that supports that organization's mission, in this case solving and subsequently prosecuting a specific crime.

5 – 2 – Investigative Task Force- Organization and Management

Law enforcement operates along a command structure similar to the military, and is referred to as a para-military organization. The rank structure is similar to the military as are the lines of authority. Within a singular law enforcement agency, the line of command authority works well as it does in the military. How does the concept of command authority work with investigators from different commands (agencies)? After all, law enforcement officers do not necessarily have to follow the orders or policies of the commander from another agency, so the concept of task force policing, if it is to be successful, must address the issue of command authority if a task force is to accomplish its mission.

No task force or similar organization will work efficiently or effectively if those assigned have to answer to more than one boss. Therefore, when creating a task force to accomplish the mission, the management concept of Unity of Command must apply. **Unity of Command** is simply defined as the principle that no subordinate in an organization should report to more than one boss. In creating a task force the issue of Unity of Command must be addressed so that those assigned to the task force do not have to answer to their home department as well as a supervisor or commander at a task force. Essentially, the command authority in

Unity of Command: The principle that no subordinate in an organization should report to more than one boss. In creating a task force the issue of Unity of Command must be addressed so that those assigned to the task force do not have to answer to their home department as well as a supervisor or commander at a task force.

the officer's home department must give operational authority of that officer(s) while that person is assigned to the task force. The officers assigned will then answer to the command authority at the task force, thus establishing clear lines of authority in the furtherance of the mission.

In the formation of a task force, the issue of **jurisdiction** is complex. A task force set up to investigate a specific crime or specific type of crime, for example a drug task force, will have members who do not have law enforcement jurisdiction where the investigation boundaries might go. For example, a city police officer assigned to a county-wide sexual assault task force would only have jurisdiction in his or her city of employment, or geographical area of employment, as sometimes this terminology is utilized in the statutes of various jurisdictions. A local law enforcement officer may be assigned to a task force investigating violations of specific federal laws where that officer would have no legal jurisdiction to enforce. How then does jurisdiction work, and how can all law enforcement officers assigned to a task force obtain the necessary jurisdiction to proceed with the investigative mission?

The term jurisdiction refers in part to:

> *a government's general power to exercise authority over all persons and things within its territory; [especially] a state's power to create interests that will be recognized under common law principles as valid in other states. 2. A court's power to decide a case or issue a decree (Garner, 2014).*

Jurisdiction is not limited to geographical boundaries but can also be legal or regulatory. Under most state laws, a law enforcement officer has enforcement powers such as the power of arrest in the geographical area of that officer's

> **Jurisdiction:** 1. A government's general power to exercise authority over all persons and things within its territory; esp., a state's power to create interests that will be recognized under common law principles as valid in other states. 2. A court's power to decide a case or issue a decree (Garner, 2014; Black's Law Dictionary 10th ed., reprinted with permission, Thomson Reuters).

employment. For example, a city police officer has law enforcement authority only in that particular city that hired him or her. Whereas a state police officer would have jurisdiction statewide. Creating a task force utilizing a number of personnel from different agencies with different jurisdictions can certainly be problematic. Fortunately, most states and the federal government have considered this dilemma and enacted laws, regulations, or have judicial opinions to addressed task force geographical jurisdiction.

It is incumbent upon all law enforcement administrators to be well versed in the issues of jurisdiction and be able to quickly mitigate any issues that would deny a task force member lawful jurisdiction. Lack of jurisdiction can not only place members of the investigative team in physical danger as they pursue leads outside of their geographical area of employment, but can also expose the investigators to potential civil liability. How, therefore, does a task force administrator address the issue of jurisdiction? The answer lies in a number of federal and state laws, regulations, case law, and formal opinions from such legal authorities as a state attorney general. Obtaining jurisdiction for these members of the task force does not have to be a complicated and bureaucratic process. It is well established that federal law enforcement agencies routinely swear-in members of state and local law enforcement as members of a federal investigative task force. An example would be the United States Marshals Service creating a fugitive task force utilizing state and local law enforcement personnel. Those non-federal investigators would be sworn-in as temporary members of the United States Marshals Service for the duration of their assignment to the task force. Another example would be Customs and Border Protection (CBP), a law enforcement agency within the United States Department of Homeland

Security. CBP routinely utilizes investigative resources from state and local law enforcement in the furtherance of a particular mission by making those members of state and local law enforcement sworn agents of CBP.

Many state and local laws authorize the temporary granting of law enforcement jurisdiction to officers who would otherwise not have it. For example, many sheriffs' and district attorneys' offices have the legal authority to grant jurisdiction within the boundaries of their own jurisdiction, a county for example. Many states have emergency management procedures guaranteeing agencies authority to provide for law enforcement jurisdiction in the case of a declared emergency. In some states, there also exists legal opinions that provide for jurisdiction. For example, in New York State, there exists an Opinion of the Attorney General that is based upon a formal agreement between municipalities, noting that law enforcement jurisdiction can be extended pursuant to the specific duties outlined in the agreement. In providing their *Informal Opinion to the City of Mechanicville, New York* (No. 97-13) on March 10, 1997, the Attorney General of the State of New York noted in part:

Read the full *Informal Opinion of the Attorney General of the State of New York to the City of Mechanicville, New York* (No. 97-13) in our online companion.

> *We note that a police officer is limited to his geographical area of employment in executing an arrest warrant, making an arrest without a warrant for a petty offense and in issuing an appearance ticket for petty offense. The Criminal Procedure Law §§ 1.20 (34-a), 120.50, 140.10, 150.20. Municipal cooperation, however, provides the extension of appropriate territorial jurisdiction necessary for the undertaking of the cooperation agreement. General Municipal Law § 119-n (c). Therefore, municipal cooperation will provide the police officers of the City of Mechanicville with full jurisdiction to make arrests and execute warrants on school property in*

the Town of Halfmoon. We conclude that a city may enter into municipal

cooperation agreement with the town for the provision of police services by

the city on city school district property located in the town.

As we have noted in part in this work, as a result of the formal and informal relationships established between law enforcement agencies before the Corr robbery-homicide, a more formalized task force was established to continue the investigation and prosecution of the case from its inception, extending the jurisdiction of many police officers well beyond their normal geographical area of employment.

Members of the Joseph D. Corr Robbery-Homicide Task Force

Members of the Joseph D. Corr Robbery-Homicide Task Force included:

1. Federal Bureau of Alcohol, Tobacco, & Firearms, Syracuse, New York

2. Federal Bureau of Investigation – Albany Field Office, Albany, New York

3. Kirkland Police Department, Clark Mills, New York

4. New Hartford Police Department, New Hartford, New York

5. New York State Police – Troop D, Oneida, New York

6. Oneida County District Attorney's Office, Utica, New York

7. Oneida County Sheriff's Office, Oriskany, New York

8. Pennsylvania State Police, Media, Pennsylvania

9. United States Attorney's Office for the Northern District of New York, Syracuse, New York

10. United States Marshals Service, Northern District of New York

11. City of Utica Police Department, Utica, New York

It is overly simplistic to think that law enforcement means only police officers. While our police officers tend to be the most public/visual representation of law enforcement, dozens of other local, county, state, and federal law enforcement personnel were not only engaged in the Corr case, but in regular, less serious cases every day. The many faces of law enforcement were all at work in the Corr case.

5 – 3 – Funding a Law Enforcement Task Force

Beyond the human toll on the many victims of the Corr robbery-homicide that was evident immediately after the events of February 27, 2006, agency administrators soon realized that this apparently local crime had state-wide and national investigative implications. This type of unforeseen

© Shutterstock.com

broad-based investigation also had significant fiscal implications for all of the agencies involved that required the pooling of local, county, state, and federal financial and personnel resources.

Numerous strategies can be employed to fund a law enforcement task force. If the task force is part of a protracted strategy to address a public safety issue, such as unlawful possession and distribution of drugs, the law enforcement and political authorities creating a task force can plan to have a budget appropriation from one or all participants in the proposed task force. The federal government, as well as state governments, may have grant programs that may fund or partially fund a proposed longer-term task force. Another innovative method to provide funding is the utilization of the asset forfeiture laws of the jurisdiction. The federal government, as well as many states have these types of specialized laws contained within their statutes. An asset forfeiture program is described by the United States department of Justice as "a program that encompasses the seizure and forfeiture of assets that represent the proceeds of, or were used to facilitate

© Shutterstock.com

federal crimes (USDOJ Asset Forfeiture Program, 2016, para. 1). These seized assets, under both state and federal laws, can be seized and subsequently sold at auction, the proceeds of which must under the law, be used for law enforcement purposes. Asset forfeiture funds can offer a sustained and reliable source of funds and other tangible assets necessary to operate a task force.

If a task force is established quickly in response to an unexpected crime, series of crimes, or other public safety need, the law enforcement administrators will need to establish or at least have an understanding of where that funding may exist to continue the operations of the task force. Many states and local governments have contingency accounts, which essentially allow a unit of government to have funds held in reserve for emergency. Law enforcement administrators should have knowledge of the existence of the emergency funds and how to access them. If there currently is no emergency reserve funds, the administrator should work with their political authorities and municipal finance personnel to properly establish such accounts, and procedures to access them quickly in an emergency. The financial operation of a law enforcement task force should also include a credit card program, backed by a strict policy of the use and documentation of said use of credit cards. Credit cards are an essential tool in the operation of a task force as they allow the flexibility for the movement and subsequent documentation of the use of authorized funds. Often, especially in an investigation, law enforcement officers will be expected to travel at a moment's notice in the furtherance of the investigation. Expenses related to the investigation such as travel, hotels, meals etc. can be easily charged to a credit card, providing for quick deployment of personnel as they follow leads. The use of a credit card by any government employee should follow a strict use and documentation policy.

Law enforcement task forces are an essential and often necessary tool to engage in a protracted or unexpected law enforcement need. Proper planning in the areas of law, finance, and jurisdiction prior to the emergency can help provide for the quick and efficient establishment of a task force and the completion of its mission.

Questions for review and further discussion

1. Does your agency or organization have a contingency fund available to fund short term emergency operations? If yes, describe how you access those funds. If no, what is holding the agency/organization back from establishing this fund?

2. Does your agency/organization have credit cards ready to be deployed to personnel at a moment's notice in the event of an emergency?

3. Explain the concept of task force policing and provide two examples where task force policing may be utilized.

4. Explain the concept of unity of command and provide an example of the use of the concept in practice.

Chapter 6

Interviews and Interrogations

~Raymond L. Philo

Outline

Keywords

1. Beyond a reasonable doubt

2. Custody

3. Interrogation

4. Interview

5. *Miranda* Rule

6. *Miranda* waiver form

7. Non-verbal behavior analysis

8. Probable cause

9. Public safety exception (to the *Miranda* rule)

10. Spontaneous statement/excited utterance

11. Sworn statement/affidavit

Expected Learning Outcomes

After reading this chapter and supplemental online materials, the reader will be able to:

1. Differentiate between an interview and an interrogation and explain each.

2. Explain when someone being interviewed must be read their *Miranda* warning.

3. Explain the public safety exception to the *Miranda* Rule.

4. Explain the different paths in criminal cases that investigators can follow without statements from defendants that still yield a successful case outcome.

5. Articulate the five steps to conducting a successful information gathering interview.

6 – 1 – The Indispensable Element?

© Shutterstock.com

Many practitioners in the criminal justice field consider that a confession is absolutely the best evidence in obtaining a conviction or plea in a criminal case. Arguably, ordinary citizens with limited exposure to the criminal justice system also consider a confession as indisputable evidence of a person's guilt. Therefore, the ability to confront a suspect and obtain a confession with all of the Constitutional protections intact is an essential skill for any criminal investigator. The ability, or skill, in obtaining a confession is often the singular element of evidence to get the investigator to the all-important threshold of **probable cause**, and the prosecutor to the evidentiary threshold of **beyond a reasonable doubt**.

When a law enforcement official is conducting a criminal investigation, he or she will have two types of encounters with individuals involved with the event; witnesses, and others that may have knowledge of, or other collateral information. These two interactions are referred to as the **interview** and the **interrogation**. Sometimes unexperienced individuals will use these two terms interchangeably; however, they are considerably different, with legal implications attached to both terms.

6 – 2 – The Interview

An interview is a discussion about a specific subject that is conducted between two people. The purpose for the interviewer is to explore the subject matter and to gather accurate information. An interview may be with a witness, victim, or others thought to have information about an event. An interview is generally not confrontational, nor is it custodial, that is to say, that the person being interviewed by law enforcement can terminate and leave the encounter at any time. When conducting an interview, the investigator should pick a location that makes the interviewee comfortable and feel confident that their contribution to the investigation is important

Probable cause: 1. *Criminal Law.* A reasonable ground to suspect that a person has committed or is committing a crime or that a place contain specific items connected with the crime. Under the Fourth Amendment, probable cause-which amounts to more than a bare suspicion but less than evidence that would justify a conviction-must be shown before an arrest warrant or search warrant may be issued. Also termed *reasonable cause; sufficient cause; reasonable grounds; reasonable excuse* (Garner, 2014; Black's Law Dictionary 10th ed., reprinted with permission, Thomson Reuters).

Beyond a reasonable doubt: [Reasonable doubt]: The doubt that prevents one from being firmly convinced of the defendant's guilt, or the belief that there is a real possibility that the defendant is not guilty. "Beyond a reasonable doubt" is the standard used by a jury to determine whether a criminal defendant is guilty. See Model Penal Code §1.12. In deciding whether guilt has been proved beyond a reasonable doubt, the jury must begin with the presumption that the defendant is innocent. Also termed *rational doubt* (Garner, 2014; Black's Law Dictionary 10th ed., reprinted with permission, Thomson Reuters).

Interview: A discussion about a specific subject that is conducted between two people. The purpose for the interviewer is to explore the subject matter and to gather accurate information.

Interrogation: The formal or systematic questioning of a person; [especially], intensive questioning by the police, [usually] of a person arrested for or suspected of committing a crime. The Supreme Court has held that, for purposes of the Fifth Amendment right against self-incrimination, interrogation includes not only express questioning but also words or action that the police should know are reasonably likely to elicit an incriminating response. *Rhode Island v. Innis*, 446 U.S. 291, 100 S.Ct. 1082 (1980) (Garner, 2014; Black's Law Dictionary 10th ed., reprinted with permission, Thomson Reuters).

and essential to the fact-finding goal of the law enforcement agency/agencies involved. Creating an atmosphere of cordiality and support often will ensure that the otherwise reluctant interviewee will divulge essential information. There are many professional standards and training courses that law enforcement officials are exposed to in order to make them better interviewers.

Five Essential Steps in Conducting a Successful Information Gathering Interview

There are five essential steps in conducting a successful information gathering interview:

1. Preparation: Determining the purpose and objective of the interview

2. Opening: Establishment of authority and development of rapport

3. Listening: Initially allowing a person to talk without interruptions

4. Specific questions: Detailing the information developed in an effort to answer outstanding questions regarding the investigation

5. Closing summary: Repeat of important assertions and review of those assertions for consistency and accuracy

Sworn statement/affidavit: A voluntary declaration of facts written down and sworn to by a declarant, [usually] before an officer authorized to administer oath's. A great deal of evidence is submitted by affidavit, [especially] in pretrial matters such as summary-judgment motions (Garner, 2014; Black's Law Dictionary 10th ed., reprinted with permission, Thomson Reuters).

Oath: 1. A solemn declaration, accompanied by a swearing to God or a revered person or thing, that one's statement is true or that one will be bound to a promise. The person making the oath implicitly invites punishment if the statement is untrue or the promise is broken. The legal effect of an oath is to subject the person to penalties for perjury if the testimony is false. 2. The statement or promise made in such a declaration. 3. The form of words used for such a declaration. 4 A formal declaration made solemn without a swearing to God or a revered person or thing (Garner, 2014; Black's Law Dictionary 10th ed., reprinted with permission, Thomson Reuters).

If the interview produces information essential to the case investigation, the investigator should be prepared to document those essential facts, usually in a **sworn statement/affidavit**. A sworn statement is a document produced by the investigator detailing the facts as stated by the interviewee (witness, victim, etc.). This document is in writing and is in the words of the interviewee, and not the investigator. This document, once produced in writing and reviewed for accuracy by the interviewee, is signed and sworn to be accurate by an **oath**, indicating accuracy under penalty of law. Many agencies will instruct their law enforcement officers to record their interviews either audibly or by video, or both if possible.

The recording of an interview, over and above the written document, provides for the ability to review the interview for accuracy and establish that no course of methods were used to obtain information not freely divulged by the interviewee.

© Shutterstock.com

It is important that the interviewer be aware of non-verbal behavior in addition to verbal statements. Often referred to as **Non-verbal Behavior Analysis**, this awareness skill allows the investigator to often detect

Non-verbal Behavior Analysis: Non-verbal behavior in addition to verbal statements made or observed by a trained interviewer to detect deception if it exists during the interview process.

deception if it exists during the interview process. Non-verbal behavior analysis is a valid scientific process. The trained interviewer can make good judgment about the truth or deception during this observation. Non-verbal behavior analysis does have its limitations, and must be conducted under interview circumstances that are not affected by outside stimuli. An interview should be conducted in a quiet, professional setting where there are no distractions. A professionally designed police station interview room is a good example. This is opposed to an interview conducted at a location not controlled by the interviewer, such as a noisy public setting, or a police vehicle. The professionally designed interview room allows the investigator to better assess the non-verbal signs of deception if they exist.

Non-verbal signs of deception can manifest themselves in many ways, or not at all. Some of the signs of deception may be unusual nervousness, the inability to sit still, inability to make eye contact, profuse sweating, etc. Verbal signs of deception may include failure to directly answer a posed question, changing the subject often, the inability to answer questions previously answered accurately, an unusual focus on time, and making excuses to terminate the interview. Investigators should be aware of these types of deceptions, and once observed, be prepared to address these non-verbal and verbal signs of possible deception.

It is important to remember that most interviews are conducted with witnesses and other non-involved individuals. The process of interviewing a person should not be confrontational, but supportive, and take place in a comfortable, professional setting that puts the interviewee at ease.

6 – 3 – The Interrogation and *Miranda*

Custody: The care and control of a thing or person for inspection, preservation, or security (Garner, 2014; Black's Law Dictionary 10th ed., reprinted with permission, Thomson Reuters).

An interrogation is the formal or systematic questioning of a person by the police, usually of a person arrested or suspected of committing a crime (Garner, 2014). The interrogation process can be either custodial, or non-custodial. Being in **custody**, or not, when an interrogation takes place is an important distinction as a number of factors, including landmark case law, attach when custody exists within an interrogation. Physical custody for the purpose of our study is defined as "custody of a person (such as an arrestee) whose freedom is directly controlled and limited" (Garner, 2014). Our laws, especially as articulated in case law, has developed over the years to guarantee that Constitutional protections are in place for those individuals who are in a situation where custody and interrogation exist. The Constitutional protections exist in response to potential coercive interrogations by the government (police) in violation of the fourth, fifth, sixth, and fourteenth amendments to the United States Constitution. The case of *Miranda v. Arizona*, 384 U.S. 436 (1966) is the landmark United States Supreme Court case on the subject and the establishment of the **Miranda Rule**. A summary of *Miranda* and its effect on police procedure during an interrogation situation is important, however, all interrogations that may produce a confession are subject to a four-part Constitutional test, only one part of which has anything to do with *Miranda* compliance. The four parts are the Fourth, Fifth, Sixth, and Fourteenth Amendment test. A statement from a defendant in violation of any of the protections guaranteed by these Amendments will hold the confession as inadmissible. The Fourth Amendment test is relative to the legal seizures, the Fifth Amendment test is relative to self-incrimination (*Miranda* test), the Sixth Amendment test relates to the right to counsel, and the Fourteenth Amendment test concerns the potential violation of due process.

> **Miranda Rule:** The doctrine that a criminal suspect in police custody must be informed of certain constitutional rights before being interrogated. The suspect must be advised of the right to remain silent, the right to have an attorney present during questioning, and the right to have an attorney appointed if the suspect cannot afford one. If the suspect is not advised of these rights or does not validly waive them, any evidence obtained during the interrogation cannot be used against the suspect at trial (except for impeachment purposes) (Garner, 2014; Black's Law Dictionary 10th ed., reprinted with permission, Thomson Reuters).

For the purposes of this chapter, we will review the *Miranda* decision and its application to law enforcement interrogations. We have previously reviewed the legal definitions of custody and interrogation as they apply to government questioning

of a potential criminal suspect, but how then do we apply them to an actual interrogation. First, one must understand that the Constitutional guarantees established by the decision only attach when both custody and interrogation exist. If one or the other does not exist, the process established by the *Miranda* decision does not apply. For example, if a police officer arrested a shoplifter on the complaint of a store employee who saw the person steal, and the police officer does not interrogate the shoplifter about the theft, the police officer does not have to evoke the procedures established by the decision such as reading the shoplifter their *Miranda* Rights. Why? Because, one of the necessary elements does not exist— interrogation. If the police officer interrogates a suspect in a setting that does not confine the suspect, or the suspect has been told they are not under arrest, the procedures set forth in the *Miranda* decision do not apply. Why? Because, there is no custody in this scenario.

Spontaneous statement/excited utterance: A statement about a startling event made under the stress and excitement of the event. An excited utterance may be admissible as a hearsay exception (Garner, 2014; Black's Law Dictionary 10th ed., reprinted with permission, Thomson Reuters).

How about the suspect who makes incriminating statements while in custody that are unsolicited by the law enforcement officer? Are these statements subject to the *Miranda* rules? The answer is no. If **spontaneous statements/excited utterances** are made by a suspect that are incriminating in nature, these statements do not enjoy the protection of the *Miranda* rule because there was no interrogation, an essential element for *Miranda* to attach. Spontaneous incriminating statements are quite common when the experienced investigator is prepared to record the statements, unimpaired by *Miranda*.

Often a suspect in a criminal investigation who is being questioned by the police while in a custodial situation will want to confess to the crime or otherwise make incriminating statements after their *Miranda* rights were administered. If this fairly common situation exists, the investigator prepares and thoroughly explains to the suspect what is called a *Miranda* waiver. The waiver encompasses two distinct protections provided by *Miranda*, the right to counsel and the right to remain silent, and the fact that these are knowingly and intelligently waived by the suspect. The burden of proof that a waiver of *Miranda* rights was the basis for incriminating statements is always on the government (prosecutor). While the *Miranda* decision does not indicate that a waiver has to be in writing, all law enforcement agencies have a ***Miranda* waiver form** that is used in the situation to further document the suspect's voluntary waiver. Many agencies have policies that require interrogations, including the waiver of rights, to be videotaped. This also provides supportive evidence that the waiver was presented and was knowingly and intelligently evoked by the defendant. The video also supports that there were no course of methods used by law enforcement in obtaining the waiver, and subsequently incriminating statements.

> **Miranda waiver form:** A document where an interviewee, in writing, voluntarily and knowledgeably waives his rights under the *Miranda* Rule.

The *Miranda* Warning

Contrary to many beliefs, the *Miranda* warning is not specifically narrated in the *Miranda* decision, and consequently there are number of versions used by law enforcement. In the *Miranda* decision, the United States Supreme Court indicated that prior to questioning, the person must be warned that he/she has the right to remain silent, that any statements he/she does make may be used against them, and that he/she has a right to the presence of an attorney, either retained or appointed. So long as the warning conveys the information above it is sufficient, and it does not have to be verbatim of the language from the decision (*Miranda v. Arizona*, 384 U.S. 436 [1966] as cited in Rutledge [2001]).

In 1981, the United States Supreme Court held in *California v. Prysock*:

> *(1) the content of* Miranda *warnings need not be a virtual incantation*
>
> *of the precise language contained in the* Miranda *opinion; such a rigid*

rule is not mandated by Miranda *or any other decision of the Supreme Court, and is not required to serve the purposes of* Miranda, *and (2) where the accused was told of his right to have a lawyer present prior to and during interrogation, and his right to have a lawyer appointed at no cost if he could not afford one, and where those warnings conveyed to him his right to have a lawyer appointed if he could not afford one prior to and during interrogation, such* Miranda *warnings were not inadequate simply because of the order in which they were given.*

*(*California v. Prysock, *453 U.S. 455, [1981])*

If the basic set of parameters meet the questioning, custody and interrogation, then the *Miranda* warnings have to be administered to the person being interrogated, adult or juvenile. If a person meeting the criteria for interrogation states, "I know my rights," the *Miranda* rights still must be administered. The United States Supreme Court decision on *Miranda* does not specify how many times the *Miranda* rights must be given and it is common practice to administer the rights only once during a routine interrogation. However, it is good practice to administer the *Miranda* warning after breaks in lengthy interrogations (*Wyrick v. Fields*, 459 U.S. 42 [1982]).

Public Safety Exception to the *Miranda* Rule: Absent actual coercion by a police officer in acting to protect himself or the public by questioning a suspect before Miranda warnings have been given, there is no constitutional imperative requiring exclusion of evidence that results from inquiry of this kind; neither do doctrinal underpinnings of Miranda require that such evidence be excluded, thus penalizing officers for asking the very questions which are the most crucial to their efforts to protect themselves and the public. *New York v. Quarles*, 467 U.S. 469 (1984)

Are there any exceptions to the *Miranda* rule when custody and interrogation exist? The United States Supreme Court has recognized one exception to the *Miranda* rule, often referred to as the "**public safety exception**." In the case of *New York v. Quarles*, 467 U.S. 469 (1984) the court ruled that when there is an immediate public safety hazard, police may question an in-custody suspect about the immediate hazard that exists, such as the location of a weapon the suspect had possessed just prior to custody. The exception was utilized during the high profile Boston Marathon Bombing when Dzhokhar A. Tsarnaev was taken into custody after hiding under a tarp which was used to cover a boat. Tsarnaev made incriminating statements while in custody and prior to *Miranda* warnings in response to police questions about the location of weapons he was thought to have immediate access to. The public safety exception to *Miranda* allows for limited pre-*Miranda* questions of an in-custody suspect to address an immediate public safety issue.

© *Shutterstock.com*

© *Shutterstock.com*

The requirement to administer the *Miranda* rights during an in-custody interrogation only applies to agents of the government (police, etc.) and not the general public. For example, if a person is taken into custody by retail store security employee, and he or she is questioned by that employee, the *Miranda* rights do not attach. Why? Because the retail store security official is an employee of the store and not working as a government law enforcement official.

The United States Supreme Court in the *Miranda* decision does not address how exactly the warning should be administered, so long as it is administered fully and intelligently. Should the *Miranda* warning be read from an agency issued format, such as a printed card, or can they be administered by memory? Once again, the *Miranda* decision does not directly indicate the method of administration. Most law enforcement agencies require that their officers administer the *Miranda* warnings directly from a written record issued by the agency. The reason for this is that it provides for substantial evidence that the warnings were recited exactly as they were printed on the card and the particular wording is consistent with the requirements of the *Miranda* decision.

Rome Sentinel, reprinted with permission

Defendant John T. Healy, (a.k.a. Toussaint Davis, a.k.a. Toussaint Martin) is escorted by deputies from the Oneida County Sheriff's Office shortly after a proceeding in the Town of New Hartford Court

WKTV, reprinted with permission

Walter Richardson, the man directly responsible for shooting/ murdering Officer Corr and car jacking/kidnapping a tow truck operator employed by Kirkland Automotive immediately after the murder, was killed in a shootout in Chester, Pennsylvania, with law enforcement officers shortly after the homicide occurred.

The Corr of *Miranda*

Interrogation techniques utilized in the Joseph D. Corr homicide case provided investigators with an interesting but common dilemma. Toussaint Davis, who is the only defendant taken into custody on the evening of the robbery/homicide, did not cooperate with police and refused to make any statement under questioning. Defendant Davis was administered his *Miranda* rights even though he did not choose to make a statement because the two conditions that attach to *Miranda* were present: custody and interrogation. While Walter Richardson, the man who killed Officer Corr, was killed in a shootout with police the next day in Chester, Pennsylvania, the two remaining suspects in the Corr homicide case invoked their rights to not cooperate with the police and therefore the provisions of the *Miranda* decision did not apply. This is quite a common occurrence in many criminal cases where the suspects refused to give a statement, either on their own or upon advice of an attorney. This is when the investigators need to rely on other types of evidence, such as eyewitnesses, forensic evidence, documentary evidence, and even circumstantial evidence to complete their case.

Questions for review and further discussion

1. Describe the differences and similarities between interviews and interrogations.

2. When is it necessary to read a person being interviewed by police their *Miranda* warnings?

3. Is it a best practice to read a suspect their *Miranda* warning from memory or from a pre-printed card/document? Defend your answer.

4. Explain the public safety exception to the *Miranda* rule and provide an example of the same.

Part 3

Adjudication

Chapter 7

The American Criminal Court Structure

~*James C. Brown*

Outline

Keywords

1. Arraignment

2. Bench Trial

3. *Brady* Hearing/Material

4. Felony hearing

5. Jurisdiction

6. *Mapp* Hearing

7. *Massiah* Hearing/Rule

8. Trial

9. *Wade* Hearing

© *Shutterstock.com*

Expected Learning Outcomes

After reading this chapter and supplemental online materials, the reader will be able to:

1. Explain how Article III of the United States Constitution exists throughout all levels of government.

2. Explain the structure of our local, county, state, and federal courts in the United States.

3. Explain the Corr courts and how the courts related to one another throughout the duration of the Corr case.

4. Explain the fundamental differences between courts of original jurisdiction and courts of appellate jurisdiction.

7 – 1 – The Charge of Our Founding Fathers

As we have briefly discussed, Article III, §1 of the Constitution of the United States of America reads in part,

> *The judicial Power of the United States, shall be vested in one supreme Court, and in such inferior Courts as the Congress may from time to time ordain and establish. The Judges, both of the supreme and inferior Courts, shall hold their Offices during good Behaviour, and shall, at stated Times, receive for their Services, a Compensation, which shall not be diminished during their Continuance in Office. (U.S. Const. art. III, § 1)*

In our American court structure, where the judiciary is one of three branches of government, there continues to be a significant amount of vertical tension that perhaps appropriately exists between the Unites States Supreme Court and the inferior courts of the local, county, state and federal judiciary. Likewise, that same tension exists horizontally across the constant check and balance between the judiciary and executive and legislative branches of government. A firm understanding of the interrelationships that exist both formally and informally between the courts throughout the United States, and the reader's own jurisdiction is fundamental to successfully navigating small and large scale operations within the American Criminal Justice System. The Founders recognized these tensions and addressed them in their collective efforts to sway their colleagues and the citizenry during the post September 17, 1787 Constitutional ratification period/process. In speaking of the judiciary in *The Federalist Papers* Number LXXVII (78), Publius (Hamilton) observed

> *There is no position which depends on clearer principles, than that every act of a delegated authority, contrary to the tenor of the commission under which it is exercised, is void. No legislative act, therefore, contrary to the Constitution, can be valid. To deny this, would be to affirm, that the deputy is greater than his principal; that the servant is above his master; that the representatives of the people are superior to the people themselves; that men acting by virtue of powers, may do not only what their powers do not authorize, but what they forbid. If it be said that the legislative body are themselves the constitutional judges of their own powers, and that the construction they put upon them is conclusive upon the other departments, it may be answered, that this cannot be the natural presumption, where it is not to be collected from any particular provisions in the Constitution. It is not otherwise to be supposed, that the Constitution could intend to enable the representatives of the people to substitute their WILL to that of their constituents. It is far more rational to suppose, that the courts were*

designed to be an intermediate body between the people and the legislature,
in order, among other things, to keep the latter within the limits assigned
to their authority. The interpretation of the laws is the proper and peculiar
province of the courts. A constitution is, in fact, and must be regarded by
the judges, as a fundamental law. It therefore belongs to them to ascertain
its meaning, as well as the meaning of any particular act proceeding from
the legislative body. If there should happen to be an irreconcilable variance
between the two, that which has the superior obligation and validity ought,
of course, to be preferred; or, in other words, the Constitution ought to be
preferred to the statute, the intention of the people to the intention of their
agents. (Kramnick, 1987)

The Corr case seemingly started at first glance with a robbery and related offenses that occurred in the jurisdiction of the Town of New Hartford, New York. Four men participated in the robbery of Lennon's W.B. Wilcox Jewelers in violation of the *New York State Penal Law,* § 160.15 et. al. From the scene of the robbery, a police chase ensued that traveled through multiple jurisdictions, ending with a vehicle crash and foot chase by law enforcement officers in the Town of Kirkland, New York. The foot chase resulted in the murder of Officer

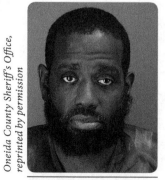

Oneida County Sheriff's Office, reprinted by permission

Toussaint Davis (a.k.a.
Toussaint Martin, a.k.a.
John T. Healy)

Oneida County Sheriff's Office, reprinted by permission

Robert Ward (a.k.a. "RB")

Oneida County Sheriff's Office, reprinted by permission

Marion Pegese (a.k.a.
"Dump," "Bill," "Amin")

Corr by Walter Richardson in the Town of Kirkland, located in Oneida County, New York, a felony offense under the *New York State Penal Law* in violation of § 125.25. After murdering Officer Corr, Walter Richardson car jacked/kidnapped a tow truck operator at Kirkland Auto, near by the murder scene, and began a several hour trip from Oneida County, New York, through many jurisdictions back to the State of Pennsylvania.

At the time of the murder, only one individual, Toussaint Davis, (a.k.a. John T. Healy et al.), was caught by local law enforcement officers at the scene of the murder. Walter Richardson, who was also in the vehicle with Davis, fled to Pennsylvania and was subsequently killed by law enforcement officers after an exchange of gunfire. The remaining two defendants involved in the case, Robert Ward (a.k.a. "RB"), Marion Pegese (a.k.a. "Dump," "Bill," "Amin"), were captured at a later time in the investigation (*U.S. v. Ward*, 505 Fed.Appx. 18 (2012)). For defendant Toussaint Davis, an initial **felony hearing (preliminary hearing)** took place at the local criminal court in the Town of New Hartford. Thereafter, the case was transferred to Oneida County Court for a jury trial, whereupon Davis was convicted by a jury **trial** of all of the original 19 counts in his indictment, including felony murder and robbery.

However, while the State of New York, through the Oneida County District Attorney's Office, had chosen to initially prosecute Davis (and Ward and Pegese) under New York State law, additional work was well underway to prosecute

> **Felony hearing (preliminary hearing):** A criminal hearing (often conducted by a magistrate) to determine whether there is sufficient evidence to prosecute an accused person; specif., A proceeding before a judge or magistrate held soon after a criminal defendant is taken into custody, usu. on felony charges, the typical prosecution having the burden to establish reasonable cause to believe that the defendant has committed a felony. If sufficient evidence exists, the case will be set for trial or bound over for grand jury review, or information will be filed in the trial court. Also termed preliminary examination; probable cause hearing; bind overhearing; examining trial; felony hearing (Garner, 2014; Black's Law Dictionary 10th ed., reprinted with permission, Thomson Reuters).
>
> **Trial:** A formal judicial examination of evidence and determination of legal claims in an adversary proceeding (Garner, 2014; Black's Law Dictionary 10th ed., reprinted with permission, Thomson Reuters).

Read the full transcript of the felony hearing in New Hartford Town Court (*People of the State of New York v. John T. Healy*, March 6, 2006) in our online companion.

Davis, Ward, and Pegese under a variety of federal laws that were far more reaching than those in New York State. While typically an act is prosecuted within the sole geographical **jurisdiction** of where the offense(s) occurred, the expansiveness of the crimes and associated actions of Davis, Pegese, Ward, and Richardson necessitated the expansion of jurisdiction and related resources of the United States Attorney for the Northern District of New York, and those related local, state, and federal resources contained within the jurisdiction of the United States Court of Appeals for the Second Circuit.

7 – 2 – Corr Courts

Regardless of how one reads the United States Constitution, the document is as much a statement of policy and direction of a nation, as it is one of practical process. Taken in tandem, Article III, and the Fifth (grand jury indictment, double-jeopardy, self-incrimination, due process, and eminent domain) and Sixth (speedy public trial by jury, arraignments/notification of charges, confronting witnesses, compulsory process/subpoena powers, and assistance of counsel) amendments to the United States Constitution serve as the fundamental and foundational blueprint of any criminal case, including the Corr case. In the final analysis, every level of our American court system was exercised in some manner, to date, in the Corr case. These included:

The Courts of the Corr Case

1. **New Hartford Town Court**, New Hartford, New York, Oneida County. Local Criminal Court. Location of the initial felony hearing for defendant John T. Healy (a.k.a. Toussaint Davis, Toussaint Martin).

2. **Oneida County Court**, Utica, New York, Oneida County. Trial court. Once the felony hearing was completed, the case was transferred for all hearings, trial, and sentencing of defendant John T. Healy (a.k.a. Toussaint Davis, Toussaint Martin).

3. **New York State Supreme Court, Appellate Division, Fourth Department**, Rochester, New York. Location for the initial appeal of eight (8) points of law from the defendant/appellant, John T. Healy (a.k.a. Toussaint Davis, Toussaint Martin).

4. **New York State Court of Appeals**, Albany, New York. New York's highest court of final appeals. Defendant/Appellant John T. Healy (a.k.a. Toussaint Davis, Toussaint

Martin) appealed ruling of the New York State Supreme Court, Appellate Division, Fourth Department. Appeal hearing denied.

5. **United States District Court for the Northern District of New York**, Syracuse, New York. Federal trial court. Location of the concurrent trial(s) and sentencing of defendants Davis, Ward, and Pegese. Convicted on all counts. Also the location of a 2015 Habeas Corpus petition by defendant Pegese. Petition denied.

6. **United States Court of Appeals for the Second Circuit**, New York, New York. Intermediate federal court of appeals. Location of the appeal(s) on various points of law from the United States Court of Appeals for the Second Circuit. Appeal denied.

7. **United States Supreme Court**, Washington, D.C. Nation's highest appeals court. Petition(s) for writ of certiorari denied.

The system, as designed by our Founding Fathers and articulated in *The Federalist Papers* and our United States Constitution, functioned as it was intended to do so in the Corr case. Readers should become familiar with every layer/structure of the court system within their local, county, state, and federal jurisdiction and understand the basic navigation of a case that starts with a seemingly simple complaint, all the way through to the appeals process. In New York State, criminal courts are specifically defined in the New York State Criminal Procedure Law. The *New York State Criminal Procedure Law* notes in part,

1. The "criminal courts" of this state are comprised of the superior courts and the local criminal courts.

FEDERAL: THE UNITED STATES COURT SYSTEM

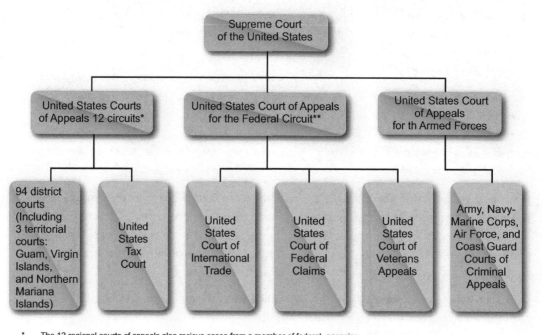

* The 12 regional courts of appeals also recieve cases from a member of federal agencies.
** The Court of Appeals for the Federal Circit also recieves cases from the International Trade Commissions, the Merit Systems Protection Board, the Patent and Trademark office, and the Board of Contract Appeals.

NEW YORK: CRIMINAL COURT STRUCTURE

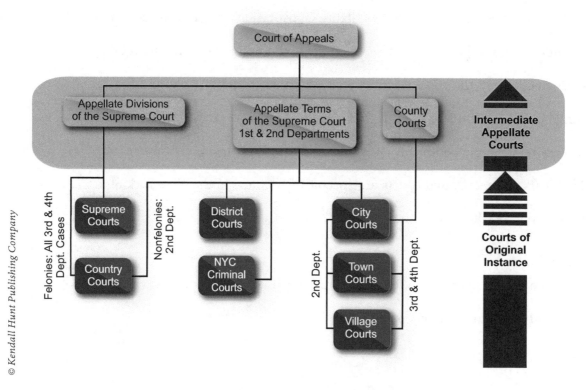

2. "Superior court" means:

   a. The supreme court; or

   b. A county court.

3. "Local criminal court" means:

   a. A district court; or

   b. The New York City criminal court; or

   c. A city court; or

   d. A town court; or

   e. A village court; or

   f. A supreme court justice sitting as a local criminal court; or

   g. A county judge sitting as a local criminal court.

4. "City court" means any court for a city, other than New York City, having trial jurisdiction of offenses of less than felony grade only committed within such city, whether such court is entitled a city court, a municipal court, a police court, a recorder's court or is known by any other name or title.

5. "Town court." A "town court" is comprised of all the town justices of a town.

6. "Village court." A "village court" is comprised of the justice of a village, or all the justices thereof if there be more than one, or, at a time when he or they are absent, an acting justice of a village who is authorized to perform the functions of a village justice during his absence.

7. Notwithstanding any other provision of this section, a court specified herein which possesses civil as well as criminal jurisdiction does not act as a criminal court when acting solely in the exercise of its civil jurisdiction, and an order or determination made by such a court in its civil capacity is not an order or determination of a criminal court even though it may

© Shutterstock.com

terminate or otherwise control or affect a criminal action or proceeding. (N.Y. Criminal Procedure Law § 10.10, 2016)

At each level of the court process, defendants are guaranteed certain rights and processes consistent with the Constitution of the United States, and the Constitution of the State of New York. The criminal courts of the State of New York, as articulated in the *New York State Criminal Procedure Law*, are all courts of original jurisdiction, also known as trial courts. These courts hear the original facts of the case and either through a trial, or through plea bargaining, look to resolve cases at this initial level. The three courts of original jurisdiction in the Corr case were:

Arraignment: The initial step in a criminal prosecution whereby the defendant is brought before the court to hear the charges and to enter a plea [Also known as preliminary hearing, or initial appearance] (Garner, 2014; Black's Law Dictionary 10th ed., reprinted with permission, Thomson Reuters).

***Mapp* hearing:** A hearing held to determine whether evidence implicating the accused was obtained as a result of an illegal search and seizure, and should therefore be suppressed. [From the landmark United States Supreme Court case of *Mapp v. Ohio*, 367 U.S. 643, 81 S.Ct. 1684 (1961) (Garner, 2014; Black's Law Dictionary 10th ed., reprinted with permission, Thomson Reuters).

***Brady* hearing/material:** Information or evidence that is favorable to a criminal defendant's case and that the prosecution has a duty to disclose. The prosecution's withholding of such information violates the defendant's due-process rights. [From the landmark United States Supreme Court case of *Brady v. Maryland* 373 U.S. 83, 83 S.Ct. 1194 (1963), also known as exculpatory evidence] (Garner, 2014; Black's Law Dictionary 10th ed., reprinted with permission, Thomson Reuters).

The Corr Courts of Original Jurisdiction

1. Town of New Hartford Local Criminal Court

2. Oneida County Court, serving as a Superior Court

3. United States District Court for the Northern District of New York, serving as the court of original jurisdiction for the federal indictment against all three defendants (Davis, Pegese, & Ward).

In courts of original jurisdiction, defendants are typically initially **arraigned** before a judge, and then prior to a trial, engage in an often lengthy series of events which typically include plea bargain discussions with the prosecution (if offered/engaged), as well as various legal hearings regarding whether or not certain processes during the investigation and arrest phase of the process were appropriately followed, and whether or not specific statements and/or evidence collected by law enforcement officials were done in a proper manner. Some of the more common hearings that typically proceed at a trial include a *Mapp* **hearing**, *Brady* **hearing/material**, *Wade* **hearing**, and a *Massiah* **hearing/rule**. Each of these hearings is as a result of the landmark United States Supreme Court case interpreting the Constitution to provide protections to criminal defendants. At the federal level in the Corr case, both a *Wade* hearing and *Massiah* hearing were held. Readers should familiarize themselves with these and other landmark cases ruled upon by the United States Supreme Court as they continue to increase their fluency in the American Criminal Justice System, and in particular in more effectively navigating the criminal courts of the United States of America. Courts of original jurisdiction, also known as trial courts, are the finders of the facts of the case. Whether a case is heard by a judge only, called the **bench trial**, or heard by a full jury, the responsibility of courts of original jurisdiction is to properly admit into evidence all of the facts and related evidence of a particular case. In the Corr case, defendant Toussaint Davis was arrested shortly after the robbery of Lennon's W.B. Wilcox Jewelry Store, and the subsequent murder of Officer Corr. Just under 11 months after the occurrence of the robbery-homicide (January 8, 2007), defendant John T. Healy

Read the full transcript of the *Wade* hearing and *Massiah* hearing(s) held before the United States District Court for the Northern District of New York, held on October 7, 2010 in the matter of the *United States of American v. Toussaint Davis, Marion Pegese, and Robert Ward*, in our online companion.

Wade **hearing:** A pretrial hearing in which the defendant contests the validity of his or her out-of-court identification. If the court finds that the identification was tainted by unconstitutional methods, the prosecution cannot use the identification and must link the defendant to the crime by other means. [From the landmark United States Supreme Court case of *U.S. v. Wade*, 388 U.S. 218, 87 S.Ct. 1926 (1967)] (Garner, 2014; Black's Law Dictionary 10th ed., reprinted with permission, Thomson Reuters).

Massiah **hearing/rule:** The principle that an attempt to elicit incriminating statements [usually not during a formal interrogation] from a suspect whose right to counsel has attached but who has not waived that right violates the sixth amendment. [From the landmark United States Supreme Court case of *Massiah v. U.S.*, 377 U.S. 201, 84 S.Ct. 1199 (1964), also known as deliberate elicitation] (Garner, 2014; Black's Law Dictionary 10th ed., reprinted with permission, Thomson Reuters).

Bench Trial: A trial before a judge without a jury. The judge decides questions of fact as well as questions of law. [Also termed *trial to the bench; nonjury trial; court trial; trial before the court; judge trial*] (Garner, 2014; Black's Law Dictionary 10th ed., reprinted with permission, Thomson Reuters).

(a.k.a. Toussaint Davis, a.k.a. Toussaint Martin) went on trial in Superior Court for the County of Oneida, also known as Oneida County Court. Davis was eventually convicted of all 19 counts of his original indictment and sentenced to life in prison for the murder of Officer Corr and subsequent sentences for the robbery that occurred at Lennon W.B. Wilcox Jewelry Store.

Subsequent to the fact-finding trial by jury that occurred in Oneida County Court, the defendant, through his attorney, filed an appeal of his case to the New York State Supreme Court for the Appellate Division, Fourth Department in Rochester, New York. Likewise, after all three defendants (Davis, Pegese, & Ward) were found guilty in the United States District Court for the Northern District of New York, in Syracuse, New York, the defendants, through their attorneys, appealed their case to the United States Court of Appeals for the Second Circuit, in New York, New York. After the court's decisions in both cases (county/state and federal), defendant Davis attempted to appeal his case to New York's highest appeals court, the New York State Court of Appeals in Albany, New York. The New York State Court of Appeals refused to hear his case. Likewise, at the federal intermediate appeals level, the defendants ultimately appealed the decision of the United States Court of Appeals for the Second Circuit to the United States Supreme Court. In similar fashion, the United States Supreme Court refused to hear their case as well.

Intermediate and senior level appellate courts are not triers of fact. Rather, the appellate court's role is strictly limited to a review of the facts,

and a review of the law and procedures/ processes followed by the trial court judge. In other words, were there errors made at the trial court level that would require the case to somehow be retried, or some aspect of the case overturned as a matter of law? Decisions of an appeals

UNITED STATES COURT OF APPEALS

© *Shutterstock.com*

court in a criminal matter either affirm (agree with) the decision of a lower court in full or in part, or, appeals courts may agree with some or all of the arguments raised by appealing parties and thus reverse and remand (send back) the case back to a lower court for reconsideration on various points of law. For example, in the Corr case, although the New York State Supreme Court for the Appellate Division, Fourth Department, dismissed seven of the eight points made by the appellant (Davis), they did agree that the sentences imposed by the trial court judge should have been ordered to be served concurrently (at the same time as other offenses), rather than consecutively (one after another) as originally ordered by the trial court judge.

The Corr case maps our entire court system in the United States of America, from a local criminal court in the Town of New Hartford, New York, then to the New York State Supreme Court Appellate Division, Fourth Department, and finally to New York's highest court, the New York State Court of Appeals. In a parallel fashion, the three surviving defendants (Davis, Pegese, & Ward) were also processed through the federal court system, beginning at the United States District Court for the Northern District of New York, then onto the United States Court of Appeals for the Second Circuit, and finally to our nation's highest court, the United States Supreme Court. The Corr case courts will forever remain an example for generations to come of the coordination and endurance of local, county, state, and federal law enforcement officials working in tandem with their judicial counterparts to seek justice within the boundaries of our Constitutionally established judicial framework at all levels of government.

Questions for review and further discussion

1. Why were so many defendant's rights landmark United States Supreme Court cases ruled upon during the era of the 1960s?

2. Identify and discuss the Corr courts in your jurisdiction. Be specific.

3. Map the courts in your jurisdiction from your local criminal courts all the way up to the United States Supreme Court.

4. Should criminal defendants be permitted unlimited chances to appeal their cases? Defend your position.

5. What statute(s) in your jurisdiction define the courts and their various functions? Be specific.

Part 4

The Aftermath

Chapter 8

Victims

~James C. Brown

Outline

Keywords

1. Pre-sentence investigation report

2. Restitution

@ *Shutterstock.com*

@ *Shutterstock.com*

After reading this chapter and supplemental online materials, the reader will be able to:

1. Explain the evolution of the voice of victims in our American criminal courts.

2. Differentiate between defendant and witness testimony and victim impact statements in court(s).

3. Experience the impact of second-hand victim impact statement(s) from the Corr case.

8 – 1 – Finding Their Voice

8 – 2 – Corr Voices

8 – 1 – Finding Their Voice

Not until the latter-half of the 20th century did crime victims have any significant official place in the American Criminal Justice System. Nowhere in the text of the United States Constitution are victims' rights eluded to. With the exception of one reference to compensation of private property owners for land taken for public use ("[a] Private property shall not be taken for public use without just compensation" [N.Y. Const art. I, § 7, 2016]), New York State's Constitution is equally void of the recognition of crime victims. One could argue that the *Bill of Rights* that are contained within each document are an effort to see the people represented by a government as being protected against unwarranted invasions by government agents or the deprivation of certain procedural/due process rights. However, if that premise is to be accepted we must also admit that both foundational documents, the former *United States Constitution* drafted in 1787 and the latter *New York State Constitution* drafted in 1938, are clearly void of any formal voice for crime victims. However, in defense of the new Constitution, and in speaking of the critical importance of the need for an independent judiciary, Publius (Hamilton) wrote in *The Federalist* LXXVIII (78):

But it is not with a view to infractions of the Constitution only, that the independence of the judges may be an essential safeguard against the effects of occasional ill humors in the society. These sometimes extend no farther than to the injury of the private rights of particular classes of citizens, by unjust and partial laws. Here also the firmness of the judicial magistracy is of vast importance in mitigating the severity and confining the operation of such laws. It not only serves to moderate the immediate mischiefs of those which may have been passed, but it operates as a check upon the legislative body in passing them; who, perceiving that obstacles to the success of iniquitous intention are to be expected from the scruples of the courts, are in a manner compelled, by the very motives of the injustice they meditate, to qualify their attempts. This is a circumstance calculated to have more influence upon the character of our governments, than but few may be aware of. The benefits of the integrity and moderation of the judiciary have already been felt in more States than one; and though they may have displeased those whose sinister expectations they may have disappointed, they must have commanded the esteem and applause of all the virtuous and disinterested. Considerate men, of every description, ought to prize whatever will tend to beget or fortify that temper in the courts: as no man can be sure that he may not be to-morrow the victim of a spirit of injustice, by which he may be a gainer to-day. *And every man must now feel, that the inevitable tendency of such a spirit is to sap the foundations of public and private confidence, and to introduce in its stead*

universal distrust and distress [emphasis added]. (Kramnick, 1987)

The federal government most notably codified crime victim's rights in 2004 with the passage of the *Crime Victims' Rights Act* as a part of the *Justice for All Act of 2004* (October 30, 2004). In part the federal government defined a crime victim as "...the person against whom the State offense is committed or, if that person is killed or incapacitated, that person's family member or other lawful representative (18 U.S.C.A. § 3771, West). Like so many pieces of legislation enacted by local, county, state, and federal legislatures, this legislation was named after five crime victims. In part, the legislation provides specifically enumerated rights for victims which include:

Federal Crime Victims' Rights Act – 2004

a. Rights of crime victims. A crime victim has the following rights:

1. The right to be reasonably protected from the accused.

2. The right to reasonable, accurate, and timely notice of any public court proceeding, or any parole proceeding, involving the crime or of any release or escape of the accused.

3. The right not to be excluded from any such public court proceeding, unless the court, after receiving clear and convincing evidence, determines that testimony by the victim would be materially altered if the victim heard other testimony at that proceeding.

4. The right to be reasonably heard at any public proceeding in the district court involving release, plea, sentencing, or any parole proceeding.

5. The reasonable right to confer with the attorney for the Government in the case.

6. The right to full and timely restitution as provided in law.

7. The right to proceedings free from unreasonable delay.

8. The right to be treated with fairness and with respect for the victim's dignity and privacy.

9. The right to be informed in a timely manner of any plea bargain or deferred prosecution agreement.

10. The right to be informed of the rights under this section and the services described in section 503(c) of the Victims' Rights and Restitution Act of 1990 (42 U.S.C. 10607(c)) and provided contact information for the Office of the Victims' Rights Ombudsman of the Department of Justice. (18 U.S.C.A. § 3771, West, 2016)

In New York State, Article 23 of the *Executive Law* is titled *Fair Treatment Standards for Crime Victims*. Like the companion federal legislation in the Crime Victims' Rights Act, the purpose of the legislation in New York, added in 1984 is:

New York State Fair Treatment Standards for Crime Victims

The object of such fair treatment standards shall be to:

1. Ensure that crime victims routinely receive emergency social and medical services as soon as possible and are given information pursuant to section six hundred twenty-five-a of this chapter on the following:

    a. availability of crime victim compensation;

    b. availability of appropriate public or private programs that provide counseling, treatment or support for crime victims, including but not limited to the following: rape crisis centers, victim/witness assistance programs, elderly victim services, victim assistance hotlines and domestic violence shelters;

    c. the role of the victims in the criminal justice process, including what they can expect from the system as well as what the system expects from them; and

    d. stages in the criminal justice process of significance to a crime victim, and the manner in which information about such stages can be obtained.

2. Ensure routine notification of a victim or witness as to steps that law enforcement officers or district attorneys can take to protect victims and witnesses from intimidation.

3. Ensure notification of victims, witnesses, relatives of those victims and witnesses who are minors, and relatives of homicide victims, if such persons provide the appropriate official with a current address and telephone number, either by phone or by mail, if possible, of judicial proceedings relating to their case, including:

    a. the arrest of an accused;

    b. the initial appearance of an accused before a judicial officer;

    c. the release of an accused pending judicial proceedings; and

    d. proceedings in the prosecution of the accused including entry of a plea of guilty, trial, sentencing, but prior to sentencing specific information shall be provided regarding the right to seek restitution and reparation, and where a term of imprisonment is imposed, specific information shall be provided regarding maximum and minimum terms of such imprisonment. (N.Y. Executive Law § 641, McKinney, 2016)

Along with the *New York State Executive Law*, the *New York State Penal Law* has evolved over time to include in the purpose of the law, victims. Specifically, the *New York State Penal Law* articulates six purposes to include:

Purpose of the New York State Penal Law

The general purposes of the provisions of this chapter are:

1. To proscribe conduct which unjustifiably and inexcusably causes or threatens substantial harm to individual or public interests;

2. To give fair warning of the nature of the conduct proscribed and of the sentences authorized upon conviction;

3. To define the act or omission and the accompanying mental state which constitute each offense;

4. To differentiate on reasonable grounds between serious and minor offenses and to prescribe proportionate penalties therefor;

5. To provide for an appropriate public response to particular offenses, **including consideration of the consequences of the offense for the victim, including the victim's family, and the community**; and

6. To insure the public safety by preventing the commission of offenses through the deterrent influence of the sentences authorized, the rehabilitation of those convicted, the promotion of their successful and productive reentry and reintegration into society, and their confinement when required in the interests of public protection [emphasis added]. (N.Y. Penal Law § 1.05, McKinney, 2016)

Within the State of New York, legislation and public sentiment over time has seen the establishment of the New York State Office of Victim Services (OVS; formerly the Crime Victim's Board prior to June, 2010), designated to serve as a clearinghouse at the state level for crime victims.

OVS has a three-tiered mission to:

1. provide compensation to innocent victims of crime in a timely, efficient and compassionate manner;

2. fund direct services to crime victims via a network of community-based programs; and

3. advocate for the rights and benefits of all innocent victims of crime. (OVS.NY.GOV)

At the local level, the Office of the Oneida County District Attorney has two dedicated positions for victim-witness coordinators. While the names may be different, prosecutors' offices around the country employ similar type positions to support victims and advocate for their rights consistent with both federal and state statutes. These positions not only coordinate the thousands of witnesses annually that participate in the judicial process through the Oneida County District Attorney's office, but they also serve as a first-hand resource to victims seeking advice regarding such issues as protection from offenders, outside support services, and compensation/**restitution** for damages as a result of criminal activity. Similarly at the federal level, major federal law enforcement agencies such as the FBI and DEA (Drug Enforcement Administration) have active victim-witness assistance programs and dedicated personnel in support of victim's rights and related issues. Readers should become familiar with both public and private crime victims services in their respective jurisdiction.

The Honorable Scott D. McNamara, Oneida County District Attorney

Restitution: ...3. Return or restoration of some specific thing to its rightful owner or status. 4. Compensation for loss [especially], full or partial compensation paid by a criminal to a victim, not awarded in a civil trial for court, but ordered as a part of a criminal sentence or as a condition of probation. [Also called criminal restitution] (Garner, 2014; Black's Law Dictionary 10th ed., reprinted with permission, Thomson Reuters).

© Shutterstock.com

8– 2 – Corr Voices

No one could ever argue that Officer Joseph D. Corr was not a crime victim. No one would argue that his wife and daughter, his mother and father, and his sisters were not crime victims. As we have noted, there are many definitions of victims, and each agency and each jurisdiction treats victims in a different manner. In the Corr case, the initial victims were those employees at Lennon's

W.B. Wilcox Jewelry Store who were robbed, and Officer Corr, who was murdered in pursuit of defendants Walter Richardson and Toussaint Davis. From the moment the defendants entered the jewelry store in New Hartford, New York on the evening of February 27, 2006, the ripple effect of growing victims commenced, like a large droplet of water violently disturbing a serene, windless pond, with seemingly no end in sight. As radio transmissions and other communications began to spin out from the center of the initial robbery in progress call, in increasingly larger concentric circles, more and more victims began to accumulate. Those public safety professionals and others engaged in the initial response to the jewelry store and subsequent vehicle chase were the next circle of victims.

Once the defendant's car had crashed at the Byrne Dairy in Kirkland, New York, fire service personnel were the next activated due to a gas pump fire caused as a result of the defendant's car crashing into the gas pump. Once Officer Corr was shot by defendant Walter Richardson, at approximately 8:28:37 p.m. (20:28:37 hours), all time was frozen for a lifetime, marked forward and backward from that moment in time. Conversations with victims over a law enforcement career has yielded the common thread of time; always marked before and after the initial victimization. For those continually victimized, such as those trapped in a cycle of domestic violence, time is often marked in different ways, but most often before and after the separation from their abuser.

Simultaneously after the crash of the defendant's vehicle, additional law enforcement officers and now emergency medical services personnel became involved in the ripple effect of victims, all within eight minutes of the initial call of a robbery in progress. After the initial involvement of public safety professionals, the process of making notifications to the family of Officer Corr as well as others, continued to see the concentric circles of victims continue to grow. Officers who were with Officer Corr moments after he was shot by defendant Walter Richardson

The crashed vehicle of Walter Richardson and Toussaint Davis (a.k.a. Toussaint Martin, a.k.a. John T. Healy) at the Byrne Dairy in Clark Mills, NY.

valiantly attempted to revive him until emergency medical personnel responded to the scene to take over life-saving measures. Officer Corr was transported to a local trauma center, where now hospital emergency services personnel became a part of the growing circles of victims, and where continued life-saving measures were applied until it could be determined that nothing else could be done to save Officer Corr's life. From these events forward, literally a handful of minutes since the defendants robbed the Lennon's W.B. Wilcox Jewelry Store, the circle of victims continued to grow and now included not only initial first responders and other public safety professionals, but direct family, extended family, friends, the greater community, and society as a whole.

Beyond the funeral for Officer Corr and select media interviews, the first official Corr voices from victims were heard in the courtroom at the sentencing of defendant Toussaint Davis, convicted in Oneida County Court of 18 counts of robbery in the first and second degree, and one count of murder in the second degree. While many of the directly impacted victims in the Corr case were called to testify at both the trial of defendant Toussaint Davis in Oneida County Court, and at the trial of all three defendants (Davis, Pegese, & Ward) at the federal court trial in the United States District Court for the Northern District of New York, their sworn testimony served more as a factual accounting of the events for the jury/court to hear, rather than relating the true impact of these crimes upon these people as individuals. While we have discussed several different laws and related organizations that support crime victim services, only within the confines of the courtroom do victims truly have an official voice. The New York State *Criminal Procedure Law* provides in part,

1. At the time of pronouncing sentence, the court must accord the prosecutor an opportunity to make a statement with respect to any matter relevant to the question of sentence. The court must then accord counsel for the defendant an opportunity to speak on behalf of the defendant. The defendant also has the right to make a statement personally in his or her

own behalf, and before pronouncing sentence the court must ask the defendant whether he or she wishes to make such a statement.

2. (a) For purposes of this section "victim" shall mean:

(1) the victim as indicated in the accusatory instrument; or

(2) if such victim is unable or unwilling to express himself or herself before the court or a person so mentally or physically disabled as to make it impracticable to appear in court in person or the victim is deceased, a member of the family of such victim, or the legal guardian or representative of the legal guardian of the victim where such guardian or representative has personal knowledge of and a relationship with the victim, unless the court finds that it would be inappropriate for such person to make a statement on behalf of the victim. (N.Y. Criminal Procedure Law § 380.50, McKinney, 2016)

At the sentencing of defendant Toussaint Davis in Oneida County Court on April 19, 2007, six victims spoke before the court prior the pronouncement of Judge Michael L. Dwyer's sentence, New Hartford Police Chief Raymond L. Philo, Officer Corr's Uncle, Robert Corr, Officer Corr's Cousin, Dan Winn, Officer Corr's Grandfather, Mr. Daniel Callan, Officer Corr's Father, Mr. David Corr, and Officer Corr's Mother, Mrs. Kathy Corr. In addition, the court heard final comments before sentencing from the prosecution, defense attorney, and the defendant, Toussaint Davis (Oneida County Court Trial Transcript, *People v. John T. Healy*, 2007). While one would normally think that the chief of police who commanded Officer Corr would be a victim, there was nonetheless significant debate/discussion on the record as to whether or not Chief Philo was actually a victim by the definition of the law. Despite the debate, the trial court judge

Read the full transcript of the sentencing in Oneida County Court (*People of the State of New York v. John T. Healy, a.k.a. Toussaint Davis, a.k.a. Toussaint Martin*, April 19, 2007) in the Appendix of this work, and in our online companion.

@ Shutterstock.com

nonetheless allowed Chief Philo to speak first prior to the pronouncement of sentence. Chief Philo's comments summarized the sentiments not only of himself and his department, but the overall community as a whole when he said, in part:

…Today marks a milestone, a sad and difficult journey we have been on for the past 14 months. Even after today our sad journey will continue for many more months, and for some of us a lifetime. As Chief of Police for the New Hartford Police Department, I was particularly impacted by the murder of Officer Corr and the horror sustained by the robbery victims. I doubt I will ever be entirely free of the private and lonely responsibility of sending a young police officer out on his last tour of duty. February 27th, 2006, is a day of infamy for us. On that Monday evening violent criminals descended upon our community and committed a series of crimes that included terrorizing innocent employees during a jewelry store robbery and murdering Officer Joseph Corr. Toussaint Davis, who sits here today convicted of robbery and murder, made a conscious decision to participate in these crimes. As a matter of record, the evidence at trial shows he played a major and significant role in planning the robbery. The facts of this case have been decided in a court of law, and, hence, are not for our discussion or debate today. Today is about the rule of law and the punishment that attaches where one is convicted of violating the law. The torrent of violent events that occurred in our community on February 27th, 2006, simply must not go under punished.

Toussaint Davis's life has been a crime in progress. I believe he is incapable of remorse or rehabilitation and he is destined to commit similar crimes if allowed to eventually go free. Therefore, since he stands convicted of 18 counts of robbery and one count of murder, I respectfully request that the Court sentence him to the maximum punishment allowed by law. (Oneida County Court Sentencing Transcript, People v. John T. Healy, a.k.a. Toussaint Davis, a.k.a. Toussaint Martin, *April 19, 2007)*

In addition to **presentence investigation reports** prepared by the probation department, victim impact statements, whether in writing, or delivered orally on the day of sentencing, provide a powerful context for the sentencing judge as they prepare to pronounce sentence. While judges typically have a sentencing matrix in mind when they take the bench on the day of sentencing, until a sentence is officially pronounced, judges retain the discretion to change a sentence based upon statements made in the courtroom on the actual day of sentencing. Among those who spoke most poignantly about the impact of the murder of Officer Corr were his father, David Corr,

> **Presentence-investigation report:** A probation officer's detailed account of a convicted defendant's educational, criminal, family, and social background, conducted at the courts request as an aid in passing sentence. [Also known as PSI; PR; PSR; PIR; PSIR, often shortened to presentence investigation or presentence report] (Garner, 2014; Black's Law Dictionary 10th ed., reprinted with permission, Thomson Reuters).

Credit: Nancy L. Ford Photography (reprinted with permission)

Mr. David Corr, Father of Officer Joseph D. Corr, addresses those gathered at his son's funeral.

and his mother Kathy Corr. Their words represent the awesome power that can be present during victim impact statements before a court and the community. Officer Corr's father, David, addressed the court and said:

For over a year now we've waited for this day to come, the criminal justice system to give our family this day. I want to thank all of the agencies, the individuals both within the law enforcement community, the legal system, the Court, to include the jury, and all those who helped in so many ways that we could not begin to list them all. We can only express our cumulative thank you. To you, Davis, you will never understand what you have taken from me. You and your cohorts, out of absolute greed, came here and showed disrespect for everyone, including yourself. You came here to victimize, terrorize, threaten, rob and steal. You think it's not your fault since you were not the shooter, but we all know it is your fault, and so does the law, and most importantly the jury says it's your fault. When you came here, you thought it would be easy pickings, but you did not plan on Joe and the New Hartford PD. You took our only son, my best friend, my granddaughter's dad, my daughters' only brother, a husband, friend; all something you wouldn't be able to relate to. I could not begin to really tell you what you have done. I look at you today and I see a person void of humanity. Your actions are proof of that, since you decided you were too smart to stay in school past the seventh grade, managed to get arrested some 50 times for literally hundreds of crimes from Hawaii to New Jersey to New York and Washington State. That's only counting the ones you were arrested for. I wonder how many more victims you had, I wonder how many more should be standing here commenting on their victims status here today. Quite a track record. It makes you a poster child for a lot more than this Court will be able to give you today. Unfortunately for now, you won't get the sentence you really deserve, no matter how much you deserve it. Ironically, even throughout the course of this trial you continued

to make a mockery of the Court by not even being truthful about your

name, and yet continuing to victimize yet another innocent man, not to

mention accepting responsibility for your actions and crime. Truly, you're a

scumbag. Today, finally, your turn has come. To the Court, I ask not only

for what he did to Joe and others at Lennon's Jewelry Store on the night

of 2/27 of last year, but also for the many other victims that still feel the

pain for that night, for the hundreds of victims and potential victims that

demand protection from this type of predator and for a civilized society, I

ask the Court to impose the maximum sentences and consecutive sentences

to this contemptible excuse for a human being. And, Davis, I sincerely

hope that you rot in prison for the rest of your life. (Oneida County Court

Sentencing Transcript, People v. John T. Healy, a.k.a. Toussaint

Davis, a.k.a. Toussaint Martin, *April 19, 2007)*

The final individual giving a victim impact statement to the court on April
19, 2007, was Officer Corr's mother, Kathy Corr. Mrs. Corr addressed the court
and said:

My name is Kathy Corr. I am Joe's mom. And this is going to be the most

difficult thing that I will ever have to do. And I'll do my best to get through

it, eventually. When you lose your parents, you lose your past. When you

lose your spouse, you lose your present. But when you lose your child, you've

lost your future. That is Joe Corr over there on that easel, that's Joe. Not

just the policeman or fireman or baseball player, but a son, a husband,

father, brother, grandson, uncle and cousin and godfather. The night my

son was murdered, I felt so numb. I'm his mother, mothers protect their

Mrs. Kathy Corr, mother of Officer Joseph D. Corr, stands next to her husband, Mr. David Corr, and her family at the funeral for her son.

children. I wish I could have jumped in front of Joe and taken the bullet myself. In the emergency room we were allowed to see him, hold him, and hug him. He looked like he was just sleeping. I rubbed his arm and held his hands; they were so cold. I wish you could've gotten blankets to warm him. But I couldn't do that because he had died, but I couldn't comprehend what that really meant. I can now say that I have experienced a parent's worst nightmare. That feeling never goes away. For 14 months I've been in counseling and on medication. I can't concentrate, I don't remember things, I don't sleep. I will be spending the rest of my life visiting memorials, planting flowers at my son's graves. It's not supposed to be that way, I'm not supposed to pick out my son's casket. We were all so excited when his dream came true and he put on a police uniform for the New Hartford Police Department. Badge 125. I truly felt he would be safe in his lifelong career and everything was perfect. I miss him calling me to watch the baby so he could run some errands. I miss our weekly family dinners. I miss seeing the dogs, Casey and Boomer. I miss his 30-minute drives from New Hartford to the Syracuse airport. I experienced all the ups and downs parents have. I now treasure every one of those memories. There is one person who can't be here and is the most affected by this senseless murder and she can't speak for herself, and that is Joe's daughter and my granddaughter. I had Joe through 30 wonderful years, but she only had her dad for one precious year. My daughter-in-law has said that Joe gave her more love in one year than other fathers give their children in a lifetime. He called her squirt. He'd rock her to sleep and didn't put her down in her crib because he said she looks so beautiful and all he wanted to do was stare at her in his arms. She won't remember him. She won't be with him and in their dream home on the hill overlooking the Mohawk Valley that they were going to build. Joe worked for years clearing the land, but is now overgrown with weeds and bushes. She can't give her dad a kiss goodbye on her first day of kindergarten. Shall miss her dad seeing her off on prom night. She won't see his proud smile as she graduates from high school and college. She won't have her dad walk her down the aisle on her wedding day. During the few days right after Joe's murder there were many New Hartford policeman coming and going at his house and they were all in uniform, the same uniform the Joe wore. I would just sit there and watch this one-year-old child, who was knee high to everyone, go from policeman, to policeman, looking for her dad. She would go and she would look up, and she would continue to go to the next policeman, look up, and try to find her dad. And she couldn't find him. And there are no more peak-a-boo games before Joe would go to work; she would look out the window and play peek-a-boo. Joe always went home for dinner and I thank God he was able to go home the night of February 27th, 2006, but he never returned home. Joe loved the outdoors and, in particular, camping. Every summer Joe and my daughter, Sheri, Flip and their friends, would all plan camping trips. They loved to go to Maine where they would hike and eat fresh lobsters. Joe's godson is three years old. He understands that Joe is not here, but he is up in the sky. At Christmas he decorated a small table-top tree with blue garland and blue ornaments, the blue standing for the blue line. A few days later he all the sudden grabbed the tree and ran out the back door and put the tree in the middle of the yard. He said he had to do that because he wanted Uncle Joe to see his tree because Uncle Joe couldn't see through the roof. Ultimately, the tree wound up on top of the swing set because the higher the tree, the better Uncle Joe could see it. One other thing my three-year-old grandson feels is that if the moon is anything but a full moon, that it is broken, and when the moon becomes full, Uncle Joe is the one that fixed it. We knew little that morning that God was going to call his name. In life we loved him dearly and in death we do the same. It broke our hearts to lose you, you did not go alone, for part of us went with you, the day God called you home. You left us peaceful memories, your love is still our guide, and though we cannot see you, you're always at our side. Our family chain is broken and nothing seems the same, but as God calls us one by one, the chain will link again. As far as you go, Mr. Toussaint Davis, you are nothing but trash from Philadelphia. You thought you had an easy heist here in New Hartford, a small town, not like Syracuse, a large city where there were two others jewelry stores that carried your Rollies, but you didn't do your homework. There was a police substation right across the street from Lennon's Jewelers and you never came upon a Joe Corr in your other crimes. Once Joe got on your tail, he would never let you go. He laid down his life so you and the other scumbag that was there couldn't hurt anybody else again. All you wanted were Rollies. You've slipped through the cracks in other states, but here in New

Hartford, New York our judicial system has you and this is the end of the road for you. You have no remorse, only arrogance, living the life of crime with many fake and stolen identities, which was your way of life, your job. I thank God that you did not have a gun in your hand and your finger on a trigger the night of February 27th because if you did, we wouldn't be mourning only the death of my son, but the death of Leslee Leisch also. You kept yelling to the person who was holding the gun to her head, kill the f-ing bitch, kill the f-ing bitch, over and over again. And again, I thank God that the N.H.P.D. came to the scene and the two other thugs out in the main part of the store yelled the cops are coming so everybody ran. You are a poor excuse for a human being. With your rap sheet, you should have been in jail a long time ago for life. Judge Dwyer, please don't let this piece of dirt slip through the cracks in the New York State Judicial System. He needs consecutive sentences. He can't have a chance to kill and destroy any other families. Mr. Toussaint Davis, you came here, you devastated my family, you assaulted our community, and for that, I will never forgive you. May you rot in hell, you son of a bitch. (Oneida County Court Sentencing Transcript, People v. John T. Healy, a.k.a. Toussaint Davis, a.k.a. Toussaint Martin, *April 19, 2007)*

Nearly four years later on July 11, 2011, defendants Davis, Pegese, and Ward were sentenced after their federal trial and convictions in the United States District Court for the Northern District of New York in Syracuse, New York. On that day, Officer Corr's mother and father, David and Kathy Corr, again spoke passionately to the court about their son and the devastation and loss that each of them continue to feel. A total of six victims spoke before the federal court. In

Read the full transcript of the sentencing in United States District Court for the Northern District of New York (*United States of America v. Toussaint Davis, Marion Pegese, & Robert Ward, July 11, 2011*) in our online companion.

addition to Officer Corr's parents, Lieutenant Timothy O'Neil of the New Hartford Police Department spoke. Ms. Leslie Liesh, an employee of Lennon's W.B. Wilcox Jewelry Store also presented a victim impact statement before the court. Ms. Pam Winn, Officer Corr's aunt, and Ms. Kelly Corr, Officer Corr's sister, also spoke at the defendants sentencing in court.

Despite the presence of our United States Constitution and a stable rule of law in the United States of America, it was not up until the latter half of the 20th century that crime victims begin to see a place in our American Criminal Justice System other than as passive observers. Despite the presence of dedicated public and private agencies and personnel within agencies and organizations passionately dedicated to crime victims' services, crime victims are often times unintentionally overlooked and/or forgotten once a criminal case has run its normal course through the criminal justice system. Crime victims, however, never forget their victimization, and most importantly never forget their loved ones and their contributions to their family, friends, and community as a whole.

Questions for review and further discussion

1. Why do you think it took so long for crime victims to have a greater/more visible role in the American Criminal Justice System?

2. Identify and discuss three resources in your community where crime victims can turn for support.

3. Discuss what types of things can be done in your community, and across the nation to enhance the role of victims in the American Criminal Justice System.

4. Discuss whether or not there should be a uniform local, county, state, and federal definition of who a victim is in the eyes of the law. If there should be a uniform definition, what would that definition look like? Be specific.

Chapter 9

In Memoriam

Outline

Expected Learning Outcomes

After reading this chapter and supplemental online materials, the reader will be able to:

1. Explain the importance of memorializing our fallen heroes with tangible memorials.

2. Articulate the differences impact between natural and sudden deaths.

3. Identify the many different ways of memorializing our fallen heroes.

    9 – 1 – Unintentionally Forgotten – Unforgiving Time

    9 – 2 – Preservation for All Time

    9 – 3 – Images for All Time

© *Shutterstock.com*

9 – 1 – Unintentionally Forgotten – Unforgiving Time

The sudden and violent death of any human being initially shocks the conscience of all of those who know that individual. As a people, we all deal with death and grieving in different ways. No one way is superior to the other, only different. History tends to be marked before and after significant personal and public events in our lives, both positive and negative. Some of those events include: the signing and ratification of our United States Constitution on September 17, 1787; the American Civil War; World War I; the horrors of the Holocaust; World War II; December 7, 1941 and Pearl Harbor; the Korean War; the assassination of President John F. Kennedy on November 22, 1963; the Vietnam War; America's bicentennial celebration in 1976; the United States Olympic Hockey Teams victory over the Soviet Union in February 1980, leading them to the gold medal after their final victory over Finland at the XIII Olympic Winter Games in Lake Placid, New York; the Space Shuttle Challenger disaster on January 28, 1986; the terrorist attacks on the United States of September 11, 2001 and the subsequent international war on terrorism; and the robbery of Lennon's W.B. Wilcox Jewelry Store and murder of New Hartford Police Officer Joseph D. Corr on February 27, 2006.

All of these events are frozen in time, marked by dates and times, and seared in the minds of those generations that ran parallel to those events. Time, however, is the only constant throughout history. Time is unforgiving. Time knows no race, color, creed, religion, or financial or social status in life. In time, memories fade, lives pass on from generation to generation, and only through the written word and the memorialization of significant events can we responsibly preserve the history for generations to come. According to world renowned grief expert, Dr. Kenneth J. Doka,

> *Sudden deaths often occur from circumstances such as an accident, suicide or homicide. While each circumstance creates unique issues for bereavement, all share complicating factors, such as a sense that the death was preventable as well as a lack of forewarning. These factors can also complicate a sudden death from natural causes such as a heart attack, aneurysm or stroke. Here, too, there is preventability and lack of forewarning. (Doka, 2005, p. 86)*

Contemporary literature in the field of sudden and violent death supports the notion that families and friends dealing with the loss of a loved one due to a homicide or related events are oftentimes subject to additional stressors caused by having their grief played out through the media, and in the criminal justice system (Ginter, 2001 as cited in Kristensen, Weisaeth, & Heir, 2012, p. 78). In such a public loss as the death of a police officer, victims go well beyond those immediate family members, close friends, and work colleagues of the deceased. Grief extends to the general public in the area where the loss occurs, and like the stone thrown in a serene pond, the victims ripple out to the larger community, and to society in general. As a society we somehow personally embrace our public servants, and in particular our public safety professionals such as those men and women who serve as police officers, firefighters, emergency medical personnel, and members of our United States Military. When a tragedy such as the murder of Officer Corr occurs, we somehow feel victimized, even though we may not be a member of the direct family, a friend, work colleague, or someone directly related to the case. In some way, society does not permit for these extended victims to grieve appropriately. Doka (1989) calls this disenfranchised grief. Dr. Doka notes,

Disenfranchised grief can be defined as the grief that persons experience when they occur loss that is not or cannot be openly acknowledged, publicly mourned, or socially supported. The concept of disenfranchised grief recognizes that societies have sets of norms-in effect, 'grieving rules' – that attempt to specify who, when, where, how, how long, and for whom people should grief. These grieving rules may be codified in personnel policies. For example, a worker may be allowed a week off for the death of a spouse or child, three days for the loss of a parent or sibling. Such policies reflect the fact that each society defines who has a legitimate right to grieve, and these definitions of right correspond to relationships, primarily familial, that are socially recognized and sanctioned. In any given society these grieving rules may not correspond to the nature of attachments, the sense of loss, or the feeling of survivors. Hence the grief of the survivors is disenfranchised. (Doka, 1989, p. 4)

Regardless of where the reader finds themselves in the concentric circle of the stone thrown into the serene pond, the acute nature of each and every sudden and violent death seemingly redefines how victims are defined in the law, a culture, and by past practice.

In 1944, eminent Boston-based psychiatrist and expert in the field of grief, Erich Lindemann, published his germinal study on the topic of acute grief, *Symptomatology and Management of Acute Grief* in the *American Journal of Psychiatry*. Dr. Lindemann conducted interviews with individuals facing actual or perceived/anticipated grief and in particular with families of the victims of the Coconut Grove Fire in Boston, Massachusetts, a tragic fire that occurred on November 28, 1942 claiming the lives of 492 people (Lindemann, 1944; The Coconut Grove Fire, 2016, para. 1). In his research, Lindemann (1944) went on to note,

> *The picture shown by persons in acute grief is remarkably uniform. Common to all is the following syndrome: sensations of somatic distress occurring in waves lasting from 20 minutes to an hour at a time, a feeling of tightness in the throat, choking with shortness of breath, need for sighing, and an empty feeling in the abdomen, lack of muscular power, and intense subjective distress described as tension or mental pain. The patient soon learns that these waves of discomfort can be precipitated by visits, by mentioning the deceased, and by receiving sympathy. There was a tendency to avoid the syndrome at any cost, to refuse visits lest they should precipitate the reaction, and to keep deliberately from thought all references to the deceased. (p. 141)*

While this work did not interview victims of the robbery-homicide involving Officer Corr, an analysis of the overall case and related victim impact statements presented in the Oneida County Court sentencing of defendant Toussaint Davis, and the sentencing of all three surviving defendants (Davis, Ward, & Pegese) in the United States District Court for the Northern District of New York, appears to support the germinal literature related to acute grief first introduced by Dr. Lindemann in 1944, and subsequent related research by Dr. Doka and others (Doka, 1989, 2005; Lindemann, 1944). As evidenced by this and related work, the Corr case is among those cases of sudden and violent death that place an additional lifetime of added stress, not only for the Corr family, but all of the parallel victims associated with this horrific robbery-homicide.

In times of grief, families tend to gather for a combination of private and public mourning which may include a private family gathering at a local funeral home, and/or public calling hours where friends and members of the community can come to pay their last respects to the deceased and their family. Services at a local funeral home may be followed by a small procession leading to a local church, and then to a local cemetery where our loved ones are laid to rest. However, in the case of a sudden and violent death involving such a public figure as a police officer such as Officer Corr, the process of grieving for a family becomes enormously more complicated as every aspect of the funeral is played out in the public eye.

While individuals such as Officer Corr always first belong to their family and closest friends, we as a collective community and society feel a strong sense of informal kinship that exists with our public servants, and in particular our public safety professionals and members of the military. The once relatively private coping, grieving, and healing process reserved for close family and friends is now exponentially magnified to include a nationwide and worldwide outpouring of grief and support from like communities of public servants. For Officer Corr's funeral, this meant literally thousands of public safety professionals from around North America who came to New Hartford, New York to pay their last respects

Credit: Nancy L. Ford Photography (reprinted with permission)

The American flag at half-staff on a brisk February day in 2006 outside of the New Hartford Volunteer Fire Department, where Officer Corr served as a volunteer firefighter.

Credit: Nancy L. Ford Photography (reprinted with permission)

A message to Officer Corr's , attached to a local business on the day of his funeral.

Credit: Nancy L. Ford Photography (reprinted with permission)

Members of the City of Utica Police Department, their shields partially covered by a black mourning band, are among the thousands of public safety professionals participating in Officer Corr's funeral.

Credit: Nancy L. Ford Photography (reprinted with permission)

The Oneida County Sheriff's Office's Honor Guard, one of dozens from around the country, marches down Oxford Road in New Hartford during Office Corr's funeral.

Credit: Nancy L. Ford Photography (reprinted with permission)

An American Hero's flag-draped casket is prepared to depart St. John the Evangelist Church in New Hartford, New York, one last time, as Officer Corr's widow, Traci Corr, and family, friends, and co-workers look on during this solemn moment. Below, Officers stand at attention as Officer Corr's casket is prepared to exit the church.

Credit: Nancy L. Ford Photography (reprinted with permission)

Officers stand at attention and salute as Officer Corr's casket makes one final visit past the New Hartford Police Department on Kellogg Road in New Hartford, New York, enroute to his final resting place.

to a fallen hero. As memories fade, and those who were most closely related to not only Officer Corr, but the case, begin to fade over unforgiving time, only the written word, the captured photograph, and those tactile objects memorializing a moment in time will live on beyond each of us, preserved for all time.

9 – 2 – Preservation for All Time

Arguably one of the greatest repositories of human knowledge and artifacts, the Smithsonian Institution, created by an Act of the United States Congress in 1846, is home to 19 museums, the National Zoo, and nine research facilities (Smithsonian Overview, 2016). Over 24.3 million visitors annually traverse through the Smithsonian Institution's museums and the National Zoo, viewing over 138,062,852 objects and specimens and having access to 2,084,587 library volumes of research materials and related documents (Smithsonian Overview, 2016). Whether objects or buildings preserved for thousands of years such as the pyramids of Egypt and the tombs of her pharaohs, or the ruins of the Parthenon in Greece, or the original copy of our own Declaration of Independence or the United States Constitution, the written word, and objects and memorials that represent the good and bad of our society are the only items that transcend time. We remain a society where the written word, and objects and symbols of our history serve as semi-permanent reminders of moments in time. We construct pyramids to honor the pharaohs, temples to honor the gods, and memorials to pay honor to individuals and events in our history.

However grand, buildings like the Smithsonian Institution and museums and historical societies around the country, and around the world, house millions of pieces of history that individuals determine as worthy of

National Law Enforcement Officer Memorial, located in Washington, D.C., contains the name of more than 20,000 fallen federal, state, and local law enforcement officers since 1791. Visitors can pay their respects and leave with a handmade etching of their family member, friend, or colleagues name.

passing along to future generations. For law enforcement officers, there is no more hallowed ground then the National Law Enforcement Officers Memorial located in Washington, D.C. dedicated on October 15, 1991; the wall holds the names of more than 20,000 fallen federal, state, and local law enforcement officers since 1791 (NLEOM, 2016). Among those inscribed on the wall for all time is the name of Joseph D. Corr. Visitors cannot only peacefully walk through the memorial, but like her companion memorials across town, the Vietnam and Korean War Memorials, visitors can take an etching of the inscribed name of their family member, friend, or colleague. This allows visitors an opportunity to take back with them a piece of the actual inscription on paper as a keepsake.

James C. Brown makes an etching of Officer Joseph D. Corr's name, inscribed at the National Law Enforcement Officer's Memorial in Washington, D.C.

Raymond L. Philo makes an etching of Officer Joseph D. Corr's name, inscribed at the National Law Enforcement Officer's Memorial in Washington, D.C.

In Memoriam   203

James C. Brown stands before the entrance to the National Law Enforcement Officer's Memorial in Washington, D.C. The inscription, as penned by one of the survivors, Vivian Eney reads, "It is not how these officers died that made them heroes it is how they lived."

Over the past more than 10 years since Officer Corr was murdered, family, friends, and colleagues continue to annually gather on February 27 of each year at the spot where Officer Corr fell. A small memorial of flowers, candles, and personal mementos marks this hallowed ground behind the Byrne Dairy Convenience Store in the Town of Kirkland, New York. Among the other permanent memorials, gestures, activities, and keepsakes created after the murder of Officer Corr were:

1. Creation of a special challenge coin depicting Officer Corr's name, shield, and date of his end of watch (EOW).

2. Creation of a special Joseph D. Corr Robbery-Homicide commemorative shield and lapel pin.

3. Creation of a service ribbon for officers to wear bearing the initials and shield number of Officer Corr.

4. Naming of a major section of New York State Route 840, the roadway which Officer Corr pursued the robbery suspects on February 27, 2006, as the Officer Joseph D. Corr Memorial Highway.

5. Renaming of the New Hartford Police Benevolent Association as the Joseph D. Corr Police Benevolent Association.

6. Naming of the baseball field on the grounds of the New Hartford High School, Officer Corr's alma mater, as Corr Memorial Field

7. Naming of a former community center building at the New Hartford Police Department as the Joseph D. Corr Command Center.

8. Annual Joseph D. Corr Softball Tournament held at Corr Memorial Field.

9. Retirement of Car 43 from the fleet of the New Hartford Police Department.

10. Creation of the Joseph D. Corr Memorial Award for Outstanding DWI Law Enforcement by the Oneida County STOP-DWI Program.

A small year-around memorial of flowers, candles, and personal mementos behind the Byrne Dairy in the Town of Kirkland, New York, marks the area where Officer Corr fell. More than 10 years after his murder, family, friends, and colleagues continue to gather each year on February 27.

Precious history cannot be left to memories and storytelling alone. Those who have lived history and fail to share the lesson's learned from events deprive future generations of their knowledge. Each of the items created, plaques placed, highways named, and memorials erected in the name of Officer Corr preserve the history of his bravery, and provide generations hence with invaluable lessons that both inform and protect future generations of law enforcement and other public safety professionals. It is incumbent upon agencies and organizations, and in particular community and educational institutions such as colleges and universities and historical societies, to participate in the effort to collectively preserve documents and related archives related to these tragedies for the benefit of future generations. The fallen lives of our public safety professionals cannot, and should not, be relegated to solely a name on a plaque hanging in an office. These heroic men and women who serve in law enforcement and other public safety professions are all, as President of the United States and former New York City Police Commissioner, Theodore Roosevelt once said, "...in the arena"

James C. Brown

Commemorative Law Enforcement Challenge Coin created for those involved in the case.

James C. Brown

Commemorative Joseph D. Corr Robbery-Homicide Joint Tast Force Shield and lapel pin created for those involved in the case.

James C. Brown

A portion of New York State Route 840, the roadway Officer Corr chased the robbery suspects on February 27, 2006 was renamed the Officer Joseph D. Corr Memorial Highway.

James C. Brown

The baseball field on the grounds of New Hartford High School, Officer Corr's alma mater, was named Corr Memorial Field.

(Roosevelt, 1910). Roosevelt said in part in his famous speech, *Citizenship in a Republic*, given at the Sorbonne in Paris, France on April 23, 1910,

© Shutterstock

> *It is not the critic who counts; not the man who points out how the strong man stumbles, or where the doer of deeds could have done them better. The credit belongs to the man who is actually in the arena, whose face is marred by dust and sweat and blood; who strives valiantly; who errs, who comes short again and again, because there is no effort without error and shortcoming; but who does actually strive to do the deeds; who knows great enthusiasms, the great devotions; who spends himself in a worthy cause; who at the best knows in the end the triumph of high achievement, and who at the worst, if he fails, at least fails while daring greatly, so that his place shall never be with those cold and timid souls who neither know victory nor defeat. (Roosevelt, 1910)*

President of the United States and former New York City Police Commissioner, Theodore Roosevelt

These heroic men and women, like Officer Corr, are worthy of a truly meaningful place in history, well beyond the memories, hearts and minds of their family, friends, and colleagues. Their place must be housed in museums, historical societies, and in the written word for all future generations to see and to learn from their stories.

9 – 3 – Images for All Time

This final section is left to a collage of final images from the Corr case; a lasting impression on a true American tragedy and a final farewell to an American hero.

Nancy L. Ford Photography, reprinted by permission

Media from multiple organizations attended many news conferences at the Clark Mills, NY Firehouse

Rome Sentinel, reprinted by permission

Black bunting is displayed for 30 days after Officer Corr's death at the New Hartford Fire Department where Officer Corr served as a firefighter.

Nancy L. Ford Photography, reprinted with permission

New Hartford Police Chief Raymond L. Philo (ret.) addresses the media at a news conference at the Clark Mills, NY Firehouse

Rome Sentinel, reprinted by permission

Law Enforcement and Fire Service Honor Guard Units prepare to march down Oxford Road in New Hartford, NY for the funeral procession for Officer Corr.

Hundreds of law enforcement officers, firefighters, and community members, friends and families wait in line for the calling hours of Officer Corr.

Thousands of law enforcement officer, firefighters, and community leaders stand at attention as they prepare for a final march from the funeral home to St. John the Evangelist Church on Oxford Road in New Hartford, NY.

The hearse carrying Officer Corr's body passes by hundreds of law enforcement officers, firefighters, and community members on its way to the cemetery, Officer Corr's final resting place.

Young and old stand in front of New Hartford High School on Oxford Road as his hearse passes by heading to St. John the Evangelist Church.

Officer Corr's Flag draped casket is carried into St. John the Evangelist Church for his funeral service.

New Hartford Police Chief Raymond L. Philo (ret.) makes a final salute to his fallen officer, Officer Joseph D. Corr, outside of St. John the Evangelist Church in New Hartford.

Officer Joseph D. Corr, his wife Tracie, and daughter Kaitlyn.

Questions for review and further discussion

1. Why is it beneficial to create memorials and memorial items for our deceased?

2. Why don't most agencies and organizations maintain comprehensive archives of their fallen members?

Appendix

The Constitution of the United States

We the People of the United States, in Order to form a more perfect Union, establish Justice, insure domestic Tranquility, provide for the common defence, promote the general Welfare, and secure the Blessings of Liberty to ourselves and our Posterity, do ordain and establish this Constitution for the United States of America

Article. I.

SECTION. 1

All legislative Powers herein granted shall be vested in a Congress of the United States, which shall consist of a Senate and House of Representatives.

SECTION. 2

The House of Representatives shall be composed of Members chosen every second Year by the People of the several States, and the Electors in each State shall have the Qualifications requisite for Electors of the most numerous Branch of the State Legislature.

No Person shall be a Representative who shall not have attained to the Age of twenty five Years, and been seven Years a Citizen of the United States, and who shall not, when elected, be an Inhabitant of that State in which he shall be chosen.

[Representatives and direct Taxes shall be apportioned among the several States which may be included within this Union, according to their respective Numbers, which shall be determined by adding to the whole Number of free Persons, including those bound to Service for a Term of Years, and excluding Indians not taxed, three fifths of all other Persons.]* The actual Enumeration shall be made within three Years after the first Meeting of the Congress of the United States, and within every subsequent Term of ten Years, in such Manner as they shall by Law direct. The Number of Representatives shall not exceed one for every thirty Thousand, but each State shall have at Least one Representative; and until such enumeration shall be made, the State of New Hampshire shall be entitled to chuse three, Massachusetts eight, Rhode-Island and Providence Plantations one, Connecticut five, New-York six, New Jersey four, Pennsylvania eight, Delaware one, Maryland six, Virginia ten, North Carolina five, South Carolina five, and Georgia three.

When vacancies happen in the Representation from any State, the Executive Authority thereof shall issue Writs of Election to fill such Vacancies.

The House of Representatives shall chuse their Speaker and other Officers; and shall have the sole Power of Impeachment.

SECTION. 3

The Senate of the United States shall be composed of two Senators from each State, [chosen by the Legislature there-of,]* for six Years; and each Senator shall have one Vote.

Immediately after they shall be assembled in Consequence of the first Election, they shall be divided as equally as may be into three Classes. The Seats of the Senators of the first Class shall be vacated at the Expiration of the second Year, of the second Class at the Expiration of the fourth Year, and of the third Class at the Expiration of the sixth Year, so that one third may be chosen every second Year; [and if Vacancies happen by Resignation, or otherwise, during the Recess of the Legislature of any State, the Executive thereof may make temporary Appointments until the next Meeting of the Legislature, which shall then fill such Vacancies.]*

No Person shall be a Senator who shall not have attained to the Age of thirty Years, and been nine Years a Citizen of the United States, and who shall not, when elected, be an Inhabitant of that State for which he shall be chosen

The Vice President of the United States shall be President of the Senate, but shall have no Vote, unless they be equally divided.

The Senate shall chuse their other Officers, and also a President pro tempore, in the Absence of the Vice President, or when he shall exercise the Office of President of the United States

The Senate shall have the sole Power to try all Impeachments. When sitting for that Purpose, they shall be on Oath or Affirmation. When the President of the United States is tried, the Chief Justice shall preside: And no Person shall be convicted without the Concurrence of two thirds of the Members present.

Judgment in Cases of Impeachment shall not extend further than to removal from Office, and disqualification to hold and enjoy any Office of honor, Trust or Profit under the United States: but the Party convicted shall nevertheless be liable and subject to Indictment, Trial, Judgment and Punishment, according to Law.

SECTION. 4

The Times, Places and Manner of holding Elections for Senators and Representatives, shall be prescribed in each State by the Legislature thereof; but the Congress may at any time by Law make or alter such Regulations, except as to the Places of chusing Senators.

The Congress shall assemble at least once in every Year, and such Meeting shall be [on the first Monday in December,]* unless they shall by Law appoint a different Day.

SECTION. 5

Each House shall be the Judge of the Elections, Returns and Qualifications of its own Members, and a Majority of each shall constitute a Quorum to do Business; but a smaller Number may adjourn from day to day, and may be authorized to compel the Attendance of absent Members, in such Manner, and under such Penalties as each House may provide.

Each House may determine the Rules of its Proceedings, punish its Members for disorderly Behaviour, and, with the Concurrence of two thirds, expel a Member.

Each House shall keep a Journal of its Proceedings, and from time to time publish the same, excepting such Parts as may in their Judgment require Secrecy; and the Yeas and Nays of the Members of either House on any question shall, at the Desire of one fifth of those Present, be entered on the Journal.

Neither House, during the Session of Congress, shall, without the Consent of the other, adjourn for more than three days, nor to any other Place than that in which the two Houses shall be sitting.

SECTION. 6

The Senators and Representatives shall receive a Compensation for their Services, to be ascertained by Law, and paid out of the Treasury of the United States. They shall in all Cases, except Treason, Felony and Breach of the Peace, be privileged from Arrest during their Attendance at the Session of their respective Houses, and in going to and returning from the same; and for any Speech or Debate in either House, they shall not be questioned in any other Place.

No Senator or Representative shall, during the Time for which he was elected, be appointed to any civil Office under the Authority of the United States, which shall have been created, or the Emoluments whereof shall have been encreased during such time; and no Person holding any Office under the United States, shall be a Member of either House during his Continuance in Office.

SECTION. 7

All Bills for raising Revenue shall originate in the House of Representatives; but the Senate may propose or concur with Amendments as on other Bills

Every Bill which shall have passed the House of Representatives and the Senate, shall, before it become a Law, be presented to the President of the United States; If he approve he shall sign it, but if not he shall return it, with his Objections to that House in which it shall have originated, who shall enter the Objections at large on their Journal, and proceed to reconsider it. If after such Reconsideration two thirds of that House shall agree to pass the Bill, it shall be sent, together with the Objections, to the other House, by which it shall likewise be reconsidered, and if approved by two thirds of that House, it shall become a Law. But in all such Cases the Votes of both Houses shall be determined by Yeas and Nays, and the Names of the Persons voting for and against the Bill shall be entered on the Journal of each House respectively, If any Bill shall not be returned by the President within ten Days (Sundays excepted) after it shall have been presented to him, the Same shall be a Law, in like Manner as if he had signed it, unless the Congress by their Adjournment prevent its Return, in which Case it shall not be a Law

Every Order, Resolution, or Vote to which the Concurrence of the Senate and House of Representatives may be necessary (except on a question of Adjournment) shall be presented to the President of the United States; and before the Same shall take Effect, shall be approved by him, or being disapproved by him, shall be repassed by two thirds of the Senate and House of Representatives, according to the Rules and Limitations prescribed in the Case of a Bill.

SECTION. 8

The Congress shall have Power To lay and collect Taxes, Duties, Imposts and Excises, to pay the Debts and provide for the common Defence and general Welfare of the United States; but all Duties, Imposts and Excises shall be uniform throughout the United States;

To borrow Money on the credit of the United States;

To regulate Commerce with foreign Nations, and among the several States, and with the Indian Tribes;

To establish an uniform Rule of Naturalization, and uniform Laws on the subject of Bankruptcies throughout the United States;

To coin Money, regulate the Value thereof, and of foreign Coin, and fix the Standard of Weights and Measures;

To provide for the Punishment of counterfeiting the Securities and current Coin of the United States;

To establish Post Offices and post Roads;

To promote the Progress of Science and useful Arts, by securing for limited Times to Authors and Inventors the exclusive Right to their respective Writings and Discoveries;

To constitute Tribunals inferior to the supreme Court;

To define and punish Piracies and Felonies committed on the high Seas, and Offenses against the Law of Nations;

To declare War, grant Letters of Marque and Reprisal, and make Rules concerning Captures on Land and Water;

To raise and support Armies, but no Appropriation of Money to that Use shall be for a longer Term than two Years;

To provide and maintain a Navy;

To make Rules for the Government and Regulation of the land and naval Forces;

To provide for calling forth the Militia to execute the Laws of the Union, suppress Insurrections and repel Invasions;

To provide for organizing, arming, and disciplining, the Militia, and for governing such Part of them as may be employed in the Service of the United States, reserving to the States respectively, the Appointment of the Officers, and the Authority of training the Militia according to the discipline prescribed by Congress;

To exercise exclusive Legislation in all Cases whatsoever, over such District (not exceeding ten Miles square) as may, by Cession of particular States, and the Acceptance of Congress, become the Seat of the Government of the United States, and to exercise like Authority over all Places purchased by the Consent of the Legislature of the State in which the Same shall be, for the Erection of Forts, Magazines, Arsenals, dock-Yards and other neeful Buildings;

-And

To make all Laws which shall be necessary and proper for carrying into Execution the foregoing Powers, and all other Powers vested by this Constitution in the Government of the United States, or in any Department or Officer thereof.

SECTION. 9

The Migration or Importation of such Persons as any of the States now existing shall think proper to admit, shall not be prohibited by the Congress prior to the Year one thousand eight hundred and eight, but a Tax or duty may be imposed on such Importation, not exceeding ten dollars for each Person

The Privilege of the Writ of Habeas Corpus shall not be suspended, unless when in Cases of Rebellion or Invasion the public Safety may require it.

No Bill of Attainder or ex post facto Law shall be passed.

[No Capitation, or other direct, Tax shall be laid, unless in Proportion to the Census or Enumeration herein before directed to be taken.]*

No Tax or Duty shall be laid on Articles exported from any State

No Preference shall be given by any Regulation of Commerce or Revenue to the Ports of one State over those of another: nor shall Vessels bound to, or from, one State, be obliged to enter, clear, or pay Duties in another.

No Money shall be drawn from the Treasury, but in Consequence of Appropriations made by Law; and a regular Statement and Account of the Receipts and Expenditures of all public Money shall be published from time to time.

No Title of Nobility shall be granted by the United States: And no Person holding any Office of Profit or Trust under them, shall, without the Consent of the Congress, accept of any present, Emolument, Office, or Title, of any kind whatever, from any King, Prince, or foreign State.

SECTION. 10

No State shall enter into any Treaty, Alliance, or Confederation; grant Letters of Marque and Reprisal; coin Money; emit Bills of Credit; make any Thing but gold and silver Coin a Tender in Payment of Debts; pass any Bill of Attainder, ex post facto Law, or Law impairing the Obligation of Contracts, or grant any Title of Nobility.

No State shall, without the Consent of the Congress, lay any Imposts or Duties on Imports or Exports, except what may be absolutely necessary for executing it's inspection Laws: and the net Produce of all Duties and Imposts, laid by any State on Imports or Exports, shall be for the Use of the Treasury of the United States; and all such Laws shall be subject to the Revision and Controul of the Congress.

No State shall, without the Consent of Congress, lay any Duty of Tonnage, keep Troops, or Ships of War in time of Peace, enter into any Agreement or Compact with another State, or with a foreign Power, or engage in War, unless actually invaded, or in such imminent Danger as will not admit of delay.

Article. II.

SECTION. 1

The executive Power shall be vested in a President of the United States of America. He shall hold his Office during the Term of four Years, and, together with the Vice President, chosen for the same Term, be elected, as follows:

Each State shall appoint, in such Manner as the Legislature thereof may direct, a Number of Electors, equal to the whole Number of Senators and Representatives to which the State may be entitled in the Congress: but no Senator or Representative, or Person holding an Office of Trust or Profit under the United States, shall be appointed an Elector.

[The Electors shall meet in their respective States, and vote by Ballot for two Persons, of whom one at least shall not be an Inhabitant of the same State with themselves. And they shall make a List of all the Persons voted for, and of the Number of Votes for each; which List they shall sign and certify, and transmit sealed to the Seat of the Government of the United States, directed to the President of the Senate. The President of the Senate shall, in the Presence of the Senate and House of Representatives, open all the Certificates, and the Votes shall then be counted. The Person having the greatest Number of Votes shall be the President, if such Number be a Majority of the whole Number of Electors appointed; and if there be more than one who have such Majority, and have an equal Number of Votes, then the House of Representatives shall immediately chuse by Ballot one of them for President; and if no Person have a Majority, then from the five highest on the List the said House shall in like Manner chuse the President.

But in chusing the President, the Votes shall be taken by States, the Representation from each State having one Vote; A quorum for this Purpose shall consist of a Member or Members from two thirds of the States, and a Majority of all the States shall be necessary to a Choice. In every Case, after the Choice of the President, the Person having the greatest Number of Votes of the Electors shall be the Vice President. But if there should remain two or more who have equal Votes, the Senate shall chuse from them by Ballot the Vice President.]*

The Congress may determine the Time of chusing the Electors, and the Day on which they shall give their Votes; which Day shall be the same throughout the United States.

No Person except a natural born Citizen, or a Citizen of the United States, at the time of the Adoption of this Constitution, shall be eligible to the Office of President; neither shall any person be eligible to that Office who shall not have attained to the Age of thirty five Years, and been fourteen Years a Resident within the United States

In Case of the Removal of the President from Office, or of his Death, Resignation, or Inability to discharge the Powers and Duties of the said Office, the Same shall devolve on the Vice President, and the Congress may by Law provide for the Case of Removal, Death, Resignation or Inability, both of the President and Vice President, declaring what Officer shall then act as President, and such Officer shall act accordingly, until the Disability be removed, or a President shall be elected.]*

The President shall, at stated Times, receive for his Services, a Compensation, which shall neither be increased nor diminished during the Period for which he shall have been elected, and he shall not receive within that Period any other Emolument from the United States, or any of them.

Before he enter on the Execution of his Office, he shall take the following Oath or Affirmation: "I do solemnly swear (or affirm) that I will faithfully execute the Office of President of the United States, and will to the best of my Ability, preserve, protect and defend the Constitution of the United States."

SECTION. 2

The President shall be Commander in Chief of the Army and Navy of the United States, and of the Militia of the several States, when called into the actual Service of the United States; he may require the Opinion, in writing, of the principal Officer in each of the executive Departments, upon any Subject relating to the Duties of their respective Offices, and he shall have Power to grant Reprieves and Pardons for Offenses against the United States, except in Cases of Impeachment.

He shall have Power, by and with the Advice and Consent of the Senate, to make Treaties, provided two thirds of the Senators present concur; and he shall nominate, and by and with the Advice and Consent of the Senate, shall appoint Ambassadors, other public Ministers and Consuls, Judges of the supreme Court, and all other Officers of the United States, whose Appointments are not herein otherwise provided for, and which shall be established by Law: but the Congress may by Law vest the Appointment of such inferior Officers, as they think proper, in the President alone, in the Courts of Law, or in the Heads of Departments.

The President shall have Power to fill up all Vacancies that may happen during the Recess of the Senate, by granting Commissions which shall expire at the End of their next Session

SECTION. 3

He shall from time to time give to the Congress Information of the State of the Union, and recommend to their Consideration such Measures as he shall judge necessary and expedient; he may, on extraordinary Occasions, convene both Houses, or either of them, and in Case of Disagreement between them, with

Respect to the Time of Adjournment, he may adjourn them to such Time as he shall think proper; he shall receive Ambassadors and other public Ministers; he shall take Care that the Laws be faithfully executed, and shall Commission all the Officers of the United States

SECTION. 4

The President, Vice President and all civil Officers of the United States, shall be removed from Office on Impeachment for, and Conviction of, Treason, Bribery, or other high Crimes and Misdemeanors.

Article. III.

SECTION. 1

The judicial Power of the United States, shall be vested in one supreme Court, and in such inferior Courts as the Congress may from time to time ordain and establish. The Judges, both of the supreme and inferior Courts, shall hold their Offices during good Behaviour, and shall at stated Times, receive for their Services, a Compensation, which shall not be diminished during their Continuance in Office.

SECTION. 2

The judicial Power shall extend to all Cases, in Law and Equity, arising under this Constitution, the Laws of the United States, and Treaties made, or which shall be made, under their Authority; -to all Cases affecting Ambassa dors, other public Ministers and Consuls; -to all Cases of admiralty and maritime Jurisdiction; -to Controversies to which the United States shall be a Party; -to Controversies between two or more States; -[between a State and Citizens of another State;-]* between Citizens of different States,

-between Citizens of the same State claiming Lands under Grants of different States, [and between a State, or the Citizens thereof;-and foreign States, Citizens or Subjects.]*

In all Cases affecting Ambassadors, other public Ministers and Consuls, and those in which a State shall be Party, the supreme Court shall have original Jurisdiction. In all the other Cases before mentioned, the supreme Court shall have appellate Jurisdiction, both as to Law and Fact, with such Exceptions, and under such Regulations as the Congress shall make.

The Trial of all Crimes, except in Cases of Impeachment; shall be by Jury; and such Trial shall be held in the State where the said Crimes shall have been committed; but when not committed within any State, the Trial shall be at such Place or Places as the Congress may by Law have directed.

SECTION. 3

Treason against the United States, shall consist only in levying War against them, or in adhering to their Enemies, giving them Aid and Comfort. No Person shall be convicted of Treason unless on the Testimony of two Witnesses to the same overt Act, or on Confession in open Court.

The Congress shall have Power to declare the Punishment of Treason, but no Attainder of Treason shall work Corruption of Blood, or Forfeiture except during the Life of the Person attainted

Article. IV.

SECTION. 1

Full Faith and Credit shall be given in each State to the public Acts, Records, and judicial Proceedings of every other State. And the Congress may by general Laws prescribe the Manner in which such Acts, Records and Proceedings shall be proved, and the Effect thereof.

SECTION. 2

The Citizens of each State shall be entitled to all Privileges and Immunities of Citizens in the several States

A Person charged in any State with Treason, Felony, or other Crime, who shall flee from Justice, and be found in another State, shall on Demand of the executive Authority of the State from which he fled, be delivered up, to be removed to the State having Jurisdiction of the Crime.

No Person held to Service or Labour in one State, under the Laws thereof, escaping into another, shall, in Consequence of any Law or Regulation therein, be discharged from such Service or Labour, but shall be delivered up on Claim of the Party to whom such Service or Labour may be due.]*

SECTION. 3

New States may be admitted by the Congress into this Union; but no new State shall be formed or erected within the Jurisdiction of any other State; nor any State be formed by the Junction of two or more States, or Parts of States, without the Consent of the Legislatures of the States concerned as well as of the Congress.

The Congress shall have Power to dispose of and make all needful Rules and Regulations respecting the Territory or other Property belonging to the United States; and nothing in this Constitution shall be so construed as to Prejudice any Claims of the United States, or of any particular State.

SECTION. 4

The United States shall guarantee to every State in this Union a Republican Form of Government, and shall protect each of them against Invasion; and on Application of the Legislature, or of the Executive (when the Legislature cannot be convened) against domestic Violence.

Article. V.

The Congress, whenever two thirds of both Houses shall deem it necessary, shall propose Amendments to this Constitution, or, on the Application of the Legislatures of two thirds of the several States, shall call a Convention for proposing Amendments, which in either Case, shall be valid to all Intents and Purposes, as Part of this Constitution, when ratified by the Legislatures of three–fourths of the several States, or by Conventions in three fourths thereof, as the one or the other Mode of Ratification may be proposed by the Congress; Provided that no Amendment which may be made prior to the Year One thousand eight hundred and eight shall in any Manner affect the first and fourth Clauses in the Ninth Section of the first Article; and that no State, without its Consent, shall be deprived of its equal Suffrage in the Senate

Article. VI.

All Debts contracted and Engagements entered into, before the Adoption of this Constitution, shall be as valid against the United States under this Constitution, as under the Confederation

This Constitution, and the Laws of the United States which shall be made in Pursuance thereof; and all Treaties made, or which shall be made, under the Authority of the United States, shall be the supreme Law of the Land; and the Judges in every State shall be bound thereby, any Thing in the Constitution or Laws of any State to the Contrary notwithstanding.

The Senators and Representatives before mentioned, and the Members of the several State Legislatures, and all executive and judicial Officers, both of the United States and of the several States, shall be bound by Oath or Affirmation, to support this Constitution; but no religious Test shall ever be required as a Qualification to any Office or public Trust under the United States

Article. VII.

The Ratification of the Conventions of nine States, shall be sufficient for the Establishment of this Constitution between the States so ratifying the Same.

Done in Convention by the Unanimous Consent of the States present the Seventeenth Day of September in the Year of our Lord one thousand seven hundred and Eighty seven and of the Independence of the United States of America the Twelfth In Witness whereof We have hereunto subscribed our Names,

Go. Washington–Presidt: and deputy from Virginia

NEW HAMPSHIRE

John Langdon Nicholas Gilman

MASSACHUSETTS

Nathaniel Gorham Rufus King

CONNECTICUT

Wm. Saml. Johnson Roger Sherman

NEW YORK

Alexander Hamilton

NEW JERSEY

Wil: Livingston David Brearley Wm. Paterson Jona: Dayton

PENNSYLVANIA

B Franklin Thomas Mifflin Robt Morris Geo. Clymer Thos. FitzSimons Jared Ingersoll James Wilson Gouv Morris

DELAWARE

Geo: Read Gunning Bedford jun John Dickinson Richard Bassett Jaco: Broom

MARYLAND

James McHenry

Dan of St. Thos. Jenifer Danl Carroll

VIRGINIA

John Blair–James Madison Jr.

NORTH CAROLINA

Wm. Blount

Richd. Dobbs Spaight Hu Williamson

SOUTH CAROLINA

J. Rutledge

Charles Cotesworth Pinckney Charles Pinckney

Pierce Butler

GEORGIA

William Few Abr Baldwin

Attest William Jackson Secretary

In Convention Monday September 17th, 1787. Present

The States of

New Hampshire, Massachusetts, Connecticut, Mr. Hamilton from New York, New Jersey, Pennsylvania, Delaware, Maryland, Virginia, North Carolina, South Carolina and Georgia.

Resolved,

That the preceeding Constitution be laid before the United States in Congress assembled, and that it is the Opinion of this Convention, that it should afterwards be submitted to a Convention of Delegates, chosen in each State by the People thereof, under the Recommendation of its Legislature, for their Assent and Ratification; and that each Convention assenting to, and ratifying the Same, should give Notice thereof to the United States in Congress assembled. Resolved,

That it is the Opinion of this Convention, that as soon as the Conventions of nine States shall have ratified this Constitution, the United States in Congress assembled should fix a Day on which Electors should be appointed by the States which shall have ratified the same, and a Day on which the Electors should assemble to vote for the President, and the Time and Place for commencing Proceedings under this Constitution

That after such Publication the Electors should be appointed, and the Senators and Representatives elected: That the Electors should meet on the Day fixed for the Election of the President, and should transmit their Votes certified, signed, sealed and directed, as the Constitution requires, to the Secretary of the United States in Congress assembled, that the Senators and Representatives should convene at the Time and Place assigned; that the Senators should appoint a President of the Senate, for the sole Purpose of receiving, opening and counting the Votes for President; and, that after he shall be chosen, the Congress, together with the President, should, without Delay, proceed to execute this Constitution

By the unanimous Order of the Convention

Go. Washington–Presidt:

W. JACKSON Secretary.

---

* Language in brackets has been changed by amendment.

The Amendments to the Constitution of the United States as Ratified by the States

Preamble to the Bill of Rights

Congress of the United States

begun and held at the City of New-York, on Wednesday the fourth of March,

THE Conventions of a number of the States, having at the time of their adopting the Constitution, expressed a desire, in order to prevent misconstruction or abuse of its powers, that further declaratory and restrictive clauses should be added: And as extending the ground of public confidence in the Government, will best ensure the beneficent ends of its institution

RESOLVED by the Senate and House of Representatives of the United States of America, in Congress assembled, two thirds of both Houses concurring, that the following Articles be proposed to the Legislatures of the several States, as amendments to the Constitution of the United States, all, or any of which Articles, when ratified by three fourths of the said Legislatures, to be valid to all intents and purposes, as part of the said Constitution; viz.

ARTICLES in addition to, and Amendment of the Constitution of the United States of America, proposed by Congress, and ratified by the Legislatures of the several States, pursuant to the fifth Article of the original Constitution.

(Note: The first 10 amendments to the Constitution were ratified December 15, 1791, and form what is known as the "Bill of Rights.")

Amendment I.

Congress shall make no law respecting an establishment of religion, or prohibiting the free exercise thereof; or abridging the freedom of speech, or of the press, or the right of the people peaceably to assemble, and to petition the Government for a redress of grievances.

Amendment II.

A well regulated Militia, being necessary to the security of a free State, the right of the people to keep and bear Arms, shall not be infringed.

Amendment III.

No Soldier shall, in time of peace be quartered in any house, without the consent of the Owner, nor in time of war, but in a manner to be prescribed by law.

Amendment IV.

The right of the people to be secure in their persons, houses, papers, and effects, against unreasonable searches and seizures, shall not be violated, and no Warrants shall issue, but upon probable cause, supported by Oath or affirmation, and particularly describing the place to be searched, and the persons or things to be seized.

Amendment V.

No person shall be held to answer for a capital, or otherwise infamous crime, unless on a presentment or indictment of a Grand Jury, except in cases arising in the land or naval forces, or in the Militia, when in actual service in time of War or public danger; nor shall any person be subject for the same offence to be twice put in jeopardy of life or limb; nor shall be compelled in any criminal case to be a witness against himself, nor be deprived of life, liberty, or property, without due process of law; nor shall private property be taken for public use, without just compensation.

Amendment VI.

In all criminal prosecutions, the accused shall enjoy the right to a speedy and public trial, by an impartial jury of the State and district wherein the crime shall have been committed, which district shall have been previously ascertained by law, and to be informed of the nature and cause of the accusation; to be confronted with the witnesses against him; to have compulsory process for obtaining witnesses in his favor, and to have the Assistance of Counsel for his defence.

Amendment VII.

In suits at common law, where the value in controversy shall exceed twenty dollars, the right of trial by jury shall be preserved, and no fact tried by a jury shall be otherwise re-examined in any Court of the United States, than according to the rules of the common law.

Amendment VIII.

Excessive bail shall not be required, nor excessive fines imposed, nor cruel and unusual punishments inflicted.

Amendment IX.

The enumeration in the Constitution, of certain rights, shall not be construed to deny or disparage others retained by the people.

Amendment X.

The powers not delegated to the United States by the Constitution, nor prohibited by it to the States, are reserved to the States respectively, or to the people.

AMENDMENTS 11–27

Amendment XI.

Passed by Congress March 4, 1794. Ratified February 7, 1795.

(Note: A portion of Article III, Section 2 of the Constitution was modified by the 11th Amendment.)

The Judicial power of the United States shall not be construed to extend to any suit in law or equity, commenced or prosecuted against one of the United States by Citizens of another State, or by Citizens or Subjects of any Foreign State.

Amendment XII.

Passed by Congress December 9, 1803. Ratified June 15, 1804.

(Note: A portion of Article II, Section 1 of the Constitution was changed by the 12th Amendment.)

The Electors shall meet in their respective states, and vote by ballot for President and Vice-President, one of whom, at least, shall not be an inhabitant of the same state with themselves; they shall name in their ballots the person voted for as President, and in distinct ballots the person voted for as Vice-President, and they shall make distinct lists of all persons voted for as President, and of all persons voted for as Vice-President, and of the number of votes for each, which lists they shall sign and certify, and transmit sealed to the seat of the government of the United States, directed to the President of the Senate; -the President of the Senate shall, in the presence of the Senate and House of Representatives, open all the certificates and the votes shall then be counted; -The person having the greatest number of votes for President, shall be the President, if such number be a majority of the whole number of Electors appointed; and if no person have such majority, then from the persons having the highest numbers not exceeding three on the list of those voted for as President, the House of Representatives shall choose immediately, by ballot, the President. But in choosing the President, the votes shall be taken by states, the representation from each state having one vote; a quorum for this purpose shall consist of a member or members from two-thirds of the states, and a majority of all the states shall be necessary to a choice. [And if the House of Representatives shall not choose a President whenever the right of choice shall devolve upon them, before the fourth day of March next following, then the Vice-President shall act as President, as in case of the death or other constitutional disability of the President.-]* The person having the greatest number of votes as Vice-President, shall be the Vice-President, if such number be a majority of the whole number of Electors appointed, and if no person have a majority, then from the two highest numbers on the list, the Senate shall choose the Vice-President; a quorum for the purpose shall consist of two-thirds of the whole number of Senators, and a majority of the whole number shall be necessary to a choice. But no person constitutionally ineligible to the office of President shall be eligible to that of Vice-President of the United States.

*Superseded by Section 3 of the 20th Amendment.

Amendment XIII.

Passed by Congress January 31, 1865. Ratified December 6, 1865.

(Note: A portion of Article IV, Section 2 of the Constitution was changed by the 13th Amendment.)

SECTION 1

Neither slavery nor involuntary servitude, except as a punishment for crime whereof the party shall have been duly convicted, shall exist within the United States, or any place subject to their jurisdiction.

SECTION 2

Congress shall have power to enforce this article by appropriate legislation.

Amendment XIV.

Passed by Congress June 13, 1866. Ratified July 9, 1868.

(Note: Article I, Section 2 of the Constitution was modified by Section 2 of the 14th Amendment.)

SECTION 1

All persons born or naturalized in the United States and subject to the jurisdiction thereof, are citizens of the United States and of the State wherein they reside. No State shall make or enforce any law which shall abridge the privileges or immunities of citizens of the United States; nor shall any State deprive any person of life, liberty, or property, without due process of law; nor deny to any person within its jurisdiction the equal protection of the laws.

SECTION 2

Representatives shall be apportioned among the several States according to their respective numbers, counting the whole number of persons in each State, excluding Indians not taxed. But when the right to vote at any election for the choice of electors for President and Vice President of the United States, Representatives in Congress, the Executive and Judicial officers of a State, or the members of the Legislature thereof, is denied to any of the male inhabitants of such State, [being twenty-one years of age,]* and citizens of the United States, or in any way abridged, except for participation in rebellion, or other crime, the basis of representation therein shall be reduced in the proportion which the number of such male citizens shall bear to the whole number of male citizens twenty-one years of age in such State.

SECTION 3

No person shall be a Senator or Representative in Congress, or elector of President and Vice President, or hold any office, civil or military, under the

United States, or under any State, who, having previously taken an oath, as a member of Congress, or as an officer of the United States, or as a member of any State legislature, or as an executive or judicial officer of any State, to support the Constitution of the United States, shall have engaged in insurrection or rebellion against the same, or given aid or comfort to the enemies thereof. But Congress may by a vote of two-thirds of each House, remove such disability.

SECTION 4

The validity of the public debt of the United States, authorized by law, including debts incurred for payment of pensions and bounties for services in suppressing insurrection or rebellion, shall not be questioned. But neither the United States nor any State shall assume or pay any debt or obligation incurred in aid of insurrection or rebellion against the United States, or any claim for the loss or emancipation of any slave; but all such debts, obligations and claims shall be held illegal and void.

SECTION 5

The Congress shall have the power to enforce, by appropriate legislation, the provisions of this article.

*Changed by Section 1 of the 26th Amendment.

Amendment XV.

Passed by Congress February 26, 1869. Ratified February 3, 1870.

SECTION 1

The right of citizens of the United States to vote shall not be denied or abridged by the United States or by any State on account of race, color, or previous condition of servitude.

SECTION 2

The Congress shall have the power to enforce this article by appropriate legislation.

Amendment XVI.

Passed by Congress July 2, 1909. Ratified February 3, 1913.

(Note: Article I, Section 9 of the Constitution was modified by the 16th Amendment.)

The Congress shall have power to lay and collect taxes on incomes, from whatever source derived, without apportionment among the several States, and without regard to any census or enumeration.

Amendment XVII.

Passed by Congress May 13, 1912. Ratified April 8, 1913.

(Note: Article I, Section 3 of the Constitution was modified by the 17th Amendment.)

The Senate of the United States shall be composed of two Senators from each State, elected by the people thereof, for six years; and each Senator shall have one vote. The electors in each State shall have the qualifications requisite for electors of the most numerous branch of the State legislatures.

When vacancies happen in the representation of any State in the Senate, the executive authority of such State shall issue writs of election to fill such vacancies: Provided, That the legislature of any State may empower the executive thereof to make temporary appointments until the people fill the vacancies by election as the legislature may direct.

This amendment shall not be so construed as to affect the election or term of any Senator chosen before it becomes valid as part of the Constitution.

Amendment XVIII.

Passed by Congress December 18, 1917. Ratified January 16, 1919. Repealed by the 21 Amendment, December 5, 1933.

SECTION 1

After one year from the ratification of this article the manufacture, sale, or transportation of intoxicating liquors within, the importation thereof into, or the exportation thereof from the United States and all territory subject to the jurisdiction thereof for beverage purposes is hereby prohibited.

SECTION 2

The Congress and the several States shall have concurrent power to enforce this article by appropriate legislation.

SECTION 3

This article shall be inoperative unless it shall have been ratified as an amendment to the Constitution by the legislatures of the several States, as provided in the Constitution, within seven years from the date of the submission hereof to the States by the Congress.

Amendment XIX.

Passed by Congress June 4, 1919. Ratified August 18, 1920.

The right of citizens of the United States to vote shall not be denied or abridged by the United States or by any State on account of sex.

Congress shall have power to enforce this article by appropriate legislation.

Amendment XX.

Passed by Congress March 2, 1932. Ratified January 23, 1933.

(Note: Article I, Section 4 of the Constitution was modified by Section 2 of this Amendment. In addition, a portion of the 12th Amendment was superseded by Section 3.)

SECTION 1

The terms of the President and the Vice President shall end at noon on the 20th day of January, and the terms of Senators and Representatives at noon on the 3d day of January, of the years in which such terms would have ended if this article had not been ratified; and the terms of their successors shall then begin.

SECTION 2

The Congress shall assemble at least once in every year, and such meeting shall begin at noon on the 3d day of January, unless they shall by law appoint a different day.

SECTION 3

If, at the time fixed for the beginning of the term of the President, the President elect shall have died, the Vice President elect shall become President. If a President shall not have been chosen before the time fixed for the beginning of his term, or if the President elect shall have failed to qualify, then the Vice President elect shall act as President until a President shall have qualified; and the Congress may by law provide for the case wherein neither a President elect nor a

Vice President shall have qualified, declaring who shall then act as President, or the manner in which one who is to act shall be selected, and such person shall act accordingly until a President or Vice President shall have qualified.

SECTION 4

The Congress may by law provide for the case of the death of any of the persons from whom the House of Representatives may choose a President whenever the right of choice shall have devolved upon them, and for the case of the death of any of the persons from whom the Senate may choose a Vice President whenever the right of choice shall have devolved upon them.

SECTION 5

Sections 1 and 2 shall take effect on the 15th day of October following the ratification of this article.

SECTION 6

This article shall be inoperative unless it shall have been ratified as an amendment to the Constitution by the legislatures of three-fourths of the several States within seven years from the date of its submission.

Amendment XXI.

Passed by Congress February 20, 1933. Ratified December 5, 1933.

SECTION 1

The eighteenth article of amendment to the Constitution of the United States is hereby repealed.

SECTION 2

The transportation or importation into any State, Territory, or possession of the United States for delivery or use therein of intoxicating liquors, in violation of the laws thereof, is hereby prohibited.

SECTION 3

This article shall be inoperative unless it shall have been ratified as an amendment to the Constitution by conventions in the several States, as provided in the Constitution, within seven years from the date of the submission hereof to the States by the Congress.

Amendment XXII.

Passed by Congress March 21, 1947. Ratified February 27, 1951.

SECTION 1

No person shall be elected to the office of the President more than twice, and no person who has held the office of President, or acted as President, for more than two years of a term to which some other person was elected President shall be elected to the office of President more than once. But this Article shall not apply to any person holding the office of President when this Article was proposed by Congress, and shall not prevent any person who may be holding the office of President, or acting as President, during the term within which this Article becomes operative from holding the office of President or acting as President during the remainder of such term.

SECTION 2

This article shall be inoperative unless it shall have been ratified as an amendment to the Constitution by the legislatures of three-fourths of the several States within seven years from the date of its submission to the States by the Congress.

Amendment XXIII.

Passed by Congress June 16, 1960. Ratified March 29, 1961.

SECTION 1

The District constituting the seat of Government of the United States shall appoint in such manner as Congress may direct:

A number of electors of President and Vice President equal to the whole number of Senators and Representatives

in Congress to which the District would be entitled if it were a State, but in no event more than the least populous State; they shall be in addition to those appointed by the States, but they shall be considered, for the purposes of the election of President and Vice President, to be electors appointed by a State; and they shall meet in the District and perform such duties as provided by the twelfth article of amendment.

SECTION 2

The Congress shall have power to enforce this article by appropriate legislation.

Amendment XXIV.

Passed by Congress August 27, 1962. Ratified January 23, 1964.

SECTION 1

The right of citizens of the United States to vote in any primary or other election for President or Vice President, for electors for President or Vice President, or for Senator or Representative in Congress, shall not be denied or abridged by the United States or any State by reason of failure to pay poll tax or other tax.

SECTION 2

The Congress shall have power to enforce this article by appropriate legislation.

Amendment XXV.

Passed by Congress July 6, 1965. Ratified February 10, 1967.

(Note: Article II, Section 1 of the Constitution was modified by the 25th Amendment.)

SECTION 1

In case of the removal of the President from office or of his death or resignation, the Vice President shall become President.

SECTION 2

Whenever there is a vacancy in the office of the Vice President, the President shall nominate a Vice President who shall take office upon confirmation by a majority vote of both Houses of Congress.

SECTION 3

Whenever the President transmits to the President pro tempore of the Senate and the Speaker of the House of Representatives his written declaration that he is unable to discharge the powers and duties of his office, and until he transmits to them a written declaration to the contrary, such powers and duties shall be discharged by the Vice President as Acting President.

SECTION 4

Whenever the Vice President and a majority of either the principal officers of the executive departments or of such other body as Congress may by law provide, transmit to the President pro tempore of the Senate and the Speaker of the House of Representatives their written declaration that the President is unable to discharge the powers and duties of his office, the Vice President shall immediately assume the powers and duties of the office as Acting President.

Thereafter, when the President transmits to the President pro tempore of the Senate and the Speaker of the House of Representatives his written declaration that no inability exists, he shall resume the powers and duties of his office unless the Vice President and a majority of either the principal officers of the executive department or of such other body as Congress may by law provide, transmit within four days to the President pro tempore of the Senate and the Speaker of the House of Representatives their written declaration that the President is unable to discharge the powers and duties of his office. Thereupon Congress shall decide the issue, assembling within forty-eight hours for that purpose if not in session. If the Congress, within twenty-one days after receipt of the latter written declaration, or, if Congress is not in session, within twenty-one days after Congress is required to assemble, determines by two-thirds vote of both Houses that the President is unable to discharge the powers and duties of his office, the Vice President shall continue to discharge the same as Acting President; otherwise, the President shall resume the powers and duties of his office.

Amendment XXVI.

Passed by Congress March 23, 1971. Ratified July 1, 1971.

(Note: Amendment 14, Section 2 of the Constitution was modified by Section 1 of the 26th Amendment.)

SECTION 1

The right of citizens of the United States, who are eighteen years of age or older, to vote shall not be denied or abridged by the United States or by any State on account of age.

SECTION 2

The Congress shall have power to enforce this article by appropriate legislation.

Amendment XXVII.

Originally proposed Sept. 25, 1789. Ratified May 7, 1992.

No law, varying the compensation for the services of the Senators and Representatives, shall take effect, until an election of representatives shall have intervened.

Appendix

The Constitution of the State of New York

New York State
Constitution

As revised, including amendments
effective January 1, 2015

ANDREW M. CUOMO
Governor

ROSSANA ROSADO
Secretary of State

THE CONSTITUTION OF
THE
STATE OF NEW YORK

As Revised, with Amendments adopted by the
Constitutional Convention of 1938 and Approved
by Vote of the People on November 8, 1938
and
Amendments subsequently adopted by the
Legislature and Approved by Vote of the People.

As Amended and in Force January 1, 2015

ARTICLE I
BILL OF RIGHTS

§1. Rights, privileges and franchise secured; power of legislature to dispense with primary elections in certain cases.
2. Trial by jury; how waived.
3. Freedom of worship; religious liberty.
4. Habeas corpus.
5. Bail; fines; punishments; detention of witnesses.
6. Grand jury; protection of certain enumerated rights; duty of public officers to sign waiver of immunity and give testimony; penalty for refusal.
7. Compensation for taking private property; private roads; drainage of agricultural lands.
8. Freedom of speech and press; criminal prosecutions for libel.
9. Right to assemble and petition; divorce; lotteries; pool-selling and gambling; laws to prevent; pari-mutuel betting on horse races permitted; games of chance, bingo or lotto authorized under certain restrictions.
10. [Repealed.]
11. Equal protection of laws; discrimination in civil rights prohibited.
12. Security against unreasonable searches, seizures and interceptions.
13. [Repealed.]
14. Common law and acts of the colonial and state legislatures.
15. [Repealed.]
16. Damages for injuries causing death.
17. Labor not a commodity; hours and wages in public work; right to organize and bargain collectively.
18. Workers' compensation.

ARTICLE II
SUFFRAGE

§1. Qualifications of voters.
2. Absentee voting.
3. Persons excluded from the right of suffrage.
4. Certain occupations and conditions not to affect residence.
5. Registration and election laws to be passed.
6. Permanent registration.
7. Manner of voting; identification of voters.
8. Bi-partisan registration and election board.
9. Presidential elections; special voting procedures authorized.

ARTICLE III
LEGISLATURE

§1. Legislative power.
2. Number and terms of senators and assemblymen.
3. Senate districts.
4. Readjustments and reapportionments; when federal census to control.
5. Apportionment of assemblymen; creation of assembly districts.

5-a. Definition of inhabitants.
5-b. Independent redistricting commission.
6. Compensation, allowances and traveling expenses of members.
7. Qualifications of members; prohibitions on certain civil appointments; acceptance to vacate seat.
8. Time of elections of members.
9. Powers of each house.
10. Journals; open sessions; adjournments.
11. Members not to be questioned for speeches.
12. Bills may originate in either house; may be amended by the other.
13. Enacting clause of bills; no law to be enacted except by bill.
14. Manner of passing bills; message of necessity for immediate vote.
15. Private or local bills to embrace only one subject, expressed in title.
16. Existing law not to be made applicable by reference.
17. Cases in which private or local bills shall not be passed.
18. Extraordinary sessions of the legislature; power to convene on legislative initiative.
19. Private claims not to be audited by legislature; claims barred by lapse of time.
20. Two-thirds bills.
21. Certain sections not to apply to bills recommended by certain commissioners or public agencies.
22. Tax laws to state tax and object distinctly; definition of income for income tax purposes by reference to federal laws authorized.
23. When yeas and nays necessary; three-fifths to constitute quorum.
24. Prison labor; contract system abolished.
25. Emergency governmental operations; legislature to provide for.

ARTICLE IV
EXECUTIVE

§1. Executive power; election and terms of governor and lieutenant-governor.
2. Qualifications of governor and lieutenant-governor.
3. Powers and duties of governor; compensation.
4. Reprieves, commutations and pardons; powers and duties of governor relating to grants of.
5. When lieutenant-governor to act as governor.
6. Duties and compensation of lieutenant-governor; succession to the governorship.
7. Action by governor on legislative bills; reconsideration after veto.
8. Departmental rules and regulations; filing; publication.

ARTICLE V
OFFICERS AND CIVIL DEPARTMENTS

§1. Comptroller and attorney-general; payment of state moneys without audit void.
2. Civil departments in the state government.
3. Assignment of functions.
4. Department heads.
5. [Repealed.]
6. Civil service appointments and promotions; veterans' credits.
7. Membership in retirement systems; benefits not to be diminished nor impaired.

1

2

3

THE CONSTITUTION

[1][**Preamble**] WE THE PEOPLE of the State of New York, grateful to Almighty God for our Freedom, in order to secure its blessings, DO ESTABLISH THIS CONSTITUTION.

ARTICLE I
BILL OF RIGHTS

[Rights, privileges and franchise secured; power of legislature to dispense with primary elections in certain cases]
Section 1. No member of this state shall be disfranchised[2], or deprived of any of the rights or privileges secured to any citizen thereof, unless by the law of the land, or the judgment of his or her peers, except that the legislature may provide that there shall be no primary election held to nominate candidates for public office or to elect persons to party positions for any political party or parties in any unit of representation of the state from which such candidates or persons are nominated or elected whenever there is no contest or contests for such nominations or election as may be prescribed by general law. (Amended by vote of the people November 3, 1959; November 6, 2001.)[3]

[Trial by jury; how waived]
§2. Trial by jury in all cases in which it has heretofore been guaranteed by constitutional provision shall remain inviolate forever; but a jury trial may be waived by the parties in all civil cases in the manner to be prescribed by law. The legislature may provide, however, by law, that a verdict may be rendered by not less than five-sixths of the jury in any civil case. A jury trial may be waived by the defendant in all criminal cases, except those in which the crime charged may be punishable by death, by a written instrument signed by the defendant in person in open court before and with the approval of a judge or justice of a court having jurisdiction to try the offense. The legislature may enact laws, not inconsistent herewith, governing the form, content, manner and time of presentation of the instrument effectuating such waiver. (Amended by Constitutional Convention of 1938 and approved by vote of the people November 8, 1938.)

[Freedom of worship; religious liberty]
§3. The free exercise and enjoyment of religious profession and worship, without discrimination or preference, shall forever be allowed in this state to all humankind; and no person shall be rendered incompetent to be a witness on account of his or her opinions on matters of religious belief; but the liberty of conscience hereby secured shall not be so construed as to excuse acts of licentiousness, or justify practices inconsistent with the peace or safety of this state. (Amended by vote of the people November 6, 2001.)

[Habeas corpus]
§4. The privilege of a writ or order of habeas corpus shall not be suspended, unless, in case of rebellion or invasion, the public safety requires it. (Amended by Constitutional Convention of 1938 and approved by vote of the people November 8, 1938.)

[Bail; fines; punishments; detention of witnesses]
§5. Excessive bail shall not be required nor excessive fines imposed, nor shall cruel and unusual punishments be inflicted, nor shall witnesses be unreasonably detained.

---

[1] Section headings and annotations [enclosed in brackets], and footnotes throughout this document are not a part of the official text.

[2] As so in original.

[3] Except where otherwise indicated, each section hereafter was re-enacted without change by the Constitutional Convention of 1938 and re-adopted by vote of the people November 8, 1938.

4

[Grand jury; protection of certain enumerated rights; duty of public officers to sign waiver of immunity and give testimony; penalty for refusal]
§6. No person shall be held to answer for a capital or otherwise infamous crime (except in cases of impeachment, and in cases of militia when in actual service, and the land, air and naval forces in time of war, or which this state may keep with the consent of congress in time of peace, and in cases of petit larceny under the regulation of the legislature), unless on indictment of a grand jury, except that a person held for the action of a grand jury upon a charge for such an offense, other than one punishable by death or life imprisonment, with the consent of the district attorney, may waive indictment by a grand jury and consent to be prosecuted on an information filed by the district attorney; such waiver shall be evidenced by written instrument signed by the defendant in open court in the presence of his or her counsel. In any trial in any court whatever the party accused shall be allowed to appear and defend in person and with counsel as in civil actions and shall be informed of the nature and cause of the accusation and be confronted with the witnesses against him or her. No person shall be subject to be twice put in jeopardy for the same offense; nor shall he or she be compelled in any criminal case to be a witness against himself or herself, providing, that any public officer who, upon being called before a grand jury to testify concerning the conduct of his or her present office or of any public office held by him or her within five years prior to such grand jury call to testify, or the performance of his or her official duties in any such present or prior offices, refuses to sign a waiver of immunity against subsequent criminal prosecution, or to answer any relevant question concerning such matters before such grand jury, shall by virtue of such refusal, be disqualified from holding any other public office or public employment for a period of five years from the date of such refusal to sign a waiver of immunity against subsequent prosecution, or to answer any relevant question concerning such matters before such grand jury, and shall be removed from his or her present office by the appropriate authority or shall forfeit his or her present office at the suit of the attorney-general.

The power of grand juries to inquire into the wilful misconduct in office of public officers, and to find indictments or to direct the filing of informations in connection with such inquiries, shall never be suspended or impaired by law. No person shall be deprived of life, liberty or property without due process of law. (Amended by Constitutional Convention of 1938 and approved by vote of the people November 8, 1938; further amended by vote of the people November 8, 1949; November 3, 1959; November 6, 1973; November 6, 2001.)

[Compensation for taking private property; private roads; drainage of agricultural lands]
§7. (a) Private property shall not be taken for public use without just compensation.

(c) Private roads may be opened in the manner to be prescribed by law; but in every case the necessity of the road and the amount of all damage to be sustained by the opening thereof shall be first determined by a jury of freeholders, and such amount, together with the expenses of the proceedings, shall be paid by the person to be benefitted.

(d) The use of property for the drainage of swamp or agricultural lands is declared to be a public use, and general laws may be passed permitting the owners or occupants of swamp or agricultural lands to construct and maintain for the drainage thereof, necessary drains, ditches and dykes upon the lands of others, under proper restrictions, on making just compensation, and such compensation together with the cost of such drainage may be assessed, wholly or partly, against any property benefitted thereby; but no special laws shall be enacted for such purposes. (Amended by Constitutional Convention of 1938 and approved by vote of the people November 8, 1938. Subdivision (e) repealed by vote of the people November 5, 1963. Subdivision (b) repealed by vote of the people November 3, 1964.)

[Freedom of speech and press; criminal prosecutions for libel]
§8. Every citizen may freely speak, write and publish his or her sentiments on all subjects, being responsible for the abuse of that right; and no law shall be passed to restrain or abridge the liberty of speech or of the press. In all criminal prosecutions or indictments for libels, the truth may be given in

evidence to the jury; and if it shall appear to the jury that the matter charged as libelous is true, and was published with good motives and for justifiable ends, the party shall be acquitted; and the jury shall have the right to determine the law and the fact. (Amended by vote of the people November 6, 2001.)

[Right to assemble and petition; divorce; lotteries; pool-selling and gambling; laws to prevent; pari-mutuel betting on horse races permitted; games of chance, bingo or lotto authorized under certain restrictions]
§9. 1. No law shall be passed abridging the rights of the people peaceably to assemble and to petition the government, or any department thereof; nor shall any divorce be granted otherwise than by due judicial proceedings; except as hereinafter provided, no lottery or the sale of lottery tickets, pool-selling, bookmaking, or any other kind of gambling, except lotteries operated by the state and the sale of lottery tickets in connection therewith as may be authorized and prescribed by the legislature, the net proceeds of which shall be applied exclusively to or in aid or support of education in this state as the legislature may prescribe, except pari-mutuel betting on horse races as may be prescribed by the legislature and from which the state shall derive a reasonable revenue for the support of government, and except casino gambling at no more than seven facilities as authorized and prescribed by the legislature shall hereafter be authorized or allowed within this state; and the legislature shall pass appropriate laws to prevent offenses against any of the provisions of this section. (Amendment approved by vote of the people November 5, 2013.)

2. Notwithstanding the foregoing provisions of this section, any city, town or village within the state may by an approving vote of the majority of the qualified electors in such municipality voting on a proposition therefor submitted at a general or special election authorize, subject to state legislative supervision and control, the conduct of one or both of the following categories of games of chance commonly known as: (a) bingo or lotto, in which prizes are awarded on the basis of designated numbers or symbols on a card conforming to numbers or symbols selected at random; (b) games in which prizes are awarded on the basis of a winning number or numbers, color or colors, or symbol or symbols determined by chance from among those previously selected or played, whether determined as the result of the spinning of a wheel, a drawing or otherwise by chance. If authorized, such games shall be subject to the following restrictions, among others which may be prescribed by the legislature: (1) only bona fide religious, charitable or non-profit organizations of veterans, volunteer firefighter and similar non-profit organizations shall be permitted to conduct such games; (2) the entire net proceeds of any game shall be exclusively devoted to the lawful purposes of such organizations; (3) no person except a bona fide member of any such organization shall participate in the management or operation of such game; and (4) no person shall receive any remuneration for participating in the management or operation of any such game. Unless otherwise provided by law, no single prize shall exceed two hundred fifty dollars, nor shall any series of prizes on one occasion aggregate more than one thousand dollars. The legislature shall pass appropriate laws to effectuate the purposes of this subdivision, ensure that such games are rigidly regulated to prevent commercialized gambling, prevent participation by criminal and other undesirable elements and the diversion of funds from the purposes authorized hereunder and establish a method by which a municipality which has authorized such games may rescind or revoke such authorization. Unless permitted by the legislature, no municipality shall have the power to pass local laws or ordinances relating to such games. Nothing in this section shall prevent the legislature from passing laws more restrictive than any of the provisions of this section. (Amendment approved by vote of the people November 7, 1939; further amended by vote of the people November 5, 1957; November 8, 1966; November 4, 1975; November 6, 1984; November 6, 2001.)

[Section 10, which dealt with ownership of lands, allodial tenures and escheats, was repealed by amendment approved by vote of the people November 6, 1962.]

[Equal protection of laws; discrimination in civil rights prohibited]
§11. No person shall be denied the equal protection of the laws of this state or any subdivision thereof. No person shall, because of race, color, creed or religion, be subjected to any discrimination in his or her civil rights by any other person or by any firm, corporation, or institution, or by the state or any agency or subdivision of the state. (New. Adopted by Constitutional Convention of 1938 and approved by vote of the people November 8, 1938; amended by vote of the people November 6, 2001.)

[Security against unreasonable searches, seizures and interceptions]
§12. The right of the people to be secure in their persons, houses, papers and effects, against unreasonable searches and seizures, shall not be violated, and no warrants shall issue, but upon probable cause, supported by oath or affirmation, and particularly describing the place to be searched, and the persons or things to be seized.

The right of the people to be secure against unreasonable interception of telephone and telegraph communications shall not be violated, and ex parte orders or warrants shall issue only upon oath or affirmation that there is reasonable ground to believe that evidence of crime may be thus obtained, and identifying the particular means of communication, and particularly describing the person or persons whose communications are to be intercepted and the purpose thereof. (New. Adopted by Constitutional Convention of 1938 and approved by vote of the people November 8, 1938.)

[Section 13, which dealt with purchase of lands of Indians, was repealed by amendment approved by vote of the people November 6, 1962.]

[Common law and acts of the colonial and state legislatures]
§14. Such parts of the common law, and of the acts of the legislature of the colony of New York, as together did form the law of the said colony, on the nineteenth day of April, one thousand seven hundred seventy-five, and the resolutions of the congress of the said colony, and of the convention of the State of New York, in force on the twentieth day of April, one thousand seven hundred seventy-seven, which have not since expired, or been repealed or altered; and such acts of the legislature of this state as are now in force, shall be and continue the law of this state, subject to such alterations as the legislature shall make concerning the same. But all such parts of the common law, and such of the said acts, or parts thereof, as are repugnant to this constitution, are hereby abrogated. (Formerly §16. Renumbered and amended by Constitutional Convention of 1938 and approved by vote of the people November 8, 1938.)

[Section 15, which dealt with certain grants of lands and of charters made by the king of Great Britain and the state and obligations and contracts not to be impaired, was repealed by amendment approved by vote of the people November 6, 1962.]

[Damages for injuries causing death]
§16. The right of action now existing to recover damages for injuries resulting in death, shall never be abrogated; and the amount recoverable shall not be subject to any statutory limitation. (Formerly §18. Renumbered by Constitutional Convention of 1938 and approved by vote of the people November 8, 1938.)

[Labor not a commodity; hours and wages in public work; right to organize and bargain collectively]
§17. Labor of human beings is not a commodity nor an article of commerce and shall never be so considered or construed.

No laborer, worker or mechanic, in the employ of a contractor or sub-contractor engaged in the performance of any public work, shall be permitted to work more than eight hours in any day or more than five days in any week, except in cases of extraordinary emergency; nor shall he or she be paid less than the rate of wages prevailing in the same trade or occupation in the locality within the state where such public work is to be situated, erected or used.

5

Employees shall have the right to organize and to bargain collectively through representatives of their own choosing. (New. Adopted by Constitutional Convention of 1938 and approved by vote of the people November 8, 1938; amended by vote of the people November 6, 2001.)

[Workers' compensation]
§18. Nothing contained in this constitution shall be construed to limit the power of the legislature to enact laws for the protection of the lives, health, or safety of employees; or for the payment, either by employers, or by employers and employees or otherwise, either directly or through a state or other system of insurance or otherwise, of compensation for injuries to employees or for death of employees resulting from such injuries without regard to fault as a cause thereof, except where the injury is occasioned by the wilful intention of the injured employee to bring about the injury or death of himself or herself or of another, or where the injury results solely from the intoxication of the injured employee while on duty; or for the adjustment, determination and settlement, with or without trial by jury, of issues which may arise under such legislation; or to provide that the right of such compensation, and the remedy therefor shall be exclusive of all other rights and remedies for injuries to employees or for death resulting from such injuries; or to provide that the amount of such compensation for death shall not exceed a fixed or determinable sum; provided that all moneys paid by an employer to his or her employees or their legal representatives, by reason of the enactment of any of the laws herein authorized, shall be held to be a proper charge in the cost of operating the business of the employer. (Formerly §19. Renumbered by Constitutional Convention of 1938 and approved by vote of the people November 8, 1938; amended by vote of the people November 6, 2001.)

ARTICLE II
SUFFRAGE

[Qualifications of voters]
Section 1. Every citizen shall be entitled to vote at every election for all officers elected by the people and upon all questions submitted to the vote of the people provided that such citizen is eighteen years of age or over and shall have been a resident of this state, and of the county, city, or village for thirty days next preceding an election. (Amended by Constitutional Convention of 1938 and approved by vote of the people November 8, 1938; further amended by vote of the people November 2, 1943; November 6, 1945; November 6, 1961; November 8, 1966; November 7, 1995.)

[Absentee voting]
§2. The legislature may, by general law, provide a manner in which, and the time and place at which, qualified voters who, on the occurrence of any election, may be absent from the county of their residence or, if residents of the city of New York, from the city, and qualified voters who, on the occurrence of any election, may be unable to appear personally at the polling place because of illness or physical disability, may vote and for the return and canvass of their votes. (Formerly §1-a. Renumbered by Constitutional Convention of 1938 and approved by vote of the people November 8, 1938; amended by vote of the people November 4, 1947; November 8, 1955; November 5, 1963.)

[Persons excluded from the right of suffrage]
§3. No person who shall receive, accept, or offer to receive, or pay, offer or promise to pay, contribute, offer or promise to contribute to another, to be paid or used, any money or other valuable thing as a compensation or reward for the giving or withholding a vote at an election, or who shall make any promise to influence the giving or withholding any such vote, or who shall make or become directly or indirectly interested in any bet or wager depending upon the result of any election, shall vote at such election; and upon challenge for such cause, the person so challenged, before the officers authorized for that purpose shall receive his or her vote, shall swear or affirm before such officers that he or she has not received or offered, does not expect to receive, has not paid, offered or promised to pay, contributed, offered or promised to contribute to another, to be paid or used, any money

or other valuable thing as a compensation or reward for the giving or withholding a vote at such election, and has not made any promise to influence the giving or withholding of any such vote, nor made or become directly or indirectly interested in any bet or wager depending upon the result of such election. The legislature shall enact laws excluding from the right of suffrage all persons convicted of bribery or of any infamous crime. (Formerly §2. Renumbered by Constitutional Convention of 1938 and approved by vote of the people November 8, 1938; amended by vote of the people November 6, 2001.)

[Certain occupations and conditions not to affect residence]
§4. For the purpose of voting, no person shall be deemed to have gained or lost a residence, by reason of his or her presence or absence, while employed in the service of the United States; nor while engaged in the navigation of the waters of this state, or of the United States, or of the high seas; nor while a student of any seminary of learning; nor while kept at any almshouse, or other asylum, or institution wholly or partly supported at public expense or by charity; nor while confined in any public prison. (Formerly §3. Renumbered by Constitutional Convention of 1938 and approved by vote of the people November 8, 1938; amended by vote of the people November 6, 2001.)

[Registration and election laws to be passed]
§5. Laws shall be made for ascertaining, by proper proofs, the citizens who shall be entitled to the right of suffrage hereby established, and for the registration of voters; which registration shall be completed at least ten days before each election. Such registration shall not be required for town and village elections except by express provision of law. (Formerly §4. Renumbered by Constitutional Convention of 1938 and approved by vote of the people November 8, 1938; amended by vote of the people November 6, 1951; further amended by vote of the people November 8, 1955; November 8, 1966; November 7, 1995.)

[Permanent registration]
§6. The legislature may provide by law for a system or systems of registration whereby upon personal application a voter may be regis- tered and his or her registration continued so long as he or she shall remain qualified to vote from an address within the jurisdiction of the board with which such voter is registered. (New. Adopted by Constitutional Convention of 1938 and approved by vote of the people November 8, 1938; amended by vote of the people November 7, 1995; November 6, 2001.)

[Manner of voting; identification of voters]
§7. All elections by the citizens, except for such town officers as may by law be directed to be otherwise chosen, shall be by ballot, or by such other method as may be prescribed by law, provided that secrecy in voting be preserved. The legislature shall provide for identification of voters through their signatures in all cases where personal registration is required and shall also provide for the signatures, at the time of voting, of all persons voting in person by ballot or voting machine, whether or not they have registered in person, save only in cases of illiteracy or physical disability. (Formerly §5. Renumbered and amended by Constitutional Convention of 1938 and approved by vote of the people November 8, 1938.)

[Bi-partisan registration and election boards]
§8. All laws creating, regulating or affecting boards or officers charged with the duty of qualifying voters, or of distributing ballots to voters, or of receiving, recording or counting votes at elections, shall secure equal representation of the two political parties which, at the general election next preceding that for which such boards or officers are to serve, cast the highest and the next highest number of votes. All such boards and officers shall be appointed or elected in such manner, and upon the nomination of such representatives of said parties respectively, as the legislature may direct. Existing laws on this subject shall continue until the legislature shall otherwise provide. This section shall not apply to town, or village elections. (Formerly §6. Renumbered and amended by Constitutional Convention of 1938 and approved by vote of the people November 8, 1938; further amended by vote of the people November 7, 1995.)

6

[Presidential elections; special voting procedures authorized]
§9. Notwithstanding the residence requirements imposed by section one of this article, the legislature may, by general law, provide special procedures whereby every person who shall have moved from another state to this state or from one county, city or village within this state to another county, city or village within this state and who shall have been an inhabitant of this state in any event for ninety days next preceding an election at which electors are to be chosen for the office of president and vice president of the United States shall be entitled to vote in this state solely for such electors, provided such person is otherwise qualified to vote in this state and is not able to qualify to vote for such electors in any other state. The legislature may also, by general law, prescribe special procedures whereby every person who is registered and would be qualified to vote in this state but for his or her removal from this state to another state within one year next preceding such election shall be entitled to vote in this state solely for such electors, provided such person is not able to qualify to vote for such electors in any other state. (New. Added by vote of the people November 5, 1963; amended by vote of the people November 6, 2001.)

ARTICLE III
LEGISLATURE

[Legislative power]
Section 1. The legislative power of this state shall be vested in the senate and assembly.

[Number and terms of senators and assemblymen]
§2. The senate shall consist of fifty members[4], except as hereinafter provided. The senators elected in the year one thousand eight hundred and ninety-five shall hold their offices for three years, and their successors shall be chosen for two years. The assembly shall consist of one hundred and fifty members. The assembly members elected in the year one thousand nine hundred and thirty-eight, and their successors, shall be chosen for two years. (Amended by vote of the people November 2, 1937; November 6, 2001.)

[Senate districts]
§3. The senate districts[5], described in section three of article three of this constitution as adopted by the people on November sixth, eighteen hundred ninety-four are hereby continued for all of the purposes of future reapportionments of senate districts pursuant to section four of this article. (Formerly §3. Repealed and replaced by new §3 amended by vote of the people November 6, 1962.)

[Readjustments and reapportionments; when federal census to control]
§4. (a) Except as herein otherwise provided, the federal census taken in the year nineteen hundred thirty and each federal census taken decennially thereafter shall be controlling as to the number of inhabitants in the state or any part thereof for the purposes of the apportionment of members of assembly and readjustment or alteration of senate and assembly districts next occurring, in so far as such census and the tabulation thereof purport to give the information necessary therefor. The legislature, by law, shall provide for the making and tabulation by state authorities of an enumeration of the inhabitants of the entire state to be used for such purposes, instead of a federal census, if the taking of a federal census in any tenth year from the year nineteen hundred thirty be omitted or if the federal census fails to show the number of aliens or Indians not taxed. If a federal census, though giving the requisite information as to the state at large, fails to give the information as to any civil or territorial divisions which is required to be known for such purposes, the legislature, by law, shall provide for such an enumeration of the inhabitants of such parts of the state only as may be necessary, which shall supersede in part the federal census and be used in connection therewith for such purposes. The legislature, by law, may provide in its discretion for an enumeration by state authorities of the inhabitants of the state, to be used

for such purposes, in place of a federal census, when the return of a decennial federal census is delayed so that it is not available at the beginning of the regular session of the legislature in the second year after the year nineteen hundred thirty or after any tenth year therefrom, or if an apportionment of members of assembly and readjustment or alteration of senate districts is not made at or before such a session. At the regular session in the year nineteen hundred thirty-two, and at the first regular session after the year nineteen hundred forty and after each tenth year therefrom the senate districts shall be readjusted or altered, but if, in any decade, counting from and including that which begins with the year nineteen hundred thirty-one, such a readjustment or alteration is not made at the time above prescribed, it shall be made at a subsequent session occurring not later than the sixth year of such decade, meaning not later than nineteen hundred thirty-six, nineteen hundred forty-six, nineteen hundred fifty-six, and so on; provided, however, that if such districts shall have been readjusted or altered by law in either of the years nineteen hundred thirty or nineteen hundred thirty-one, they shall remain unaltered until the first regular session after the year nineteen hundred forty. No town, except a town having more than a full ratio of apportionment, and no block in a city inclosed by streets or public ways, shall be divided in the formation of senate districts. In the reapportionment of senate districts, no district shall contain a greater excess in population over an adjoining district in the same county, than the population of a town or block therein adjoining such district. Counties, towns or blocks which, from their location, may be included in either of two districts, shall be so placed as to make said districts most nearly equal in number of inhabitants, excluding aliens.

No county shall have four or more senators unless it shall have a full ratio for each senator. No county shall have more than one-third of all the senators; and no two counties or the territory thereof as now organized, which are adjoining counties, or which are separated only by public waters, shall have more than one-half of all the senators.

(b) The independent redistricting commission established pursuant to section five-b of this article shall prepare a redistricting plan to establish senate, assembly, and congressional districts every ten years commencing in two thousand twenty-one, and shall submit to the legislature such plan and the implementing legislation therefor on or before January first or as soon as practicable thereafter but no later than January fifteenth in the year ending in two beginning in two thousand twenty-two. The redistricting plans for the assembly and the senate shall be contained in and voted upon by the legislature in a single bill, and the congressional district plan may be included in the same bill if the legislature chooses to do so. The implementing legislation shall be voted upon, without amendment, by the senate or the assembly and if approved by the first house voting upon it, such legislation shall be delivered to the other house immediately to be voted upon without amendment. If approved by both houses, such legislation shall be presented to the governor for action.

If either house shall fail to approve the legislation implementing the first redistricting plan, or the governor shall veto such legislation and the legislature shall fail to override such veto, each house or the governor if he or she vetoes it, shall notify the commission that such legislation has been disapproved. Within fifteen days of such notification and in no case later than February twenty-eighth, the redistricting commission shall prepare and submit to the legislature a second redistricting plan and the necessary implementing legislation for such plan. Such legislation shall be voted upon, without amendment, by the senate or the assembly and, if approved by the first house voting upon it, such legislation shall be delivered to the other house immediately to be voted upon without amendment. If approved by both houses, such legislation shall be presented to the governor for action.

If either house shall fail to approve the legislation implementing the second redistricting plan, or the governor shall veto such legislation and the legislature shall fail to override such veto, each house shall introduce such implementing legislation with any amendments each house of the legislature deems necessary. All such amendments shall comply with the provisions of this article. If approved by both houses, such legislation shall be presented to the governor for action.

All votes by the senate or assembly on any redistricting plan legislation pursuant to this article shall be conducted in accordance with the following rules:

---

[4] State Law §123 sets forth current number of senators.

[5] State Law §124 currently sets forth 63 senate districts.

7

(1) In the event that the speaker of the assembly and the temporary president of the senate are members of two different political parties, approval of legislation submitted by the independent redistricting commission pursuant to subdivision (f) of section five-b of this article shall require the vote in support of its passage by at least a majority of the members elected to each house.

(2) In the event that the speaker of the assembly and the temporary president of the senate are members of two different political parties, approval of legislation submitted by the independent redistricting commission pursuant to subdivision (g) of section five-b of this article shall require the vote in support of its passage by at least sixty percent of the members elected to each house.

(3) In the event that the speaker of the assembly and the temporary president of the senate are members of the same political party, approval of legislation submitted by the independent redistricting commission pursuant to subdivision (f) or (g) of section five-b of this article shall require the vote in support of its passage by at least two-thirds of the members elected to each house.

(c) Subject to the requirements of the federal constitution and statutes and in compliance with state constitutional requirements, the following principles shall be used in the creation of state senate and state assembly districts and congressional districts:

(1) When drawing district lines, the commission shall consider whether such lines would result in the denial or abridgement of racial or language minority voting rights, and districts shall not be drawn to have the purpose of, nor shall they result in, the denial or abridgement of such rights. Districts shall be drawn so that, based on the totality of the circumstances, racial or minority language groups do not have less opportunity to participate in the political process than other members of the electorate and to elect representatives of their choice.

(2) To the extent practicable, districts shall contain as nearly as may be an equal number of inhabitants. For each district that deviates from this requirement, the commission shall provide a specific public explanation as to why such deviation exists.

(3) Each district shall consist of contiguous territory.

(4) Each district shall be as compact in form as practicable.

(5) Districts shall not be drawn to discourage competition or for the purpose of favoring or disfavoring incumbents or other particular candidates or political parties. The commission shall consider the maintenance of cores of existing districts, of pre-existing political subdivisions, including counties, cities, and towns, and of communities of interest.

(6) In drawing senate districts, towns or blocks which, from their location may be included in either of two districts, shall be so placed as to make said districts most nearly equal in number of inhabitants. The requirements that senate districts not divide counties or towns, as well as the 'block-on-border' and 'town-on-border' rules, shall remain in effect.

During the preparation of the redistricting plan, the independent redistricting commission shall conduct not less than one public hearing on proposals for the redistricting of congressional and state legislative districts in each of the following (i) cities: Albany, Buffalo, Syracuse, Rochester, and White Plains; and (ii) counties: Bronx, Kings, New York, Queens, Richmond, Nassau, and Suffolk. Notice of all such hearings shall be widely published using the best available means and media a reasonable time before every hearing. At least thirty days prior to the first public hearing and in any event no later than September fifteenth of the year ending in one or as soon as practicable thereafter, the independent redistricting commission shall make widely available to the public, in print form and using the best available technology, its draft redistricting plans, relevant data, and related information. Such plans, data, and information shall be in a form that allows and facilitates their use by the public to review, analyze, and comment upon such plans and to develop alternative redistricting plans for presentation to the commission at the public hearings. The independent redistricting commission shall report the findings of all such hearings to the legislature upon submission of a redistricting plan.

(d) The ratio for apportioning senators shall always be obtained by dividing the number of inhabitants, excluding aliens, by fifty, and the senate shall always be composed of fifty members, except that if any county having three or more senators at the time of any apportionment shall be entitled on such ratio to an additional senator or senators, such additional senator or senators shall be given to such county in addition to the fifty senators, and the whole number of senators shall be increased to that extent.

The senate districts, including the present ones, as existing immediately before the enactment of a law readjusting or altering the senate districts, shall continue to be the senate districts of the state until the expirations of the terms of the senators then in office, except for the purpose of an election of senators for full terms beginning at such expirations, and for the formation of assembly districts.

(e) The process for redistricting congressional and state legislative districts established by this section and sections five and five-b of this article shall govern redistricting in this state except to the extent that a court is required to order the adoption of, or changes to, a redistricting plan as a remedy for a violation of law.

A reapportionment plan and the districts contained in such plan shall be in force until the effective date of a plan based upon the subsequent federal decennial census taken in a year ending in zero unless modified pursuant to court order. (Amended by vote of the people November 6, 1945; further amended by vote of the people November 4, 2014.)

[Apportionment of assemblymen; creation of assembly districts]
§5. The members of the assembly shall be chosen by single districts and shall be apportioned pursuant to this section and sections four and five-b of this article at each regular session at which the senate districts are readjusted or altered, and by the same law, among the several counties of the state, as nearly as may be according to the number of their respective inhabitants, excluding aliens. Every county heretofore established and separately organized, except the county of Hamilton, shall always be entitled to one member of assembly, and no county shall hereafter be erected unless its population shall entitle it to a member. The county of Hamilton shall elect with the county of Fulton, until the population of the county of Hamilton shall, according to the ratio, entitle it to a member. But the legislature may abolish the said county of Hamilton and annex the territory thereof to some other county or counties.

The quotient obtained by dividing the whole number of inhabitants of the state, excluding aliens, by the number of members of assembly, shall be the ratio for apportionment, which shall be made as follows: One member of assembly shall be apportioned to every county, including Fulton and Hamilton as one county, containing less than the ratio and one-half over. Two members shall be apportioned to every other county. The remaining members of assembly shall be apportioned to the counties having more than two ratios according to the number of inhabitants, excluding aliens. Members apportioned on remainders shall be apportioned to the counties having the highest remainders in the order thereof respectively. No county shall have more members of assembly than a county having a greater number of inhabitants, excluding aliens.

The assembly districts[6], including the present ones, as existing immediately before the enactment of a law making an apportionment of members of assembly among the counties, shall continue to be the assembly districts of the state until the expiration of the terms of members then in office, except for the purpose of an election of members of assembly for full terms beginning at such expirations.

In any county entitled to more than one member, the board of supervisors, and in any city embracing an entire county and having no board of supervisors, the common council, or if there be none, the body exercising the powers of a common council, shall assemble at such times as the legislature making an apportionment shall prescribe, and divide such counties into assembly districts as nearly equal in number of inhabitants, excluding aliens, as may be, of convenient and contiguous territory in as compact form as practicable, each of which shall be wholly within a senate district formed under the same apportionment, equal to the number of members of assembly to which such county shall be entitled, and shall cause to be filed in the office of the secretary of state and of the clerk of such county, a description of such districts, specifying the number of each district and of the inhabitants thereof, excluding aliens, according to the census or enumeration used as the population basis for the formation of such districts; and such apportionment

---

[6] State Law §121 sets forth 150 assembly districts.

8

and districts shall remain unaltered until after the next reapportionment of members of assembly, except that the board of supervisors of any county containing a town having more than a ratio of apportionment and one-half over may alter the assembly districts in a senate district containing such town at any time on or before March first, nineteen hundred forty-six. In counties having more than one senate district, the same number of assembly districts shall be put in each senate district, unless the assembly districts cannot be evenly divided among the senate districts of any county, in which case one more assembly district shall be put in the senate district in such county having the largest, or one less assembly district shall be put in the senate district in such county having the smallest number of inhabitants, excluding aliens, as the case may require. Nothing in this section shall prevent the division, at any time, of counties and towns and the erection of new towns by the legislature.

An apportionment by the legislature, or other body, shall be subject to review by the supreme court, at the suit of any citizen, under such reasonable regulations as the legislature may prescribe; and any court before which a cause may be pending involving an apportionment, shall give precedence thereto over all other causes and proceedings, and if said court be not in session it shall convene promptly for the disposition of the same. The court shall render its decision within sixty days after a petition is filed. In any judicial proceeding relating to redistricting of congressional or state legislative districts, any law establishing congressional or state legislative districts found to violate the provisions of this article shall be invalid in whole or in part. In the event that a court finds such a violation, the legislature shall have a full and reasonable opportunity to correct the law's legal infirmities. (Amended by vote of the people November 6, 1945; further amended by vote of the people November 4, 2014.)

[Definition of inhabitants]
§5-a. For the purpose of apportioning senate and assembly districts pursuant to the foregoing provisions of this article, the term "inhabitants, excluding aliens" shall mean the whole number of persons. (New. Added by vote of the people November 4, 1969.)

[Independent redistricting commission]
§5-b. (a) On or before February first of each year ending with a zero and at any other time a court orders that congressional or state legislative districts be amended, an independent redistricting commission shall be established to determine the district lines for congressional and state legislative offices. The independent redistricting commission shall be composed of ten members, appointed as follows:

(1) two members shall be appointed by the temporary president of the senate;

(2) two members shall be appointed by the speaker of the assembly;

(3) two members shall be appointed by the minority leader of the senate;

(4) two members shall be appointed by the minority leader of the assembly;

(5) two members shall be appointed by the eight members appointed pursuant to paragraphs (1) through (4) of this subdivision by a vote of not less than five members in favor of such appointment, and these two members shall not have been enrolled in the preceding five years in either of the two political parties that contain the largest or second largest number of enrolled voters within the state;

(6) one member shall be designated chair of the commission by a majority of the members appointed pursuant to paragraphs (1) through (5) of this subdivision to convene and preside over each meeting of the commission.

(b) The members of the independent redistricting commission shall be registered voters in this state. No member shall within the last three years:

(1) be or have been a member of the New York state legislature or United States Congress or a statewide elected official;

(2) be or have been a state officer or employee or legislative employee as defined in section seventy-three of the public officers law;

(3) be or have been a registered lobbyist in New York state;

(4) be or have been a political party chairman, as defined in paragraph (k) of subdivision one of section seventy-three of the public officers law;

(5) be the spouse of a statewide elected official or of any member of the United States Congress, or of the state legislature.

(c) To the extent practicable, the members of the independent redistricting commission shall reflect the diversity of the residents of this state with regard to race, ethnicity, gender, language, and geographic residence and to the extent practicable the appointing authorities shall consult with organizations devoted to protecting the voting rights of minority and other voters concerning potential appointees to the commission.

(d) Vacancies in the membership of the commission shall be filled within thirty days in the manner provided for in the original appointments.

(e) The legislature shall provide by law for the compensation of the members of the independent redistricting commission, including compensation for actual and necessary expenses incurred in the performance of their duties.

(f) A minimum of five members of the independent redistricting commission shall constitute a quorum for the transaction of any business or the exercise of any power of such commission prior to the appointment of the two commission members appointed pursuant to paragraph (5) of subdivision (a) of this section, and a minimum of seven members shall constitute a quorum after such members have been appointed, and no exercise of any power of the independent redistricting commission shall occur without the affirmative vote of at least a majority of the members, provided that, in order to approve any redistricting plan and implementing legislation, the following rules shall apply:

(1) In the event that the speaker of the assembly and the temporary president of the senate are members of the same political party, approval of a redistricting plan and implementing legislation by the commission for submission to the legislature shall require the vote in support of its approval by at least seven members including at least one member appointed by each of the legislative leaders.

(2) In the event that the speaker of the assembly and the temporary president of the senate are members of two different political parties, approval of a redistricting plan by the commission for submission to the legislature shall require the vote in support of its approval by at least seven members including at least one member appointed by the speaker of the assembly and one member appointed by the temporary president of the senate.

(g) In the event that the commission is unable to obtain seven votes to approve a redistricting plan on or before January first in the year ending in two or as soon as practicable thereafter, the commission shall submit to the legislature that redistricting plan and implementing legislation that garnered the highest number of votes in support of its approval by the commission with a record of the votes taken. In the event that more than one plan received the same number of votes for approval, and such number was higher than that for any other plan, then the commission shall submit all plans that obtained such number of votes. The legislature shall consider and vote upon such implementing legislation in accordance with the voting rules set forth in subdivision (b) of section four of this article.

(h) (1) The independent redistricting commission shall appoint two co-executive directors by a majority vote of the commission in accordance with the following procedure:

(i) In the event that the speaker of the assembly and the temporary president of the senate are members of two different political parties, the co-executive directors shall be approved by a majority of the commission that includes at least one appointee by the speaker of the assembly and at least one appointee by the temporary president of the senate.

(ii) In the event that the speaker of the assembly and the temporary president of the senate are members of the same political party, the co-executive directors shall be approved by a majority of the commission that includes at least one appointee by each of the legislative leaders.

(2) One of the co-executive directors shall be enrolled in the political party with the highest number of enrolled members in the state and one shall be enrolled in the political party with the second highest number of enrolled

9

members in the state. The co-executive directors shall appoint such staff as are necessary to perform the commission's duties, except that the commission shall review a staffing plan prepared and provided by the co-executive directors which shall contain a list of the various positions and the duties, qualifications, and salaries associated with each position.

(3) In the event that the commission is unable to appoint one or both of the co-executive directors within forty-five days of the establishment of a quorum of seven commissioners, the following procedure shall be followed:

(i) In the event that the speaker of the assembly and the temporary president of the senate are members of two different political parties, within ten days the speaker's appointees on the commission shall appoint one co-executive director, and the temporary president's appointees on the commission shall appoint the other co-executive director. Also within ten days the minority leader of the assembly shall select a co-deputy executive director, and the minority leader of the senate shall select the other co-deputy executive director.

(ii) In the event that the speaker of the assembly and the temporary president of the senate are members of the same political party, within ten days the speaker's and temporary president's appointees on the commission shall together appoint one co-executive director, and the two minority leaders' appointees on the commission shall together appoint the other co-executive director.

(4) In the event of a vacancy in the offices of co-executive director or co-deputy executive director, the position shall be filled within ten days of its occurrence by the same appointing authority or authorities that appointed his or her predecessor.

(i) The state budget shall include necessary appropriations for the expenses of the independent redistricting commission, provide for compensation and reimbursement of expenses for the members and staff of the commission, assign to the commission any additional duties that the legislature may deem necessary to the performance of the duties stipulated in this article, and require other agencies and officials of the state of New York and its political subdivisions to provide such information and assistance as the commission may require to perform its duties. (New. Added by vote of the people November 4, 2014.)

[Compensation, allowances and traveling expenses of members]
§6. Each member of the legislature shall receive for his or her services a like annual salary, to be fixed by law. He or she shall also be reimbursed for his or her actual traveling expenses in going to and returning from the place in which the legislature meets, not more than once each week while the legislature is in session. Senators, when the senate alone is convened in extraordinary session, or when serving as members of the court for the trial of impeachments, and such members of the assembly, not exceeding nine in number, as shall be appointed managers of an impeachment, shall receive an additional per diem allowance, to be fixed by law. Any member, while serving as an officer of his or her house or in any other special capacity therein or directly connected therewith not hereinbefore in this section specified, may also be paid and receive, in addition, any allowance which may be fixed by law for the particular and additional services appertaining to or entailed by such office or special capacity. Neither the salary of any member nor any other allowance so fixed may be increased or diminished during, and with respect to, the term for which he or she shall have been elected, nor shall he or she be paid or receive any other extra compensation. The provisions of this section and laws enacted in compliance therewith shall govern and be exclusively controlling, according to their terms. Members shall continue to receive such salary and additional allowance as heretofore fixed and provided in this section, until changed by law pursuant to this section. (Amended by Constitutional Convention of 1938 and approved by vote of the people November 8, 1938; further amended by vote of the people November 4, 1947; November 3, 1964; November 6, 2001.)

[Qualifications of members; prohibitions on certain civil appointments; acceptance to vacate seat]
§7. No person shall serve as a member of the legislature unless he or she is a citizen of the United States and has been a resident of the state of New

York for five years, and, except as hereinafter otherwise prescribed, of the assembly or senate district for the twelve months immediately preceding his or her election; if elected a senator or member of assembly at the first election next ensuing after a readjustment or alteration of the senate or assembly districts becomes effective, a person, to be eligible to serve as such, must have been a resident of the county in which the senate or assembly district is contained for the twelve months immediately preceding his or her election. No member of the legislature shall, during the time for which he or she was elected, receive any civil appointment from the governor, the governor and the senate, the legislature or from any city government, to an office which shall have been created, or the emoluments whereof shall have been increased during such time. If a member of the legislature be elected to congress, or appointed to any office, civil or military, under the government of the United States, the state of New York, or under any city government except as a member of the national guard or naval militia of the state, or of the reserve forces of the United States, his or her acceptance thereof shall vacate his or her seat in the legislature, providing, however, that a member of the legislature may be appointed commissioner of deeds or to any office in which he or she shall receive no compensation. (New. Derived in part from former §§7 and 8. Adopted by Constitutional Convention of 1938 and approved by vote of the people November 8, 1938; amended by vote of the people November 2, 1943.)

[Time of elections of members]
§8. The elections of senators and members of assembly, pursuant to the provisions of this constitution, shall be held on the Tuesday succeeding the first Monday of November, unless otherwise directed by the legislature. (Formerly §9. Renumbered by Constitutional Convention of 1938 and approved by vote of the people November 8, 1938.)

[Powers of each house]
§9. A majority of each house shall constitute a quorum to do business. Each house shall determine the rules of its own proceedings, and be the judge of the elections, returns and qualifications of its own members; shall choose its own officers; and the senate shall choose a temporary president and the assembly shall choose a speaker. (Formerly §10. Renumbered by Constitutional Convention of 1938 and approved by vote of the people November 8, 1938. Amended by vote of the people November 5, 1963.)

[Journals; open sessions; adjournments]
§10. Each house of the legislature shall keep a journal of its proceedings, and publish the same, except such parts as may require secrecy. The doors of each house shall be kept open, except when the public welfare shall require secrecy. Neither house shall, without the consent of the other, adjourn for more than two days. (Formerly §11. Renumbered and amended by Constitutional Convention of 1938 and approved by vote of the people November 8, 1938.)

[Members not to be questioned for speeches]
§11. For any speech or debate in either house of the legislature, the members shall not be questioned in any other place. (Formerly §12. Renumbered by Constitutional Convention of 1938 and approved by vote of the people November 8, 1938.)

[Bills may originate in either house; may be amended by the other]
§12. Any bill may originate in either house of the legislature, and all bills passed by one house may be amended by the other. (Formerly §13. Renumbered by Constitutional Convention of 1938 and approved by vote of the people November 8, 1938.)

[Enacting clause of bills; no law to be enacted except by bill]
§13. The enacting clause of all bills shall be "The People of the State of New York, represented in Senate and Assembly, do enact as follows," and no law shall be enacted except by bill. (Formerly §14. Renumbered by Constitutional Convention of 1938 and approved by vote of the people November 8, 1938.)

10

[Manner of passing bills; message of necessity for immediate vote]

§14. No bill shall be passed or become a law unless it shall have been printed and upon the desks of the members, in its final form, at least three calendar legislative days prior to its final passage, unless the governor, or the acting governor, shall have certified, under his or her hand and the seal of the state, the facts which in his or her opinion necessitate an immediate vote thereon, in which case it must nevertheless be upon the desks of the members in final form, not necessarily printed, before its final passage; nor shall any bill be passed or become a law, except by the assent of a majority of the members elected to each branch of the legislature; and upon the last reading of a bill, no amendment thereof shall be allowed, and the question upon its final passage shall be taken immediately thereafter, and the ayes and nays entered on the journal.

For purposes of this section, a bill shall be deemed to be printed and upon the desks of the members if: it is set forth in a legible electronic format by electronic means, and it is available for review in such format at the desks of the members. For purposes of this section "electronic means" means any method of transmission of information between computers or other machines designed for the purpose of sending and receiving such transmissions and which: allows the recipient to reproduce the information transmitted in a tangible medium of expression; and does not permit additions, deletions or other changes to be made without leaving an adequate record thereof. (Formerly §15. Renumbered and amended by Constitutional Convention of 1938 and approved by vote of the people November 8, 1938; further amended by vote of the people: November 6, 2001; November 4, 2014.)

[Private or local bills to embrace only one subject, expressed in title]

§15. No private or local bill, which may be passed by the legislature, shall embrace more than one subject, and that shall be expressed in the title. (Formerly §16. Renumbered by Constitutional Convention of 1938 and approved by vote of the people November 8, 1938.)

[Existing law not to be made applicable by reference]

§16. No act shall be passed which shall provide that any existing law, or any part thereof, shall be made or deemed a part of said act, or which shall enact that any existing law, or part thereof, shall be applicable, except by inserting it in such act. (Formerly §17. Renumbered by Constitutional Convention of 1938 and approved by vote of the people November 8, 1938.)

[Cases in which private or local bills shall not be passed]

§17. The legislature shall not pass a private or local bill in any of the following cases:

Changing the names of persons.

Laying out, opening, altering, working or discontinuing roads, highways or alleys, or for draining swamps or other low lands. Locating or changing county seats.

Providing for changes of venue in civil or criminal cases.

Incorporating villages.

Providing for election of members of boards of supervisors.

Selecting, drawing, summoning or empaneling grand or petit jurors.

Regulating the rate of interest on money.

The opening and conducting of elections or designating places of voting.

Creating, increasing or decreasing fees, percentages or allowances of public officers, during the term for which said officers are elected or appointed.

Granting to any corporation, association or individual the right to lay down railroad tracks.

Granting to any private corporation, association or individual any exclusive privilege, immunity or franchise whatever.

Granting to any person, association, firm or corporation, an exemption from taxation on real or personal property.

Providing for the building of bridges, except over the waters forming a part of the boundaries of the state, by other than a municipal or other public corporation or a public agency of the state. (Formerly §18. Renumbered and amended by Constitutional Convention of 1938 and approved by vote of the people November 8, 1938; further amended by vote of the people November 3, 1964.)

[Extraordinary sessions of the legislature; power to convene on legislative initiative]

§18. The members of the legislature shall be empowered, upon the presentation to the temporary president of the senate and the speaker of the assembly of a petition signed by two-thirds of the members elected to each house of the legislature, to convene the legislature on extraordinary occasions to act upon the subjects enumerated in such petition. (New. Added by vote of the people November 4, 1975.)

[Private claims not to be audited by legislature; claims barred by lapse of time]

§19. The legislature shall neither audit nor allow any private claim or account against the state, but may appropriate money to pay such claims as shall have been audited and allowed according to law.

No claim against the state shall be audited, allowed or paid which, as between citizens of the state, would be barred by lapse of time. But if the claimant shall be under legal disability, the claim may be presented within two years after such disability is removed. (Derived in part from former §6 of Art. 7. Amended by Constitutional Convention of 1938 and approved by vote of the people November 8, 1938; further amended by vote of the people November 3, 1964.)

[Two-thirds bills]

§20. The assent of two-thirds of the members elected to each branch of the legislature shall be requisite to every bill appropriating the public moneys or property for local or private purposes.

[Certain sections not to apply to bills recommended by certain commissioners or public agencies]

§21. Sections 15, 16 and 17 of this article shall not apply to any bill, or the amendments to any bill, which shall be recommended to the legislature by commissioners or any public agency appointed or directed pursuant to law to prepare revisions, consolidations or compilations of statutes. But a bill amending an existing law shall not be excepted from the provisions of sections 15, 16 and 17 of this article unless such amending bill shall itself be recommended to the legislature by such commissioners or public agency. (Formerly §23. Renumbered and amended by Constitutional Convention of 1938 and approved by vote of the people November 8, 1938.)

[Tax laws to state tax and object distinctly; definition of income for income tax purposes by reference to federal laws authorized]

§22. Every law which imposes, continues or revives a tax shall distinctly state the tax and the object to which it is to be applied, and it shall not be sufficient to refer to any other law to fix such tax or object.

Notwithstanding the foregoing or any other provision of this constitution, the legislature, in any law imposing a tax or taxes on, in respect to or measured by income, may define the income on, in respect to or by which such tax or taxes are imposed or measured, by reference to any provision of the laws of the United States as the same may be or become effective at any time or from time to time, and may prescribe exceptions or modifications to any such provision. (Formerly §24. Renumbered by Constitutional Convention of 1938 and approved by vote of the people November 8, 1938; amended by vote of the people November 3, 1959.)

[When yeas and nays necessary; three-fifths to constitute quorum]

§23. On the final passage, in either house of the legislature, of any act which imposes, continues or revives a tax, or creates a debt or charge, or makes, continues or revives any appropriation of public or trust money or property, or releases, discharges or commutes any claim or demand of the state, the question shall be taken by yeas and nays, which shall be duly entered upon the journals, and three-fifths of all the members elected to either house shall, in all such cases, be necessary to constitute a quorum therein. (Formerly §25. Renumbered by Constitutional Convention of 1938 and approved by vote of the people November 8, 1938.)

[Prison labor; contract system abolished]

§24. The legislature shall, by law, provide for the occupation and employment of prisoners sentenced to the several state prisons,

11

penitentiaries, jails and reformatories in the state; and no person in any such prison, penitentiary, jail or reformatory, shall be required or allowed to work, while under sentence thereto, at any trade, industry or occupation, wherein or whereby his or her work, or the product or profit of his or her work, shall be farmed out, contracted, given or sold to any person, firm, association or corporation, provided that the legislature may provide by law that such prisoners may voluntarily perform work for nonprofit organizations. As used in this section, the term "nonprofit organization" means an organization operated exclusively for religious, charitable, or educational purposes, no part of the net earnings of which inures to the benefit of any private shareholder or individual. This section shall not be construed to prevent the legislature from providing that convicts may work for, and that the products of their labor may be disposed of to, the state or any political division thereof, or for or to any public institution owned or managed and controlled by the state, or any political division thereof. (Formerly §29. Renumbered and amended by Constitutional Convention of 1938 and approved by vote of the people November 8, 1938; further amended by vote of the people November 6, 2001; November 3, 2009.)

[Emergency governmental operations; legislature to provide for]
§25. Notwithstanding any other provision of this constitution, the legislature, in order to insure continuity of state and local governmental operations in periods of emergency caused by enemy attack or by disasters (natural or otherwise), shall have the power and the immediate duty (1) to provide for prompt and temporary succession to the powers and duties of public offices, of whatever nature and whether filled by election or appointment, the incumbents of which may become unavailable for carrying on the powers and duties of such offices, and (2) to adopt such other measures as may be necessary and proper for insuring the continuity of governmental operations.

Nothing in this article shall be construed to limit in any way the power of the state to deal with emergencies arising from any cause. (New. Added by vote of the people November 5, 1963.)

ARTICLE IV
EXECUTIVE

[Executive power; election and terms of governor and lieutenant-governor]
Section 1. The executive power shall be vested in the governor, who shall hold office for four years; the lieutenant-governor shall be chosen at the same time, and for the same term. The governor and lieutenant-governor shall be chosen at the general election held in the year nineteen hundred thirty-eight, and each fourth year thereafter. They shall be chosen jointly, by the casting by each voter of a single vote applicable to both offices, and the legislature by law shall provide for making such choice in such manner. The respective persons having the highest number of votes cast jointly for them for governor and lieutenant-governor respectively shall be elected. (Amended by Constitutional Convention of 1938 and approved by vote of the people November 8, 1938; further amended by vote of the people November 3, 1953; November 6, 2001.)

[Qualifications of governor and lieutenant-governor]
§2. No person shall be eligible to the office of governor or lieutenant-governor, except a citizen of the United States, of the age of not less than thirty years, and who shall have been five years next preceding the election a resident of this state. (Amended by vote of the people November 6, 2001.)

[Powers and duties of governor; compensation]
§3. The governor shall be commander-in-chief of the military and naval forces of the state. The governor shall have power to convene the legislature, or the senate only, on extraordinary occasions. At extraordinary sessions convened pursuant to the provisions of this section no subject shall be acted upon, except such as the governor may recommend for consideration. The governor shall communicate by message to the legislature at every session the condition of the state, and recommend such matters to it as he or she shall judge expedient. The governor shall expedite all such measures as may be resolved

12

upon by the legislature, and shall take care that the laws are faithfully executed. The governor shall receive for his or her services an annual salary to be fixed by joint resolution of the senate and assembly, and there shall be provided for his or her use a suitable and furnished executive residence. (Formerly §4. Renumbered and amended by Constitutional Convention of 1938 and approved by vote of the people November 8, 1938; further amended by vote of the people November 3, 1953; November 5, 1963; November 6, 2001.)

[Reprieves, commutations and pardons; powers and duties of governor relating to grants of]
§4. The governor shall have the power to grant reprieves, commutations and pardons after conviction, for all offenses except treason and cases of impeachment, upon such conditions and with such restrictions and limitations, as he or she may think proper, subject to such regulations as may be provided by law relative to the manner of applying for pardons. Upon conviction for treason, the governor shall have power to suspend the execution of the sentence, until the case shall be reported to the legislature at its next meeting, when the legislature shall either pardon, or commute the sentence, direct the execution of the sentence, or grant a further reprieve. The governor shall annually communicate to the legislature each case of reprieve, commutation or pardon granted, stating the name of the convict, the crime of which the convict was convicted, the sentence and its date, and the date of the commutation, pardon or reprieve. (Formerly §5. Renumbered by Constitutional Convention of 1938 and approved by vote of the people November 8, 1938; further amended by vote of the people November 6, 2001.)

[When lieutenant-governor to act as governor]
§5. In case of the removal of the governor from office or of his or her death or resignation, the lieutenant-governor shall become governor for the remainder of the term.

In case the governor-elect shall decline to serve or shall die, the lieutenant-governor-elect shall become governor for the full term.

In case the governor is impeached, is absent from the state or is otherwise unable to discharge the powers and duties of the office of governor, the lieutenant-governor shall act as governor until the inability shall cease or until the term of the governor shall expire.

In case of the failure of the governor-elect to take the oath of office at the commencement of his or her term, the lieutenant-governor-elect shall act as governor until the governor shall take the oath. (Formerly §6. Renumbered and amended by Constitutional Convention of 1938 and approved by vote of the people November 8, 1938; further amended by vote of the people November 8, 1949; November 5, 1963; November 6, 2001.)

[Duties and compensation of lieutenant-governor; succession to the governorship]
§6. The lieutenant-governor shall possess the same qualifications of eligibility for office as the governor. The lieutenant-governor shall be the president of the senate but shall have only a casting vote therein.
The lieutenant-governor shall receive for his or her services an annual salary to be fixed by joint resolution of the senate and assembly.

In case of vacancy in the offices of both governor and lieutenant-governor, a governor and lieutenant-governor shall be elected for the remainder of the term at the next general election happening not less than three months after both offices shall have become vacant. No election of a lieutenant-governor shall be had in any event except at the time of electing a governor.

In case of vacancy in the offices of both governor and lieutenant-governor or if both of them shall be impeached, absent from the state or otherwise unable to discharge the powers and duties of the office of governor, the temporary president of the senate shall act as governor until the inability shall cease or until a governor shall be elected.

In case of vacancy in the office of lieutenant-governor alone, or if the lieutenant-governor shall be impeached, absent from the state or otherwise unable to discharge the duties of office, the temporary president of the senate shall perform all the duties of lieutenant-governor during such vacancy or inability.

If, when the duty of acting as governor devolves upon the temporary president of the senate, there be a vacancy in such office or the temporary president of the senate shall be absent from the state or otherwise unable to discharge the duties of governor, the speaker of the assembly shall act as governor during such vacancy or inability.

The legislature may provide for the devolution of the duty of acting as governor in any case not provided for in this article. (Formerly §§7 and 8. Renumbered and amended by Constitutional Convention of 1938 and approved by vote of the people November 8, 1938; further amended by vote of the people November 6, 1945; November 3, 1953; November 5, 1963; November 6, 2001.)

[Action by governor on legislative bills; reconsideration after veto]
§7. Every bill which shall have passed the senate and assembly shall, before it becomes a law, be presented to the governor; if the governor approve, he or she shall sign it; but if not, he or she shall return it with his or her objections to the house in which it shall have originated, which shall enter the objections at large on the journal, and proceed to reconsider it. If after such reconsideration, two-thirds of the members elected to that house shall agree to pass the bill, it shall be sent together with the objections, to the other house, by which it shall likewise be reconsidered; and if approved by two-thirds of the members elected to that house, it shall become a law notwithstanding the objections of the governor. In all such cases the votes in both houses shall be determined by yeas and nays, and the names of the members voting shall be entered by yeas and nays, and the names of the members voting shall be entered on the journal of each house respectively. If any bill shall not be returned by the governor within ten days (Sundays excepted) after it shall have been presented to him or her, the same shall be a law in like manner as if he or she had signed it, unless the legislature shall, by their adjournment, prevent its return, in which case it shall not become a law without the approval of the governor. No bill shall become a law after the final adjournment of the legislature, unless approved by the governor within thirty days after such adjournment. If any bill presented to the governor contain several items of appropriation of money, the governor may object to one or more of such items while approving of the other portion of the bill. In such case the governor shall append to the bill, at the time of signing it, a statement of the items to which he or she objects; and the appropriation so objected to shall not take effect. If the legislature be in session, he or she shall transmit to the house in which the bill originated a copy of such statement, and the items objected to shall be separately reconsidered. If on reconsideration one or more of such items be approved by two-thirds of the members elected to each house, the same shall be part of the law, notwithstanding the objections of the governor. All the provisions of this section, in relation to bills not approved by the governor, shall apply in cases in which he or she shall withhold approval from any item or items contained in a bill appropriating money. (Formerly §9. Renumbered by Constitutional Convention of 1938 and approved by vote of the people November 8, 1938; further amended by vote of the people November 6, 2001.)

[Departmental rules and regulations; filing; publication]
§8. No rule or regulation made by any state department, board, bureau, officer, authority or commission, except such as relates to the organization or internal management of a state department, board, bureau, authority or commission shall be effective until it is filed in the office of the department of state. The legislature shall provide for the speedy publication of such rules and regulations, by appropriate laws. (New. Adopted by Constitutional Convention of 1938 and approved by vote of the people November 8, 1938.)

ARTICLE V
OFFICERS AND CIVIL DEPARTMENTS

[Comptroller and attorney-general; payment of state moneys without audit void]
Section 1. The comptroller and attorney-general shall be chosen at the same general election as the governor and hold office for the same term, and shall possess the qualifications provided in section 2 of article IV. The legislature shall provide for filling vacancies in the office of comptroller and of attorney-general. No election of a comptroller or an attorney-general shall be had except at the time of electing a governor. The comptroller shall be required: (1) To audit all vouchers before payment and all official accounts; (2) to audit the accrual and collection of all revenues and receipts; and (3) to prescribe such methods of accounting as are necessary for the performance of the foregoing duties. The payment of any money of the state, or of any money under its control, or the refund of any money paid to the state, except upon audit by the comptroller, shall be void, and may be restrained upon the suit of any taxpayer with the consent of the supreme court in appellate division on notice to the attorney-general. In such respect the legislature shall define the powers and duties and may also assign to him or her: (1) supervision of the accounts of any political subdivision of the state; and (2) powers and duties pertaining to or connected with the assessment and taxation of real estate, including determination of ratios which the assessed valuation of taxable real property bears to the full valuation thereof, but not including any of those powers and duties reserved to officers of a county, city, town or village by virtue of sections seven and eight of article nine of this constitution. The legislature shall assign to him or her no administrative duties, excepting such as may be incidental to the performance of these functions, any other provision of this constitution to the contrary notwithstanding. (Amended by Constitutional Convention of 1938 and approved by vote of the people November 8, 1938; further amended by vote of the people November 3, 1953; November 8, 1955; November 6, 2001.)

[Civil departments in the state government]
§2. There shall be not more than twenty civil departments in the state government, including those referred to in this constitution. The legislature may by law change the names of the departments referred to in this constitution. (Amended by Constitutional Convention of 1938 and approved by vote of the people November 8, 1938; further amended by vote of the people November 2, 1943; November 3, 1959; November 7, 1961.)

[Assignment of functions]
§3. Subject to the limitations contained in this constitution, the legislature may from time to time assign by law new powers and functions to departments, officers, boards, commissions or executive offices of the governor, and increase, modify or diminish their powers and functions. Nothing contained in this article shall prevent the legislature from creating temporary commissions for special purposes or executive offices of the governor and from reducing the number of departments as provided for in this article, by consolidation or otherwise. (Amended by Constitutional Convention of 1938 and approved by vote of the people November 8, 1938; further amended by vote of the people November 7, 1961.)

[Department heads]
§4. The head of the department of audit and control shall be the comptroller and of the department of law, the attorney-general. The head of the department of education shall be The Regents of the University of the State of New York, who shall appoint and at pleasure remove a commissioner of education to be the chief administrative officer of the department. The head of the department of agriculture and markets shall be appointed in a manner to be prescribed by law. Except as otherwise provided in this constitution, the heads of all other departments and the members of all boards and commissions, excepting temporary commissions for special purposes, shall be appointed by the governor by and with the advice and consent of the senate and may be removed by the governor, in a manner to be prescribed by law. (Amended by Constitutional Convention of 1938 and approved by vote of the people November 8, 1938; further amended by vote of the people November 7, 1961.)

[Section 5, which abolished certain offices, was repealed by amendment approved by vote of the people November 6, 1962.]

[Civil service appointments and promotions; veterans' credits]
§6. Appointments and promotions in the civil service of the state and all of the civil divisions thereof, including cities and villages, shall be made according to merit and fitness to be ascertained, as far as practicable, by examination which, as far as practicable, shall be competitive; provided,

13

however, that any member of the armed forces of the United States who served therein in time of war, and who, at the time of such member's appointment or promotion, is a citizen or an alien lawfully admitted for permanent residence in the United States and a resident of this state and is honorably discharged or released under honorable circumstances from such service, shall be entitled to receive five points additional credit in a competitive examination for original appointment and two and one-half points additional credit in an examination for promotion or, if such member was disabled in the actual performance of duty in any war and his or her disability is certified by the United States department of veterans affairs to be in existence at the time of application for appointment or promotion, he or she shall be entitled to receive ten points additional credit in a competitive examination for original appointment and five points additional credit in an examination for promotion. Such additional credit shall be added to the final earned rating of such member after he or she has qualified in an examination and shall be granted only at the time of establishment of an eligible list. No such member shall receive the additional credit granted by this section after he or she has received one appointment, either original entrance or promotion, from an eligible list on which he or she was allowed the additional credit granted by this section, except where a member has been appointed or promoted from an eligible list on which he or she was allowed additional credit for military service and subsequent to such appointment he or she is disabled as provided in this section, such member shall be entitled to ten points additional credit less the number of points of additional credit allowed for the prior appointment. (Formerly §6. Repealed and new section approved by vote of the people November 8, 1949; further amended by vote of the people November 3, 1964; November 3, 1987; November 4, 1997; November 6, 2001; November 4, 2008; November 5, 2013.)

[Membership in retirement systems; benefits not to be diminished nor impaired]

§7. After July first, nineteen hundred forty, membership in any pension or retirement system of the state or of a civil division thereof shall be a contractual relationship, the benefits of which shall not be diminished or impaired. (New. Adopted by Constitutional Convention of 1938 and approved by vote of the people November 8, 1938.)

ARTICLE VI[7]
JUDICIARY

[Unified court system; organization; process]

Section 1. a. There shall be a unified court system for the state. The state-wide courts shall consist of the court of appeals, the supreme court including the appellate divisions thereof, the court of claims, the county court, the surrogate's court and the family court, as hereinafter provided. The legislature shall establish in and for the city of New York, as part of the unified court system for the state, a single, city-wide court of civil jurisdiction and a single, city-wide court of criminal jurisdiction, as hereinafter provided, and may upon the request of the mayor and the local legislative body of the city of New York, merge the two courts into one city-wide court of both civil and criminal jurisdiction. The unified court system for the state shall also include the district, town, city and village courts outside the city of New York, as hereinafter provided.

b. The court of appeals, the supreme court including the appellate divisions thereof, the court of claims, the county court, the surrogate's court, the family court, the courts or court of civil and criminal jurisdiction of the city of New York, and such other courts as the legislature may determine shall be courts of record.

c. All processes, warrants and other mandates of the court of appeals, the supreme court including the appellate divisions thereof, the court of claims, the county court, the surrogate's court and the family court may be served and executed in any part of the state. All processes, warrants and other mandates of the courts or court of civil and criminal jurisdiction of the city of New York may, subject to such limitation as may be prescribed by the

legislature, be served and executed in any part of the state. The legislature may provide that processes, warrants and other mandates of the district court may be served and executed in any part of the state and that processes, warrants and other mandates of town, village and city courts outside the city of New York may be served and executed in any part of the county in which such courts are located or in any part of any adjoining county.

[Court of appeals; organization; designations; vacancies, how filled; commission on judicial nomination]

§2. a. The court of appeals is continued. It shall consist of the chief judge and the six elected associate judges now in office, who shall hold their offices until the expiration of their respective terms, and their successors, and such justices of the supreme court as may be designated for service in said court as hereinafter provided. The official terms of the chief judge and the six associate judges shall be fourteen years.

Five members of the court shall constitute a quorum, and the concurrence of four shall be necessary to a decision; but no more than seven judges shall sit in any case. In case of the temporary absence or inability to act of any judge of the court of appeals, the court may designate any justice of the supreme court to serve as associate judge of the court during such absence or inability to act. The court shall have power to appoint and to remove its clerk. The powers and jurisdiction of the court shall not be suspended for want of appointment when the number of judges is sufficient to constitute a quorum.

b. Whenever and as often as the court of appeals shall certify to the governor that the court is unable, by reason of the accumulation of causes pending therein, to hear and dispose of the same with reasonable speed, the governor shall designate such number of justices of the supreme court as may be so certified to be necessary, but not more than four, to serve as associate judges of the court of appeals. The justices so designated shall be relieved, while so serving, from their duties as justices of the supreme court, and shall serve as associate judges of the court of appeals until the court shall certify that the need for the services of any such justices no longer exists, whereupon they shall return to the supreme court. The governor may fill vacancies among such designated judges. No such justices shall serve as associate judge of the court of appeals except while holding the office of justice of the supreme court. The designation of a justice of the supreme court as an associate judge of the court of appeals shall not be deemed to affect his or her existing office any longer than until the expiration of his or her designation as such associate judge, nor to create a vacancy.

c. There shall be a commission on judicial nomination to evaluate the qualifications of candidates for appointment to the court of appeals and to prepare a written report and recommend to the governor those persons who by their character, temperament, professional aptitude and experience are well qualified to hold such judicial office. The legislature shall provide by law for the organization and procedure of the judicial nominating commission.

d. (1) The commission on judicial nomination shall consist of twelve members of whom four shall be appointed by the governor, four by the chief judge of the court of appeals, and one each by the speaker of the assembly, the temporary president of the senate, the minority leader of the senate, and the minority leader of the assembly. Of the four members appointed by the governor, no more than two shall be enrolled in the same political party, two shall be members of the bar of the state, and two shall not be members of the bar of the state. Of the four members appointed by the chief judge of the court of appeals, no more than two shall be enrolled in the same political party, two shall be members of the bar of the state, and two shall not be members of the bar of the state. No member of the commission shall hold or have held any judicial office or hold any elected public office for which he or she receives compensation during his or her period of service, except that the governor and the chief judge may each appoint no more than one former judge or justice of the unified court system to such commission. No member of the commission shall hold any office in any political party. No member of the judicial nominating commission shall be eligible for appointment to judicial office in any court of the state during the member's period of service or within one year thereafter.

(2) The members first appointed by the governor shall have respectively one, two, three and four year terms as the governor shall designate. The

---

[7] New article, adopted by vote of the people November 7, 1961; repealed and replaced former article adopted November 3, 1925, as amended.

14

members first appointed by the chief judge of the court of appeals shall have respectively one, two, three and four year terms as the chief judge shall designate. The member first appointed by the temporary president of the senate shall have a one-year term. The member first appointed by the minority leader of the senate shall have a two-year term. The member first appointed by the speaker of the assembly shall have a four-year term. The member first appointed by the minority leader of the assembly shall have a three-year term. Each subsequent appointment shall be for a term of four years.

(3) The commission shall designate one of their number to serve as chairperson.

(4) The commission shall consider the qualifications of candidates for appointment to the offices of judge and chief judge of the court of appeals and, whenever a vacancy in those offices occurs, shall prepare a written report and recommend to the governor persons who are well qualified for those judicial offices.

e. The governor shall appoint, with the advice and consent of the senate, from among those recommended by the judicial nominating commission, a person to fill the office of chief judge or associate judge, as the case may be, whenever a vacancy occurs in the court of appeals; provided, however, that no person may be appointed a judge of the court of appeals unless such person is a resident of the state and has been admitted to the practice of law in this state for at least ten years. The governor shall transmit to the senate the written report of the commission on judicial nomination relating to the nominee.

f. When a vacancy occurs in the office of chief judge or associate judge of the court of appeals and the senate is not in session to give its advice and consent to an appointment to fill the vacancy, the governor shall fill the vacancy by interim appointment upon the recommendation of a commission on judicial nomination as provided in this section. An interim appointment shall continue until the senate shall pass upon the governor's selection. If the senate confirms an appointment, the judge shall serve a term as provided in subdivision a of this section commencing from the date of his or her interim appointment. If the senate rejects an appointment, a vacancy in the office shall occur sixty days after such rejection. If an interim appointment to the court of appeals be made from among the justices of the supreme court or the appellate divisions thereof, that appointment shall not affect the justice's existing office, nor create a vacancy in the supreme court, or the appellate division thereof, unless such appointment is confirmed by the senate and the appointee shall assume such office. If an interim appointment of chief judge of the court of appeals be made from among the associate judges, an interim appointment of associate judge shall be made in like manner; in such case, the appointment as chief judge shall not affect the existing office of associate judge, unless such appointment as chief judge is confirmed by the senate and the appointee shall assume such office.

g. The provisions of subdivisions c, d, e and f of this section shall not apply to temporary designations or assignments of judges or justices. (Subdivision a amended, subdivision c repealed and new subdivisions c through g added by vote of the people November 8, 1977; further amended by vote of the people November 6, 2001.)

[Court of appeals; jurisdiction]
§3. a. The jurisdiction of the court of appeals shall be limited to the review of questions of law except where the judgment is of death, or where the appellate division, on reversing or modifying a final or interlocutory judgment in an action or a final or interlocutory order in a special proceeding, finds new facts and a final judgment or a final order pursuant thereto is entered; but the right to appeal shall not depend upon the amount involved.

b. Appeals to the court of appeals may be taken in the classes of cases hereafter enumerated in this section;

In criminal cases, directly from a court of original jurisdiction where the judgment is of death, and in other criminal cases from an appellate division or otherwise as the legislature may from time to time provide.

In civil cases and proceedings as follows:

(1) As of right, from a judgment or order entered upon the decision of an appellate division of the supreme court which finally determines an action or special proceeding wherein is directly involved the construction of the constitution of the state or of the United States, or where one or more of the justices of the appellate division dissents from the decision of the court, or where the judgment or order is one of reversal or modification.

(2) As of right, from a judgment or order of a court of record of original jurisdiction which finally determines an action or special proceeding where the only question involved on the appeal is the validity of a statutory provision of the state or of the United States under the constitution of the state or of the United States; and on any such appeal only the constitutional question shall be considered and determined by the court.

(3) As of right, from an order of the appellate division granting a new trial in an action or a new hearing in a special proceeding where the appellant stipulates that, upon affirmance, judgment absolute or final order shall be rendered against him or her.

(4) From a determination of the appellate division of the supreme court in any department, other than a judgment or order which finally determines an action or special proceeding, where the appellate division allows the same and certifies that one or more questions of law have arisen which, in its opinion, ought to be reviewed by the court of appeals, but in such case the appeal shall bring up for review only the question or questions so certified; and the court of appeals shall certify to the appellate division its determination upon such question or questions.

(5) From an order of the appellate division of the supreme court in any department, in a proceeding instituted by or against one or more public officers or a board, commission or other body of public officers or a court or tribunal, other than an order which finally determines such proceeding, where the court of appeals shall allow the same upon the ground that, in its opinion, a question of law is involved which ought to be reviewed by it, and without regard to the availability of appeal by stipulation for final order absolute.

(6) From a judgment or order entered upon the decision of an appellate division of the supreme court which finally determines an action or special proceeding but which is not appealable under paragraph (1) of this subdivision where the appellate division or the court of appeals shall certify that in its opinion a question of law is involved which ought to be reviewed by the court of appeals. Such an appeal may be allowed upon application (a) to the appellate division, and in case of refusal, to the court of appeals, or (b) directly to the court of appeals. Such an appeal shall be allowed when required in the interest of substantial justice.

(7) No appeal shall be taken to the court of appeals from a judgment or order entered upon the decision of an appellate division of the supreme court in any civil case or proceeding where the appeal to the appellate division was from a judgment or order entered in an appeal from another court, including an appellate or special term of the supreme court, unless the construction of the constitution of the state or of the United States is directly involved therein, or unless the appellate division of the supreme court shall certify that in its opinion a question of law is involved which ought to be reviewed by the court of appeals.

(8) The legislature may abolish an appeal to the court of appeals as of right in any or all of the cases or classes of cases specified in paragraph (1) of this subdivision wherein no question involving the construction of the constitution of the state or of the United States is directly involved, provided, however, that appeals in any such case or class of cases shall thereupon be governed by paragraph (6) of this subdivision.

(9) The court of appeals shall adopt and from time to time may amend a rule to permit the court to answer questions of New York law certified to it by the Supreme Court of the United States, a court of appeals of the United States or an appellate court of last resort of another state, which may be determinative of the cause then pending in the certifying court and which in the opinion of the certifying court are not controlled by precedent in the decisions of the courts of New York. (Paragraph (9) added by vote of the people November 5, 1985; further amended by vote of the people November 6, 2001.)

[Judicial departments; appellate divisions, how constituted; governor to designate justices; temporary assignments; jurisdiction]
§4. a. The state shall be divided into four judicial departments. The first department shall consist of the counties within the first judicial district of the state. The second department shall consist of the counties within the second, ninth, tenth and eleventh judicial districts of the state. The third

15

department shall consist of the counties within the third, fourth and sixth judicial districts of the state. The fourth department shall consist of the counties within the fifth, seventh and eighth judicial districts of the state. Each department shall be bounded by the lines of judicial districts. Once every ten years the legislature may alter the boundaries of the judicial departments, but without changing the number thereof.

b. The appellate divisions of the supreme court are continued, and shall consist of seven justices of the supreme court in each of the first and second departments, and five justices in each of the other departments. In each appellate division, four justices shall constitute a quorum, and the concurrence of three shall be necessary to a decision. No more than five justices shall sit in any case.

c. The governor shall designate the presiding justice of each appellate division, who shall act as such during his or her term of office and shall be a resident of the department. The other justices of the appellate divisions shall be designated by the governor, from all the justices elected to the supreme court, for terms of five years or the unexpired portions of their respective terms of office, if less than five years.

d. The justices heretofore designated shall continue to sit in the appellate divisions until the terms of their respective designations shall expire. From time to time as the terms of the designations expire, or vacancies occur, the governor shall make new designations. The governor may also, on request of any appellate division, make temporary designations in case of the absence or inability to act of any justice in such appellate division, for service only during such absence or inability to act.

e. In case any appellate division shall certify to the governor that one or more additional justices are needed for the speedy disposition of the business before it, the governor may designate an additional justice or additional justices; but when the need for such additional justice or justices shall no longer exist, the appellate division shall so certify to the governor, and thereupon service under such designation or designations shall cease.

f. A majority of the justices designated to sit in any appellate division shall at all times be residents of the department.

g. Whenever the appellate division in any department shall be unable to dispose of its business within a reasonable time, a majority of the presiding justices of the several departments, at a meeting called by the presiding justice of the department in arrears, may transfer any pending appeals from such department to any other department for hearing and determination.

h. A justice of the appellate division of the supreme court in any department may be temporarily designated by the presiding justice of his or her department to the appellate division in another judicial department upon agreement by the presiding justices of the appellate division of the departments concerned.

i. In the event that the disqualification, absence or inability to act of justices in any appellate division prevents there being a quorum of justices qualified to hear an appeal, the justices qualified to hear the appeal may transfer it to the appellate division in another department for hearing and determination. In the event that the justices in any appellate division qualified to hear an appeal are equally divided, said justices may transfer the appeal to the appellate division in another department for hearing and determination. Each appellate division shall have power to appoint and remove its clerk.

j. No justice of the appellate division shall, within the department to which he or she may be designated to perform the duties of an appellate justice, exercise any of the powers of a justice of the supreme court, other than those of a justice out of court, and those pertaining to the appellate division, except that the justice may decide causes or proceedings theretofore submitted, or hear and decide motions submitted by consent of counsel, but any such justice, when not actually engaged in performing the duties of such appellate justice in the department to which he or she is designated, may hold any term of the supreme court and exercise any of the powers of a justice of the supreme court in any judicial district in any other department of the state.

k. The appellate divisions of the supreme court shall have all the jurisdiction possessed by them on the effective date of this article and such additional jurisdiction as may be prescribed by law, provided, however, that the right to appeal to the appellate divisions from a judgment or order

16

which does not finally determine an action or special proceeding may be limited or conditioned by law. (Subdivision e amended by vote of the people November 8, 1977; further amended by vote of the people November 6, 2001.)

[Appeals from judgment or order; new trial]
§5. a. Upon an appeal from a judgment or an order, any appellate court to which the appeal is taken which is authorized to review such judgment or order may reverse or affirm, wholly or in part, or may modify the judgment or order appealed from, and each interlocutory judgment or intermediate or other order which it is authorized to review, and as to any or all of the parties. It shall thereupon render judgment of affirmance, judgment of reversal and final judgment upon the right of any or all of the parties, or judgment of modification thereon according to law, except where it may be necessary or proper to grant a new trial or hearing, when it may grant a new trial or hearing.

b. If any appeal is taken to an appellate court which is not authorized to review such judgment or order, the court shall transfer the appeal to an appellate court which is authorized to review such judgment or order.

[Judicial districts; how constituted; supreme court][8]
§6. a. The state shall be divided into eleven judicial districts. The first judicial district shall consist of the counties of Bronx and New York. The second judicial district shall consist of the counties of Kings and Richmond. The third judicial district shall consist of the counties of Albany, Columbia, Greene, Rensselaer, Schoharie, Sullivan, and Ulster. The fourth judicial district shall consist of the counties of Clinton, Essex, Franklin, Fulton, Hamilton, Montgomery, St. Lawrence, Saratoga, Schenectady, Warren and Washington. The fifth judicial district shall consist of the counties of Herkimer, Jefferson, Lewis, Oneida, Onondaga, and Oswego. The sixth judicial district shall consist of the counties of Broome, Chemung, Chenango, Cortland, Delaware, Madison, Otsego, Schuyler, Tioga and Tompkins. The seventh judicial district shall consist of the counties of Cayuga, Livingston, Monroe, Ontario, Seneca, Steuben, Wayne and Yates. The eighth judicial district shall consist of the counties of Allegany, Cattaraugus, Chautauqua, Erie, Genesee, Niagara, Orleans and Wyoming. The ninth judicial district shall consist of the counties of Dutchess, Orange, Putnam, Rockland and Westchester. The tenth judicial district shall consist of the counties of Nassau and Suffolk. The eleventh judicial district shall consist of the county of Queens.

b. Once every ten years the legislature may increase or decrease the number of judicial districts or alter the composition of judicial districts and thereupon re-apportion the justices to be thereafter elected in the judicial districts so altered. Each judicial district shall be bounded by county lines.

c. The justices of the supreme court shall be chosen by the electors of the judicial district in which they are to serve. The terms of justices of the supreme court shall be fourteen years from and including the first day of January next after their election.

d. The supreme court is continued. It shall consist of the number of justices of the supreme court including the justices designated to the appellate divisions of the supreme court, judges of the county court of the counties of Bronx, Kings, Queens and Richmond and judges of the court of general sessions of the county of New York authorized by law on the thirty-first day of August next after the approval and ratification of this amendment by the people, all of whom shall be justices of the supreme court for the remainder of their terms. The legislature may increase the number of justices of the supreme court in any judicial district, except that the number in any district shall not be increased to exceed one justice for fifty thousand, or fraction over thirty thousand, of the population thereof as shown by the last federal census or state enumeration. The legislature may decrease the number of justices of the supreme court in any judicial district, except that the number in any district shall not be less than the number of justices of the supreme court authorized by law on the effective date of this article.

e. The clerks of the several counties shall be clerks of the supreme court, with such powers and duties as shall be prescribed by law.

---

[8] Judiciary Law §140 currently sets forth 13 judicial districts.

[Supreme court; jurisdiction]

§7. a. The supreme court shall have general original jurisdiction in law and equity and the appellate jurisdiction herein provided. In the city of New York, it shall have exclusive jurisdiction over crimes prosecuted by indictment, provided, however, that the legislature may grant to the city-wide court of criminal jurisdiction of the city of New York jurisdiction over misdemeanors prosecuted by indictment and to the family court in the city of New York jurisdiction over crimes and offenses by or against minors or between spouses or between parent and child or between members of the same family or household.

b. If the legislature shall create new classes of actions and proceedings, the supreme court shall have jurisdiction over such classes of actions and proceedings, but the legislature may provide that another court or other courts shall also have jurisdiction and that actions and proceedings of such classes may be originated in such other court or courts. (Subdivision b repealed and subdivision c relettered b by vote of the people November 8, 1977.)

[Appellate terms; composition; jurisdiction]

§8. a. The appellate division of the supreme court in each judicial department may establish an appellate term in and for such department or in and for a judicial district or districts or in and for a county or counties within such department. Such an appellate term shall be composed of not less than three nor more than five justices of the supreme court who shall be designated from time to time by the chief administrator of the courts with the approval of the presiding justice of the appropriate appellate division, and who shall be residents of the department or of the judicial district or districts as the case may be and the chief administrator of the courts shall designate the place or places where such appellate terms shall be held.

b. Any such appellate term may be discontinued and re-established as the appellate division of the supreme court in each department shall determine from time to time and any designation to service therein may be revoked by the chief administrator of the courts with the approval of the presiding justice of the appropriate appellate division.

c. In each appellate term no more than three justices assigned thereto shall sit in any action or proceeding. Two of such justices shall constitute a quorum and the concurrence of two shall be necessary to a decision.

d. If so directed by the appellate division of the supreme court establishing an appellate term, an appellate term shall have jurisdiction to hear and determine appeals now or hereafter authorized by law to be taken to the supreme court or to the appellate division other than appeals from the supreme court, a surrogate's court, the family court or appeals in criminal cases prosecuted by indictment or by information as provided in section six of article one.

e. As may be provided by law, an appellate term shall have jurisdiction to hear and determine appeals from the district court or a town, village or city court outside the city of New York. (Subdivisions a, b and d amended by vote of the people November 8, 1977.)

[Court of claims; jurisdiction]

§9. The court of claims is continued. It shall consist of the eight judges now authorized by law, but the legislature may increase such number and may reduce such number to six or seven. The judges shall be appointed by the governor by and with the advice and consent of the senate and their terms of office shall be nine years. The court shall have jurisdiction to hear and determine claims against the state or by the state against the claimant or between conflicting claimants as the legislature may provide.

[County courts; judges]

§10. a. The county court is continued in each county outside the city of New York. There shall be at least one judge of the county court in each county and such number of additional judges in each county as may be provided by law. The judges shall be residents of the county and shall be chosen by the electors of the county.

b. The terms of the judges of the county court shall be ten years from and including the first day of January next after their election.

[County court; jurisdiction]

§11. a. The county court shall have jurisdiction over the following classes of actions and proceedings which shall be originated in such county court in the manner provided by law, except that actions and proceedings within the jurisdiction of the district court or a town, village or city court outside the city of New York may, as provided by law, be originated therein: actions and proceedings for the recovery of money, actions and proceedings for the recovery of chattels and actions and proceedings for the foreclosure of mechanics liens and liens on personal property where the amount sought to be recovered or the value of the property does not exceed twenty-five thousand dollars exclusive of interest and costs; over all crimes and other violations of law; over summary proceedings to recover possession of real property and to remove tenants therefrom; and over such other actions and proceedings, not within the exclusive jurisdiction of the supreme court, as may be provided by law.

b. The county court shall exercise such equity jurisdiction as may be provided by law and its jurisdiction to enter judgment upon a counterclaim for the recovery of money only shall be unlimited.

c. The county court shall have jurisdiction to hear and determine all appeals arising in the county in the following actions and proceedings: as of right, from a judgment or order of the district court or a town, village or city court which finally determines an action or proceeding and, as may be provided by law, from a judgment or order of any such court which does not finally determine an action or proceeding. The legislature may provide, in accordance with the provisions of section eight of this article, that any or all of such appeals be taken to an appellate term of the supreme court instead of the county court.

d. The provisions of this section shall in no way limit or impair the jurisdiction of the supreme court as set forth in section seven of this article. (Subdivision b repealed and subdivisions c, d and e relettered b, c and d by vote of the people November 8, 1977; subdivision a amended by vote of the people November 8, 1983.)

[Surrogate's courts; judges; jurisdiction]

§12. a. The surrogate's court is continued in each county in the state. There shall be at least one judge of the surrogate's court in each county and such number of additional judges of the surrogate's court as may be provided by law.

b. The judges of the surrogate's court shall be residents of the county and shall be chosen by the electors of the county.

c. The terms of the judges of the surrogate's court in the city of New York shall be fourteen years, and in other counties ten years, from and including the first day of January next after their election.

d. The surrogate's court shall have jurisdiction over all actions and proceedings relating to the affairs of decedents, probate of wills, administration of estates and actions and proceedings arising thereunder or pertaining thereto, guardianship of the property of minors, and such other actions and proceedings, not within the exclusive jurisdiction of the supreme court, as may be provided by law.

e. The surrogate's court shall exercise such equity jurisdiction as may be provided by law.

f. The provisions of this section shall in no way limit or impair the jurisdiction of the supreme court as set forth in section seven of this article.

[Family court; organization; jurisdiction]

§13. a. The family court of the state of New York is hereby established. It shall consist of at least one judge in each county outside the city of New York and such number of additional judges for such counties as may be provided by law. Within the city of New York it shall consist of such number of judges as may be provided by law. The judges of the family court within the city of New York shall be residents of such city and shall be appointed by the mayor of the city of New York for terms of ten years. The judges of the family court outside the city of New York, shall be chosen by the electors of the counties wherein they reside for terms of ten years.

b. The family court shall have jurisdiction over the following classes of actions and proceedings which shall be originated in such family court in the manner provided by law: (1) the protection, treatment, correction and commitment of those minors who are in need of the exercise of the authority

17

of the court because of circumstances of neglect, delinquency or dependency, as the legislature may determine; (2) the custody of minors except for custody incidental to actions and proceedings for marital separation, divorce, annulment of marriage and dissolution of marriage; (3) the adoption of persons; (4) the support of dependents except for support incidental to actions and proceedings in this state for marital separation, divorce, annulment of marriage or dissolution of marriage; (5) the establishment of paternity; (6) proceedings for conciliation of spouses; and (7) as may be provided by law: the guardianship of the person of minors and, in conformity with the provisions of section seven of this article, crimes and offenses by or against minors or between spouses or between parent and child or between members of the same family or household. Nothing in this section shall be construed to abridge the authority or jurisdiction of courts to appoint guardians in cases originating in those courts.

c. The family court shall also have jurisdiction to determine, with the same powers possessed by the supreme court, the following matters when referred to the family court from the supreme court: habeas corpus proceedings for the determination of the custody of minors; and in actions and proceedings for marital separation, divorce, annulment of marriage and dissolution of marriage, applications to fix temporary or permanent support and custody, or applications to enforce judgments and orders of support and of custody, or applications to modify judgments and orders of support and of custody which may be granted only upon the showing to the family court that there has been a subsequent change of circumstances and that modification is required.

d. The provisions of this section shall in no way limit or impair the jurisdiction of the supreme court as set forth in section seven of this article. (Amended by vote of the people November 6, 1973.)

[Discharge of duties of more than one judicial office by same judicial officer]
§14. The legislature may at any time provide that outside the city of New York the same person may act and discharge the duties of county judge and surrogate or of judge of the family court and surrogate, or of county judge and judge of the family court, or of all three positions in any county.

[New York city; city-wide courts; jurisdiction]
§15. a. The legislature shall by law establish a single court of city-wide civil jurisdiction and a single court of city-wide criminal jurisdiction in and for the city of New York and the legislature may, upon the request of the mayor and the local legislative body of the city of New York, merge the two courts into one city-wide court of both civil and criminal jurisdiction. The said city-wide courts shall consist of such number of judges as may be provided by law. The judges of the court of city-wide civil jurisdiction shall be residents of such city and shall be chosen for terms of ten years by the electors of the counties included within the city of New York from districts within such counties established by law. The judges of the court of city-wide criminal jurisdiction shall be residents of such city and shall be appointed for terms of ten years by the mayor of the city of New York.

b. The court of city-wide civil jurisdiction of the city of New York shall have jurisdiction over the following classes of actions and proceedings which shall be originated in such court in the manner provided by law: actions and proceedings for the recovery of money, actions and proceedings for the recovery of chattels and actions and proceedings for the foreclosure of mechanics liens and liens on personal property where the amount sought to be recovered or the value of the property does not exceed twenty-five thousand dollars exclusive of interest and costs, or such smaller amount as may be fixed by law; over summary proceedings to recover possession of real property and to remove tenants therefrom and over such other actions and proceedings, not within the exclusive jurisdiction of the supreme court, as may be provided by law. The court of city-wide civil jurisdiction shall further exercise such equity jurisdiction as may be provided by law and its jurisdiction to enter judgment upon a counterclaim for the recovery of money only shall be unlimited.

c. The court of city-wide criminal jurisdiction of the city of New York shall have jurisdiction over crimes and other violations of law, other than those prosecuted by indictment, provided, however, that the legislature may grant to said court jurisdiction over misdemeanors prosecuted by indictment;

and over such other actions and proceedings, not within the exclusive jurisdiction of the supreme court, as may be provided by law.

d. The provisions of this section shall in no way limit or impair the jurisdiction of the supreme court as set forth in section seven of this article. (Subdivision b amended by vote of the people November 8, 1983; further amended by vote of the people November 7, 1995.)

[District courts; jurisdiction; judges]
§16. a. The district court of Nassau county may be continued under existing law and the legislature may, at the request of the board of supervisors or other elective governing body of any county outside the city of New York, establish the district court for the entire area of such county or for a portion of such county consisting of one or more cities, or one or more towns which are contiguous, or of a combination of such cities and such towns provided at least one of such cities is contiguous to one of such towns.

b. No law establishing the district court for an entire county shall become effective unless approved at a general election on the question of the approval of such law by a majority of the votes cast thereon by the electors within the area of any cities in the county considered as one unit and by a majority of the votes cast thereon by the electors within the area outside of cities in the county considered as one unit.

c. No law establishing the district court for a portion of a county shall become effective unless approved at a general election on the question of the approval of such law by a majority of the votes cast thereon by the electors within the area of any cities included in such portion of the county considered as one unit and by a majority of the votes cast thereon by the electors within the area outside of cities included in such portion of the county considered as one unit.

d. The district court shall have such jurisdiction as may be provided by law, but not in any respect greater than the jurisdiction of the courts for the city of New York as provided in section fifteen of this article, provided, however, that in actions and proceedings for the recovery of money, actions and proceedings for the recovery of chattels and actions and proceedings for the foreclosure of mechanics liens and liens on personal property, the amount sought to be recovered or the value of the property shall not exceed fifteen thousand dollars exclusive of interest and costs.

e. The legislature may create districts of the district court which shall consist of an entire county or of an area less than a county.

f. There shall be at least one judge of the district court for each district and such number of additional judges in each district as may be provided by law.

g. The judges of the district court shall be apportioned among the districts as may be provided by law, and to the extent practicable, in accordance with the population and the volume of judicial business.

h. The judges shall be residents of the district and shall be chosen by the electors of the district. Their terms shall be six years from and including the first day of January next after their election.

i. The legislature may regulate and discontinue the district court in any county or portion thereof. (Subdivision d amended by vote of the people November 8, 1983.)

[Town, village and city courts; jurisdiction; judges]
§17. a. Courts for towns, villages and cities outside the city of New York are continued and shall have the jurisdiction prescribed by the legislature but not in any respect greater than the jurisdiction of the district court as provided in section sixteen of this article.

b. The legislature may regulate such courts, establish uniform jurisdiction, practice and procedure for city courts outside the city of New York and may discontinue any village or city court outside the city of New York existing on the effective date of this article. The legislature may discontinue any town court existing on the effective date of this article only with the approval of a majority of the total votes cast at a general election on the question of a proposed discontinuance of the court in each such town affected thereby.

c. The legislature may abolish the legislative functions on town boards of justices of the peace and provide that town councilmen be elected in their stead.

18

d. The number of the judges of each of such town, village and city courts and the classification and duties of the judges shall be prescribed by the legislature. The terms, method of selection and method of filling vacancies for the judges of such courts shall be prescribed by the legislature, provided, however, that the justices of town courts shall be chosen by the electors of the town for terms of four years from and including the first day of January next after their election.

[Trial by jury; trial without jury; claims against state]
§18. a. Trial by jury is guaranteed as provided in article one of this constitution. The legislature may provide that in any court of original jurisdiction a jury shall be composed of six or of twelve persons and may authorize any court which shall have jurisdiction over crimes and other violations of law, other than crimes prosecuted by indictment, to try such matters without a jury, provided, however, that crimes prosecuted by indictment shall be tried by a jury composed of twelve persons, unless a jury trial has been waived as provided in section two of article one of this constitution.

b. The legislature may provide for the manner of trial of actions and proceedings involving claims against the state.

[Transfer of actions and proceedings]
§19. a. The supreme court may transfer any action or proceeding, except one over which it shall have exclusive jurisdiction which does not depend upon the monetary amount sought, to any other court having jurisdiction of the subject matter within the judicial department provided that such other court has jurisdiction over the classes of persons named as parties. As may be provided by law, the supreme court may transfer to itself any action or proceeding originated or pending in another court within the judicial department other than the court of claims upon a finding that such a transfer will promote the administration of justice.

b. The county court shall transfer to the supreme court or surrogate's court or family court any action or proceeding which has not been transferred to it from the supreme court or surrogate's court or family court and over which the county court has no jurisdiction. The county court may transfer any action or proceeding, except a criminal action or proceeding involving a felony prosecuted by indictment or an action or proceeding required by this article to be dealt with in the surrogate's court or family court, to any court, other than the supreme court, having jurisdiction of the subject matter within the county provided that such other court has jurisdiction over the classes of persons named as parties.

c. As may be provided by law, the supreme court or the county court may transfer to the county court any action or proceeding originated or pending in the district court or a town, village or city court outside the city of New York upon a finding that such a transfer will promote the administration of justice.

d. The surrogate's court shall transfer to the supreme court or the county court or the family court or the courts for the city of New York established pursuant to section fifteen of this article any action or proceeding which has not been transferred to it from any of said courts and over which the surrogate's court has no jurisdiction.

e. The family court shall transfer to the supreme court or the surrogate's court or the county court or the courts for the city of New York established pursuant to section fifteen of this article any action or proceeding which has not been transferred to it from any of said courts and over which the family court has no jurisdiction.

f. The courts for the city of New York established pursuant to section fifteen of this article shall transfer to the supreme court or the surrogate's court or the family court any action or proceeding which has not been transferred to them from any of said courts and over which the said courts for the city of New York have no jurisdiction.

g. As may be provided by law, the supreme court shall transfer any action or proceeding to any other court having jurisdiction of the subject matter in any other judicial district or county provided that such other court has jurisdiction over the classes of persons named as parties.

h. As may be provided by law, the county court, the surrogate's court, the family court and the courts for the city of New York established pursuant to section fifteen of this article may transfer any action or proceeding, other than one which has previously been transferred to it, to any other court, except the supreme court, having jurisdiction of the subject matter in any other judicial district or county provided that such other court has jurisdiction over the classes of persons named as parties.

i. As may be provided by law, the district court or a town, village or city court outside the city of New York may transfer any action or proceeding, other than one which has previously been transferred to it, to any court, other than the county court or the surrogate's court or the family court or the supreme court, having jurisdiction of the subject matter in the same or an adjoining county provided that such other court has jurisdiction over the classes of persons named as parties.

j. Each court shall exercise jurisdiction over any action or proceeding transferred to it pursuant to this section.

k. The legislature may provide that the verdict or judgment in actions and proceedings so transferred shall not be subject to the limitation of monetary jurisdiction of the court to which the actions and proceedings are transferred if that limitation be lower than that of the court in which the actions and proceedings were originated.

[Judges and justices; qualifications; eligibility for other office or service; restrictions]
§20. a. No person, other than one who holds such office at the effective date of this article, may assume the office of judge of the court of appeals, justice of the supreme court, or judge of the court of claims unless he or she has been admitted to practice law in this state at least ten years. No person, other than one who holds such office at the effective date of this article, may assume the office of judge of the county court, surrogate's court, family court, a court for the city of New York established pursuant to section fifteen of this article, district court or city court outside the city of New York unless he or she has been admitted to practice law in this state at least five years or such greater number of years as the legislature may determine.

b. A judge of the court of appeals, justice of the supreme court, judge of the court of claims, judge of a county court, judge of the surrogate's court, judge of the family court or judge of a court for the city of New York established pursuant to section fifteen of this article who is elected or appointed after the effective date of this article may not:

(1) hold any other public office or trust except an office in relation to the administration of the courts, member of a constitutional convention or member of the armed forces of the United States or of the state of New York in which latter event the legislature may enact such legislation as it deems appropriate to provide for a temporary judge or justice to serve during the period of the absence of such judge or justice in the armed forces;

(2) be eligible to be a candidate for any public office other than judicial office or member of a constitutional convention, unless he or she resigns from judicial office; in the event a judge or justice does not so resign from judicial office within ten days after his or her acceptance of the nomination of such other office, his or her judicial office shall become vacant and the vacancy shall be filled in the manner provided in this article;

(3) hold any office or assume the duties or exercise the powers of any office of any political organization or be a member of any governing or executive agency thereof;

(4) engage in the practice of law, act as an arbitrator, referee or compensated mediator in any action or proceeding or matter or engage in the conduct of any other profession or business which interferes with the performance of his or her judicial duties.

Judges and justices of the courts specified in this subdivision shall also be subject to such rules of conduct as may be promulgated by the chief administrator of the courts with the approval of the court of appeals.

c. Qualifications for and restrictions upon the judges of district, town, village or city courts outside the city of New York, other than such qualifications and restrictions specifically set forth in subdivision a of this section, shall be prescribed by the legislature, provided, however, that the legislature shall require a course of training and education to be completed by justices of town and village courts selected after the effective date of this article who have not been admitted to practice law in this state. Judges of such courts shall also be subject to such rules of conduct not inconsistent with laws as may be promulgated by the chief administrator of the courts

19

with the approval of the court of appeals. (Amended by vote of the people November 8, 1977; November 6, 2001.)

[Vacancies; how filled]

§21. a. When a vacancy shall occur, otherwise than by expiration of term, in the office of justice of the supreme court, of judge of the county court, of judge of the surrogate's court or judge of the family court outside the city of New York, it shall be filled for a full term at the next general election held not less than three months after such vacancy occurs and until the vacancy shall be so filled, the governor by and with the advice and consent of the senate, if the senate shall be in session, or, if the senate not be in session, the governor may fill such vacancy by an appointment which shall continue until and including the last day of December next after the election at which the vacancy shall be filled.

b. When a vacancy shall occur, otherwise than by expiration of term, in the office of judge of the court of claims, it shall be filled for the unexpired term in the same manner as an original appointment.

c. When a vacancy shall occur, otherwise than by expiration of term, in the office of judge elected to the city-wide court of civil jurisdiction of the city of New York, it shall be filled for a full term at the next general election held not less than three months after such vacancy occurs and, until the vacancy shall be so filled, the mayor of the city of New York may fill such vacancy by an appointment which shall continue until and including the last day of December next after the election at which the vacancy shall be filled. When a vacancy shall occur, otherwise than by expiration of term on the last day of December of any year, in the office of judge appointed to the family court within the city of New York or the city-wide court of criminal jurisdiction of the city of New York, the mayor of the city of New York shall fill such vacancy by an appointment for the unexpired term.

d. When a vacancy shall occur, otherwise than by expiration of term, in the office of judge of the district court, it shall be filled for a full term at the next general election held not less than three months after such vacancy occurs and, until the vacancy shall be so filled, the board of supervisors or the supervisor or supervisors of the affected district if such district consists of a portion of a county or, in counties with an elected county executive officer, such county executive officer may, subject to confirmation by the board of supervisors or the supervisor or supervisors of such district, fill such vacancy by an appointment which shall continue until and including the last day of December next after the election at which the vacancy shall be filled.

[Commission on judicial conduct; composition; organization and procedure; review by court of appeals; discipline of judges or justices]

§22. a. There shall be a commission on judicial conduct. The commission on judicial conduct shall receive, initiate, investigate and hear complaints with respect to the conduct, qualifications, fitness to perform or performance of official duties of any judge or justice of the unified court system, in the manner provided by law; and, in accordance with subdivision d of this section, may determine that a judge or justice be admonished, censured or removed from office for cause, including, but not limited to, misconduct in office, persistent failure to perform his or her duties, habitual intemperance, and conduct, on or off the bench, prejudicial to the administration of justice, or that a judge or justice be retired for mental or physical disability preventing the proper performance of his or her judicial duties. The commission shall transmit an[9] such determination to the chief judge of the court of appeals who shall cause written notice of such determination to be given to the judge or justice involved. Such judge or justice may either accept the commission's determination or make written request to the chief judge, within thirty days after receipt of such notice, for a review of such determination by the court of appeals.

b. (1) The commission on judicial conduct shall consist of eleven members, of whom four shall be appointed by the governor, one by the temporary president of the senate, one by the minority leader of the senate, one by the speaker of the assembly, one by the minority leader of the assembly and three by the chief judge of the court of appeals. Of the

members appointed by the governor one person shall be a member of the bar of the state but not a judge or justice, two shall not be members of the bar, justices or judges or retired justices or judges of the unified court system, and one shall be a judge or justice of the unified court system. Of the members appointed by the chief judge one person shall be a justice of the appellate division of the supreme court and two shall be judges or justices of a court or courts other than the court of appeals or appellate divisions. None of the persons to be appointed by the legislative leaders shall be justices or judges or retired justices or judges.

(2) The persons first appointed by the governor shall have respectively one, two, three, and four-year terms as the governor shall designate. The persons first appointed by the chief judge of the court of appeals shall have respectively two, three, and four-year terms as the governor shall designate. The person first appointed by the temporary president of the senate shall have a one-year term. The person first appointed by the minority leader of the senate shall have a two-year term. The person first appointed by the speaker of the assembly shall have a four-year term. The person first appointed by the minority leader of the assembly shall have a three-year term. Each member of the commission shall be appointed thereafter for a term of four years. Commission membership of a judge or justice appointed by the governor or the chief judge shall terminate if such member ceases to hold the judicial position which qualified him or her for such appointment. Membership shall also terminate if a member attains a position which would have rendered him or her ineligible for appointment at the time of appointment. A vacancy shall be filled by the appointing officer for the remainder of the term.

c. The organization and procedure of the commission on judicial conduct shall be as provided by law. The commission on judicial conduct may establish its own rules and procedures not inconsistent with law. Unless the legislature shall provide otherwise, the commission shall be empowered to designate one of its members or any other person as a referee to hear and report concerning any matter before the commission.

d. In reviewing a determination of the commission on judicial conduct, the court of appeals may admonish, censure, remove or retire, for the reasons set forth in subdivision a of this section, any judge of the unified court system. In reviewing a determination of the commission on judicial conduct, the court of appeals shall review the commission's findings of fact and conclusions of law on the record of the proceedings upon which the commission's determination was based. The court of appeals may impose a less or more severe sanction prescribed by this section than the one determined by the commission, or impose no sanction.

e. The court of appeals may suspend a judge or justice from exercising the powers of his or her office while there is pending a determination by the commission on judicial conduct for his or her removal or retirement, or while the judge or justice is charged in this state with a felony by an indictment or an information filed pursuant to section six of article one. The suspension shall continue upon conviction and, if the conviction becomes final, the judge or justice shall be removed from office. The suspension shall be terminated upon reversal of the conviction and dismissal of the accusatory instrument. Nothing in this subdivision shall prevent the commission on judicial conduct from determining that a judge or justice be admonished, censured, removed, or retired pursuant to subdivision a of this section.

f. Upon the recommendation of the commission on judicial conduct or on its own motion, the court of appeals may suspend a judge or justice from office when he or she is charged with a crime punishable as a felony under the laws of this state, or any other crime which involves moral turpitude. The suspension shall continue upon conviction and, if the conviction becomes final, the judge or justice shall be removed from office. The suspension shall be terminated upon reversal of the conviction and dismissal of the accusatory instrument. Nothing in this subdivision shall prevent the commission on judicial conduct from determining that a judge or justice be admonished, censured, removed, or retired pursuant to subdivision a of this section.

g. A judge or justice who is suspended from office by the court of appeals shall receive his or her judicial salary during such period of suspension, unless the court directs otherwise. If the court has so directed

---

[9] As so in original ("an should be "any").

20

and such suspension is thereafter terminated, the court may direct that the judge or justice shall be paid his or her salary for such period of suspension.

h. A judge or justice retired by the court of appeals shall be considered to have retired voluntarily. A judge or justice removed by the court of appeals shall be ineligible to hold other judicial office.

i. Notwithstanding any other provision of this section, the legislature may provide by law for review of determinations of the commission on judicial conduct with respect to justices of town and village courts by an appellate division of the supreme court. In such event, all references in this section to the court of appeals and the chief judge thereof shall be deemed references to an appellate division and the presiding justice thereof, respectively.

j. If a court on the judiciary shall have been convened before the effective date of this section and the proceeding shall not be concluded by that date, the court on the judiciary shall have continuing jurisdiction beyond the effective date of this section to conclude the proceeding. All matters pending before the former commission on judicial conduct on the effective date of this section shall be disposed of in such manner as shall be provided by law. (Former §22 repealed and new §22 added by November 6, 2001.)

[Removal of judges]
§23. a. Judges of the court of appeals and justices of the supreme court may be removed by concurrent resolution of both houses of the legislature, if two-thirds of all the members elected to each house concur therein.

b. Judges of the court of claims, the county court, the surrogate's court, the family court, the courts for the city of New York established pursuant to section fifteen of this article, the district court and such other courts as the legislature may determine may be removed by the senate, on the recommendation of the governor, if two-thirds of all the members elected to the senate concur therein.

c. No judge or justice shall be removed by virtue of this section except for cause, which shall be entered on the journals, nor unless he or she shall have been served with a statement of the cause alleged, and shall have had an opportunity to be heard. On the question of removal, the yeas and nays shall be entered on the journal. (Amended by vote of the people November 6, 2001.)

[Court for trial of impeachments; judgment]
§24. The assembly shall have the power of impeachment by a vote of a majority of all the members elected thereto. The court for the trial of impeachments shall be composed of the president of the senate, the senators, or the major part of them, and the judges of the court of appeals, or the major part of them. On the trial of an impeachment against the governor or lieutenant-governor, neither the lieutenant-governor nor the temporary president of the senate shall act as a member of the court. No judicial officer shall exercise his or her office after articles of impeachment against him or her shall have been preferred to the senate, until he or she shall have been acquitted. Before the trial of an impeachment, the members of the court shall take an oath or affirmation truly and impartially to try the impeachment according to the evidence, and no person shall be convicted without the concurrence of two-thirds of the members present. Judgment in cases of impeachment shall not extend further than to removal from office, or removal from office and disqualification to hold and enjoy any public office of honor, trust, or profit under this state; but the party impeached shall be liable to indictment and punishment according to law. (Amended by vote of the people November 6, 2001.)

[Judges and justices; compensation; retirement]
§25. a. The compensation of a judge of the court of appeals, a justice of the supreme court, a judge of the court of claims, a judge of the county court, a judge of the surrogate's court, a judge of the family court, a judge of a court for the city of New York established pursuant to section fifteen of this article, a judge of the district court or of a retired judge or justice shall be established by law and shall not be diminished during the term of office for which he or she was elected or appointed. Any judge or justice of a court abolished by section thirty-five of this article, who pursuant to that section becomes a judge or justice of a court established or continued by this article, shall receive without interruption or diminution for the remainder of the term

for which he or she was elected or appointed to the abolished court the compensation he or she had been receiving upon the effective date of this article together with any additional compensation that may be prescribed by law.

b. Each judge of the court of appeals, justice of the supreme court, judge of the court of claims, judge of the county court, judge of the surrogate's court, judge of the family court, judge of a court for the city of New York established pursuant to section fifteen of this article and judge of the district court shall retire on the last day of December in the year in which he or she reaches the age of seventy. Each such former judge thereafter perform the duties of a justice of the supreme court, with power to hear and determine actions and proceedings, provided, however, that it shall be certificated in the manner provided by law that the services of such judge or justice are necessary to expedite the business of the court and that he or she is mentally and physically able and competent to perform the full duties of such office. Any such certification shall be valid for a term of two years and may be extended as provided by law for additional terms of two years. A retired judge or justice shall serve no longer than until the last day of December in the year in which he or she reaches the age of seventy-six. A retired judge or justice shall be subject to assignment by the appellate division of the supreme court of the judicial department of his or her residence. Any retired justice of the supreme court who had been designated to and served as a justice of any appellate division immediately preceding his or her reaching the age of seventy shall be eligible for designation by the governor as a temporary or additional justice of the appellate division. A retired judge or justice shall not be counted in determining the number of justices in a judicial district for purposes of subdivision d of section six of this article.

c. The provisions of this section shall also be applicable to any judge or justice who has not reached the age of seventy-six and to whom it would otherwise have been applicable but for the fact that he or she reached the age of seventy and retired before the effective date of this article. (Subdivision b amended by vote of the people November 8, 1966; further amended by vote of the people November 6, 2001.)

[Temporary assignments of judges and justices]
§26. a. A justice of the supreme court may perform the duties of office or hold court in any county and may be temporarily assigned to the supreme court in any judicial district or to the court of claims. A justice of the supreme court in the city of New York may be temporarily assigned to the family court in the city of New York or to the surrogate's court in any county within the city of New York when required to dispose of the business of such court.

b. A judge of the court of claims may perform the duties of office or hold court in any county and may be temporarily assigned to the supreme court in any judicial district.

c. A judge of the county court may perform the duties of office or hold court in any county and may be temporarily assigned to the supreme court in the judicial department of his or her residence or to the county court or the family court in any county or to the surrogate's court in any county outside the city of New York or to a court for the city of New York established pursuant to section fifteen of this article.

d. A judge of the surrogate's court in any county within the city of New York may perform the duties of office or hold court in any county and may be temporarily assigned to the supreme court in the judicial department of his or her residence.

e. A judge of the surrogate's court in any county outside the city of New York may perform the duties of office or hold court in any county and may be temporarily assigned to the supreme court in the judicial department of his or her residence or to the county court or the family court in any county or to a court for the city of New York established pursuant to section fifteen of this article.

f. A judge of the family court may perform the duties of office or hold court in any county and may be temporarily assigned to the supreme court in the judicial department of his or her residence or to the county court or the family court in any county or to the surrogate's court in any county outside the city of New York or to a court for the city of New York established pursuant to section fifteen of this article.

g. A judge of a court for the city of New York established pursuant to section fifteen of this article may perform the duties of office or hold court in

21

any county and may be temporarily assigned to the supreme court in the judicial department of his or her residence or to the county court or the family court in any county or to the other court for the city of New York established pursuant to section fifteen of this article.

h. A judge of the district court in any county may perform the duties of office or hold court in any county and may be temporarily assigned to the county court in the judicial department of his or her residence or to a court for the city of New York established pursuant to section fifteen of this article or to the district court in any county.

i. Temporary assignments of all the foregoing judges or justices listed in this section, and of judges of the city courts pursuant to paragraph two of subdivision j of this section, shall be made by the chief administrator of the courts in accordance with standards and administrative policies established pursuant to section twenty-eight of this article.

j. (1) The legislature may provide for temporary assignments within the county of residence or any adjoining county, of judges of town, village or city courts outside the city of New York.

(2) In addition to any temporary assignments to which a judge of a city court may be subject pursuant to paragraph one of this subdivision, such judge also may be temporarily assigned by the chief administrator of the courts to the county court, the family court or the district court within his or her county of residence or any adjoining county provided he or she is not permitted to practice law.

k. While temporarily assigned pursuant to the provisions of this section, any judge or justice shall have the powers, duties and jurisdiction of a judge or justice of the court to which assigned. After the expiration of any temporary assignment, as provided in this section, the judge or justice assigned shall have all the powers, duties and jurisdiction of a judge or justice of the court to which he or she was assigned with respect to matters pending before him or her during the term of such temporary assignment. (Subdivision i amended by vote of the people November 8, 1977; subdivision f amended by vote of the people November 8, 1983; further amended by vote of the people November 6, 2001.)

[Supreme court; extraordinary terms]
§27. The governor may, when in his or her opinion the public interest requires, appoint extraordinary terms of the supreme court. The governor shall designate the time and place of holding the term and the justice who shall hold the term. The governor may terminate the assignment of the justice and may name another justice in his or her place to hold the term. (Amended by vote of the people November 6, 2001.)

[Administrative supervision of court system]
§28. a. The chief judge of the court of appeals shall be the chief judge of the state of New York and shall be the chief judicial officer of the unified court system. There shall be an administrative board of the courts which shall consist of the chief judge of the court of appeals as chairperson and the presiding justice of the appellate division of the supreme court of each judicial department. The chief judge shall, with the advice and consent of the administrative board of the courts, appoint a chief administrator of the courts who shall serve at the pleasure of the chief judge.

b. The chief administrator, on behalf of the chief judge, shall supervise the administration and operation of the unified court system. In the exercise of such responsibility, the chief administrator of the courts shall have such powers and duties as may be delegated to him or her by the chief judge and such additional powers and duties as may be provided by law.

c. The chief judge, after consultation with the administrative board, shall establish standards and administrative policies for general application throughout the state, which shall be submitted by the chief judge to the court of appeals, together with the recommendations, if any, of the administrative board. Such standards and administrative policies shall be promulgated after approval by the court of appeals. (Formerly §28. Repealed and new §28 added by vote of the people November 8, 1977; amended by vote of the people November 6, 2001.)

[Expenses of courts]
§29. a. The legislature shall provide for the allocation of the cost of operating and maintaining the court of appeals, the appellate division of the supreme court in each judicial department, the supreme court, the court of claims, the county court, the surrogate's court, the family court, the courts for the city of New York established pursuant to section fifteen of this article and the district court, among the state, the counties, the city of New York and other political subdivisions.

b. The legislature shall provide for the submission of the itemized estimates of the annual financial needs of the courts referred to in subdivision a of this section to the chief administrator of the courts to be forwarded to the appropriating bodies with recommendations and comment.

c. Insofar as the expense of the courts is borne by the state or paid by the state in the first instance, the final determination of the itemized estimates of the annual financial needs of the courts shall be made by the legislature and the governor in accordance with articles four and seven of this constitution.

d. Insofar as the expense of the courts is not paid by the state in the first instance and is borne by counties, the city of New York or other political subdivisions, the final determination of the itemized estimates of the annual financial needs of the courts shall be made by the appropriate governing bodies of such counties, the city of New York or other political subdivisions. (Subdivision b amended by vote of the people November 8, 1977.)

[Legislative power over jurisdiction and proceedings; delegation of power to regulate practice and procedure]
§30. The legislature shall have the same power to alter and regulate the jurisdiction and proceedings in law and in equity that it has heretofore exercised. The legislature may, on such terms as it shall provide and subject to subsequent modification, delegate, in whole or in part, to a court, including the appellate division of the supreme court, or to the chief administrator of the courts, any power possessed by the legislature to regulate practice and procedure in the courts. The chief administrator of the courts shall exercise any such power delegated to him or her with the advice and consent of the administrative board of the courts. Nothing herein contained shall prevent the adoption of regulations by individual courts consistent with the general practice and procedure as provided by statute or general rules. (Amended by vote of the people November 8, 1977.)

[Inapplicability of article to certain courts]
§31. This article does not apply to the peacemakers courts or other Indian courts, the existence and operation of which shall continue as may be provided by law.

[Custodians of children to be of same religious persuasion]
§32. When any court having jurisdiction over a child shall commit it or remand it to an institution or agency or place it in the custody of any person by parole, placing out, adoption or guardianship, the child shall be committed or remanded or placed, when practicable, in an institution or agency governed by persons, or in the custody of a person, of the same religious persuasion as the child.

[Existing laws; duty of legislature to implement article]
§33. Existing provisions of law not inconsistent with this article shall continue in force until repealed, amended, modified or superseded in accordance with the provisions of this article. The legislature shall enact appropriate laws to carry into effect the purposes and provisions of this article, and may, for the purpose of implementing, supplementing or clarifying any of its provisions, enact any laws, not inconsistent with the provisions of this article, necessary or desirable in promoting the objectives of this article.

[Pending appeals, actions and proceedings; preservation of existing terms of office of judges and justices]
§34. a. The court of appeals, the appellate division of the supreme court, the supreme court, the court of claims, the county court in counties outside the city of New York, the surrogate's court and the district court of Nassau county shall hear and determine all appeals, actions and proceedings pending therein on the effective date of this article except that the appellate division of the supreme court in the first and second judicial departments or the appellate term in such departments, if so directed by the appropriate appellate division of the supreme court, shall hear and determine all appeals

22

pending in the appellate terms of the supreme court in the first and second judicial departments and in the court of special sessions of the city of New York and except that the county court or an appellate term shall, as may be provided by law, hear and determine all appeals pending in the county court or the supreme court other than an appellate term. Further appeal from a decision of the county court, the appellate term or the appellate division of the supreme court, rendered on or after the effective date of this article, shall be governed by the provisions of this article.

b. The justices of the supreme court in office on the effective date of this article shall hold their offices as justices of the supreme court until the expiration of their respective terms.

c. The judges of the court of claims in office on the effective date of this article shall hold their offices as judges of the court of claims until the expiration of their respective terms.

d. The surrogates, and county judges outside the city of New York, including the special county judges of the counties of Erie and Suffolk, in office on the effective date of this article shall hold office as judges of the surrogate's court or county judge, respectively, of such counties until the expiration of their respective terms.

e. The judges of the district court of Nassau county in office on the effective date of this article shall hold their offices until the expiration of their respective terms.

f. Judges of courts for towns, villages and cities outside the city of New York in office on the effective date of this article shall hold their offices until the expiration of their respective terms.

[Certain courts abolished; transfer of judges, court personnel, and actions and proceedings to other courts]

§35. a. The children's courts, the court of general sessions of the county of New York, the county courts of the counties of Bronx, Kings, Queens and Richmond, the city court of the city of New York, the domestic relations court of the city of New York, the municipal court of the city of New York, the court of special sessions of the city of New York and the city magistrates' courts of the city of New York are abolished from and after the effective date of this article and thereupon the seals, records, papers and documents of or belonging to such courts shall, unless otherwise provided by law, be deposited in the offices of the clerks of the several counties in which these courts now exist.

b. The judges of the county court of the counties of Bronx, Kings, Queens and Richmond and the judges of the court of general sessions of the county of New York in office on the effective date of this article appointed, be justices of the supreme court in and for the judicial district which includes the county in which they resided on that date. The salaries of such justices shall be the same as the salaries of the other justices of the supreme court residing in the same judicial district and shall be paid in the same manner. All actions and proceedings pending in the county court of the counties of Bronx, Kings, Queens and Richmond and in the court of general sessions of the county of New York on the effective date of this article shall be transferred to the supreme court in the county in which the action or proceedings was pending, or otherwise as may be provided by law.

c. The legislature shall provide by law that the justices of the city court of the city of New York and the justices of the municipal court of the city of New York in office on the date such courts are abolished shall, for the remainder of the term for which each was elected or appointed, be judges of the city-wide court of civil jurisdiction of the city of New York established pursuant to section fifteen of this article and for such district as the legislature may determine.

d. The legislature shall provide by law that the justices of the court of special sessions and the magistrates of the city magistrates' courts of the city of New York in office on the date such courts are abolished shall, for the remainder of the term for which each was appointed, be judges of the city-wide court of criminal jurisdiction of the city of New York established pursuant to section fifteen provided, however, that each term shall expire on the last day of the year in which it would have expired except for the provisions of this article.

e. All actions and proceedings pending in the city court of the city of New York and the municipal court in the city of New York on the date such courts are abolished shall be transferred to the city-wide court of civil jurisdiction of the city of New York established pursuant to section fifteen of this article or as otherwise provided by law.

f. All actions and proceedings pending in the court of special sessions of the city of New York and the city magistrates' courts of the city of New York on the date such courts are abolished shall be transferred to the city-wide court of criminal jurisdiction of the city of New York established pursuant to section fifteen of this article or as otherwise provided by law.

g. The special county judges of the counties of Broome, Chautauqua, Jefferson, Oneida and Rockland and the judges of the children's courts in all counties outside the city of New York in office on the effective date of this article shall, for the remainder of the terms for which they were elected or appointed, be judges of the family court in and for the county in which they hold office. Except as otherwise provided in this section, the office of special county judge and the office of special surrogate is abolished from and after the effective date of this article and the terms of the persons holding such offices shall terminate on that date.

h. All actions and proceedings pending in the children's courts in counties outside the city of New York on the effective date of this article shall be transferred to the family court in the respective counties.

i. The justices of the domestic relations court of the city of New York in office on the effective date of this article shall, for the remainder of the terms for which they were appointed, be judges of the family court within the city of New York.

j. All actions and proceedings pending in the domestic relations court of the city of New York on the effective date of this article shall be transferred to the family court in the city of New York.

k. The office of official referee is abolished, provided, however, that official referees in office on the effective date of this article shall, for the remainder of the terms for which they were appointed or certified, be official referees of the court in which appointed or certified or the successor court, as the case may be. At the expiration of the term of any official referee, his or her office shall be abolished and thereupon such former official referee shall be subject to the relevant provisions of section twenty-five of this article.

l. As may be provided by law, the non-judicial personnel of the courts affected by this article in office on the effective date of this article shall, to the extent practicable, be continued without diminution of salaries and with the same status and rights in the courts established or continued by this article; and especially skilled, experienced and trained personnel shall, to the extent practicable, be assigned to like functions in the courts which exercise the jurisdiction formerly exercised by the courts in which they were employed. In the event that the adoption of this article shall require or make possible a reduction in the number of non-judicial personnel, or in the number of certain categories of such personnel, such reduction shall be made, to the extent practicable, by provision that the death, resignation, removal or retirement of an employee shall not create a vacancy until the reduced number of personnel has been reached.

m. In the event that a judgment or order was entered before the effective date of this article and a right of appeal existed and notice of appeal therefrom is filed after the effective date of this article, such appeal shall be taken from the supreme court, the county courts, the surrogate's courts, the children's courts, the court of general sessions of the county of New York and the domestic relations court of the city of New York to the appellate division of the supreme court in the judicial department in which such court was located; from the court of claims to the appellate division of the supreme court in the third judicial department, except for those claims which arose in the fourth judicial department, in which case the appeal shall be to the appellate division of the supreme court in the fourth judicial department; from the city court of the city of New York, the municipal court of the city of New York, the court of special sessions of the city of New York and the city magistrates' courts of the city of New York to the appellate division of the supreme court in the judicial department in which such court was located, provided, however, that such appellate division of the supreme court may transfer any such appeal to an appellate term, if such appellate term be established; and from the district court, town, village and city courts outside the city of New York to the county court in the county in which such court was located, provided, however, that the legislature may require the transfer of any such appeal to an appellate term, if such appellate term be

23

established. Further appeal from a decision of a county court or an appellate term or the appellate division of the supreme court shall be governed by the provisions of this article. However, if in any action or proceeding decided prior to the effective date of this article, a party had a right of direct appeal from a court of original jurisdiction to the court of appeals, such appeal may be taken directly to the court of appeals.

n. In the event that an appeal was decided before the effective date of this article and a further appeal could be taken as of right and notice of appeal therefrom is filed after the effective date of this article, such appeal may be taken from the appellate division of the supreme court to the court of appeals and from any other court to the appellate division of the supreme court. Further appeal from a decision of the appellate division of the supreme court shall be governed by the provisions of this article. If a further appeal could not be taken as of right, such appeal shall be governed by the provisions of this article. (Amended by vote of the people November 6, 2001.)

[Pending civil and criminal cases]
§36. No civil or criminal appeal, action or proceeding pending before any court or any judge or justice on the effective date of this article shall abate but such appeal, action or proceeding so pending shall be continued in the courts as provided in this article and, for the purposes of the disposition of such actions or proceedings only, the jurisdiction of any court to which any such action or proceeding is transferred by this article shall be coextensive with the jurisdiction of the former court from which the action or proceeding was transferred. Except to the extent inconsistent with the provisions of this article, subsequent proceedings in such appeal, action or proceeding shall be conducted in accordance with the laws in force on the effective date of this article until superseded in the manner authorized by law.

[Effective date of certain amendments to articles VI and VII]
§36-a. The amendments to the provisions of sections two, four, seven, eight, eleven, twenty, twenty-two, twenty-six, twenty-eight, twenty-nine and thirty of article six and to the provisions of section one of article seven, as first proposed by a concurrent resolution passed by the legislature in the year nineteen hundred seventy-six and entitled "Concurrent Resolution of the Senate and Assembly proposing amendments to articles six and seven of the constitution, in relation to the manner of selecting judges of the court of appeals, creation of a commission on judicial conduct and administration of the unified court system, providing for the effectiveness of such amendments and the repeal of subdivision c of section two, subdivision b of section seven, subdivision b of section eleven, section twenty-two and section twenty-eight of article six thereof relating thereto", shall become a part of the constitution on the first day of January next after the approval and ratification of the amendments proposed by such concurrent resolution by the people but the provisions thereof shall not become operative and the repeal of subdivision c of section two, section twenty-two and section twenty-eight shall not become effective until the first day of April next thereafter which date shall be deemed the effective date of such amendments and the chief judge and the associate judges of the court of appeals in office on such effective date shall hold their offices until the expiration of their respective terms. Upon a vacancy in the office of any such judge, such vacancy shall be filled in the manner provided in section two of article six. (New. Added by vote of the people November 8, 1977.)

[No section 36-b]

[Effective date of certain amendments to article VI, section 22]
§36-c. The amendments to the provisions of section twenty-two of article six as first proposed by a concurrent resolution passed by the legislature in the year nineteen hundred seventy-four and entitled "Concurrent Resolution of the Senate and Assembly proposing an amendment to section twenty-two of article six and adding section thirty-six-c to such article of the constitution, in relation to the powers of and reconstituting the court on the judiciary and creating a commission on judicial conduct", shall become a part of the constitution on the first day of January next after the approval and ratification of the amendments proposed by such concurrent resolution by the people but the provisions thereof shall not become operative until the first day of September next thereafter which date shall be deemed the effective date

24

of such amendments. (New. Added by vote of the people November 4, 1975.)

[Effective date of article]
§37. This article shall become a part of the constitution on the first day of January next after the approval and ratification of this amendment by the people but its provisions shall not become operative until the first day of September next thereafter which date shall be deemed the effective date of this article.

ARTICLE VII
STATE FINANCES

[Estimates by departments, the legislature and the judiciary of needed appropriations; hearings]
Section 1. For the preparation of the budget, the head of each department of state government, except the legislature and judiciary, shall furnish the governor such estimates and information in such form and at such times as the governor may require, copies of which shall forthwith be furnished to the appropriate committees of the legislature. The governor shall hold hearings thereon at which the governor may require the attendance of heads of departments and their subordinates. Designated representatives of such committees shall be entitled to attend the hearings thereon and to make inquiry concerning any part thereof.

Itemized estimates of the financial needs of the legislature, certified by the presiding officer of each house, and of the judiciary, approved by the court of appeals and certified by the chief judge of the court of appeals, shall be transmitted to the governor not later than the first day of December in each year for inclusion in the budget without revision but with such recommendations as the governor may deem proper. Copies of the itemized estimates of the financial needs of the judiciary also shall forthwith be transmitted to the appropriate committees of the legislature. (Amended by vote of the people November 8, 1977; November 6, 2001.)

[Executive budget]
§2. Annually, on or before the first day of February in each year following the year fixed by the constitution for the election of governor and lieutenant governor, and on or before the second Tuesday following the first day of the annual meeting of the legislature, in all other years, the governor shall submit to the legislature a budget containing a complete plan of expenditures proposed to be made before the close of the ensuing fiscal year and all moneys and revenues estimated to be available therefor, together with an explanation of the basis of such estimates and recommendations as to proposed legislation, if any, which the governor may deem necessary to provide moneys and revenues sufficient to meet such proposed expenditures. It shall also contain such other recommendations and information as the governor may deem proper and such additional information as may be required by law. (New. Derived in part from former §2 of Art. 4-a. Adopted by Constitutional Convention of 1938 and approved by vote of the people November 8, 1938; amended by vote of the people November 2, 1965; November 6, 2001.)

[Budget bills; appearances before legislature]
§3. At the time of submitting the budget to the legislature the governor shall submit a bill or bills containing all the proposed appropriations and reappropriations included in the budget and the proposed legislation, if any, recommended therein.

The governor may at any time within thirty days thereafter and, with the consent of the legislature, at any time before the adjournment thereof, amend or supplement the budget and submit amendments to any bills submitted by him or her or submit supplemental bills.

The governor and the heads of departments shall have the right, and it shall be the duty of the heads of departments when requested by either house of the legislature or an appropriate committee thereof, to appear and be heard in respect to the budget during the consideration thereof, and to answer inquiries relevant thereto. The procedure for such appearances and inquiries shall be provided by law. (New. Derived in part from former §§2 and 3 of

Art. 4-a. Adopted by Constitutional Convention of 1938 and approved by vote of the people November 8, 1938; amended by vote of the people November 6, 2001.)

[Action on budget bills by legislature; effect thereof]
§4. The legislature may not alter an appropriation bill submitted by the governor except to strike out or reduce items therein, but it may add thereto items of appropriation provided that such additions are stated separately and distinctly from the original items of the bill and refer each to a single object or purpose. None of the restrictions of this section, however, shall apply to appropriations for the legislature or judiciary.

Such an appropriation bill shall when passed by both houses be a law immediately without further action by the governor, except that appropriations for the legislature and judiciary and separate items added to the governor's bills by the legislature shall be subject to approval of the governor as provided in section 7 of article IV. (New. Derived in part from former §3 of Art. 4-a. Adopted by Constitutional Convention of 1938 and approved by vote of the people November 8, 1938; amended by vote of the people November 6, 2001.)

[Restrictions on consideration of other appropriations]
§5. Neither house of the legislature shall consider any other bill making an appropriation until all the appropriation bills submitted by the governor shall have been finally acted on by both houses, except on message from the governor certifying to the necessity of the immediate passage of such a bill. (New. Derived in part from former §4 of Art. 4-a. Adopted by Constitutional Convention of 1938 and approved by vote of the people November 8, 1938.)

[Restrictions on content of appropriation bills]
§6. Except for appropriations contained in the bills submitted by the governor and in a supplemental appropriation bill for the support of government, no appropriations shall be made except by separate bills each for a single object or purpose. All such bills and such supplemental appropriation bill shall be subject to the governor's approval as provided in section 7 of article IV.

No provision shall be embraced in any appropriation bill submitted by the governor or in such supplemental appropriation bill unless it relates specifically to some particular appropriation in the bill, and any such provision shall be limited in its operation to such appropriation. (New. Derived in part from former §22 of Art. 3 and former §4 of Art. 4-a. Adopted by Constitutional Convention of 1938 and approved by vote of the people November 8, 1938.)

[Appropriation bills]
§7. No money shall ever be paid out of the state treasury or any of its funds, or any of the funds under its management, except in pursuance of an appropriation by law; nor unless such payment be made within two years next after the passage of such appropriation act; and every such law making a new appropriation or continuing or reviving an appropriation, shall distinctly specify the sum appropriated, and the object or purpose to which it is to be applied; and it shall not be sufficient for such law to refer to any other law to fix such sum. (New. Derived in part from former §21 of Art. 3. Adopted by Constitutional Convention of 1938 and approved by vote of the people November 8, 1938.)

[Gift or loan of state credit or money prohibited; exceptions for enumerated purposes]
§8. 1. The money of the state shall not be given or loaned to or in aid of any private corporation or association, or private undertaking; nor shall the credit of the state be given or loaned to or in aid of any individual, or public or private corporation or association, or private undertaking, but the foregoing provisions shall not apply to any fund or property now held or which may hereafter be held by the state for educational, mental health or mental retardation purposes.

2. Subject to the limitations on indebtedness and taxation, nothing in this constitution contained shall prevent the legislature from providing for the aid, care and support of the needy directly or through subdivisions of the state; or for the protection by insurance or otherwise, against the hazards of unemployment, sickness and old age; or for the education and support of the blind, the deaf, the dumb, the physically handicapped, the mentally ill, the emotionally disturbed, the mentally retarded or juvenile delinquents as it may deem proper; or for health and welfare services for all children, either directly or through subdivisions of the state, including school districts; or for the aid, care and support of neglected and dependent children and of the needy sick, through agencies and institutions authorized by the state board of social welfare or other state department having the power of inspection thereof, by payments made on a per capita basis directly or through the subdivisions of the state; or for the increase in the amount of pensions of any member of a retirement system of the state, or of a subdivision of the state; or for an increase in the amount of pension benefits of any widow or widower of a retired member of a retirement system of the state or of a subdivision of the state to whom payable as beneficiary under an optional settlement in connection with the pension of such member. The enumeration of legislative powers in this paragraph shall not be taken to diminish any power of the legislature hitherto existing.

3. Nothing in this constitution contained shall prevent the legislature from authorizing the loan of the money of the state to a public corporation to be organized for the purpose of making loans to non-profit corporations or for the purpose of guaranteeing loans made by banking organizations, as that term shall be defined by the legislature, to finance the construction of new industrial or manufacturing plants, the construction of new buildings to be used for research and development, the construction of other eligible business facilities, and for the purchase of machinery and equipment related to such new industrial or manufacturing plants, research and development buildings, and other eligible business facilities in this state or the acquisition, rehabilitation or improvement of former or existing industrial or manufacturing plants, buildings to be used for research and development, other eligible business facilities, and machinery and equipment in this state, including the acquisition of real property therefor, and the use of such money by such public corporation for such purposes, to improve employment opportunities in any area of the state, provided, however, that any such plants, buildings or facilities or machinery and equipment therefor shall not be (i) primarily used in making retail sales of goods or services to customers who personally visit such facilities to obtain such goods or services or (ii) used primarily as a hotel, apartment house or other place of business which furnishes dwelling space or accommodations to either residents or transients, and provided further that any loan by such public corporation shall not exceed sixty per centum of the cost of any such project and the repayment of which shall be secured by a mortgage thereon which shall not be a junior encumbrance thereon by more than fifty per centum of such cost or by a security interest if personalty, and that the amount of any guarantee of a loan made by a banking organization shall not exceed eighty per centum of the cost of any such project. (Formerly §1. Derived in part from former §9 of Art. 8. Renumbered and amended by Constitutional Convention of 1938 and approved by vote of the people November 8, 1938; further amended by vote of the people November 6, 1951; November 7, 1961; November 8, 1966; November 6, 1973; November 8, 1977; November 5, 1985; November 6, 2001.)

[Short term state debts in anticipation of taxes, revenues and proceeds of sale of authorized bonds]
§9. The state may contract debts in anticipation of the receipt of taxes and revenues, direct or indirect, for the purposes and within the amounts of appropriations theretofore made. Notes or other obligations for the moneys so borrowed shall be issued as may be provided by law, and shall with the interest thereon be paid from such taxes and revenues within one year from the date of issue.

The state may also contract debts in anticipation of the receipt of the proceeds of the sale of bonds theretofore authorized, for the purpose and within the amounts of the bonds so authorized. Notes or obligations for the money so borrowed shall be issued as may be provided by law, and shall with the interest thereon be paid from the proceeds of the sale of such bonds within two years from the date of issue, except as to bonds issued or to be issued for any of the purposes authorized by article eighteen of this constitution, in which event the notes or obligations shall with the interest thereon be paid from the proceeds of the sale of such bonds within five years from the date of issue. (Formerly §2. Renumbered and amended by Constitutional

25

Convention of 1938 and approved by vote of the people November 8, 1938; further amended by vote of the people November 4, 1958; November 7, 1995.)

[State debts on account of invasion, insurrection, war and forest fires]

§10. In addition to the above limited power to contract debts, the state may contract debts to repel invasion, suppress insurrection, or defend the state in war, or to suppress forest fires; but the money arising from the contracting of such debts shall be applied for the purpose for which it was raised, or to repay such debts, and to no other purpose whatever. (Formerly §3. Renumbered by Constitutional Convention of 1938 and approved by vote of the people November 8, 1938.)

[State debts generally; manner of contracting; referendum]

§11. Except the debts or refunding debts specified in sections 9, 10 and 13 of this article, no debt shall be hereafter contracted by or in behalf of the state, unless such debt shall be authorized by law, for some single work or purpose, to be distinctly specified therein. No such law shall take effect until it shall, at a general election, have been submitted to the people, and have received a majority of all the votes cast for and against it at such election nor shall it be submitted to be voted on within three months after its passage nor at any general election when any other law or any bill shall be submitted to be voted for or against.

The legislature may, at any time after the approval of such law by the people, if no debt shall have been contracted in pursuance thereof, repeal the same; and may at any time, by law, forbid the contracting of any further debt or liability under such law. (Formerly §4. Renumbered and amended by Constitutional Convention of 1938 and approved by vote of the people November 8, 1938; further amended by vote of the people November 2, 1993.)

[State debts generally; how paid; contribution to sinking funds; restrictions on use of bond proceeds]

§12. Except the debts or refunding debts specified in sections 9, 10 and 13 of this article, all debts contracted by the state and each portion of any such debt from time to time so contracted shall be subject to the following rules:

1. The principal of each debt or any portion thereof shall either be paid in equal annual installments or in installments that result in substantially level or declining debt service payments such as shall be authorized by law, or, in the alternative, contributions of principal in the amount that would otherwise be required to be paid annually shall be made to a sinking fund.

2. When some portions of the same debt are payable annually while other portions require contributions to a sinking fund, the entire debt shall be structured so that the combined amount of annual installments of principal paid and/or annual contributions of principal made in each year shall be equal to the amount that would be required to be paid if the entire debt were payable in annual installments.

3. When interest on state obligations is not paid at least annually, there shall also be contributed to a sinking fund at least annually, the amount necessary to bring the balance thereof, including income earned on contributions, to the accreted value of the obligations to be paid therefrom on the date such contribution is made, less the sum of all required future contributions of principal, in the case of sinking fund obligations, or payments of principal, in the case of serial obligations. Notwithstanding the foregoing, nothing contained in this subdivision shall be deemed to require contributions for interest to sinking funds if total debt service due on the debt or portion thereof in the year such interest is due will be substantially the same as the total debt service due on such debt or portion thereof in each other year or if the total amount of debt service due in each subsequent year on such debt or portion thereof shall be less than the total debt service due in each prior year.

4. The first annual installment on such debt shall be paid, or the first annual contribution shall be made to a sinking fund, not more than one year, and the last installment shall be paid, or contribution made not more than forty years, after such debt or portion thereof shall have been contracted, provided, however, that in contracting any such debt the privilege of paying all or any part of such debt prior to the date on which the same shall be due may be reserved to the state in such manner as may be provided by law.

5. No such debt shall be contracted for a period longer than that of the probable life of the work or purpose for which the debt is to be contracted, or in the alternative, the weighted average period of probable life of the works or purposes for which such indebtedness is to be contracted. The probable lives of such works or purposes shall be determined by general laws, which determination shall be conclusive.

6. The money arising from any loan creating such debt or liability shall be applied only to the work or purpose specified in the act authorizing such debt or liability, or for the payment of such debt or liability, including any notes or obligations issued in anticipation of the sale of bonds evidencing such debt or liability.

7. Any sinking funds created pursuant to this section shall be maintained and managed by the state comptroller or an agent or trustee designated by the state comptroller, and amounts in sinking funds created pursuant to this section, and earnings thereon, shall be used solely for the purpose of retiring the obligations secured thereby except that amounts in excess of the required balance on any contribution date and amounts remaining in such funds after all of the obligations secured thereby have been retired shall be deposited in the general fund.

8. No appropriation shall be required for disbursement of money, or income earned thereon, from any sinking fund created pursuant to this section for the purpose of paying principal of and interest on the obligations for which such fund was created, except that interest shall be paid from any such fund only if, and to the extent that, it is not payable annually and contributions on account of such interest were made thereto.

9. The provisions of section 15 of this article shall not apply to sinking funds created pursuant to this section.

10. When state obligations are sold at a discount, the debt incurred for purposes of determining the amount of debt issued or outstanding pursuant to a voter approved bond referendum or other limitation on the amount of debt that may be issued or outstanding for a work or purpose shall be deemed to include only the amount of money actually received by the state notwithstanding the face amount of such obligations. (Derived in part from former §4. Renumbered and amended by Constitutional Convention of 1938 and approved by vote of the people November 8, 1938; further amended by vote of the people, November 2, 1993.)

[Refund of state debts]

§13. The legislature may provide means and authority whereby any state debt or debts, or any portion or combination thereof, may be refunded in accordance with the following provisions:

1. State debts may be refunded at any time after they are incurred provided that the state will achieve a debt service savings on a present value basis as a result of the refunding transaction, and further provided that no maturity shall be called for redemption unless the privilege to pay prior to the maturity date was reserved to the state. The legislature may provide for the method of computation of present value for such purpose.

2. In no event shall refunding obligations be issued in an amount exceeding that necessary to provide sufficient funds to accomplish the refunding of the obligations to be refunded including paying all costs and expenses related to the refunding transaction and, in no event, shall the proceeds of refunding obligations be applied to any purpose other than accomplishing the refunding of the debt to be refunded and paying costs and expenses related to the refunding.

3. Proceeds of refunding obligations shall be deposited in escrow funds which shall be maintained and managed by the state comptroller or by an agent or trustee designated by the state comptroller and no legislative appropriation shall be required for disbursement of money, or income earned thereon, from such escrow funds for the purposes enumerated in this section.

4. Refunding obligations may be refunded pursuant to this section.

5. Refunding obligations shall either be paid in annual installments or annual contributions shall be made to a sinking fund in amounts sufficient to retire the refunding obligations at their maturity. No annual installments or contributions of principal need be made with respect to all or any portion of an issue of refunding obligations in years when debt service on such refunding obligations or portion thereof is paid or contributed

26

entirely from an escrow fund created pursuant to subdivision 3 of this section or in years when no installments or contributions would have been due on the obligations to be refunded. So long as any of the refunding obligations remain outstanding, installments or contributions shall be made in any years that installments or contributions would have been due on the obligations to be refunded.

6. In no event shall the last annual installment or contribution on any portion of refunding debt, including refunding obligations issued to refund other refunding obligations, be made after the termination of the period of probable life of the projects financed with the proceeds of the relevant portion of the debt to be refunded, or any debt previously refunded with the refunding obligations to be refunded, determined as of the date of issuance of the original obligations pursuant to section 12 of this article to finance such projects, or forty years from such date, if earlier; provided, however, that in lieu of the foregoing, an entire refunding issue or portion thereof may be structured to mature over the remaining weighted average useful life of all projects financed with the obligations being refunded.

7. Subject to the provisions of subdivision 5 of this section, each annual installment or contribution of principal of refunding obligations shall be equal to the amount that would be required by subdivision 1 of section 12 of this article if such installments or contributions were required to be made from the year that the next installment or contribution would have been due on the obligations to be refunded, if they had not been refunded, until the final maturity of the refunding obligations but excluding any year in which no installment or contribution would have been due on the obligations to be refunded or, in the alternative, the total payments of principal and interest on the refunding bonds shall be less in each year to their final maturity than the total payments of principal and interest on the bonds to be refunded in each such year.

8. The provisions of subdivision 3 and subdivisions 7 through 9 of section 12 of this article shall apply to sinking funds created pursuant to this section for the payment at maturity of refunding obligations. (New. Adopted by Constitutional Convention of 1938 and approved by vote of the people November 8, 1938; further amended by vote of the people November 2, 1993.)

[State debt for elimination of railroad crossings at grade; expenses; how borne; construction and reconstruction of state highways and parkways]
§14. The legislature may authorize by law the creation of a debt or debts of the state, not exceeding in the aggregate three hundred million dollars, to provide moneys for the elimination, under state supervision, of railroad crossings at grade within the state, and for incidental improvements connected therewith as authorized by this section. The provisions of this article, not inconsistent with this section, relating to the issuance of bonds for a debt or debts of the state and the maturity and payment thereof, shall apply to a state debt or debts created pursuant to this section; except that the law authorizing the contracting of such debt or debts shall take effect without submission to the people pursuant to section 11 of this article. The aggregate amount of a state debt or debts which may be created pursuant to this section shall not exceed the difference between the amount of the debt or debts heretofore created or authorized by law, under the provisions of section 14 of article VII of the constitution in force on July first, nineteen hundred thirty-eight, and the sum of three hundred million dollars.

The expense of any grade crossing elimination the construction work for which was not commenced before January first, nineteen hundred thirty-nine, including incidental improvements connected therewith as authorized by this section, whether or not an order for such elimination shall theretofore have been made, shall be paid by the state in the first instance, but the state shall be entitled to recover from the railroad company or companies, by way of reimbursement (1) the entire amount of the railroad improvements not an essential part of elimination, and (2) the amount of the net benefit to the company or companies from the elimination exclusive of such railroad improvements, the amount of such net benefit to be adjudicated after the completion of the work in the manner to be prescribed by law, and in no event to exceed fifteen per centum of the expense of the elimination, exclusive of all incidental improvements. The reimbursement by the railroad companies shall be payable at such times, in such manner and with interest at such rate as the legislature may prescribe.

The expense of any grade crossing elimination the construction work for which was commenced before January first, nineteen hundred thirty-nine, shall be borne by the state, railroad companies, and the municipality or municipalities in the proportions formerly prescribed by section 14 of article VII of the constitution in force on July first, nineteen hundred thirty-eight, and the law or laws enacted pursuant to its provisions, applicable to such elimination, and subject to the provisions of such former section and law or laws, including advances in aid of any railroad company or municipality, although such elimination shall not be completed until after January first, nineteen hundred thirty-nine.

A grade crossing elimination the construction work for which shall be commenced after January first, nineteen hundred thirty-nine, shall include incidental improvements rendered necessary or desirable because of such elimination, and reasonably included in the engineering plans therefor. Out of the balance of all moneys authorized to be expended under section 14 of article VII of the constitution in force on July first, nineteen hundred thirty-eight, and remaining unexpended and unobligated on such date, fifty million dollars shall be deemed segregated for grade crossing eliminations and incidental improvements in the city of New York and shall be available only for such purposes until such eliminations and improvements are completed and paid for.

Notwithstanding any of the foregoing provisions of this section the legislature is hereby authorized to appropriate, out of the proceeds of bonds now or hereafter sold to provide moneys for the elimination of railroad crossings at grade and incidental improvements pursuant to this section, sums not exceeding in the aggregate sixty million dollars for the construction and reconstruction of state highways and parkways. (Amended by Constitutional Convention of 1938 and approved by vote of the people November 8, 1938; further amended by vote of the people November 4, 1941.)

[Sinking funds; how kept and invested; income therefrom and application thereof]
§15. The sinking funds provided for the payment of interest and the extinguishment of the principal of the debts of the state heretofore contracted shall be continued; they shall be separately kept and safely invested, and neither of them shall be appropriated or used in any manner other than for such payment and extinguishment as hereinafter provided. The comptroller shall each year appraise the securities held for investment in each of such funds at their fair market value not exceeding par. The comptroller shall then determine and certify to the legislature the amount of each of such funds and the amounts which, if thereafter annually contributed to each such fund, would, with the fund and with the accumulations thereon and upon the contributions thereto, computed at the rate of three per centum per annum, produce at the date of maturity the amount of the debt to retire which such fund was created, and the legislature shall thereupon appropriate as the contribution to each such fund for such year at least the amount thus certified.

If the income of any such fund in any year is more than a sum which, if annually added to such fund would, with the fund and its accumulations as aforesaid, retire the debt at maturity, the excess income may be applied to the interest on the debt for which the fund was created.

After any sinking fund shall equal in amount the debt for which it was created no further contribution shall be made thereto except to make good any losses ascertained at the annual appraisals above mentioned, and the income thereof shall be applied to the payment of the interest on such debt. Any excess in such income not required for the payment of interest may be applied to the general fund of the state. (Formerly §5. Renumbered and amended by Constitutional Convention of 1938 and approved by vote of the people November 8, 1938; further amended by vote of the people November 6, 2001.)

[Payment of state debts; when comptroller to pay without appropriation]
§16. The legislature shall annually provide by appropriation for the payment of the interest upon and installments of principal of all debts or refunding debts created on behalf of the state except those contracted under section 9 of this article, as the same shall fall due, and for the contribution to all of the sinking funds created by law, of the amounts annually to be

27

contributed under the provisions of section 12, 13 or 15 of this article. If at any time the legislature shall fail to make any such appropriation, the comptroller shall set apart from the first revenues thereafter received, applicable to the general fund of the state, a sum sufficient to pay such interest, installments of principal, or contributions to such sinking fund, as the case may be, and shall so apply the moneys thus set apart. The comptroller may be required to set aside and apply such revenues as aforesaid, at the suit of any holder of such bonds.

Notwithstanding the foregoing provisions of this section, the comptroller may covenant with the purchasers of any state obligations that they shall have no further rights against the state for payment of such obligations or any interest thereon after an amount or amounts determined in accordance with the provisions of such covenant is deposited in a described fund or with a named or described agency or trustee. In such case, this section shall have no further application with respect to payment of such obligations or any interest thereon after the comptroller has complied with the prescribed conditions of such covenant. (Formerly §11. Renumbered and amended by Constitutional Convention of 1938 and approved by vote of the people November 8, 1938; further amended by vote of the people November 2, 1993.)

[Authorizing the legislature to establish a fund or funds for tax revenue stabilization reserves; regulating payments thereto and withdrawals therefrom]

§17. The legislature may establish a fund or funds to aid in the stabilization of the tax revenues of the state available for expenditure or distribution. Any law creating such a fund shall specify the tax or taxes to which such fund relates, and shall prescribe the method of determining the amount of revenue from any such tax or taxes which shall constitute a norm of each fiscal year. Such part as shall be prescribed by law of any revenue derived from such tax or taxes during a fiscal year in excess of such norm shall be paid into such fund. No moneys shall at any time be withdrawn from such fund unless the revenue derived from such tax or taxes during a fiscal year shall fall below the norm for such year; in which event such amount as may be prescribed by law, but in no event an amount exceeding the difference between such revenue and such norm, shall be paid from such fund into the general fund.

No law changing the method of determining a norm or prescribing the amount to be paid into such a fund or to be paid from such a fund into the general fund may become effective until three years from the date of its enactment. (Added by amendment approved by vote of the people November 2, 1943.)

[Bonus on account of service of certain veterans in World War II]

§18. The legislature may authorize by law the creation of a debt or debts of the state to provide for the payment of a bonus to each male and female member of the armed forces of the United States, still in the armed forces, or separated or discharged under honorable conditions, for service while on active duty with the armed forces at any time during the period from December seventh, nineteen hundred forty-one to and including September second, nineteen hundred forty-five, who was a resident of this state for a period of at least six months immediately prior to his or her enlistment, induction or call to active duty. The law authorizing the creation of the debt shall provide for payment of such bonus to the next of kin of each male and female member of the armed forces who, having been a resident of this state for a period of six months immediately prior to his or her enlistment, induction or call to active duty, died while on active duty at any time during the period from December seventh, nineteen hundred forty-one to and including September second, nineteen hundred forty-five; or who died while on active duty subsequent to September second, nineteen hundred forty-five, or after his or her separation or discharge under honorable conditions, prior to receiving payment of such bonus. An apportionment of the moneys on the basis of the periods and places of service of such members of the armed forces shall be provided by general laws. The aggregate of the debts authorized by this section shall not exceed four hundred million dollars. The provisions of this article, not inconsistent with this section, relating to the issuance of bonds for a debt or debts of the state and the maturity and payment thereof, shall apply to a debt or debts created

pursuant to this section; except that the law authorizing the contracting of such debt or debts shall take effect without submission to the people pursuant to section eleven of this article.

Proceeds of bonds issued pursuant to law, as authorized by this section as in force prior to January first, nineteen hundred fifty shall be available and may be expended for the payment of such bonus to persons qualified therefor as now provided by this section. (Added by amendment approved by vote of the people November 4, 1947; further amended by vote of the people November 8, 1949.)

[State debt for expansion of state university]

§19. The legislature may authorize by law the creation of a debt or debts of the state, not exceeding in the aggregate two hundred fifty million dollars, to provide moneys for the construction, reconstruction, rehabilitation, improvement and equipment of facilities for the expansion and development of the program of higher education provided and to be provided at institutions now or hereafter comprised within the state university, for acquisition of real property therefor, and for payment of the state's share of the capital costs of locally sponsored institutions of higher education approved and regulated by the state university trustees. The provisions of this article, not inconsistent with this section, relating to the issuance of bonds for a debt or debts of the state and the maturity and payment thereof, shall apply to a state debt or debts created pursuant to this section; except that the law authorizing the contracting of such debt or debts shall take effect without submission to the people pursuant to section eleven of this article. (New. Added by vote of the people November 5, 1957.)

ARTICLE VIII
LOCAL FINANCES

[Gift or loan of property or credit of local subdivisions prohibited; exceptions for enumerated purposes]

Section 1. No county, city, town, village or school district shall give or loan any money or property to or in aid of any individual, or private corporation or association, or private undertaking, or become directly or indirectly the owner of stock in, or bonds of, any private corporation or association; nor shall any county, city, town, village or school district give or loan its credit to or in aid of any individual, or public or private corporation or association, or private undertaking, except that two or more such units may join together pursuant to law in providing any municipal facility, service, activity or undertaking which each of such units has the power to provide separately. Each such unit may be authorized by the legislature to contract joint or several indebtedness, pledge its or their faith and credit for the payment of such indebtedness for such joint undertaking and levy real estate or other authorized taxes or impose charges therefor subject to the provisions of this constitution otherwise restricting the power of such units to contract indebtedness or to levy taxes on real estate. The legislature shall have power to provide by law for the manner and the proportion in which indebtedness arising out of such joint undertakings shall be incurred by such units and shall have power to provide a method by which such indebtedness shall be determined, allocated and apportioned among such units and such indebtedness treated for purposes of exclusion from applicable constitutional limitations, provided that in no event shall more than the total amount of indebtedness incurred for such joint undertaking be included in ascertaining the power of all such participating units to incur indebtedness. Such law may provide that such determination, allocation and apportionment shall be conclusive if made or approved by the comptroller. This provision shall not prevent a county from contracting indebtedness for the purpose of advancing to a town or school district, pursuant to law, the amount of unpaid taxes returned to it.

Subject to the limitations on indebtedness and taxation applying to any county, city, town or village nothing in this constitution contained shall prevent a county, city or town from making such provision for the aid, care and support of the needy as may be authorized by law, nor prevent any such county, city or town from providing for the care, support, maintenance and secular education of inmates of orphan asylums, homes for dependent children or correctional institutions and of children placed in family homes

28

by authorized agencies, whether under public or private control, or from providing health and welfare services for all children, nor shall anything in this constitution contained prevent a county, city, town or village from increasing the pension benefits payable to retired members of a police department or fire department or to widows, dependent children or dependent parents of members or retired members of a police department or fire department; or prevent the city of New York from increasing the pension benefits payable to widows, dependent children or dependent parents of members or retired members of the relief and pension fund of the department of street cleaning of the city of New York. Payments by counties, cities or towns to charitable, eleemosynary, correctional and reformatory institutions and agencies, wholly or partly under private control, for care, support and maintenance, may be authorized, but shall not be required, by the legislature. No such payments shall be made for any person cared for by any such institution or agency, nor for a child placed in a family home, who is not received and retained therein pursuant to rules established by the state board of social welfare or other state department having the power of inspection thereof. (Formerly §10. Renumbered and amended by Constitutional Convention of 1938 and approved by vote of the people November 8, 1938; further amended by vote of the people November 3, 1959; November 5, 1963; November 2, 1965.)

[Restrictions on indebtedness of local subdivisions; contracting and payment of local indebtedness; exceptions]

§2. No county, city, town, village or school district shall contract any indebtedness except for county, city, town, village or school district purposes, respectively. No indebtedness shall be contracted for longer than the period of probable usefulness of the object or purpose for which such indebtedness is to be contracted, or, in the alternative, the weighted average period of probable usefulness of the several objects or purposes for which such indebtedness is to be contracted, to be determined by the governing body of the county, city, town, village or school district contracting such indebtedness pursuant to general or special laws of the state legislature, which determination shall be conclusive, and in no event for longer than forty years. Indebtedness or any portion thereof may be refunded within either such period of probable usefulness, or average period of probable usefulness, as may be determined by such governing body computed from the date such indebtedness was contracted.

No indebtedness shall be contracted by any county, city, town, village or school district unless such county, city, town, village or school district shall have pledged its faith and credit for the payment of the principal thereof and the interest thereon. Except for indebtedness contracted in anticipation of the collection of taxes actually levied and uncollected or to be levied for the year when such indebtedness is contracted and indebtedness contracted to be paid in one of the two fiscal years immediately succeeding the fiscal year in which such indebtedness was contracted, all such indebtedness and each portion thereof from time to time contracted, including any refunding thereof, shall be paid in annual installments, the first of which, except in the case of refunding of indebtedness heretofore contracted, shall be paid not more than two years after such indebtedness or portion thereof shall have been contracted, and no installment, except in the case of refunding of indebtedness heretofore contracted, shall be more than fifty per centum in excess of the smallest prior installment, unless the governing body of the county, city, town, village or school district contracting such indebtedness provides for substantially level or declining debt service payments as may be authorized by law.

Notwithstanding the foregoing provisions, indebtedness contracted by the city of New York and each portion of any such indebtedness from time to time so contracted for the supply of water, including the acquisition of land in connection with such purpose, may be financed either by serial bonds with a maximum maturity of fifty years, in which case such indebtedness shall be paid in annual installments as hereinbefore provided, or by sinking fund bonds with a maximum maturity of fifty years, which shall be redeemed through annual contributions to sinking funds established and maintained for the purpose of amortizing the indebtedness for which such bonds are issued. Notwithstanding the foregoing provisions, indebtedness hereafter contracted by the city of New York and each portion of any such indebtedness from time to time so contracted for (a) the acquisition, construction or equipment of rapid transit railroads, or (b) the construction of docks, including the acquisition of land in connection with any of such purposes, may be financed either by serial bonds with a maximum maturity of forty years, in which case such indebtedness shall be paid in annual installments as hereinbefore provided, or by sinking fund bonds with a maximum maturity of forty years, which shall be redeemed through annual contributions to sinking funds established and maintained for the purpose of amortizing the indebtedness for which such bonds are issued.

Notwithstanding the foregoing provisions, but subject to such requirements as the legislature shall impose by general or special law, indebtedness contracted by any county, city, town, village or school district and each portion thereof from time to time contracted for any object or purpose for which indebtedness may be contracted may also be financed by sinking fund bonds with a maximum maturity of fifty years, which shall be redeemed through annual contributions to sinking funds established by such county, city, town, village or school district, provided, however, that each such annual contribution shall be at least equal to the amount required, if any, to enable the sinking fund to redeem, on the date of the contribution, the same amount of such indebtedness as would have been paid and then be payable if such indebtedness had been financed entirely by the issuance of serial bonds, except, if an issue of sinking fund bonds is combined for sale with an issue of serial bonds, for the same object or purpose, then the amount of each annual sinking fund contribution shall be at least equal to the amount required, if any, to enable the sinking fund to redeem, on the date of each such annual contribution, (i) the amount which would be required to be paid annually if such indebtedness had been issued entirely as serial bonds, less (ii) the amount of indebtedness, if any, to be paid during such year on the portion of such indebtedness actually issued as serial bonds. Sinking funds established on or after January first, nineteen hundred eighty-six pursuant to the preceding sentence shall be maintained and managed by the state comptroller pursuant to such requirements and procedures as the legislature shall prescribe, including provisions for reimbursement by the issuer of bonds payable from such sinking funds for the expenses related to such maintenance and management.

Provisions shall be made annually by appropriation by every county, city, town, village and school district for the payment of interest on all indebtedness and for the amounts required for (a) the amortization and redemption of term bonds, sinking fund bonds and serial bonds, (b) the redemption of certificates or other evidence of indebtedness (except those issued in anticipation of the collection of taxes or other revenues, or renewals thereof, and which are described in paragraph A of section five of this article and those issued in anticipation of the receipt of the proceeds of the sale of bonds theretofore authorized) contracted to be paid in such year out of the tax levy or other revenues applicable to a reduction thereof, and (c) the redemption of certificates or other evidence of indebtedness issued in anticipation of the collection of taxes or other revenues, or renewals thereof, which are not retired within five years after their date of original issue. If at any time the respective appropriating authorities shall fail to make such appropriations, a sufficient sum shall be set apart from the first revenues thereafter received and shall be applied to such purposes. The fiscal officer of any county, city, town, village or school district may be required to set apart and apply such revenues as aforesaid at the suit of any holder of obligations issued for any such indebtedness.

Notwithstanding the foregoing, all interest need not be paid annually on an issue of indebtedness provided that either (a) substantially level or declining debt service payments (including all payments of interest) shall be made over the life of such issue of indebtedness, or (b) there shall annually be contributed to a sinking fund created pursuant to this section, the amount necessary to bring the balance thereof, including income earned on contributions, to the accreted value of the obligations to be paid therefrom on the date such contribution is made, less the sum of all required future contributions of principal, in the case of sinking fund obligations, or payments of principal, in the case of serial obligations. When obligations are sold by a county, city, town, village or school district at a discount, the debt incurred for the purposes of any debt limitation contained in this constitution, shall be deemed to include only the amount of money actually received by the county, city, town, village or school district, irrespective of the face amount

29

of the obligations. (New. Adopted by Constitutional Convention of 1938 and approved by vote of the people November 8, 1938; further amended by vote of the people November 8, 1949; November 3, 1953; November 5, 1985; November 2, 1993.)

[Local indebtedness for water supply, sewage and drainage facilities and purposes; allocations and exclusions of indebtedness]

§2-a. Notwithstanding the provisions of section one of this article, the legislature by general or special law and subject to such conditions as it shall impose:

A. May authorize any county, city, town or village or any county or town on behalf of an improvement district to contract indebtedness to provide a supply of water, in excess of its own needs, for sale to any other public corporation or improvement district;

B. May authorize two or more public corporations and improvement districts to provide for a common supply of water and may authorize any such corporation, or any county or town on behalf of an improvement district, to contract joint indebtedness for such purpose or to contract indebtedness for specific proportions of the cost;

C. May authorize any county, city, town or village or any county or town on behalf of an improvement district to contract indebtedness to provide facilities, in excess of its own needs, for the conveyance, treatment and disposal of sewage from any other public corporation or improvement district;

D. May authorize two or more public corporations and improvement districts to provide for the common conveyance, treatment and disposal of sewage and may authorize any such corporation, or any county or town on behalf of an improvement district, to contract joint indebtedness for such purpose or to contract indebtedness for specific proportions of the cost;

E. May authorize any county, city, town or village or any county or town on behalf of an improvement district to contract indebtedness to provide facilities, in excess of its own needs, for drainage purposes from any other public corporation or improvement district.

F. May authorize two or more public corporations and improvement districts to provide for a common drainage system and may authorize any such corporation, or any county or town on behalf of an improvement district, to contract joint indebtedness for such purpose or to contract indebtedness for specific proportions of the cost.

Indebtedness contracted by a county, city, town or village pursuant to this section shall be for a county, city, town or village purpose, respectively. In ascertaining the power of a county, city, town or village to contract indebtedness, any indebtedness contracted pursuant to paragraphs A and B of this section shall be excluded.

The legislature shall provide the method by which a fair proportion of joint indebtedness contracted pursuant to paragraphs D and F of this section shall be allocated to any county, city, town or village.

The legislature by general law in terms and in effect applying alike to all counties, to all cities, to all towns and/or to all villages also may provide that all or any part of indebtedness contracted or proposed to be contracted by any county, city, town or village pursuant to paragraphs D and F of this section for a revenue producing public improvement or service may be excluded periodically in ascertaining the power of such county, city, town or village to contract indebtedness. The amount of any such exclusion shall have a reasonable relation to the extent to which such public improvement or service shall have yielded or is expected to yield revenues sufficient to provide for the payment of the interest on and amortization of or payment of indebtedness contracted or proposed to be contracted for such public improvement or service, after deducting all costs of operation, maintenance and repairs thereof. The legislature shall provide the method by which a fair proportion of joint indebtedness proposed to be contracted pursuant to paragraphs D and F of this section shall be allocated to any county, city, town or village for the purpose of determining the amount of any such exclusion. The provisions of paragraph C of section five and section ten-a of this article shall not apply to indebtedness contracted pursuant to paragraphs D and F of this section.

The legislature may provide that any allocation of indebtedness, or determination of the amount of any exclusion of indebtedness, made pursuant to this section shall be conclusive if made or approved by the state

30

comptroller. (Section added by vote of the people November 3, 1953. Paragraphs C-F added, next unnumbered paragraph amended, and three concluding unnumbered paragraphs added by amendment approved by vote of the people November 8, 1955.)

[Restrictions on creation and indebtedness of certain corporations]

§3. No municipal or other corporation (other than a county, city, town, village, school district or fire district, or a river improvement, river regulating, or drainage district, established by or under the supervision of the department of conservation) possessing the power (a) to contract indebtedness and (b) to levy taxes or benefit assessments upon real estate or to require the levy of such taxes or assessments, shall hereafter be established or created, but nothing herein shall prevent the creation of improvement districts in counties and towns, provided that the county or town or towns in which such districts are located shall pledge its or their faith and credit for the payment of the principal of and interest on all indebtedness to be contracted for the purposes of such districts, and in ascertaining the power of any such county or town to contract indebtedness, such indebtedness shall be included, unless such indebtedness would, under the provisions of this article, be excluded in ascertaining the power of a county or town to contract indebtedness. No such corporation now existing shall hereafter contract any indebtedness without the consent, granted in such manner as may be prescribed by general law, of the city or village within which, or of the town within any unincorporated area of which any real estate may be subject to such taxes or assessments. If the real estate subject to such taxes or assessments is wholly within a city, village or the unincorporated area of a town, in ascertaining the power of such city, village or town to contract indebtedness, there shall be included any indebtedness hereafter contracted by such corporation, unless such indebtedness would, under the provisions of this article, be excluded if contracted by such city, village or town. If only part of the real estate subject to such taxes or assessments is within a city, village or the unincorporated area of a town, in ascertaining the power of such city, village or town to contract indebtedness, there shall be included the proportion, determined as prescribed by general law, of any indebtedness hereafter contracted by such corporation, unless such indebtedness would, under the provisions of this article, be excluded if contracted by such city, village or town. (New. Adopted by Constitutional Convention of 1938 and approved by vote of the people November 8, 1938.)

[Limitations on local indebtedness]

§4. Except as otherwise provided in this constitution, no county, city, town, village or school district described in this section shall be allowed to contract indebtedness for any purpose or in any manner which, including existing indebtedness, shall exceed an amount equal to the following percentages of the average full valuation of taxable real estate of such county, city, town, village or school district:

(a) the county of Nassau, for county purposes, ten per centum;

(b) any county, other than the county of Nassau, for county purposes, seven per centum;

(c) the city of New York, for city purposes, ten per centum;

(d) any city, other than the city of New York, having one hundred twenty-five thousand or more inhabitants according to the latest federal census, for city purposes, nine per centum;

(e) any city having less than one hundred twenty-five thousand inhabitants according to the latest federal census, for city purposes, excluding education purposes, seven per centum;

(f) any town, for town purposes, seven per centum;

(g) any village for village purposes, seven per centum; and

(h) any school district which is coterminous with, or partly within, or wholly within, a city having less than one hundred twenty-five thousand inhabitants according to the latest federal census, for education purposes, five per centum; provided, however, that such limitation may be increased in relation to indebtedness for specified objects or purposes with (1) the approving vote of sixty per centum or more of the duly qualified voters of such school district voting on a proposition therefor submitted at a general or special election, (2) the consent of The Regents of the University of the State of New York and (3) the consent of the state comptroller. The legislature shall prescribe by law the qualifications for voting at any such election.

Except as otherwise provided in this constitution, any indebtedness contracted in excess of the respective limitations prescribed in this section shall be void.

In ascertaining the power of any city having less than one hundred twenty-five thousand inhabitants according to the latest federal census to contract indebtedness, indebtedness heretofore contracted by such city for education purposes shall be excluded. Such indebtedness so excluded shall be included in ascertaining the power of a school district which is coterminous with, or partly within, or wholly within, such city to contract indebtedness. The legislature shall prescribe by law the manner by which the amount of such indebtedness shall be determined and allocated among such school districts. Such law may provide that such determinations and allocations shall be conclusive if made or approved by the state comptroller.

In ascertaining the power of a school district described in this section to contract indebtedness, certificates or other evidences of indebtedness described in paragraph A of section five of this article shall be excluded.

The average full valuation of taxable real estate of any such county, city, town, village or school district shall be determined in the manner prescribed in section ten of this article.

Nothing contained in this section shall be deemed to restrict the powers granted to the legislature by other provisions of this constitution to further restrict the powers of any county, city, town, village or school district to contract indebtedness. (New. Approved by vote of the people November 6, 1951. Substituted for §4, derived in part from former §10, renumbered and amended by Constitutional Convention of 1938 and approved by vote of the people November 8, 1938.)

[Ascertainment of debt-incurring power of counties, cities, towns and villages; certain indebtedness to be excluded]

§5. In ascertaining the power of a county, city, town or village to contract indebtedness, there shall be excluded:

A. Certificates or other evidences of indebtedness (except serial bonds of an issue having a maximum maturity of more than two years) issued for purposes other than the financing of capital improvements and contracted to be redeemed in one of the two fiscal years immediately succeeding the year of their issue, and certificates or other evidences of indebtedness issued in any fiscal year in anticipation of (a) the collection of taxes on real estate for amounts theretofore actually levied and uncollected or to be levied in such year and payable out of such taxes, (b) moneys receivable from the state which have theretofore been apportioned by the state or which are to be so apportioned within one year after their issue and (c) the collection of any other taxes due and payable or to become due and payable within one year or of other revenues to be received within one year after their issue; excepting any such certificates or other evidences of indebtedness or renewals thereof which are not retired within five years after their date of original issue.

B. Indebtedness heretofore or hereafter contracted to provide for the supply of water.

C. Indebtedness heretofore or hereafter contracted by any county, city, town or village for a public improvement or part thereof, or service, owned or rendered by such county, city, town or village, annually proportionately to the extent that the same shall have yielded to such county, city, town or village net revenue; provided, however, that such net revenue shall be twenty-five per centum or more of the amount required in such year for the payment of the interest on, amortization of, or payment of, such indebtedness. Such exclusion shall be granted only if the revenues of such public improvement or part thereof, or service, are applied to and actually used for payment of all costs of operation, maintenance and repairs, and payment of the amounts required in such year for interest on and amortization of or redemption of such indebtedness, or such revenues are deposited in a special fund to be used solely for such payments. Any revenues remaining after such payments are made may be used for any lawful purpose of such county, city, town or village, respectively.

Net revenue shall be determined by deducting from gross revenues of the preceding year all costs of operation, maintenance and repairs for such year, or the legislature may provide that net revenue shall be determined by deducting from the average of the gross revenues of not to exceed five of the preceding years during which the public improvement or part thereof, or

service, has been in operation, the average of all costs of operation, maintenance and repairs for the same years.

A proportionate exclusion of indebtedness contracted or proposed to be contracted also may be granted for the period from the date when such indebtedness is first contracted or to be contracted for such public improvement or part thereof, or service, through the first year of operation of such public improvement or part thereof, or service. Such exclusion shall be computed in the manner provided in this section on the basis of estimated net revenue which shall be determined by deducting from the gross revenues estimated to be received during the first year of operation of such public improvement or part thereof, or service, all estimated costs of operation, maintenance and repairs for such year. The amount of any such proportionate exclusion shall not exceed seventy-five per centum of the amount which would be excluded if the computation were made on the basis of net revenue instead of estimated net revenue.

Except as otherwise provided herein, the legislature shall prescribe the method by which and the terms and conditions under which the proportionate amount of any such indebtedness to be so excluded shall be determined and no proportionate amount of such indebtedness shall be excluded except in accordance with such determination. The legislature may provide that the state comptroller shall make such determination or it may confer appropriate jurisdiction on the appellate division of the supreme court in the judicial departments in which such counties, cities, towns or villages are located for the purpose of determining the proportionate amount of any such indebtedness to be so excluded.

The provisions of this paragraph C shall not affect or impair any existing exclusions of indebtedness, or the power to exclude indebtedness, granted by any other provision of this constitution.

D. Serial bonds, issued by any county, city, town or village which now maintains a pension or retirement system or fund which is not on an actuarial reserve basis with current payments to the reserve adequate to provide for all current accruing liabilities. Such bonds shall not exceed in the aggregate an amount sufficient to provide for the payment of the liabilities of such system or fund, accrued on the date of issuing such bonds, both on account of pensioners on the pension roll on that date and prospective pensions to dependents of such pensioners and on account of prior service of active members of such system or fund on that date. Such bonds or the proceeds thereof shall be deposited in such system or fund. Each such pension or retirement system or fund thereafter shall be maintained on an actuarial reserve basis with current payments to the reserve adequate to provide for all current accruing liabilities.

E. Indebtedness contracted on or after January first, nineteen hundred sixty-two and prior to January first, two thousand twenty-four, for the construction or reconstruction of facilities for the conveyance, treatment and disposal of sewage. The legislature shall prescribe the method by which and the terms and conditions under which the amount of any such indebtedness to be excluded shall be determined, and no such indebtedness shall be excluded except in accordance with such determination. (Derived in part from former §10. Renumbered and amended by Constitutional Convention of 1938 and approved by vote of the people November 8, 1938; paragraph C further amended by vote of the people November 8, 1949, and November 6, 1951; paragraph A amended by vote of the people November 3, 1953; paragraph E added by vote of the people November 5, 1963 and amended November 6, 1973; further amended by vote of the people November 8, 1983; November 2, 1994; November 4, 2003, November 5, 2013.)

[Debt-incurring power of Buffalo, Rochester and Syracuse; certain additional indebtedness to be excluded]

§6. In ascertaining the power of the cities of Buffalo, Rochester and Syracuse to contract indebtedness, in addition to the indebtedness excluded by section 5 of this article, there shall be excluded:

Indebtedness not exceeding in the aggregate the sum of ten million dollars, heretofore or hereafter contracted by the city of Buffalo or the city of Rochester and indebtedness not exceeding in the aggregate the sum of five million dollars heretofore or hereafter contracted by the city of Syracuse for so much of the cost and expense of any public improvement as may be required by the ordinance or other local law therein assessing the same to be

31

raised by assessment upon local property or territory. (Derived in part from former §10. Renumbered and amended by Constitutional Convention of 1938 and approved by vote of the people November 8, 1938.)

[Debt-incurring power of New York city; certain additional indebtedness to be excluded]

§7. In ascertaining the power of the city of New York to contract indebtedness, in addition to the indebtedness excluded by section 5 of this article, there shall be excluded:

A. Indebtedness contracted prior to the first day of January, nineteen hundred ten, for dock purposes proportionately to the extent to which the current net revenues received by the city therefrom shall meet the interest on and the annual requirements for the amortization of such indebtedness. The legislature shall prescribe the method by which and the terms and conditions under which the amount of any such indebtedness to be so excluded shall be determined, and no such indebtedness shall be excluded except in accordance with such determination. The legislature may confer appropriate jurisdiction on the appellate division of the supreme court in the first judicial department for the purpose of determining the amount of any such indebtedness to be so excluded.

B. The aggregate of indebtedness initially contracted from time to time after January first, nineteen hundred twenty-eight, for the construction or equipment, or both, of new rapid transit railroads, not exceeding the sum of three hundred million dollars. Any indebtedness thereafter contracted in excess of such sum for such purposes shall not be so excluded, but this provision shall not be construed to prevent the refunding of any of the indebtedness excluded hereunder.

C. The aggregate of indebtedness initially contracted from time to time after January first, nineteen hundred fifty, for the construction, reconstruction and equipment of city hospitals, not exceeding the sum of one hundred fifty million dollars. Any indebtedness thereafter contracted in excess of such sum for such purposes, other than indebtedness contracted to refund indebtedness excluded pursuant to this paragraph, shall not be so excluded.

D. The aggregate of indebtedness initially contracted from time to time after January first, nineteen hundred fifty-two, for the construction and equipment of new rapid transit railroads, including extensions of and interconnections with and between existing rapid transit railroads or portions thereof, and reconstruction and equipment of existing rapid transit railroads, not exceeding the sum of five hundred million dollars. Any indebtedness thereafter contracted in excess of such sum for such purposes, other than indebtedness contracted to refund indebtedness excluded pursuant to this paragraph, shall not be so excluded.

E. Indebtedness contracted for school purposes, evidenced by bonds, to the extent to which state aid for common schools, not exceeding two million five hundred thousand dollars, shall meet the interest and the annual requirements for the amortization and payment of part or all of one or more issues of such bonds. Such exclusion shall be effective only during a fiscal year of the city in which its expense budget provides for the payment of such debt service from such state aid. The legislature shall prescribe by law the manner by which the amount of any such exclusion shall be determined and such indebtedness shall not be excluded hereunder except in accordance with the determination so prescribed. Such law may provide that any such determination shall be conclusive if made or approved by the state comptroller. (Derived in part from former §10. Renumbered and amended by Constitutional Convention of 1938 and approved by vote of the people November 8, 1938. Paragraph D added by amendment approved by vote of the people November 8, 1949; paragraphs E and F added by vote of the people November 6, 1951. Former paragraph A deleted; subsequent paragraphs re-lettered A to E by amendment approved by vote of the people November 3, 1953.)

[Debt-incurring power of New York city; certain indebtedness for railroads and transit purposes to be excluded]

§7-a. In ascertaining the power of the city of New York to contract indebtedness, in addition to the indebtedness excluded under any other section of this constitution, there shall be excluded:

A. The aggregate of indebtedness initially contracted from time to time by the city for the acquisition of railroads and facilities or properties used in connection therewith or rights therein or securities of corporations owning such railroads, facilities or rights, not exceeding the sum of three hundred fifteen million dollars. Provision for the amortization of such indebtedness shall be made either by the establishment and maintenance of a sinking fund therefor or by annual payment of part thereof, or by both such methods. Any indebtedness thereafter contracted in excess of such sum for such purposes shall not be so excluded, but this provision shall not be construed to prevent the refunding of any such indebtedness.

Notwithstanding any other provision of the constitution, the city is hereby authorized to contract indebtedness for such purposes and to deliver its obligations evidencing such indebtedness to the corporations owning the railroads, facilities, properties or rights acquired, to the holders of securities of such owning corporations, to the holders of securities of corporations holding the securities of such owning corporations, or to the holders of securities to which such acquired railroads, facilities, properties or rights are now subject.

B. Indebtedness contracted by the city for transit purposes, and not otherwise excluded, proportionately to the extent to which the current net revenue received by the city from all railroads and facilities and properties used in connection therewith and rights therein owned by the city and securities of corporations owning such railroads, facilities, properties or rights, owned by the city, shall meet the interest and the annual requirements for the amortization and payment of such non-excluded indebtedness.

In determining whether indebtedness for transit purposes may be excluded under this paragraph of this section, there shall first be deducted from the current net revenue received by the city from such railroads and facilities and properties used in connection therewith and rights therein and securities owned by the city: (a) an amount equal to the interest and amortization requirements on indebtedness for rapid transit purposes heretofore excluded by order of the appellate division, which exclusion shall not be terminated by or under any provision of this section; (b) an amount equal to the interest on indebtedness contracted pursuant to this section and of the annual requirements for amortization on any sinking fund bonds and for redemption of any serial bonds evidencing such indebtedness; (c) an amount equal to the sum of all taxes and bridge tolls accruing to the city in the fiscal year of the city preceding the acquisition of the railroads or facilities or properties or rights therein or securities acquired by the city hereunder, from such railroads, facilities and properties; and (d) the amount of net operating revenue derived by the city from the independent subway system during such fiscal year. The legislature shall prescribe the method by which and the terms and conditions under which the amount of any indebtedness to be excluded hereunder shall be determined, and no indebtedness shall be excluded except in accordance with the determination so prescribed. The legislature may confer appropriate jurisdiction on the appellate division of the supreme court in the first judicial department for the purpose of determining the amount of any debt to be so excluded. (New. Adopted by Constitutional Convention of 1938 and approved by vote of the people November 8, 1938.)

[Indebtedness not to be invalidated by operation of this article]

§8. No indebtedness of a county, city, town, village or school district valid at the time of its inception shall thereafter become invalid by reason of the operation of any of the provisions of this article. (Derived in part from former §10. Renumbered and amended by Constitutional Convention of 1938 and approved by vote of the people November 8, 1938.)

[When debt-incurring power of certain counties shall cease]

§9. Whenever the boundaries of any city are the same as those of a county, or when any city includes within its boundaries more than one county, the power of any county wholly included within such city to contract indebtedness shall cease, but the indebtedness of such county shall not, for the purposes of this article, be included as a part of the city indebtedness. (Derived in part from former §10. Renumbered and amended by Constitutional Convention of 1938 and approved by vote of the people November 8, 1938.)

32

[Limitations on amount to be raised by real estate taxes for local purposes; exceptions]

§10. Hereafter, in any county, city, village or school district described in this section, the amount to be raised by tax on real estate in any fiscal year, in addition to providing for the interest on and the principal of all indebtedness, shall not exceed an amount equal to the following percentages of the average full valuation of taxable real estate of such county, city, village or school district, less the amount to be raised by tax on real estate in such year for the payment of the interest on and redemption of certificates or other evidence of indebtedness described in paragraphs A and D of section five of this article, or renewals thereof:

(a) any county, for county purposes, one and one-half per centum; provided, however, that the legislature may prescribe a method by which such limitation may be increased to not to exceed two per centum;

(b) any city of one hundred twenty-five thousand or more inhabitants according to the latest federal census, for city purposes, two per centum;

(c) any city having less than one hundred twenty-five thousand inhabitants according to the latest federal census, for city purposes, two per centum;

(d) any village, for village purposes, two per centum;

(e) Notwithstanding the provisions of sub-paragraphs (a) and (b) of this section, the city of New York and the counties therein, for city and county purposes, a combined total of two and one-half per centum.

The average full valuation of taxable real estate of such county, city, village or school district shall be determined by taking the assessed valuations of taxable real estate on the last completed assessment rolls and the four preceding rolls of such county, city, village or school district, and applying thereto the ratio which such assessed valuation on each of such rolls bears to the full valuation, as determined by the state tax commission or by such other state officer or agency as the legislature shall by law direct. The legislature shall prescribe the manner by which such ratio shall be determined by the state tax commission or by such other state officer or agency.

Nothing contained in this section shall be deemed to restrict the powers granted to the legislature by other provisions of this constitution to further restrict the powers of any county, city, town, village or school district to levy taxes on real estate. (Derived in part from former §10. Renumbered and amended by Constitutional Convention of 1938 and approved by vote of the people November 8, 1938; further amended by vote of the people November 8, 1949; November 3, 1953; subparagraph (f) added by separate amendment approved by vote of the people November 3, 1953. Former subparagraph (e) repealed and former subparagraph (f) relettered (e) by amendment approved by vote of the people November 5, 1985.)

[Application and use of revenues: certain public improvements]

§10-a. For the purpose of determining the amount of taxes which may be raised on real estate pursuant to section ten of this article, the revenues received in each fiscal year by any county, city or village from a public improvement or part thereof, or service, owned or rendered by such county, city or village for which bonds or capital notes are issued after January first, nineteen hundred fifty, shall be applied first to the payment of all costs of operation, maintenance and repairs thereof, and then to the payment of the amounts required in such fiscal year to pay the interest on and the amortization of, or payment of, indebtedness contracted for such public improvement or part thereof, or service. The provisions of this section shall not prohibit the use of excess revenues for any lawful county, city or village purpose. The provisions of this section shall not be applicable to a public improvement or part thereof constructed to provide for the supply of water. (New section added by amendment approved by vote of the people November 8, 1949. Amended by vote of the people November 3, 1953.)

[Taxes for certain capital expenditures to be excluded from tax limitation]

§11. (a) Whenever the city of New York is required by law to pay for all or any part of the cost of capital improvements by direct budgetary appropriation in any fiscal year or by the issuance of certificates or other evidence of indebtedness (except serial bonds of an issue having a maximum maturity of more than two years) to be redeemed in one of the two immediately succeeding fiscal years, taxes required for such appropriation or for the redemption of such certificates or other evidence of indebtedness may be excluded in whole or in part by such city from the tax limitation prescribed by section ten of this article, in which event the total amount so required for such appropriation and for the redemption of such certificates or other evidence of indebtedness shall be deemed to be indebtedness to the same extent and in the same manner as if such amount had been financed through indebtedness payable in equal annual installments over the period of the probable usefulness of such capital improvement, as determined by law. The fiscal officer of such city shall determine the amount to be deemed indebtedness pursuant to this section, and the legislature, in its discretion, may provide that such determination, if approved by the state comptroller, shall be conclusive. Any amounts determined to be deemed indebtedness of any county, city, other than the city of New York, village or school district in accordance with the provisions of this section as in force and effect prior to January first, nineteen hundred fifty-two, shall not be deemed to be indebtedness on and after such date.

(b) Whenever any county, city, other than the city of New York, village or school district which is coterminous with, or partly within, or wholly within, a city having less than one hundred twenty-five thousand inhabitants according to the latest federal census provides by direct budgetary appropriation for any fiscal year for the payment in such fiscal year or in any future fiscal year or years of all or any part of the cost of an object or purpose for which a period of probable usefulness has been determined by law, the taxes required for such appropriation shall be excluded from the tax limitation prescribed by section ten of this article unless the legislature otherwise provides. (New. Adopted by Constitutional Convention of 1938 and approved by vote of the people November 8, 1938; amended by vote of the people November 8, 1949, and by vote of the people November 6, 1951.)

[Powers of local governments to be restricted; further limitations on contracting local indebtedness authorized]

§12. It shall be the duty of the legislature, subject to the provisions of this constitution, to restrict the power of taxation, assessment, borrowing money, contracting indebtedness, and loaning the credit of counties, cities, towns and villages, so as to prevent abuses in taxation and assessments and in contracting of indebtedness by them. Nothing in this article shall be construed to prevent the legislature from further restricting the powers herein specified of any county, city, town, village or school district to contract indebtedness or to levy taxes on real estate. The legislature shall not, however, restrict the power to levy taxes on real estate for the payment of interest on or principal of indebtedness theretofore contracted. (New. Adopted by Constitutional Convention of 1938 and approved by vote of the people November 8, 1938. Amended by vote of the people November 5, 1963.)

ARTICLE IX[10]
LOCAL GOVERNMENTS

[Bill of rights for local governments]

Section 1. Effective local self-government and intergovernmental cooperation are purposes of the state. In furtherance thereof, local governments shall have the following rights, powers, privileges and immunities in addition to those granted by other provisions of this constitution:

(a) Every local government, except a county wholly included within a city, shall have a legislative body elective by the people thereof. Every local government shall have power to adopt local laws as provided by this article.

(b) All officers of every local government whose election or appointment is not provided for by this constitution shall be elected by the people of the local government, or of some division thereof, or appointed by such officers of the local government as may be provided by law.

---

[10] New article, adopted by amendment approved by vote of the people November 5, 1963. Former Article IX repealed, except sections 5, 6 and 8, which were relettered subdivisions (a), (b) and (c) respectively of new section 13 of Article XIII.

33

(c) Local governments shall have power to agree, as authorized by act of the legislature, with the federal government, a state or one or more other governments within or without the state, to provide cooperatively, jointly or by contract any facility, service, activity or undertaking which each participating local government has the power to provide separately. Each such local government shall have power to apportion its share of the cost thereof upon such portion of its area as may be authorized by act of the legislature.

(d) No local government or any part of the territory thereof shall be annexed to another until the people, if any, of the territory proposed to be annexed shall have consented thereto by majority vote on a referendum and until the governing board of each local government, the area of which is affected, shall have consented thereto upon the basis of a determination that the annexation is in the over-all public interest. The consent of the governing board of a county shall be required only where a boundary of the county is affected. On or before July first, nineteen hundred sixty-four, the legislature shall provide, where such consent of a governing board is not granted, for adjudication and determination, on the law and the facts, in a proceeding initiated in the supreme court, of the issue of whether the annexation is in the over-all public interest.

(e) Local governments shall have power to take by eminent domain private property within their boundaries for public use together with excess land or property but no more than is sufficient to provide for appropriate disposition or use of land or property which abuts on that necessary for such public use, and to sell or lease that not devoted to such use. The legislature may authorize and regulate the exercise of the power of eminent domain and excess condemnation by a local government outside its boundaries.

(f) No local government shall be prohibited by the legislature (1) from making a fair return on the value of the property used and useful in its operation of a gas, electric or water public utility service, over and above costs of operation and maintenance and necessary and proper reserves, in addition to an amount equivalent to taxes which such service, if privately owned, would pay to such local government, or (2) from using such profits for payment of refunds to consumers or for any other lawful purpose.

(g) A local government shall have power to apportion its cost of a governmental service or function upon any portion of its area, as authorized by act of the legislature.

(h) (1) Counties, other than those wholly included within a city, shall be empowered by general law, or by special law enacted upon county request pursuant to section two of this article, to adopt, amend or repeal alternative forms of county government provided by the legislature or to prepare, adopt, amend or repeal alternative forms of their own. Any such form of government or any amendment thereof, by act of the legislature or by local law, may transfer one or more functions or duties of the county or of the cities, towns, villages, districts or other units of government wholly contained in such county to each other or when authorized by the legislature to the state, or may abolish one or more offices, departments, agencies or units of government provided, however, that no such form or amendment, except as provided in paragraph (2) of this subdivision, shall become effective unless approved on a referendum by a majority of the votes cast thereon in the area of the county outside of cities, and in the cities of the county, if any, considered as one unit. Where an alternative form of county government or any amendment thereof, by act of the legislature or by local law, provides for the transfer of any function or duty to or from any village or the abolition of any office, department, agency or unit of government of a village wholly contained in such county, such form or amendment shall not become effective unless it shall also be approved on the referendum by a majority of the votes cast thereon in all the villages so affected considered as one unit.

(2) After the adoption of an alternative form of county government by a county, any amendment thereof by act of the legislature or by local law which abolishes or creates an elective county office, changes the voting or veto power of or the method of removing an elective county officer during his or her term of office, abolishes, curtails or transfers to another county officer or agency any power of an elective county officer or changes the form or composition of the county legislative body shall be subject to a permissive referendum as provided by the legislature. (Amended by vote of the people November 6, 2001.)

34

Powers and duties of legislature; home rule powers of local governments; statute of local governments.

§2. (a) The legislature shall provide for the creation and organization of local governments in such manner as shall secure to them the rights, powers, privileges and immunities granted to them by this constitution.

(b) Subject to the bill of rights of local governments and other applicable provisions of this constitution, the legislature:

(1) Shall enact, and may from time to time amend, a statute of local governments granting to local governments powers including but not limited to those of local legislation and administration in addition to the powers vested in them by this article. A power granted in such statute may be repealed, diminished, impaired or suspended only by enactment of a statute by the legislature with the approval of the governor at its regular session in one calendar year and the re-enactment and approval of such statute in the following calendar year.

(2) Shall have the power to act in relation to the property, affairs or government of any local government only by general law, or by special law only (a) on request of two-thirds of the total membership of its legislative body or on request of its chief executive officer concurred in by a majority of such membership, or (b) except in the case of the city of New York, on certificate of necessity from the governor reciting facts which in the judgment of the governor constitute an emergency requiring enactment of such law and, in such latter case, with the concurrence of two-thirds of the members elected to each house of the legislature.

(3) Shall have the power to confer on local governments powers not relating to their property, affairs or government including but not limited to those of local legislation and administration, in addition to those otherwise granted by or pursuant to this article, and to withdraw or restrict such additional powers.

(c) In addition to powers granted in the statute of local governments or any other law, (i) every local government shall have power to adopt and amend local laws not inconsistent with the provisions of this constitution or any general law relating to its property, affairs or government and, (ii) every local government shall have power to adopt and amend local laws not inconsistent with the provisions of this constitution or any general law relating to the following subjects, whether or not they relate to the property, affairs or government of such local government, except to the extent that the legislature shall restrict the adoption of such a local law relating to other than the property, affairs or government of such local government:

(1) The powers, duties, qualifications, number, mode of selection and removal, terms of office, compensation, hours of work, protection, welfare and safety of its officers and employees, except that cities and towns shall not have such power with respect to members of the legislative body of the county in their capacities as county officers.

(2) In the case of a city, town or village, the membership and composition of its legislative body.

(3) The transaction of its business.

(4) The incurring of its obligations, except that local laws relating to financing by the issuance of evidences of indebtedness by such local government shall be consistent with laws enacted by the legislature.

(5) The presentation, ascertainment and discharge of claims against it.

(6) The acquisition, care, management and use of its highways, roads, streets, avenues and property.

(7) The acquisition of its transit facilities and the ownership and operation thereof.

(8) The levy, collection and administration of local taxes authorized by the legislature and of assessments for local improvements, consistent with laws enacted by the legislature.

(9) The wages or salaries, the hours of work or labor, and the protection, welfare and safety of persons employed by any contractor or sub-contractor performing work, labor or services for it.

(10) The government, protection, order, conduct, safety, health and well-being of persons or property therein.

(d) Except in the case of a transfer of functions under an alternative form of county government, a local government shall not have power to adopt local laws which impair the powers of any other local government.

(e) The rights and powers of local governments specified in this section insofar as applicable to any county within the city of New York shall be vested in such city. (Amended by vote of the people November 6, 2001.)

Existing laws to remain applicable; construction; definitions.
§3. (a) Except as expressly provided, nothing in this article shall restrict or impair any power of the legislature in relation to:

(1) The maintenance, support or administration of the public school system, as required or provided by article XI of this constitution, or any retirement system pertaining to such public school system,

(2) The courts as required or provided by article VI of this constitution, and

(3) Matters other than the property, affairs or government of a local government.

(b) The provisions of this article shall not affect any existing valid provisions of acts of the legislature or of local legislation and such provisions shall continue in force until repealed, amended, modified or superseded in accordance with the provisions of this constitution.

(c) Rights, powers, privileges and immunities granted to local governments by this article shall be liberally construed.

(d) Whenever used in this article the following terms shall mean or include:

(1) "General law." A law which in terms and in effect applies alike to all counties, all counties other than those wholly included within a city, all cities, all towns or all villages.

(2) "Local government." A county, city, town or village.

(3) "People." Persons entitled to vote as provided in section one of article two of this constitution.

(4) "Special law." A law which in terms and in effect applies to one or more, but not all, counties, counties other than those wholly included within a city, cities, towns or villages.

ARTICLE X
CORPORATIONS

[Corporations; formation of]
Section 1. Corporations may be formed under general law; but shall not be created by special act, except for municipal purposes, and in cases where, in the judgment of the legislature, the objects of the corporation cannot be attained under general laws. All general laws and special acts passed pursuant to this section may be altered from time to time or repealed. (Formerly §1 of Art. 8. Renumbered by Constitutional Convention of 1938 and approved by vote of the people November 8, 1938.)

[Dues of corporations]
§2. Dues from corporations shall be secured by such individual liability of the corporators and other means as may be prescribed by law. (Formerly §2 of Art. 8. Renumbered by Constitutional Convention of 1938 and approved by vote of the people November 8, 1938.)

[Savings bank charters; savings and loan association charters; special charters not to be granted]
§3. The legislature shall, by general law, conform all charters of savings banks, savings and loan associations, or institutions for savings, to a uniformity of powers, rights and liabilities, and all charters hereafter granted for such corporations shall be made to conform to such general law, and to such amendments as may be made thereto. The legislature shall have no power to pass any act granting any special charter for banking purposes; but corporations or associations may be formed for such purposes under general laws. (Formerly §4 of Art. 8. Renumbered by Constitutional Convention of 1938 and approved by vote of the people November 8, 1938; amended by vote of the people November 8, 1983.)

[Corporations; definition; right to sue and be sued]
§4. The term corporations as used in this section, and in sections 1, 2 and 3 of this article shall be construed to include all associations and joint-stock companies having any of the powers or privileges of corporations not possessed by individuals or partnerships. And all corporations shall have the right to sue and shall be subject to be sued in all courts in like cases as natural persons. (Formerly §3 of Art. 8. Renumbered and amended by Constitutional Convention of 1938 and approved by vote of the people November 8, 1938.)

[Public corporations; restrictions on creation and powers; accounts; obligations of]
§5. No public corporation (other than a county, city, town, village, school district or fire district or an improvement district established in a town or towns) possessing both the power to contract indebtedness and the power to collect rentals, charges, rates or fees for the services or facilities furnished or supplied by it shall hereafter be created except by special act of the legislature.

No such public corporation (other than a county or city) shall hereafter be given both the power to contract indebtedness and the power, within any city, to collect rentals, charges, rates or fees from the owners of real estate, or the occupants of real estate (other than the occupants of premises owned or controlled by such corporation or by the state or any civil division thereof), for services or facilities furnished or supplied in connection with such real estate, if such services or facilities are of a character or nature then or formerly furnished or supplied by the city, unless the electors of the city shall approve the granting to such corporation of such powers by a majority vote at a general or special election in such city; but this paragraph shall not apply to a corporation created pursuant to an interstate compact.

The accounts of every such public corporation heretofore or hereafter created shall be subject to the supervision of the state comptroller, or, if the member or members of such public corporation are appointed by the mayor of a city, to the supervision of the comptroller of such city; provided, however, that this provision shall not apply to such a public corporation created pursuant to agreement or compact with another state or with a foreign power, except with the consent of the parties to such agreement or compact.

Neither the state nor any political subdivision thereof shall at any time be liable for the payment of any obligations issued by such a public corporation heretofore or hereafter created, nor may the legislature accept, authorize acceptance of or impose such liability upon the state or any political subdivision thereof; but the state or a political subdivision thereof may, if authorized by the legislature, acquire the properties of any such corporation and pay the indebtedness thereof. (New. Adopted by Constitutional Convention of 1938 and approved by vote of the people November 8, 1938.)

[Liability of state for payment of bonds of public corporation to construct state thruways; use of state canal lands and properties]
§6. Notwithstanding any provision of this or any other article of this constitution, the legislature may by law, which shall take effect without submission to the people:

(a) make or authorize making the state liable for the payment of the principal of and interest on bonds of a public corporation created to construct state thruways, in a principal amount not to exceed five hundred million dollars, maturing in not to exceed forty years after their respective dates, and for the payment of the principal of and interest on notes of such corporation issued in anticipation of such bonds, which notes and any renewals thereof shall mature within five years after the respective dates of such notes; and

(b) authorize the use of any state canal lands and properties by such a public corporation for so long as the law may provide. To the extent payment is not otherwise made or provided for, the provisions of section sixteen of article seven shall apply to the liability of the state incurred pursuant to this section, but the powers conferred by this section shall not be subject to the limitations of this or any other article. (New. Added by vote of the people November 6, 1951.)

[Liability of state for obligations of the port of New York authority for railroad commuter cars; limitations]
§7. Notwithstanding any provision of this or any other article of this constitution, the legislature may by law, which shall take effect without submission to the people, make or authorize making the state liable for the payment of the principal of and interest on obligations of the port of New

35

York authority issued pursuant to legislation heretofore or hereafter enacted, to purchase or refinance the purchase of, or to repay advances from this state made for the purpose of purchasing, railroad passenger cars, including self-propelled cars, and locomotives and other rolling stock used in passenger transportation, for the purpose of leasing such cars to any railroad transporting passengers between municipalities in the portion of the port of New York district within the state, the majority of the trackage of which within the port of New York district utilized for the transportation of passengers shall be in the state; provided, however, that the total amount of obligations with respect to which the state may be made liable shall not exceed one hundred million dollars at any time, and that all of such obligations shall be due not later than thirty-five years after the effective date of this section.

To the extent payment is not otherwise made or provided for, the provisions of section sixteen of article seven shall apply to the liability of the state incurred pursuant to this section, but the powers conferred by this section shall not be subject to the limitations of this or any other article. (New. Added by vote of the people November 7, 1961.)

[Liability of state on bonds of a public corporation to finance new industrial or manufacturing plants in depressed areas]
§8. Notwithstanding any provision of this or any other article of this constitution, the legislature may by law, which shall take effect without submission to the people, make or authorize making the state liable for the payment of the principal of and interest on bonds of a public corporation to be created pursuant to and for the purposes specified in the last paragraph of section eight of article seven of this constitution, maturing in not to exceed thirty years after their respective dates, and for the principal of and interest on notes of such corporation issued in anticipation of such bonds, which notes and any renewals thereof shall mature within seven years after the respective dates of such notes, provided that the aggregate principal amount of such bonds with respect to which the state shall be so liable shall not at any one time exceed nine hundred million dollars, excluding bonds issued to refund outstanding bonds. (New. Added by vote of the people November 7, 1961. Formerly duplicate §7 added by vote of the people November 7, 1961; renumbered and amended by vote of the people November 4, 1969; further amended by vote of the people November 3, 1981; November 5, 1985; November 5, 1991.)

ARTICLE XI
EDUCATION

[Common schools]
Section 1. The legislature shall provide for the maintenance and support of a system of free common schools, wherein all the children of this state may be educated. (Formerly §1 of Art. 9. Renumbered by Constitutional Convention of 1938 and approved by vote of the people November 8, 1938.)

[Regents of the University]
§2. The corporation created in the year one thousand seven hundred eighty-four, under the name of The Regents of the University of the State of New York, is hereby continued under the name of The University of the State of New York. It shall be governed and its corporate powers, which may be increased, modified or diminished by the legislature, shall be exercised by not less than nine regents. (Formerly §2 of Art. 9. Renumbered and amended by Constitutional Convention of 1938 and approved by vote of the people November 8, 1938.)

[Use of public property or money in aid of denominational schools prohibited; transportation of children authorized]
§3. Neither the state nor any subdivision thereof, shall use its property or credit or any public money, or authorize or permit either to be used, directly or indirectly, in aid or maintenance, other than for examination or inspection, of any school or institution of learning wholly or in part under the control or direction of any religious denomination, or in which any denominational tenet or doctrine is taught, but the legislature may provide for the transportation of children to and from any school or institution of learning. (Formerly §4 of Art. 9. Renumbered and amended by Constitutional Convention of 1938 and approved by vote of the people November 8, 1938.

Formerly §4, renumbered §3 without change by amendment approved by vote of the people November 6, 1962; former § 4 repealed by same amendment.)

ARTICLE XII[11]
DEFENSE

[Defense; militia]
Section 1. The defense and protection of the state and of the United States is an obligation of all persons within the state. The legislature shall provide for the discharge of this obligation and for the maintenance and regulation of an organized militia.

ARTICLE XIII
PUBLIC OFFICERS

[Oath of office; no other test for public office]
Section 1. Members of the legislature, and all officers, executive and judicial, except such inferior officers as shall be by law exempted, shall, before they enter on the duties of their respective offices, take and subscribe the following oath or affirmation: "I do solemnly swear (or affirm) that I will support the constitution of the United States, and the constitution of the State of New York, and that I will faithfully discharge the duties of the office of ......, according to the best of my ability;" and no other oath, declaration or test shall be required as a qualification for any office of public trust, except that any committee of a political party may, by rule, provide for equal representation of the sexes on any such committee, and a state convention of a political party, at which candidates for public office are nominated, may, by rule, provide for equal representation of the sexes on any committee of such party. (Amended by Constitutional Convention of 1938 and approved by vote of the people November 8, 1938.)

[Duration of term of office]
§2. When the duration of any office is not provided by this constitution it may be declared by law, and if not so declared, such office shall be held during the pleasure of the authority making the appointment. (Formerly §3 of Art. 10. Renumbered by Constitutional Convention of 1938 and approved by vote of the people November 8, 1938. Formerly §6, renumbered §2 without change by amendment approved by vote of the people November 6, 1962; former §2 repealed by same amendment.)

[Vacancies in office; how filled; boards of education]
§3. The legislature shall provide for filling vacancies in office, and in case of elective officers, no person appointed to fill a vacancy shall hold his or her office by virtue of such appointment longer than the commencement of the political year next succeeding the first annual election after the happening of the vacancy; provided, however, that nothing contained in this article shall prohibit the filling of vacancies on boards of education, including boards of education of community districts in the city school district of the city of New York, by appointment until the next regular school district election, whether or not such appointment shall extend beyond the thirty-first day of December in any year. (Formerly §5 of Art. 10. Renumbered by Constitutional Convention of 1938 and approved by vote of the people November 8, 1938. Formerly §8, renumbered §3 without change by amendment approved by vote of the people November 6, 1962; former §3 repealed by same amendment. Amended by vote of the people November 8, 1977; November 6, 2001.)

[Political year and legislative term]
§4. The political year and legislative term shall begin on the first day of January; and the legislature shall, every year, assemble on the first Wednesday after the first Monday in January. (Formerly §6 of Art. 10. Renumbered and amended by Constitutional Convention of 1938 and

---

[11] New article, adopted by vote of the people November 6, 1962; repealing and replacing former article adopted November 8, 1938.

approved by vote of the people November 8, 1938. Formerly §9, renumbered §4 without change by amendment approved by vote of the people November 6, 1962; former §4 repealed by same amendment.)

[Removal from office for misconduct]
§5. Provision shall be made by law for the removal for misconduct or malversation in office of all officers, except judicial, whose powers and duties are not local or legislative and who shall be elected at general elections, and also for supplying vacancies created by such removal. (Formerly §7 of Art. 10. Renumbered by Constitutional Convention of 1938 and approved by vote of the people November 8, 1938. Formerly §10, renumbered §5 without change by amendment approved by vote of the people November 6, 1962; former §5 repealed by same amendment.)

[When office to be deemed vacant; legislature may declare]
§6. The legislature may declare the cases in which any office shall be deemed vacant when no provision is made for that purpose in this constitution. (Formerly §8 of Art. 10. Renumbered by Constitutional Convention of 1938 and approved by vote of the people November 8, 1938. Formerly §11, renumbered §6 without change by amendment approved by vote of the people November 6, 1962; former §6 repealed by same amendment.)

[Compensation of officers]
§7. Each of the state officers named in this constitution shall, during his or her continuance in office, receive a compensation, to be fixed by law, which shall not be increased or diminished during the term for which he or she shall have been elected or appointed; nor shall he or she receive to his or her use any fees or perquisites of office or other compensation. (Formerly §9 of Art. 10. Renumbered and amended by Constitutional Convention of 1938 and approved by vote of the people November 8, 1938. Formerly §12, renumbered §7 without change by amendment approved by vote of the people November 6, 1962; former §7 repealed by same amendment; further amended as §12 by vote of the people November 5, 1963; further amended by vote of the people November 6, 2001.)

[Election and term of city and certain county officers]
§8. All elections of city officers, including supervisors, elected in any city or part of a city, and of county officers elected in any county wholly included in a city, except to fill vacancies, shall be held on the Tuesday succeeding the first Monday in November in an odd-numbered year, and the term of every such officer shall expire at the end of an odd-numbered year. This section shall not apply to elections of any judicial officer. (New. Added by amendment approved by vote of the people November 2, 1965.)

[No sections 9-12; former 9-12 renumbered 4-7]

[Law enforcement and other officers]
§13. (a) Except in counties in the city of New York and except as authorized in section one of article nine of this constitution, registers in counties having registers shall be chosen by the electors of the respective counties once in every three years and whenever the occurring of vacancies shall require; the sheriff and the clerk of each county shall be chosen by the electors once in every three or four years as the legislature shall direct. Sheriffs shall hold no other office. They may be required by law to renew their security, from time to time; and in default of giving such new security, their offices shall be deemed vacant. The governor may remove any elective sheriff, county clerk, district attorney or register within the term for which he or she shall have been elected; but before so doing the governor shall give to such officer a copy of the charges against him or her and an opportunity of being heard in his or her defense. In each county a district attorney shall be chosen by the electors once in every three or four years as the legislature shall direct. The clerk of each county in the city of New York shall be appointed, and be subject to removal, by the appellate division of the supreme court in the judicial department in which the county is located. In addition to his or her powers and duties as clerk of the supreme court, he or she shall have power to select, draw, summon and empanel grand and petit jurors in the manner and under the conditions now or hereafter prescribed by

law, and shall have such other powers and duties as shall be prescribed by the city from time to time by local law.

(b) Any district attorney who shall fail faithfully to prosecute a person charged with the violation in his or her county of any provision of this article which may come to his or her knowledge, shall be removed from office by the governor, after due notice and an opportunity of being heard in his or her defense. The expenses which shall be incurred by any county, in investigating and prosecuting any charge of bribery or attempting to bribe any person holding office under the laws of this state, within such county, or of receiving bribes by any such person in said county, shall be a charge against the state, and their payment by the state shall be provided for by law.

(c) The city of New York is hereby vested with power from time to time to abolish by local law, as defined by the legislature, the office of any county officer within the city other than judges, clerks of counties and district attorneys, and to assign any or all functions of such officers to city officers, courts or clerks of counties, and to prescribe the powers, duties, qualifications, number, mode of selection and removal, terms of office and compensation of the persons holding such offices and the employees therein, and to assign to city officers any powers or duties of clerks of counties not assigned by this constitution. The legislature shall not pass any law affecting any such matters in relation to such offices within the city of New York except on message from the governor declaring that an emergency exists and the concurrent action of two-thirds of the members of each house, except that existing laws regarding each such office shall continue in force, and may be amended or repealed by the legislature as heretofore, until the power herein granted to the city has been exercised with respect to that office. The provisions of article nine shall not prevent the legislature from passing general or special laws prescribing or affecting powers and duties of such city officers or such courts or clerks to whom or which functions of such county officers shall have been so assigned, in so far as such powers or duties embrace subjects not relating to property, affairs or government of such city. (Added by vote of the people November 5, 1963. Subdivisions (a), (b) and (c), formerly §§5, 6 and 8 of Art. 9. Subdivision (a) amended by vote of the people November 7, 1972; subdivision (a) further amended by vote of the people November 6, 1984; November 7, 1989; further amended by vote of the people November 6, 2001.)

[Employees of, and contractors for, the state and local governments; wages, hours and other provisions to be regulated by legislature]
§14. The legislature may regulate and fix the wages or salaries and the hours of work or labor, and make provisions for the protection, welfare and safety, of persons employed by the state or by any county, city, town, village or other civil division of the state, or by any contractor or subcontractor performing work, labor or services for the state or for any county, city, town, village or other civil division thereof. (New. Added by amendment approved by vote of the people November 5, 1963.)

ARTICLE XIV
CONSERVATION

[Forest preserve to be forever kept wild; authorized uses and exceptions]
Section 1. The lands of the state, now owned or hereafter acquired, constituting the forest preserve as now fixed by law, shall be forever kept as wild forest lands. They shall not be leased, sold or exchanged, or be taken by any corporation, public or private, nor shall the timber thereon be sold, removed or destroyed. Nothing herein contained shall prevent the state from constructing, completing and maintaining any highway heretofore specifically authorized by constitutional amendment, nor from constructing and maintaining to federal standards federal aid interstate highway route five hundred two from a point in the vicinity of the city of Glens Falls, thence northerly to the vicinity of the villages of Lake George and Warrensburg, the hamlets of South Horicon and Pottersville and thence northerly in a generally straight line on the west side of Schroon Lake to the vicinity of the hamlet of Schroon, then continuing northerly to the vicinity of Schroon Falls, Schroon River and North Hudson, and to the east of Makomis Mountain, east of the

37

hamlet of New Russia, east of the village of Elizabethtown and continuing northerly in the vicinity of the hamlet of Towers Forge, and east of Poke-O-Moonshine Mountain and continuing northerly to the vicinity of the village of Keeseville and the city of Plattsburgh, all of the aforesaid taking not to exceed a total of three hundred acres of state forest preserve land, nor from constructing and maintaining not more than twenty-five miles of ski trails thirty to two hundred feet wide, together with appurtenances thereto, provided that no more than five miles of such trails shall be in excess of one hundred twenty feet wide, on the north, east and northwest slopes of Whiteface Mountain in Essex county, nor from constructing and maintaining not more than twenty-five miles of ski trails thirty to two hundred feet wide, together with appurtenances thereto, provided that no more than two miles of such trails shall be in excess of one hundred twenty feet wide, on the slopes of Belleayre Mountain in Ulster and Delaware counties and not more than forty miles of ski trails thirty to two hundred feet wide, together with appurtenances thereto, provided that no more than eight miles of such trails shall be in excess of one hundred twenty feet wide, on the slopes of Gore and Pete Gay mountains in Warren county, nor from relocating, reconstructing and maintaining a total of not more than fifty miles of existing state highways for the purpose of eliminating the hazards of dangerous curves and grades, provided a total of no more than four hundred acres of forest preserve land shall be used for such purpose and that no single relocated portion of any highway shall exceed one mile in length. Notwithstanding the foregoing provisions, the state may convey to the village of Saranac Lake ten acres of forest preserve land adjacent to the boundaries of such village for public use in providing for refuse disposal and in exchange therefore the village of Saranac Lake shall convey to the state thirty acres of certain true forest land owned by such village on Roaring Brook in the northern half of Lot 113, Township 11, Richards Survey. Notwithstanding the foregoing provisions, the state may convey to the town of Arietta twenty-eight acres of forest preserve land within such town for public use in providing for the extension of the runway and landing strip of the Piseco airport and in exchange therefor the town of Arietta shall convey to the state thirty acres of certain land owned by such town in the town of Arietta. Notwithstanding the foregoing provisions and subject to legislative approval of the tracts to be exchanged prior to the actual transfer of title, the state, in order to consolidate its land holdings for better management, may convey to International Paper Company approximately eight thousand five hundred acres of forest preserve land located in townships two and three of Totten and Crossfield Purchase and township nine of the Moose River Tract, Hamilton county, and in exchange therefore International Paper Company shall convey to the state for incorporation into the forest preserve approximately the same number of acres of land located within such townships and such County on condition that the legislature shall determine that the lands to be received by the state are at least equal in value to the lands to be conveyed by the state. Notwithstanding the foregoing provisions and subject to legislative approval of the tracts to be exchanged prior to the actual transfer of title and the conditions herein set forth, the state, in order to facilitate the preservation of historic buildings listed on the national register of historic places by rejoining an historic grouping of buildings under unitary ownership and stewardship, may convey to Sagamore Institute, Inc., a not-for-profit educational organization, approximately ten acres of land and buildings thereon adjoining the real property of the Sagamore Institute, Inc. and located on Sagamore Road, near Racquette Lake Village, in the Town of Long Lake, county of Hamilton, and in exchange therefor; Sagamore Institute, Inc. shall convey to the state for incorporation into the forest preserve approximately two hundred acres of wild forest land located within the Adirondack Park on condition that the legislature shall determine that the lands to be received by the state are at least equal in value to the lands and buildings to be conveyed by the state and that the natural and historic character of the lands and buildings conveyed by the state will be secured by appropriate covenants and restrictions and that the lands and buildings conveyed by the state will reasonably be available for public visits according to agreement between Sagamore Institute, Inc. and the state. Notwithstanding the foregoing provisions the state may convey to the town of Arietta fifty acres of forest preserve land within such town for public use in providing for the extension of the runway and landing strip of the Piseco airport and providing for the maintenance of a clear zone around such runway, and in exchange therefor,

the town of Arietta shall convey to the state fifty-three acres of true forest land located in lot 2 township 2 Totten and Crossfield's Purchase in the town of Lake Pleasant.

Notwithstanding the foregoing provisions and subject to legislative approval prior to actual transfer of title, the state may convey to the town of Keene, Essex county, for public use as a cemetery owned by such town, approximately twelve acres of forest preserve land within such town and, in exchange therefor, the town of Keene shall convey to the state for incorporation into the forest preserve approximately one hundred forty-four acres of land, together with an easement over land owned by such town including the riverbed adjacent to the land to be conveyed to the state that will restrict further development of such land, on condition that the legislature shall determine that the property to be received by the state is at least equal in value to the land to be conveyed by the state.

Notwithstanding the foregoing provisions and subject to legislative approval prior to actual transfer of title, because there is no viable alternative to using forest preserve lands for the siting of drinking water wells and necessary appurtenances and because such wells are necessary to meet drinking water quality standards, the state may convey to the town of Long Lake, Hamilton county, one acre of forest preserve land within such town for public use as the site of such drinking water wells and necessary appurtenances for the municipal water supply for the hamlet of Raquette Lake. In exchange therefor, the town of Long Lake shall convey to the state at least twelve acres of land located in Hamilton county for incorporation into the forest preserve that the legislature shall determine is at least equal in value to the land to be conveyed by the state. The Raquette Lake surface reservoir shall be abandoned as a drinking water supply source.

Notwithstanding the foregoing provisions and subject to legislative approval prior to actual transfer of title, the state may convey to National Grid up to six acres adjoining State Route 56 in St. Lawrence County where it passes through Forest Preserve in Township 5, Lots 1, 2, 5 and 6 that is necessary and appropriate for National Grid to construct a new 46kV power line and in exchange therefore National Grid shall convey to the state for incorporation into the forest preserve at least 10 acres of forest land owned by National Grid in St. Lawrence county, on condition that the legislature shall determine that the property to be received by the state is at least equal in value to the land conveyed by the state.

Notwithstanding the foregoing provisions, the legislature may authorize the settlement, according to terms determined by the legislature, of title disputes in township forty, Totten and Crossfield purchase in the town of Long Lake, Hamilton county, to resolve longstanding and competing claims of title between the state and private parties in said township, provided that prior to, and as a condition of such settlement, land purchased without the use of state-appropriated funds, and suitable for incorporation in the forest preserve within the Adirondack park, shall be conveyed to the state on the condition that the legislature shall determine that the property to be conveyed to the state shall provide a net benefit to the forest preserve as compared to the township forty lands subject to such settlement.

Notwithstanding the foregoing provisions, the state may authorize NYCO Minerals, Inc. to engage in mineral sampling operations, solely at its expense, to determine the quantity and quality of wollastonite on approximately 200 acres of forest preserve land contained in lot 8, Stowers survey, town of Lewis, Essex county provided that NYCO Minerals, Inc. shall provide the data and information derived from such drilling to the state for appraisal purposes. Subject to legislative approval of the tracts to be exchanged prior to the actual transfer of the title, the state may subsequently convey said lot 8 to NYCO Minerals, Inc., and, in exchange therefor, NYCO Minerals, Inc. shall convey to the state for incorporation into the forest preserve not less than the same number of acres of land, on condition that the legislature shall determine that the lands to be received by the state are equal to or greater than the value of the land to be conveyed by the state and on condition that the assessed value of the land to be conveyed to the state shall total not less than one million dollars. When NYCO Minerals, Inc. terminates all mining operations on such lot 8 it shall remediate the site and convey title to such lot back to the state of New York for inclusion in the forest preserve. In the event that lot 8 is not conveyed to NYCO Minerals, Inc. pursuant to this paragraph, NYCO Minerals, Inc. nevertheless shall convey to the state for incorporation into the forest preserve not less than the

38

same number of acres of land that is disturbed by any mineral sampling operations conducted on said lot 8 pursuant to this paragraph on condition that the legislature shall determine that the lands to be received by the state are equal to or greater than the value of the lands disturbed by the mineral sampling operations. (Formerly §7 of Art. 7. Renumbered and amended by Constitutional Convention of 1938 and approved by vote of the people November 8, 1938; further amended by vote of the people November 4, 1941; November 4, 1947; November 5, 1957; November 3, 1959; November 5, 1963; November 2, 1965; November 6, 1979; November 8, 1983; November 3, 1987; November 5, 1991; November 7, 1995; November 6, 2007; November 3, 2009; November 5, 2013.)

[Reservoirs]
§2. The legislature may by general laws provide for the use of not exceeding three per centum of such lands for the construction and maintenance of reservoirs for municipal water supply, and for the canals of the state. Such reservoirs shall be constructed, owned and controlled by the state, but such work shall not be undertaken until after the boundaries and high flow lines thereof shall have been accurately surveyed and fixed, and after public notice, hearing and determination that such lands are required for such public use. The expense of any such improvements shall be apportioned on the public and private property and municipalities benefited to the extent of the benefits received. Any such reservoir shall always be operated by the state and the legislature shall provide for a charge upon the property and municipalities benefited for a reasonable return to the state upon the value of the rights and property of the state used and the services of the state rendered, which shall be fixed for terms of not exceeding ten years and be readjustable at the end of any term. Unsanitary conditions shall not be created or continued by any such public works. (Derived in part from former §7 of Art. 7. Renumbered and amended by Constitutional Convention of 1938 and approved by vote of the people November 8, 1938; further amended by vote of the people November 3, 1953.)

[Forest and wild life conservation; use or disposition of certain lands authorized]
§3. 1. Forest and wild life conservation are hereby declared to be policies of the state. For the purpose of carrying out such policies the legislature may appropriate moneys for the acquisition by the state of land, outside of the Adirondack and Catskill parks as now fixed by law, for the practice of forest or wild life conservation. The prohibitions of section 1 of this article shall not apply to any lands heretofore or hereafter acquired or dedicated for such purposes within the forest preserve counties but outside of the Adirondack and Catskill parks as now fixed by law, except that such lands shall not be leased, sold or exchanged, or be taken by any corporation, public or private.

2. As to any other lands of the state, now owned or hereafter acquired, constituting the forest preserve referred to in section one of this article, but outside of the Adirondack and Catskill parks as now fixed by law, and consisting in any case of not more than one hundred contiguous acres entirely separated from any other portion of the forest preserve, the legislature may by appropriate legislation, notwithstanding the provisions of section one of this article, authorize: (a) the dedication thereof for the practice of forest or wild life conservation; or (b) the use thereof for public recreational or other state purposes or the sale, exchange or other disposition thereof; provided, however, that all moneys derived from the sale or other disposition of any of such lands shall be paid into a special fund of the treasury and be expended only for the acquisition of additional lands for such forest preserve within either such Adirondack or Catskill park. (Formerly §16 of Art. 7. Renumbered and amended by Constitutional Convention of 1938 and approved by vote of the people November 8, 1938; further amended by vote of the people November 5, 1957; November 6, 1973.)

[Protection of natural resources; development of agricultural lands]
§4. The policy of the state shall be to conserve and protect its natural resources and scenic beauty and encourage the development and improvement of its agricultural lands for the production of food and other agricultural products. The legislature, in implementing this policy, shall include adequate provision for the abatement of air and water pollution and of excessive and unnecessary noise, the protection of agricultural

lands, wetlands and shorelines, and the development and regulation of water resources. The legislature shall further provide for the acquisition of lands and waters, including improvements thereon and any interest therein, outside the forest preserve counties, and the dedication of properties so acquired or now owned, which because of their natural beauty, wilderness character, or geological, ecological or historical significance, shall be preserved and administered for the use and enjoyment of the people. Properties so dedicated shall constitute the state nature and historical preserve and they shall not be taken or otherwise disposed of except by law enacted by two successive regular sessions of the legislature. (New. Added by vote of the people November 4, 1969.)

[Violations of article; how restrained]
§5. A violation of any of the provisions of this article may be restrained at the suit of the people or, with the consent of the supreme court in appellate division, on notice to the attorney-general at the suit of any citizen. (New. Derived from former §7 of Art. 7. Adopted by Constitutional Convention of 1938 and approved by vote of the people November 8, 1938. Renumbered §5 by vote of the people November 4, 1969.)

ARTICLE XV
CANALS

[Disposition of canals and canal properties prohibited]
Section 1. The legislature shall not sell, abandon or otherwise dispose of the now existing or future improved barge canal, the divisions of which are the Erie canal, the Oswego canal, the Champlain canal, and the Cayuga and Seneca canals, or of the terminals constructed as part of the barge canal system; nor shall it sell, abandon or otherwise dispose of any portion of the canal system existing prior to the barge canal improvement which portion forms a part of, or functions as a part of, the present barge canal system; but such canals and terminals shall remain the property of the state and under its management and control forever. This prohibition shall not prevent the legislature, by appropriate laws, from authorizing the granting of revocable permits or leases for periods of time as authorized by the legislature for the occupancy or use of such lands or structures. (Formerly §8 of Art. 7. Renumbered and amended by Constitutional Convention of 1938 and approved by vote of the people November 8, 1938; November 5, 1991.)

[Prohibition inapplicable to lands and properties no longer useful; disposition authorized]
§2. The prohibition of sale, abandonment or other disposition contained in section 1 of this article shall not apply to barge canal lands, barge canal terminals or barge canal terminal lands which have or may become no longer necessary or useful for canal or terminal purposes; nor to any canal lands and appertaining structures constituting the canal system prior to the barge canal improvement which have or may become no longer necessary or useful in conjunction with the now existing barge canal. The legislature may by appropriate legislation authorize the sale, exchange, abandonment or other disposition of any barge canal lands, barge canal terminals, barge canal terminal lands or other canal lands and appertaining structures which have or may become no longer necessary or useful as a part of the barge canal system, as an aid to navigation thereon, or for barge canal terminal purposes. (Formerly duplicate §8 of Art. 7. Renumbered and amended by Constitutional Convention of 1938 and approved by vote of the people November 8, 1938; November 5, 1991.)

[Contracts for work and materials; special revenue fund]
§3. All boats navigating the canals and the owners and masters thereof, shall be subject to such laws and regulations as have been or may hereafter be enacted concerning the navigation of the canals. The legislature shall annually make provision for the expenses of the superintendence and repairs of the canals, and may provide for the improvement of the canals in such manner as shall be provided by law notwithstanding the creation of a special revenue fund as provided in this section. All contracts for work or materials on any canal shall be made with the persons who shall offer to do or provide the same at the lowest responsible price, with adequate security for their performance as provided by law.

39

All funds that may be derived from any sale or other disposition of any barge canal lands, barge canal terminals, barge canal terminal lands or other canal lands and appertaining structures and any other funds collected for the use of the canals or canal lands shall be paid into a special revenue fund of the treasury. Such funds shall only be expended for the maintenance, construction, reconstruction, development or promotion of the canal, canal lands, or lands adjacent to the canal as provided by law. (Formerly §9 of Art. 7. Renumbered and amended by Constitutional Convention of 1938 and approved by vote of the people November 8, 1938; November 5, 1991.)

[Lease or transfer to federal government of barge canal system authorized]
§4. Notwithstanding the prohibition of sale, abandonment or other disposition contained in section one of this article, the legislature may authorize by law the lease or transfer to the federal government of the barge canal, consisting of the Erie, Oswego, Champlain, Cayuga and Seneca divisions and the barge canal terminals and facilities for purposes of operation, improvement and inclusion in the national system of inland waterways. Such lease or transfer to the federal government for the purposes specified herein may be made upon such terms and conditions as the legislature may determine with or without compensation to the state. Nothing contained herein shall prevent the legislature from providing annual appropriations for the state's share, if any, of the cost of operation, maintenance and improvement of the barge canal, the divisions thereof, terminals and facilities in the event of the transfer of the barge canal in whole to the federal government whether by lease or transfer.

The legislature, in determining the state's share of the annual cost of operation, maintenance and improvement of the barge canal, the several divisions, terminals and facilities, shall give consideration and evaluate the benefits derived from the barge canal for purposes of flood control, conservation and utilization of water resources. (Added by vote of the people November 3, 1959.)

ARTICLE XVI[12]
TAXATION

[Power of taxation; exemptions from taxation]
Section 1. The power of taxation shall never be surrendered, suspended or contracted away, except as to securities issued for public purposes pursuant to law. Any laws which delegate the taxing power shall specify the types of taxes which may be imposed thereunder and provide for their review.

Exemptions from taxation may be granted only by general laws. Exemptions may be altered or repealed except those exempting real or personal property used exclusively for religious, educational or charitable purposes as defined by law and owned by any corporation or association organized or conducted exclusively for one or more of such purposes and not operating for profit.

[Assessments for taxation purposes]
§2. The legislature shall provide for the supervision, review and equalization of assessments for purposes of taxation. Assessments shall in no case exceed full value.

Nothing in this constitution shall be deemed to prevent the legislature from providing for the assessment, levy and collection of village taxes by the taxing authorities of those subdivisions of the state in which the lands comprising the respective villages are located, nor from providing that the respective counties of the state may loan or advance to any village located in whole or in part within such county the amount of any tax which shall have been levied for village purposes upon any lands located within such county and remaining unpaid.

[Situs of intangible personal property; taxation of]
§3. Moneys, credits, securities and other intangible personal property within the state not employed in carrying on any business therein by the owner shall

be deemed to be located at the domicile of the owner for purposes of taxation, and, if held in trust, shall not be deemed to be located in this state for purposes of taxation because of the trustee being domiciled in this state, provided that if no other state has jurisdiction to subject such property held in trust to death taxation, it may be deemed property having a taxable situs within this state for purposes of death taxation. Intangible personal property shall not be taxed ad valorem nor shall any excise tax be levied solely because of the ownership or possession thereof, except that the income therefrom may be taken into consideration in computing any excise tax measured by income generally. Undistributed profits shall not be taxed.

[Certain corporations not to be discriminated against]
§4. Where the state has power to tax corporations incorporated under the laws of the United States there shall be no discrimination in the rates and method of taxation between such corporations and other corporations exercising substantially similar functions and engaged in substantially similar business within the state.

[Compensation of public officers and employees subject to taxation]
§5. All salaries, wages and other compensation, except pensions, paid to officers and employees of the state and its subdivisions and agencies shall be subject to taxation. (Amended by vote of the people November 6, 2001.)

[Public improvements or services; contract of indebtedness; creation of public corporations]
§6. Notwithstanding any provision of this or any other article of this constitution to the contrary, the legislature may by law authorize a county, city, town or village, or combination thereof acting together, to undertake the development of public improvements or services, including the acquisition of land, for the purpose of redevelopment of economically unproductive, blighted or deteriorated areas and, in furtherance thereof, to contract indebtedness. Any such indebtedness shall be contracted by any such county, city, town or village, or combination thereof acting together, without the pledge of its faith and credit, or the faith and credit of the state, for the payment of the principal thereof and the interest thereon, and such indebtedness may be paid without restriction as to the amount or relative amount of annual installments. The amount of any indebtedness contracted under this section may be excluded in ascertaining the power of such county, city, town or village to contract indebtedness within the provisions of this constitution relating thereto. Any county, city, town or village contracting indebtedness pursuant to this section for redevelopment of an economically unproductive, blighted or deteriorated area shall pledge to the payment thereof that portion of the taxes raised by it on real estate in such area which, in any year, is attributed to the increase in value of taxable real estate resulting from such redevelopment. The legislature may further authorize any county, city, town or village, or combination thereof acting together, to carry out the powers and duties conferred by this section by means of a public corporation created therefor. (New. Added by vote of the people November 8, 1983; amended by vote of the people November 6, 2001.)

ARTICLE XVII
SOCIAL WELFARE

[Public relief and care]
Section 1. The aid, care and support of the needy are public concerns and shall be provided by the state and by such of its subdivisions, and in such manner and by such means, as the legislature may from time to time determine. (New. Adopted by Constitutional Convention of 1938 and approved by vote of the people November 8, 1938.)

[State board of social welfare; powers and duties]
§2. The state board of social welfare shall be continued. It shall visit and inspect, or cause to be visited and inspected by members of its staff, all public and private institutions, whether state, county, municipal, incorporated or not incorporated, which are in receipt of public funds and which are of a charitable, eleemosynary, correctional or reformatory character, including all reformatories for juveniles and institutions or agencies exercising

---

[12] Entire new article, adopted by Constitutional Convention of 1938 and approved by vote of the people November 8, 1938.

40

custody of dependent, neglected or delinquent children, but excepting state institutions for the education and support of the blind, the deaf and the dumb, and excepting also such institutions as are hereinafter made subject to the visitation and inspection of the department of mental hygiene or the state commission of correction. As to institutions, whether incorporated or not incorporated, having inmates, but not in receipt of public funds, which are of a charitable, eleemosynary, correctional or reformatory character, and agencies, whether incorporated or not incorporated, not in receipt of public funds, which exercise custody of dependent, neglected or delinquent children, the state board of social welfare shall make inspections, or cause inspections to be made by members of its staff, but solely as to matters directly affecting the health, safety, treatment and training of their inmates, or of the children under their custody. Subject to the control of the legislature and pursuant to the procedure prescribed by general law, the state board of social welfare may make rules and regulations, not inconsistent with this constitution, with respect to all of the functions, powers and duties with which the department and the state board of social welfare are herein or shall be charged. (New. Derived in part from former §11 of Art. 8. Adopted by Constitutional Convention of 1938 and approved by vote of the people November 8, 1938.)

[Public health]
§3. The protection and promotion of the health of the inhabitants of the state are matters of public concern and provision therefor shall be made by the state and by such of its subdivisions and in such manner, and by such means as the legislature shall from time to time determine. (New. Adopted by Constitutional Convention of 1938 and approved by vote of the people November 8, 1938.)

[Care and treatment of persons suffering from mental disorder or defect; visitation of institutions for]
§4. The care and treatment of persons suffering from mental disorder or defect and the protection of the mental health of the inhabitants of the state may be provided by state and local authorities and in such manner as the legislature may from time to time determine. The head of the department of mental hygiene shall visit and inspect, or cause to be visited and inspected by members of his or her staff, all institutions either public or private used for the care and treatment of persons suffering from mental disorder or defect. (New. Adopted by Constitutional Convention of 1938 and approved by vote of the people November 8, 1938; amended by vote of the people November 6, 2001.)

[Institutions for detention of criminals; probation; parole; state commission of correction]
§5. The legislature may provide for the maintenance and support of institutions for the detention of persons charged with or convicted of crime and for systems of probation and parole of persons convicted of crime. There shall be a state commission of correction, which shall visit and inspect or cause to be visited and inspected by members of its staff, all institutions used for the detention of sane adults charged with or convicted of crime. (New. Derived in part from former §11 of Art. 8. Adopted by Constitutional Convention of 1938 and approved by vote of the people November 8, 1938. Amended by vote of the people November 6, 1973.)

[Visitation and inspection]
§6. Visitation and inspection as herein authorized, shall not be exclusive of other visitation and inspection now or hereafter authorized by law. (New. Derived from former §13 of Art. 8. Adopted by Constitutional Convention of 1938 and approved by vote of the people November 8, 1938.)

[Loans for hospital construction]
§7. Notwithstanding any other provision of this constitution, the legislature may authorize the state, a municipality or a public corporation acting as an instrumentality of the state or municipality to lend its money or credit to or in aid of any corporation or association, regulated by law as to its charges, profits, dividends, and disposition of its property or franchises, for the purpose of providing such hospital or other facilities for the prevention, diagnosis or treatment of human disease, pain, injury, disability, deformity

or physical condition, and for facilities incidental or appurtenant thereto as may be prescribed by law. (New. Added by vote of the people November 4, 1969.)

ARTICLE XVIII[13]
Housing

[Housing and nursing home accommodations for persons of low income; slum clearance]
Section 1. Subject to the provisions of this article, the legislature may provide in such manner, by such means and upon such terms and conditions as it may prescribe for low rent housing and nursing home accommodations for persons of low income as defined by law, or for the clearance, replanning, reconstruction and rehabilitation of substandard and insanitary areas, or for both such purposes, and for recreational and other facilities incidental or appurtenant thereto. (Amended by vote of the people November 2, 1965.)

[*Idem*; powers of legislature in aid of]
§2. For and in aid of such purposes, notwithstanding any provision in any other article of this constitution, but subject to the limitations contained in this article, the legislature may: make or contract to make or authorize to be made or contracted capital or periodic subsidies by the state to any city, town, village, or public corporation, payable only with moneys appropriated therefor from the general fund of the state; authorize any city, town or village to make or contract to make such subsidies to any public corporation, payable only with moneys locally appropriated therefor from the general or other fund available for current expenses of such municipality; authorize the contracting of indebtedness for the purpose of providing moneys out of which it may make or contract to make or authorize to be made or contracted loans by the state to any city, town, village or public corporation; authorize any city, town or village to make or contract to make loans to any public corporation; authorize any city, town or village to guarantee the principal of and interest on, or only the interest on, indebtedness contracted by a public corporation; authorize and provide for loans by the state and authorize loans by any city, town or village to or in aid of corporations regulated by law as to rents, profits, dividends and disposition of their property or franchises and engaged in providing housing facilities or nursing home accommodations; authorize any city, town or village to make loans to the owners of existing multiple dwellings for the rehabilitation and improvement thereof for occupancy by persons of low income as defined by law; grant or authorize tax exemptions in whole or in part, except that no such exemption may be granted or authorized for a period of more than sixty years; authorize cooperation with and the acceptance of aid from the United States; grant the power of eminent domain to any city, town or village, to any public corporation and to any corporation regulated by law as to rents, profits, dividends and disposition of its property or franchises and engaged in providing housing facilities.

As used in this article, the term "public corporation" shall mean any corporate governmental agency (except a county or municipal corporation) organized pursuant to law to accomplish any or all of the purposes specified in this article. (Amended by vote of the people November 2, 1965.)

[Article VII to apply to state debts under this article, with certain exceptions; amortization of state debts; capital and periodic subsidies]
§3. The provisions of article VII, not inconsistent with this article, relating to debts of the state shall apply to all debts contracted by the state for the purpose of providing moneys out of which to make loans pursuant to this article, except (a) that any law or laws authorizing the contracting of such debt, not exceeding in the aggregate three hundred million dollars, shall take effect without submission to the people, and the contracting of a greater amount of debt may not be authorized prior to January first, nineteen hundred forty-two; (b) that any such debt and each portion thereof, except as

---

[13] Entire new article, adopted by Constitutional Convention of 1938 and approved by vote of the people November 8, 1938.

41

hereinafter provided, shall be paid in equal annual installments, the first of which shall be payable not more than three years, and the last of which shall be payable not more than fifty years, after such debt or portion thereof shall have been contracted; and (c) that any law authorizing the contracting of such debt may be submitted to the people at a general election, whether or not any other law or bill shall be submitted to be voted for or against at such election.

Debts contracted by the state for the purpose of providing money out of which to make loans to or in aid of corporations regulated by law as to rents, profits, dividends and disposition of their property or franchises and engaged in providing housing facilities pursuant to this article may be paid in such manner that the total annual charges required for the payment of principal and interest are approximately equal and constant for the entire period in which any of the bonds issued therefor are outstanding.

Any law authorizing the making of contracts for capital or periodic subsidies to be paid with moneys currently appropriated from the general fund of the state shall take effect without submission to the people, and the amount to be paid under such contracts shall not be included in ascertaining the amount of indebtedness which may be contracted by the state under this article; provided, however, (a) that such periodic subsidies shall not be paid for a period longer than the life of the projects assisted thereby, but in any event for not more than sixty years; (b) that no contracts for periodic subsidies shall be entered into in any one year requiring payments aggregating more than one million dollars in any one year; and (c) that there shall not be outstanding at any one time contracts for periodic subsidies requiring payments exceeding an aggregate of thirty-four million dollars in any one year, unless a law authorizing contracts in excess of such amounts shall have been submitted to and approved by the people at a general election; and any such law may be submitted to the people at a general election, whether or not any other law or bill shall be submitted to be voted for or against at such election. (Amended by vote of the people November 8, 1955; further amended by vote of the people November 5, 1957.)

[Powers of cities, towns and villages to contract indebtedness in aid of low rent housing and slum clearance projects; restrictions thereon]

§4. To effectuate any of the purposes of this article, the legislature may authorize any city, town or village to contract indebtedness to an amount which shall not exceed two per centum of the average assessed valuation of the real estate of such city, town or village subject to taxation, as determined by the last completed assessment roll and the four preceding assessment rolls of such city, town or village, for city, town or village taxes prior to the contracting of such indebtedness. In ascertaining the power of a city, or village having a population of five thousand or more as determined by the last federal census, to contract indebtedness pursuant to this article there may be excluded any such indebtedness if the project or projects aided by guarantees representing such indebtedness or by loans for which such indebtedness was contracted shall have yielded during the preceding year net revenue to be determined annually by deducting from the gross revenues, including periodic subsidies therefor, received from such project or projects, all costs of operation, maintenance, repairs and replacements, and the interest on such indebtedness and the amounts required in such year for the payment of such indebtedness; provided that in the case of guarantees such interest and such amounts shall have been paid, and in the case of loans an amount equal to such interest and such amounts shall have been paid to such city or village. The legislature shall prescribe the method by which the amount of any such indebtedness to be excluded shall be determined, and no such indebtedness shall be excluded except in accordance with such determination. The legislature may confer appropriate jurisdiction on the appellate division of the supreme court in the judicial departments in which such cities or villages are located for the purpose of determining the amount of any such indebtedness to be so excluded.

The liability of a city, town or village on account of any contract for capital or periodic subsidies to be paid subsequent to the then current year shall, for the purpose of ascertaining the power of such city, town or village to contract indebtedness, be deemed indebtedness in the amount of the commuted value of the total of such capital or periodic subsidies remaining unpaid, calculated on the basis of an annual interest rate of four per centum. Such periodic subsidies shall not be contracted for a period longer than the life of the projects assisted thereby, and in no event for more than sixty years. Indebtedness contracted pursuant to this article shall be excluded in ascertaining the power of a city or such village otherwise to create indebtedness under any other section of this constitution. Notwithstanding the foregoing the legislature shall not authorize any city or village having a population of five thousand or more to contract indebtedness hereunder in excess of the limitations prescribed by any other article of this constitution unless at the same time it shall by law require such city or village to levy annually a tax or taxes other than an ad valorem tax on real estate to an extent sufficient to provide for the payment of the principal of and interest on any such indebtedness. Nothing herein contained, however, shall be construed to prevent such city or village from pledging its faith and credit for the payment of such principal and interest nor shall any such law prevent recourse to an ad valorem tax on real estate to the extent that revenue derived from such other tax or taxes in any year, together with revenues from the project or projects aided by the proceeds of such indebtedness, shall become insufficient to provide fully for payment of such principal and interest in that year. (Amended by vote of the people November 8, 1949.)

[Liability for certain loans made by the state to certain public corporations]

§5. Any city, town or village shall be liable for the repayment of any loans and interest thereon made by the state to any public corporation, acting as an instrumentality of such city, town or village. Such liability of a city, town or village shall be excluded in ascertaining the power of such city, town or village to become indebted pursuant to the provisions of this article, except that in the event of a default in payment under the terms of any such loan, the unpaid balance thereof shall be included in ascertaining the power of such city, town or village to become so indebted. No subsidy, in addition to any capital or periodic subsidy originally contracted for in aid of any project or projects authorized under this article, shall be paid by the state to a city, town, village or public corporation, acting as an instrumentality thereof, for the purpose of enabling such city, town, village or corporation to remedy an actual default or avoid an impending default in the payment of principal or interest on a loan which has been theretofore made by the state to such city, town, village or corporation pursuant to this article. (Amended by vote of the people November 5, 1957.)

[Loans and subsidies; restrictions on and preference in occupancy of projects]

§6. No loan, or subsidy shall be made by the state to aid any project unless such project is in conformity with a plan or undertaking for the clearance, replanning and reconstruction or rehabilitation of a substandard and unsanitary area or areas and for recreational and other facilities incidental or appurtenant thereto. The legislature may provide additional conditions to the making of such loans or subsidies consistent with the purposes of this article. The occupancy of any such project shall be restricted to persons of low income as defined by law and preference shall be given to persons who live or shall have lived in such area or areas.

[Liability arising from guarantees to be deemed indebtedness; method of computing]

§7. The liability arising from any guarantee of the principal of and interest on indebtedness contracted by a public corporation shall be deemed indebtedness in the amount of the face value of the principal thereof remaining unpaid. The liability arising from any guarantee of only the interest on indebtedness contracted by a public corporation shall be deemed indebtedness in the amount of the commuted value of the total interest guaranteed and remaining unpaid, calculated on the basis of an annual interest rate of four per centum.

[Excess condemnation]

§8. Any agency of the state, or any city, town, village, or public corporation, which is empowered by law to take private property by eminent domain for any of the public purposes specified in section one of this article, may be empowered by the legislature to take property necessary for any such purpose but in excess of that required for public use after such purpose shall have been accomplished; and to improve and utilize such excess, wholly or

42

partly for any other public purpose, or to lease or sell such excess with restrictions to preserve and protect such improvement or improvements.

[Acquisition of property for purposes of article]

§9. Subject to any limitation imposed by the legislature, the state, or any city, town, village or public corporation, may acquire by purchase, gift, eminent domain or otherwise, such property as it may deem ultimately necessary or proper to effectuate the purposes of this article, or any of them, although temporarily not required for such purposes.

[Power of legislature; construction of article]

§10. The legislature is empowered to make all laws which it shall deem necessary and proper for carrying into execution the foregoing powers. This article shall be construed as extending powers which otherwise might be limited by other articles of this constitution and shall not be construed as imposing additional limitations; but nothing in this article contained shall be deemed to authorize or empower the state, or any city, town, village or public corporation to engage in any private business or enterprise other than the building and operation of low rent dwelling houses for persons of low income as defined by law, or the loaning of money to owners of existing multiple dwellings as herein provided.

ARTICLE XIX
AMENDMENTS TO CONSTITUTION

[Amendments to constitution; how proposed, voted upon and ratified; failure of attorney-general to render opinion not to affect validity]

Section 1. Any amendment or amendments to this constitution may be proposed in the senate and assembly whereupon such amendment or amendments shall be referred to the attorney-general whose duty it shall be within twenty days thereafter to render an opinion in writing to the senate and assembly as to the effect of such amendment or amendments upon other provisions of the constitution. Upon receiving such opinion, if the amendment or amendments as proposed or as amended shall be agreed to by a majority of the members elected to each of the two houses, such proposed amendment or amendments shall be entered on their journals, and the ayes and noes taken thereon, and referred to the next regular legislative session convening after the succeeding general election of members of the assembly, and shall be published for three months previous to the time of making such choice; and if in such legislative session, such proposed amendment or amendments shall be agreed to by a majority of all the members elected to each house, then it shall be the duty of the legislature to submit each proposed amendment or amendments to the people for approval in such manner and at such times as the legislature shall prescribe; and if the people shall approve and ratify such amendment or amendments by a majority of the electors voting thereon, such amendment or amendments shall become a part of the constitution on the first day of January next after such approval. Neither the failure of the attorney-general to render an opinion concerning such a proposed amendment nor his or her failure to do so timely shall affect the validity of such proposed amendment or legislative action thereon. (Formerly §1 of Art. 14. Renumbered and amended by Constitutional Convention of 1938 and approved by vote of the people November 8, 1938; further amended by vote of the people November 4, 1941; November 6, 2001.)

[Future constitutional conventions; how called; election of delegates; compensation; quorum; submission of amendments; officers; employees; rules; vacancies]

§2. At the general election to be held in the year nineteen hundred fifty-seven, and every twentieth year thereafter, and also at such times as the legislature may by law provide, the question "Shall there be a convention to revise the constitution and amend the same?" shall be submitted to and decided by the electors of the state; and in case a majority of the electors voting thereon shall decide in favor of a convention for such purpose, the electors of every senate district of the state, as then organized, shall elect three delegates at the next ensuing general election, and the electors of the state voting at the same election shall elect fifteen delegates-at-large. The delegates so elected shall convene at the capitol on the first Tuesday of April next ensuing after their election, and shall continue their session until the business of such convention shall have been completed. Every delegate shall receive for his or her services the same compensation as shall then be annually payable to the members of the assembly and be reimbursed for actual traveling expenses, while the convention is in session, to the extent that a member of the assembly would then be entitled thereto in the case of a session of the legislature. A majority of the convention shall constitute a quorum for the transaction of business, and no amendment to the constitution shall be submitted for approval to the electors as hereinafter provided, unless by the assent of a majority of all the delegates elected to the convention, the ayes and noes being entered on the journal to be kept. The convention shall have the power to appoint such officers, employees and assistants as it may deem necessary, and fix their compensation and to provide for the printing of its documents, journal, proceedings and other expenses of said convention. The convention shall determine the rules of its own proceedings, choose its own officers, and be the judge of the election, returns and qualifications of its members. In case of a vacancy, by death, resignation or other cause, of any district delegate elected to the convention, such vacancy shall be filled by a vote of the remaining delegates representing the district in which such vacancy occurs. If such vacancy occurs in the office of a delegate-at-large, such vacancy shall be filled by a vote of the remaining delegates-at-large. Any proposed constitution or constitutional amendment which shall have been adopted by such convention, shall be submitted to a vote of the electors of the state at the time and in the manner provided by such convention, at an election which shall be held not less than six weeks after the adjournment of such convention. Upon the approval of such constitution or constitutional amendments, in the manner provided in the last preceding section, such constitution or constitutional amendment, shall go into effect on the first day of January next after such approval. (Formerly §2 of Art. 14. Renumbered and amended by Constitutional Convention of 1938 and approved by vote of the people November 8, 1938; further amended by vote of the people November 6, 2001.)

[Amendments simultaneously submitted by convention and legislature]

§3. Any amendment proposed by a constitutional convention relating to the same subject as an amendment proposed by the legislature, coincidently submitted to the people for approval shall, if approved, be deemed to supersede the amendment so proposed by the legislature. (Formerly §3 of Art. 14. Renumbered and amended by Constitutional Convention of 1938 and approved by vote of the people November 8, 1938.)

ARTICLE XX
WHEN TO TAKE EFFECT

[Time of taking effect]

Section 1. This constitution shall be in force from and including the first day of January, one thousand nine hundred thirty-nine, except as herein otherwise provided. (Formerly §1 of Art. 15. Renumbered and amended by Constitutional Convention of 1938 and approved by vote of the people November 8, 1938.)

★ ★ ★

DONE in Convention at the Capitol in the city of Albany, the twenty-fifth day of August, in the year one thousand nine hundred thirty-eight, and of the Independence of the United States of America the one hundred and sixty-third.
IN WITNESS WHEREOF, we have hereunto subscribed our names.

FREDERICK E. CRANE,
President and Delegate-at-Large

U.H. Boyden, *Secretary*

43

Appendix

Articles of Confederation

Articles of Confederation, 1777

To all to whom these Presents shall come, we the undersigned Delegates of the States affixed to our Names send greeting.

Articles of Confederation and perpetual Union between the states of New Hampshire, Massachusetts-bay Rhode Island and Providence Plantations, Connecticut, New York, New Jersey, Pennsylvania, Delaware, Maryland, Virginia, North Carolina, South Carolina and Georgia.

I.

The Stile of this Confederacy shall be **"The United States of America"**.

II.

Each state retains its sovereignty, freedom, and independence, and every power, jurisdiction, and right, which is not by this Confederation expressly delegated to the United States, in Congress assembled.

III.

The said States hereby severally enter into a firm league of friendship with each other, for their common defense, the security of their liberties, and their mutual and general welfare, binding themselves to assist each other, against all force offered to, or attacks made upon them, or any of them, on account of religion, sovereignty, trade, or any other pretense whatever.

IV.

The better to secure and perpetuate mutual friendship and intercourse among the people of the different States in this Union, the free inhabitants of each of these States, paupers, vagabonds, and fugitives from justice excepted, shall be entitled to all privileges and immunities of free citizens in the several States; and the people of each State shall free ingress and regress to and from any other State, and shall enjoy therein all the privileges of trade and commerce, subject to the same duties, impositions, and restrictions as the inhabitants thereof respectively, provided that such restrictions shall not extend so far as to prevent the removal of property imported into any State, to any other State, of which the owner is an inhabitant; provided also that no imposition, duties or restriction shall be laid by any State, on the property of the United States, or either of them.

If any person guilty of, or charged with, treason, felony, or other high misdemeanor in any State, shall flee from justice, and be found in any of the United States, he shall, upon demand of the Governor or executive power of the State from which he fled, be delivered up and removed to the State having jurisdiction of his offense.

Full faith and credit shall be given in each of these States to the records, acts, and judicial proceedings of the courts and magistrates of every other State.

V.

For the most convenient management of the general interests of the United States, delegates shall be annually appointed in such manner as the legislatures of each State shall direct, to meet in Congress on the first Monday in November, in every year, with a powerreserved to each State to recall its delegates, or any of them, at any time within the year, and to send others in their stead for the remainder of the year.

No State shall be represented in Congress by less than two, nor more than seven members; and no person shall be capable of being a delegate for more than three years in any term of six years; nor shall any person, being a delegate, be capable of holding any office under the United States, for which he, or another for his benefit, receives any salary, fees or emolument of any kind.

Each State shall maintain its own delegates in a meeting of the States, and while they act as members of the committee of the States.

In determining questions in the United States in Congress assembled, each State shall have one vote.

Freedom of speech and debate in Congress shall not be impeached or questioned in any court or place out of Congress, and the members of Congress shall be protected in their persons from arrests or imprisonments, during the time of their going to and from, and attendence on Congress, except for treason, felony, or breach of the peace.

VI.

No State, without the consent of the United States in Congress assembled, shall send any embassy to, or receive any embassy from, or enter into any conference, agreement, alliance or treaty with any King, Prince or State; nor shall any person holding any office of profit or trust under the United States, or any of them, accept any present, emolument, office or title of any kind whatever from any King, Prince or foreign State; nor shall the United States in Congress assembled, or any of them, grant any title of nobility.

No two or more States shall enter into any treaty, confederation or alliance whatever between them, without the consent of the United States in Congress assembled, specifying accurately the purposes for which the same is to be entered into, and how long it shall continue.

No State shall lay any imposts or duties, which may interfere with any stipulations in treaties, entered into by the United States in Congress assembled, with any King, Prince or State, in pursuance of any treaties already proposed by Congress, to the courts of France and Spain.

No vessel of war shall be kept up in time of peace by any State, except such number only, as shall be deemed necessary by the United States in Congress assembled, for the defense of such State, or its trade; nor shall any body of forces be kept up by any State in time of peace, except such number only, as in the judgement of the United States in Congress assembled, shall be deemed requisite to garrison the forts necessary for the defense of such State; but every State shall always keep up a well-regulated and disciplined militia, sufficiently armed and accoutered, and shall provide and constantly have ready for use, in public stores, a due number of filed pieces and tents, and a proper quantity of arms, ammunition and camp equipage.

No State shall engage in any war without the consent of the United States in Congress assembled, unless such State be actually invaded by enemies, or shall have received certain advice of a resolution being formed by some nation of

Indians to invade such State, and the danger is so imminent as not to admit of a delay till the United States in Congress assembled can be consulted; nor shall any State grant commissions to any ships or vessels of war, nor letters of marque or reprisal, except it be after a declaration of war by the United States in Congress assembled, and then only against the Kingdom or State and the subjects thereof, against which war has been so declared, and under such regulations as shall be established by the United States in Congress assembled, unless such State be infested by pirates, in which case vessels of war may be fitted out for that occasion, and kept so long as the danger shall continue, or until the United States in Congress assembled shall determine otherwise.

VII.

When land forces are raised by any State for the common defense, all officers of or under the rank of colonel, shall be appointed by the legislature of each State respectively, by whom such forces shall be raised, or in such manner as such State shall direct, and all vacancies shall be filled up by the State which first made the appointment.

VIII.

All charges of war, and all other expenses that shall be incurred for the common defense or general welfare, and allowed by the United States in Congress assembled, shall be defrayed out of a common treasury, which shall be supplied by the several States in proportion to the value of all land within each State, granted or surveyed for any person, as such land and the buildings and improvements thereon shall be estimated according to such mode as the United States in Congress assembled, shall from time to time direct and appoint.

The taxes for paying that proportion shall be laid and levied by the authority and direction of the legislatures of the several States within the time agreed upon by the United States in Congress assembled.

IX.

The United States in Congress assembled, shall have the sole and exclusive right and power of determining on peace and war, except in the cases mentioned in the sixth article—of sending and receiving ambassadors—entering into treaties and alliances, provided that no treaty of commerce shall be made whereby the legislative power of the respective States shall be restrained from imposing such imposts and duties on foreigners, as their own people are subjected to, or from prohibiting the exportation or importation of any species of goods or commodities whatsoever –of establishing rules for deciding in all cases, what captures on land or water shall be legal, and in what manner prizes taken by land or naval forces in the service of the United States shall be divided or appropriated –of granting letters of marque and reprisal in times of peace –appointing courts for the trial of piracies and felonies commited on the high seas and establishing courts for receiving and determining finally appeals in all cases of captures, provided that no member of Congress shall be appointed a judge of any of the said courts.

The United States in Congress assembled shall also be the last resort on appeal in all disputes and differences now subsisting or that hereafter may arise between two or more States concerning boundary, jurisdiction or any other causes whatever; which authority shall always be exercised in the manner following. Whenever the legislative or executive authority or lawful agent of any State in controversy with another shall present a petition to Congress stating the matter in question and praying for a hearing, notice thereof shall be given by order of

Congress to the legislative or executive authority of the other State in controversy, and a day assigned for the appearance of the parties by their lawful agents, who shall then be directed to appoint by joint consent, commissioners or judges to constitute a court for hearing and determining the matter in question: but if they cannot agree, Congress shall name three persons out of each of the United States, and from the list of such persons each party shall alternately strike out one, the petitioners beginning, until the number shall be reduced to thirteen; and from that number not less than seven, nor more than nine names as Congress shall direct, shall in the presence of Congress be drawn out by lot, and the persons whose names shall be so drawn or any five of them, shall be commissioners or judges, to hear and finally determine the controversy, so always as a major part of the judges who shall hear the cause shall agree in the determination: and if either party shall neglect to attend at the day appointed, without showing reasons, which Congress shall judge sufficient, or being present shall refuse to strike, the Congress shall proceed to nominate three persons out of each State, and the secretary of Congress shall strike in behalf of such party absent or refusing; and the judgement and sentence of the court to be appointed, in the manner before prescribed, shall be final and conclusive; and if any of the parties shall refuse to submit to the authority of such court, or to appear or defend their claim or cause, the court shall nevertheless proceed to pronounce sentence, or judgement, which shall in like manner be final and decisive, the judgement or sentence and other proceedings being in either case transmitted to Congress, and lodged among the acts of Congress for the security of the parties concerned: provided that every commissioner, before he sits in judgement, shall take an oath to be administered by one of the judges of the supreme or superior court of the State, where the cause shall be tried, 'well and truly to hear and determine the matter in question, according to the best of his judgement, without favor, affection or hope of reward': provided also, that no State shall be deprived of territory for the benefit of the United States.

All controversies concerning the private right of soil claimed under different grants of two or more States, whose jurisdictions as they may respect such lands, and the States which passed such grants are adjusted, the said grants or either of them being at the same time claimed to have originated antecedent to such settlement of jurisdiction, shall on the petition of either party to the Congress of the United States, be finally determined as near as may be in the same manner as is before presecribed for deciding disputes respecting territorial jurisdiction between different States.

The United States in Congress assembled shall also have the sole and exclusive right and power of regulating the alloy and value of coin struck by their own authority, or by that of the respective States—fixing the standards of weights and measures throughout the United States—regulating the trade and managing all affairs with the Indians, not members of any of the States, provided that the legislative right of any State within its own limits be not infringed or violated—establishing or regulating post offices from one State to another, throughout all the United States, and exacting such postage on the papers passing through the same as may be requisite to defray the expenses of the said office—appointing all officers of the land forces, in the service of the United States, excepting regimental officers—appointing all the officers of the naval forces, and commissioning all officers whatever in the service of the

United States—making rules for the government and regulation of the said land and naval forces, and directing their operations.

The United States in Congress assembled shall have authority to appoint a committee, to sit in the recess of Congress, to be denominated 'A Committee of the States', and to consist of one delegate from each State; and to appoint such other committees and civil officers as may be necessary for managing the general affairs of the United States under their direction—to appoint one of their members to preside, provided that no person be allowed to serve in the office of president more than one year in any term of three years; to ascertain the necessary sums of money to be raised for the service of the United States, and to appropriate and apply the same for defraying the public expenses—to borrow money, or emit bills on the credit of the United States, transmitting every half-year to the respective States an account of the sums of money so borrowed or emitted—to build and equip a navy—to agree upon the number of land forces, and to make requisitions from each State for its quota, in proportion to the number of white inhabitants in such State; which requisition shall be binding, and thereupon the legislature of each State shall appoint the regimental officers, raise the men and cloath, arm and equip them in a solid-like manner, at the expense of the United States; and the officers and men so cloathed, armed and equipped shall march to the place appointed, and within the time agreed on by the United States in Congress assembled. But if the United States in Congress assembled shall, on consideration of circumstances judge proper that any State should not raise men, or should raise a smaller number of men than the quota thereof, such extra number shall be raised, officered, cloathed, armed and equipped in the same manner as the quota of each State, unless the legislature of such State shall judge that such extra number cannot be safely spread out in the same, in which case they shall raise, officer, cloath, arm and equip as many of such extra number as they judeg can be safely spared. And the officers and men so cloathed, armed, and equipped, shall march to the place appointed, and within the time agreed on by the United States in Congress assembled.

The United States in Congress assembled shall never engage in a war, nor grant letters of marque or reprisal in time of peace, nor enter into any treaties or alliances, nor coin money, nor regulate the value thereof, nor ascertain the sums and expenses necessary for the defense and welfare of the United States, or any of them, nor emit bills, nor borrow money on the credit of the United States, nor appropriate money, nor agree upon the number of vessels of war, to be built or purchased, or the number of land or sea forces to be raised, nor appoint a commander in chief of the army or navy, unless nine States assent to the same: nor shall a question on any other point, except for adjourning from day to day be determined, unless by the votes of the majority of the United States in Congress assembled.

The Congress of the United States shall have power to adjourn to any time within the year, and to any place within the United States, so that no period of adjournment be for a longer duration than the space of six months, and shall publish the journal of their proceedings monthly, except such parts thereof relating to treaties, alliances or military operations, as in their judgement require secrecy; and the yeas and nays of the delegates of each State on any question shall be entered on the journal, when it is desired by any delegates of a State, or any of them, at his or their request shall be furnished with a transcript of the said journal, except such parts as are above excepted, to lay before the legislatures of the several States.

X.

The Committee of the States, or any nine of them, shall be authorized to execute, in the recess of Congress, such of the powers of Congress as the United States in Congress assembled, by the consent of the nine States, shall from time to time think expedient to vest them with; provided that no power be delegated to the said Committee, for the exercise of which, by the Articles of Confederation, the voice of nine States in the Congress of the United States assembled be requisite.

XI.

Canada acceding to this confederation, and adjoining in the measures of the United States, shall be admitted into, and entitled to all the advantages of this Union; but no other colony shall be admitted into the same, unless such admission be agreed to by nine States.

XII.

All bills of credit emitted, monies borrowed, and debts contracted by, or under the authority of Congress, before the assembling of the United States, in pursuance of the present confederation, shall be deemed and considered as a charge against the United States, for payment and satisfaction whereof the said United States, and the public faith are hereby solemnly pleged.

XIII.

Every State shall abide by the determination of the United States in Congress assembled, on all questions which by this confederation are submitted to them. And the Articles of this Confederation shall be inviolably observed by every State, and the Union shall be perpetual; nor shall any alteration at any time hereafter be made in any of them; unless such alteration be agreed to in a Congress of the United States, and be afterwards confirmed by the legislatures of every State.

And Whereas it hath pleased the Great Governor of the World to incline the hearts of the legislatures we respectively represent in Congress, to approve of, and to authorize us to ratify the said Articles of Confederation and perpetual Union. Know Ye that we the undersigned delegates, by virtue of the power and authority to us given for that purpose, do by these presents, in the name and in behalf of our respective constituents, fully and entirely ratify and confirm each and every of the said Articles of Confederation and perpetual Union, and all and singular the matters and things therein contained: And we do further solemnly plight and engage the faith of our respective constituents, that they shall abide by the determinations of the United States in Congress assembled, on all questions, which by the said Confederation are submitted to them. And that the Articles thereof shall be inviolably observed by the States we respectively represent, and that the Union shall be perpetual.

In Witness whereof we have hereunto set our hands in Congress. Done at Philadelphia in the State of Pennsylvania the ninth day of July in the Year of our Lord One Thousand Seven Hundred and Seventy-Eight, and in the Third Year of the independence of America.

Agreed to by Congress 15 November 1777 In force after ratification by Maryland, 1 March 1781

Appendix

The Declaration of Independence: A Transcription

United States Declaration of Independence, 1776

IN CONGRESS, July 4, 1776.

The unanimous Declaration of the thirteen united States of America,

When in the Course of human events, it becomes necessary for one people to dissolve the political bands which have connected them with another, and to assume among the powers of the earth, the separate and equal station to which the Laws of Nature and of Nature's God entitle them, a decent respect to the opinions of mankind requires that they should declare the causes which impel them to the separation.

We hold these truths to be self-evident, that all men are created equal, that they are endowed by their Creator with certain unalienable Rights, that among these are Life, Liberty and the pursuit of Happiness.—That to secure these rights, Governments are instituted among Men, deriving their just powers from the consent of the governed,—That whenever any Form of Government becomes destructive of these ends, it is the Right of the People to alter or to abolish it, and to institute new Government, laying its foundation on such principles and organizing its powers in such form, as to them shall seem most likely to effect their Safety and Happiness. Prudence, indeed, will dictate that Governments long established should not be changed for light and transient causes; and accordingly all experience hath shewn, that mankind are more disposed to suffer, while evils are sufferable, than to right themselves by abolishing the forms to which they are accustomed. But when a long train of abuses and usurpations, pursuing invariably the same Object evinces a design to reduce them under absolute Despotism, it is their right, it is their duty, to throw off such Government, and to provide new Guards for their future security. –Such has been the patient sufferance of these Colonies; and such is now the necessity which constrains them to alter their former Systems of Government. The history of the present King of Great Britain is a history of repeated injuries and usurpations, all having in direct object the establishment of an absolute Tyranny over these States. To prove this, let Facts be submitted to a candid world.

He has refused his Assent to Laws, the most wholesome and necessary for the public good.

He has forbidden his Governors to pass Laws of immediate and pressing importance, unless suspended in their operation till his Assent should be obtained; and when so suspended, he has utterly neglected to attend to them.

He has refused to pass other Laws for the accommodation of large districts of people, unless those people would relinquish the right of Representation in the Legislature, a right inestimable to them and formidable to tyrants only.

He has called together legislative bodies at places unusual, uncomfortable, and distant from the depository of their public Records, for the sole purpose of fatiguing them into compliance with his measures.

He has dissolved Representative Houses repeatedly, for opposing with manly firmness his invasions on the rights of the people.

He has refused for a long time, after such dissolutions, to cause others to be elected; whereby the Legislative powers, incapable of Annihilation, have returned to the People at large for their exercise; the State remaining in the mean time exposed to all the dangers of invasion from without, and convulsions within.

He has endeavoured to prevent the population of these States; for that purpose obstructing the Laws for Naturalization of Foreigners; refusing to pass others to encourage their migrations hither, and raising the conditions of new Appropriations of Lands.

He has obstructed the Administration of Justice, by refusing his Assent to Laws for establishing Judiciary powers.

He has made Judges dependent on his Will alone, for the tenure of their offices, and the amount and payment of their salaries.

He has erected a multitude of New Offices, and sent hither swarms of Officers to harrass our people, and eat out their substance.

He has kept among us, in times of peace, Standing Armies without the Consent of our legislatures.

He has affected to render the Military independent of and superior to the Civil power.

He has combined with others to subject us to a jurisdiction foreign to our constitution, and unacknowledged by our laws; giving his Assent to their Acts of pretended Legislation:

For Quartering large bodies of armed troops among us:

For protecting them, by a mock Trial, from punishment for any Murders which they should commit on the Inhabitants of these States:

For cutting off our Trade with all parts of the world:

For imposing Taxes on us without our Consent:

For depriving us in many cases, of the benefits of Trial by Jury:

For transporting us beyond Seas to be tried for pretended offences

For abolishing the free System of English Laws in a neighbouring Province, establishing therein an Arbitrary government, and enlarging its Boundaries so as to render it at once an example and fit instrument for introducing the same absolute rule into these Colonies:

For taking away our Charters, abolishing our most valuable Laws, and altering fundamentally the Forms of our Governments:

For suspending our own Legislatures, and declaring themselves invested with power to legislate for us in all cases whatsoever.

He has abdicated Government here, by declaring us out of his Protection and waging War against us.

He has plundered our seas, ravaged our Coasts, burnt our towns, and destroyed the lives of our people.

He is at this time transporting large Armies of foreign Mercenaries to compleat the works of death, desolation and tyranny, already begun with circumstances of Cruelty & perfidy scarcely paralleled in the most barbarous ages, and totally unworthy the Head of a civilized nation.

He has constrained our fellow Citizens taken Captive on the high Seas to bear Arms against their Country, to become the executioners of their friends and Brethren, or to fall themselves by their Hands.

He has excited domestic insurrections amongst us, and has endeavoured to bring on the inhabitants of our frontiers, the merciless Indian Savages, whose known rule of warfare, is an undistinguished destruction of all ages, sexes and conditions.

In every stage of these Oppressions We have Petitioned for Redress in the most humble terms: Our repeated Petitions have been answered only by repeated injury. A Prince whose character is thus marked by every act which may define a Tyrant, is unfit to be the ruler of a free people.

Nor have We been wanting in attentions to our Brittish brethren. We have warned them from time to time of attempts by their legislature to extend an unwarrantable jurisdiction over us. We have reminded them of the circumstances of our emigration and settlement here. We have appealed to their native justice and magnanimity, and we have conjured them by the ties of our common kindred to disavow these usurpations, which, would inevitably interrupt our connections and correspondence. They too have been deaf to the voice of justice and of consanguinity. We must, therefore, acquiesce in the necessity, which denounces our Separation, and hold them, as we hold the rest of mankind, Enemies in War, in Peace Friends.

We, therefore, the Representatives of the united States of America, in General Congress, Assembled, appealing to the Supreme Judge of the world for the rectitude of our intentions, do, in the Name, and by Authority of the good People of these Colonies, solemnly publish and declare, That these United Colonies are, and of Right ought to be Free and Independent States; that they are Absolved from all Allegiance to the British Crown, and that all political connection between them and the State of Great Britain, is and ought to be totally dissolved; and that as Free and Independent States, they have full Power to levy War, conclude Peace, contract Alliances, establish Commerce, and to do all other Acts and Things which Independent States may of right do. And for the support of this Declaration, with a firm reliance on the protection of divine Providence, we mutually pledge to each other our Lives, our Fortunes and our sacred Honor.

The 56 signatures on the Declaration appear in the positions indicated:

Column 1

Georgia:

  Button Gwinnett

  Lyman Hall

  George Walton

Column 2

North Carolina:

  William Hooper

  Joseph Hewes

  John Penn

South Carolina:

  Edward Rutledge

  Thomas Heyward, Jr.

  Thomas Lynch, Jr.

  Arthur Middleton

Column 3

Massachusetts:

  John Hancock

Maryland:

Samuel Chase

William Paca

Thomas Stone

Charles Carroll of Carrollton

Virginia:

George Wythe

Richard Henry Lee

Thomas Jefferson

Benjamin Harrison

Thomas Nelson, Jr.

Francis Lightfoot Lee

Carter Braxton

Column 4

Pennsylvania:

Robert Morris

Benjamin Rush

Benjamin Franklin

John Morton

George Clymer

James Smith

George Taylor

James Wilson

George Ross

Delaware:

Caesar Rodney

George Read

Thomas McKean

Column 5

New York:

William Floyd

Philip Livingston

Francis Lewis

Lewis Morris

New Jersey:

Richard Stockton

John Witherspoon

Francis Hopkinson

John Hart

Abraham Clark

Column 6

New Hampshire:

Josiah Bartlett

William Whipple

Massachusetts:

Samuel Adams

John Adams

Robert Treat Paine

Elbridge Gerry

Rhode Island:

Stephen Hopkins

William Ellery

Connecticut:

Roger Sherman

Samuel Huntington

William Williams

Oliver Wolcott

New Hampshire:

Matthew Thornton

Magna Carta
June 15, 1215

The British Library

John, by the grace of God, king of England, lord of Ireland, duke of Normandy and Aquitaine, and count of Anjou, to the archbishops, bishops, abbots, earls, barons, justiciars, foresters, sheriffs, stewards, servants, and to all his bailiffs and liege subjects, greeting. Know that, having regard to God and for the salvation of our soul, and those of all our ancestors and heirs, and unto the honor of God and the advancement of holy church, and for the reform of our realm, by advice of our venerable fathers, Stephen archbishop of Canterbury, primate of all England and cardinal of the holy Roman Church, Henry archbishop of Dublin, William of London, Peter of Winchester, Jocelyn of Bath and Glastonbury, Hugh of Lincoln, Walter of Worcester, William of Coventry, Benedict of Rochester, bishops; of master Pandulf, subdeacon and member of the household of our lord the Pope, of brother Aymeric (master of the Knights of the Temple in England), and of the illustrious men William Marshall earl of Pembroke, William earl of Salisbury, William earl of Warenne, William earl of Arundel, Alan of Galloway (constable of Scotland), Waren Fitz Gerald, Peter Fits Herbert, Hubert de Burgh (seneschal of Poitou), Hugh de Neville, Matthew Fitz Herbert, Thomas Basset,

Alan Basset, Philip d'Aubigny, Robert of Roppesley, John Marshall, John Fitz Hugh, and others, our liegemen.

1. In the first place we have granted to God, and by this our present charter confirmed for us and our heirs for ever that the English church shall be free, and shall have her rights entire, and her liberties inviolate; and we will that it be thus observed; which is apparent from this that the freedom of elections, which is reckoned most important and very essential to the English church, we, of our pure and unconstrained will, did grant, and did by our charter confirm and did obtain the ratification of the same from our lord, Pope Innocent III., before the quarrel arose between us and our barons: and this we will observe, and our will is that it be observed in good faith by our heirs for ever. We have also granted to all freemen of our kingdom, for us and our heirs for ever, all the underwritten liberties, to be had and held by them and their heirs, of us and our heirs for ever.

2. If any of our earls or barons, or others holding of us in chief by military service shall have died, and at the time of his death his heir shall be of full age and owe "relief" he shall have his inheritance on payment of the ancient relief, namely the heir or heirs of an earl, 100 pounds for a whole earl's barony; the heir or heirs of a baron, 100 pounds for a whole barony; the heir or heirs of a knight, 100 shillings at most for a whole knight's fee; and whoever owes less let him give less, according to the ancient custom officers.

3. If, however, the heir of any of the aforesaid has been under age and in wardship, let him have his inheritance without relief and without fine when he comes of age.

4. The guardian of the land of an heir who is thus under age, shall take from the land of the heir nothing but reasonably produce, reasonable customs, and reasonable services, and that without destruction or waste of men or goods; and if we have committed the wardship of the lands of any such minor to the sheriff, or to any other who is responsible to us for its issues, and he has made destruction or waste of what he holds in wardship, we will take of him amends, and the land shall be committed to two lawful and discreet men of that fee, who shall be responsible for the issues to us or to him to whom we shall assign them; and if we have given or sold the wardship of any such land to anyone and he has there in made destruction or waste, he shall lose that wardship, and it shall be transferred to two lawful and discreet men of that fief, who shall be responsible to us in like manner as aforesaid.

5. The guardian, moreover, so long as he has the wardship of the land, shall keep up the houses, parks, fishponds, stanks, mills, and other things pertaining to the land, out of the issues of the same land; and he shall restore to the heir, when he has come to full age, all his land, stocked with ploughs and "waynage," according as the season of husbandry shall require, and the issues of the land can reasonably bear.

6. Heirs shall be married without disparagement, yet so that before the marriage takes place the nearest in blood to that heir shall have notice.

7. A widow, after the death of her husband, shall forthwith and without difficulty have her marriage portion and inheritance; nor shall she give anything for her dower, or for her marriage portion, or for the inheritance which her husband and she held on the day of the death of that husband;

and she may remain in the house of her husband for forty days after his death, within which time her dower shall be assigned to her.

8. No widow shall be compelled to marry, so long as she prefers to live without a husband; provided always that she gives security not to marry without our consent, if she holds of us, or without the consent of the lord of whom she holds, if she holds of another.

9. Neither we nor our bailiffs shall seize any land or rent for any debt, so long as the chattels of the debtor are sufficient to repay the debt; nor shall the sureties of the debtor be distrained so long as the principal debtor is able to satisfy the debt; and if the principal debtor shall fail to pay the debt, having nothing wherewith to pay it, then the sureties shall answer for the debt; and let them have the lands and rents of the debtor, if they desire them, until they are indemnified for the debt which they have paid for him, unless the principal debtor can show proof that he is discharged thereof as against the said sureties.

10. If one who has borrowed from the Jews any sum, great or small, die before that loan can be repaid, the debt shall not bear interest while the heir is under age, of whomsoever he may hold; and if the debt fall into our hands, we will not take anything except the principal sum contained in the bond.

11. And if any one die indebted to the Jews, his wife shall have her dower and pay nothing of that debt; and if any children of the deceased are left underage, necessaries shall be provided for them in keeping with the holding of the deceased; and out of the residue the debt shall be paid, reserving, however, service due to feudal lords; in like manner let it be done touching debts due to others than Jews.

12. No scutage nor aid shall be imposed on our kingdom, unless by common counsel of our kingdom, except for ransoming our person, for making our eldest son a knight, and for once marrying our eldest daughter; and for these there shall not be levied more than a reasonable aid. In like manner it shall be done concerning aids from the city of London.

13. And the city of London shall have all its ancient liberties and free customs, as well by land as by water; furthermore, we decree and grant that all other cities, boroughs, towns, and ports shall have all their liberties and free customs.

14. And for obtaining the common counsel of the kingdom anent the assessing of an aid (except in the three cases aforesaid) or of a scutage, we will cause to be summoned the archbishops, bishops, abbots, earls, and greater barons, severally by our letters; and we will moreover cause to be summoned generally, through our sheriffs and bailiffs, all others who hold of us in chief, for a fixed date, namely, after the expiry of at least forty days, and at a fixed place; and in all letters of such summons we will specify the reason of the summons. And when the summons has thus been made, the business shall proceed on the day appointed, according to the counsel of such as are present, although not all who were summoned have come.

15. We will not for the future grant to any one license to take an aid from his own free tenants, except to ransom his body, to make his eldest son a knight, and once to marry his eldest daughter; and on each of these occasions there shall be levied only a reasonable aid.

16. No one shall be distrained for performance of greater service for a knight's fee, or for any other free tenement, than is due therefrom.

17. Common pleas shall not follow our court, but shall be held in some fixed place.

18. Inquests of novel disseisin, of mort d'ancester, and of darrein presentment, shall not be held elsewhere than in their own county courts and that in manner following,—We, or, if we should be out of the realm, our chief justiciar, will send two justiciars through every county four times a year, who shall, along with four knights of the county chosen by the county, hold the said assize in the county court, on the day and in the place of meeting of that court.

19. And if any of the said assizes cannot be taken on the day of the county court, let there remain of the knights and freeholders, who were present at the county court on that day, as many as may be required for the efficient making of judgments, according as the business be more or less.

20. A freeman shall not be amerced for a slight offense, except in accordance with the degree of the offense; and for a grave offense he shall be amerced in accordance with the gravity of the offense, yet saving always his "contentment;" and a merchant in the same way, saving his "merchandise;" and a villein shall be amerced in the same way, saving his "wainage"—if they have fallen into our mercy: and none of the aforesaid amercements shall be impsed except by the oath of honest men of the neighborhood.

21. Earls and barons shall not be amerced except through their peers, and only in accordance with the degree of the offense.

22. A clerk shall not be amerced in respect of his lay holding except after the manner of the others aforesaid; further, he shall not be amerced in accordance with the extent of his ecclesiastical benefice.

23. No village or individual shall be compelled to make bridges at river-banks, except those who from of old were legally bound to do so.

24. No sheriff, constable, coroners, or others of our bailiffs, shall hold pleas of our Crown.

25. All counties, hundreds, wapentakes, and trithings (except our demesne manors) shall remain at old rents, and without any additional payment.***here may be an error

26. If any one holding of us a lay fief shall die, and our sheriff or bailiff shall exhibit our letters patent of summons for a debt which the deceased owed to us, it shall be lawful for our sheriff or bailiff to attach and catalogue chattels of the deceased, found upon the lay fief, to the value of that debt, at the sight of law-worthy men, provided always that nothing whatever be then be removed until the debt which is evident shall be fully paid to us; and the residue shall be left to the executors to fulfil the will of the deceased; and if there be nothing due from him to us, all the chattels shall go to the deceased, saving to his wife and children their reasonable shares.

27. If any freeman shall die intestate, his chattels shall be distributed by the hands of his nearest kinsfolk and friends, under supervision of the church, saving to every one the debts which the deceased owed to him.

28. No constable or other bailiff of ours shall take corn or other provisions from any one without immediately tendering money therefor, unless he can have postponement thereof by permission of the seller.

29. No constable shall compel any knight to give money in lieu of castle-guard, when he is willing to perform it in his own person, or (if he cannot do it from any reasonable cause) then by another responsible man. Further, if we

have led or sent him upon military service, he shall be relieved from guard in proportion to the time during which he has been on service because of us.

30. No sheriff or bailiff of ours, or other person, shall take the horses or carts of any freeman for transport duty, against the will of the said freeman.

31. Neither we nor our bailiffs shall take, for our castles or for any other work of ours, wood which is not ours, against the will of the owner of that wood.

32. We will not retain beyond one year and one day, the lands of those who have been convicted of felony, and the lands shall thereafter be handed over to the lords of the fiefs.

33. All kiddles for the future shall be removed altogether from Thames and Medway, and throughout all England, except upon the seashore.

34. The writ which is called praecipe shall not for the future be issued to any one, regarding any tenement whereby a freeman may lose his court.

35. Let there be one measure of wine throughout our whole realm; and one measure of ale; and one measure of corn, to wit, "the London quarter;" and one width of cloth (whether dyed, or russet, or "halberget"), to wit, two ells within the selvages; of weights also let it be as of measures.

36. Nothing in future shall be given or taken for a writ of inquisition of life or limbs, but freely it shall be granted, and never denied.

37. If any one holds of us by fee-farm, by socage, or by burgage, and holds also land of another lord by knight's service, we will not (by reason of that fee-farm, socage, or burgage) have the wardship of the heir, or of such land of his as is of the fief of that other; nor shall we have wardship of that fee-farm, socage, or burgage, unless such fee-farm owes knight's service. We will not by reason of any small serjeanty which any one may hold of us by

the service of rendering to us knives, arrows, or the like, have wardship of his heir of the land which he holds of another lord by knight's service.

38. No bailiff for the future shall, upon his own unsupported complaint, put any one to his "law," without credible witnesses brought for this purpose.

39. No freeman shall be taken or imprisoned or disseised or exiled or in anyway destroyed, nor will we go upon him nor send upon him, except by the lawful judgment of his peers or by the law of the land.

40. To no one will we sell, to no one will we refuse or delay, right or justice.

41. All merchants shall have safe and secure exit from England, and entry to England, with the right to tarry there and to move about as well by land as by water, for buying and selling by the ancient and right customs, quit from all evil tolls, except (in time of war) such merchants as are of the land at war with us. And if such are found in our land at the beginning of the war, they shall be detained, without injury to their bodies or goods, until information be received by us, or by our chief justiciar, how the merchants of our land found in the land at war with us are treated; and if our men are safe there, the others shall be safe in our land.

42. It shall be lawful in future for any one (excepting always those imprisoned or outlawed in accordance with the law of the kingdom, and natives of any country at war with us, and merchants, who shall be treated as is above provided) to leave our kingdom and to return, safe and secure by land and water, except for a short period in time of war, on grounds of public policy—reserving always the allegiance due to us.

43. If any one holding of some escheat (such as the honor of Wallingford, Nottingham, Boulogne, Lancaster, or of other escheats which are in our

hands and are baronies) shall die, his heir shall give no other relief, and perform no other service to us than he would have done to the baron, if that barony had been in the baron's hand; and we shall hold it in the same manner in which the baron held it.

44. Men who dwell without the forest need not henceforth come before our justiciars of the forest upon a general summons, except those who are impleaded, or who have become sureties for any person or persons attached for forest offenses.

45. We will appoint as justices, constables, sheriffs, or bailiffs only such as know the law of the realm and mean to observe it well.

46. All barons who have founded abbeys, concerning which they hold charters from the kings of England, or of which they have long-continued possession, shall have the wardship of them, when vacant, as they ought to have.

47. All forests that have been made such in our time shall forthwith be disafforested; and a similar course shall be followed with regard to river-banks that have been placed "in defense" by us in our time.

48. All evil customs connected with forests and warrens, foresters and warreners, sheriffs and their officers, river-banks and their wardens, shall immediately be inquired into in each county by twelve sworn knights of the same county chosen by the honest men of the same county, and shall, within forty days of the said inquest, be utterly abolished, so as never to be restored, provided always that we previously have intimation thereof, or our justiciar, if we should not be in England.

49. We will immediately restore all hostages and charters delivered to us by Englishmen, as sureties of the peace or of faithful service.

50. We will entirely remove from their bailiwicks, the relations of Gerard Athee (so that in future they shall have no bailiwick in England); namely, Engelard of Cigogne, Peter, Guy, and Andrew of Chanceaux, Guy of Cigogne, Geofrrey of Martigny with his brothers, Philip Mark with his brothers and his nephew Geoffrey, and the whole brood of the same.

51. As soon as peace is restored, we will banish from the kingdom all foreign-born knights, cross-bowmen, serjeants, and mercenary soldiers, who have come with horses and arms to the kingdom's hurt.

52. If any one has been dispossessed or removed by us, without the legal judgment of his peers, from his lands, castles, franchises, or from his right, we will immediately restore them to him; and if a dispute arise over this, then let it be decided by the five-and-twenty barons of whom mention is made below in the clause for securing the peace. Moreover, for all those possessions, from which any one has, without the lawful judgment of his peers, be endisseised or removed, by our father, King Henry, or by our brother, King Richard, and which we retain in our hand (or which are possessed by others, to whom we are bound to warrant them) we shall have respite until the usual term of crusaders; excepting those things about which a plea has been raised, or an inquest made by our order, before our taking of the cross; but as soon as were turn from our expedition (or if perchance we desist from the expedition) we will immediately grant full justice therein.

53. We shall have, moreover, the same respite and in the same manner in rendering justice concerning the disafforestation or retention of those forests which Henry our father and Richard our brother afforested, and concerning wardship of lands which are of the fief of another (namely, such

wardships as we have hitherto had by reason of a fief which any one held of us by knight's service), and concerning abbeys founded on other fiefs than our own, in which the lord of the fief claims to have right; and when we have returned, or if we desist from our expedition, we will immediately grant full justice to all who complain of such things.

54. No one shall be arrested or imprisoned upon the appeal of a woman, for the death of any other than her husband.

55. All fines made with us unjustly and against the law of the land, and all amercements imposed unjustly and against the law of the land, shall be entirely remitted, or else it shall be done concerning them according to the decision of the five-and-twenty barons of whom mention is made below in the clause for securing the peace, or according to the judgment of the majority of the same, along with the aforesaid Stephen, archbishop of Canterbury, if he can be present, and such others as he may wish to bring with him for this purpose, and if he cannot be present the business shall nevertheless proceed without him, provided always that if any one or more of the aforesaid five-and-twenty barons are in a similar suit, they shall be removed as far as concerns this particular judgment, others being substituted in their places after having been selected by the rest of the same five-and-twenty for this purpose only, and after having been sworn.

56. If we have disseised or removed Welshmen from lands or liberties, or other things, without the legal judgment of their peers in England or in Wales, they shall be immediately restored to them; and if a dispute arise over this, then let it be decided in the marches by the judgment of their peers; for tenements in England according to the law of England, for tenements in

Wales according to the law of Wales, and for tenements in the marches according to the law of the marches. Welshmen shall do the same to us and ours.

57. Further, for all those possessions from which any Welshman has, without the lawful judgment of his peers, been disseised or removed by King Henry our father or King Richard our brother, and which we retain in our hand (or which are possessed by others, to whom we are bound to warrant them) we shall have respite until the usual term of crusaders; excepting those things about which a plea has been raised or an inquest made by our order before we took the cross; but as soon as we return (or if perchance we desist from our expedition), we will immediately grant full justice in accordance with the laws of the Welsh and in relation to the foresaid regions.

58. We will immediately give up the son of Llywelyn and all the hostages of Wales, and the charters delivered to us as security for the peace.

59. We will do toward Alexander, King of Scots, concerning the return of his sisters and his hostages, and concerning his franchises, and his right, in the same manner as we shall do toward our other barons of England, unless it ought to be otherwise according to the charters which we hold from William his father, formerly King of Scots; and this shall be according to the judgment of his peers in our court.

60. Moreover, all these aforesaid customs and liberties, the observance of which we have granted in our kingdom as far as pertains to us toward our men, shall be observed by all of our kingdom, as well clergy as laymen, as far as pertains to them toward their men.

61. Since, moreover, for God and the amendment of our kingdom and for the better allaying of the quarrel that has arisen between us and our barons, we have granted all these concessions, desirous that they should enjoy them in complete and firm endurance for ever, we give and grant to them the underwritten security, namely, that the barons choose five-and-twenty barons of the kingdom, whomsoever they will, who shall be bound with all their might, to observe and hold, and cause to be observed, the peace and liberties we have granted and confirmed to them by this our present Charter, so that if we, or our justiciar, or our bailiffs or any one of our officers, shall in anything be at fault toward any one, or shall have broken any one of the articles of the peace or of this security, and the offense be notified to four barons of the foresaid five-and-twenty, the said four barons shall repair to us (or our justiciar, if we are out of the realm) and, laying the transgression before us, petition to have that transgression redressed without delay. And if we shall not have corrected the transgression (or, in the event of our being out of the realm, if our justiciar shall not have corrected it) within forty days, reckoning from the time it has been intimated to us (or to our justiciar, if we should be out of the realm), the four barons aforesaid shall refer that matter to the rest of the five-and-twenty barons, and those five-and-twenty barons shall, together with the community of the whole land, distrain and distress us in all possible ways, namely, by seizing our castles, lands, possessions, and in any other way they can, until redress has been obtained as they deem fit, saving harmless our own person, and the persons of our queen and children; and when redress has been obtained, they shall resume their old relations toward us. And let whoever in the country desires it, swear to

obey the orders of the said five-and-twenty barons for the execution of all the aforesaid matters, and along with them, to molest us to the utmost of his power; and we publicly and freely grant leave to every one who wishes to swear, and we shall never forbid any one to swear. All those, moreover, in the land who of themselves and of their own accord are unwilling to swear to the twenty-five to help them in constraining and molesting us, we shall by our command compel the same to swear to the effect aforesaid. And if any one of the five-and-twenty barons shall have died or departed from the land, or be incapacitated in any other manner which would prevent the foresaid provisions being carried out, those of the said twenty-five barons who are left shall choose another in his place according to their own judgment, and he shall be sworn in the same way as the others. Further, in all matters, the execution of which is intrusted to these twenty-five barons, if perchance these twenty-five are present, that which the majority of those present ordain or command shall be held as fixed and established, exactly as if the whole twenty-five had concurred in this; and the said twenty-five shall swear that they will faithfully observe all that is aforesaid, and cause it to be observed with all their might. And we shall procure nothing from any one, directly or indirectly, whereby any part of these concessions and liberties might be revoked or diminished; and if any such thing has been procured, let it be void and null, and we shall never use it personally or by another.

62. And all the ill-will, hatreds, and bitterness that have arisen between us and our men, clergy and lay, from the date of the quarrel, we have completely remitted and pardoned every one. Moreover, all trespasses occasioned by the said quarrel, from Easter in the sixteenth year of our reign till the

restoration of peace, we have fully remitted to all, both clergy and laymen, and completely forgiven, as far as pertains to us. And, on this head, we have caused to be made for them letters testimonial patent of the lord Stephen, archbishop of Canterbury, of the lord Henry, archbishop of Dublin, of the bishops aforesaid, and of Master Pandulf as touching this security and the concessions aforesaid.

63. Wherefore it is our will, and we firmly enjoin, that the English Church be free, and that the men in our kingdom have and hold all the aforesaid liberties, rights, and concessions, well and peaceably, freely and quietly, fully and wholly, for themselves and their heirs, of us and our heirs, in all respects and in all places for ever, as is aforesaid. An oath, moreover, has been taken, as well on our part as on the part of the barons, that all these conditions aforesaid shall be kept in good faith and without evil intent. Given under our hand–the above-named and many others being witnesses–in the meadow which is called Runnymede, between Windsor and Staines, on the fifteenth day of June, in the seventeenth year of our reign.

Appendix

Judiciary Act of 1789

Library of Congress

CHAP. XX.—*An Act to establish the Judicial Courts of the United States.*(a)

STATUTE I.
Sept. 24, 1789.

SECTION 1. *Be it enacted by the Senate and House of Representatives of the United States of America in Congress assembled*, That the supreme court of the United States shall consist of a chief justice and five associate justices,(b) any four of whom shall be a quorum, and shall hold annually at the seat of government two sessions, the one commencing the first Monday of February, and the other the first Monday of August. That the associate justices shall have precedence according to the date of their commissions, or when the commissions of two or more of them bear date on the same day, according to their respective ages.

Supreme court to consist of a chief justice, and five associates.
Two sessions annually.
Precedence.

SEC. 2. *And be it further enacted*, That the United States shall be, and they hereby are divided into thirteen districts, to be limited and called as follows, to wit: one to consist of that part of the State of Massachusetts which lies easterly of the State of New Hampshire, and to be called Maine District; one to consist of the State of New Hampshire, and to be called New Hampshire District;(c) one to consist of the remaining part of the State of Massachusetts, and to be called Massachusetts district; one to consist of the State of Connecticut, and to be called Connecticut District; one to consist of the State of New York, and to be called New York District; one to consist of the State of New Jersey, and to be called New Jersey District; one to consist of the State of Pennsylvania, and to be called Pennsylvania District; one to consist of the State of Delaware, and to be called Delaware District; one to consist of the State of Maryland, and to be called Maryland District; one to consist of the State of Virginia, except that part called the District of Kentucky, and to be called Virginia District; one to consist of the remaining part of the State of Virginia, and to be called Kentucky District; one to consist of the State of South Carolina, and to be called South Carolina District; and one to consist of the State of Georgia, and to be called Georgia District.

Thirteen districts.

Maine.
N. Hampshire.
Massachusetts.

Connecticut.
New York.
New Jersey.
Pennsylvania.
Delaware.
Maryland.

Virginia.
Kentucky.

South Carolina.
Georgia.

SEC. 3. *And be it further enacted*, That there be a court called a District Court, in each of the afore mentioned districts, to consist of one judge, who shall reside in the district for which he is appointed, and shall be called a District Judge, and shall hold annually four

A district court in each district.

(a) The 3d article of the Constitution of the United States enables the judicial department to receive jurisdiction to the full extent of the constitution, laws and treaties of the United States, when any question respecting them shall assume such a form that the judicial power is capable of acting on it. That power is capable of acting only where the subject is submitted to it by a party who asserts his right in a form presented by law. It then becomes a case. Osborn et al. *v.* The Bank of the United States, 9 Wheat. 738; 5 Cond. Rep. 741.

(b) By the act of April 29, 1802, chap. 31, the Supreme Court was declared to consist of a Chief Justice and six associate Justices, and by the act of March 3, 1837, chap. 32, it was made to consist of a Chief Justice and eight associate Justices.

By the act of April 29, 1802, chap. 31, the provision of the act of September 24, 1789, requiring two annual sessions of the Supreme Court, was repealed, and the 2d section of that act required that the associate Justice of the fourth circuit should attend at Washington on the first Monday of August annually, to make all necessary rules and orders, touching suits and actions depending in the court. This section was repealed by the 7th section of the act of February 28, 1839, chap. 36.

By an act passed May 4, 1826, chap. 37, the sessions of the Supreme Court were directed to commence on the second Monday in January annually, instead of the first Monday in February; and by an act passed June 17, 1844, the sessions of the Supreme Court were directed to commence on the first Monday in December annually.

(c) The jurisdiction and powers of the District Courts have been declared and established by the following acts of Congress: Act of September 24, 1789; act of June 5, 1794, sec. 6; act of May 10, 1800; act of December 31, 1814; act of April 16, 1816; act of April 20, 1818; act of May 15, 1820; act of March 3, 1793.

The decisions of the Courts of the United States on the jurisdiction of the District Courts have been: The Thomas Jefferson, 10 Wheat. 428; 6 Cond. Rep. 173. M'Donough *v.* Danery, 3 Dall. 188; 1 Cond. Rep. 94. United States *v.* La Vengeance, 3 Dall. 297; 1 Cond. Rep. 132. Glass et al. *v.* The Betsey, 3 Dall. 6; 1 Cond. Rep. 10. The Alerta *v.* Blas Moran, 9 Cranch, 359; 3 Cond. Rep. 425. The Merino et al., 9 Wheat. 391; 5 Cond. Rep. 623. The Josefa Segunda, 10 Wheat. 312; 6 Cond. Rep. 111. The Bolina, 1 Gallis' C. C. R. 75. The Robert Fulton, Paine's C. C. R. 620. Jansen *v.* The Vrow Christiana Magdalena, Bee's D. C. R. 11. Jennings *v.* Carson, 4 Cranch, 2; 2 Cond. Rep. 2. The Sarah, 8 Wheat. 391; 5 Cond. Rep. 472. Penhallow et al. *v.* Doane's Adm'rs, 3 Dall. 54; 1 Cond. Rep. 21. The United States *v.* Richard Peters, 3 Dall. 121; 1 Cond. Rep. 60. M'Lellan *v.* the United States,

Four sessions
annually in a
district; and
when held.
sessions, the first of which to commence as follows, to wit: in the districts of New York and of New Jersey on the first, in the district of Pennsylvania on the second, in the district of Connecticut on the third, and in the district of Delaware on the fourth, Tuesdays of November next; in the districts of Massachusetts, of Maine, and of Maryland, on the first, in the district of Georgia on the second, and in the districts of New Hampshire, of Virginia, and of Kentucky, on the third Tuesdays of December next; and the other three sessions progressively in the respective districts on the like Tuesdays of every third calendar month afterwards, and in the district of South Carolina, on the third Monday in March and September, the first Monday in July, and the second Monday in December of each and every year, commencing in December next; and that the District Judge shall have power to hold special courts at his discretion. That the stated District Court shall be held at the places following, to wit: in the district of Maine, at Portland and Pownalsborough alternately, beginning at the first; in the district of New Hampshire, at Exeter and Portsmouth alternately, beginning at the first; in the district of Massachusetts, at Boston and Salem alternately, beginning at the first; in the district of Connecticut, alternately at Hartford and New Haven, beginning at the first; in the district of New York, at New York; in the district of New Jersey, alternately at New Brunswick and Burlington, beginning at the first; in the district of Pennsylvania, at Philadelphia and York Town alternately, beginning at the first; in the district of Delaware, alternately at Newcastle and Dover, beginning at the first; in the district of Maryland, alternately at Baltimore and Easton, beginning at the first; in the district of Virginia, alternately at Richmond and Williamsburgh, beginning at the first; in the district of Kentucky, at Harrodsburgh; in the district of South Carolina, at Charleston; and in the district of Georgia, alternately at Savannah and Augusta, beginning at the first; and that the special courts shall be held at the same place in each district as the stated courts, or in districts that have two, at either of them, in the discretion of the judge, or at such other place in the district, as the nature of the business and his discretion shall direct. And that in the districts that have but one place for holding the District Court, the records thereof shall be kept at that place; and in districts that have two, at that place in each district which the judge shall appoint.

Special district courts.

Stated district courts; when holden.

Special courts, where held.

Where records kept.

Three circuits, and how divided. [Obsolete.]

SEC. 4. *And be it further enacted,* That the before mentioned districts, except those of Maine and Kentucky, shall be divided into three circuits, and be called the eastern, the middle, and the southern circuit. That the eastern circuit shall consist of the districts of New Hampshire, Massachusetts, Connecticut and New York; that the middle circuit shall consist of the districts of New Jersey, Pennsylvania, Delaware, Maryland and Virginia; and that the southern circuit shall consist of the districts of South Carolina and Georgia, and that there shall be held annually in each district of said circuits, two courts, which shall be called Circuit Courts, and shall consist of any two justices of

---

1 Gallis' C. C. R. 227. Hudson et al. v. Guestier, 6 Cranch, 281; 2 Cond. Rep. 374. Brown v. The United States, 8 Cranch, 110; 3 Cond. Rep. 56. De Lovio v. Boit et al., 2 Gallis' Rep. 398. Burke v. Trevitt, 1 Mason, 96. The Amiable Nancy, 3 Wheat. 546; 4 Cond. Rep. 322. The Abby, 1 Mason, 360. The Little Ann, Paine's C. C. R. 40. Slocum v. Maybury et al., 2 Wheat. 1; 4 Cond. Rep. 1. Southwick v. The Postmaster General, 2 Peters, 442. Davis v. A New Brig, Gilpin's D. C. R. 473. Smith v. The Pekin, Gilpin's D. C. R. 203. Peters' Digest, "Courts," "District Courts of the United States."

The 3d section of the act of Congress of 1789, to establish the Judicial Courts of the United States, which provides that no summary writ, return of process, judgment, or other proceedings in the courts of the United States shall be abated, arrested or quashed for any defect or want of form, &c., although it does not include verdicts, eo nomine, but judgments are included; and the language of the provision, "writ, declaration, judgment or other proceeding, in court causes," and further "such writ, declaration, pleading, process, judgment or other proceeding whatsoever," is sufficiently comprehensive to embrace every conceivable step to be taken in a court, from the emanation of the writ, down to the judgment. Roach v. Hulings, 16 Peters, 319.

the Supreme Court, and the district judge of such districts, any two of whom shall constitute a quorum : *Provided,* That no district judge shall give a vote in any case of appeal or error from his own decision; but may assign the reasons of such his decision.

Sec. 5. *And be it further enacted,* That the first session of the said circuit court in the several districts shall commence at the times following, to wit: in New Jersey on the second, in New York on the fourth, in Pennsylvania on the eleventh, in Connecticut on the twenty-second, and in Delaware on the twenty-seventh, days of April next; in Massachusetts on the third, in Maryland on the seventh, in South Carolina on the twelfth, in New Hampshire on the twentieth, in Virginia on the twenty-second, and in Georgia on the twenty-eighth, days of May next, and the subsequent sessions in the respective districts on the like days of every sixth calendar month afterwards, except in South Carolina, where the session of the said court shall commence on the first, and in Georgia where it shall commence on the seventeenth day of October, and except when any of those days shall happen on a Sunday, and then the session shall commence on the next day following. And the sessions of the said circuit court shall be held in the district of New Hampshire, at Portsmouth and Exeter alternately, beginning at the first; in the district of Massachusetts, at Boston; in the district of Connecticut, alternately at Hartford and New Haven, beginning at the last; in the district of New York, alternately at New York and Albany, beginning at the first; in the district of New Jersey, at Trenton; in the district of Pennsylvania, alternately at Philadelphia and Yorktown, beginning at the first; in the district of Delaware, alternately at New Castle and Dover, beginning at the first; in the district of Maryland, alternately at Annapolis and Easton, beginning at the first; in the district of Virginia, alternately at Charlottesville and Williamsburgh, beginning at the first; in the district of South Carolina, alternately at Columbia and Charleston, beginning at the first; and in the district of Georgia, alternately at Savannah and Augusta, beginning at the first. And the circuit courts shall have power to hold special sessions for the trial of criminal causes at any other time at their discretion, or at the discretion of the Supreme Court.(*a*)

First session of the circuit courts; when holden.
[Obsolete.]

Where holden.

Circuit courts. Special sessions.

(*a*) The sessions of the Circuit Courts have been regulated by the following acts : In ALABAMA—act of March 3, 1837. In ARKANSAS—act of March 3, 1837. In CONNECTICUT—act of September 24, 1789; act of April 13, 1792; act of March 2, 1793; act of March 3, 1797; act of April 29, 1802; act of May 13, 1826. In DELAWARE—act of September 24, 1789; act of March 3, 1797; act of April 29, 1802; act of March 24, 1804; act of March 3, 1837. In GEORGIA—act of September 24, 1789; act of August 11, 1790; act of April 13, 1792; act of March 3, 1797; act of April 29, 1802; act of May 13, 1826; act of Jan. 21, 1829. KENTUCKY—act of March 3, 1801; act of March 8, 1802; act of March 2, 1803; act of Feb. 27, 1807; act of March 22, 1808; April 22, 1824. LOUISIANA—act of March 3, 1837. MAINE—act of March 3, 1801; act of March 8, 1802; act of March 30, 1820. MARYLAND—act of Sept. 24, 1789; act of March 3, 1797; act of April 29, 1802; act of Feb. 11, 1830; act of March 3, 1837. MASSACHUSETTS—act of Sept. 24, 1789; act of March 3, 1791; act of June 9, 1794; act of March 2, 1793; act of March 3, 1797; act of March 3, 1801; act of March 8, 1802; act of April 29, 1802; act of March 26, 1812. MISSOURI—act of March 3, 1837. MISSISSIPPI—act of March 3, 1839. NEW HAMPSHIRE—act of Sept. 24, 1789; act of March 3, 1791; act of April 13, 1792; act of March 2, 1793; act of March 3, 1797; act of March 3, 1801; act of April 29, 1802; act of March 6, 1812. NEW JERSEY—act of September 24, 1789; act of March 3, 1797; act of April 2, 1802. NEW YORK—act of September 24, 1789; act of March 3, 1791; act of April 13, 1792; act of March 2, 1793; act of March 3, 1797; act of April 29, 1802; act of March 3, 1825; act of February 10, 1832; act of May 13, 1836; act of March 3, 1837. NORTH CAROLINA—act of September 24, 1789; act of April 13, 1792; act of March 2, 1793; act of March 31, 1796; act of March 3, 1797; act of July 5, 1797; act of April 29, 1802; act of March 8, 1806; act of February 4, 1807. OHIO—act of February 24, 1807; act of March 22, 1808; act of April 22, 1824; act of May 20, 1826. PENNSYLVANIA—act of September 24, 1789; act of May 12, 1796; act of March 3, 1797; act of December 24, 1799; act of April 29, 1802; act of March 3, 1837. RHODE ISLAND—act of June 23, 1790; act of March 3, 1791; act of March 2, 1793; act of May 22, 1796; act of March 3, 1797; act of March 3, 1801; act of March 8, 1802; act of April 29, 1802; act of March 26, 1812. SOUTH CAROLINA—act of September 24, 1789; act of August 11, 1790; act of March 3, 1797; act of April 29, 1802; act of April 14, 1816; act of May 25, 1824; act of March 3, 1825; act of May 4, 1826; act of February 5, 1829. TENNESSEE—act of February 24, 1807; act of March 22, 1808; act of March 10, 1812; act of January 13, 1831. VERMONT—act of March 2, 1791; act of March 2, 1793; act of May 27, 1796; act of March 3, 1797; act of April 29, 1802; act of March 22, 1816. VIRGINIA—act of September 24, 1789; act of March 3, 1791; act of April 13, 1792; act of March 3, 1797; act of April 29, 1802; act of March 2, 1837.

Supreme court adjourned by one or more justices; circuit courts adjourned.

Sec. 6. *And be it further enacted,* That the Supreme Court may, by any one or more of its justices being present, be adjourned from day to day until a quorum be convened; and that a circuit court may also be adjourned from day to day by any one of its judges, or if none are present, by the marshal of the district until a quorum be convened;(a) and that a district court, in case of the inability of the judge to attend at the commencement of a session, may by virtue of a written order from the

District courts adjourned.

said judge, directed to the marshal of the district, be adjourned by the said marshal to such day, antecedent to the next stated session of the said court, as in the said order shall be appointed; and in case of the death of the said judge, and his vacancy not being supplied, all process, pleadings and proceedings of what nature soever, pending before the said court, shall be continued of course until the next stated session after the appointment and acceptance of the office by his successor.

The courts have power to appoint clerks.

Sec. 7. *And be it [further] enacted,* That the Supreme Court, and the district courts shall have power to appoint clerks for their respective courts,(b) and that the clerk for each district court shall be clerk also of the circuit court in such district, and each of the said clerks shall, before he enters upon the execution of his office, take the following oath

Their oath or affirmation.

or affirmation, to wit: "I, A. B., being appointed clerk of   , do solemnly swear, or affirm, that I will truly and faithfully enter and record all the orders, decrees, judgments and proceedings of the said court, and that I will faithfully and impartially discharge and perform all the duties of my said office, according to the best of my abilities and understanding. So help me God." Which words, so help me God, shall be omitted in all cases where an affirmation is admitted instead of an oath. And the said clerks shall also severally give bond, with sufficient sureties, (to be approved of by the Supreme and district courts respectively) to the United States, in the sum of two thousand dollars, faithfully to discharge the duties of his office, and seasonably to record the decrees, judgments and determinations of the court of which he is clerk.

Sec. 8. *And be it further enacted,* That the justices of the Supreme Court, and the district judges, before they proceed to execute the duties of their respective offices, shall take the following oath or affirmation, to

Oath of justices of supreme court and judges of the district court.

wit: " I, A. B., do solemnly swear or affirm, that I will administer justice without respect to persons, and do equal right to the poor and to the rich, and that I will faithfully and impartially discharge and perform all the duties incumbent on me as   , according to the best of my abilities and understanding, agreeably to the constitution and laws of the United States. So help me God."

District courts exclusive jurisdiction.

Sec. 9. *And be it further enacted,* That the district courts(c) shall have, exclusively of the courts of the several States, cognizance of all crimes and offences that shall be cognizable under the authority of the United States, committed within their respective districts, or upon the

---

By the act of March 10, 1838, the Justice of the Supreme Court is required to attend but one circuit in the districts of Indiana, Illinois, and Michigan.

By an act passed in 1844, the Justices of the Supreme Court are empowered to hold but one session of the Circuit Court in each district in their several circuits. The Judges of the District Courts hold the other sessions of the Circuit Court in their several districts.

(a) The provisions of law on the subject of the adjournments of the Supreme Court in addition to the 6th section of this act, are, that in case of epidemical disease, the court may be adjourned to some other place than the seat of government. Act of February 25, 1799.

(b) By the 2d section of the act entitled "an act in amendment of the acts respecting the judicial system of the United States," passed February 28, 1839, chap. 36, it is provided "that all the circuit courts of the United States shall have the appointment of their own clerks, and in case of disagreement between the judges, the appointment shall be made by the presiding judge of the court." See ex parte Duncan N. Hennen, 13 Peters, 230.

(c) The further legislation on the subject of the jurisdiction and powers of the District Courts are : the act of June 5, 1794, ch. 50, sec. 6; act of May 10, 1800, chap. 51, sec. 5; act of February 24, 1807, chap. 13; act of February 24, 1807, chap. 16; act of March 3, 1815; act of April 16, 1816, chap. 56, sec. 6; act of April 20, 1818, chap. 103; act of May 15, 1820, chap. 106, sec. 4; act of March 3, 1823, chap. 71.

high seas; where no other punishment than whipping, not exceeding thirty stripes, a fine not exceeding one hundred dollars, or a term of imprisonment not exceeding six months, is to be inflicted; and shall also have exclusive original cognizance of all civil causes of admiralty and maritime jurisdiction, including all seizures under laws of impost, navigation or trade of the United States, where the seizures are made, on waters which are navigable from the sea by vessels of ten or more tons burthen, within their respective districts as well as upon the high seas;(*a*) saving to suitors, in all cases, the right of a common law remedy, where the common law is competent to give it; and shall also have exclusive original cognizance of all seizures on land, or other waters than as aforesaid, made, and of all suits for penalties and forfeitures incurred, under the laws of the United States.(*b*)   And shall also have cognizance, concurrent with the courts of the several States, or the circuit courts, as the case may be, of all causes where an alien sues for a tort only in violation of the law of nations or a treaty of the United States.(*c*) And shall also have cognizance, concurrent as last mentioned, of all suits at common law where the United States sue, and the matter in dispute amounts, exclusive of costs, to the sum or value of one hundred dollars. And shall also have jurisdiction exclusively of the courts of the several States, of all suits against consuls or vice-consuls, except for offences above the description aforesaid.(*d*) And the trial of issues in fact, in the district courts, in all causes except civil causes of admiralty and maritime jurisdiction, shall be by jury.

Sec. 10. *And be it further enacted,* That the district court in Kentucky district shall, besides the jurisdiction aforesaid, have jurisdiction of all other causes, except of appeals and writs of error, hereinafter made cognizable in a circuit court, and shall proceed therein in the same

[Margin notes:]
[Acts of June 5, 1794, sect. 6; act of Feb. 13, 1807; act of March 3, 1815, sect. 4.]
Original cognizance in maritime causes and of seizure under the laws of the United States.

Concurrent jurisdiction.

Trial of fact by jury.

Kentucky district court.
[Obsolete.]

(*a*) Jurisdiction of the District Courts in cases of admiralty seizures, under laws of impost, navigation and trade. M'Donough *v.* Danery, 3 Dall. 188; 1 Cond. Rep. 94. The United States *v.* La Vengeance, 3 Dall. 297; 1 Cond. Rep. 132. Glass et al. *v.* The Betsey, 3 Dall. 6; 1 Cond. Rep. 10. The Alerta, 3 Cranch, 359; 3 Cond. Rep. 425. The Merino et al., 9 Wheat. 391; 5 Cond. Rep. 623. The Josefa Segunda, 10 Wheat. 312; 6 Cond. Rep. 111. Jennings *v.* Carson, 4 Cranch, 2; 2 Cond. Rep. 2. The Sarah, 8 Wheat. 691; 5 Cond. Rep. 472. Penhallow et al. *v.* Doane's Adm'rs, 3 Dall. 54; 1 Cond. Rep. 21. United States *v.* Richard Peters, 3 Dall. 121; 1 Cond. Rep. 60. Hudson et al. *v.* Guestier, 6 Cranch, 281; 2 Cond. Rep. 374. Brown *v.* The United States, 8 Cranch, 110; 3 Cond. Rep. 56. The Sarah, 8 Wheat. 391; 5 Cond. Rep. 472. The Amiable Nancy, 3 Wheat. 546; 4 Cond. Rep. 322. Slocum *v.* Maybury, 2 Wheat. 1; 4 Cond. Rep. 1. Gelston et al. *v.* Hoyt, 3 Wheat. 246; 4 Cond. Rep. 244. The Bolina, 1 Gallis' C. C. R. 75. The Robert Fulton, 1 Paine's C. C. R. 620; Bee's D. C. R. 11. De Lovio *v.* Boit et al., 2 Gallis' C. C. R. 398. The Abby, 1 Mason's Rep. 360. The Little Ann, Paine's C. C. R. 40. The Catharine, 1 Adm. Decis. 104.

(*b*) An information against a vessel under the act of Congress of May 22, 1794, on account of an alleged exportation of arms, is a case of admiralty and maritime jurisdiction; and an appeal from the District to the Circuit Court, in such a case is sustainable. It is also a civil cause, and triable without the intervention of a jury, under the 9th section of the judicial act. The United States *v.* La Vengeance, 3 Dall. 297; 1 Cond. Rep. 132. The Sarah, 8 Wheat. 691; 5 Cond. Rep. 472. The Abby, 1 Mason, 360. The Little Ann, Paine's C. C. R. 40.

When the District and State courts have concurrent jurisdiction, the right to maintain the jurisdiction attaches to that tribunal which first exercises it, and obtains possession of the thing. The Robert Fulton, Paine's C. C. R. 620.

(*c*) Burke *v.* Trevitt, 1 Mason, 96. The courts of the United States have exclusive jurisdiction of all seizures made on land or water, for a breach of the laws of the United States, and any intervention of State authority, which by taking the thing seized out of the hands of the officer of the United States, might obstruct the exercise of this jurisdiction, is unlawful. Slocum *v.* Mayberry et al., 2 Wheat. 1; 4 Cond. Rep. 1.

(*d*) Davis *v.* Packard, 6 Peters, 41. As an abstract question, it is difficult to understand on what ground a State court can claim jurisdiction of civil suits against foreign consuls. By the Constitution, the judicial power of the United States extends to all cases affecting ambassadors, other public ministers and consuls; and the judiciary act of 1789 gives to the district courts of the United States, exclusively of the courts of the several States, jurisdiction of all suits against consuls and vice consuls, except for certain offences enumerated in this act. Davis *v.* Packard, 7 Peters, 276.

If a consul, being sued in a State court, omits to plead his privilege of exemption from the suit, and afterwards, on removing the judgment of the inferior court to a higher court by writ of error, claims the privilege, such an omission is not a waiver of the privilege. If this was to be viewed merely as a personal privilege, there might be grounds for such a conclusion. But it cannot be so considered; it is the privilege of the country or government which the consul represents. This is the light in which foreign ministers are considered by the law of nations; and our constitution and law seem to put consuls on the same footing in this respect. *Ibid.*

G 2

manner as a circuit court, and writs of error and appeals shall lie from decisions therein to the Supreme Court in the same causes, as from a circuit court to the Supreme Court, and under the same regulations.(a)

Maine district court.
[Obsolete.]

And the district court in Maine district shall, besides the jurisdiction herein before granted, have jurisdiction of all causes, except of appeals and writs of error herein after made cognizable in a circuit court, and shall proceed therein in the same manner as a circuit court: And writs of error shall lie from decisions therein to the circuit court in the district of Massachusetts in the same manner as from other district courts to their respective circuit courts.

Circuit courts original cognizance where the matter in dispute exceeds five hundred dollars.

Sec. 11. *And be it further enacted*, That the circuit courts shall have original cognizance, concurrent with the courts of the several States, of all suits of a civil nature at common law or in equity, where the matter in dispute exceeds, exclusive of costs, the sum or value of five hundred dollars, and the United States are plaintiffs, or petitioners; or an alien is a party, or the suit is between a citizen of the State where the suit is brought, and a citizen of another State.(b)   And shall have

---

(a) By an act passed February 24, 1807, the Circuit Court jurisdiction of the District Court of Kentucky was abolished.

(b) The amount laid in the declaration is the sum in controversy. If the plaintiff receive less than the amount so claimed, the jurisdiction of the court is not affected. Green *v.* Liter, 8 Cranch, 229. Gordon *v.* Longest, 16 Peters, 97. Lessee of Hartshorn *v.* Wright, Peters' C. C. R. 64.

By the 5th section of the act of February 21, 1794, "an act to promote the progress of the useful arts," &c., jurisdiction in actions for violations of patent rights, is given to the Circuit Courts. Also by the act of February 15, 1819, original cognizance, as well in equity as at law, is given to the Circuit Courts of all actions, and for the violation of copy rights. In such cases appeals lie to the Supreme Court of the United States. So also in cases of interest, or disability of a district judge. Act of May 8, 1792, sec. 11; act of March 2, 1809, sec. 1; act of March 3, 1821.

Jurisdiction in cases of injunctions on Treasury warrants of distress. Act of May 15, 1820, sec. 4.

Jurisdiction in cases removed from State courts. Act of February 4, 1815, sec. 8; act of March 3, 1815, sec. 6.

Jurisdiction in cases of assigned debentures. Act of March 2, 1799.

Jurisdiction of crimes committed within the Indian territories. Act of March 30, 1830, sec. 15; act of April 30, 1816, sec. 4; act of March 3, 1817, sec. 2.

Jurisdiction in bankruptcy. Act of August 19, 1841, chap. 9, [repealed.]

Jurisdiction in cases where citizens of the same State claim title to land under a grant from a State other than that in which the suit is pending in a State court. Act of September 24, 1789, sec. 12. See Colson *v.* Lewis, 2 Wheat. 377; 4 Cond. Rep. 168.

Jurisdiction where officers of customs are parties. Act of February 4, 1815, sec. 8; act of March 3, 1815, sec. 6; act of March 3, 1817, sec. 2.

A circuit court though an inferior court in the language of the constitution, is not so in the language of the common law; nor are its proceedings subject to the scrutiny of those narrow rules, which the caution or jealousy of the courts at Westminster long applied to courts of that denomination; but are entitled to as liberal intendments and presumptions in favour of their regularity, as those of any supreme court. Turner *v.* The Bank of North America, 4 Dall. 8; 1 Cond. Rep. 205.

The Circuit Courts of the United States have cognizance of all offences against the United States. What those offences are depends upon the common law applied to the sovereignty and authorities confided to the United States. The United States *v.* Coolidge, 1 Gallis' C. C. R. 488, 495.

Where the jurisdiction of the federal courts has once attached, no subsequent change in the relation or condition of the parties in the progress of the cause, will oust that jurisdiction. The United States *v.* Meyers, 2 Brocken, C. C. R. 516.

All the cases arising under the laws of the United States are not, per se, among the cases comprised within the jurisdiction of the Circuit Court, under the provisions of the 11th section of the judiciary act of 1789. The Postmaster General *v.* Stockton and Stokes, 12 Peters, 524.

Jurisdiction of the Circuit Courts of the United States in suits between aliens and citizens of another State than that in which the suit is brought:

The courts of the United States will entertain jurisdiction of a cause where all the parties are aliens, if none of them object to it. Mason et al. *v.* The Blaireau, 2 Cranch, 240; 1 Cond. Rep. 397.

The Supreme Court understands the expressions in the act of Congress, giving jurisdiction to the courts of the United States "where an alien is a party, or the suit is between a citizen of the State where the suit is brought, and a citizen of another State," to mean that each distinct interest should be represented by persons, all of whom have a right to sue, or may be sued in the federal courts: that is, when the interest is joint, each of the persons concerned in that interest must be competent to sue or be liable to be sued in those courts. Strawbridge *v.* Curtis, 3 Cranch, 267; 1 Cond. Rep. 523.

Neither the Constitution nor the act of Congress regards the subject of the suit, but the parties to it. Mossman's Ex'ors *v.* Higginson, 4 Dall. 12; 1 Cond. Rep. 210.

When the jurisdiction of the Circuit Court depends on the character of the parties, and such party consists of a number of individuals, each one must be competent to sue in the courts of the United States, or jurisdiction cannot be entertained. Ward *v.* Arredendo et al., Paine's C. C. R. 410. Strawbridge *v.* Curtis, 3 Cranch, 267; 1 Cond. Rep. 523.

The courts of the United States have not jurisdiction, unless it appears by the record that it belongs

exclusive cognizance of all crimes and offences cognizable under the authority of the United States,(a) except where this act otherwise provides, or the laws of the United States shall otherwise direct, and concurrent jurisdiction with the district courts of the crimes and offences cognizable therein.   But no person shall be arrested in one district for trial in another, in any civil action before a circuit or district court.(b) And no civil suit shall be brought before either of said courts against an inhabitant of the United States, by any original process in any other district than that whereof he is an inhabitant, or in which he shall be found at the time of serving the writ, nor shall any district or circuit court have cognizance of any suit to recover the contents of any promissory note or other chose in action in favour of an assignee, unless a suit might have been prosecuted in such court to recover the said contents if no assignment had been made, except in cases of foreign bills of exchange.(c)   And the circuit courts shall also have appellate jurisdiction from the district courts under the regulations and restrictions herein after provided.(d)

SEC. 12. *And be it further enacted,* That if a suit be commenced in any state court against an alien, or by a citizen of the state in which the suit is brought against a citizen of another state, and the matter in dispute exceeds the aforesaid sum or value of five hundred dollars, exclusive of costs, to be made to appear to the satisfaction of the court; and the defendant shall, at the time of entering his appearance in such state court, file a petition for the removal of the cause for trial into the next circuit court, to be held in the district where the suit is pending, or if in the district of Maine to the district court next to be holden therein, or if in Kentucky district to the district court next to be holden therein, and offer good and sufficient surety for his entering in such court, on the first day of its session, copies of said process against him, and also for his there appearing and entering special bail in the cause, if special bail was originally requisite therein, it shall then be the duty of the state court to accept the surety, and proceed no further in the cause, and any bail that may have been originally taken shall be discharged, and the said copies being entered as aforesaid, in such court of the United States, the cause shall there proceed in the same manner as if it had been brought there by original process.(e)   And any attach-

Sidenotes:
Exclusive cognizance of crimes and offences cognizable under the laws of the United States.
No person to be arrested in one district for trial in another on any civil suit.
Limitation as to civil suits.
Actions on promissory notes.
Circuit courts shall also have appellate jurisdiction.
Matter in dispute above 500 dollars.
Removal of causes from state courts.
Special bail.

---

to them, as that the parties are citizens of different States. Wood v. Wagnon, 2 Cranch, 9; 1 Cond. Rep. 335.

Where the parties to a suit are such as to give the federal courts jurisdiction, it is immaterial that they are administrators or executors, and that those they represent were citizens of the same State. Chappedelaine et al. v. Decheneaux, 4 Cranch, 306; 2 Cond. Rep. 116. Childress et al. v. Emory et al., 8 Wheat. 642; 5 Cond. Rep. 547. See also Brown v. Strode, 5 Cranch, 303; 2 Cond. Rep. 265. Bingham v. Cabot, 3 Dall. 382; 1 Cond. Rep. 170. Gracie v. Palmer, 8 Wheat. 699; 5 Cond. Rep. 561. Massie v. Watts, 6 Cranch, 148; 2 Cond. Rep. 332. Sere et al. v. Pitot et al., 6 Cranch, 332; 2 Cond. Rep. 389. Shute v. Davis, Peters' C. C. R. 431. Flanders v. The Ætna Ins. Com., 3 Mason, C. C. R. 158. Kitchen v. Sullivan et al., 4 Wash. C. C. R. 84. Briggs v. French, 2 Sumner's C. C. R. 252.

(a) The Circuit Courts of the United States have jurisdiction of a robbery committed on the high seas under the 8th section of the act of April 30, 1790, although such robbery could not, if committed on land, be punished with death. The United States v. Palmer et al., 3 Wheat. 610; 4 Cond. Rep. 352. See The United States v. Coolidge et al., 1 Gallis' C. C. R. 488, 495. The United States v. Coombs, 12 Peters, 72.

The Circuit Courts have no original jurisdiction in suits for penalties and forfeitures arising under the laws of the United States, but the District Courts have exclusive jurisdiction. Ketland v. The Cassius, 2 Dall. 365.

(b) The petitioner was arrested in Pennsylvania, by the marshal of the district of Pennsylvania, under an attachment from the Circuit Court of Rhode Island, for a contempt in not appearing in that court after a monition, served upon him in the State of Pennsylvania, to answer in a prize cause as to a certain bale of goods condemned to the captors, which had come into the possession of Peter Graham, the petitioner. Held, that the circuit and district courts of the United States cannot, either in suits at law or equity, send their process into another district, except where specially authorized so to do by some act of Congress. Ex parte Peter Graham, 3 Wash. C. C. R. 456.

(c) Bean v. Smith, 2 Mason's C. C. R. 252. Young v. Bryan, 6 Wheat. 146; 5 Cond. Rep. 44. Mollan v. Torrance, 9 Wheat. 537; 5 Cond. Rep. 666.

(d) Smith v. Jackson, Paine's C. C. R. 453.

(e) The Judge of a State Court to which an application is made for the removal of a cause into a court of the United States must exercise a legal discretion as to the right claimed to remove the cause;

Attachment of goods holden to final judgment.

ment of the goods or estate of the defendant by the original process, shall hold the goods or estate so attached, to answer the final judgment in the same manner as by the laws of such state they would have been holden to answer final judgment, had it been rendered by the court in which the suit commenced. And if in any action commenced in a state court, the title of land be concerned, and the parties are citizens of the same state, and the matter in dispute exceeds the sum or value of five hundred dollars, exclusive of costs, the sum or value being made to appear to the satisfaction of the court, either party, before the trial, shall state to the court and make affidavit if they require it, that he claims and shall rely upon a right or title to the land, under a grant from a state other than that in which the suit is pending, and produce the original grant or an exemplification of it, except where the loss of public records shall put it out of his power, and shall move that the adverse party inform the court, whether he claims a right or title to the land under a grant from the state in which the suit is pending; the said adverse [party] shall give such information, or otherwise not be allowed to plead such grant, or give it in evidence upon the trial, and if he informs that he does claim under such grant, the party claiming under the grant first mentioned may then, on motion, remove the cause for trial to the next circuit court to be holden in such district, or if in the district of Maine, to the court next to be holden therein; or if in Kentucky district, to the district court next to be holden therein; but if he is the defendant, shall do it under the same regulations as in the beforementioned case of the removal of a cause into such court by an alien; and neither party removing the cause, shall be allowed to plead or give evidence of any other title than that by him stated as aforesaid, as the ground of his claim; and the trial of issues in fact in the circuit courts shall, in all suits, except those of equity, and of admiralty, and maritime jurisdiction, be by jury.(a.)

Title of land where value exceeds 500 dollars.

If in Maine and Kentucky, where causes are removable. [Obsolete.]

Issues in fact by jury.

Supreme court exclusive jurisdiction.

Sec. 13. *And be it further enacted,* That the Supreme Court shall have exclusive jurisdiction of all controversies of a civil nature, where a state is a party, except between a state and its citizens; and except also between a state and citizens of other states, or aliens, in which latter case it shall have original but not exclusive jurisdiction.(b.) And shall have exclusively all such jurisdiction of suits or proceedings against ambassadors, or other public ministers, or their domestics, or domestic servants, as a court of law can have or exercise consistently with the law of nations; and original, but not exclusive jurisdiction of all suits brought by ambassadors, or other public ministers, or in which a consul,

Proceedings against public ministers.

the defendant being entitled to the right to remove the cause under the law of the United States, on the facts of the case, (the judge of the State court could not legally prevent the removal;) the application for the removal having been made in proper form, it was the duty of the State court to proceed no further in the cause. Gordon *v.* Longest, 16 Peters, 97.

One great object in the establishment of the courts of the United States, and regulating their jurisdiction, was to have a tribunal in each State presumed to be free from local influence, and to which all who were non-residents or aliens, might resort for legal redress; and this object would be defeated if a judge in the exercise of any other than a legal discretion, may deny to the party entitled to it, a removal of his cause. *Ibid.*

(a) The provisions of the laws of the United States relating to juries, and trials by jury are:—*Trial by jury*—act of September 24, 1789, chap. 20, sec. 10, sec. 12, sec. 15.—*Exemption from attending on juries*—act of May 7, 1800, chap. 46, sec. 4. *Choice of jurors and qualification of juries*—act of September 24, 1789, chap. 20, sec. 29; act of May 13, 1800; act of July 20, 1840; act of March 3, 1841, chap. 19. Expired as to juries in Pennsylvania. Special jury act of April 29, 1802, chap. 31, sec. 30. —*Jury in criminal cases*—act of September 24, 1789, chap. 20, sec. 29; act of April 30, 1790, chap. 9. *Manner of summoning jurors*—act of September 24, 1789, sec. 29; act of April 29, 1802, chap. 31. *Jurymen de talibus*—act of September 24, 1789, chap. 20.

(b) As to cases in which States, or alleged States, are parties, the following cases are referred to : The Cherokee Nation *v.* The State of Georgia, 5 Peters, 1. New Jersey *v.* The State of New York, 5 Peters, 284. Ex parte Juan Madrazzo, 7 Peters, 627. The State of Rhode Island *v.* The State of Massachusetts, 12 Peters, 651. Cohens *v.* The State of Virginia, 6 Wheat. 264; 5 Cond. Rep. 90. New York *v.* Connecticut, 4 Dall. 3. Fowler *v.* Lindsay et al., 3 Dall. 411.

or vice consul, shall be a party.(a)   And the trial of issues in fact in the Supreme Court, in all actions at law against citizens of the United States, shall be by jury.   The Supreme Court shall also have appellate jurisdiction from the circuit courts and courts of the several states, in the cases herein after specially provided for ;(b) and shall have power to issue writs of prohibition(c) to the district courts, when proceeding as courts of admiralty and maritime jurisdiction, and writs of *mandamus*,(d) in cases warranted by the principles and usages of law, to any courts appointed, or persons holding office, under the authority of the United States.

> Sup. Court appellate jurisdiction.
>
> Writs of Prohibition.
>
> Of Mandamus.

Sec. 14. *And be it further enacted,* That all the before-mentioned courts of the United States, shall have power to issue writs of *scire facias, habeas corpus*,(e) and all other writs not specially provided for

> Courts may issue writs scire facias, habeas corpus, &c.

(a) The United States *v.* Ortega, 11 Wheat. 467; 6 Cond. Rep. 394.   Davis *v.* Packard, 6 Peters, 41.

(b) As to the appellate jurisdiction of the Supreme Court, see the cases collected in Peters's Digest, "Supreme Court," "Appellate Jurisdiction of the Supreme Court," and the following cases : The United States *v.* Goodwin, 7 Cranch, 108; 2 Cond. Rep. 434.   Wiscart *v.* Dauchy, 3 Dall. 321; 1 Cond. Rep. 144.   United States *v.* Moore, 3 Cranch, 159; 1 Cond. Rep. 480.   Owings *v.* Norwood's Lessee, 5 Cranch, 344; 2 Cond. Rep. 275.   Martin *v.* Hunter's Lessee, 1 Wheat. 304; 3 Cond. Rep. 575.   Gordon *v.* Caldcleugh, 3 Cranch, 268; 1 Cond. Rep. 524.   Ex parte Kearney, 7 Wheat. 38; 5 Cond. Rep. 225.   Smith *v.* The State of Maryland, 6 Cranch, 286; 2 Cond. Rep. 377.   Inglee *v.* Coolidge, 2 Wheat. 363; 4 Cond. Rep. 155.   Nicholls et al. *v.* Hodges Ex'ors, 1 Peters, 562.   Buel et al. *v.* Van Ness, 8 Wheat. 312; 5 Cond. Rep. 445.   Miller *v.* Nicholls, 4 Wheat. 311; 4 Cond. Rep. 465.   Matthews *v.* Zane et al., 7 Wheat. 164; 5 Cond. Rep. 265.   M'Cluny *v.* Silliman, 6 Wheat. 598; 5 Cond. Rep. 197.   Houston *v.* Moore, 3 Wheat. 433; 3 Cond. Rep. 286.   Montgomery *v.* Hernandez et al., 12 Wheat. 129; 6 Cond. Rep. 475.   Cohens *v.* Virginia, 6 Wheat. 264; 5 Cond. Rep. 90.   Gibbons *v.* Ogden, 6 Wheat. 448; 5 Cond. Rep. 134.   Weston et al. *v.* The City Council of Charleston, 2 Peters, 449.   Hickie *v.* Starke et al., 1 Peters, 94.   Satterlee *v.* Matthewson, 2 Peters, 380.   M'Bride *v.* Hoey, 11 Peters, 167.   Ross *v.* Barland et. al., 1 Peters, 655.   The City of New Orleans *v.* De Armas, 9 Peters, 224.   Crowell *v.* Randell, 10 Peters, 368.   Williams *v.* Norris, 12 Wheat. 117; 6 Cond. Rep. 462.   Menard *v.* Aspasia, 5 Peters, 505.   Worcester *v.* The State of Georgia, 6 Wheat. 515.   The United States *v.* Moore, 3 Cranch, 159; 1 Cond. Rep. 480.

(c) Prohibition.   Where the District Court of the United States has no jurisdiction of a cause brought before it, a prohibition will be issued from the Supreme Court to prevent proceedings.   The United States *v.* Judge Peters, 3 Dall. 121; 1 Cond. Rep. 60.

(d) Mandamus.   The following cases have been decided on the power of the Supreme Court to issue a mandamus.   Marbury *v.* Madison, 1 Cranch, 137; 1 Cond. Rep. 267.   M'Cluny *v.* Silliman, 2 Wheat. 369; 4 Cond. Rep. 162.   United States *v.* Lawrence, 3 Dall. 42; 1 Cond. Rep. 19.   United States *v.* Peters, 3 Dall. 121; 1 Cond. Rep. 60.   Ex parte Burr, 9 Wheat. 529; 5 Cond. Rep. 660.   Parker *v.* The Judges of the Circuit Court of Maryland, 12 Wheat. 561; 6 Cond. Rep. 644.   Ex parte Roberts et al., 6 Peters, 216.   Ex parte Davenport, 6 Peters, 661.   Ex parte Bradstreet, 12 Peters, 174; 7 Peters, 634; 8 Peters, 588.   Life and Fire Ins. Comp. of New York *v.* Wilson's heirs, 8 Peters, 291.

On a mandamus a superior court will never direct in what manner the discretion of the inferior tribunal shall be exercised; but they will, in a proper case, require an inferior court to decide.   *Ibid.*   Life and Fire Ins. Comp. of New York *v.* Adams, 9 Peters, 571.   Ex parte Story, 12 Peters, 339.   Ex parte Jesse Hoyt, collector, &c., 13 Peters, 279.

A writ of mandamus is not a proper process to correct an erroneous judgment or decree rendered in an inferior court.   This is a matter which is properly examinable on a writ of error, or an appeal to a proper appellate tribunal.   *Ibid.*

Writs of mandamus from the Circuit Courts of the United States.   A Circuit Court of the United States has power to issue a mandamus to a collector, commanding him to grant a clearance.   Gilchrist et al. *v.* Collector of Charleston, 1 Hall's Admiralty Law Journal, 429.

The power of the Circuit Court to issue the writ of mandamus is confined exclusively to those cases in which it may be necessary to the exercise of their jurisdiction.   M'Intire *v.* Wood, 7 Cranch, 504; 2 Cond. Rep. 588.

The Circuit Courts of the United States have no power to issue writs of mandamus after the practice of the King's Bench; but only where they are necessary for the exercise of their jurisdiction.   Smith *v.* Jackson, Paine's C. C. R. 453.

(e) Habeas corpus.   Ex parte Burford, 3 Cranch, 448; 1 Cond. Rep. 594; Ex parte Bollman, 4 Cranch, 75; 2 Cond. Rep. 33.

The writ of habeas corpus does not lie to bring up a person confined in the prison bounds upon a capias ad satisfaciendum, issued in a civil suit.   Ex parte Wilson, 6 Cranch, 52; 2 Cond. Rep. 300.   Ex parte Kearney, 7 Wheat. 38; 5 Cond. Rep. 225.

The power of the Supreme Court to award writs of habeas corpus is conferred expressly on the court by the 14th section of the judicial act, and has been repeatedly exercised.   No doubt exists respecting the power.   No law of the United States prescribes the cases in which this great writ shall be issued, nor the power of the court over the party brought up by it.   The term used in the constitution is one which is well understood, and the judicial act authorizes the court, and all other courts of the United States and the judges thereof to issue the writ " for the purpose of inquiring into the cause of commitment."   Ex parte Tobias Watkins, 3 Peters, 201.

As the jurisdiction of the Supreme Court is appellate, it must be shown to the court that the court has power to award a habeas corpus, before one will be granted.   Ex parte Milburn, 9 Peters, 704.

Vol. I.—11

Act of 1793, ch. 22; act of 1807, ch. 13; act of 1818, ch. 83; act of Feb. 1819; act of May 20, 1826, ch. 124.

Limitation of writs of habeas corpus.

by statute, which may be necessary for the exercise of their respective jurisdictions, and agreeable to the principles and usages of law. And that either of the justices of the supreme court, as well as judges of the district courts, shall have power to grant writs of *habeas corpus* for the purpose of an inquiry into the cause of commitment.—*Provided,* That writs of *habeas corpus* shall in no case extend to prisoners in gaol, unless where they are in custody, under or by colour of the authority of the United States, or are committed for trial before some court of the same, or are necessary to be brought into court to testify.

Parties shall produce books and writings.

Sec. 15. *And be it further enacted,* That all the said courts of the United States, shall have power in the trial of actions at law, on motion and due notice thereof being given, to require the parties to produce books or writings in their possession or power, which contain evidence pertinent to the issue, in cases and under circumstances where they might be compelled to produce the same by the ordinary rules of proceeding in chancery; and if a plaintiff shall fail to comply with such order, to produce books or writings, it shall be lawful for the courts respectively, on motion, to give the like judgment for the defendant as in cases of nonsuit; and if a defendant shall fail to comply with such order, to produce books or writings, it shall be lawful for the courts respectively on motion as aforesaid, to give judgment against him or her by default.(*a*)

Suits in equity limited.

Sec. 16. *And be it further enacted,* That suits in equity shall not be sustained in either of the courts of the United States, in any case where plain, adequate and complete remedy may be had at law.(*b*)

The act of Congress authorizing the writ of habeas corpus to be issued "for the purpose of inquiring into the cause of commitment," applies as well to cases of commitment under civil as those of criminal process. See Chief Justice Marshall, 2 Brocken C. C. R. 447. Ex parte Cabrera, 1 Wash. C. C. R. 232. United States *v.* French, 1 Gallis's C. C. R. 2. Holmes *v.* Jennison, Governor of the State of Vermont, 14 Peters, 540.

(*a*) It is sufficient for one party to suggest that the other is in possession of a paper, which he has, under the act of Congress, given him notice to produce at the trial, without offering other proof of the fact; and the party so called upon must discharge himself of the consequences of not producing it, by affidavit or other proof that he has it not in his power to produce it. Hylton *v.* Brown, 1 Wash. C. C. R. 298.

The court will not, upon a notice of the defendant to the plaintiff to produce a title paper to the land in dispute, which is merely to defeat the plaintiff's title, compel him to do so; unless the defendant first shows title to the land. Merely showing a right of possession is not sufficient to entitle him to the aid of a court of chancery, or of the Supreme Court, to compel a discovery of papers which are merely to defeat the plaintiff's title without strengthening the defendant's. It is sufficient, in order to entitle him to call for papers to show the title to the land, although none is shown in the papers. *Ibid.*

Where one party in a cause wishes the production of papers supposed to be in the possession of the other, he must give notice to produce them : if not produced, he may give inferior evidence of their contents. But if it is his intention to nonsuit the plaintiff, or if the plaintiff requiring the papers means to obtain a judgment by default, under the 15th section of the judicial act, he is bound to give the opposite party notice that he means to move the court for an order upon him to produce the papers, or on a failure so to do, to award a nonsuit or judgment, as the case may be. Bas *v.* Steele, 3 Wash. C. C. R. 381.

No advantage can be taken of the non-production of papers, unless ground is laid for presuming that the papers were, at the time notice was given, in the possession or power of the party to whom notice was given, and that they were pertinent to the issue. In either of the cases, the party to whom notice was given may be required to prove, by his own oath, that the papers are not in his possession or power; which oath may be met by contrary proof according to the rules of equity. *Ibid.*

To entitle the defendant to nonsuit the plaintiff for not obtaining papers which he was noticed to produce, the defendant must first obtain an order of the court, under a rule that they should be produced. But this order need not be absolute when moved for, but may be nisi, unless cause be shown at the trial. Dunham *v.* Riley, 4 Wash. C. C. R. 126.

Notice to the opposite party to produce on the trial all letters in his possession, relating to monies received by him under the award of the commissioners under the Florida treaty, is sufficiently specific as they described their subject matter. If to such notice the party answer on oath that he has not a particular letter in his possession, and after diligent search could find none such, it is sufficient to prevent the offering of secondary proof of its contents. The party cannot be asked or compelled to answer whether he ever had such a letter in his possession. Vasse *v.* Mifflin, 4 Wash. C. C. R. 519.

(*b*) The equity jurisdiction of the courts of the United States is independent of the local law of any State, and is the same in nature and extent as the equity jurisdiction of England from which it is derived. Therefore it is no objection to this jurisdiction, that there is a remedy under the local law. Gordon *v.* Hobart, 2 Sumner's C. C. R. 401.

If a case is cognizable at common law, the defendant has a right of trial by jury, and a suit upon it cannot be sustained in equity. Baker *v.* Biddle, 1 Baldwin's C. C. R. 405.

Sec. 17. *And be it further enacted,* That all the said courts of the United States shall have power to grant new trials, in cases where there has been a trial by jury for reasons for which new trials have usually been granted in the courts of law ;(*a*) and shall have power to impose and administer all necessary oaths or affirmations, and to punish by fine or imprisonment, at the discretion of said courts, all contempts of authority in any cause or hearing before the same ;(*b*) and to make and establish all necessary rules for the orderly conducting business in the said courts, provided such rules are not repugnant to the laws of the United States.

Courts may grant new trials.

Act of March 2, 1831, ch. 99.

Sec. 18. *And be it further enacted,* That when in a circuit court, judgment upon a verdict in a civil action shall be entered, execution may on motion of either party, at the discretion of the court, and on such conditions for the security of the adverse party as they may judge proper, be stayed forty-two days from the time of entering judgment, to give time to file in the clerk's office of said court, a petition for a new trial. And if such petition be there filed within said term of forty-two days, with a certificate thereon from either of the judges of such court, that he allows the same to be filed, which certificate he may make or refuse at his discretion, execution shall of course be further stayed to the next session of said court.(*c*) And if a new trial be granted, the former judgment shall be thereby rendered void.

Execution may be stayed on conditions.

Sec. 19. *And be it further enacted,* That it shall be the duty of circuit courts, in causes in equity and of admiralty and maritime jurisdiction, to cause the facts on which they found their sentence or decree, fully to appear upon the record either from the pleadings and decree itself, or a state of the case agreed by the parties, or their counsel, or if they disagree by a stating of the case by the court.

Facts to appear on record.

Altered by act of March 3, 1803, chap. 40.

Sec. 20. *And be it further enacted,* That where in a circuit court, a plaintiff in an action, originally brought there, or a petitioner in equity, other than the United States, recovers less than the sum or value of five hundred dollars, or a libellant, upon his own appeal, less than the sum or value of three hundred dollars, he shall not be allowed, but at the discretion of the court, may be adjudged to pay costs.

Costs not allowed unless 500 dollars recovered.

Sec. 21. *And be it further enacted,* That from final decrees in a district court in causes of admiralty and maritime jurisdiction, where the matter in dispute exceeds the sum or value of three hundred dollars, exclusive of costs, an appeal shall be allowed to the next circuit court,

Appeals from the district to the circuit court where matter in dispute exceeds 300 dolls.

There cannot be concurrent jurisdiction at law and equity, where the right and remedy are the same ; but equity may proceed in aid of the remedy at law, by incidental and auxiliary relief; if the remedy at law is complete. Its jurisdiction is special, limited and defined ; not as in England, where it depends on usage. *Ibid.*

The 16th section of the judiciary law is a declaratory act settling the law as to cases of equity jurisdiction, in the nature of a proviso, limitation or exception to its exercise. If the plaintiff have a plain, adequate and complete remedy at law, the case is not a suit in equity, under the constitution, or the judiciary act. *Ibid.*

Though the rules and principles established in English Chancery at the revolution, are adopted in the federal courts, the changes introduced there since, are not followed here ; especially in matters of jurisdiction, as to which the 16th section of the act of 1789 is imperative. *Ibid.*

(*a*) New trials. Calder *v.* Bull and Wife, 3 Dall. 386 ; 1 Cond. Rep. 172. Arnold *v.* Jones, Bee's Rep. 104.

(*b*) Contempt of court. The courts of the United States have no common law jurisdiction of crimes against the United States. But independent of statutes, the courts of the United States have power to fine for contempts, and imprison for contumacy, and to enforce obedience to their orders, &c. The United States *v.* Hudson et al., 7 Cranch, 32 ; 2 Cond. Rep. 405.

By an act passed March 2, 1831, chap. 99, it is enacted, that the power of the courts of the United States to punish for contempts shall not extend to any cases, except to misbehaviour in the presence of the court, or so near to the court as to obstruct the administration of justice, or the misbehaviour of the officers of the court in their official transactions, and disobedience or resistance by any officer of the court, party, juror, witness or any person to any writ, process, order or decree of the court. Indictments may be presented against persons impeding the proceedings of the court, &c. See the statute.

(*c*) Execution. The 14th section of the Judiciary act of September 24, 1789, chap. 20, authorizes the courts of the United States to issue writs of execution upon judgments which have been rendered. This section provides only for the issuing of the writ, and directs no mode of proceeding by the officer obeying its command. Bank of the United States *v.* Halstead, 10 Wheat. 51 ; 6 Cond. Rep. 22.

Altered by the 2d section of the act of March 3, 1803, chap. 40. [Obsolete.]

to be held in such district. *Provided nevertheless,* That all such appeals from final decrees as aforesaid, from the district court of Maine, shall be made to the circuit court, next to be holden after each appeal in the district of Massachusetts.

Final decrees re-examined above 50 dollars.

Sec. 22. *And be it further enacted,* That final decrees and judgments in civil actions in a district court, where the matter in dispute exceeds the sum or value of fifty dollars, exclusive of costs, may be re-examined, and reversed or affirmed in a circuit court, holden in the

Altered by the 2d section of the act of March 3, 1803, chap. 40.

same district, upon a writ of error, whereto shall be annexed and returned therewith at the day and place therein mentioned, an authenticated transcript of the record, an assignment of errors, and prayer for reversal, with a citation to the adverse party, signed by the judge of such district court, or a justice of the Supreme Court, the adverse party

And suits in equity, exceeding 2000 dollars in value.

having at least twenty days' notice.(*a*) And upon a like process, may final judgments and decrees in civil actions, and suits in equity in a circuit court, brought there by original process, or removed there from courts of the several States, or removed there by appeal from a district court where the matter in dispute exceeds the sum or value of two thousand dollars, exclusive of costs, be re-examined and reversed or affirmed in the Supreme Court, the citation being in such case signed by a judge of such circuit court, or justice of the Supreme Court, and the adverse party having at least thirty days' notice.(*b*) But there shall be no rever-

---

(*a*) The rules, regulations and restrictions contained in the 21st and 22d sections of the judiciary act of 1789, respecting the time within which a writ of error shall be brought, and in what instances it shall operate as a supersedeas, the citation to the opposite party, the security to be given by the plaintiff in error, and the restrictions on the appellate court as to reversals in certain enumerated cases, are applicable to the act of 1803, and are to be substantially observed; except that where the appeal is prayed for at the same time when the decree or sentence is pronounced, a citation is not necessary. The San Pedro, 2 Wheat. 132; 4 Cond. Rep. 65.

By the 2d section of the act of March 3, 1803, chap. 40, appeals are allowed from all final judgments or decrees in any of the District courts, where the matter in dispute, exclusive of costs, shall exceed the sum or value of fifty dollars. Appeals from the Circuit Court to the Supreme Court are allowed when the sum or value, exclusive of costs exceeds $2000. This section repeals so much of the 19th and 20th sections of the act of 1789, as comes within the purview of those provisions.

By the provisions of the act of April 2, 1816, chap. 39, appeals from the Circuit Court of the United States for the District of Columbia, are allowed when the matter in dispute in the cause exceeds $1000, exclusive of costs.

(*b*) The following cases have been decided on the questions which have arisen as to the value in controversy, in a case removed by writ of error or appeal.

The verdict and judgment do not ascertain the matter in dispute between the parties. To determine this, recurrence must be had to the original controversy; to the matter in dispute when the action was instituted. Wilson *v.* Daniel, 3 Dall. 401; 1 Cond. Rep. 185.

Where the value of the matter in dispute did not appear in the record, in a case brought by writ of error, the court allowed affidavits to be taken to prove the same, on notice to the opposite party. The writ of error not to be a supersedeas. Course *v.* Stead's Ex'ors, 4 Dall. 22; 1 Cond. Rep. 217; 4 Dall. 20; 1 Cond. Rep. 215.

The Supreme Court will permit viva voce testimony to be given of the value of the matter in dispute, in a case brought up by a writ of error or by appeal. The United States *v.* The Brig Union et al., 4 Cranch, 216; 2 Cond. Rep. 91.

The plaintiff below claimed more than $2000 in his declaration, but obtained a verdict for a less sum. The appellate jurisdiction of the Supreme Court depends on the sum or value in dispute between the parties, as the case stands on the writ of error in the Supreme Court; not on that which was in dispute in the Circuit Court. If the writ of error be brought by the plaintiff below, then the sum the declaration shows to be due may still be recovered, should the judgment for a smaller sum be reversed; and consequently the whole sum claimed is in dispute. Smith *v.* Honey, 3 Peters, 469; Gordon *v.* Ogden, 3 Peters, 33.

In cases where the demand is not for money, and the nature of the action does not require the value of the thing to be stated in the declaration, the practice of the courts of the United States has been to allow the value to be given in evidence. Ex parte Bradstreet, 7 Peters, 634.

The onus probandi of the amount in controversy, to establish the jurisdiction of the Supreme Court in a case brought before it by writ of error, is upon the party seeking to obtain the revision of the case. He may prove that the value exceeds $2000, exclusive of costs. Hagan *v.* Foison, 10 Peters, 160.

The Supreme Court has no jurisdiction in a case in which separate decrees have been entered in the Circuit Court for the wages of seamen, the decree in no one case amounting to $2000, although the amount of the several decrees exceed that sum, and the seamen in each case claimed under the same contract. Oliver *v.* Alexander, 6 Peters, 143. See Scott *v.* Lunt's Adm'rs, 6 Peters, 349.

The Supreme Court will not compel the hearing of a cause unless the citation be served thirty days before the first day of the term. Welsh *v.* Mandeville, 5 Cranch, 321; 2 Cond. Rep. 268.

A citation must accompany the writ of error. Lloyd *v.* Alexander, 1 Cranch, 365; 1 Cond. Rep. 334.

When an appeal is prayed during the session of the court, a citation to the appellee is not necessary. Riley, appellant, *v.* Lamar et al., 2 Cranch, 344; 1 Cond. Rep. 419.

sal in either court on such writ of error for error in ruling any plea in abatement, other than a plea to the jurisdiction of the court, or such plea to a petition or bill in equity, as is in the nature of a demurrer, or for any error in fact. And writs of error shall not be brought but within five years after rendering or passing the judgment or decree complained of, or in case the person entitled to such writ of error be an infant, *feme covert, non compos mentis*, or imprisoned, then within five years as aforesaid, exclusive of the time of such disability.(*a*)　And every justice or judge signing a citation on any writ of error as aforesaid, shall take good and sufficient security, that the plaintiff in error shall prosecute his writ to effect, and answer all damages and costs if he fail to make his plea good.(*b*)

Writs of error limited.

Plaintiff to give security.
Act of December 12, 1794, chap. 3.

Sec. 23. *And be it further enacted,* That a writ of error as aforesaid shall be a supersedeas and stay execution in cases only where the writ of error is served, by a copy thereof being lodged for the adverse party in the clerk's office where the record remains, within ten days, Sundays exclusive, after rendering the judgment or passing the decree complained of. Until the expiration of which term of ten days, executions shall not issue in any case where a writ of error may be a supersedeas; and whereupon such writ of error the Supreme or a circuit court shall affirm a judgment or decree, they shall adjudge or decree to the respondent in error just damages for his delay, and single or double costs at their discretion.(*c*)

Writ of error a supersedeas.

Sec. 24. *And be it further enacted,* That when a judgment or decree shall be reversed in a circuit court, such court shall proceed to render such judgment or pass such decree as the district court should have rendered or passed; and the Supreme Court shall do the same on reversals therein, except where the reversal is in favour of the plaintiff, or petitioner in the original suit, and the damages to be assessed, or matter to be decreed, are uncertain, in which case they shall remand the cause for a final decision. And the Supreme Court shall not issue execution in causes that are removed before them by writs of error, but shall send a special mandate to the circuit court to award execution thereupon.

Judgment or decree reversed.

Supreme court not to issue execution but mandate.

Sec. 25. *And be it further enacted,* That a final judgment or decree in any suit, in the highest court of law or equity of a State in which a decision in the suit could be had, where is drawn in question the validity of a treaty or statute of, or an authority exercised under the United States, and the decision is against their validity; or where is drawn in question the validity of a statute of, or an authority exercised under any State, on the ground of their being repugnant to the constitution, treaties or laws of the United States, and the decision is in favour of such their validity,(*d*) or where is drawn in question the construction of any

Cases in which judgment and decrees of the highest court of a state may be examined by the supreme court, on writ of error.

(*a*) An appeal under the judiciary acts of 1789 and 1803, was prayed for and allowed within five years; held to be valid, although the security was not given within five years. The mode of taking the security and the time of perfecting it, are exclusively within the control of the court below. The Dos Hermanos, 10 Wheat. 306; 6 Cond. Rep. 109.

(*b*) By the act of December 12, 1794, chap. 3, the security required to be taken on signing a citation on any writ of error which shall not be a supersedeas, and stay execution, shall only be for an amount which will be sufficient to answer for costs.

(*c*) Supersedeas. The Supreme Court will not quash an execution issued by the court below to enforce its decree, pending a writ of error, if the writ be not a supersedeas to the decree. Wallen *v.* Williams, 7 Cranch, 278; 2 Cond. Rep. 491.

(*d*) In delivering the opinion of the Supreme Court in the case of Fisher *v.* Cockrell, 5 Peters, 248, Mr. Chief Justice Marshall said: " In the argument the court has been admonished of the jealousy with which the States of the Union view the revising power entrusted by the constitution and laws to this tribunal. To observations of this character the answer uniformly has been that the course of the judicial department is marked out by law. We must tread the direct and narrow path prescribed for us. As this court has never grasped at ungranted jurisdiction, so it never will, we trust, shrink from that which is conferred upon it."

The appellate power of the Supreme Court of the United States extends to cases pending in the State courts; and the 25th section of the judiciary act, which authorizes the exercise of this jurisdiction in the specified cases by writ of error, is supported by the letter and spirit of the constitution. Martin *v.* Hunter's Lessee, 1 Wheat. 304; 3 Cond. Rep. 575.

Under the 25th section of the judiciary act of 1789, where the construction of any clause in the con-

H

clause of the constitution, or of a treaty, or statute of, or commission held under the United States, and the decision is against the title, right, privilege or exemption specially set up or claimed by either party, under such clause of the said Constitution, treaty, statute or commission, may be re-examined and reversed or affirmed in the Supreme Court of the United States upon a writ of error, the citation being signed by the chief justice, or judge or chancellor of the court rendering or passing the judgment or decree complained of, or by a justice of the Supreme Court of the United States, in the same manner and under the same regulations, and the writ shall have the same effect, as if the judgment or decree complained of had been rendered or passed in a circuit court, and the proceeding upon the reversal shall also be the same, except that the Supreme Court, instead of remanding the cause for a final decision as before provided, may at their discretion, if the cause shall have been once remanded before, proceed to a final decision of the same, and award execution.   But no other error shall be assigned or regarded as a ground of reversal in any such case as aforesaid, than such as appears on the face of the record, and immediately respects the before men-

Proceedings on reversal.

No writs of error but as above mentioned.

---

stitution or any statute of the United States is drawn in question, in any suit in a State court, the decision must be against the title or right set up by the party under such clause in the constitution or statute; otherwise the Supreme Court has no appellate jurisdiction in the case. It is not sufficient that the construction of the statute was drawn in question, and that the decision was against the title. It must appear that the title set up depended on the statute. Williams v. Norris, 12 Wheat. 117; 6 Cond. Rep. 462.

If the construction or validity of a treaty of the United States is drawn in question in the State courts, and the decision is against its validity, or against the title set up by either party under the treaty, the Supreme Court has jurisdiction to ascertain that title, and to determine its legal meaning; and is not confined to the abstract construction of the treaty itself. *Ibid.*

The 2d article of the constitution of the United States enables the Supreme Court to receive jurisdiction to the full extent of the constitution, laws and treaties of the United States, when any question respecting them shall assume such form that the judicial power is capable of acting upon it. That power is capable of acting only when the subject is submitted to it by a party who asserts his right in the form prescribed by law. It then becomes a case. Osborn v. The Bank of the United States, 6 Wheat. 738; 5 Cond. Rep. 741.

The Supreme Court has no jurisdiction under the 25th section of the act of 1789, unless the judgment or decree of the State court be a final judgment or decree. A judgment reversing that of an inferior court, and awarding a scire facias de novo, is not a final judgment. Houston v. Moore, 3 Wheat. 433; 4 Cond. Rep. 286.

The Supreme Court has no appellate jurisdiction under the 25th section of the judiciary act, unless the right, title, privilege, or exemption under a statute or commission of the United States be specially set up by the party claiming it in the State court, and the decision be against the same. Montgomery v. Hernandez, 12 Wheat. 129; 6 Cond. Rep. 475.

It is no objection to the exercise of the appellate jurisdiction under this section, that one party is a State, and the other a citizen of that State. Cohens v. The State of Virginia, 6 Wheat. 264; 5 Cond. Rep. 90.

In order to bring a case for a writ of error or an appeal to the Supreme Court from the highest court of a State within the 25th section of the judiciary act, it must appear on the face of the record: 1. That some of the questions stated in that section did arise in the State court. 2. That the question was decided in the State court as required in the section.

It is not necessary that the question shall appear in the record to have been raised, and the decision made in direct and positive terms, ipsissimis verbis; but it is sufficient if it appears by clear and necessary intendment that the question must have been raised, and must have been decided, in order to induce the judgment. It is not sufficient to show that a question might have arisen and been applicable to the case, unless it is further shown, on the record, that it did arise and was applied by the State Court to the case. Crowell v. Randall, 10 Peters, 368. See also Williams v. Norris, 12 Wheat. 117; 6 Cond. Rep. 462. Jackson v. Lamphire, 3 Peters, 280. Menard v. Aspasia, 5 Peters, 505. Fisher v. Cockrell, 5 Peters, 248. Gelston v. Hoyt, 3 Wheat. 246; 4 Cond. Rep. 244. Gordon v. Caldcleugh et al., 3 Cranch, 268; 1 Cond. Rep. 524. Owings v. Norwood's Lessee, 5 Cranch, 344; 2 Cond. Rep. 275. Buel et al. v. Van Ness, 8 Wheat. 312; 5 Cond. Rep. 445. Miller v. Nicholls, 4 Wheat. 311; 4 Cond. Rep. 465. Matthews v. Zane et al., 7 Wheat. 164; 5 Cond. Rep. 265. Gibbons v. Ogden, 6 Wheat. 448; 5 Cond. Rep. 134.

Under the 25th section of the judiciary act of 1789, three things are necessary to give the Supreme Court jurisdiction of a case brought up by writ of error or appeal: 1. The validity of a statute of the United States, or of authority exercised under a State, must be drawn in question. 2. It must be drawn in question on the ground that it is repugnant to the constitution, treaties and laws of the United States. 3. The decision of the State court must be in favour of its validity. The Commonwealth Bank of Kentucky v. Griffith et al., 14 Peters, 46. See also Pollard's heirs v. Kibbe, 14 Peters, 353. M'Cluny v. Silliman, 6 Wheat. 598; 5 Cond. Rep. 197. Weston et al. v. The City Council of Charleston, 2 Peters, 449. Hickie v. Starke et al., 1 Peters, 94. Satterlee v. Matthewson, 2 Peters, 380. Wilson et al. v. The Blackbird Creek Marsh Association, 2 Peters, 245. Harris v. Dennie, 3 Peters, 292. M'Bride v. Hoey, 11 Peters, 167. Winn's heirs v. Jackson et al., 12 Wheat. 135; 6 Cond. Rep. 479. City of New Orleans v. De Armas, 9 Peters, 224. Davis v. Packard, 6 Peters, 41.

tioned questions of validity or construction of the said constitution, treaties, statutes, commissions, or authorities in dispute.(*a*)

SEC. 26. *And be it further enacted,* That in all causes brought before either of the courts of the United States to recover the forfeiture annexed to any articles of agreement, covenant, bond, or other speciality, where the forfeiture, breach or non-performance shall appear, by the default or confession of the defendant, or upon demurrer, the court before whom the action is, shall render judgment therein for the plaintiff to recover so much as is due according to equity. And when the sum for which judgment should be rendered is uncertain, the same shall, if either of the parties request it, be assessed by a jury.

SEC. 27. *And be it further enacted,* That a marshal shall be appointed in and for each district for the term of four years, but shall be removable from office at pleasure, whose duty it shall be to attend the district and circuit courts when sitting therein, and also the Supreme Court in the district in which that court shall sit.(*b*) And to execute throughout the district, all lawful precepts directed to him, and issued under the authority of the United States, and he shall have power to command all necessary assistance in the execution of his duty, and to appoint as there shall be occasion, one or more deputies,(*c*) who shall be removable from office by the judge of the district court, or the circuit court sitting within the district, at the pleasure of either; and before he enters on the duties of his office, he shall become bound for the faithful performance of the same, by himself and by his deputies before the judge of the district court to the United States, jointly and severally, with two good and sufficient sureties, inhabitants and freeholders of such district, to be approved by the district judge, in the sum of twenty thousand dollars, and shall take before said judge, as shall also his deputies, before they enter on the duties of their appointment, the following oath of office: "I, A. B., do solemnly swear or affirm, that I will faithfully execute all lawful precepts directed to the marshal of the district of
under the authority of the United States, and true returns make, and in all things well and truly, and without malice or partiality, perform the duties of the office of marshal (or marshal's deputy, as the case may be) of the district of   , during my continuance in said office, and take only my lawful fees. So help me God."

SEC. 28. *And be it further enacted,* That in all causes wherein the marshal or his deputy shall be a party, the writs and precepts therein shall be directed to such disinterested person as the court, or any justice or judge thereof may appoint, and the person so appointed, is hereby authorized to execute and return the same. And in case of the death of any marshal, his deputy or deputies shall continue in office, unless otherwise specially removed; and shall execute the same in the name of the deceased, until another marshal shall be appointed and sworn: And the defaults or misfeasances in office of such deputy or deputies in the mean time, as well as before, shall be adjudged a breach of the condition of the bond given, as before directed, by the marshal who appointed

Margin notes:
In cases of forfeiture the courts may give judgment according to equity.

Jury to assess damages when the sum is uncertain.

Marshal to be appointed.
Duration of office.
Act of May 15, 1820, ch. 101, 106, sec. 8.

Deputies removable by the district and circuit courts.

Sureties.

Oath of marshal, and of his deputies.

If marshal, or his deputy, a party to a suit, process to be directed to a person selected by the court.
Deputies to continue in office on the death of the marshal.
Defaults of deputies.

(*a*) Williams *v.* Norris, 6 Wheat. 117; 6 Cond. Rep. 462.

(*b*) A marshal is not removed by the appointment of a new one, until he receives notice of such appointment. All acts done by the marshal after the appointment of a new one, before notice, are good; but his acts subsequent to notice are void. Wallace's C. C. R. 119.

It is the duty of a marshal of a court of the United States to execute all process which may be placed in his hand, but he performs this duty at his peril, and under the guidance of law. He must, of course, exercise some judgment in the performance. Should he fail to obey the exegit of the writ without a legal excuse, or should he in its letter violate the rights of others, he is liable to the action of the injured party. Life and Fire Ins. Comp. of New York *v.* Adams, 9 Peters, 573.

(*c*) A marshal is liable on his official bond for the failure of his deputies to serve original process, but the measure of his liability is the extent of the injury received by the plaintiff, produced by his negligence. If the loss of the debt be the direct legal consequence of a failure to serve the process, the amount of the debt is the measure of the damages; but not so if otherwise. The United States *v.* Moore's Adm'rs, 2 Brocken's C. C. R. 317. See San Jose Indiano, 2 Gallis. C. C. R. 311. Ex parte Jesse Hoyt, collector, &c., 13 Peters, 279.

Powers of the executor or administrator of deceased marshals.

them; and the executor or administrator of the deceased marshal shall have like remedy for the defaults and misfeasances in office of such deputy or deputies during such interval, as they would be entitled to if the marshal had continued in life and in the exercise of his said office, until his successor was appointed, and sworn or affirmed: And every marshal or his deputy when removed from office, or when the term for which the marshal is appointed shall expire, shall have power notwithstanding to execute all such precepts as may be in their hands respectively at the time of such removal or expiration of office; and the marshal shall be held answerable for the delivery to his successor of all prisoners which may be in his custody at the time of his removal, or when the term for which he is appointed shall expire, and for that purpose may retain such prisoners in his custody until his successor shall be appointed and qualified as the law directs.(a)

Marshal's power after removal.

Trial of cases punishable with death to be had in county.

SEC. 29. *And be it further enacted,* That in cases punishable with death, the trial shall be had in the county where the offence was committed, or where that cannot be done without great inconvenience, twelve petit jurors at least shall be summoned from thence.(b) And jurors in all cases to serve in the courts of the United States shall be designated by lot or otherwise in each State respectively according to the mode of forming juries therein now practised, so far as the laws of the same shall render such designation practicable by the courts or marshals of the United States; and the jurors shall have the same qualifications as are requisite for jurors by the laws of the State of which they are citizens, to serve in the highest courts of law of such State, and shall be returned as there shall be occasion for them, from such parts of the district from time to time as the court shall direct, so as shall be most favourable to an impartial trial, and so as not to incur an unnecessary expense, or unduly to burthen the citizens of any part of the district with such services. And writs of *venire facias* when directed by the court shall issue from the clerk's office, and shall be served and returned by the marshal in his proper person, or by his deputy, or in case the marshal or his deputy is not an indifferent person, or is interested in the event of the cause, by such fit person as the court shall specially appoint for that purpose, to whom they shall administer an oath or affirmation that he will truly and impartially serve and return such writ. And when from challenges or otherwise there shall not be a jury to determine any civil or criminal cause, the marshal or his deputy shall, by order of the court where such defect of jurors shall happen, return jurymen *de talibus circumstantibus* sufficient to complete the pannel; and when the marshal or his deputy are disqualified as aforesaid, jurors may be returned by such disinterested person as the court shall appoint.

Jurors by lot. Act of May 13, 1800, ch. 61.

Writs of venire facias from clerk's office.

Juries de talibus, &c.

Mode of proof.

Act of April 29, 1802, ch.31, § 25.

SEC. 30. *And be it further enacted,* That the mode of proof by oral testimony and examination of witnesses in open court shall be the same in all the courts of the United States, as well in the trial of causes in equity and of admiralty and maritime jurisdiction, as of actions at common law. And when the testimony of any person shall be necessary in any civil cause depending in any district in any court of the United States, who shall live at a greater distance from the place of trial than one hundred miles, or is bound on a voyage to sea, or is about to go out of the United States, or out of such district, and to a greater distance from the place of trial than as aforesaid, before the time of trial, or is ancient or very infirm, the deposition of such person may be taken *de bene esse* before any justice or judge of any of the courts of the United States,

Depositions de bene esse.

(a) If a debtor committed to the State jail under process of the courts of the United States escapes, the marshal is not liable. Randolph *v.* Donnaldson, 9 Cranch, 76; 3 Cond. Rep. 280.

(b) The Circuit Courts of the United States are bound to try all crimes committed within the district, which are duly presented before it; but not to try them in the county where they have been committed. The United States *v.* Wilson and Porter, Baldwin's C. C. R. 78.

or before any chancellor, justice or judge of a supreme or superior court, mayor or chief magistrate of a city, or judge of a county court or court of common pleas of any of the United States, not being of counsel or attorney to either of the parties, or interested in the event of the cause, provided that a notification from the magistrate before whom the deposition is to be taken to the adverse party, to be present at the taking of the same, and to put interrogatories, if he think fit, be first made out and served on the adverse party or his attorney as either may be nearest, if either is within one hundred miles of the place of such caption, allowing time for their attendance after notified, not less than at the rate of one day, Sundays exclusive, for every twenty miles travel.(a) And in causes of admiralty and maritime jurisdiction, or other cases of seizure when a libel shall be filed, in which an adverse party is not named, and depositions of persons circumstanced as aforesaid shall be taken before a claim be put in, the like notification as aforesaid shall be given to the person having the agency or possession of the property libelled at the time of the capture or seizure of the same, if known to the libellant. And every person deposing as aforesaid shall be carefully examined and cautioned, and sworn or affirmed to testify the whole truth, and shall subscribe the testimony by him or her given after the same shall be reduced to writing, which shall be done only by the magistrate taking the deposition, or by the deponent in his presence. And the depositions so taken shall be retained by such magistrate until he deliver the same with his own hand into the court for which they are taken, or shall, together with a certificate of the reasons as aforesaid of their being taken, and of the notice if any given to the adverse party, be by him the said magistrate sealed up and directed to such court, and remain under his seal until opened in court.(b) And any person may be compelled to appear and depose as aforesaid in the same manner as to appear and testify in court. And in the trial of any cause of admiralty or maritime jurisdiction in a district court, the decree in which may be appealed from, if either party shall suggest to and satisfy the court that probably it will not be in his power to produce the witnesses there testifying before the circuit court should an appeal be had, and shall move that their testimony be taken down in writing, it shall be so done by the clerk of the court.(c) And

Adverse party to be notified.

Notice in admiralty and maritime causes.

Agent notified.

Depositions retained.

Persons may be compelled to appear and testify.

Appeal allowed.

(a) The following cases have been decided relating to depositions taken under the provisions of this act:

That the deponent is a seaman on board a gun-boat in the harbour, and liable to be ordered to some other place, and not to be able to attend the court at the time of sitting, is not a sufficient reason for taking his deposition under the act of September 24, 1789, chap. 20.

If it appear on the face of the deposition taken under the act of Congress, that the officer taking the same, was authorized by the act, it is sufficient in the first instance, without any proof that he was such officer. Ruggles v. Bucknor, 1 Paine's C. C. R. 358.

Objections to the competency of the witness whose deposition is taken under the act of 1789, should be made at the time of taking the deposition, if the party attend, and the objections are known to him, in order that they may be removed : otherwise he will be presumed to waive them. United States v. Hairpencils, 1 Paine's C. C. R. 400.

A deposition taken under the 30th section of the act of 1789 cannot be made on evidence, unless the judge before whom it was taken, certify that it was reduced to writing by himself, or by the witness in his presence. Pettibone v. Derringer, 4 Wash. C. C. R. 215. See United States v. Smith, 4 Day, 121. North Carolina Cases, 81.

The authority given by the act of 1789, to take depositions of witnesses in the absence of the opposite party, is in derogation of the rules of common law, and has always been construed strictly ; and therefore it is necessary to establish that all the requisites have been complied with, before such testimony can be admitted. Bell v. Morrison et al., 1 Peters, 351. The Patapsco Ins. Comp. v. Southgate, 5 Peters, 604. The United States v. Coolidge, 1 Gallis. C. C. R. 488. Evans v. Hettick, 3 Wash. C. C. R. 408. Thomas and Henry v. The United States, 1 Brockeb's C. C. R. 367.

The provisions of the 30th section of the act of 1789, as to taking depositions, de bene esse, does not apply to cases pending in the Supreme Court, but only to cases in the Circuit and District Courts. The Argo, 2 Wheat. 287; 4 Cond. Rep. 119.

Where there is an attorney on record, notice must in all cases be given to him. Ibid.

The deposition of a person residing out of the State, and more than one hundred miles from the place of trial, cannot be read in evidence. Bleeker v. Bond, 3 Wash. C. C. R. 529. See Buddicum v. Kirke, 3 Cranch, 293; 1 Cond. Rep. 535.

(b) It is a fatal objection to a deposition taken under the 30th section of the act of 1789, that it was opened out of court. Beale v. Thompson, 8 Cranch, 70; 3 Cond. Rep. 35.

(c) Since the act of March 3, 1803, chap. 40, in admiralty as well as in equity cases carried up to the

Act of March
3, 1803, ch. 40.

if an appeal be had, such testimony may be used on the trial of the same, if it shall appear to the satisfaction of the court which shall try the appeal, that the witnesses are then dead or gone out of the United States, or to a greater distance than as aforesaid from the place where the court is sitting, or that by reason of age, sickness, bodily infirmity or imprisonment, they are unable to travel and appear at court, but not otherwise. And unless the same shall be made to appear on the trial of any cause, with respect to witnesses whose depositions may have been taken therein, such depositions shall not be admitted or used in the cause. *Provided*, That nothing herein shall be construed to prevent any court of the United States from granting a *dedimus potestatem* to take depositions according to common usage, when it may be necessary to prevent a failure or delay of justice,(*a*) which power they shall severally possess, nor to extend to depositions taken in *perpetuam rei memoriam*, which if they relate to matters that may be cognizable in any court of the United States, a circuit court on application thereto made as a court of equity, may, according to the usages in chancery direct to be taken.

Depositions
used in case of
sickness, death,
&c.

Dedimus po-
testatem as
usual.

Executor or
administrator
may prosecute
and defend.

Neglect of
executor or ad-
ministrator to
become a party
to the suit,
judgment to be
rendered.

Executor and
administrator
may have con-
tinuance.

Two plaintiffs.
Surviving
plaintiff may
continue suit.

Sec. 31. *And be it [further] enacted*, That where any suit shall be depending in any court of the United States, and either of the parties shall die before final judgment, the executor or administrator of such deceased party who was plaintiff, petitioner, or defendant, in case the cause of action doth by law survive, shall have full power to prosecute or defend any such suit or action until final judgment; and the defendant or defendants are hereby obliged to answer thereto accordingly; and the court before whom such cause may be depending, is hereby empowered and directed to hear and determine the same, and to render judgment for or against the executor or administrator, as the case may require. And if such executor or administrator having been duly served with a *scire facias* from the office of the clerk of the court where such suit is depending, twenty days beforehand, shall neglect or refuse to become a party to the suit, the court may render judgment against the estate of the deceased party, in the same manner as if the executor or administrator had voluntarily made himself a party to the suit.(*b*) And the executor or administrator who shall become a party as aforesaid, shall, upon motion to the court where the suit is depending, be entitled to a continuance of the same until the next term of the said court. And if there be two or more plaintiffs or defendants, and one or more of them shall die, if the cause of action shall survive to the surviving plaintiff or plaintiffs, or against the surviving defendant or defendants, the writ or action shall not be thereby abated; but such death being suggested upon the record, the action shall proceed at the suit of the surviving plaintiff or plaintiffs against the surviving defendant or defendants.(*c*)

Supreme Court by appeal, the evidence goes with the cause, and it must consequently be in writing. 1 Gallis. C. C. R. 25; 1 Sumner's C. C. R. 328.

(*a*) When a foreign government refuses to suffer the commission to be executed within its jurisdiction, the Circuit Court may issue letters rogatory for the purpose of obtaining testimony according to the forms and practice of the civil law. Nelson et al. *v.* The United States, Peters' C. C. R. 255. See Buddicum *v.* Kirke, 3 Cranch, 293; 1 Cond. Rep. 535.

Depositions taken according to the proviso in the 30th section of the judiciary act of 1789, under a dedimus potestatem, according to common usage, when it may be necessary to prevent a failure or delay of justice, are, under no circumstances, to be considered as taken de bene esse. Sergeant's Lessee *v.* Biddle, 4 Wheat. 508; 4 Cond. Rep. 522.

(*b*) This statute embraces all cases of death before final judgment, and of course is more extensive than the 17 Car. 2, and 8 and 9 W. 3. The death may happen before or after plea pleaded, before or after issue joined, before or after verdict, or before or after interlocutory judgment; and in all these cases the proceedings are to be exactly as if the executor or administrator were a voluntary party to the suit. Hatch *v.* Eustis, 1 Gallis. C. C. R. 160.

(*c*) In real and personal actions at common law, the death of the parties before judgment abates the suit, and it requires the aid of some statutory provision to enable the suit to be prosecuted by or against the personal representatives of the deceased, where the cause of action survives. This is effected by the 31st section of the judiciary act of 1789, chap. 20. Green *v.* Watkins, 6 Wheat. 260; 5 Cond. Rep. 87.

In real actions the death of either party before judgment, abates the suit. The 31st section of the judiciary act of 1789, which enables the action to be prosecuted by or against the representatives of the

Sec. 32. *And be it further enacted*, That no summons, writ, declaration, return, process, judgment, or other proceedings in civil causes in any of the courts of the United States, shall be abated, arrested, quashed or reversed, for any defect or want of form, but the said courts respectively shall proceed and give judgment according as the right of the cause and matter in law shall appear unto them, without regarding any imperfections, defects, or want of form in such writ, declaration, or other pleading, return, process, judgment, or course of proceeding whatsoever, except those only in cases of demurrer, which the party demurring shall specially sit down and express together with his demurrer as the cause thereof. And the said courts respectively shall and may, by virtue of this act, from time to time, amend all and every such imperfections, defects and wants of form, other than those only which the party demurring shall express as aforesaid, and may at any time permit either of the parties to amend any defect in the process or pleadings, upon such conditions as the said courts respectively shall in their discretion, and by their rules prescribe.(*a*)

Sec. 33. *And be it further enacted*, That for any crime or offence against the United States, the offender may, by any justice or judge of the United States, or by any justice of the peace, or other magistrate of any of the United States where he may be found agreeably to the usual mode of process against offenders in such state, and at the expense of the United States, be arrested, and imprisoned or bailed, as the case may be, for trial before such court of the United States as by this act has cognizance of the offence.(*b*) And copies of the process shall be returned as speedily as may be into the clerk's office of such court, together with the recognizances of the witnesses for their appearance to testify in the case; which recognizances the magistrate before whom the examination shall be, may require on pain of imprisonment. And if such commitment of the offender, or the witnesses shall be in a district other than that in which the offence is to be tried, it shall be the duty of the judge of that district where the delinquent is imprisoned, seasonably to issue, and of the marshal of the same district to execute, a warrant for the removal of the offender, and the witnesses, or either of them, as the case may be, to the district in which the trial is to be had. And upon all arrests in criminal cases, bail shall be admitted, except where the punishment may be death, in which cases it shall not be admitted but by the supreme or a circuit court, or by a justice of the supreme court, or a judge of a district court, who shall exercise their discretion therein, regarding the nature and circumstances of the offence, and of the evidence, and the usages of law. And if a person committed by a justice of the supreme or a judge of a district court for an offence not punishable with death, shall afterwards procure bail, and there be no judge

Marginal notes:

Writs shall not abate for defect of form.

Exceptions.

Courts may amend imperfections.

Criminals against U. S. arrested by any justice of the peace.
Act of March 2, 1793, ch. 22.
Act of July 16, 1798, ch. 83.
Recognizance to be returned to the clerk's office.

Offender may be removed by warrant.

Bail admitted.

Bail, how taken.

---

deceased, when the cause of action survives, is clearly confined to personal actions. Macker's heirs v. Thomas, 7 Wheat. 530; 5 Cond. Rep. 334.

(*a*) The 32d section of the act of 1789, allowing amendments, is sufficiently comprehensive to embrace causes of appellate as well as original jurisdiction; and there is nothing in the nature of an appellate jurisdiction, proceeding according to the common law, which forbids the granting of amendments. 1 Gallis. C. C. R. 22.

If the amendment is made in the Circuit Court, the cause is heard and adjudicated in that court, and upon appeal by the Supreme Court on the new allegation. But if the amendment is allowed by the Supreme Court, the cause is remanded to the Circuit Court, with directions to allow the amendment to be made. The Mariana Flora, 11 Wheat. 1; 6 Cond. Rep. 201.

By the provisions of the act of Congress a variance which is merely matter of form may be amended at any time. Scull v. Biddle, 2 Wash. C. C. R. 200. See Smith v. Jackson, 1 Paine's C. C. R. 486. Ex parte Bradstreet, 7 Peters, 634. Randolph v. Barrett, 16 Peters, 136. Hozey v. Buchanan, 18 Peters, 215. Woodward v. Brown, 13 Peters, 1.

(*b*) The Supreme Court of the United States has jurisdiction, under the constitution and laws of the United States, to bail a person committed for trial on a criminal charge by a district judge of the United States. The United States v. Hamilton, 3 Dall. 13.

The circumstances of the case must be very strong, which will, at any time, induce a court to admit a person to bail, who stands charged with high treason. The United States v. Stewart, 2 Dall. 345.

of the United States in the district to take the same, it may be taken by any judge of the supreme or superior court of law of such state.

Laws of States rules of decision.

SEC. 34. *And be it further enacted,* That the laws of the several states, except where the constitution, treaties or statutes of the United States shall otherwise require or provide, shall be regarded as rules of decision in trials at common law in the courts of the United States in cases where they apply.(*a*)

Parties may manage their own cause.

SEC. 35. *And be it further enacted,* That in all the courts of the United States, the parties may plead and manage their own causes personally or by the assistance of such counsel or attorneys at law as by the rules of the said courts respectively shall be permitted to manage and conduct causes therein. And there shall be appointed in each district a meet

Attorney of the U. S. for each district.

person learned in the law to act as attorney for the United States in such district, who shall be sworn or affirmed to the faithful execution of his

His duties.

office, whose duty it shall be to prosecute in such district all delinquents for crimes and offences, cognizable under the authority of the United States, and all civil actions in which the United States shall be concerned, except before the supreme court in the district in which that

Compensation.

court shall be holden. And he shall receive as a compensation for his

---

(*a*) The 34th section of the judiciary act of 1799, does not apply to the process and practice of the courts. It merely furnishes a decision, and is not intended to regulate the remedy. Wyman *v.* Southard, 10 Wheat. 1 ; 6 Cond. Rep. 1.

In construing the statutes of a State, infinite mischief would ensue, should the federal courts observe a different rule from that which has long been established in the State. M'Keen *v.* Delancy's lessee, 5 Cranch, 22 ; 2 Cond. Rep. 179.

In cases depending on the statutes of a State, and more especially in those respecting the titles to land, the federal courts adopt the construction of the State, where that construction is settled or can be ascertained. Polk's Lessee *v.* Wendall, 9 Cranch, 87 ; 3 Cond. Rep. 286.

The Supreme Court uniformly acts under a desire to conform its decisions to the State courts on their local law. Mutual Assurance Society *v.* Watts, 1 Wheat. 279 ; 3 Cond. Rep. 570.

The Supreme Court holds in the highest respect, decisions of State Courts upon local laws, forming rules of property. Shipp et al. *v.* Miller's heirs, 2 Wheat. 316 ; 4 Cond. Rep. 132.

When the construction of the statute of the State relates to real property, and has been settled by any judicial decision of the State where the land lies, the Supreme Court, upon the principles uniformly adopted by it, would recognize the decision as part of the local law. Gardner *v.* Collins, 2 Peters, 58.

In construing local statutes respecting real property, the courts of the Union are governed by the decisions of State tribunals. Thatcher et al. *v.* Powell, 6 Wheat. 119 ; 5 Cond. Rep. 28.

The courts of the United States, in cases depending on the laws of a particular State, will in general adopt the construction given by the courts of the State, to those laws. Elmendorf *v.* Taylor, 10 Wheat. 152 ; 6 Cond. Rep. 47.

Under the 34th section of the judiciary act of 1789, the acts of limitation of the several States where no special provision has been made by Congress, form rules of the decision in the courts of the United States; and the same effect is given to them as is given in the State courts. M'Cluny *v.* Silliman, 3 Peters, 277.

The statute laws of the States must furnish the rules of decision to the federal courts, as far as they comport with the laws of the United States, in all cases arising within the respective States; and a fixed and received construction of these respective statute laws in their own courts, makes a part of such statute law. Shelby et al. *v.* Guy, 11 Wheat. 361 ; 6 Cond. Rep. 345.

The Supreme Court adopts the local law of real property as ascertained by the decisions of State courts; whether those decisions are grounded on the construction of the statutes of the State, or from a part of the unwritten law of the State, which has become a fixed rule of property. Jackson *v.* Chew, 12 Wheat. 153; 6 Cond. Rep. 489.

Soon after the decision of a case in the Circuit Court for the district of Virginia, a case was decided in the court of appeals of the State, on which the question on the execution laws of Virginia was elaborately argued, and deliberately decided. The Supreme Court, according to its uniform course, adopts the construction of the act, which is made by the highest court of the State. The United States *v.* Morrison, 4 Peters, 124.

The Supreme Court has uniformly adopted the decisions of the State tribunals, respectively, in all cases where the decision of a State court has become a rule of property. Green *v.* Neal, 6 Peters, 291.

In all cases arising under the constitution and laws of the United States, the Supreme Court may exercise a revising power, and its decisions are final and obligatory on all other tribunals, State as well as federal. A State tribunal has a right to examine any such questions, and to determine thereon, but its decisions must conform to those of the Supreme Court, or the corrective power of that court may be exercised. But the case is very different when the question arises under a local law. The decision of this question by the highest tribunal of a State, should be considered as final by the Supreme Court; not because the State tribunal has power, in such a case, to bind the Supreme Court, but because, in the language of the court in Shelby *v.* Guy, 11 Wheat. 361, a fixed and received construction by a State, in its own courts, makes a part of the statute law. *Ibid.* See also Smith *v.* Clapp, 15 Peters, 125. Watkins *v.* Holman et al., 16 Peters, 25. Long *v.* Palmer, 16 Peters, 65. Golden *v.* Price, 3 Wash. C. C. R. 313. Campbell *v.* Claudius, Peters' C. C. R. 484. Henderson and Wife *v.* Griffin, 5 Peters, 151. Coates' executrix *v.* Muse's adm'or., 1 Brocken's C. C. R. 539. Parsons *v.* Bedford et al., 3 Peters, 433.

services such fees as shall be taxed therefor in the respective courts before which the suits or prosecutions shall be.   And there shall also be appointed a meet person, learned in the law, to act as attorney-general for the United States, who shall be sworn or affirmed to a faithful execution of his office; whose duty it shall be to prosecute and conduct all suits in the Supreme Court in which the United States shall be concerned, and to give his advice and opinion upon questions of law when required by the President of the United States, or when requested by the heads of any of the departments, touching any matters that may concern their departments, and shall receive such compensation for his services as shall by law be provided.(*a*)

Approved, September 24, 1789.

Attorney General of the U. S.

Duties.

Act of May 29, 1830, ch. 153.

Compensation.

Statute I.

Chap. XXI.—*An Act to regulate Processes in the Courts of the United States.*

Sept. 29, 1789.

Section 1. *Be it enacted by the Senate and House of Representatives of the United States of America in Congress assembled,* That all writs and processes issuing from a supreme or a circuit court shall bear test of the chief justice of the supreme court, and if from a district court, shall bear test of the judge of such court, and shall be under the seal of the court from whence they issue; and signed by the clerk thereof. The seals of the supreme and circuit courts to be provided by the supreme court, and of the district courts, by the respective judges of the same.

Sec. 2. *And be it further enacted,* That until further provision shall be made, and except where by this act or other statutes of the United States is otherwise provided, the forms of writs and executions, except their style, and modes of process and rates of fees, except fees to judges, in the circuit and district courts, in suits at common law, shall be the same in each state respectively as are now used or allowed in the supreme courts of the same.(*b*)   And the forms and modes of proceedings in

Act of May 26, 1790. Obsolete.
Act of February 18, 1791. Repealed.
Writs to bear test of the Chief Justice.
To be under the seal of the Court from which they issue.
Act of May 8, 1792.
Act of May 19, 1828.
Forms of writs and executions

(*a*) The acts relating to the compensation of the Attorney General of the United States are: Act of March 2, 1797; act of March 2, 1799, chap. 38; act of February 20, 1804, chap. 12; act of February 20, 1819, chap. 27; act of May 29, 1830, chap. 153, sec. 10.

(*b*) The 34th section of the judiciary act of 1789, authorizes the courts of the United States to issue writs of execution as well as other writs. Wayman *v.* Southard, 10 Wheat. 1; 6 Cond. Rep. 1.

Whenever, by the state laws in force in 1789, a capias might issue from a state court, the acts of 1789 and 1792, extending in terms to that species of writ, must be understood to have adopted its use permanently in the federal courts.   Bank of the United States *v.* January, 10 Wheat. 66—in note.

The process act of 1792, chap. 36, is the law which regulates executions issuing from the courts of the United States, and it adopts the practice of the supreme courts of the States existing in 1789, as the rule for governing proceedings on such executions, subject to such alterations as the Supreme Court of the United States may make; but not subject to the alterations which have since taken place in the State laws and practice. Wayman *v.* Southard, 10 Wheat. 1; 6 Cond. Rep. 1.

At an early period after the organization of the federal courts, the rules of practice in the State courts, which were similar to the English practice, were adopted by the judges of the Circuit Court.   A subsequent change in the practice of the State courts will not authorize a departure from the rules first adopted in the Circuit Court.   1 Peters' C. C. R. 1.

Whenever by the laws of the United States a defendant may be arrested, the process of arrest employed in the State may be adopted.   Burr's trial, 431.

The process act of 1828 was passed shortly after the decision of the Supreme Court of the United States, in the case of Wayman *v.* Southard, and the Bank of the United States *v.* Halstead, and was intended as a legislative sanction of the opinions of the court in those cases.   The power given to the courts of the United States to make rules and regulations on final process, so as to conform the same to the laws of the States on the same subject, extends to future legislation; and as well to the modes of proceeding on executions as to the forms of writs.   Ross and King *v.* Duval et al., 13 Peters, 45.

The first judiciary act of 1789, chap. 20, does not contemplate compulsive process against any person, in any district, unless he be an inhabitant of, or found within the same district at the time of serving the writ.   Picquet *v.* Swann, 5 Mason's C. C. R. 35.

Congress have by the constitution, exclusive authority to regulate proceedings in the courts of the United States, and the States have no authority to control those proceedings, except so far as the State process acts are adopted by Congress, or by the courts of the United States under the authority of Congress. Wayman *v.* Southard, 10 Wheat. 1; 6 Cond. Rep. 1.

The laws of the United States authorize the courts of the United States so to alter the form of process of execution used in the Supreme Court of the United States in 1789, as to subject to executions

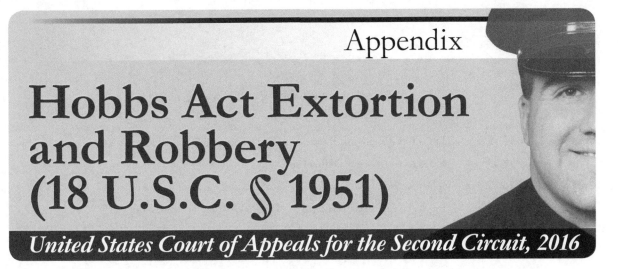

Appendix

Hobbs Act Extortion and Robbery (18 U.S.C. § 1951)

United States Court of Appeals for the Second Circuit, 2016

Hobbs Act Extortion and Robbery *(18 U.S.C. § 1951)*

6.18.1951 Hobbs Act - Elements of the Offense (18 U.S.C. § 1951)

In order to sustain its burden of proof for the crime of interfering with interstate commerce by *(robbery)(extortion)* as charged in Count *(No.)* of the indictment, the government must prove the following three (3) essential elements beyond a reasonable doubt:

First: That Defendant *(name)* took from *(the victim alleged in the indictment)* the property described in Count *(No.)* of the indictment;

Second: That *(name)* did so knowingly and willfully by *(robbery) (extortion)*; and

Third: That as a result of *(name)*'s actions, interstate commerce *(an item moving in interstate commerce)* was obstructed, delayed, or affected.

Comment

Kevin F. O'Malley, Jay E. Grenig, & Hon. William C. Lee, 1A Federal Jury Practice and Instructions § 53.03 [hereinafter O'Malley et al., *supra*].

18 U.S.C. § 1951(a) provides:

Whoever in any way or degree obstructs, delays, or affects commerce or the movement of any article or commodity in commerce, by robbery or extortion or attempts or conspires so to do, or commits or threatens physical violence to any person or property in furtherance of a plan or purpose to do anything in violation of this section shall be fined under this title or imprisoned not more than twenty years, or both.

If the defendant is charged with attempt the court should adapt this instruction and should also give Instruction 7.01 (Attempt).

Likewise, if the defendant is charged with conspiracy to violate this statute, the appropriate instructions on conspiracy should be given. *See* Instruction 6.18.371A et seq.

ˇ2ˇ

It should be noted that a Hobbs Act conspiracy does not require proof of an overt act. *See United States v. Salahuddin,* 765 F.3d 329 (3d Cir. 2014). Further, if the defendant is charged with conspiracy to obtain something of value under color of official right, the government is not required to establish that the defendant actually obtained something of value. *See United States v. Salahuddin,* 765 F.3d 329 (3d Cir. 2014). The Third Circuit also held that "the specific benefits that the members of the conspiracy sought to obtain is not a required element of Hobbs Act conspiracy;" accordingly, the trial court does not have to instruct the jury specifically as to unanimity as to the benefit sought. *Salahuddin,* 765 F.3d 329.

The Third Circuit has held:

> [A] conviction under the Hobbs Act requires proof beyond a reasonable doubt that (1) the defendant knowingly or willfully committed, or attempted or conspired to commit, robbery or extortion, and (2) the defendant's conduct affected interstate commerce.

See United States v. Powell, 693 F.3d 398 (3d Cir. 2012).

In *United States v. Traitz,* 871 F.2d 368, 380-81 (3d Cir. 1989), the trial court gave the following instruction:

> In order to meet its burden of proving that the defendants committed extortion under the Hobbs Act, the Government must prove each of the following elements:
>
> First, that the defendants induced or attempted to induce others to part with their property;
>
> Second, that the defendants did so with the victims' consent, but that this consent was compelled by the wrongful use or threat of force, violence or fear;
>
> Third, that interstate commerce or an item moving in interstate commerce was delayed, obstructed or affected in any way or degree; and
>
> Fourth, that the defendants acted knowingly and willfully.

The Third Circuit quoted the instructions but remarked only that the defendants did not challenge the trial court's "general recitation of the essential elements of the Hobbs Act." *Traitz,* 871 F.2d at 381. *See also United States v. Driggs,* 823 F.2d 52 (3d Cir. 1987). In *Driggs,* the court noted:

> The essential elements that the government must prove are that the

˅3˅

defendant obstructed, delayed or affected commerce or attempted to do so; by extortion ("the obtaining of property from another, with his consent, . . . under color of official right"); and that the defendant acted knowingly and willfully.

823 F.2d at 54.

(Revised 2014)

6.18.1951-1 Hobbs Act - Robbery Defined

Robbery is the unlawful taking or obtaining of personal property from the person or in the presence of another, against *(his)(her)* will, by means of actual or threatened force, or violence, or fear of injury, whether immediately or in the future, to *(his)(her)* person or property, or property in *(his)(her)* custody or possession, or the person or property of a relative or member of *(his)(her)* family or of anyone in *(his)(her)* company at the time of the taking or obtaining.

Comment

O'Malley et al., supra, § 53-05.

18 U.S.C. § 1951(b)(1) provides:

As used in this section--

(1) The term "robbery" means the unlawful taking or obtaining of personal property from the person or in the presence of another, against his will, by means of actual or threatened force, or violence, or fear of injury, immediate or future, to his person or property, or property in his custody or possession, or the person or property of a relative or member of his family or of anyone in his company at the time of the taking or obtaining.

˘5˘

6.18.1951-2 Hobbs Act - Extortion by Force, Violence, or Fear

Extortion is the obtaining of another person's property or money, with *(his)(her)* consent when this consent is induced or brought about through the use of actual or threatened force, violence or fear.

[In order for (name) to have obtained the property of another there must have been a transfer of possession of, or a legal interest in, that property from that other person to (name) or a designee of (name).]

Comment

Hon. Leonard Sand, John S. Siffert, Walter P. Loughlin, Steven A. Reiss & Nancy Batterman, Modern Federal Jury Instructions - Criminal Volumes 50-9 (Matthew Bender 2003) [hereinafter, Sand et al., supra]; O'Malley et al., supra, § 53.09.

18 U.S.C. § 1951(b)(2) provides:

As used in this section-
* * *
(2) The term "extortion" means the obtaining of property from another, with his consent, induced by wrongful use of actual or threatened force, violence, or fear, or under color of official right.

The court should use this instruction when the defendant is charged with extortion through force, violence, or fear. The court should also give Instructions 6.18.1951-3 (Hobbs Act - "Unlawful Taking by Force, Violence or Fear" Defined), 6.18.1951-4 (Hobbs Act - "Fear of Injury" Defined), and 6.18.1951-5 (Hobbs Act - Property Defined). If the defendant is charged with extortion under color of official right, the court should give Instruction 6.18.1951-6 (Hobbs Act - Extortion Under Color of Official Right).

The bracketed language should be included if there is a question concerning whether the defendant acquired property rather than simply depriving the victim of property. Mere deprivation of property or interference with the use of property is not sufficient under the statute. In *Scheidler v. National Organization for Women, Inc.*, 537 U.S. 393 (2003), the Court addressed the definition of "extortion" under § 1951. The Court stated, "we have construed the extortion provision of the Hobbs Act at issue in these cases to require not only the deprivation of but also the acquisition of property." *Id.* at 404.

˘6˘

6.18.1951-3 Hobbs Act - "Unlawful Taking by Force, Violence or Fear" Defined

The government must prove beyond a reasonable doubt that *(name)* unlawfully took *(the alleged victim)*'s property against *(his)(her)* will by actual or threatened force, violence, or fear of injury, whether immediately or in the future. You must determine whether *(name)* obtained the property by using any of these unlawful means, as set forth in the indictment. The government does not need to prove that force, violence, and fear were all used or threatened. The government satisfies its burden of proving an unlawful taking if you unanimously agree that *(name)* employed any of these methods; that is, the government satisfies its burden only if you all agree concerning the particular method used by *(name)*.

In considering whether *(name)* used, or threatened to use force, violence or fear, you should give those words their common and ordinary meaning, and understand them as you normally would. A threat may be made verbally or by physical gesture. Whether a statement or physical gesture by *(name)* actually was a threat depends upon the surrounding facts.

Comment

Sand et al., supra, 50-5.

If the defendant is charged with attempt the court should modify this instruction accordingly. *See United States v. Parkin*, 319 F. App'x. 101 (3d Cir. 2009) (non-precedential) (holding that where defendant was charged with attempted extortion, the government did not need to establish that the defendant actually caused fear). (revised 12/09)

ˇ7ˇ

6.18.1951-4   Hobbs Act - "Fear of Injury" Defined

Fear exists if a victim experiences anxiety, concern, or worry over expected personal *(physical)(economic)* harm. The fear must be reasonable under the circumstances existing at the time of the defendant's actions.

Your decision whether *(name)* used or threatened fear of injury involves a decision about *(the alleged victim)*'s state of mind at the time of *(name)*'s actions. It is obviously impossible to prove directly a person's subjective feeling. You cannot look into a person's mind to see what *(his)(her)* state of mind is or was. But a careful consideration of the circumstances and evidence should enable you to decide whether *(the alleged victim)* was in fear and whether this fear was reasonable.

Looking at the overall situation and the actions of the person in question may help you determine what *(his)(her)* state of mind was. You can consider this kind of evidence - which is called "circumstantial evidence" - in deciding whether *(name)* obtained property through the use of threat or fear.

You have also heard the testimony of *(the alleged victim)* describing *(his)(her)* state of mind - that is, how *(he)(she)* felt about giving up the property. This testimony was allowed to help you decide whether the property was obtained by fear. You should consider this testimony for that purpose only.

You may also consider the relationship between *(name)* and *(the alleged*

˘8˘

victim) **in deciding whether the element of fear exists. However, even a friendly relationship between the parties does not preclude you from finding that fear exists.**

Comment

Sand et al., supra, 50-6. *See also United States v. Provenzano*, 334 F.2d 678, 687 (3d Cir. 1964) (citing *United States v. Tolub*, 309 F.2d 286 (2d Cir. 1962) (fear experienced by the victim must be reasonable)); *United States v. Addonizio*, 451 F.2d 49, 72 (3d Cir. 1972) (fear may be of economic or physical harm).

6.18.1951-5 Hobbs Act - Property Defined

The term "property" includes money and other tangible and intangible things of value.

Comment

Sand et al., supra, 50-4.

In many cases, there will be no need to instruct the jury on the meaning of the term "property." When intangible property is involved, the court should include this instruction. In *Scheidler v. National Organization for Women, Inc.*, 537 U.S. 393, 402 (2003), the Supreme Court recognized that the term property includes intangible as well as tangible things of value. However, the property must be transferrable. *Sekhar v. United States*, 133 S. Ct. 2720, 2725 (2013). In *Sekhar*, the jury convicted the defendant of Hobbs Act extortion because he sought to force the general counsel of the New York State Comptroller to recommend approval of a commitment to purchase shares in a fund managed by the defendant's firm on behalf of a retirement fund for state employees. *Sekhar*, 133 S. Ct. at 2724. The Court held that the recommendation did not qualify as obtainable property and therefore could not support a conviction under the Hobbs Act. *Sekhar*, 133 S. Ct. at 2726.

(Revised 11/2013)

˘10˘

6.18.1951-6 Hobbs Act - Extortion Under Color of Official Right

The government alleges that *(name)* committed extortion under color of official right. A public *(official)(employee)* commits "extortion under color of official right" if *(he)(she)* uses the power and authority of *(his)(her)* office in order to obtain money, property, or something of value from another to which neither that public *(official)(employee)* nor that government office has an official right.

Extortion under color of official right means that a public official induced, obtained, accepted, or agreed to accept a payment to which he or she was not entitled, knowing that the payment was made in return for taking, withholding, or influencing official acts. *[The government may show that the benefit was meant to be given to the public official directly, or to a third party who is not a public official.l]*

The government is not required to prove an explicit promise to perform the official acts in return for the payment. Passive acceptance of a benefit by a public official is a sufficient basis for this type of extortion, if the official knows that *(he)(she)* is being offered payment in exchange for *(his)(her)* ability to do official acts.

The government is not required to prove that *(name)* made any specific threat or used force or fear to cause *(the victim alleged in the indictment)* to part with the property that the indictment alleges *(name)* obtained by

˘11˘

extortion under color of right. However, the government must prove beyond a reasonable doubt that *(name)* **knowingly and deliberately used** *(his)(her)* **official position in order to obtain something of value, to which** *(name)* **had no right.**

[The government is not required to prove that (name) actually possessed the official power to guarantee, deny, or influence any actions. It is enough to show that (victim alleged in indictment) reasonably believed that (name) had the actual, residual, or anticipated official power to help (him)(her) with respect to matters pending before a government agency.]

[In order for (name) to have obtained the property of another there must have been a transfer of possession of, or a legal interest in, that property from that other person to (name) or a designee of (name).]

Comment

Sand et al., supra, 50-9; O'Malley et al., supra, § 53.09. *See also United States v. Munchak*, 2013 WL 2382618 (3d Cir. 2013) (non-precedential) (discussing instructions).

18 U.S.C. § 1951(b)(2) provides:

As used in this section-
* * *
(2) The term "extortion" means the obtaining of property from another, with his consent, induced by wrongful use of actual or threatened force, violence, or fear, or under color of official right.

This instruction and the one that follows address extortion by color of official right, which is distinct from extortion through force, violence, or fear, and may only be committed by a public official (although a non-public official may be guilty of aiding and abetting extortion by color of official right). If the defendant is charged with conspiracy

˘12˘

to obtain something of value under color of official right, the government is not required to establish that the defendant actually obtained something of value. *See United States v. Salahuddin,* 765 F.3d 329 (3d Cir. 2014).

In *United States v. Kenny*, 462 F.2d 1205, 1229 (3d Cir. 1972), the Third Circuit held that the following instruction properly defined extortion under the statute:

> The term 'extortion' means the obtaining of property from another with his consent induced either by wrongful use of fear or under color of official right. The term 'fear,' as used in the statute, has the commonly accepted meaning. It is a state of anxious concern, alarm, apprehension of anticipated harm to a business or of a threatened loss.
>
> * * *
>
> Extortion under color of official right is the wrongful taking by a public officer of money not due him or his office, whether or not the taking was accomplished by force, threats or use of fear. You will note that extortion as defined by Federal Law is committed when property is obtained by consent of the victim by wrongful use of fear, or when it is obtained under color of official right, and in either instance the offense of extortion is committed.

The defendant complained that the instruction defined extortion disjunctively, allowing the jury to find extortion if the defendant obtained money or property either by use of fear or under color of official right. The Third Circuit rejected the defendant's argument and explained:

> [W]hile private persons may violate the statute only by use of fear and public officials may violate the act by use of fear, persons holding public office may also violate the statute by a wrongful taking under color of official right. The term "extortion" is defined in § 1951(b)(2): "The term 'extortion' means the obtaining of property from another, with his consent, induced by wrongful use of actual or threatened force, violence, or fear, or under color of official right." The "under color of official right" language plainly is disjunctive. That part of the definition repeats the common law definition of extortion, a crime which could only be committed by a public official, and which did not require proof of threat, fear, or duress. The disjunctive charge on § 1951 extortion was correct.

Id. at 1229 (citations omitted). In *United States v. Urban*, 404 F.3d 754, 768 (3d Cir. 2005), the Third Circuit explained that, "[i]n order to prove Hobbs Act extortion 'under color of official right,' 'the Government need only show that a public official has obtained a payment to which he was not entitled, knowing that the payment was made in return for official acts.'"

˘13˘

There need not be one benefit for one official act. Instead, a conviction may be based on proof that the official accepted a "stream of benefits" in exchange for one or more official acts. *See United States v. Donna*, 366 F. App'x. 441 (3d Cir. 2010) (non-precedential) (citing *United States v. Kemp*, 500 F.3d 257, 282 (3d Cir. 2007)).

The government may show that the benefit was meant to be given to the public official directly, or to a third party who is not a public official. *See generally United States v. Antico*, 275 F.3d 245, 255-56 (3d Cir. 2001); *United States v. Bradley*, 173 F.3d 225, 231-32 (3d Cir. 1999); *United States v. Margiotta*, 688 F.2d 108, 133 (2d Cir. 1982) ("A Hobbs Act prosecution may lie where the extorted payments are transferred to third parties, including political allies and political parties, rather than to the public official who has acted under color of official right.").1

The offense of extortion under color of official right does not have to involve force or threat on the part of the public official. The coercive element is provided by the existence of the public office itself. *Evans v. United States*, 504 U.S. 255, 265 (1992); *Antico*, 275 F.3d at 255 n.14; *United States v. Jannotti*, 673 F.2d 578, 594 (3d Cir. 1982).

The government need not prove that the defendant acted exclusively with corrupt intent. *See United States v. Donna*, 366 F. App'x. 441 (3d Cir. 2010) (non-precedential) (remarking that trial court's "dual motive" instruction stating that a person commits extortion under color of official right when that person has "a partly corrupt intent and a partly neutral intent" constituted a correct statement of the law).

In *McCormick v. United States*, 500 U.S. 257 (1991), the Court held that, when an elected official is charged with extorting campaign contributions, the government must prove "an explicit promise or undertaking" by the public official. In other cases, an explicit promise to perform the official acts in return for the payment is not required. *See Evans*, 504 U.S. at 268; *United States v. Salahuddin*, 765 F.3d 329 (3d Cir. 2014); *Antico*, 275 F.3d at 255-56; *Bradley*, 173 F.3d at 231. Passive acceptance of a benefit by a public official is a sufficient basis for this type of extortion, if the official knows that he or she is being offered payment in exchange for his ability to do official acts. The government need not prove that the public official first suggested or solicited the giving of money or property. *Evans*, 504 U.S. at 259; *United States v. Blandford*, 33 F.3d 685, 698-99 n.15 (6th Cir. 1994). Extortion occurs if the official knows that the payment or benefit is motivated by a hope that it will influence the official in the exercise of his or her office, or influence any action that the official takes because of the official position, and if, knowing this, the official accepts or agrees to accept the payment or benefit or have it accepted by another person. *United States v. Holzer*, 816 F.2d 304, 311 (7th Cir. 1987);

---

1 As originally published, the instruction included the additional requirement that the third party was acting in concert with the public official. In *United States v. Salahuddin*, 765 F.3d 329 (3d Cir. 2014), although the issue was not before the court, the Third Circuit questioned in footnote 7 of the opinion whether proof of action in concert is required. That language was removed from the instruction.

United States v. Butler, 618 F.2d 411, 417-19 (6th Cir. 1980); *United States v. Trotta*, 525 F.2d 1096, 1101 (2d Cir. 1975) ("To repeat, it is the use of the power of public office itself to procure the payments of money not owed to the public official or his office that constitutes the offense."); *United States v. Braasch*, 505 F.2d 139, 151 (7th Cir. 1974).

It is not necessary for the government to prove that the defendant actually misused or attempted to misuse the power of his/her office insofar as the defendant granted some benefit or favor to the payors. Though the payors may not have gotten any more than their due in the defendant's performance of his office, the defendant's acceptance of money or a benefit, in return for the use of, or the attempted use of, his/her office is extortion. *See Antico*, 275 F.3d at 255-58; *United States v. Evans*, 30 F.3d 1015, 1019 (8th Cir. 1994); *United States v. Loftus*, 992 F.2d 793, 797 (8th Cir. 1993); *Holzer*, 816 F.2d at 308; *United States v. Paschall*, 772 F.2d 68, 71, 74 (4th Cir. 1985) (citing *United States v. Manton*, 107 F.2d 834 (2d Cir. 1939)); *United States v. Bibby*, 752 F.2d 1116, 1128 (6th Cir. 1985) ("[I]t is not essential that a [public] official be able to guarantee a certain result before his acceptance of money to bring about that result will run afoul of the law."); *United States v. Butler,* 618 F.2d 411, 420 (6th Cir. 1980).

The public official's agreement to take or refrain from taking an action on behalf of the payor need not be express. *Antico,* 275 F.3d at 255-57; *United States v. Donna*, 366 F. App'x. 441 (3d Cir. 2010) (non-precedential).

The official need not actually possess the power to provide, deny, or influence the particular action. *United States v. Mazzei*, 521 F.2d 639, 645 (3d Cir. 1975); *United States v. Nedza*, 880 F.2d 896, 902 (7th Cir. 1989); *United States v. Braasch*, 505 F.2d 139, 151 (7th Cir. 1974). It is the payor's reasonable belief in such power which is relevant. *Mazzei*, 521 F.2d at 643; *United States v. McDonough,* 56 F.3d 381, 388 (2d Cir. 1995); *Nedza*, 880 F.2d at 902; *see United States v. Brown*, 540 F.2d 364, 372 (8th Cir. 1976). The mere agreement to exercise influence will suffice. *See United States v. Bencivengo*, 749 F.3d 205, 212 (3d Cir. 2014).

The bracketed language in the last paragraph should be included if there is a question concerning whether the defendant acquired property rather than simply depriving the victim of property. Mere deprivation of property or interference with the use of property is not sufficient under the statute. In *Scheidler v. National Organization for Women, Inc.*, 537 U.S. 393 (2003), the Court addressed the definition of "extortion" under § 1951. The Court stated, "we have construed the extortion provision of the Hobbs Act at issue in these cases to require not only the deprivation of but also the acquisition of property." *Id.* at 404.

If the public official plays a role in more than one aspect of government, the court may want to specify the particular office that the extortion threatened to corrupt. *See, e.g., United States v. Mister*, 2010 WL 1006693 (3d Cir. 2010) (non-precedential) (rejecting defendant's variance argument in part because jury instructions clearly stated

˘15˘

the corruption at issue in the case).

(Revised 2014)

6.18.1951-7   Hobbs Act - Affecting Interstate Commerce

The third element that the government must prove beyond a reasonable doubt is that *(name)*'s conduct affected or could have affected interstate commerce. Conduct affects interstate commerce if it in any way interferes with, changes, or alters the movement or transportation or flow of goods, merchandise, money, or other property in commerce between or among the states. The effect can be minimal.

It is not necessary to prove that *(name)* intended to obstruct, delay or interfere with interstate commerce or that the purpose of the alleged crime was to affect interstate commerce. Further, you do not have to decide whether the effect on interstate commerce was to be harmful or beneficial to a particular business or to commerce in general. You do not even have to find that there was an actual effect on commerce. All that is necessary to prove this element is that the natural consequences of the offense potentially caused an effect on interstate commerce to any degree, however minimal or slight.

Comment

Sand et al., supra, 50-7 and 50-15.

18 U.S.C. § 1951(b) provides:

As used in this section--

(3) The term "commerce" means commerce within the District of Columbia, or any Territory or Possession of the United States; all

˘17˘

commerce between any point in a State, Territory, Possession, or the District of Columbia and any point outside thereof; all commerce between points within the same State through any place outside such State; and all other commerce over which the United States has jurisdiction.

The government need not prove that the defendant intended to affect interstate commerce but only that it was one natural effect of the defendant's conduct. *See United States v. Powell*, 693 F.3d 398 (3d Cir. 2012) (citing model instructions as reflecting circuit precedent). *See also United States v. Ligon*, --- F. App'x. ----, 2014 WL 4783721 (2014) (non-precedential) (stating approval of model instruction); *United States v. Addonizio*, 451 F.2d 49, 77 (3d Cir. 1972); *United States v. Reyes*, 363 F. App'x. 192 (3d Cir. 2010) (non-precedential).

In *United States v. Haywood*, 363 F.3d 200, 209-10 (3d Cir. 2004), the Third Circuit addressed the interstate commerce element:

> To sustain a conviction for interference with commerce by robbery under § 1951, the government must prove the element of interference with interstate or foreign commerce by robbery. "The charge that interstate commerce is affected is critical since the Federal Government's jurisdiction of this crime rests only on that interference." However, "[i]f the defendants' conduct produces any interference with or effect upon interstate commerce, whether slight, subtle or even potential, it is sufficient to uphold a prosecution under [§ 1951]." Moreover, "[a] jury may infer that interstate commerce was affected to some minimal degree from a showing that the business assets were depleted." (citations omitted).

See also United States v. Ligon, --- F. App'x. ----, 2014 WL 4783721 (2014) (non-precedential) (rejecting argument that instruction allowing conviction based on *de minimis* or potential effect on interstate commerce was error); *United States v. Shavers*, 693 F.3d 363 (3d Cir. 2012) (holding that the government is not required to show substantial effect on interstate commerce, and it is sufficient if the government establishes some interference with or effect upon interstate commerce, even if it is only slight). In *Haywood*, the court held that the following instruction was proper:

> if the government proves beyond a reasonable doubt that this business purchased goods or services that came from outside St. Thomas, Virgin Islands, and that, therefore, all or part of the personal property obtained from this business, because of the alleged robbery, came from outside St. Thomas, Virgin Islands, then you are instructed that you may find that the defendants obtained, delayed or affected commerce as this term is used in these instructions.

˘18˘

The court held further that the government satisfied its burden on this element by introducing the testimony of a police officer that the victim business sold some beers that were not manufactured in the Virgin Islands, but came instead from the mainland United States. *Haywood,* 363 F.3d at 210. *See also United States v. Powell,* 693 F.3d 398 (3d Cir. 2012) (stating that conviction requires only *de minimis* effect on commerce); *United States v. Clausen,* 328 F.3d 708, 710-11 (3d Cir. 2003) (stating that effect on commerce may be minimal); *United States v. Berroa,* 2010 WL 827617 (3d Cir. 2010) (non-precedential) (affirming conviction where robbery targeted store with inventory purchased in interstate commerce and store closed for part of day as a result of robbery); *United States v. McNeill,* 360 F. App'x. 363, 365 (3d Cir. 2010) (non-precedential) (concluding that evidence defendant robbed business that purchases goods in interstate commerce and had customers who traveled in interstate commerce is sufficient).

In *Powell,* the Third Circuit held that evidence that the defendants targeted store owners, "seeking to steal the stores' earnings and assets," provided sufficient evidence of effect on interstate commerce, even though the defendants robbed the individual store owners rather than the businesses. *Powell,* 693 F.3d at 405-06. In *Shavers,* the Third Circuit declined to adopt "a heightened interstate commerce requirement when the victim of the alleged crime is an individual rather than a business." 693 F.3d at 376.

In *United States v. Urban,* 404 F.3d 754, 762 (3d Cir. 2005), the Third Circuit held that the following instruction properly conveyed the way in which the government could establish effect on commerce through a depletion of assets theory:

> You do not even have to find that there was an actual effect on commerce. All that is necessary to prove this element is that the natural consequences of the extortion--of the money payment, potentially caused an effect on interstate commerce to any degree, however minimal or slight. Payment from a business engaged in interstate commerce satisfies the requirement of an effect on interstate commerce. If the resources of a business are expended or diminished as a result of the payment of money, then interstate commerce is affected by such payment and may reduce the assets available for purchase of goods, services or other things originating in other states.

In *United States v. Powell,* 693 F.3d 398 (3d Cir. 2012), the court held that the evidence was sufficient to establish effect on commerce through depletion of assets and that the trial court did not commit error when it supplemented the Model Instruction with the following language explaining depletion of assets:

> You can, but are not required to, find an effect on interstate commerce if the defendant's actions reduced the assets of a business engaged or purchasing goods or services in interstate commerce, which assets would otherwise have been available for conducting the purchase of such goods

˅19˅

or services in interstate commerce.

The instruction served "to exemplify one way the required nexus can be established."

In *United States v. Reyes*, 363 F. App'x. 192 (3d Cir. 2010) (non-precedential), the court noted that the government need not show actual effect on interstate commerce and held that the following instruction was correct:

> The defendant need not have intended or anticipated an effect on interstate commerce. You may find the effect as a natural consequence of his actions. If you find that the defendant intended to take certain actions, that is, he did the acts charged in the indictment in order to obtain property, and you find those actions have either caused or would probably cause an effect on interstate commerce no matter how minimal, then you may find the requirements of this element satisfied.

See also United States v. Ligon, --- F. App'x. ---, 2014 WL 4783721 (2014) (non-precedential); *United States v. Powell*, 693 F.3d 398 (3d Cir. 2012) (stating that effect may be potential not actual).

(Revised 2014)

˘20˘

Appendix

Actual Reproduction/Images of Oneida County Court Indictment for Toussaint Davis (a.k.a. John T. Healy, a.k.a. Toussaint Martin)

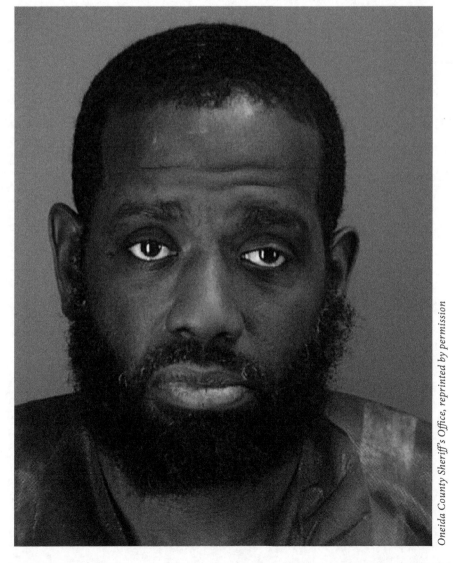

Oneida County Sheriff's Office, reprinted by permission

STATE OF NEW YORK)

                              SS:

COUNTY OF ONEIDA   )

I, JEANNE NATALE , Associate Court Clerk of the County

Court, County of Oneida, being a Court of Record, do certify that I

have compared this copy of Indictment I06-113 with the original filed

4/12/06 and entered in this office and that the same is a true copy

thereof.

IN WITNESS WHEREOF, I have hereunto set my hand and

affixed the seal of said County and said Court.

July 29, 2016
   DATE   JEANNE NATALE
                                    ASSOCIATE COURT CLERK
                                    Oneida County Combined Court

INDICTMENT
(ORIGINAL)

STATE OF NEW YORK
COUNTY COURT   ONEIDA COUNTY

THE PEOPLE OF THE STATE OF NEW YORK

Against

John T. Healy,

Defendant.

INDICTMENT

IND. NO. I 2006-113

Filed April 12, 2006

FIRST COUNT

THE GRAND JURY OF ONEIDA COUNTY, do hereby accuse John T. Healy, defendant, of the offense of **Murder in the Second Degree** in violation of Section 125.25, subdivision 3, of the Penal Law of the State of New York, a felony, committed as follows: The said defendant, on or about February 27, 2006, in the County of Oneida, Towns of New Hartford and Kirkland, did commit or attempt to commit robbery, and, in the course of and in furtherance of such crime or of immediate flight therefrom, he, or another participant caused the death of a person, to wit: Patrolman Joseph D. Corr, a sworn officer of the New Hartford Police Department, who was not a participant in the crime, by shooting him with a loaded firearm.

SECOND COUNT

THE GRAND JURY OF ONEIDA COUNTY, do hereby accuse John T. Healy, defendant, of the offense of **Robbery in the First Degree** in violation of Section 160.15, subdivision 1, of the Penal Law of the State of New York, a felony, committed as follows: The said defendant, on or about February 27, 2006, in the County of Oneida, Towns of New Hartford and Kirkland, did forcibly steal property, to wit: jewelry, watches and precious gems, from Gary M. Lennon, an employee of Lennon's-W.B. Wilcox Jewelers, and in the course of the commission of the crime or of immediate flight therefrom, he or another participant in the crime caused serious physical injury, to wit: death, to Patrolman Joseph D. Corr, a sworn officer of the New Hartford Police Department, who was not a participant in the crime.

THIRD COUNT

THE GRAND JURY OF ONEIDA COUNTY, do hereby accuse John T. Healy, defendant, of the offense of **Robbery in the First Degree** in violation of Section 160.15, subdivision 2, of the Penal Law of the State of New York, an armed felony, committed as follows: The said defendant, on or about February 27, 2006, in the County of Oneida, Towns of New Hartford and Kirkland, did forcibly steal property, to wit: jewelry, watches and precious gems, from Gary M. Lennon, an employee of Lennon's-W.B. Wilcox Jewelers, and in the course of the commission of the crime or of immediate flight therefrom, he or another participant in the crime was armed with a deadly weapon, to wit: a loaded firearm.

FOURTH COUNT

THE GRAND JURY OF ONEIDA COUNTY, do hereby accuse John T. Healy, defendant, of the offense of **Robbery in the Second Degree** in violation of Section 160.10, subdivision 1, of the Penal Law of the State of New York, a felony, committed as follows: The said defendant, while aided by another person who was actually present, on or about February 27, 2006, in the County of Oneida, Town of New Hartford, did forcibly steal property, to wit: jewelry, watches and precious gems, from Gary M. Lennon, an employee of Lennon's-W.B. Wilcox Jewelers.

FIFTH COUNT

THE GRAND JURY OF ONEIDA COUNTY, do hereby accuse John T. Healy, defendant, of the offense of **Robbery in the First Degree** in violation of Section 160.15, subdivision 1, of the Penal Law of the State of New York, a felony, committed as follows: The said defendant, on or about February 27, 2006, in the County of Oneida, Towns of New Hartford and Kirkland, did forcibly steal property, to wit: jewelry, watches and precious gems, from Stephen C. Lennon, an employee of Lennon's-W.B. Wilcox Jewelers, and in the course of the commission of the crime or of immediate flight therefrom, he or another participant in the crime caused serious physical injury, to wit: death, to Patrolman Joseph D. Corr, a sworn officer of the New Hartford Police Department, who was not a participant in the crime

SIXTH COUNT

THE GRAND JURY OF ONEIDA COUNTY, do hereby accuse John T. Healy, defendant, of the offense of **Robbery in the First Degree** in violation of Section 160.15, subdivision 2, of the Penal Law of the State of New York, an armed felony, committed as follows: The said defendant, on or about February 27, 2006, in the County of Oneida, Towns of New Hartford and Kirkland, did forcibly steal property, to wit: jewelry, watches and precious gems, from Stephen C. Lennon, an employee of Lennon's-W.B. Wilcox Jewelers, and in the course of the commission of the crime or of immediate flight therefrom, he or another participant in the crime was armed with a deadly weapon, to wit: a loaded firearm.

SEVENTH COUNT

THE GRAND JURY OF ONEIDA COUNTY, do hereby accuse John T. Healy, defendant, of the offense of **Robbery in the Second Degree** in violation of Section 160.10, subdivision 1, of the Penal Law of the State of New York, a felony, committed as follows: The said defendant, while aided by another person who was actually present, on or about February 27, 2006, in the County of Oneida, Town of New Hartford, did forcibly steal property, to wit: jewelry, watches and precious gems, from Stephen C. Lennon, an employee of Lennon's-W.B. Wilcox Jewelers.

EIGHTH COUNT

THE GRAND JURY OF ONEIDA COUNTY, do hereby accuse John T. Healy, defendant, of the offense of **Robbery in the First Degree** in violation of Section 160.15, subdivision 1, of the Penal Law of the State of New York, a felony, committed as follows: The said defendant, on or about February 27, 2006, in the County of Oneida, Towns of New Hartford and Kirkland, did forcibly steal property, to wit: jewelry, watches and precious gems, from Linda J. Gozy, an employee of Lennon's-W.B. Wilcox Jewelers, and in the course of the commission of the crime or of immediate flight therefrom, he or another participant in the crime caused serious physical injury, to wit: death, to Patrolman Joseph D. Corr, a sworn officer of the New Hartford Police Department, who was not a participant in the crime.

NINTH COUNT

THE GRAND JURY OF ONEIDA COUNTY, do hereby accuse John T. Healy, defendant, of the offense of **Robbery in the First Degree** in violation of Section 160.15, subdivision 2, of the Penal Law of the State of New York, an armed felony, committed as follows: The said defendant, on or about February 27, 2006, in the County of Oneida, Towns of New Hartford and Kirkland, did forcibly steal property, to wit: jewelry, watches and precious gems, from Linda J. Gozy, an employee of Lennon's-W.B. Wilcox Jewelers, and in the course of the commission of the crime or of immediate flight therefrom, he or another participant in the crime was armed with a deadly weapon, to wit: a loaded firearm.

TENTH COUNT

THE GRAND JURY OF ONEIDA COUNTY, do hereby accuse John T. Healy, defendant, of the offense of **Robbery in the Second Degree** in violation of Section 160.10, subdivision 1, of the Penal Law of the State of New York, a felony, committed as follows: The said defendant, while aided by another person who was actually present, on or about February 27, 2006, in the County of Oneida, Town of New Hartford, did forcibly steal property, to wit: jewelry, watches and precious gems, from Linda J. Gozy, an employee of Lennon's-W.B. Wilcox Jewelers.

ELEVENTH COUNT

THE GRAND JURY OF ONEIDA COUNTY, do hereby accuse John T. Healy, defendant, of the offense of **Robbery in the First Degree** in violation of Section 160.15, subdivision 1, of the Penal Law of the State of New York, a felony, committed as follows: The said defendant, on or about February 27, 2006, in the County of Oneida, Towns of New Hartford and Kirkland, did forcibly steal property, to wit: jewelry, watches and precious gems, from Wendy L. Daniels, an employee of Lennon's-W.B. Wilcox Jewelers, and in the course of the commission of the crime or of immediate flight therefrom, he or another participant in the crime caused serious physical injury to wit: death, to Patrolman Joseph D. Corr, a sworn officer of the New Hartford Police Department, who was not a participant in the crime.

TWELFTH COUNT

THE GRAND JURY OF ONEIDA COUNTY, do hereby accuse John T. Healy, defendant, of the offense of **Robbery in the First Degree** in violation of Section 160.15, subdivision 2, of the Penal Law of the State of New York, an armed felony, committed as follows: The said defendant, on or about February 27, 2006, in the County of Oneida, Towns of New Hartford and Kirkland, did forcibly steal property, to wit: jewelry, watches and precious gems, from Wendy L. Daniels, an employee of Lennon's-W.B. Wilcox Jewelers, and in the course of the commission of the crime or of immediate flight therefrom, he or another participant in the crime was armed with a deadly weapon, to wit: a loaded firearm.

THIRTEENTH COUNT

THE GRAND JURY OF ONEIDA COUNTY, do hereby accuse John T. Healy, defendant, of the offense of **Robbery in the Second Degree** in violation of Section 160.10, subdivision 1, of the Penal Law of the State of New York, a felony, committed as follows: The said defendant, while aided by another person who was actually present, on or about February 27, 2006, in the County of Oneida, Town of New Hartford, did forcibly steal property, to wit: jewelry, watches and precious gems, from Wendy L. Daniels, an employee of Lennon's-W.B. Wilcox Jewelers.

FOURTEENTH COUNT

THE GRAND JURY OF ONEIDA COUNTY, do hereby accuse John T. Healy, defendant, of the offense of **Robbery in the First Degree** in violation of Section 160.15, subdivision 1, of the Penal Law of the State of New York, a felony, committed as follows: The said defendant, on or about February 27, 2006, in the County of Oneida, Towns of New Hartford and Kirkland, did forcibly steal property, to wit: jewelry, watches and precious gems, from Kimberly A. Suriano, an employee of Lennon's-W.B. Wilcox Jewelers, and in the course of the commission of the crime or of immediate flight therefrom, he or another participant in the crime caused serious physical injury, to wit: death, to Patrolman Joseph D. Corr, a sworn officer of the New Hartford Police Department, who was not a participant in the crime.

FIFTEENTH COUNT

THE GRAND JURY OF ONEIDA COUNTY, do hereby accuse John T. Healy, defendant, of the offense of **Robbery in the First Degree** in violation of Section 160.15, subdivision 2, of the Penal Law of the State of New York, an armed felony, committed as follows: The said defendant, on or about February 27, 2006, in the County of Oneida, Towns of New Hartford and Kirkland, did forcibly steal property, to wit: jewelry, watches and precious gems, from Kimberly A. Suriano, an employee of Lennon's-W.B. Wilcox Jewelers, and in the course of the commission of the crime or of immediate flight therefrom, he or another participant in the crime was armed with a deadly weapon, to wit: a loaded firearm.

SIXTEENTH COUNT

THE GRAND JURY OF ONEIDA COUNTY, do hereby accuse John T. Healy, defendant, of the offense of **Robbery in the Second Degree** in violation of Section 160.10, subdivision 1, of the Penal Law of the State of New York, a felony, committed as follows: The said defendant, while aided by another person who was actually present, on or about February 27, 2006, in the County of Oneida, Town of New Hartford, did forcibly steal property, to wit: jewelry, watches and precious gems, from Kimberly A. Suriano, an employee of Lennon's-W.B. Wilcox Jewelers.

SEVENTEENTH COUNT

THE GRAND JURY OF ONEIDA COUNTY, do hereby accuse John T. Healy, defendant, of the offense of **Robbery in the First Degree** in violation of Section 160.15, subdivision 1, of the Penal Law of the State of New York, a felony, committed as follows: The said defendant, on or about February 27, 2006, in the County of Oneida, Towns of New Hartford and Kirkland, did forcibly steal property, to wit: jewelry, watches and precious gems, from Leslee A. Liesch, an employee of Lennon's-W.B. Wilcox Jewelers, and in the course of the commission of the crime or of immediate flight therefrom, he or another participant in the crime caused serious physical injury, to wit: death, to Patrolman Joseph D. Corr, a sworn officer of the New Hartford Police Department, who was not a participant in the crime.

EIGHTEENTH COUNT

THE GRAND JURY OF ONEIDA COUNTY, do hereby accuse John T. Healy, defendant, of the offense of **Robbery in the First Degree** in violation of Section 160.15, subdivision 2, of the Penal Law of the State of New York, an armed felony, committed as follows: The said defendant, on or about February 27, 2006, in the County of Oneida, Towns of New Hartford and Kirkland, did forcibly steal property, to wit: jewelry, watches and precious gems, from Leslee A. Liesch, an employee of Lennon's-W.B. Wilcox Jewelers, and in the course of the commission of the crime or of immediate flight therefrom, he or another participant in the crime was armed with a deadly weapon, to wit: a loaded firearm.

NINETEENTH COUNT

THE GRAND JURY OF ONEIDA COUNTY, do hereby accuse John T. Healy, defendant, of the offense of **Robbery in the Second Degree** in violation of Section 160.10, subdivision 1, of the Penal Law of the State of New York, a felony, committed as follows: The said defendant, while aided by another person who was actually present, on or about February 27, 2006, in the County of Oneida, Town of New Hartford, did forcibly steal property, to wit: jewelry, watches and precious gems, from Leslee A. Liesch, an employee of Lennon's-W.B. Wilcox Jewelers.

[signature] : Oneida County District Attorney,

[signature] : Foreperson, Oneida County Grand Jury.

COUNTY COURT

COUNTY OF ONEIDA

THE PEOPLE OF THE STATE OF NEW YORK

vs.

John T. Healy

INDICTMENT FOR

STATE OF NEW YORK
COUNTY COURT   ONEIDA COUNTY
_____

THE PEOPLE OF THE STATE OF NEW YORK

Against

Marion Pegeses, a/k/a "Dump," a/k/a "Ameen,"

Defendant.
_____

INDICTMENT

IND. NO. I 2006-200

Filed June 29, 2006

FIRST COUNT

THE GRAND JURY OF ONEIDA COUNTY, do hereby accuse Marion Pegeses, a/k/a "Dump," a/k/a "Ameen," defendant, of the offense of **Murder in the Second Degree** in violation of Section 125.25, subdivision 3, of the Penal Law of the State of New York, a felony, committed as follows: The said defendant, on or about February 27, 2006, in the County of Oneida, Towns of New Hartford and Kirkland, did commit or attempt to commit robbery, and, in the course of and in furtherance of such crime or of immediate flight therefrom, he, or another participant caused the death of a person, to wit: Patrolman Joseph D. Corr, a sworn officer of the New Hartford Police Department, who was not a participant in the crime, by shooting him with a loaded firearm.

SECOND COUNT

THE GRAND JURY OF ONEIDA COUNTY, do hereby accuse Marion Pegeses, a/k/a "Dump," a/k/a "Ameen," defendant, of the offense of **Robbery in the First Degree** in violation of Section 160.15, subdivision 1, of the Penal Law of the State of New York, a felony, committed as follows: The said defendant, on or about February 27, 2006, in the County of Oneida, Towns of New Hartford and Kirkland, did forcibly steal property, to wit: jewelry, watches and precious gems, from Gary M. Lennon, an employee of Lennon's-W.B. Wilcox Jewelers, and in the course of the commission of the crime or of immediate flight therefrom, he or another participant in the crime caused serious physical injury, to wit: death, to Patrolman

Joseph D. Corr, a sworn officer of the New Hartford Police Department, who was not a participant in the crime.

THIRD COUNT

THE GRAND JURY OF ONEIDA COUNTY, do hereby accuse Marion Pegeses, a/k/a "Dump," a/k/a "Ameen," defendant, of the offense of **Robbery in the First Degree** in violation of Section 160.15, subdivision 2, of the Penal Law of the State of New York, an armed felony, committed as follows: The said defendant, on or about February 27, 2006, in the County of Oneida, Towns of New Hartford and Kirkland, did forcibly steal property, to wit: jewelry, watches and precious gems, from Gary M. Lennon, an employee of Lennon's-W.B. Wilcox Jewelers, and in the course of the commission of the crime or of immediate flight therefrom, he or another participant in the crime was armed with a deadly weapon, to wit: a loaded firearm.

FOURTH COUNT

THE GRAND JURY OF ONEIDA COUNTY, do hereby accuse Marion Pegeses, a/k/a "Dump," a/k/a "Ameen," defendant, of the offense of **Robbery in the Second Degree** in violation of Section 160.10, subdivision 1, of the Penal Law of the State of New York, a felony, committed as follows: The said defendant, while aided by another person who was actually present, on or about February 27, 2006, in the County of Oneida, Town of New Hartford, did forcibly steal property, to wit: jewelry, watches and precious gems, from Gary M. Lennon, an employee of Lennon's-W.B. Wilcox Jewelers.

FIFTH COUNT

THE GRAND JURY OF ONEIDA COUNTY, do hereby accuse Marion Pegeses, a/k/a "Dump," a/k/a "Ameen," defendant, of the offense of **Robbery in the First Degree** in violation of Section 160.15, subdivision 1, of the Penal Law of the State of New York, a felony, committed as follows: The said defendant, on or about February 27, 2006, in the County of Oneida, Towns of New Hartford and Kirkland, did forcibly steal property, to wit: jewelry, watches and precious gems, from Stephen C. Lennon, an employee of Lennon's-W.B. Wilcox Jewelers, and in the course of the commission of the crime or of immediate flight therefrom, he or another participant in the crime caused serious physical injury, to wit: death, to Patrolman Joseph D. Corr, a sworn officer of the New Hartford Police Department, who was not a participant in the crime.

SIXTH COUNT

THE GRAND JURY OF ONEIDA COUNTY, do hereby accuse Marion Pegeses, a/k/a "Dump," a/k/a "Ameen," defendant, of the offense of **Robbery in the First Degree** in violation of Section 160.15, subdivision 2, of the Penal Law of the State of New York, an armed felony, committed as follows: The said defendant, on or about February 27, 2006, in the County of Oneida, Towns of New Hartford and Kirkland, did forcibly steal property, to wit: jewelry, watches and precious gems, from Stephen C. Lennon, an employee of Lennon's-W.B. Wilcox Jewelers, and in the course of the commission of the crime or of immediate flight therefrom, he or another participant in the crime was armed with a deadly weapon, to wit: a loaded firearm.

SEVENTH COUNT

THE GRAND JURY OF ONEIDA COUNTY, do hereby accuse Marion Pegeses, a/k/a "Dump," a/k/a "Ameen," defendant, of the offense of **Robbery in the Second Degree** in violation of Section 160.10, subdivision 1, of the Penal Law of the State of New York, a felony, committed as follows: The said defendant, while aided by another person who was actually present, on or about February 27, 2006, in the County of Oneida, Town of New Hartford, did forcibly steal property, to wit: jewelry, watches and precious gems, from Stephen C. Lennon, an employee of Lennon's-W.B. Wilcox Jewelers.

EIGHTH COUNT

THE GRAND JURY OF ONEIDA COUNTY, do hereby accuse Marion Pegeses, a/k/a "Dump," a/k/a "Ameen," defendant, of the offense of **Robbery in the First Degree** in violation of Section 160.15, subdivision 1, of the Penal Law of the State of New York, a felony, committed as follows: The said defendant, on or about February 27, 2006, in the County of Oneida, Towns of New Hartford and Kirkland, did forcibly steal property, to wit: jewelry, watches and precious gems, from Linda J. Gozy, an employee of Lennon's-W.B. Wilcox

Jewelers, and in the course of the commission of the crime or of immediate flight therefrom, he or another participant in the crime caused serious physical injury, to wit: death, to Patrolman Joseph D. Corr, a sworn officer of the New Hartford Police Department, who was not a participant in the crime.

NINTH COUNT

THE GRAND JURY OF ONEIDA COUNTY, do hereby accuse Marion Pegeses, a/k/a "Dump," a/k/a "Ameen," defendant, of the offense of **Robbery in the First Degree** in violation of Section 160.15, subdivision 2, of the Penal Law of the State of New York, an armed felony, committed as follows: The said defendant, on or about February 27, 2006, in the County of Oneida, Towns of New Hartford and Kirkland, did forcibly steal property, to wit: jewelry, watches and precious gems, from Linda J. Gozy, an employee of Lennon's-W.B. Wilcox Jewelers, and in the course of the commission of the crime or of immediate flight therefrom, he or another participant in the crime was armed with a deadly weapon, to wit: a loaded firearm.

TENTH COUNT

THE GRAND JURY OF ONEIDA COUNTY, do hereby accuse Marion Pegeses, a/k/a "Dump," a/k/a "Ameen," defendant, of the offense of **Robbery in the Second Degree** in violation of Section 160.10, subdivision 1, of the Penal Law of the State of New York, a felony, committed as follows: The said defendant, while aided by another person who was actually present, on or about February 27, 2006, in the County of Oneida, Town of New Hartford, did forcibly steal property, to wit: jewelry, watches and precious gems, from Linda J. Gozy, an employee of Lennon's-W.B. Wilcox Jewelers.

ELEVENTH COUNT

THE GRAND JURY OF ONEIDA COUNTY, do hereby accuse Marion Pegeses, a/k/a "Dump," a/k/a "Ameen," defendant, of the offense of **Robbery in the First Degree** in violation of Section 160.15, subdivision 1, of the Penal Law of the State of New York, a felony, committed as follows: The said defendant, on or about February 27, 2006, in the County of Oneida, Towns of New Hartford and Kirkland, did forcibly steal property, to wit: jewelry, watches and precious gems, from Wendy L. Daniels, an employee of Lennon's-W.B. Wilcox Jewelers, and in the course of the commission of the crime or of immediate flight therefrom, he or another participant in the crime caused serious physical injury to wit: death, to Patrolman Joseph D. Corr, a sworn officer of the New Hartford Police Department, who was not a participant in the crime.

TWELFTH COUNT

THE GRAND JURY OF ONEIDA COUNTY, do hereby accuse Marion Pegeses, a/k/a "Dump," a/k/a "Ameen," defendant, of the offense of **Robbery in the First Degree** in violation of Section 160.15, subdivision 2, of the Penal Law of the State of New York, an armed felony, committed as follows: The said defendant, on or about February 27, 2006, in the County of Oneida, Towns of New Hartford and Kirkland, did forcibly steal property, to wit: jewelry, watches and precious gems, from Wendy L. Daniels, an employee of Lennon's-W.B. Wilcox Jewelers, and in the course of the commission of the crime or of immediate flight therefrom, he or another participant in the crime was armed with a deadly weapon, to wit: a loaded firearm.

THIRTEENTH COUNT

THE GRAND JURY OF ONEIDA COUNTY, do hereby accuse Marion Pegeses, a/k/a "Dump," a/k/a "Ameen," defendant, of the offense of **Robbery in the Second Degree** in violation of Section 160.10, subdivision 1, of the Penal Law of the State of New York, a felony, committed as follows: The said defendant, while aided by another person who was actually present, on or about February 27, 2006, in the County of Oneida, Town of New Hartford, did forcibly steal property, to wit: jewelry, watches and precious gems, from Wendy L. Daniels, an employee of Lennon's-W.B. Wilcox Jewelers.

FOURTEENTH COUNT

THE GRAND JURY OF ONEIDA COUNTY, do hereby accuse Marion Pegeses, a/k/a "Dump," a/k/a "Ameen," defendant, of the offense of **Robbery in the First Degree** in violation of Section 160.15, subdivision 1, of the Penal Law of the State of New York, a felony, committed as follows: The said defendant, on or about February 27, 2006, in the County of

Oneida, Towns of New Hartford and Kirkland, did forcibly steal property, to wit: jewelry, watches and precious gems, from Kimberly A. Suriano, an employee of Lennon's-W.B. Wilcox Jewelers, and in the course of the commission of the crime or of immediate flight therefrom, he or another participant in the crime caused serious physical injury, to wit: death, to Patrolman Joseph D. Corr, a sworn officer of the New Hartford Police Department, who was not a participant in the crime.

FIFTEENTH COUNT

THE GRAND JURY OF ONEIDA COUNTY, do hereby accuse Marion Pegeses, a/k/a "Dump," a/k/a "Ameen," defendant, of the offense of **Robbery in the First Degree** in violation of Section 160.15, subdivision 2, of the Penal Law of the State of New York, an armed felony, committed as follows: The said defendant, on or about February 27, 2006, in the County of Oneida, Towns of New Hartford and Kirkland, did forcibly steal property, to wit: jewelry, watches and precious gems, from Kimberly A. Suriano, an employee of Lennon's-W.B. Wilcox Jewelers, and in the course of the commission of the crime or of immediate flight therefrom, he or another participant in the crime was armed with a deadly weapon, to wit: a loaded firearm.

SIXTEENTH COUNT

THE GRAND JURY OF ONEIDA COUNTY, do hereby accuse Marion Pegeses, a/k/a "Dump," a/k/a "Ameen," defendant, of the offense of **Robbery in the Second Degree** in violation of Section 160.10, subdivision 1, of the Penal Law of the State of New York, a felony, committed as follows: The said defendant, while aided by another person who was actually present, on or about February 27, 2006, in the County of Oneida, Town of New Hartford, did forcibly steal property, to wit: jewelry, watches and precious gems, from Kimberly A. Suriano, an employee of Lennon's-W.B. Wilcox Jewelers.

SEVENTEENTH COUNT

THE GRAND JURY OF ONEIDA COUNTY, do hereby accuse Marion Pegeses, a/k/a "Dump," a/k/a "Ameen," defendant, of the offense of **Robbery in the First Degree** in violation of Section 160.15, subdivision 1, of the Penal Law of the State of New York, a felony, committed as follows: The said defendant, on or about February 27, 2006, in the County of Oneida, Towns of New Hartford and Kirkland, did forcibly steal property, to wit: jewelry, watches and precious gems, from Leslee A. Liesch, an employee of Lennon's-W.B. Wilcox Jewelers, and in the course of the commission of the crime or of immediate flight therefrom, he or another participant in the crime caused serious physical injury, to wit: death, to Patrolman Joseph D. Corr, a sworn officer of the New Hartford Police Department, who was not a participant in the crime.

EIGHTEENTH COUNT

THE GRAND JURY OF ONEIDA COUNTY, do hereby accuse Marion Pegeses, a/k/a "Dump," a/k/a "Ameen," defendant, of the offense of **Robbery in the First Degree** in violation of Section 160.15, subdivision 2, of the Penal Law of the State of New York, an armed felony, committed as follows: The said defendant, on or about February 27, 2006, in the County of Oneida, Towns of New Hartford and Kirkland, did forcibly steal property, to wit: jewelry, watches and precious gems, from Leslee A. Liesch, an employee of Lennon's-W.B. Wilcox Jewelers, and in the course of the commission of the crime or of immediate flight therefrom, he or another participant in the crime was armed with a deadly weapon, to wit: a loaded firearm.

NINETEENTH COUNT

THE GRAND JURY OF ONEIDA COUNTY, do hereby accuse Marion Pegeses, a/k/a "Dump," a/k/a "Ameen," defendant, of the offense of **Robbery in the Second Degree** in violation of Section 160.10, subdivision 1, of the Penal Law of the State of New York, a felony, committed as follows: The said defendant, while aided by another person who was actually present, on or about February 27, 2006, in the County of Oneida, Town of New Hartford, did forcibly steal property, to wit: jewelry, watches and precious gems, from Leslee A. Liesch, an employee of Lennon's-W.B. Wilcox Jewelers.

_____ : **Oneida County District Attorney,**

_____ : **Foreperson, Oneida County Grand Jury.**

Actual Reproduction/ Images of Oneida County Court Indictment for Robert Ward

Oneida County Sheriff's Office, reprinted by permission

STATE OF NEW YORK
COUNTY COURT   ONEIDA COUNTY

THE PEOPLE OF THE STATE OF NEW YORK

Against

Robert Ward, a/k/a "RB",

Defendant.

INDICTMENT

IND. NO. I 2006-130

Filed April 25, 2006

FIRST COUNT

THE GRAND JURY OF ONEIDA COUNTY, do hereby accuse Robert Ward, a/k/a "RB", defendant, of the offense of **Murder in the Second Degree** in violation of Section 125.25, subdivision 3, of the Penal Law of the State of New York, a felony, committed as follows: The said defendant, on or about February 27, 2006, in the County of Oneida, Towns of New Hartford and Kirkland, did commit or attempt to commit robbery, and, in the course of and in furtherance of such crime or of immediate flight therefrom, he, or another participant caused the death of a person, to wit: Patrolman Joseph D. Corr, a sworn officer of the New Hartford Police Department, who was not a participant in the crime, by shooting him with a loaded firearm.

SECOND COUNT

THE GRAND JURY OF ONEIDA COUNTY, do hereby accuse Robert Ward, a/k/a "RB", defendant, of the offense of **Robbery in the First Degree** in violation of Section 160.15, subdivision 1, of the Penal Law of the State of New York, a felony, committed as follows: The said defendant, on or about February 27, 2006, in the County of Oneida, Towns of New Hartford and Kirkland, did forcibly steal property, to wit: jewelry, watches and precious gems, from Gary M. Lennon, an employee of Lennon's-W.B. Wilcox Jewelers, and in the course of the commission of the crime or of immediate flight therefrom, he or another participant in the crime caused serious physical injury, to wit: death, to Patrolman Joseph D. Corr, a sworn officer of the New Hartford Police Department, who was not a participant in the crime.

THIRD COUNT

THE GRAND JURY OF ONEIDA COUNTY, do hereby accuse Robert Ward, a/k/a "RB", defendant, of the offense of **Robbery in the First Degree** in violation of Section 160.15, subdivision 2, of the Penal Law of the State of New York, an armed felony, committed as follows: The said defendant, on or about February 27, 2006, in the County of Oneida, Towns of New Hartford and Kirkland, did forcibly steal property, to wit: jewelry, watches and precious gems, from Gary M. Lennon, an employee of Lennon's-W.B. Wilcox Jewelers, and in the course of the commission of the crime or of immediate flight therefrom, he or another participant in the crime was armed with a deadly weapon, to wit: a loaded firearm.

FOURTH COUNT

THE GRAND JURY OF ONEIDA COUNTY, do hereby accuse Robert Ward, a/k/a "RB", defendant, of the offense of **Robbery in the Second Degree** in violation of Section 160.10, subdivision 1, of the Penal Law of the State of New York, a felony, committed as follows: The said defendant, while aided by another person who was actually present, on or about February 27, 2006, in the County of Oneida, Town of New Hartford, did forcibly steal property, to wit: jewelry, watches and precious gems, from Gary M. Lennon, an employee of Lennon's-W.B. Wilcox Jewelers.

FIFTH COUNT

THE GRAND JURY OF ONEIDA COUNTY, do hereby accuse Robert Ward, a/k/a "RB", defendant, of the offense of **Robbery in the First Degree** in violation of Section 160.15, subdivision 1, of the Penal Law of the State of New York, a felony, committed as follows: The said defendant, on or about February 27, 2006, in the County of Oneida, Towns of New Hartford and Kirkland, did forcibly steal property, to wit: jewelry, watches and precious gems, from Stephen C. Lennon, an employee of Lennon's-W.B. Wilcox Jewelers, and in the course of the commission of the crime or of immediate flight therefrom, he or another participant in the crime caused serious physical injury, to wit: death, to Patrolman Joseph D. Corr, a sworn officer of the New Hartford Police Department, who was not a participant in the crime.

SIXTH COUNT

THE GRAND JURY OF ONEIDA COUNTY, do hereby accuse Robert Ward, a/k/a "RB", defendant, of the offense of **Robbery in the First Degree** in violation of Section 160.15, subdivision 2, of the Penal Law of the State of New York, an armed felony, committed as follows: The said defendant, on or about February 27, 2006, in the County of Oneida, Towns of New Hartford and Kirkland, did forcibly steal property, to wit: jewelry, watches and precious gems, from Stephen C. Lennon, an employee of Lennon's-W.B. Wilcox Jewelers, and in the course of the commission of the crime or of immediate flight therefrom, he or another participant in the crime was armed with a deadly weapon, to wit: a loaded firearm.

SEVENTH COUNT

THE GRAND JURY OF ONEIDA COUNTY, do hereby accuse Robert Ward, a/k/a "RB", defendant, of the offense of **Robbery in the Second Degree** in violation of Section 160.10, subdivision 1, of the Penal Law of the State of New York, a felony, committed as follows: The said defendant, while aided by another person who was actually present, on or about February 27, 2006, in the County of Oneida, Town of New Hartford, did forcibly steal property, to wit: jewelry, watches and precious gems, from Stephen C. Lennon, an employee of Lennon's-W.B. Wilcox Jewelers.

EIGHTH COUNT

THE GRAND JURY OF ONEIDA COUNTY, do hereby accuse Robert Ward, a/k/a "RB", defendant, of the offense of **Robbery in the First Degree** in violation of Section 160.15, subdivision 1, of the Penal Law of the State of New York, a felony, committed as follows: The said defendant, on or about February 27, 2006, in the County of Oneida, Towns of New Hartford and Kirkland, did forcibly steal property, to wit: jewelry, watches and precious gems, from Linda J. Gozy, an employee of Lennon's-W.B. Wilcox Jewelers, and in the course of the commission of the crime or of immediate flight therefrom, he or another participant in the crime caused serious physical injury, to wit: death, to Patrolman Joseph D. Corr, a sworn officer of the New Hartford Police Department, who was not a participant in the crime.

NINTH COUNT

THE GRAND JURY OF ONEIDA COUNTY, do hereby accuse Robert Ward, a/k/a "RB", defendant, of the offense of **Robbery in the First Degree** in violation of Section 160.15, subdivision 2, of the Penal Law of the State of New York, an armed felony, committed as follows: The said defendant, on or about February 27, 2006, in the County of Oneida, Towns of New Hartford and Kirkland, did forcibly steal property, to wit: jewelry, watches and precious gems, from Linda J. Gozy, an employee of Lennon's-W.B. Wilcox Jewelers, and in the course of the commission of the crime or of immediate flight therefrom, he or another participant in the crime was armed with a deadly weapon, to wit: a loaded firearm.

TENTH COUNT

THE GRAND JURY OF ONEIDA COUNTY, do hereby accuse Robert Ward, a/k/a "RB", defendant, of the offense of **Robbery in the Second Degree** in violation of Section 160.10, subdivision 1, of the Penal Law of the State of New York, a felony, committed as follows: The said defendant, while aided by another person who was actually present, on or about February 27, 2006, in the County of Oneida, Town of New Hartford, did forcibly steal property, to wit: jewelry, watches and precious gems, from Linda J. Gozy, an employee of Lennon's-W.B. Wilcox Jewelers.

ELEVENTH COUNT

THE GRAND JURY OF ONEIDA COUNTY, do hereby accuse Robert Ward, a/k/a "RB", defendant, of the offense of **Robbery in the First Degree** in violation of Section 160.15, subdivision 1, of the Penal Law of the State of New York, a felony, committed as follows: The said defendant, on or about February 27, 2006, in the County of Oneida, Towns of New Hartford and Kirkland, did forcibly steal property, to wit: jewelry, watches and precious gems, from Wendy L. Daniels, an employee of Lennon's-W.B. Wilcox Jewelers, and in the course of the commission of the crime or of immediate flight therefrom, he or another participant in the crime caused serious physical injury to wit: death, to Patrolman Joseph D. Corr, a sworn officer of the New Hartford Police Department, who was not a participant in the crime.

TWELFTH COUNT

THE GRAND JURY OF ONEIDA COUNTY, do hereby accuse Robert Ward, a/k/a "RB", defendant, of the offense of **Robbery in the First Degree** in violation of Section 160.15, subdivision 2, of the Penal Law of the State of New York, an armed felony, committed as follows: The said defendant, on or about February 27, 2006, in the County of Oneida, Towns of New Hartford and Kirkland, did forcibly steal property, to wit: jewelry, watches and precious gems, from Wendy L. Daniels, an employee of Lennon's-W.B. Wilcox Jewelers, and in the course of the commission of the crime or of immediate flight therefrom, he or another participant in the crime was armed with a deadly weapon, to wit: a loaded firearm.

THIRTEENTH COUNT

THE GRAND JURY OF ONEIDA COUNTY, do hereby accuse Robert Ward, a/k/a "RB", defendant, of the offense of **Robbery in the Second Degree** in violation of Section 160.10, subdivision 1, of the Penal Law of the State of New York, a felony, committed as follows: The said defendant, while aided by another person who was actually present, on or about February 27, 2006, in the County of Oneida, Town of New Hartford, did forcibly steal property, to wit: jewelry, watches and precious gems, from Wendy L. Daniels, an employee of Lennon's-W.B. Wilcox Jewelers.

FOURTEENTH COUNT

THE GRAND JURY OF ONEIDA COUNTY, do hereby accuse Robert Ward, a/k/a "RB", defendant, of the offense of **Robbery in the First Degree** in violation of Section 160.15, subdivision 1, of the Penal Law of the State of New York, a felony, committed as follows: The said defendant, on or about February 27, 2006, in the County of Oneida, Towns of New Hartford and Kirkland, did forcibly steal property, to wit: jewelry, watches and precious gems, from Kimberly A. Suriano, an employee of Lennon's-W.B. Wilcox Jewelers, and in the course of the commission of the crime or of immediate flight therefrom, he or another participant in the crime caused serious physical injury, to wit: death, to Patrolman Joseph D. Corr, a sworn officer of the New Hartford Police Department, who was not a participant in the crime.

FIFTEENTH COUNT

THE GRAND JURY OF ONEIDA COUNTY, do hereby accuse Robert Ward, a/k/a "RB", defendant, of the offense of **Robbery in the First Degree** in violation of Section 160.15, subdivision 2, of the Penal Law of the State of New York, an armed felony, committed as follows: The said defendant, on or about February 27, 2006, in the County of Oneida, Towns of New Hartford and Kirkland, did forcibly steal property, to wit: jewelry, watches and precious gems, from Kimberly A. Suriano, an employee of Lennon's-W.B. Wilcox Jewelers, and in the course of the commission of the crime or of immediate flight therefrom, he or another participant in the crime was armed with a deadly weapon, to wit: a loaded firearm.

SIXTEENTH COUNT

THE GRAND JURY OF ONEIDA COUNTY, do hereby accuse Robert Ward, a/k/a "RB", defendant, of the offense of **Robbery in the Second Degree** in violation of Section 160.10, subdivision 1, of the Penal Law of the State of New York, a felony, committed as follows: The said defendant, while aided by another person who was actually present, on or about February 27, 2006, in the County of Oneida, Town of New Hartford, did forcibly steal property, to wit: jewelry, watches and precious gems, from Kimberly A. Suriano, an employee of Lennon's-W.B. Wilcox Jewelers.

SEVENTEENTH COUNT

THE GRAND JURY OF ONEIDA COUNTY, do hereby accuse Robert Ward, a/k/a "RB", defendant, of the offense of **Robbery in the First Degree** in violation of Section 160.15, subdivision 1, of the Penal Law of the State of New York, a felony, committed as follows: The said defendant, on or about February 27, 2006, in the County of Oneida, Towns of New Hartford and Kirkland, did forcibly steal property, to wit: jewelry, watches and precious gems, from Leslee A. Liesch, an employee of Lennon's-W.B. Wilcox Jewelers, and in the course of the commission of the crime or of immediate flight therefrom, he or another participant in the crime caused serious physical injury, to wit: death, to Patrolman Joseph D. Corr, a sworn officer of the New Hartford Police Department, who was not a participant in the crime.

EIGHTEENTH COUNT

THE GRAND JURY OF ONEIDA COUNTY, do hereby accuse Robert Ward, a/k/a "RB", defendant, of the offense of **Robbery in the First Degree** in violation of Section 160.15, subdivision 2, of the Penal Law of the State of New York, an armed felony, committed as follows: The said defendant, on or about February 27, 2006, in the County of Oneida, Towns of New Hartford and Kirkland, did forcibly steal property, to wit: jewelry, watches and precious gems, from Leslee A. Liesch, an employee of Lennon's-W.B. Wilcox Jewelers, and in the course of the commission of the crime or of immediate flight therefrom, he or another participant in the crime was armed with a deadly weapon, to wit: a loaded firearm.

NINETEENTH COUNT

THE GRAND JURY OF ONEIDA COUNTY, do hereby accuse Robert Ward, a/k/a "RB", defendant, of the offense of **Robbery in the Second Degree** in violation of Section 160.10, subdivision 1, of the Penal Law of the State of New York, a felony, committed as follows: The said defendant, while aided by another person who was actually present, on or about February 27, 2006, in the County of Oneida, Town of New Hartford, did forcibly steal property, to wit: jewelry, watches and precious gems, from Leslee A. Liesch, an employee of Lennon's-W.B. Wilcox Jewelers.

: Oneida County District Attorney,

: Foreperson, Oneida County Grand Jury.

Appendix

Actual Reproduction/ Images of Federal Grand Jury Indictment (Davis, Pegese, Ward)

U.S. DISTRICT COURT - N.D. OF N.Y.
FILED
JUL 16 2009
AT_____ O'CLOCK
Lawrence K. Baerman, Clerk - Syracuse

IN THE UNITED STATES DISTRICT COURT
FOR THE NORTHERN DISTRICT OF NEW YORK

UNITED STATES OF AMERICA :	CRIMINAL NO. 5:09-cr-390 (NAM)
v. :	
	VIOLATIONS:
MARION PEGESE, :	18 U.S.C. § 1951(a) (Conspiracy to
a/k/a "Dump,"	Interfere with Interstate Commerce by
a/k/a "Bill," :	Robbery - 1 count)
a/k/a "Amein,"	
:	18 U.S.C. § 1951(a) (Interference with
ROBERT WARD,	Interstate Commerce by Robbery - 1
a/k/a "RB," and :	count); 18 U.S.C. § 2 (Aiding and
	Abetting)
TOUSSAINT DAVIS, :	
a/k/a "Toot,"	18 U.S.C. § 924 (j)(1) (Murder as a Result
a/k/a "John Healy," :	of Possession and Discharge of a Firearm
a/k/a "Toussaint Martin,"	in Furtherance of a Crime of Violence-1
	count)
Defendants	

INDICTMENT

THE GRAND JURY CHARGES:

COUNT ONE

At all times material to this indictment:

1.   The Lennon's-W.B. Wilcox Jewelers store located at Commercial Drive, New Hartford, New York ["Lennon's Jewelers"], was a business engaged in the retail sale of jewelry and watches in and affecting interstate and foreign commerce.

2.   The Ballew Jewelers store located at West Main Street, Freehold, New Jersey ["Ballew Jewelers"], was a business engaged in the retail sale of jewelry and watches in and affecting interstate and foreign commerce.

THE ROBBERY CONSPIRACY

3.   From in or about August 2005 until on or about May 2006, in Oneida County in the Northern District of New York, and elsewhere, defendants

MARION PEGESE,
a/k/a " Dump,"
a/k/a "Bill,"
a/k/a "Amein,"

ROBERT WARD,
a/k/a "RB,"

TOUSSAINT DAVIS,
a/k/a "Toot,"
a/k/a "John Healy,"
a/k/a "Toussaint Martin,"

did combine, conspire, confederate, and agree, with each other and others known and unknown to the grand jury, including Walter R. Richardson, Jr., to commit robberies, which robberies would unlawfully obstruct, delay, and affect commerce, and the movement of articles and commodities in such commerce, in that defendants MARION PEGESE, ROBERT WARD and TOUSSAINT DAVIS conspired to unlawfully take and obtain jewelry and Rolex watches from the person and presence of

2

others and against their will, by means of actual and threatened force, violence, and immediate fear of injury to their person and property, all in violation of Title 18, United States Code, Section 1951(a).

MANNER AND MEANS

It was part of the conspiracy that:

4.   Defendants MARION PEGESE, ROBERT WARD, and TOUSSAINT DAVIS, along with Walter R. Richardson, Jr. and others known and unknown to the grand jury, engaged in robberies to steal jewelry and Rolex watches from jewelry stores during regular business hours.

5.   The group traveled in one or more vehicles from Philadelphia, Pennsylvania to locations in New York and New Jersey to commit the robberies.

6.   The group would commit "takeover-style" robberies of victim jewelry stores by holding store employees hostage at gunpoint while seizing Rolex watches and jewelry, which they put into bags before fleeing.

7.   The defendants robbed the two victim stores listed in paragraphs 1 and 2 above and stole jewelry and Rolex watches with a retail value in excess of $2 million.

OVERT ACTS

8. In furtherance of the conspiracy, defendants MARION PEGESE, ROBERT WARD, and TOUSSAINT DAVIS committed the following overt acts in the Northern District of New York and elsewhere:

Ballew Jewelers

a.   On or about August 26, 2005, defendant MARION PEGESE entered Ballew Jewelers posing as a prospective customer, examined jewelry and watches in display cases, and engaged store employees in conversation.

3

b.   On or about August 26, 2005, defendants ROBERT WARD and TOUSSAINT DAVIS, along with Eric Lane, entered Ballew Jewelers carrying bags a short time after defendant MARION PEGESE entered.

c.   Defendant MARION PEGESE and Eric Lane displayed handguns and ordered the employees of Ballew Jewelers to enter a back room.

d.   Defendant MARION PEGESE and Eric Lane unsuccessfully sought to disable the video surveillance system in Ballew Jewelers.

e.   Defendants MARION PEGESE, ROBERT WARD, and TOUSSAINT DAVIS, along with Eric Lane, took Rolex watches and jewelry from their cases and put them into bags.

f.   Defendants MARION PEGESE, ROBERT WARD, and TOUSSAINT DAVIS, along with Eric Lane, tied the hands and feet of the employees of Ballew Jewelers with duct tape and moved them to the basement of the store.

g.   Defendants MARION PEGESE, ROBERT WARD, and TOUSSAINT DAVIS, along with Eric Lane, escaped through a rear door of Ballew Jewelers with stolen watches and jewelry worth in excess of $1 million.

Lennon's Jewelers

h.   On or about February 22, 2006, defendant TOUSSAINT DAVIS used a personal computer located at 1307 West Wishart, Philadelphia, Pennsylvania to obtain driving directions from that location to Lennon's Jewelers in New Hartford, New York.

i.   On or about February 23, 2006, defendants TOUSSAINT DAVIS, MARION PEGESE, and ROBERT WARD, along with Walter R. Richardson, Jr., traveled from Philadelphia, Pennsylvania to New Hartford, New York in multiple vehicles.

4

j.   While traveling to New Hartford, New York on or about February 23, 2006, defendants TOUSSAINT DAVIS, MARION PEGESE, and ROBERT WARD, along with Walter R. Richardson, Jr., remained in communication with each other through the use of mobile telephones.

k.   Upon arriving in New Hartford, New York, on or about February 23, 2006, defendants TOUSSAINT DAVIS, MARION PEGESE, and ROBERT WARD, along with Walter R. Richardson, Jr., went to the vicinity of Commercial Drive and the Sangertown Mall, near Lennon's Jewelers, where they remained for approximately one to one and half hours, after which they returned to Philadelphia, Pennsylvania.

l.   On or about February 27, 2006, defendants TOUSSAINT DAVIS, MARION PEGESE, and ROBERT WARD, along with Walter R. Richardson, Jr., traveled from Philadelphia, Pennsylvania to New Hartford, New York in more than one vehicle, remaining in communication with each other through the use of mobile telephones.

m.   At approximately 8:15 p.m. on or about February 27, 2006, defendants TOUSSAINT DAVIS, MARION PEGESE, and ROBERT WARD, along with Walter R. Richardson, Jr., wearing masks and carrying at least one firearm, entered Lennon's Jewelers and ordered five employees of Lennon's Jewelers to the ground and secured their hands with handcuffs.

n.   On or about February 27, 2006, one or more of the co-conspirators took the owner of Lennon's Jewelers at gun point to a vault area and ordered him to identify the video surveillance system, which one of the co-conspirators then disabled.

o.   On or about February 27, 2006, defendants TOUSSAINT DAVIS, MARION PEGESE, and ROBERT WARD, along with Walter R. Richardson, Jr., stole jewelry and 31 Rolex watches worth approximately $1 million dollars from Lennon's Jewelers.

5

p.   On or about February 27, 2006, after police came to the scene of the robbery based on telephone calls made by a Lennon's Jewelry store employee who was hiding during the robbery, defendant TOUSSAINT DAVIS and Walter R. Richardson, Jr. fled from the scene in a blue Buick automobile driven by Richardson.

q.   On or about February 27, 2006, after police came to the scene of the robbery in response to telephone calls made by a Lennon's Jewelry store employee who was hiding during the robbery, defendants MARION PEGESE and ROBERT WARD escaped undetected in WARD'S Cadillac.

r.   On or about February 27, 2006, while being pursued by police, conspirator Walter R. Richardson, Jr., crashed a Buick automobile into gasoline pumps in front of a Byrne Dairy Store in the Town of Kirkland, New York.

s.   On or about February 27, 2006, defendant TOUSSAINT DAVIS got out of a blue Buick automobile and unsuccessfully attempted to flee from police.

t.   At approximately 8:27 p.m. on or about February 27, 2006, as Town of New Hartford Police Officer Joseph Corr conducted a search for suspects in the rear of a Byrne Dairy Store in Kirkland, New York, coconspirator Walter R. Richardson, Jr. shot and killed Officer Corr.

COUNT TWO

1.   Paragraphs 1 through 8 and overt acts 8(a) through 8(t) of Count One are incorporated here.

2.   On or about February 27, 2006, in the Northern District of New York and elsewhere, defendants,

6

MARION PEGESE,
a/k/a " Dump,"
a/k/a "Bill,"
a/k/a "Amein,"

ROBERT WARD,
a/k/a "RB,"

TOUSSAINT DAVIS,
a/k/a "Toot,"
a/k/a "John Healy,"
a/k/a "Toussaint Martin,"

aiding and abetting one another, did unlawfully obstruct, delay, and affect and attempt to obstruct,

delay, and affect commerce, and the movement of articles and commodities in commerce, by robbery,

in that defendants MARION PEGESE, ROBERT WARD, and TOUSSAINT DAVIS unlawfully took

and obtained property, and aided and abetted the unlawful taking and obtaining of property, that is,

jewelry and Rolex watches valued at approximately $1 million, from the person and presence of

employees of Lennon's Jewelry store against their will, by means of actual and threatened force,

violence, and fear of immediate injury to their person and property, and property in their custody and

possession belonging to the store, that is, by taking and obtaining jewelry and Rolex watches.

In violation of Title 18, United States Code, Sections 1951(a) and 2.

COUNT THREE

1.   Paragraphs 1 through 8 and overt acts 8(a) through 8(t) of Count One are incorporated

here.

2.   On or about February 27, 2006 in the Northern District of New York and elsewhere,

defendants,

MARION PEGESE,
a/k/a " Dump,"

7

a/k/a "Bill,"
a/k/a "Amein,"

ROBERT WARD,
a/k/a "RB,"

TOUSSAINT DAVIS,
a/k/a "Toot,"
a/k/a "John Healy,"
a/k/a "Toussaint Martin,"

during and in relation to a crime of violence for which they could be prosecuted in a court of the United States, specifically: (a) conspiracy to commit robbery which would unlawfully obstruct, delay, and affect commerce, and the movement of articles and commodities in commerce, in violation of Title 18, United States Code, Sections 1951, as charged in Count One of this indictment; and (b) robbery which would unlawfully obstruct, delay, and affect commerce, and the movement of articles and commodities in commerce, in violation of Title 18, United States Code, Section 1951, as charged in Count Two of this indictment, used and carried a firearm, specifically, a .40 caliber Smith & Wesson pistol, and, in furtherance of such crime of violence, possessed such firearm, and, through the use of that firearm, caused the death of New Hartford Police Officer Joseph Corr, which unlawful killing was murder in that the defendants acted with malice aforethought, and the killing was willful, deliberate, and premeditated, and committed during the perpetration of a robbery.

All in violation of Title 18, United States Code, Sections 924(c)(1), 924(j)(1), and Pinkerton v. United States, 328 U.S. 640 (1946) ("Pinkerton liability").

Dated: July 16 , 2009

A TRUE BILL,

_____

Foreperson

8

ANDREW T. BAXTER
UNITED STATES ATTORNEY
NORTHERN DISTRICT OF NEW YORK

By: _____
John G. Duncan
Executive Assistant U.S. Attorney
Bar Roll #601100

By: _____
Richard R. Southwick
Assistant U.S. Attorney
Bar Roll #506265

9

Appendix

Actual Reproduction of Sentencing Transcripts & Victim Impact Statements, *People v. John T. Healy*

```
 1   STATE OF NEW YORK  :  FIFTH JUDICIAL DISTRICT
     COUNTY COURT       :  COUNTY OF ONEIDA
 2   -----------------------------------------------X
     THE PEOPLE OF STATE OF NEW YORK        :
 3                                          :
                                            :
 4                                          :  IND. 06-113
     -v-                                    :  NYSID#0493904R
 5                                          :
     JOHN T. HEALY, a/k/a  TOUSSAINT DAVIS a/k/a:
 6   TOUSSAINT MARTIN,                      :
                                            :
 7                     Defendant.           :
     -----------------------------------------------X
 8
                             SENTENCING
 9                           APRIL 19, 2007

10                           Oneida County Courthouse
                             Elizabeth Street
11                           Utica, New York 13501

12   B E F O R E:

13             THE HONORABLE MICHAEL L. DWYER,
                   ONEIDA COUNTY COURT JUDGE
14
     A P P E A R A N C E S:
15
          For the People:
16
               SCOTT D. MCNAMARA, ESQ.
17             Acting District Attorney, County of Oneida
                   KURT D. HAMELINE, ESQ.
18             PAUL J. HERNON, ESQ.
               Assistant District Attorneys
19

20        For the Defendant:

21             REBECCA WITTMAN, ESQ.
               P.O. Box 8485
22             Utica, New York 13504

23
               Defendant present
24
                              Deborah A. Rose
25                            Senior Court Reporter
```

1   THE COURT: All right, this is the matter of

2 People versus John H. Healy under Indictment

3 2006-143. This matter was the subject of a jury

4 trial that took place between the dates of January

5 4th, of 2007, and January the 22nd, of 2007, after

6 which the defendant was found guilty of all 19

7 counts of the indictment. We are here today for the

8 handling of a 330 motion, and also for the purpose

9 of sentencing.

10   Prior to getting to those two matters, Mr.

11 Hameline, is there anything that the People want to

12 state for the record?

13   MR. HAMELINE: At this time, your Honor, we

14 would make a motion to amend the indictment with

15 respect to the defendant's name. We would ask that

16 the indictment be amended to read People of the

17 State of New York versus Toussaint Davis. That's

18 T-O-U-S-S-A-I-N-T, Davis. That would be the primary

19 name, that is his given name and date of birth. We

20 would also add an a/k/a, an alias known as Toussaint

21 Martin, same spelling on Toussaint, last name

22 Martin, M-A-R-T-I-N, and a second alias, which would

23 be John T. Healy, the original name that he provided

24 to the police department, the name he was indicted

25 under, and the name he went to trial on. So the

1   indictment would read Toussaint Davis, also known as

2   Toussaint Martin, also known as John T. Healy.

3   We would ask that the Court records also be

4   deemed to reflect his true date of birth, April

5   19th, 1968, and that his social security number is

6   184-50-3748. And I can put on the record, if you

7   want, some information that we have obtained to back

8   that up.

9   THE COURT: Okay, please do so.

10   MR. HAMELINE: Among the things that we have

11   acquired, your Honor, is his birth certificate,

12   which indicates that he was born under the name, or

13   given the name of Toussaint Davis at birth, that his

14   date of birth is 4/19/68. We have the original

15   application for a social security number, which was

16   at the request of his mother, who was a Loretta

17   Davis, the father is a Gaddis Martin, G-A-D-D-I-S.

18   This was the original application in 1973 for a

19   social security number.

20   We also have the defendant's own application

21   for re-issuance of a replacement card, that was on

22   September 30th, 2003, in which he indicated he was

23   Toussaint Davis, gave the date of birth that we've

24   already mentioned, the same parents, Loretta Davis,

25   Gaddis Martin.

We also have his application for a State of
Pennsylvania drivers license, it has the same basic
information, it also has a photograph that was
submitted or taken by the Department of Motor
Vehicles in Pennsylvania. This application and
license was used as verification when he applied for
the re-issuance of his social security card.

We have talked to family members, talked to his
former girlfriend, all of whom indicate his name is
Toussaint Davis. He was arrested and has been
previously arrested under the name Toussaint Davis,
fingerprinted with the name Toussaint Davis. He --
right now he's on probation in Montgomery County,
Pennsylvania under the name of Toussaint Davis. We
have plenty of back-up information, there's no doubt
in our minds he's Toussaint Davis, not John
T. Healy, John T. Healy being an identity that was
stolen from the real John T. Healy in Pennsylvania.

THE COURT: Miss Wittman, do you want to be
heard on that motion?

MS. WITTMAN: Thank you, your Honor.

I appreciate what the People are trying to
accomplish, that being clear up Mr. Healy's issues
down in Pennsylvania. I would have to object to the
current motion being made. First of all, I was not

1   aware that that motion was being made today. I was

2   aware that the People were investigating the

3   underlying issues, but I was not aware that that

4   motion was going to be made today.

5   I see that the People have some documentation

6   here. My client's position is that he's not

7   Toussaint Davis, his family has -- I just actually

8   just spoke with them this morning to confirm they

9   had sent out documentation, which I would expect I'm

10   going to receive today, that confirms that he is not

11   Toussaint Davis.

12   THE COURT: Does it confirm who he is?

13   MS. WITTMAN: I am hoping that it will. Well,

14   it's going to conflict with what the People have.

15   However, I guess my main grounds for objecting is

16   the fact that if the Court reads the presentence

17   report, or if the Court were to review his rap

18   sheets, there's many, many aliases, and I'm not

19   aware of anything that occurred at the time of the

20   arrest or any conversations with police officers

21   where either the name Toussaint Davis or Toussaint

22   Martin was used by my client during the, either

23   during the incident or during the arrest or booking

24   process, so why the People should be allowed, out of

25   the laundry list of 10 or 15 aliases, to say we'd

1   like to pick those two names and we'd like to attach

2   them to the indictment, and the name that was

3   presented or that was -- that law enforcement used,

4   that being John Healy, that that becomes the third

5   a/k/a. I would think the indictment, if it were

6   going to be amended, would have to read John

7   T. Healy, the name that was used, a/k/a Martin or

8   Davis, but I don't know why we should be picking

9   those two, those two aliases from the numerous that

10   are submitted.

11   THE COURT: Well I think he's just told you why

12   he's picked the one Toussaint Davis because their

13   investigation has revealed that he is, in fact,

14   Toussaint Davis.

15   MS. WITTMAN: I appreciate --

16   THE COURT: It wasn't picked at random.

17   MS. WITTMAN: I appreciate what their

18   investigation has revealed, which was just revealed

19   to me today. My client tells me he's not Toussaint

20   Davis, his family says he's not and claims they are

21   giving me documentation to that effect. If I knew

22   that we were going to be presented with this this

23   morning as opposed to at the Grand Jury, I would

24   have been prepared to have that documentation this

25   morning, or in advance of this morning.

1   THE COURT: All right. I will grant the

2   People's motion and the indictment will be amended

3   to read People of the State of New York against

4   Toussaint Davis, also known as Toussaint Martin,

5   also known as John Healy.

6   Okay, subject to the jury verdicts, Miss

7   Wittman, on the date of April 4th, of this year,

8   filed a motion pursuant to Criminal Procedure Law

9   Section 330.30, asking the Court to set aside the

10   verdict due to alleged errors that she said occurred

11   in the trial. I also have an answering affirmation

12   that was filed by Mr. Hameline on the date of April

13   16th. We are here today, this morning, for oral

14   argument and the decision of the Court.

15   Miss Wittman, do you wish to be heard orally in

16   support of the request that you've made in your

17   moving papers?

18   MS. WITTMAN: No, thank you, your Honor.

19   THE COURT: Mr. Hameline, do you wish to be

20   heard?

21   MR. HAMELINE: No, we'll rely on our papers,

22   your Honor.

23   THE COURT: Then the Court has considered the

24   arguments of counsel. The Court is going to deny

25   the defendant's motion to set aside the verdict of

1   the jury.

2   Miss Wittman, any legal cause why sentence

3   should not be imposed on today's date?

4   MS. WITTMAN: No, your Honor.

5   THE COURT: Do have the People wish to be heard

6   with respect to sentence?

7   MR. HAMELINE: Your Honor, the People do, but

8   first there are certain family members and Chief

9   Philo who wishes to address the Court at this time.

10   THE COURT: Okay, if you would go ahead.

11   MR. HAMELINE: Chief Philo first.

12   Your Honor, if I could be heard, I did receive

13   notice and I did receive, in a timely fashion, did

14   receive notice relative to people speaking, I just

15   would note I'm not sure if Chief Philo falls under

16   the statutory definition of victim who would be

17   allowed to speak.

18   THE COURT: Okay. I will allow Chief Philo to

19   address the Court.

20   CHIEF PHILO: Judge Dwyer, thank you for

21   allowing me to address the Court today at the

22   sentencing of Toussaint Davis for his conviction for

23   the robbery of the Lennon's W.B. Wilcox Jewelry

24   Store and the subsequent murder of New Hartford

25   Police Officer Joseph Corr.

1   Today marks a milestone, a sad and difficult

2   journey we have been on for the past 14 months.

3   Even after today our sad journey will continue for

4   many more months, and for some of us a lifetime.

5   As Chief of Police for the New Hartford Police

6   Department, I was particularly impacted by the

7   murder of Officer Corr and the horror sustained by

8   the robbery victims. I doubt I will ever be

9   entirely free of the private and lonely

10   responsibility of sending a young police officer out

11   on his last tour of duty.

12   February 27th, 2006, is a day of infamy for us.

13   On that Monday evening violent criminals descended

14   upon our community and committed a series of crimes

15   that included terrorizing innocent employees during

16   a jewelry store robbery and murdering Officer Joseph

17   Corr. Toussaint Davis, who sits here today

18   convicted of robbery and murder, made a conscious

19   decision to participate in these crimes. As a

20   matter of record, the evidence at trial shows he

21   played a major and significant role in planning the

22   robbery.

23   The facts of this case have been decided in a

24   court of law, and, hence, are not for our discussion

25   or debate today. Today is about the rule of law and

1   the punishment that attaches where one is convicted

2   of violating the law. The torrent of violent events

3   that occurred in our community on February 27th,

4   2006, simply must not go under punished.

5   Toussaint Davis's life has been a crime in

6   progress. I believe he is incapable of remorse or

7   rehabilitation and he is destined to commit similar

8   crimes if allowed to eventually go free. Therefore,

9   since he stands convicted of 18 counts of robbery

10   and one count of murder, I respectfully request that

11   the Court sentence him to the maximum punishment

12   allowed by law.

13   Thank you.

14   THE COURT: Good morning. If you could just

15   please state your name for the record prior to

16   starting your statement.

17   ROBERT CORR: Good morning, Judge. My name is

18   Robert Corr. I am Joseph Corr's uncle and

19   godfather. Thank you, your Honor, for your time.

20   As I look back on the events that led to Joe's

21   death, my thoughts turn to the pain felt by those

22   closest to him, particularly my brother, Dave, and

23   Kathy. And, of course, Tracie. And perhaps, worst

24   of all, little Kaitlyn, who will never remember the

25   love of her father. She will never hear his words

of advice, his gentle cautions or parental directives.

I think about how Cindy, my wife, and I tried to tell our daughters that night. How could we somehow ease the pain of the news we had to give them when they were both hundreds of miles away. It was too far for us to be there and comfort them when they learned the news. As parents we always try to protect our children, I guess shelter them from the pains of life. It has been very difficult for both of them. Joe was like a big brother to my daughter, Terry.

Joe and Tracie had just bought land up the street from us to build a new home. They were going to be our new neighbors. It was really something that Cindy and I were looking forward to. Joe would drive up to the lot of land with his dogs to let them go out and run, and whenever he did he would stop, pull in the driveway and make sure that everything was okay. He was ever the protector, that was Joe.

But the list of victims is very, very long. Joe's sisters, Kelly and Sheri, Joe's best friend, Dennis, cousins, aunts, uncles, all affected. And, of course, Joe's brothers on the police department.

I have felt this very seriously. Aside from family, we witness the tears of complete strangers caught up in the horror of the moment. A whole community that was stunned and injured by this tragedy. People who realized that this little town was never going to be the same.

I think about the people that Joe helped every day as he patrolled the town. I think about the people that will never receive the help he would have provided them. And I think about how much easier it would have been for Dennis to finish that addition with Joe's help. It makes me ask myself how senseless, selfish acts of a few impact literally tens of thousands of people.

Just think about it for a moment: A few guys get together, they decide they have a quick answer to getting rich. Not by benefitting society, but by attacking it, by taking from it. As they go about their blundering, they leave a reckless path of destruction and fear in their wake. They don't look back, they just continue their tour of devastation until finally they get brought in.

I think about Leslee Leisch and the other employees at Lennon's Jewelers who feared for their lives, thinking they were about to breathe their

1   last breath at the hands of four selfish, greedy,

2   career criminals. I think about the real John

3   T. Healy who will spend the rest of his life

4   explaining that he isn't the cop killer. I think

5   about the untold endless victims of this life of

6   crime.

7   We are here today somehow seeking justice. The

8   anger and rage I felt a year ago has been replaced

9   by a sadness that will never go away. But it is a

10   sadness on many levels because I think about the

11   society that creates these criminals. How is it

12   that the same society that creates this loving and

13   caring community that we live in also creates

14   greedy, self-centered killers like Toussaint Davis?

15   The purpose today is to impose a sentence that

16   is just. Mr. Davis would surely have you believe he

17   is the victim because he didn't pull the trigger.

18   But he made career choices that took him down a path

19   of his own choosing. With that path, this is the

20   inevitable conclusion.

21   Today is not about revenge. Yes, to some

22   degree it is about retribution, justice and

23   punishment. But I see today as protection. I don't

24   know what it is about our society that creates

25   people like Walter Richardson and Toussaint Davis,

1 but I do know that once these criminals like

2 Mr. Davis are identified, we have a responsibility

3 to permanently end any possibility that they ever

4 have an opportunity to inflict this type of damage

5 on anyone ever again. It is all about protection.

6 That is really why we are here today. It is the

7 only proactive thing we can do. We cannot change

8 the past, but as a responsible -- as a responsible

9 society, we can protect the future.

10 I believe the state has no greater obligation

11 than to protect its citizens from the likes of Mr.

12 Davis. That is why, your Honor, I ask that today

13 you protect the future from this man. I ask that

14 you make sure he never has the opportunity to steal,

15 injure, assault, or kill anyone again. I ask that

16 you do what others before you did not or could not

17 do. I ask that you make sure there are no future

18 victims. As surely as night follows day, given the

19 opportunity, this man will return to a life of

20 creating new victims. There is nothing we can do to

21 bring Joe back or to undo the damage and pain

22 inflicted on society by this life of crime, but

23 today you can honor Joe's sacrifice by making sure

24 Mr. Davis never has the opportunity to create

25 another victim.

1   Thank you.

2   MR. WINN: Good morning, Judge Dwyer. My name

3 is Dan Winn and I am Joe Corr's cousin. I'm here

4 today to talk to you about how Joe was a big part of

5 my life and how his untimely death has affected me.

6   While growing up, the Winn/Corr kids were

7 inseparable. We did just about everything together.

8 With Joe having two older sisters and not having a

9 brother, I'd like to think he thought about me as

10 his younger brother. He sure acted like an older

11 brother to me by constantly picking on me, bullying

12 me, and telling me he was always right.

13   One of our favorite things to do was to go

14 hunting and fishing. My father, my brother George,

15 Uncle Dave and Joe and I were all in competition

16 with each other to see who caught the biggest fish

17 and who was the better hunter.

18   As we grew older we still were close. It was

19 Joe and Tracie who introduced me to my wife, Annie.

20 If it had not been for Joe and Tracie, I would not

21 have my four beautiful children. Watching Joe play

22 around with my kids, I knew that some day he would

23 be a great father. When Joe's daughter was born he

24 proved me right and was a fantastic dad to his

25 little princess.

1   The last day I spent with Joe was on February

2   26th, at Paul's house, redoing his basement. On the

3   way back to my house we talked about how I was going

4   to repay him by helping him build his dream house

5   that summer. I told him that it was the least I

6   could do for all the things that he has done for me.

7   The next night my life was shattered. All my dreams

8   of raising our children together and bringing them

9   hunting and fishing like we used to were gone.

10   Since that night my family's been left with an

11   emptiness in our hearts that can never be filled.

12   Yesterday, having taken part in Utica Police

13   Officer's Thomas Lindsay's funeral, I was shocked to

14   see that our community was once again dealing with

15   the loss of another hero taken from us so

16   tragically.

17   Judge Dwyer, if you decided to hand out the

18   maximum sentence to Mr. Davis, you will show

19   everyone that the justice system is doing everything

20   they can to prove that taking the life of our heroes

21   is not acceptable and that the people held

22   responsible will never see the light of day again.

23   Thank you.

24   MR. CALLAN: Your Honor, I stand here today --

25   I stand here today as a proud grandfather of Police

1   Officer Joseph Daniel Corr. My purpose here is to

2   inform the Court of the impact that this vicious

3   crime had on my entire family, the despair, the

4   destruction and the terror inflicted by this

5   convicted criminal.

6   They say every story begins on page one. In

7   our family that was true. When my wife, Mary Ruth,

8   gave birth to our first child, a baby girl, we named

9   her Kathleen. Joe's mother. And of course, like it

10   is true in the Irish families, we were off to the

11   races then. They kept coming and coming and they

12   grew up and they followed the same tradition and

13   blessed us with 15 grandchildren, one of which is

14   Joe Corr. And then those 15 polluted the world a

15   little further and they come up with 18

16   grandchildren, and the youngest one is named Joe.

17   Our family is huge and is large. And it sort

18   of was all going good, everybody was having a good

19   time, when all of the sudden one night our world

20   came crashing down upon us. Our brother, Joe, was

21   gone. So all 54 of us grieved and we were touched

22   by Joe's death. Tracie's husband never came home

23   from work. And Tracie (sic) lost her daddy.

24   A Rolex dealer and a little jewelry store with

25   a town police department and it was all plotted.

1 That would be cake for these four varmints. Until
2 they ran across the New Hartford Police Department
3 and that was their downfall, led by Chief Philo,
4 people are well equipped, well trained, well
5 motivated and heroic. They also lost their brother.
6 And also sort of ironic that this man with the
7 beautiful background he has were to really be done
8 in by a little girl that sits right out here today.
9 Her name is Leslee. As it was reported at the trial
10 she is, in height, probably five foot. I don't know
11 if she's gained any weight since then, but she was
12 about a hundred pounds then, and this guy took his
13 foot and squashed her into the pavement, into the
14 hard floor, and screamed at his companion, to use
15 her words at the trial, he said, "Shoot the bitch.
16 Shoot the bitch." A victim, she is a victim. We
17 are all victims by this action.
18   But you know, some things happened that are a
19 little strange. In our family we had one of the
20 dogs die, one of -- one of my grandson's, and their
21 three little kids were there. His name was Cody,
22 and Cody and I were great friends, I loved Cody.
23 The poor fellow was ridden by those kids, they
24 pulled his tail, they put their finger in his ears,
25 and he never complained a bit. So I figured I'll go

1   down there and be the consoler. And little Jake's

2   four years old -- says he's five, but he's really

3   only four -- and I said to all the people I said it

4   to, Jake, Jake, I'm awful sorry about Cody. He

5   looked at me and said pop, don't worry, he's in

6   heaven with Uncle Joe and Uncle Joe is watching over

7   him.

8   One last thing I have to say here is that our

9   family was bent, but it was not broken. We have a

10 very proud family and we will survive. We were

11 deeply shocked, hurt, but -- and we were wounded.

12 But we will recover. With the help of almighty God.

13 And we will never, ever forget.

14   Thank you.

15   DAVID CORR: My name is David Corr and I'm

16 Joe's father.

17   For over a year now we've waited for this day

18 to come, the criminal justice system to give our

19 family this day. I want to thank all of the

20 agencies, the individuals both within the law

21 enforcement community, the legal system, the Court,

22 to include the jury, and all those who helped in so

23 many ways that we could not begin to list them all.

24 We can only express our cumulative thank you.

25   To you, Davis, you will never understand what

you have taken from me. You and your cohorts, out
of absolute greed, came here and showed disrespect
for everyone, including yourself. You came here to
victimize, terrorize, threaten, rob and steal. You
think it's not your fault since you were not the
shooter, but we all know it is your fault, and so
does the law, and most importantly the jury says
it's your fault.

When you came here, you thought it would be
easy pickings, but you did not plan on Joe and the
New Hartford PD. You took our only son, my best
friend, my granddaughter's dad, my daughters' only
brother, a husband, friend; all something you
wouldn't be able to relate to. I could not begin to
really tell you what you have done.

I look at you today and I see a person void of
humanity. Your actions are proof of that, since you
decided you were too smart to stay in school past
the seventh grade, managed to get arrested some 50
times for literally hundreds of crimes from Hawaii
to New Jersey to New York and Washington State.
That's only counting the ones you were arrested for,
I wonder how many more victims you had, I wonder how
many more should be standing here commenting on
their victims status here today. Quite a track

1   record. It makes you a poster child for a lot more

2   than this Court will be able to give you today.

3   Unfortunately for now, you won't get the

4   sentence you really deserve, no matter how much you

5   deserve it. Ironically, even throughout the course

6   of this trial you continued to make a mockery of the

7   Court by not even being truthful about your name,

8   and yet continuing to victimize yet another innocent

9   man, not to mention accepting responsibility for

10   your actions and crime. Truly, you're a scumbag.

11   Today, finally, your turn has come.

12   To the Court, I ask not only for what he did to

13   Joe and others at Lennon's Jewelry Store on the

14   night of 2/27 of last year, but also for the many

15   other victims that still feel the pain for that

16   night, for the hundreds of victims and potential

17   victims that demand protection from this type of

18   predator and for a civilized society, I ask the

19   Court to impose the maximum sentences and

20   consecutive sentences to this contemptible excuse

21   for a human being.

22   And, Davis, I sincerely hope that you rot in

23   prison for the rest of your life.

24   Thank you.

25   MRS. CORR: My name is Kathy Corr. I am Joe's

mom. And this is going to be the most difficult thing that I will ever have to do. And I'll do my best to get through it, eventually.

When you lose your parents, you lose your past. When you lose your spouse, you lose your present. But when you lose your child, you've lost your future.

That is Joe Corr over there on that easel, that's Joe. Not just the policeman or fireman or baseball player, but a son, a husband, father, brother, grandson, uncle and cousin and godfather. The night my son was murdered, I felt so numb. I'm his mother, mother's protect their children. I wish I could have jumped in front of Joe and taken the bullet myself. In the emergency room we were allowed to see him, hold him and hug him. He looked like he was just sleeping. I rubbed his arm and held his hands; they were so cold. I wish I could have gotten blankets to warm him. But I couldn't do that because he had died, but I couldn't comprehend what that really meant.

I can now say that I have experienced a parent's worst nightmare. That feeling never goes away. For 14 months I have been in counseling and on medication. I can't concentrate, I don't

1   remember things, I don't sleep. I will be spending

2   the rest of my life visiting memorials, planting

3   flowers at my son's graves. It's not supposed to be

4   that way, I'm not supposed to pick out my son's

5   casket.

6   We were all so excited when his dream came true

7   and he put on a police uniform for the New Hartford

8   Police Department. Badge 125. I truly felt he

9   would be safe in his lifelong career and everything

10   was perfect.

11   I miss him calling me to watch the baby so he

12   could run some errands. I miss our weekly family

13   dinners. I miss seeing the dogs, Casey and Boomer.

14   I miss his 30-minute drives from New Hartford to the

15   Syracuse airport. I experienced all the ups and

16   downs parents have. I now treasure every one of

17   those memories.

18   There is one person who can't be here and is

19   the most affected by this senseless murder and she

20   can't speak for herself, and that is Joe's daughter

21   and my granddaughter. I had Joe through 30

22   wonderful years, but she only had her dad for one

23   precious year. My daughter-in-law has said that Joe

24   gave her more love in one year than other fathers

25   give their children in a lifetime. He called her

1   squirt. He'd rock her to sleep but didn't put her

2   down in her crib because he said she looked so

3   beautiful and all he wanted to do was stare at her

4   in his arms. She won't remember him. She won't be

5   with him in their dream home on a hill overlooking

6   the Mohawk Valley that they were going to build.

7   Joe worked for years clearing the land, but it is

8   now overgrown with weeds and bushes. She can't give

9   her dad a kiss goodbye on her first day of

10   kindergarten. She'll miss her dad seeing her off on

11   prom night. She won't see his proud smile as she

12   graduates from high school and college. She won't

13   have her dad walk her down the aisle on her wedding

14   day.

15   During the few days right after Joe's murder

16   there were many New Hartford policemen coming and

17   going at his house and they were all in uniform, the

18   same uniform that Joe wore. I would just sit there

19   and watch this one-year-old child, who was knee high

20   to everyone, go from policeman, to policeman,

21   looking for her dad. She would go and she would

22   look up, and she would continue to go to the next

23   policeman, look up, and try to find her dad. And

24   she couldn't find him. And there are no more

25   peek-a-boo games before Joe would go to work; she

1   would look out the window and play peek-a-boo.   Joe

2   always went home for dinner and I thank God he was

3   able to go home the night of February 27th, 2006,

4   but he never returned home.

5   Joe loved the outdoors and, in particular,

6   camping.   Every summer Joe and my daughter, Sheri,

7   Flip and their friends, would all plan camping

8   trips.   They loved to go to Maine where they would

9   hike and eat fresh lobsters.

10   Joe's godson is three years old.   He

11   understands that Joe is not here, but he is up in

12   the sky.   At Christmas he decorated a small

13   table-top tree with blue garland and blue ornaments,

14   the blue standing for the blue line.   A few days

15   later he all the sudden grabbed the tree and ran out

16   the back door and put the tree in the middle of the

17   yard.   He said he had to do that because he wanted

18   Uncle Joe to see his tree because Uncle Joe couldn't

19   see through the roof.   Ultimately, the tree wound up

20   on top of the swing set because the higher the tree,

21   the better Uncle Joe could see it.

22   One other thing my three-year-old grandson

23   feels is that if the moon is anything but a full

24   moon, that it is broken, and when the moon becomes

25   full, Uncle Joe is the one that fixed it.

1   We knew little that morning that God was going

2   to call his name. In life we loved him dearly and

3   in death we do the same. It broke our hearts to

4   lose you, you did not go alone, for part of us went

5   with you, the day God called you home. You left us

6   peaceful memories, your love is still our guide, and

7   though we cannot see you, you're always at our side.

8   Our family chain is broken and nothing seems the

9   same, but as God calls us one by one, the chain will

10   link again.

11   As far as you go, Mr. Toussaint Davis, you are

12   nothing but trash from Philadelphia. You thought

13   you had an easy heist here in New Hartford, a small

14   town, not like Syracuse, a large city where there

15   were two others jewelry stores that carried your

16   Rollies, but you didn't do your homework. There was

17   a police substation right across the street from

18   Lennon's Jewelers and you never came upon a Joe Corr

19   in your other crimes. Once Joe got on your tail, he

20   would never let you go. He laid down his life so

21   you and the other scumbag that was there couldn't

22   hurt anybody else again. All you wanted were

23   Rollies. You've slipped through the cracks in other

24   states, but here in New Hartford, New York our

25   judicial system has you and this is the end of the

1   road for you.

2   You have no remorse, only arrogance, living the

3   life of crime with many fake and stolen identities,

4   which was your way of life, your job. I thank God

5   that you did not have a gun in your hand and your

6   finger on a trigger the night of February 27th

7   because if you did, we wouldn't be mourning only the

8   death of my son, but the death of Leslee Leisch

9   also. You kept yelling to the person who was

10   holding the gun to her head, kill the f-ing bitch,

11   kill the f-ing bitch, over and over again. And

12   again, I thank God that the N.H.P.D. came to the

13   scene and the two other thugs out in the main part

14   of the store yelled the cops are coming so everybody

15   ran.

16   You are a poor excuse for a human being. With

17   your rap sheet, you should have been in jail a long

18   time ago for life.

19   Judge Dwyer, please don't let this piece of

20   dirt slip through the cracks in the New York State

21   Judicial System. He needs consecutive sentences.

22   He can't have a chance to kill and destroy any other

23   families.

24   Mr. Toussaint Davis, you came here, you

25   devastated my family, you assaulted our community,

and for that, I will never forgive you. May you rot
in hell, you son of a bitch.

MR. HAMELINE: Your Honor, what more can be
said I guess. As has been amply stated before you
now today, Mr. Davis's life can only be
characterized as one of a criminal rampage. It was
the life of crime. He has slipped through the
cracks previously, some by his own doing, his lies
and his deceit, and some because the system failed.
There is no question that the system failed in this
case. He should not have been on the street the
evening of February 27th, of 2006.

Even though Mr. Davis did not pull the trigger,
it is clear from the testimony that the Court heard
and all that we've learned about that night that he
played a major, major role. He planned, he came to
New Hartford, New York to scout their endeavor, he
was a complete accomplice in every sense of the
word. There is no doubt in my mind that he was the
person in that store yelling for Mr. Richardson to
shoot Leslee Liesch in the head. That's the kind of
person that we have before the Court today, and I'm
sure Mrs. Corr is correct, if he had a gun, he would
have done it himself.

Even to this very day he continues with his

1   lies and his deceit by providing false information

2   to the probation department in the presentence

3   investigation. It doesn't stop. It never stops.

4   He has continually put his own self-interest ahead

5   of society and today it's time for society to put

6   their interest first.

7   I have learned a lot about Mr. Davis through

8   the course of the investigation, the trial and after

9   the trial, and I can honestly say I have not found

10   one redeeming aspect in his entire life. Not one.

11   Nothing. Compare that or contrast that to what we

12   lost in Officer Corr.

13   By your sentence today, we implore you to send

14   a message not only with the sentence, but words when

15   you sentence Mr. Davis, that he should never, ever

16   be even considered to return to a civilized society,

17   that he never, ever breathe the fresh air of freedom

18   again in his life.

19   THE COURT: Miss Wittman, is there anything

20   that you want to say prior to the sentencing of your

21   client?

22   MS. WITTMAN: Your Honor, there are a couple

23   things that I want to say with respect to the

24   presentence report. I know that seems awfully

25   mundane and nit-picky after listening to the

1   comments of the family, however the fact that

2   there's an audience doesn't mean I can do anything

3   less than my job.

4   I have reviewed the presentence report, it is

5   very lengthy, prepared by Mr. Lawrence. I had a

6   couple of matters that I wondered if the Court would

7   consider deleting from the probation report. I

8   don't know if the Court has the report here, or?

9   THE COURT: Yes, I do.

10 MS. WITTMAN: The notes that I took, and

11 there's really just a couple matters, one of those

12 was on page ten. The probation officer, apparently

13 based on a review of the D.A.'s file, goes through a

14 pretty lengthy recitation of the issue of identity,

15 Mr. Healy, purchase of a vehicle, provides

16 documentation, specific information about the

17 purchase of that vehicle, why that probation officer

18 believes that to have been a fraudulent transaction.

19 I don't know what that information, although the

20 probation officer sets it forth as fact, I don't

21 know where he got the information or what place it

22 has in this probation report. It has nothing to do

23 with the crimes for which my client has been

24 convicted. It may be appropriate in some future

25 probation report. But he states a number of facts

1   as conclusions which are -- they're just not

2   relevant at all to this probation report.

3   THE COURT: Go ahead. Anything else?

4   MS. WITTMAN: The other matter that I'm sure

5   the Court won't make this correction, but at page

6   12, and I believe at a couple of other points in the

7   report, I appreciate that the conclusion that was

8   reached by the jury was that my client must

9   necessarily have been the person who said to shoot

10   the bitch in the head, referring to Miss Leisch,

11   however, if the Court reads the way the probation

12   officer characterizes that, he actually sort of

13   correctly characters it and says there was no

14   testimony at trial where anybody said it was

15   Mr. Healy, at the time Mr. Healy. There was no

16   testimony at trial where anybody said that he's the

17   person who uttered those words, however, he's the

18   guy who uttered the words, and that appears two or

19   three times throughout the report. And so I do

20   object to that characterization because although

21   that conclusion could be drawn, it mis -- Well

22   actually it accurately states it, there was no such

23   testimony, so I would ask that that be omitted.

24   Additionally, I appreciate the fact that I'm

25   sure the entire New Hartford Police Department has

an opinion about the sentence and I'm sure it is not

favorable, however, in the section of the probation

report regarding the arresting officer's comment, it

initially refers to the comments of, I guess it's

Sergeant Inserra, who, in fact, was the arresting

officer, and I think that's fair as far as the

probation report is concerned. However, there are

then pages and pages and pages of interviews, I

don't know whether it was personal interviews or

over the phone or what, but information gathered

from I believe how six separate members of the New

Hartford Police Department feel about my client and

what their thoughts are as far as sentencing is

concerned. And I know that it sounds awfully cold

of me to make this argument, but it's a legal one as

opposed to an emotional one. Just as I argued that

Chief Philo is not, I don't know, technically falls

under the definition of a victim, although the Court

allowed him to speak, I also don't think that the

members of the New Hartford Police Department,

although they have an opinion, I don't believe that

they're -- each individual's personal opinion on

this subject is appropriate for the probation

report, and they don't, they don't fall under the

definition of a victim whose statement should be

1   included, although emotionally they fall under the

2   common sense definition. And as far as an arresting

3   officer, I mean there can't be six arresting

4   officers, there's one officer who's interviewed. I

5   may have missed something, but he certainly did not

6   testify at trial and I don't know if he was even

7   involved in the investigation, he's just interviewed

8   for his thoughts. I would ask the Court to omit all

9   of the other officers' feelings, with the exception

10 of the arresting officer's commentary, which is

11 typically included in the probation report.

12   My notes also, when I reference page ten

13 regarding the information about John T. Healy,

14 that's also at 18 and 19, my same objection. So I

15 don't know if the Court wants to --

16   THE COURT: Your objections are noted for the

17 record. I am not, at this point, going to delete

18 anything that's contained in the presentence report.

19   MS. WITTMAN: Okay. Thank you, your Honor.

20   And with respect to any further statement, I

21 would be very brief. I'm sure no one in the room is

22 really interested in what I have to -- what I'm

23 thinking or what I have to say anyway. I just

24 wanted it to be clear because the family and the

25 public at large may not be aware of the fact that --

1   I think they look at it and they say, you know, this

2   guy wanted to be a pain in the neck right to the

3   end, he insisted on having a trial, he insisted on

4   doing this; there was never any offer for my client

5   to consider, there was -- essentially our hand was

6   forced into having to go to trial, with the

7   exception of saying let me plead guilty to the

8   entire 19 or 20-count indictment. So, a trial was

9   inevitable, and although we had raised many, many

10   issues prior to trial, which are actually the

11   ordinary course of business on a case, both my

12   client and myself, although we had to go to trial,

13   wanted to be as accommodating as we could be to the

14   People as far as stipulating to what we could, tried

15   to do what we could so that the testimony that the

16   family was forced to hear would be as, I won't say

17   the least upsetting as possible, it was going to be

18   upsetting, but we certainly tried to streamline the

19   process.

20   So, I know the Court -- I mean there was no

21   question after conviction that the Court was going

22   to impose the maximum sentence, however, I would ask

23   the Court -- Having researched the case law on the

24   issue of consecutive versus concurrent, my reading

25   of the cases seems to be that all of the robbery

1   counts must necessarily run concurrently and it

2   also, the case law also seems to be very clear that

3   where there's a felony murder count, that the

4   underlying felony must run concurrently with the

5   felony murder charge. So there's no question in my

6   mind that the Court will be imposing the maximum

7   sentence, however I would ask the Court to impose

8   that sentence in accordance with the law, which, I

9   believe, would be a 25-to-life sentence.

10   Thank you.

11   THE COURT: Mr. Healy, anything that you want

12 to say to me before I impose sentence?

13   MR. HEALY: Yes, I would like -- yes.

14   THE COURT: Okay, you can stand up.

15   MR. HEALY: I would like to speak to the

16 family, if possible, Philo.

17   THE COURT: Do you want him to go -- Why don't

18 you go over to the microphone.

19   MR. HEALY: All right.

20   THE COURT: Try to get as close to the

21 microphone as you can.

22   MR. HEALY: All right.

23   I loathe standing before you today, knowing

24 that I'm expected to sum up the whole impact of

25 events of February 27th, 2006, in a single

1 statement, but I must say that it can't be done.

2 But what I'll try to do today is clear up the

3 misunderstandings and false accusations that's been

4 circulating unchecked for the last 14 months. I

5 will challenge you, Mr. Dwyer, as the decision

6 maker, to be responsible for fairness and to have

7 patience with me today, as these matters must be

8 addressed uninterrupted.

9   First I would like to say that there is no

10 Robert Ward or Marion Pegese within these events as

11 the People claim. They are not participants of the

12 events of February 27th, 2006. It's just a matter

13 of plain guilt by association, and the husband and

14 wife fabrication team of the Shkane. But I won't

15 comment on that further.

16   I'm here today to let the Corr family know that

17 in no way do I condone Richardson's actions, and

18 also I do not in any way feel responsible for the

19 death of Officer Corr. And I also want to let the

20 family know that the explanation that was given by

21 Kurt in his closing summation was a hundred percent

22 false, as far as Kurt stating that Richardson was

23 waiting in the bushes for me when Officer Corr was

24 killed and give the impression that I was like

25 ordering the murder. No, that was false. He was

```
 1        going his way and I was going my way.  Kurt also
 2        said in his summation that no apologies would be
 3        accepted by the family, so today no apology will be
 4        given by me.  And I know that you all came here
 5        today looking to get blood, sweat and tears out of
 6        me, so if it's blood that you're looking for, it's
 7        blood that I don't have to give, and if it's sweat
 8        that you're looking for, it's sweat that I do not
 9        have to give, and if it's tears that you're looking
10        for, know that I'll choose death before I shed a
11        tear.
12            Today it's about three individuals being held
13        accountable for their actions on February 27th,
14        2006, for the death of Officer Corr.  These
15        individuals are Walter Richardson, Toussaint Martin
16        and Raymond Philo.  As we all know, Walter
17        Richardson was held accountable for his actions when
18        he was massacred on March the 1st.  Today the Court
19        will hold me accountable for my actions, and I
20        wholeheartedly welcome it.  When I heard that
21        Raymond Philo was going to address the Court, I
22        prayed that he would take this opportunity to accept
23        responsibility for his actions for not teaching
24        Officer Corr the basics of policing and how to
25        apprehend a armed felon and how to respond to an
```

1   armed robbery. So, Philo, promise the Corr family

2   that you will better prepare your officers so this

3   will not happen again.

4   I hope that that's understood, so now let me

5   give you understanding of myself, so this way nobody

6   will leave this courtroom today with any

7   misconceptions about this.

8   For one, I'm a principled man and I was taught

9   that principled men are born with identifiable

10   characteristics, meaning true men of principles are

11   not born, but -- are born and not made. Principled

12   men do not fold or run when faced with difficulties,

13   we analyze and determine the best course of action.

14   We understand that the actions we choose has

15   consequences, and I do, I understand that.

16   Therefore, before we act, we first settle within our

17   hearts and minds that we can handle the

18   consequences, whether it be beneficial or

19   detrimental to ourselves and the lives of those that

20   we risk our life and freedom for.

21   As a man I'll walk out of this courtroom with

22   my head up, knowing that I'm going to prison forever

23   for a crime that you and I know that I knowingly

24   never committed. All I can do is stand tall. But

25   most of all I'll never entertain the thought of

giving up because life and all its ups and downs means nothing unless you accept all the challenges in your life in order to receive that which is destined to you.

I have been the target of a relentless attack. My name has been besmirched, my integrity has been impugned and my character has been assassinated. Never have so many lies been told in a criminal matter. Although the jury has reached its verdict unanimously, I have every intention of continuing my quest to bring the full truth of this matter to the surface because now I should say that I am not only innocent of the charges of second degree murder pertaining to Officer Corr, I have never committed a violent crime in my life. Though crimes, never violence. I have never killed and I have never spilled blood.

I sometimes wonder how people wrong their souls to say all these terrible things about someone they do not know. You best believe that I am not unhappy and I am not tormented. And God would not allow me to be tormented, okay. I live with no secrets. So if you want to persecute me, I guess fine, you know, it's the same type of people that persecuted Jesus. It's the same government that persecuted Martin

1   Luther King. This is the government that allowed

2   blacks to be enslaved. This is the same government

3   that allowed my ancestors to be raped. This is

4   nothing new.

5   Most likely my sentence today will be

6   tantamount to a death sentence. But my father once

7   told me it doesn't matter where a man dies, as long

8   as he dies as man. I'll do that standing up as a

9   man and accepting the consequences of the illicit

10 acts, which are the reasons behind the death

11 sentence that I will definitely receive today, but

12 it is definitely not the end of the world.

13 There is three realities to this life:

14 freedom, prison and death. And the odds are

15 negatively stacked against all of the participants

16 of this life, but this is something we know and

17 accept before we get involved in this life. I

18 pushed so hard so that the people that I care about

19 and love wouldn't have to follow in my footsteps and

20 experience all of the struggles and hardships I did.

21 Sometimes it's accomplished and sometimes it isn't.

22 Whether it is or isn't, I'm more than willing to

23 accept the hand that's dealt to me, simply because I

24 do not live a lie. I honestly have no faith for

25 justice, but then this is the judicial, or should I

1 say political system.

2   I have come to terms with the lifestyle I chose

3 years ago. I take responsibility for my actions and

4 the choices that I made. I am not going to blame

5 the system, the environment, and no one else. I

6 blame myself. But I don't accept everything that's

7 happened to me, especially this unjust murder

8 conviction. I did anticipate a verdict. So I'll

9 trust in Allah to punish me, give me justice, pardon

10 me.

11   But throughout everything all is as well as

12 can be expected under these circumstances. You

13 spared no expenses to eliminate me. But I remain

14 undaunted and resolute in my stance. Head up and

15 chest out. I've been in solitary confinement for 14

16 months, a long time, and I'm so glad that it's

17 finally ended. And I've been tortured immensely.

18 That's what it's supposed to do. I'm placed in a

19 hole, I'm in solitary confinement. But I guess you

20 all agree and you tell me I'll remain indefinitely.

21 But it only strengthens my resolve. You're

22 saying -- Oneida County do not shape me or mold me,

23 so you cannot control me.

24   This is what I say: I will not wish this to a

25 dog or to a snake or to the most low and unfortunate

creatures of this earth. I would not wish this on
any of them and I have suffered things I am not
guilty of. But my conviction is I am suffering for
things that I am guilty of. I truly believe I am
suffering because I am different, and indeed I am
different. I am suffering because I am black, and
indeed I am black. I am suffering more for my
family than myself, but I am so convinced to be
right in this situation that if you could execute me
two times and if I could be reborn two more times, I
would live again and to do what I have already done.

I have finished.

THE COURT: Thank you, Mr. Davis, for making
that statement. And I am glad that you made it
because if anyone had any doubt in their minds that
there was any self-worth within your body, you made
sure that they fully understand just who you are and
what you're about. You are a coward, and you
remember that for the rest of your life.

MR. HEALY: I will.

THE COURT: You are incapable of standing up
and facing the truth. You will see the truth
through your own eyes, through your own lies, from
now 'til the day you die. You should have been able
to witness how much pain and suffering you have

1 caused for this family, for the New Hartford Police

2 Department, and for this whole community, but you're

3 not capable of even doing that. You cannot even

4 realize the amount of pain, the amount of

5 devastation that you have caused this entire

6 community, and so now I have one purpose with my

7 sentence: As long as this family suffers, and that

8 includes the grandparents, the parents, the wife,

9 the aunts and uncles, the children, as long as they

10 suffer, as long as every member of the New Hartford

11 Police Department suffers, that's how long I want

12 you punished. For the rest of your natural life. I

13 will do everything in my power to keep you behind

14 bars, as you described, like an animal. Because

15 that's how you act and that's how you deserve to be

16 treated. Everything I can do I will do to make sure

17 you are never, ever released again. And you richly

18 deserve it, especially after the statements you just

19 made. So, thank you.

20 MR. HEALY: You're welcome.

21 THE COURT: It will be the sentence of this

22 Court, as to the defendant's conviction for murder

23 in the second degree, that he will receive the

24 maximum sentence, that is 25 years to life in

25 prison. And I want to state for the record right

1   now that I may not be here in 25 years, I may be

2   dead myself, and if that, in fact, does happen, I

3   want the Department of Parole to know, and the

4   Department of Corrections, that under no

5   circumstances should you ever be released from

6   confinement in a state prison facility. There would

7   be no excuses, no exceptions for you to be released.

8   As to counts three, six, nine, twelve, fifteen

9   and eighteen, where you were convicted of robbery in

10   the first degree, that being armed with a deadly

11   weapon, the Court will impose the maximum sentence,

12   twenty-five years in state prison, on each of those

13   convictions, with five years of post-release

14   supervision as to each.

15   As to counts four, seven, ten, thirteen,

16   sixteen and nineteen, where you were convicted of

17   six counts of robbery in the second degree, that

18   being aided by another person that was actually

19   present, the Court will also impose the maximum

20   sentence of fifteen years in state prison, with five

21   years of post-release supervision.

22   As to counts two, five, eight, eleven, fourteen

23   and seventeen, where you were convicted of six

24   counts of robbery in the first degree, that being

25   for causing serious physical injury to Police

1   Officer Joseph Corr, the Court will also impose a

2   maximum sentence, twenty-five years in state prison,

3   with five years of post-release supervision.

4   I do not agree with all of the rules and

5   regulations concerning concurrent and consecutive

6   sentences that are currently in the New York State

7   Penal Law. And there is ample case law that finds

8   gray areas in many of these statutes. I do not feel

9   that a person should be sentenced to the same

10   sentence whether there's one person in the store or

11   whether there's six people in the store. In my

12   estimation, every one of those six individuals in

13   that Lennon's Jewelry Store on the night of this

14   robbery were separately robbed, threatened, and

15   harassed. And so I am going to order that all of

16   those robbery in the first degree sentences be

17   imposed consecutively. That would be for a total of

18   150 years. And I will freely admit -- I will freely

19   admit that I am not sure, I have great doubts as to

20   whether an Appellate Court will ever approve of this

21   decision, but if anybody deserves it, Mr. Martin, it

22   is -- or Mr. Davis, it is you.

23   I am also going to order, based on the case of

24   People versus *Ramirez*, cited at *89 NY2d 444*, that

25   the six counts of robbery in the first degree, those

1   being under counts two, five, eight, eleven,

2   fourteen and seventeen, I am also going to order

3   that those six counts be served consecutively to the

4   murder conviction and to the other robbery

5   convictions. On the basis of the reasoning of that

6   Court of Appeals case, I feel that the original two

7   robberies were of -- that you had left the store,

8   and that by going to the Byrne Dairy and causing

9   serious physical injury, which resulted in death to

10   Officer Corr, that was at a separate time and

11   changed it from a single transaction to a

12   transaction where you can receive consecutive

13   sentences. The case itself states, "Even if the

14   statutory elements of multiple offenses overlap,

15   sentences may be imposed to run consecutively when

16   multiple offenses are committed through separate and

17   distinct acts, though they are part of a single

18   transaction." It is the Court's determination that

19   when you got into the get-away car and then you went

20   to the Byrne Dairy in Kirkland where the crash

21   occurred and then the serious physical injury was

22   caused to Officer Corr resulting in his death, that

23   that was a separate and distinct act, which makes it

24   separate and apart from the robberies that were

25   completed in the jewelry store. So I do have

```
 1       confidence that the Appellate Courts will uphold at

 2       least this part of the sentence, and I will order

 3       that those six counts of robbery in the first

 4       degree, based on the theory of causing serious

 5       physical injury, be served consecutively to that of

 6       the murder and that of the robbery in the first

 7       degree and the second degree.

 8              In addition to that, the Court has to impose a

 9       $270.00 surcharge, a $50.00 DNA surcharge.

10              Again, at the end of this I want to make it

11       clear to the Department of Parole and the Department

12       of Corrections that, in my estimation, this man

13       should never, ever be released from custody as long

14       as he lives.

15              Mr. Davis, or Mr. Martin, or Mr. Healy, by

16       whichever you want to go by, you have a right to

17       appeal this judgment of conviction. You do that by

18       filing a notice of appeal with the clerk of this

19       court. I want to warn you and your attorney that if

20       you don't file that notice of appeal within 30 days

21       of today's date, you could waive or give up your

22       right to appeal this conviction.

23              Take him out of the courtroom before anybody

24       else leaves.

25                     (End of proceedings)
```

1

2

3

4

5

6   REPORTER'S CERTIFICATE

7

8

9   I, Deborah A. Rose, an official reporter of the State of

10   New York, do hereby certify that I recorded stenographically

11   the foregoing proceeding, and that the preceding is a true

12   and correct transcript of my stenographic minutes to the best

13   of my knowledge and ability.

14

15   Dated: July 27, 2007.

16

17   _____

18   Deborah A. Rose
                        Sr. Court Reporter

19

20

21

22

23

24

25

Appendix

Habeas Corpus Memorandum-Decision, Hon. Norman A. Mordue, November 30, 2015

UNITED STATES DISTRICT COURT
NORTHERN DISTRICT OF NEW YORK
◆◇

MARION PEGESE,

                              Petitioner,

              -v-   **5:09-CR-390-1 (NAM)**
                                                     5:14-CV-218 (NAM)
UNITED STATES OF AMERICA,

                              Respondent.

◆◇

APPEARANCES:

Office of J. Scott Porter
J. Scott Porter, Esq., of counsel
78 Cayuga Street
Seneca Falls, New York 13148
Attorney for Petitioner

Hon. Richard S. Hartunian, United States Attorney
Richard Southwick, Esq., Assistant United States Attorney
100 South Clinton Street
Syracuse, New York 13261
Attorney for Respondent

Hon. Norman A. Mordue, Senior U.S. District Judge:

MEMORANDUM-DECISION AND ORDER

INTRODUCTION

On November 5, 2010, a jury convicted petitioner Marion Pegese ("Pegese") and

codefendants Robert Ward and Toussaint Davis on all counts of a three-count indictment

charging conspiracy to interfere with interstate commerce by robbery, in violation of the Hobbs

Act, 18 U.S.C. § 1951(a); interference with interstate commerce by robbery, in violation of 18

U.S.C. §§ 1951(a) and 2; and murder as a result of possession and discharge of a firearm in

furtherance of a crime of violence, in violation of 18 U.S.C. § 924(c)(1) and (j)(1), and pursuant to *Pinkerton v. United States*, 328 U.S. 640 (1946). The Court sentenced each defendant to

concurrent terms of 240 months' imprisonment on the two robbery counts and life imprisonment

on the murder count. The Second Circuit affirmed the conviction and sentence, *United States v.*

Ward (Pegese), 505 F.App'x 18 (2d Cir. 2012), and the Supreme Court denied certiorari. *Pegese*

v. United States, 133 S.Ct. 1512 (2013).

In this *habeas corpus* proceeding under 28 U.S.C. § 2255 ("section 2255") (Dkt. Nos. 250,

255),[1] Pegese, who is represented by counsel, claims he received ineffective assistance of trial

counsel. In a separate motion (Dkt. No. 269), he requests investigative services and discovery to

support his section 2255 motion. As set forth below, the Court denies the motions, dismisses the

proceeding, and denies a certificate of appealability.

FACTUAL BACKGROUND

This Court set forth an exhaustive review of the trial evidence in its decision (Dkt. No.

216) denying defendants' motions for judgments of acquittal and new trials pursuant to Rules 29

and 33 of the Federal Rules of Criminal Procedure. The Court refers the reader thereto and does

not review the evidence in detail herein. The Second Circuit's brief summary of the factual

background of the crimes of conviction is as follows:

> On August 26, 2005, at 3:45 p.m., the three defendants and another man, Eric
> Lane, entered Ballew Jewelers in Freehold, New Jersey, forced the store's
> employees into a back room at gunpoint, bound their hands and feet, and
> robbed the store of approximately $1.8 million dollars worth of diamonds and
> Rolex watches. Nearly six months later, in late February, 2006, the defendants
> conducted Internet research on jewelry stores in Utica, New York and took a
> daylong trip from Philadelphia, Pennsylvania to New Hartford, a suburb of
> Utica. On February 27, 2006, the defendants again traveled to New Hartford,
> this time accompanied by a fourth man, Walter Richardson ("Richardson").

---

[1] All citations to the docket herein refer to the criminal case, 5:09-CR-390(1).

-2-

While en route to New Hartford, the four men, traveling in two vehicles, pulled into a gas station and asked two other customers, Louis and Julie Shkane, for directions to Commercial Drive, some four miles away. Within about a half hour, a number of masked men entered Lennon's Jewelers, on Commercial Drive, and robbed it at gunpoint. At trial, Gary Lennon ("Lennon"), one of the store owners, testified to the presence of at least three men, but was unsure of the exact number. Lennon also testified that one of the men held a gun a few feet from his head and handcuffed his left wrist to his right ankle. Leslie Liesch ("Liesch"), another employee, testified that she alerted the police by phone, after which two of the robbers discovered her lying on the floor, and stood over her while one pointed a gun at her head and the other repeatedly yelled, "shoot the bitch in the head." At this time, Liesch heard someone else shout, "the cops are here," and the robbers fled the store in two separate vehicles, absconding with nearly a million dollars worth of merchandise.

Two officers responding to the robbery, Joseph Corr and Ronald Fontaine, pursued one of these vehicles until it crashed, at a high speed, into a gasoline pump. Davis and Richardson then exited the vehicle and fled on foot. Officer Fontaine testified at trial that as he pursued and arrested Davis, Officer Corr was shot and killed by Richardson. Evading arrest, Richardson then hijacked a truck at gunpoint and fled to Chester, Pennsylvania. Richardson was killed the next morning in a firefight with law enforcement agents who had tracked him to that location and attempted to arrest him.

Ward and Pegese, who fled from the robbery in a separate vehicle [a Cadillac], were arrested later in 2006. While incarcerated pending trial, Ward and Pegese approached a fellow inmate, David Carroway ("Carroway"), and discussed the Lennon robbery with him. Carroway later approached law enforcement agents with the details of these conversations.

At trial, the government presented the testimony of fifty-six witnesses and introduced more than 150 exhibits into evidence. Among the witnesses were Carroway, and Louis and Julie Shkane. On November 5, 2010, the jury returned a verdict finding the defendants guilty on all counts.

Id., 505 F.App'x at 21-22. Relevant to the issues on the instant motion, the evidence shows that on the night of February 27, 2006, after fleeing from Lennon's Jewelers in the Cadillac, Pegese and Ward drove to the Genesee Grande Hotel in Syracuse, checked in at around 10 p.m. using a falsified driver's license bearing Tarik Hooks' name and Pegese's photograph, went out for pizza,

-3-

checked out of the hotel at 3:05 a.m., and drove to Philadelphia.

APPLICABLE LAW

The Sixth Amendment right to counsel is "the right to the effective assistance of counsel." *McMann v. Richardson*, 397 U.S. 759, 771, n.14 (1970). To establish a claim of ineffective assistance of counsel supporting a *habeas corpus* petition, a petitioner must show (1) that counsel's performance was deficient, and (2) that the deficiency prejudiced the defense. *See Strickland v. Washington*, 466 U.S. 668, 687 (1984). To show deficient performance, a petitioner must show that counsel's performance fell below an objective standard of reasonableness. *Id.* at 688. To show prejudice, a petitioner must show a reasonable probability that, but for counsel's mistakes, the outcome of the trial would have been different. *Id.* at 694. A "reasonable probability" is one that "undermine[s] confidence in the outcome." *Id.* Thus, when assessing prejudice, a court "must consider the totality of the evidence" before the jury. *Id.* at 695. The court's review "must be highly deferential" and "indulge a strong presumption" that counsel's action might be considered sound trial strategy. *Id.* at 689. The petitioner has the burden of proof by a preponderance of the evidence. *See Triana v. United States*, 205 F.3d 36, 40 (2d Cir. 2000).

Under section 2255, "[u]nless the motion and the files and records of the case conclusively show that the [petitioner] is entitled to no relief, the court shall ... grant a prompt hearing thereon, determine the issues and make findings of fact and conclusions of law with respect thereto." 28 U.S.C. § 2255(b). "To warrant a hearing on an ineffective assistance of counsel claim, the [petitioner] need establish only that he has a plausible claim of ineffective assistance of counsel, not that he will necessarily succeed on the claim." *Puglisi v. United States*, 586 F.3d 209, 213 (2d Cir. 2009) (citations and quotation marks omitted). If it "plainly appears

-4-

from the motion, any attached exhibits, and the record of prior proceedings that the moving party

is not entitled to relief, the judge must dismiss the motion." *Id.*

Under Rule 6(a) of the Rules Governing Section 2255 Proceedings for the United States

District Courts, "[a] judge may, for good cause, authorize a party to conduct discovery under the

Federal Rules of Criminal Procedure or Civil Procedure, or in accordance with the practices and

principles of law." A petitioner has shown good cause "where specific allegations before the

court show reason to believe that the petitioner may, if the facts are fully developed, be able to

demonstrate that he is ... entitled to relief." *Bracy v. Gramley*, 520 U.S. 899, 908-09 (1997).

THE MOTION

In arguing that he received ineffective assistance of counsel, Pegese contends that his trial

counsel, Jeffrey DeRoberts, Esq., failed to investigate and obtain evidence from alibi witnesses

who would have established that he was in Philadelphia at the time of the Lennon's Jewelers

robbery.[2] Pegese submits affidavits from two purported alibi witnesses, Larry and Brandon

Guilford. In an affidavit sworn on January 16, 2014, Larry Guilford states that he lives at 51-49

Parrish Street, Philadelphia, Pennsylvania. He continues:

> I am acquainted with Mr. Marian Pegese and have known him for many years.
> Mr. Pegese is presently incarcerated at East Jersey State Prison, Rahway, NJ.
> He has been sentenced on two Robberies, one in New Jersey and one in New
> York State.
>
> In February 2006 Marian Pegese explained to me that he had a problem in
> New Jersey having to do with a Jewelry Store robbery and wanted to stay
> away from everyone and keep out of trouble. At the same time I had a bout
> with diabetes and was laid up. I decided to invite Mr. Pegese to stay at my
> house. He moved in on February 19, 2006 and remained until the second week
> of March 2006. Mr. Pegese would help me shop, pick up my step son, Aaron,

---

[2] Pegese does not deny that he participated in the Ballew Jewelers robbery.

-5-

from school and overall be a help to me. My little brother, Brandon, was shot in the street some time ago in Philadelphia. As a result, my brother had a portion of his leg amputated. Mr. Pegese would carry Brandon up and down the stairs during the time period that Marian Pegese stayed with us. When Marian left, the second week of March, he left with his sister.

Brandon Guilford signed an affidavit on February 21, 2014, stating that he is acquainted with Pegese. He writes:

In September 2005, I had my leg amputated and stayed with my brother, Larry Guilford, at 51-49 Parrish St., Philadelphia, Pa. I had another operation at the end of January 2006, so, I stayed with my brother for several months after that.

Mr. Marian Pegese also stayed with us. He would help me every day, sometimes carrying me up and down the stairs. I know he lived there with us from the second week of February until the second week of March 2006. Besides helping me on a daily basis, he did a lot for my brother, Larry. Pegese would go shopping and even helped my brother by picking up his step-son, Aaron, from school.

In his own declaration, Pegese states that he gave Attorney DeRoberts the names of the Guilfords as well as three other potential alibi witnesses – Anita Hampton, Sandra Dickerson, and Treva Harris – but that Attorney DeRoberts did not interview or obtain statements from them. Pegese does not present affidavits from Hampton, Dickerson, or Harris or describe what evidence they would have given.

In addition, Pegese argues that counsel failed to investigate and obtain evidence that would have undermined the identification evidence at trial and established that it was Tony Grooms, not Pegese, who was involved in the Lennon's Jewelers robbery.[3] Pegese avers that counsel should have obtained a statement from codefendant Toussaint Davis' brother Yousef

---

[3] Codefendant Toussaint Davis took the stand at trial, and testified that it was Grooms, not Pegese, who was involved in the Lennon's Jewelers robbery.

-6-

Davis, who would have testified to receiving a telephone call from Tony Grooms in which Grooms implicated himself in the Lennon's Jewelers robbery. Pegese further states that the cell phone attributed to him contained text messages from Tony Grooms' daughter Lateefah Davis and other people connected to Grooms. Further, he asserts, trial counsel should have shown the jury the surveillance video recorded the night of February 27, 2006 at the pizzeria near the Genesee Grande Hotel in Syracuse. According to Pegese, the video depicted a black male more closely resembling Grooms than Pegese. Finally, Pegese argues that trial counsel failed to secure forensic evidence from the Cadillac in which Pegese and Ward fled the scene of the Lennon's Jewelers robbery.

In a separate motion, Pegese asks the Court to assign an investigator to interview and obtain statements from Anita Hampton, Sandra Dickerson, and Treva Harris; obtain a photograph of Tony Grooms for comparison with the pizzeria's surveillance video; and obtain fingerprint and other forensic evidence from the Cadillac.

In opposition, the Government submits an affidavit from Attorney DeRoberts.[4] He states that in preparing for trial, he met with Pegese on numerous occasions. He "retained a highly experienced former Assistant U.S. Attorney, Kevin McCormack, Esq . as associate counsel, and a veteran former Onondaga County Probation Officer, Mary Richardson, to assist [him] in reviewing the vast discovery materials and investigate any potential defenses that might be raised." They thoroughly reviewed approximately 40,000 pages of discovery material provided by the Government. Attorney DeRoberts adds:

---

[4] Pegese voluntarily signed a Waiver and Authorization waiving any attorney-client privilege as to Attorney DeRoberts (Dkt. No. 268).

-7-

As part of my efforts to find weaknesses in the prosecution's case, approximately one month prior to the trial, my investigator, Mary Richardson, and I traveled to Philadelphia to interview witnesses who might be of assistance to our defense. Mr. Pegese was aware that we were going to Philadelphia and had provided us with a list of names of individuals we should contact, including Tarik Hooks, Cheryl Brown, Malika Wilson, Jay Fitzgerald, and Yousef Davis. We were assisted by Mr. Pegese's brother in locating these people. Despite our efforts, most of these individuals provided no useful information or refused to speak with us. Contrary to his assertion, at no time did Mr. Pegese mention or request that I contact any persons by the names of Larry Guilford, Brandon Guilford, Anita Hampton, or Sandra Dickerson nor did their names surface in our examination of all the investigative reports. Mr. Pegese's assertion that he told me these witnesses could verify that he was in Philadelphia at the time of the Lennon's robbery is simply untrue. I have spoken with my investigator, Mary Richardson, and she confirms that we were never told about these individuals.

Attorney DeRoberts' affidavit also describes his investigation concerning the cell phone linked to Pegese. He found no evidence linking the cell phone number to Grooms. Regarding the surveillance video from the pizzeria, he points out that the facial features and heights of the males present are not readily discernable.[5] He explains that he made a strategic decision not to introduce the video "because it may have hurt our defense if the jury believed it appeared to show Mr. Pegese to be in the pizzeria." He adds: "In my judgment, the video simply does not support Mr. Pegese's present claim that it pointed to Grooms, not defendant[.]" Counsel also describes his unsuccessful efforts to locate the Cadillac and any reports of forensic testing of the vehicle, and adds that there are no wiretaps of Carroway or audible recordings from the body wire Carroway wore during conversations with Pegese. The Government confirms that there is no forensic evidence from the Cadillac and no audible recordings involving Carroway and Pegese.

DISCUSSION

---

[5] Having reviewed the surveillance video, the Court agrees that it does not depict facial features and heights with sufficient clarity to assist the jury in determining the identities of the people present.

-8-

The record of the pretrial, trial, and post-trial proceedings shows that, in the course of representing Pegese, Attorney DeRoberts conducted a thorough investigation, including retaining an associate attorney and an investigator. He moved to suppress identification evidence and participated in hearings under *United States v. Wade*, 388 U.S. 218 (1967), and *Massiah v. United States*, 377 U.S. 201 (1964). At trial, he conducted extensive cross-examination of Government witnesses. In an effort to cast doubt on the Government's contention that the cell phone attributed to Pegese was in his possession at the time of the Lennon's Jewelers robbery on February 27, 2006, Attorney DeRoberts called as a defense witness a New York State Police Senior Investigator, Michael Hulihan, who established that as of March 21, 2006, the cell phone was in the possession of Lateefah Davis in Utah.[6] In his closing statement, Attorney DeRoberts argued that, immediately after the Lennon's Jewelers robbery and Officer Corr's murder, the police "targeted" Pegese, although they lacked evidence linking him to the crimes. Counsel vigorously challenged the identification testimony, Carroway's testimony about Pegese's admissions, and the cell phone evidence. His closing clearly articulated the defense position that Pegese's participation in the Lennon's Jewelers robbery had not been proven beyond a reasonable doubt. After the verdict, Attorney DeRoberts filed a post-trial motion for a judgment of acquittal or a new trial, and, with regard to the sentencing, challenged the Guidelines calculation and argued against a life sentence for Pegese. Attorney DeRoberts' representation met an objective standard

---

[6] In his affidavit in opposition to this motion, Attorney DeRoberts states that discovery materials revealed that three weeks after the Lennon's Jewelers robbery, a cell phone with the same number as the one attributed to Pegese was recovered by investigators in Salt Lake City, Utah in the possession of Lateefah Davis, "a young Philadelphia woman," and that she reported that she had bought it from a man in Philadelphia. Attorney DeRoberts states: "Despite our investigative efforts, no evidence or witnesses were found to support Mr. Pegese's claim that the phone was utilized by Tony Grooms in connection with the robbery."

-9-

of reasonableness.

The Court rejects Pegese's argument that Attorney DeRoberts was ineffective because he failed to investigate, obtain, and present testimony and evidence that would have helped raise a reasonable doubt about his identity as a participant in the Lennon's Jewelers's robbery. As noted, in addition to his own declaration, Pegese relies on the affidavits of Larry and Brandon Guilford. The Guilfords, who allegedly were sufficiently close friends of Pegese to invite him to live with them for a few weeks, gave no explanation for their failure to come forward at any time since his arraignment in this case in July 2009. Nor does Pegese give any explanation for the fact that throughout the pretrial, trial, and sentencing proceedings, he did nothing about his attorney's failure to call these two witnesses, despite the fact that their testimony, if believed by the jury, would have exculpated him completely from the Lennon's Jewelers robbery and Officer Corr's murder.[7] Neither the Guilford affidavits nor Pegese's conclusory allegations on this motion regarding the other alleged alibi witnesses raise a plausible challenge to the adequacy of Attorney DeRoberts' investigation and defense, particularly in view of the strong prosecution evidence against Pegese, including his inculpatory admissions to David Carroway and Cheryl Brown, the evidence that he checked in to the Genesee Grande Hotel in Syracuse on the night of February 27, 2006, and the cell phone evidence. The surveillance video does not support Pegese's claim that it was Grooms, not Pegese, in the pizzeria, and counsel's decision not to introduce the video at trial constituted sound strategy. There was no available forensic evidence from the Cadillac or audible recordings of Pegese's conversations with Carraway. Moreover, Attorney DeRoberts' affidavit

---

[7] Indeed, Pegese did not refer to an alibi or mention the Guilfords, Sandra Dickerson, Anita Hampton, or Treva Harris in his lengthy allocution at sentencing, at which he repeatedly proclaimed his innocence and attacked the testimony given by Cheryl Brown, the Shkanes, David Carroway, and Cathy Vang, the clerk at the Genesee Grande Hotel.

-10-

on this motion is wholly consistent with the record. Viewed in the context of the entire record,

Pegese's declaration and the Guilfords' affidavits lack credibility and do not support a plausible

claim that Attorney DeRoberts' representation was deficient.

Pegese received a fair trial. He was convicted not through any lapse in his defense but

because the evidence against him was overwhelming. Indeed, in affirming, the Second Circuit

wrote:

> Upon our review of the record, there is no doubt that there was sufficient evidence for the jury to have found all three defendants guilty of Count Three based upon a *Pinkerton* theory of liability, as well as guilty of Counts One and Two. While it is unnecessary to restate in detail the evidence presented at trial, which Judge Mordue thoroughly discussed in his Memorandum and Order dated July 8, 2011, we note that the government's case included cell-phone and site records demonstrating the defendants' communications and their whereabouts; a videotape of one of the robberies; the testimony of informants and cooperating witnesses, including Davis's former girlfriend, who identified the defendants in a videotape of the Ballew robbery; the testimony of Tarik Hooks, a lifelong friend of Pegese whose identity he usurped during the Lennon robbery; testimony by witnesses of the Lennon robbery; and the testimony of Carroway.

505 F.App'x at 23 (footnote omitted).

The Court has considered the totality of the evidence. It plainly appears from the motion,

exhibits, and record of prior proceedings that Pegese cannot show that the representation he

received fell below an objective standard of reasonableness or that he was prejudiced by

counsel's decisions as to how best to defend against the Government's case. To the contrary,

petitioner received a thorough and competent defense and can have sustained no prejudice.

Because the record conclusively shows that Pegese is entitled to no relief, there is no basis for a

hearing. Finally, Pegese's submissions fail to suggest the existence of relevant exculpatory

evidence or otherwise to support a finding that, if the facts were fully developed, he might be able

-11-

to demonstrate that he is entitled to section 2255 relief. Therefore, Pegese has not shown good cause for discovery or investigative services. Pegese is entitled to no relief in this section 2255 proceeding.

CONCLUSION

A certificate of appealability may be issued "only if the applicant has made a substantial showing of the denial of a constitutional right." 28 U.S.C. § 2253(c)(2). Since petitioner has failed to make such a showing herein, the Court declines to issue a certificate of appealability in this matter. *See Hohn v. United States*, 524 U.S. 236, 239-40 (1998).

It is therefore

ORDERED that the motion (Dkt. No. 269) for discovery and investigative services is denied; and it is further

ORDERED that the motion (Dkt. No. 250, 255) for relief under 28 U.S.C. § 2255 is denied and the proceeding (5:14-CV-218) is dismissed; and it is further

ORDERED that a certificate of appealability is denied; and it is further

ORDERED that the Clerk is directed to serve this Memorandum-Decision and Order in accordance with the Local Rules.

IT IS SO ORDERED.

Date: November 30, 2015
       Syracuse, New York

Norman A. Mordue
Senior U.S. District Judge

-12-

Appendix

Online Resources

1. All Power Point presentations by chapter/section

2. All items contained in the printed Appendix

3. Full Transcript of the Felony Hearing for *People v. John T. Healy*, New Hartford Town Court, March 6, 2006

4. Full Transcript (PDF) of the *People v. John Healy* (state prosecution) and associated grand jury indictment.

5. Full Transcript (PDF) of *People v. All Defendants* (federal prosecution) and associated grand jury indictment.

6. Habeas Corpus Memorandum-Decision, The Honorable Norman A. Mordue, November 30, 2015 (PDF)

7. Audio/radio transmissions of February 27, 2006

8. Video footage of key events.

9. Test bank by chapter

10. Link to *The Federalist Papers* from Congress.gov (https://www.congress.gov/resources/display/content/The+Federalist+Papers)

11. Link to Official Site of United States Federal Courts: http://www.uscourts.gov/

12. *Informal Opinion to the City of Mechanicville, New York*, No. 97-13 (March 10, 1997) of the Attorney General of the State of New York

13. New York State Supreme Court, Appellate Division, Fourth Department; Brief for the Appellant, *People v. Toussaint Davis*

14. New York State Supreme Court, Appellate Division, Fourth Department; Brief for the Respondent, *People v. Toussaint Davis*

15. New York State Supreme Court, Appellate Division, Fourth Department; Decision of the Court, *People v. Toussaint Davis*

16. New York State Court of Appeals, Opinion, *People v. Toussaint Davis*

17. United States Court of Appeals for the Second Circuit, Opinion of the Court

18. United States Supreme Court, Opinion denying certiorari

Appendix

References

Brown, J.C., Philo, R.L., Callisto, A., & Smith, P.J. (2016). Command transitions in public administration: A quantitative and qualitative analysis of proactive strategies. *Springer Briefs in Policing, 1*(1), 1–57. doi: 10.1007/978-3-319-27844-5

BusinessDictionary.com. (2016). *Task force*. Retrieved from http://www.businessdictionary.com/definition/task-force.html

Carson, E.A. (2015). *Prisoners 2014*. Bureau of Justice Statistics (September 2015, NCJ 248955). Retrieved from http://www.bjs.gov

Cole, J.D. (1997). *Informal opinion of the attorney general of the State of New York to the City of Mechanicville, New York* (No. 97-13 of March 10, 1997. Retrieved from https://www.ag.ny.gov

Doka, K.J. (1989). Disenfranchised grief: Recognizing hidden sorrow. Lexington, Massachusetts/Toronto: Lexington Books.

Doka, K.J. (2005). Ethics, end-of-life decisions and grief. *Mortality, 10*(1), 83–90, Retrieved from http://web.a.ebscohost.com.

Federal Bureau of Investigation. (2016). Uniform crime report: Crime in United

States 2014. Retrieved from https://ucr.fbi.gov

Federal Bureau of Investigation. (2016). Uniform crime reporting statistics:

About the uniform crime reporting program. Retrieved from

http://www.ucrdatatool.gov/

Florida Statutes Annnotated. (2016). § 775.012, West.

Fuller, J.R. (2014). *Criminal justice: mainstream and crosscurrents* (3rd ed.).

New York: Oxford University Press.

Garner, B.A. (Ed.). (2014). *Black's Law Dictionary* (10th ed.). St. Paul, MD:

Thomson Reuters.

Holmes, O., & White, G. (2009). *The Common Law*. Harvard University Press.

Retrieved from http://www.jstor.org/stable/j.ctt13x0kkk

Kramnick, I. (Ed) (1987). *The Federalist Papers*. London: Penguin Books.

Kristensen, P, Weisaeth, L, & Heir, T. (2012). Bereavement and mental health after

sudden and violent losses: A review. *Psychiatry, 75*(1), 76–97, Retrieved from

http://search.proquest.com

Lindemann, E. (1944). Symptomatology and management of acute grief. *The

American Journal of Psychiatry, 101*(2), 141–148. Retrieved from http://nyu.edu.

Minton, T.D. & Zeng, Z. (2015). *Jail inmates at midyear 2014*. Bureau of Justice

Statistics (June 2015, NCJ 248629). Retrieved from http://www.bjs.gov

National Law Enforcement Officers Memorial (NLEOM). (2016). *The Memorial*.

Retrieved From http://www.nleomf.org/

N.Y. Penal Law. (2016). § 10, McKinneys.

Peak, K. J. & Everett, P.M. (2017). *Introduction to criminal justice: practice and process.* Sage: Thousand Oaks. ISBN-978-1-5063-0592-9

Pegese v. United States of America, Memorandum-Decision & Order of the Honorable Norman A. Mordue, U.S. Dist. Ct. Case 5:09-cr-00390-NAM, Document 278, November 30, 2015

Raadschelders, J.C.N. (1999). A coherent framework for the study of public administration. *Journal of Public Administration, 9*(2), 281–303. Retrieved from http://jpart.oxfordjournals.org/

Roosevelt, T. (1910). *Citizenship in a republic.* Retrieved from http://www.theodore-roosevelt.com/trsorbonnespeech.html

Ross, J.E. (2006). The entrenched position of plea bargaining in United States legal practice. *American Journal of Comparative Law (54)*, 717–732. Retrieved from https://1.next.westlaw.com

Rutledge, D. (2001). Criminal interrogation: law and tactics (4th ed.). Belmont, CA: Thomaon Learning Academic Resources Center.

Schmalleger, F. (2015). *Criminal justice today: An introductory text for the 21st century* (13th ed.). Boston: Pearson. ISBN-13: 978-0-13-346004-9

Smithsonian Institution. (2016). *Smithsonian overview.* Retrieved from https://www.si.edu/About

U.S. Census Bureau. (2016). *Quick facts: Oneida County, New York.* Retrieved August 13, 2016 from http://www.census.gov/quickfacts/table/PST045215/36065

U.S. Const. art. I, § 1

U.S. Const. art. I, § 8, §§ 18

U.S. Const. art. VI, § 2

U.S. Const. amend. X

U.S. Const. Preamble

U.S. Department of Justice, Bureau of Justice Statistics. (2011). *Law enforcement management and administrative statistics, 2007.* Ann Arbor, MI: Inter-university Consortium for Political and Social Research. Retrieved from http://www.icpsr.umich.edu/icpsrweb/ICPSR/studies/31161

U. S. Department of Justice (2016). *Asset forfeiture program.* Retrieved from https://www.justice.gov/afp

U. S. Department of Justice (2015). *U.S. Attorney's Manual: Title 9 – Criminal.* Retrieved from http://www.justice.gov/usam/usam-9-131000-hobbs-act-18-usc-1951

U.S. Department of Justice, Bureau of Justice Statistics. (2014). *Law enforcement.* Retrieved from http://www.bjs.gov/index.cfm?ty=tp&tid=7

U.S. District Court: Northern District of New York. (2015). *Judge Biographies: Honorable Glenn T. Suddaby.* Retrieved from http://www.nynd.uscourts.gov/judge-biographies

U. S. Government Printing Office. (2007). *The Constitution of the United States of America: As Amended, Unratified Amendments, Analytical Index (Document #110-50).* Washington, DC: Publisher.

United States of America v. Marion Pegese, Robert Ward & Toussaint Davis.

(July 16, 2009). Indictment #5:09-cr-00390. Retrieved from: www.pacer.gov.

U.S. v. Ward, 505 Fed.Appx. 18 (2012)

United States Sentencing Commission. (2016). *Mission*. Retrieved from

http://www.ussc.gov/

Glossary

Appeal: … A proceeding undertaken to have a decision reconsidered by a higher court [especially], the submission of a lower court's or agency's decision to a higher court for review and possible reversal (Garner, 2014; Black's Law Dictionary 10th ed., reprinted with permission, Thomson Reuters).

Appellant: A party who appeals a lower court's decision [usually] seeking reversal of that decision (Garner, 2014; Black's Law Dictionary 10th ed., reprinted with permission, Thomson Reuters).

Appellate Division of the Supreme Court: There are four Appellate Divisions of the Supreme Court, one in each of the State's four Judicial Departments. These Courts resolve appeals from judgments or orders of the superior courts of original jurisdiction in civil and criminal cases, and review civil appeals taken from the Appellate Terms and the County Courts acting as appellate courts (NYCourts. gov, 2016).

Appellate Jurisdiction: The power of the court to review and revise a lower court's decision. For example, U.S. Const. art. III, § 2 vests appellate jurisdiction in the Supreme Court, while 28 USCA §§ 1291-1295 grant appellate jurisdiction to lower federal courts of appeals (Garner, 2014; Black's Law Dictionary 10th ed., reprinted with permission, Thomson Reuters). [The same structures/rules apply at the state level as well].

Appellee: A party against whom an appeal is taken and whose role is to respond to that appeal [usually] seeking affirmance of the lower court's decision [also known as Respondent] (Garner, 2014; Black's Law Dictionary 10th ed., reprinted with permission, Thomson Reuters).

Arraignment: The initial step in a criminal prosecution whereby the defendant is brought before the court to hear the charges and to enter a plea (Garner, 2014; Black's Law Dictionary 10th ed., reprinted with permission, Thomson Reuters).

Arrest: 1. A seizure or forcible restraint, [especially] by legal authority. 2. The taking or keeping of a person in custody by legal authority, [especially] in response to a criminal charge; [specifically], the apprehension of someone for the purpose of securing the administration of the law, [especially] of bringing that person before a court (Garner, 2014; Black's Law Dictionary 10th ed., reprinted with permission, Thomson Reuters).

Bench Trial: A trial before a judge without a jury. The judge decides questions of fact as well as questions of law. [Also termed *trial to the bench; nonjury trial; court trial; trial before the court; judge trial*] (Garner, 2014; Black's Law Dictionary 10th ed., reprinted with permission, Thomson Reuters).

Beyond a Reasonable Doubt: [Reasonable doubt]: The doubt that prevents one from being firmly convinced of the defendant's guilt, or the belief that there is a real possibility that the defendant is not guilty. "Beyond a reasonable doubt" is the standard used by a jury to determine whether a criminal defendant is guilty. See Model Penal Code §1.12. In deciding whether guilt has been proved beyond a reasonable doubt, the jury must begin with the presumption that the defendant is innocent. Also termed *rational doubt* (Garner, 2014; Black's Law Dictionary 10th ed., reprinted with permission, Thomson Reuters).

Binding Authority: [also called binding precedent]. A precedent that a court must follow. For example, a lower court is bound by an applicable holding of a higher court in the same jurisdiction. -Also termed authoritative precedent; binding authority (Garner, 2014; Black's Law Dictionary 10th ed., reprinted with permission, Thomson Reuters).

***Brady* Hearing/Material:** Information or evidence that is favorable to a criminal defendant's case and that the prosecution has a duty to disclose. The prosecution's withholding of such information violates the defendant's due-process rights. [From the landmark United States Supreme Court case of *Brady v. Maryland* 373 U.S. 83, 83 S.Ct. 1194 (1963), also known as exculpatory evidence] (Garner, 2014; Black's Law Dictionary 10th ed., reprinted with permission, Thomson Reuters).

Certiorari: An extraordinary writ issued by an appellate court, at its discretion, directing a lower court to deliver the record in the case for review. The writ evolved from one of the prerogative writs of the English Court of Kings Bench, and in the United States it became a general appellate remedy. The US Supreme Court uses certiorari to review most of the cases that it decides to hear. Also termed *writ of certiorari* (Garner, 2014; Black's Law Dictionary 10th ed., reprinted with permission, Thomson Reuters).

Circumstantial Evidence: 1. Evidence based on inference and not on personal knowledge or observation. Also termed indirect evidence; oblique evidence.

2. All evidence that is not given by eyewitness testimony (Garner, 2014; Black's Law Dictionary 10th ed., reprinted with permission, Thomson Reuters).

Command Post: (also known as an incident command post) is "the field location at which the primary tactical-level, on-scene incident command functions are performed (Federal Emergency Management Agency [FEMA], 2008).

Concurrent Jurisdiction: 1. Jurisdiction that might be exercised simultaneously by more than one court over the same subject matter and within the same territory, a litigant having the right to choose the court in which to file the action. 2. Jurisdiction shared by two or more states, [especially] over the physical boundaries (such as rivers or other bodies of water) between them [also termed coordinate jurisdiction; overlapping jurisdiction]. (Garner, 2014; Black's Law Dictionary 10th ed., reprinted with permission, Thomson Reuters).

Coroner: A public official whose duty it is to investigate the causes and circumstances of any death that occurs suddenly, suspiciously, or by only. [See also Medical Examiner] (Garner, 2014; Black's Law Dictionary 10th ed., reprinted with permission, Thomson Reuters).

Custody: The care and control of a thing or person for inspection, preservation, or security (Garner, 2014; Black's Law Dictionary 10th ed., reprinted with permission, Thomson Reuters).

Defense: A defendant's stated reason why the plaintiff or prosecutor has no valid case; [especially] a defendant's answer, denial, or plea [her defense was that she was 25 miles away in the building at the time of the robbery] (Garner, 2014; Black's Law Dictionary 10th ed., reprinted with permission, Thomson Reuters).

Defense Counsel: An attorney hired/appointed to represent a defendant. Typically this individual is a member of a Public Defender's Office, or an assigned attorney, frequently called an assigned counsel. These are typically local members of a Bar Association who are a part of a pool of attorneys available in a rotation to defend accused individuals in criminal matters.

District Attorney: The district attorney, sometimes referred to as the prosecutor, is the representative of the government, the People of the State of New York (or other state). District Attorney's are typically elected by the people of their jurisdiction (usually a county), as is the case in New York State. A public official appointed or elected to represent the state in criminal cases in a particular judicial district; prosecutor [abbreviated DA]-Also termed *public prosecutor; states attorney; prosecuting attorney, United States Attorney* (Garner, 2014; Black's Law Dictionary 10th ed., reprinted with permission, Thomson Reuters).

Exhibit: 1. A document, record, or other tangible object formally introduced as evidence in court. 2. A document attached to and made part of a pleading, motion, contract, or other instrument (Garner, 2014; Black's Law Dictionary 10th ed., reprinted with permission, Thomson Reuters).

Felony Hearing (Preliminary Hearing): a criminal hearing (often conducted by a magistrate) to determine whether there is sufficient evidence to prosecute an accused person; specif., A proceeding before a judge or magistrate held soon after a criminal defendant is taken into custody, usu. on felony charges, the typical prosecution having the burden to establish reasonable cause to believe that the defendant has committed a felony. If sufficient evidence exists, the case will be set for trial or bound over for grand jury review, or information will be filed in the trial court. Also termed preliminary examination; probable cause hearing; bind overhearing; examining trial; felony hearing (Garner, 2014; Black's Law Dictionary 10th ed., reprinted with permission, Thomson Reuters).

Foundation: The basis on which something is supported; [especially] evidence or testimony that establishes the admissibility of other evidence [laying the foundation] (Garner, 2014; Black's Law Dictionary 10th ed., reprinted with permission, Thomson Reuters).

Grand Jury: A body of [usually 16 to 23] people were chosen to sit permanently for at least a month-and sometimes a year-and who, in ex parte proceedings, decide whether to issue indictments. If the grand jury decides the evidence is strong enough to hold the suspect for trial, it returns the bill of indictment (a true bill) charging the suspect with a specific crime. Also termed *accusing jury; presenting jury; jury of indictment* (Garner, 2014; Black's Law Dictionary 10th ed., reprinted with permission, Thomson Reuters).

Hobbs Act: Title 18 of the United States Code (U.S.C) § 1951 has come to be known as The Hobbs Act. The Hobbs Act was enacted in 1946 and takes its name from the sponsor of the legislation Congressman Sam Hobbs of Alabama. The legislation was enacted in an attempt to aggressively address racketeering in labor management disputes. Among other things, the Act prohibits actual or attempted robbery or extortion affecting interstate or foreign commerce. § 1951 also proscribes conspiracy to commit robbery or extortion without reference to the conspiracy statute at 18 U.S.C. § 371. Although the Hobbs Act was enacted as a statute to combat racketeering in labor-management disputes, the statute is frequently used in connection with cases involving public corruption, commercial disputes, and corruption directed at members of labor unions (United States Department of Justice, 2015, § 9-131.010).

Indictment: 1. The formal written accusation of a crime, made by a grand jury and presented to a court for prosecution against the accused person. 2. The act or process of preparing or bringing forward such a formal written accusation (Garner, 2014; Black's Law Dictionary 10th ed., reprinted with permission, Thomson Reuters).

Interrogation: The formal or systematic questioning of a person; [especially], intensive questioning by the police, [usually] of a person arrested for or suspected of committing a crime. The Supreme Court has held that, for purposes of the Fifth Amendment right against self-incrimination, interrogation includes not only express questioning but also words or action that the police should know are reasonably likely to elicit an incriminating response. *Rhode Island v. Innis*, 446 U.S. 291, 100 S.Ct. 1082 (1980) (Garner, 2014; Black's Law Dictionary 10th ed., reprinted with permission, Thomson Reuters).

Interview: A discussion about a specific subject that is conducted between two people. The purpose for the interviewer is to explore the subject matter and to gather accurate information.

Judiciary Act of 1789: The Judiciary Act of 1789, officially titled "An Act to Establish the Judicial Courts of the United States," was signed into law by President George Washington on September 24, 1789. Article III of the Constitution established a Supreme Court, but left to Congress the authority to create lower federal courts as needed. Principally authored by Senator Oliver Ellsworth of Connecticut, the Judiciary Act of 1789 established the structure and jurisdiction of the federal court system and created the position of attorney general. Although amended throughout the years by Congress, the basic outline of the federal court system established by the First Congress remains largely intact today (United States Library of Congress, 2016).

Jurisdiction: 1. A government's general power to exercise authority over all persons and things within its territory; [especially] a state's power to create interests that will be recognized under common law principles as valid and other states. 2. A court's power to decide a case or issue a decree (Garner, 2014; Black's Law Dictionary 10th ed., reprinted with permission, Thomson Reuters).

Jury: A group of persons selected according to law and given the power to decide questions of fact and return a verdict in the case submitted to them. In certain contexts, jury embraces any fact-trier, including an arbitrator or a trial judge sitting in a nonjury proceeding -Also termed *empaneled jury; impaneled jury* (Garner, 2014; Black's Law Dictionary 10th ed., reprinted with permission, Thomson Reuters).

Lead Desk: A physical location, usually at a law enforcement command post, where all leads and other case management information and activities are received, assigned, and systematically cataloged for a specific investigation.

Lead Index System: A case management tool (system) utilized by law enforcement to track leads and other activities relative to a specific investigation.

***Mapp* Hearing:** A hearing held to determine whether evidence implicating the accused was obtained as a result of an illegal search and seizure, and should therefore be suppressed. [From the landmark United States Supreme Court case of *Mapp v. Ohio*, 367 U.S. 643, 81 S.Ct. 1684 (1961) (Garner, 2014; Black's Law Dictionary 10th ed., reprinted with permission, Thomson Reuters).

***Massiah* Hearing/Rule:** The principle that an attempt to elicit incriminating statements [usually not during a formal interrogation] from a suspect whose right to counsel has attached but who has not waived that right violates the sixth amendment. [From the landmark United States Supreme Court case of *Massiah* *v. U.S.*, 377 U.S. 201, 84 S.Ct. 1199 (1964), also known as deliberate elicitation] (Garner, 2014; Black's Law Dictionary 10th ed., reprinted with permission, Thomson Reuters).

Medical Examiner: A public official who investigates deaths, conduct autopsies, and helps the state prosecute homicide cases. Medical examiners have replaced corners in many states [sometimes shortened to examiner] (Garner, 2014; Black's Law Dictionary 10th ed., reprinted with permission, Thomson Reuters).

Miranda **Rule:** The doctrine that a criminal suspect in police custody must be informed of certain constitutional rights before being interrogated. The suspect must be advised of the right to remain silent, the right to have an attorney present during questioning, and the right to have an attorney appointed if the suspect cannot afford one. If the suspect is not advised of these rights or does not validly waive them, any evidence obtained during the interrogation cannot be used against the suspect at trial (except for impeachment purposes) (Garner, 2014; Black's Law Dictionary 10th ed., reprinted with permission, Thomson Reuters).

Miranda **Waiver Form:** A document where an interviewee, in writing, voluntarily and knowledgeably waives his rights under the *Miranda* Rule.

New York State Court of Appeals: The Court of Appeals, New York's highest-level court, hears civil and criminal appeals from the state's intermediate appellate courts, and, in some instances, directly from the trial courts. The Court also hears appeals from determinations by the State Commission on Judicial Conduct, which is responsible for reviewing allegations of misconduct brought against judges (NYCourts.gov, 2016).

New York State Court of Claims: The New York State Court of Claims is the exclusive forum for civil litigation seeking damages against the State of New

York or certain other State-related entities such as the New York State Thruway Authority, the City University of New York, the Olympic Regional Development Authority, the Roswell Park Cancer Institute Corporation and the New York State Power Authority (claims for the appropriation of real property only). The Court of Claims has no jurisdiction over any city, county or town government, or over any individual defendant (NYCourts.gov, 2016).

Non-verbal Behavior Analysis: Non-verbal behavior in addition to verbal statements made or observed by a trained interviewer to detect deception if it exists during the interview process.

Notice of Appeal: A document filed with the court and served on the other parties, stating in intention to appeal the trial court's judgment or order. In most jurisdictions, filing a notice of appeal is the act by which the appeal is perfected. For instance, the Federal Rules of Appellate Procedure provide that an appeal is taken by filing a notice of appeal with the clerk of the District Court from which the appeal is taken and that the clerk is to send copies of the notice to all of the other party's attorneys, as well as the Court of Appeals (Garner, 2014; Black's Law Dictionary 10th ed., reprinted with permission, Thomson Reuters).

Oath: 1. A solemn declaration, accompanied by a swearing to God or a revered person or thing, that one statement is true or that one will be bound to a promise. The person making the oath implicitly invites punishment if the statement is untrue or the promise is broken. The legal effect of an oath is to subject the person to penalties for perjury if the testimony is faults. 2. The statement or promise made in such a declaration. 3. The form of words used for such a declaration. 4 A formal declaration made solemn without a swearing to

God or a revered person or thing (Garner, 2014; Black's Law Dictionary 10th ed., reprinted with permission, Thomson Reuters).

Oath of Office: An oath or affirmation taken by a person to enter into the duties of public office, by which the person promises to perform the duties of that office in good faith (Garner, 2014; Black's Law Dictionary 10th ed., reprinted with permission, Thomson Reuters).

Objection: A formal statement opposing something that has occurred, or is about to occur, in court and seeking the judge's immediate ruling on the point. The party objecting must [usually] state the basis for the objection to preserve the right to appeal an adverse ruling (Garner, 2014; Black's Law Dictionary 10th ed., reprinted with permission, Thomson Reuters).

Original Jurisdiction: A court's power to hear and decide a matter before any other court can review the matter (Garner, 2014; Black's Law Dictionary 10th ed., reprinted with permission, Thomson Reuters).

Plea: 1. Criminal law. An accused person's formal response of "guilty," "not guilty," or "no contest" to a criminal charge – Also termed *criminal plea* (Garner, 2014; Black's Law Dictionary 10th ed., reprinted with permission, Thomson Reuters).

Presentence-investigation report: A probation officer's detailed account of a convicted defendant's educational, criminal, family, and social background, conducted at the courts request as an aid in passing sentence. [Also known as PSI; PR; PSR; PIR; PSIR, often shortened to presentence investigation or presentence report] (Garner, 2014; Black's Law Dictionary 10th ed., reprinted with permission, Thomson Reuters).

Presentence Investigation: A probation officer's detailed account of the convicted defendants educational, criminal, family, and social background, conducted at the courts request as an aid in passing sentence (Garner, 2014; Black's Law Dictionary 10th ed., reprinted with permission, Thomson Reuters).

Probable Cause: 1. *Criminal Law.* A reasonable ground to suspect that a person has committed or is committing a crime or that a place contain specific items connected with the crime. Under the Fourth Amendment, probable cause-which amounts to more than a bare suspicion but less than evidence that would justify a conviction-must be shown before an arrest warrant or search warrant may be issued. Also termed *reasonable cause; sufficient cause; reasonable grounds; reasonable excuse* (Garner, 2014; Black's Law Dictionary 10th ed., reprinted with permission, Thomson Reuters).

Public Safety Exception to the *Miranda* Rule: Absent actual coercion by police officer in acting to protect himself or public by questioning a suspect before *Miranda* warnings have been given, there is no constitutional imperative requiring exclusion of evidence that results from inquiry of this kind; neither do doctrinal underpinnings of *Miranda* require that such evidence be excluded, thus penalizing officers for asking the very questions which are the most crucial to their efforts to protect themselves and the public. *New York v. Quarles*, 467 U.S. 469 (1984)

Respondent: 1. The party against whom an appeal is taken; Appellee. In some appellate courts, the parties are designated as petitioner and respondent. In most appellate courts in the United States, the parties are designated as appellant and appellee. Often the designations depend on whether the appeal is taken by writ of certiorari (or writ of error) or by direct appeal. 2. The party against whom a motion or petition is filed. 3. At common law, the defendant in an equity proceeding. 4. Civil law. Someone who answers for another or acts as another security (Garner, 2014; Black's Law Dictionary 10th ed., reprinted)

Restitution: 3. Return or restoration of some specific thing to its rightful owner or status. 4. Compensation for loss [especially], full or partial compensation paid by a criminal to a victim, not awarded in a civil trial for court, but ordered as a part of a criminal sentence or as a condition of probation. [Also called criminal restitution] (Garner, 2014; Black's Law Dictionary 10th ed., reprinted with permission, Thomson Reuters).

Search Warrant: A judge's written order authorizing a law enforcement officer to conduct a search of a specified place and to seize evidence (Garner, 2014; Black's Law Dictionary 10th ed., reprinted with permission, Thomson Reuters).

Sentence: The judgment that a court formally pronounces after finding a criminal defendant guilty; the punishment imposed on a criminal wrongdoer... Also termed *judgment of conviction* (Garner, 2014; Black's Law Dictionary 10th ed., reprinted with permission, Thomson Reuters).

Spontaneous Statement/Excited Utterance: A statement about a startling event made under the stress and excitement of the event. An excited utterance may be admissible as a hearsay exception (Garner, 2014; Black's Law Dictionary 10th ed., reprinted with permission, Thomson Reuters).

Stare Decisis: Latin, "to standby things decided." The doctrine of precedent, under which a court must follow earlier judicial decisions when the same points arise again in litigation (Garner, 2014; Black's Law Dictionary 10th ed., reprinted with permission, Thomson Reuters).

Subpoena: A writ or order commanding a person to appear before a court or other tribunal, subject to a penalty for failing to comply... [also] 1. To serve with a subpoena to appear before a court or other tribunal, <subpoena the material witness>. 2. To order the production of (documents or other things) by subpoena duces tecum <subpoena the corporate records> (Garner, 2014; Black's Law Dictionary 10th ed., reprinted with permission, Thomson Reuters).

Sworn Statement/Affidavit: A voluntary declaration of facts written down and sworn to by a declarant, [usually] before an officer authorized to administer oath's. A great deal of evidence is submitted by affidavit, [especially] in pretrial matters such as summary-judgment motions (Garner, 2014; Black's Law Dictionary 10th ed., reprinted with permission, Thomson Reuters).

Task Force: A temporary group of people formed to carry out a specific mission or project, or to solve a problem that requires a multi-disciplinary approach (BusinessDictionary.com, 2016).

Task Force Policing: A temporary group of law enforcement and other related practitioners whose mission is directed at a specific public safety need that requires focused attention.

The U.S. Sentencing Commission: is an independent agency in the judicial branch of government created by the Sentencing Reform Act of 1984. Congress enacted the SRA in response to widespread disparity in federal sentencing, ushering in a new era of federal sentencing through the creation of the Commission and the promulgation of federal sentencing guidelines (USSC, 2016).

Trial: A formal judicial examination of evidence and determination of legal claims in an adversary proceeding (Garner, 2014; Black's Law Dictionary 10th ed., reprinted with permission, Thomson Reuters).

Uniform Crime Report: The FBI's Uniform Crime Reporting (UCR) Program is a nationwide, cooperative statistical effort of nearly 18,000 city, university and college, county, state, tribal, and federal law enforcement agencies voluntarily reporting data on crimes brought to their attention. Since 1930, the FBI has administered the UCR Program and continued to assess and monitor the nature and type of crime in the nation. The program's primary objective is to generate reliable information for use in law enforcement administration, operation, and management; however, its data have over the years become one of the country's leading social indicators. Criminologists, sociologists, legislators, municipal planners, the media, and other students of criminal justice use the data for varied research and planning purposes (FBI Uniform Crime Reporting Statistics, 2016).

United States Attorney for the Northern District of New York: Like a local district attorney, state's attorney, or prosecutor, the United States Attorney and his/her assistant are charged with representing the People of the United States in regards to violations of federal criminal laws/prosecutions. There are 94 federal districts in the United States, each represented by one appointed United States Attorney (USA), and many other Assistant United States Attorneys (AUSA).

United States Court of Appeals: There are 13 appellate courts that sit below the U.S. Supreme Court, and they are called the U.S. Courts of Appeals. The 94 federal judicial districts are organized into 12 regional circuits, each of which has a court of appeals. The appellate court's task is to determine whether or not the law was applied correctly in the trial court. Appeals courts consist of three judges and do not use a jury. A court of appeals hears challenges to district court decisions from courts located within its circuit, as well as appeals from decisions of federal administrative agencies. In addition, the Court of Appeals for the Federal Circuit has nationwide jurisdiction to hear appeals in specialized cases, such as those involving patent laws, and cases decided by the U.S. Court of International Trade and the U.S. Court of Federal Claims (USCourts.gov, 2016).

United States District Court: The nation's 94 district or trial courts are called U.S. District Courts. District courts resolve disputes by determining the facts and applying legal principles to decide who is right. Trial courts include the district judge who tries the case and a jury that decides the case. Magistrate judges assist district judges in preparing cases for trial. They may also conduct trials in misdemeanor cases. There is at least one district court in each state, and the District of Columbia. Each district includes a U.S. bankruptcy court as a unit of the district court. Four territories of the United States have U.S. district courts that hear federal cases, including bankruptcy cases: Puerto Rico, the Virgin Islands, Guam, and the Northern Mariana Islands. There are also two special trial courts. The Court of International Trade addresses cases involving international trade and customs laws. The U.S. Court of Federal Claims deals with most claims for money damages against the U.S. government (USCourts. gov, 2016).

United States Supreme Court: The Supreme Court is the highest court in the United States. Article III of the U.S. Constitution created the Supreme Court and authorized Congress to pass laws establishing a system of lower courts. In the federal court system's present form, 94 district level trial courts and 13 courts of appeals sit below the Supreme Court (USCourts.gov, 2016).

Unity of Command: The principle that no subordinate in an organization should report to more than one boss. In creating a task force the issue of Unity of Command must be addressed so that those assigned to the task force do not have to answer to their home department as well as a supervisor or commander at a task force.

Wade Hearing: A pretrial hearing in which the defendant contests the validity of his or her out-of-court identification. If the court finds that the identification was tainted by unconstitutional methods, the prosecution cannot use the identification and must link the defendant to the crime by other means. [From the landmark United States Supreme Court case of _U.S. v. Wade_, 388 U.S. 218, 87 S.Ct. 1926 (1967)] (Garner, 2014; Black's Law Dictionary 10th ed., reprinted with permission, Thomson Reuters).

Warrant: A judge's written order authorizing a law enforcement officer to conduct a search of a specified place and to seize evidence (Garner, 2014; Black's Law Dictionary 10th ed., reprinted with permission, Thomson Reuters).

Index

L

M